BASIC COMPUTING
CONCEPTS

All-In-One Beginner's Guide To Computer Proficiency

4TH EDITION

LILIAN UKADIKE

Page Solutions
541 Buttermilk Pike
Crescent Springs, KY 41017

Copyright © 2025 by Lilian Ukadike.

ISBN 979-8-89633-063-9 (softcover)
ISBN 979-8-89633-062-2 (ebook)

All rights reserved. No part of this book may be reproduced or transmitted in any form or by any means, electronic or mechanical, including photocopying, recording, or by any information storage and retrieval system without express written permission from the author, except in the case of brief quotations embodied in critical reviews and certain other noncommercial uses permitted by copyright law.

Printed in the United States of America.

CONTENTS

Overview & Preface 7
Chapter Synopsis 9
Message to the Instructor 14

Chapter 1 17
Introduction to Basic Computer Concepts 17
Basic Computer Concepts 18
The two main components of computer 19
Contents of the motherboard 20
Data Storage Devices 21
Hardware And Peripherals 23
The Keyboard – Terms And Definitions 28
Computer Input And Output Devices 38
Differences Between Crt And Lcd Monitors 39
The Computer Memory 40
Common Facts About Computer Viruses, Spyware, And Adware 42
Protecting Your Privacy And Computer From Viruses, Spyware, And Adware 46
Chapter Summary & Key Terms 48
Demonstrate Your Knowledge & Skill 50
Chapter 1 Practice Exercises: Basic Computer Concepts 51
Chapter I Skill-Based Practice: Projects Basic Computer Concepts 61

Chapter 2 63
Introduction to Microsoft Windows 10 63
Explore, Navigate, And Understand Windows 10 Desktop Features 68
Personalize & Customize Windows 10 74
Manage User Accounts 81
Improve Programs In Your Computer Using Microsoft Windows Updates 84

Take Care Of Your Computer With Routine System Maintenance 85
Managing Files In Windows 10 89
Windows 10 Basic Shortcut Keys 106
Chapter Summary & Key Terms 107
Demonstrate Your Knowledge & Skill 109
Chapter 2 Practice Exercises: Introduction to Windows 10 110
Chapter 2 Skill-Based Practice Projects: Introduction to Windows 10 118

Chapter 3 121
Overview of Microsoft Office Software 121
Ms Office 2019 Vs. Office 365 What's The Difference? 123
New Features Of Ms Office 2019 125
Overview & Summary Of Office 2019 Package 126
Install, Run, And Uninstall Software 133
Activate Microsoft Office Programs 136
Find Contents You Need In Microsoft Office Help Window 141
Chapter Summary & Key Terms 143
Demonstrate Your Knowledge & Skill 144
Chapter 3 Practice Exercises: Overview of Microsoft Office Software 145
Chapter 3 Skill-Based Practice Projects: Overview of Microsoft Office Software 151

Chapter 4 155
Introduction to Microsoft Office Word 2019 155
New Features Of Microsoft Word 2019 156
Formatting Documents – Change Page Margins, Text Size, Page Orientation & Line Spacing 166
Move, Cut, Or Copy Text To A New Location In A Document 174
Spelling And Grammar Check 176
Insert & Format A Table In A Word Document 178
Insert Header, Footer, & Page Number In A Document 184
Save A Word 2019 Document In Word Earlier Versions (97-2003) 188
Chapter Summary & Key Terms 192
Demonstrate Your Knowledge & Skill 194
Chapter 4 Practice Exercises: Introduction to Microsoft Word 2019 195
Chapter 4 Skill-Based Practice Projects: Introduction to Microsoft Word 2019 204

Chapter 5 209

Welcome to Microsoft Excel 2019 209
What's New In Ms Excel 2019 210
Create A Workbook & Format A Worksheet Within The Workbook 213
Insert/Delete Rows/Columns & Adjust Row Height & Column Width 219
Basic Excel Worksheet Formatting Options 227
Excel References, Constants, & Operators 238
Create Excel Formulas Into Cells & Copy To Other Worksheet 240
Link A Worksheet Formula To Another Worsheet 244
Insert Headers & Footer In A Worksheet 250
Working With Charts & Graphs 256
Chapter Summary & Key Terms 269
Demonstrate Your Knowledge & Skill 271
Chapter 5 Practice Exercises: Introduction to MS Excel 2019 272
Chapter 5 Skill-Based Practice Projects: Introduction to MS Microsoft Excel 2019 279

Chapter 6 284

Welcome to Microsoft Powerpoint 2019 284
New Features Of Powerpoint 2019 285
Work With Powerpoint Slides & Create A New Ppt Presentation 290
Change Slide Background Themes 313
Insert Header & Footer In Presentation Handouts 316
Chapter Summary & Key Terms 321
Demonstrate Your Knowledge & Skill 323
Chapter 6 Practice Exercises: Introduction to MS PowerPoint 324
Chapter 6 Skill-Based Practice Projects: Introduction to MS PowerPoint 2019 332

Chapter 7 338

Introduction to Internet Explorer 11 & Electronic Communication 338
Login To Internet Explorer And Navigate The Window 340
Connecting To The Internet & Types Of Internet Connections 343
Factors Affecting Internet Connection Speed 345
Perform Basic Tasks On The Internet 351
Basic Internet Explorer Terms & Definitions 362
Tips For Performing Searches On The Internet 364

Other Internet Features & How To Use Them To Perform Basic Online Tasks...........................367
Sharing Files & Printers On The Internet...370
The Emailing Process 378
Free Web-Based E-Mail Service 379
Create And Send Messages Online 382
Chapter Summary & Key Terms 391
Demonstrate Your Knowledge & Skill..394
Chapter 7 Practice Exercises: Introduction to Internet Explorer & Electronic Communication..............395
Chapter 7 Skill-Based Practice Projects: Introduction to Internet Explorer 11 & Electronic Communication... 407

Chapter 8 411
Introduction to Remote Online Learning...411
What Is Virtual Online Education & How Does It Work? 413
Some Types Of Online Learning Management Systems..414
Video Conferencing Services & The Most Commonly Used Types In Today's Business.........416
Advantages & Disadvantages Of Online Learning..426
Technology Requirements For Online Learning 428
Overview Of Online Course Management Tools 430
How To Participate In An Online Course..431
Overview Of Online Discussion Boards & How To Use Them 437
Is Online Learning For Everyone?...441
On-Line Interaction & Communication 443
The Six Main Netiquette Rules Of On-Line Communication 444
Conduct Online Research Effectively 447
Locate Resources For Your Research 449
Manage Your Time In An Online Course..452
effective test-taking tips for online learning 455
Introduction To Social Networking 457
Etiquettes Of Social Networking Communications...459
Chapter Summary & Key Terms 464
Demonstrate Your Knowledge & Skill...466
Chapter 8 Skill-Based Practice Projects: Introduction to Remote Online Learning 467
Glossary Of Terms & Definitions..468
References 492
About The Author...493

OVERVIEW & PREFACE

This book, *Basic Computing Concepts – All-in-One Beginner's Guide to Computer Proficiency" 4th Edition* is intended to offer beginners in computer technology a way to build strong foundation through grassroot learning techniques that will effectively empower them to become proficient in basic computing. In addition, the contents of the book incorporates general knowledge of daily computing up to basic concepts in Microsoft Office products (Word, Excel, and PowerPoint). Specifically, with this book, a beginner can learn computer concepts in general from Windows 10, and move on to beginner's guide to Microsoft Office application programs. The book is a "Combo" people don't have to buy one book to learn Computer Basics, another Microsoft Word book for beginners, MS Excel for beginners, and MS PowerPoint for beginners. The book comes as All-in-One package with everything a new beginner needs to become computer proficient from beginner's computer concepts to Microsoft Office beginner's guide, including a bonus chapter on distance online learning which has become our new normal in today's world necessitated by the 2020 COVID-19 pandemic. Contents of this book are proven techniques in computer system functionalities that have brought great success to my former students at Piedmont Technical College (PTC), Greenwood South Carolina 10 years ago. With current updates in today's technology, I have used the teaching/learning techniques myself for many years, tested, taught new employees on my previous job as organizational policy writer and Microsoft Office application program trainer. I know that the teaching and learning techniques in this book are very effective. Therefore, I feel compelled to share this knowledge with the world, especially with new beginners as I watch them still struggling with computer literacy in this 21st century with all the technological advancements available to everyone.

The computer industry is very dynamic as technology creators and program designers continue to introduce new and updated program features for school, home, and business computing. In this constantly changing technological environment, new beginner continue to struggle to learn how to perform basic computer tasks and face the challenge of adapting to this ever changes computing world. In reviewing many computer beginner's guide in the market today, such as *Computer for Dummies, Computer Basics for Beginners, Absolute Beginner's Guide, Basic Guide to Home Computing,* and the list goes on, I found a common flaw in many of these books. Something is missing – these books have incomplete steps. First and foremost, I found that the instructional steps for performing various basic computer tasks are not complete. For example, if you are proving instructions for a beginner on how to save a file in a flash drive, you should not only state: *"Insert flash drive in the computer USB Port and save your document."* Instead, the instruction should read: (1) *Insert flash drive in the computer USB Port located at the back of a PC or side of a laptop. (2) In the open Explorer window of your computer drive, navigate the left pane to locate your flash drive name. (3) Double-click the flash drive to open it. (4) Then on your open document, click* **File** *tab at top ribbon. (5) Select* **Save As***, name your file, and click* **Save** *to save the document as a file in your flash drive."* Without complete instructions, there is no way a new beginner in computer technology will know where to find the USB Port or what to do after inserting flash drive into the computer USB Port. This same flaw has continued to be the same problem I encountered as an Instructor of Business & Information Technology (2007-2012) at Piedmont Technical College (PTC) Greenwood, South Carolina. The purpose of *Basic Computing Concepts 4th Edition* is to fill the gap (the missing link), and provide what is missing in most computer beginner's guide in today's technology marketplace.

Many young people in our society today especially students, often referred to as Wiz Kids can quickly manipulate technologies and gadgets such as cell phones, surf the Internet, use Instagram, twitter, and hack into other people's devices. However, when you ask the question: *"How much do they really know about basic computing and application programs?* You find out that they have no clue. Based on my research, majority of public high schools students do not know how to create a new folder, save a document in the new folder, or even change page margins in a Word document. My 5-year experience as an Instructor of Developmental Technology and Business at a 2-year community college, PTC, Greenwood, SC made me realize that most of these so called Wiz Kids don't know anything about basic computing and application programs. I strongly believe that my book can help beginners in computer literacy, individuals struggling to perform basic computer tasks on their own, college students, and high school seniors to gain new knowledge or improve their computer skills to become proficient and master the necessary skills required to prepare for college and effectively compete in today's technological job market.

This textbook is intended to serve as a learning solution targeted specifically to beginners in computer technology at 2-year colleges, universities (sophomores & juniors), and high school seniors (8-12 graders). The book also comes with some supplemental teaching aids to help teachers facilitate classroom lectures. The goal is to provide a strong foundation on which beginners in computer technology can build upon as they move toward intermediate and advance levels of computer competencies. *Basic Computing Concepts* contains everything a beginner needs to know (All-in-One) to become proficient with basic computer concepts and fundamental guide to Microsoft Office applications. This is why I changed the subtitle from *"A Simplified Approach"* on the 1st, 2nd & 3rd Editions to *"All-in-One Beginner's Guide to Computer Proficiency"* in this 4th Edition.

CHAPTER SYNOPSIS

The main objective of this textbook is to systematically break down the barriers that prevent beginners from quickly learning or becoming proficient with computer technology. The ultimate goal is to educate the students to levels of proficiency that will enable them compete effectively in today's business world. The method, format, style, and layout of the book contents provide a comfortable foundation for a beginner to learn without feeling intimidated. The instructions contained in the book per chapter are presented in a simple step-by-step, easy-to-follow format to facilitate hands-on practice with the keyboard. Also included at the end of the book after chapter 8, is a glossary list of key terms and definitions covered throughout the book, listed in alphabetical order.

Each chapter begins with one or two paragraphs providing introduction, an overview of the chapter describing its purpose, general information about the topic to be covered, including updates on newer technologies on the chapter topics that a new beginner in computer technology should know. The introductory paragraph(s) is followed by a list of learning objectives to be covered in each chapter. The learning objectives are further broken down into several headings and subheadings throughout the book with more detailed topics relevant to each chapter's learning objectives. Throughout the book, the materials covered in each chapter, the format used on the graphics, and the language used on the step-by-step instructions for performing basic computer tasks are all presented in a user-friendly pattern that beginners can easily understand. The format and layout of each chapter will make beginners in computer technology feel very excited and eager to learn new things. Each chapter contains multiple choices, true/false, or matching questions, including practice projects aimed at assessing the students' understanding of the basic concepts in computer technology such as definitions of key words and terms. Included at the end of the book is a glossary containing definitions of key words throughout the book listed in alphabetical order.

CHAPTER 1 – INTRODUCTION TO BASIC COMPUTER CONCEPTS

A discussion of the importance of computer technology is presented in this chapter. Students learn the definition of a computer, the various types of computers available in today's homes, businesses, and schools. They also learn the basic parts of a computer and their functions. In addition, this chapter discusses basic mouse skills and how to use the mouse correctly. Students are also trained on how to perform regular maintenance on their home computers, basic trouble-shooting techniques, how to protect their computers from viruses, and protect their personal privacy from hackers.

CHAPTER 2 – INTRODUCTION TO MICROSOFT WINDOWS 10

This chapter provides an overview of the new Microsoft Windows 10 as an operating system; various parts of its components; how to use it to perform basic computer tasks; and some simple troubleshooting techniques. It introduces students to new features included in this new version of Windows, and how they differ from Windows 7. Student also learn the difference between an operating system and an application software. These are the two terms in basic computing that many students find very confusing. In this chapter, students will learn that Windows 10 is similar to Windows 7 in some ways but contain faster functionalities that allow them to get things done quicker than if they were using Windows 7. The new Explorer interface accessible through the "Personalized" context menu item on the desktop allows one to customize and switch between themes, as well as download more themes from Microsoft's web site.

CHAPTER 3 – OVERVIEW OF MICROSOFT OFFICE SOFTWARE

Chapter 3 introduces students to the most commonly used software programs available in today's marketplace. The chapter begins with the definition of software, and how it works in a computer as powered by the operating system. Students learn that software needs to be installed on a computer, usually from a CD or downloaded from online before it can work on a computer. They are also trained on how to install and uninstall software in the computer, including downloading/installing Windows Updates for regular system maintenance. This chapter also provides students with a list of what programs are included in a Microsoft Office package such as Microsoft Outlook, MS Word, MS Excel, MS Access, MS PowerPoint, and MS Publisher. A brief description of each program is also included along with their functions. The chapter also discusses the similarities and differences between Microsoft Office 2019 and Office 365. However, the focus of MS Office programs in this textbook is on beginner's guide to Microsoft 2019 – Word, Excel, and PowerPoint.

CHAPTER 4 – INTRODUCTION TO MICROSOFT WORD 2019

In this chapter, students are taught that word processing is similar to using a typewriter to type a document except that you can edit text, copy/paste, and move/delete text. They learn that word processing program comes in the form of software that is installed on a computer and used to create documents. The chapter introduces students to the newest features of Microsoft Word 2019 as the program commonly found on most personal computers and may be the program frequently used by almost everyone. It teaches beginners how to create various types of documents, format, type, save, and print the document. They will also learn how to edit documents, copy, paste, and much more. By following simple steps, getting started with a basic document in Microsoft Office Word 2019 is very easy.

CHAPTER 5 – INTRODUCTION TO MICROSOFT EXCEL 2019

This chapter introduces beginners to the use of Excel spreadsheet as a supplemental accounting program. It teaches students the general uses of Excel as an accounting program. They learn to view the program as the most widely used program in businesses, schools, and homes to manage finances and budgets. Although business organizations have their primary accounting systems, they use Excel in conjunction with their primary accounting programs to process, research, calculate, and manage data produced by their primary systems that enable them make informed business decisions. In this chapter, students will learn how easy it is to calculate numbers using Excel formula feature. They will learn how to streamline data entry with AutoFill, create and format worksheets, create formulas, link worksheets, insert graphs into a worksheet and much more.

CHAPTER 6 – INTRODUCTION TO MICROSOFT POWERPOINT 2019

To beginners in computer technology, this chapter introduces them to the world of making a presentation to an audience using PowerPoint program. Students learn the general uses of PowerPoint and why it is a very important tool in business, schools, public relations, and a variety of projects that require making presentations to an audience. Specifically, this chapter teaches students that if they have an idea to sell, they have to make it very convincing to get people on board the idea. Students will learn how to plan, perform the necessary research, organize their facts, create presentation from scratch, and present to their audience. Beginners will learn that PowerPoint is basically a presentation creation tool that produces slideshows with text, images, shapes, animations, audio, and much more.

CHAPTER 7 – WELCOME TO INTERNET EXPLORER & ELECTRONIC COMMUNICATION

This chapter introduces beginners to Internet Explorer 11, the latest version. It provides a basic overview of the features, and shows them how to use those features to explore the Internet. Students are trained on how to use the Built-in IntelliSense technology to save time in completing routine Web tasks. They also learn how to use basic search engine techniques to find information on the website, bookmark favorite Internet sites, and create their favorite lists of Web sites they visit most often, including general navigation of Web browser, or simply "surfing the Internet." Learning the techniques for using Internet search engines to perform researches required to write school term paper is one of the most important tools of this chapter to beginners. The knowledge and use of Internet **Free Web-based Emailing** services offered by such companies as Yahoo, Gmail, Hotmail, MSN, etc. is also incorporated in this chapter. It educates beginners on how to effectively communicate electronically using the free web-based email service found on the Internet. Students will learn how to setup an e-mail account; how emailing works, including how to create and send an email message to anywhere worldwide; attach a file to an email message; create contact list in the address book; and much more.

CHAPTER 8 – INTRODUCTION TO REMOTE ONLINE LEARNING

In our society today, remote online learning has become our new normal; a new way of life necessitated by the 2020 COVID-19 pandemic. The idea of online learning often referred to as **"computer-mediated distance education"** is not new, but in today's world, this idea has become almost imperative as students globally struggled to learn remotely online while on lockdown in the face of the deadly coronavirus. Despite the popularity of online learning, many students still struggle to use it in this brave new world. The purpose of this chapter is to help such students navigate their way through remote online learning and ensure that they have all the tools they need to become successful. Currently, advancements in computer technology, instructional technologies, and curriculum development along with learning assessment have made distant education through online learning a desirable and efficient way of learning for students worldwide. This chapter introduces students to the use of technology in distant education and gives them a choice of either schooling in a traditional classroom setting or online using technology. In addition, for adult professionals who want to further their education, learning does not have to stop just because work schedule cannot accommodate schooling. Knowledge gained from this chapter would provide such students a strong platform on which to build their strengths and develop the necessary computing skills required for a successful online education. Depending on which learning management system in use at any school, such as Blackboard, Illuminate, D2L (Desire to Learn), etc. beginners in online learning will learn what they need to know in order to successfully participate in online education. They will learn how to use the discussion board, download assignment files, submit completed assignments, conduct online research effectively, take online exams, and all other learning activities required in an online classroom.

MESSAGE TO THE INSTRUCTOR

The 1st Edition of this book, "*Basic Computing Concepts: A Simplified Approach*" published 2011 (a custom book) grew out of my strong desire to help my students learn basic computer concepts and become proficient. I am a former Instructor of Developmental Technology & Business at Piedmont Technical College (PTC), Greenwood, South Carolina (2007-2012). Before I proceed with my message to you, I want to use this opportunity to provide you with a brief history and origin of the current 4th Edition – *"Basic Computing Concepts: All-in-One Beginner's Guide to Computer Proficiency"* to help you understand why I am so passionate about it.

During my time at PTC, in delivering my daily lectures, I saw first-hand, how my students struggled with the current text book in use at the time. They often complained to me: "*When I followed all the steps in the book, the system doesn't produce the result the book says it would.*" In response to my students' complaints, I began testing a sample of steps in each chapter myself, and found that the students had valid reasons to complain – the steps in the book were incomplete. To help the students understand things better and facilitate learning, I began breaking down each chapter of my lecture into easy-to-follow format, and adding all the missing steps to ensure that the students have the complete instructional steps they need to perform basic computer tasks. At the beginning of each class lecture, I provided them with handouts/notes for that chapter with detailed complete instructions to help them do their homework and project assignments. Some of these students, especially the older (non-traditional) students had never touched or used a computer before. Some of them were a bit advanced in age (in their 50s and older); they did not even know how to use the mouse. Teaching this group of students required a great deal of patience with a grass-root and building-block approach. This concept involved breaking down the teaching materials into smaller units with very detailed steps to make the subject matters easier for students to grasp. As I used my simplified teaching notes in classroom lectures, and provided students with handouts, I noticed a significant improvement in the way they understood the basic concepts of technology in general. Over time, they were able to perform some basic tasks on the computer independently with very minimal supervision using my handout notes. As they learn new things, their excitement grew, and they remained fully engaged at each 75 minutes class lecture.

My students spread the news of the effectiveness of my handout notes all the way to the office of the Dean of Business and Information Technology, who after her thorough review and reviews by my peers, authorized me to write a custom book on computer basics for the college (PTC). Eventually, the teaching notes I had written and maintained over a 2-year period, modified and presented in proper format for a textbook became the 1st Edition of *"Basic Computing Concepts–A Simplified Approach"* based on Windows XP. The book was published in 2011 by McGraw-Hill Learning Solutions. This was how I became a writer of beginner's manual in computer technology; inspired by my strong desire to help my students learn and succeed. In early 2012, at the request of the college, I upgraded the custom book to Windows 7, the 2nd Edition also published by McGraw-Hill Learning Solutions for PTC. Essentially, the 1st and 2nd Editions of *"Basic Computing Concepts"* were inspired by my students and written for my students at PTC as custom books for the college.

I relocated to New Mexico in July 2012 and worked with New Mexico Taxation & Revenue Department (NMTRD) first as Cash Control Manager (Dec.2012 – Feb. 2015) and lastly as Assistant Bureau Chief from Feb. 2015 to retiring in Dec. 2022. During my first year in NM, unbeknown to me, the two custom books I wrote for PTC in SC were already generating so much interest from a representative at Tate Publishing Enterprise in Mustang, Oklahoma who wondered why such good books should be confined to one college alone while many beginners in our society continue to struggle with computer literacy. Consequently, I was contacted by the publisher and persuaded to write a 3rd edition of the book for US national market. With such high interest, I was compelled to upgrade the book to a 3rd Edition published by Tate Publishing Enterprise in 2014.

I have a Master's Degree in Business Administration and a Bachelor's Degree in Accounting with extensive knowledge/experience of research in information technology, business application programs over the years, and strong background in technical writing. I am an Accountant by profession, a job I love and have enjoyed doing for the past 27 years. However, I also have a strong passion for writing and teaching, empowering people to acquire new knowledge and get excited about learning. The fulfillment I enjoy when I can help people learn new things, make them feel empowered; and get excited about acquiring new knowledge is priceless to me. At the onset of my employment with NMTRD in Dec. 2012, senior management quickly recognized my writing skills after reading some of the reports I had written during my first year. They decided to designate me as the official policies/procedures (Standard Operating Procedures) writer for the department, in addition to my primary function. I continued to function in this role until my retirement in

2022. Additionally, with my classroom teaching experience, the department also allowed me to participate in providing employee trainings for the agency during implementation of new technologies and new work processes. Blessed with these multiple talents – an accountant, a teacher, and a writer, I want to share my knowledge with the world and help improve computer literacy in our society to the best of my abilities. As a former teacher who has observed how individuals struggle with computer technology firsthand, I had to see learning from the eyes of a new beginner. With this empathy, I poured my heart and soul into this book to ensure that beginners can learn with enthusiasm, excitement, and feel empowered with the knowledge and proficiency acquired in learning basic computer technology.

I hope that after reading my story, you the Instructor can learn to teach with empathy, if you are not already doing so. Put yourself in the "shoes" of your students; try to see learning new things from the eyes of new beginners; teach from your heart; and keep them fully engaged. Finally, my advice for teaching any developmental course is to start from the scratch – a grassroot approach. Do not assume anything about the level of knowledge your students already have before coming into your class. When I write and teach new beginners, I start from scratch as if they've never had any prior knowledge of the subject matter. I do not assume that they probably know a little bit, so I'll start from the middle; this will create incomplete knowledge of the topic being discussed. With my grass-root approach to teaching, and detailed instructional steps, students with some knowledge of the subject matter prior to attending my class will have improved knowledge; and students with no idea of the topic will gain a new knowledge. It's a win-win situation. I have gone to great lengths to include training materials (PowerPoint presentation, Lecture notes, Answer key and solution guide to practice questions and skilled-based practice projects) to facilitate classroom teaching of this beginner's computer course. I hope you would find them very helpful and enjoy teaching this course as much as I have enjoyed it over the years.

Sincerely,

Lilian N. Ukadike

CHAPTER 1

INTRODUCTION TO BASIC COMPUTER CONCEPTS

In this new world of information technology, computers have become an integral part of our lives. They are found in homes, offices, schools, stores, hospitals, and many other places. They enable us to quickly communicate with people around the world through the internet and email, shop online, and access our bank accounts from home. It will be difficult to find a business or occupation that does not rely on computers to operate daily. Since computers are always around us and will continue to be for a long time, it is important to learn the basic skills and gain the knowledge necessary to make someone a responsible user. The knowledge gained is what makes a person **computer proficient**. This section is designed for beginners or people with very limited experience in computer technology. The focus is on getting new learners to be familiar with the basic parts of a computer, and show them how to perform basic task such as surf the Internet, send e-mail, and type text. This chapter takes a look at the most commonly used types of computers and their functions; including computer hardware and software.

Learning Objectives:

After completing this chapter, you will be able to:

- Define a computer and describe the types of computer used in business today.
- Identify basic parts of a computer, understand their functions, peripherals, input, and output devices.
- Understand the computer memory, and identify various types of data storage devices.

- Understand keyboard function keys, definitions, and how to use them to perform basic computer tasks.
- Learn common facts about computer viruses; identify the most commonly used antivirus, spyware, and adware software programs in the market today.
- Learn what Cookies are and how to remove them from your computer system.
- Learn how to protect your personal privacy, and your computer from viruses.
- Protect and maintain your computer system using Windows updates.

BASIC COMPUTER CONCEPTS

What is a Computer?

A **compute**r is a programmable electronic device that can input, process, output, and store data. A computer processes data and converts it into information. The definition of a computer is derived from its four basic functions also known as **information processing cycle (IPC).**

The Four Basic Functions of a Computer

1. **Input** – The computer collects data or allows a user to enter data using two types of input device called **Keyboard** and **Mouse.**
2. **Process** – Data collected is converted into information. Data processing takes place in the **central processing unit (CPU)** located in the operating system within the PC which is the computer brain.
3. **Output** – The processed data, which now becomes information, is retrieved from the computer through an output device known as **Printer.** Information you view on your computer screen is **Soft Copy.** When the information is printed, it is called a **Hard Copy.**
4. **Storage** – The data or information is stored for future use by using storage devices such as **CD, Flash Drive**, or stored on **C Drive** inside the PC.

THE TWO MAIN COMPONENTS OF COMPUTER

The CPU

The CPU is the brain of the computer that is responsible for controlling the commands and tasks performed by the computer. The CPU consists of two main parts – the **control unit** and the **arithmetic logic unit (ALU).** The control unit is responsible for obtaining instructions from the computer memory, interpreting the instructions, executing them, and coordinating the activities of all other parts of the computer components. The arithmetic logic unit (ALU) performs all the arithmetic and logic functions of the computer which includes addition, subtraction, multiplication, division and also makes logical comparison decisions. The functions of the ALU enables the CPU to perform tasks such as sorting data alphabetically or numerically and filtering data to locate specific data.

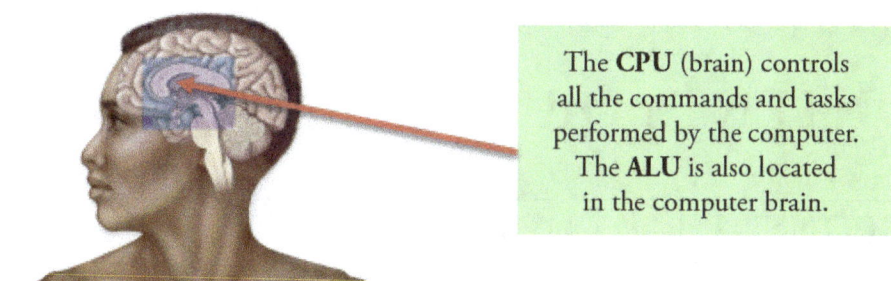

The **CPU** (brain) controls all the commands and tasks performed by the computer. The **ALU** is also located in the computer brain.

Fig. 1.1   CPU -Computer Brain

System Unit

This is the computer itself with its entire components referred to as the **system unit,** also known as the tower, box, or console. The four basic functions of the computer – input, process, output, and storage, are performed within the system unit. One of the most essential components found within the system unit is the microprocessor chip, also known as the **central processing unit (CPU).** The CPU is housed in the **microprocessor** located on the **motherboard** – a large printed circuit board to which all other circuits within the computer are connected to. The speed of the CPU is measured in **megahertz (MHz)** or **gigahertz (GHz)**, with a speed in excess of **3 GHz**. There are three important factors that determine how quickly a computer processes data – processor (CPU) speed, size of memory, video, and graphics cards.

All-in-One Beginners Guide to Computer Proficiency

Fig. 1.2 System Unit – Motherboard

CONTENTS OF THE MOTHERBOARD

COMPONENT	DESCRIPTION
Motherboard /System Board	The main computer circuit board that connects all computer components.
CPU	The central processing unit that obtains data from memory and performs mathematical or logical operations to process data.
Memory (RAM) Chips	The temporary holding area inside the computer where data is stored electronically and made available for processing. For the processor to process data, the data must first be stored in the **Random-Access Memory (RAM).**
Memory (RAM) Slots	Tiny slots on the motherboard used to hold the RAM chips in place.
Expansion Cards	Removable circuit boards used to add new peripherals or increase capabilities.
Expansion Slots	The slots used to hold expansion cards.

Table 1.1

DATA STORAGE DEVICES

Drives: Drives are different places on your computer where you can save information.

- **C Drive:** This is the hard drive, computer's largest internal storage device. Its storage space is usually measured in gigabytes (GB) with new computers ranging in sizes from **400** to **500 GB**.
- **D & E Drives:** These drives are used for inserting CDs and DVDs. D drive is used to install software in the computer.

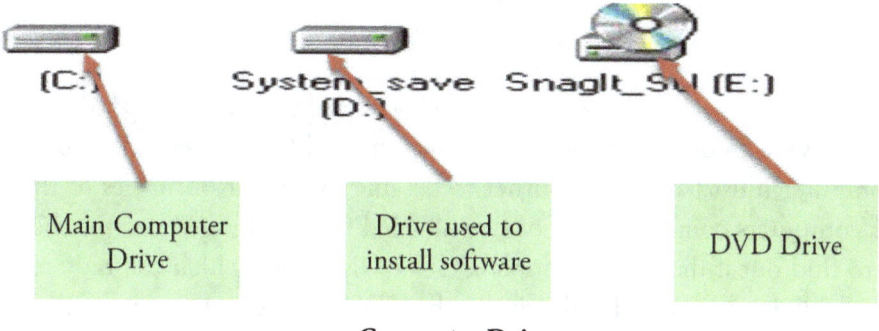

Fig. 1.3   **Computer Drives**

Disks

External storage devices used to store information from a computer. Disks serve as backup of data and information on your computer in the case of an accidental data loss allowing you to replace lost data back into your computer. The two types of disks commonly used to store data include:

1. Flash Drives: These are removable storage devices that use flash memory and connect to the computer by a USB port. Flash drives are often referred to as thumb drives, **universal serial bus (USB)** drives, or simply jump drives. It is typically a device small enough to fit on a keychain or in a pocket. The flash drive is built with circuitry and contains no moving parts which makes it extremely durable. It is available in several storage sizes ranging from **16 MB** to **64 GB** and is the quickest way to save and transport files.

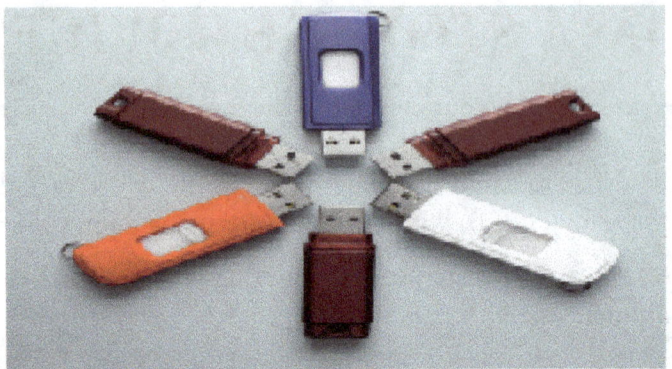

Fig .1.4 **Flash Drive**

2. CD ROM and/or DVD Drives: Today's computers are equipped with at least a CD or CD/DVD drive to provide an option for portable storage if need be. However, in order to save information on a CD, the computer must have a CD burner to be able to save or burn files to the CD. The software we install on our computers comes in a CD or downloaded from online. When purchasing a new computer, it is important to find out if the drive is simply a CD-ROM drive, which can only read CDs or if it is a CD RW drive, which allows you to read and write on the CD. Most computers come with either CD burner only or both CD and DVD writer. Although both items look alike, DVDs are capable of holding much more information than CDs. While a CD can hold up to **700 MB** of data, a DVD can store almost **10 GB**. This is why a CD drive is unable to read DVDs, but a DVD drive can read CDs.

Figs. 1.5   CD/DVD   DVD Burner   CD/DVD in a Protective Case

Why Burn Data on a CD Instead of Simply Saving on it?

CDs are optical storage devices made up of flat plastic discs coated in a special reflective material that saves data by using a laser beam to burn tiny pits into the storage medium. The leaser reads, saves, and organizes data using tracks and sensors similar to those used in magnetic medium.

Two Types of CDs:

1. **CD-R:** A record-only disc that allows you to record or burn information to the disc one time only. Information saved this way cannot be deleted or rewritten.
2. **CD-RW:** A rewritable CD that allows information to be recorded, revised, updated, or deleted. New data can also be written on the disc just as with magnetic media.

Two Types of DVDs:

1. **DVD-R/RW**: Also known as "DVD dash" can be used to read information only. It cannot rewrite the information.
2. **DVD+R/RW:** Also known as "DVD plus." The +RW suffix indicates that the DVD can be used to record and can also be rewritten. Although most DVDs in the market today can play either format, if you want to record to a DVD, make sure you know the format the DVD recorder requires.

HARDWARE AND PERIPHERALS

Hardware is the name for the physical parts of your computer. Hardware consists of CPU, Monitor, Keyboard, Mouse, Speakers, and Printer. Printers and speakers are often called **peripheral** devices attached to the computer. Speakers help you hear sounds from your computer, such as listening to music.

Central Processing Unit (CPU)

Also called the CPU or simply, the PC. This is what makes a computer work. It is like the brain of the computer and comes with hard drives that processes data into information. It also contains disk drives, and USB Ports to facilitate external data storage on a CD or flash drive. The power switch must be turned on for the computer to work.

Laptop

This is a small, portable personal computer with a "clamshell" form factor; it typically comes with built-in CPU, combined with LCD or LED computer screen mounted on the inside of the upper cover, including keyboard, built-in mouse (located on the flat surface of the keyboard), and USB Port. A typical laptop is displayed on **Fig. 1.7** below. To use laptop mouse, press the flat surface (left-click or right-click). Laptops are folded shut for transportation, and thus are suitable for mobile use. As the name suggests, it is meant to be placed on a person's lap when in use. During 2014, there seemed to be a distinction between laptops and notebooks; currently, you really can't tell the difference. Today, laptops are commonly used in a variety of settings, such as at work, in education, for playing games, web browsing, for personal multimedia, and general home use.

Monitor

Looks like a TV screen where the document you type is displayed for your view. A document viewed on the monitor is called **soft copy**.

- **Desktop:** This is the first screen you see when the computer starts up and the monitor is turned on. A typical desktop with complete computer package is shown in **Fig. 1.8** below. You can also save your files created with any MS office program or information downloaded from the website on a desktop. It can contain folders and documents.
- **Folders and Documents:** Folders help organize the things you save on the computer and can be found on the desktop monitor. Desktop is a drive where folders and files can be saved and may be opened at any time on the monitor.

Keyboard

An input device used to enter data into the computer; and consists of Arrow Keys, Caps Lock, Shift, Back Space/ Delete, and Enter or Return keys. The keyboard also contains function keys labeled **F1** to **F12** located at the top of the keyboard, including other function keys. When you press any of these keys, they produce specific actions in the programs.

Mouse

A device used to navigate around and across the computer screen by moving the cursor to desired locations. It allows you to – click, double-click, click, and drag, and right-click. The mouse is also an input device used to copy information and paste into your document.

Speakers

Computer peripherals that allow you to hear sounds from your computer, such as music. With advancements in technologies within the past 20 years, new computers now come with built-in speakers and microphones. Today's new computers no longer have attached speakers.

Printer

This is an output device attached to your computer PC that prints information displayed on your monitor screen (soft copy) that you cannot touch, and produces a hard copy (printed copy) that you can touch or hold. There are three main types of printers available in the market:

1. **Ink Jet Printers**
    - Inexpensive but ink cartridges are costly
    - Prints in black/white and color
2. **Laser Printers**
    - Highest quality
    - Prints fast in black/white and color
    - Less expensive to operate
3. **Multifunction Printers**
    - Printer, photocopier, fax, scanner in one unit
    - Popular for home and small office
    - Somewhat expensive depending on the size

Fig. 1.6 **Multifunction Printer**

Fig. 1.7 **A Typical Laptop**

Fig. 1.8 **Desktop Computer Package**

Basic Computing Concepts

Figs. 1.9 Speakers (Output Device) Printer (Output Device)

Newer Technologies in Computing

Within the last decades, we have seen tremendous advancements in computer technology particularly in the design and processing capabilities of computers. Today's computers are much faster; the functionalities are built to handle more work at a faster rate, and the retail prices are much better than we had in the late 1990s. Computer PCs, monitors, and laptops now look smaller in size than before making them very easy to carry; we even have wireless mouse. Once upon a time, computers were owned by only the privilege few. Today, the average household in America with young school-aged children can own up to 3 desktop computers or laptops. Computers are everywhere and many people own them now than before. **Table 1.2** below shows new designs of the computers, accessories, and laptops currently sold in the new market economy.

Designs of Newer Computer Technologies

Fig. 1.10 Delll PC

Fig. 1.11 Monitor

All-in-One Beginners Guide to Computer Proficiency | 27

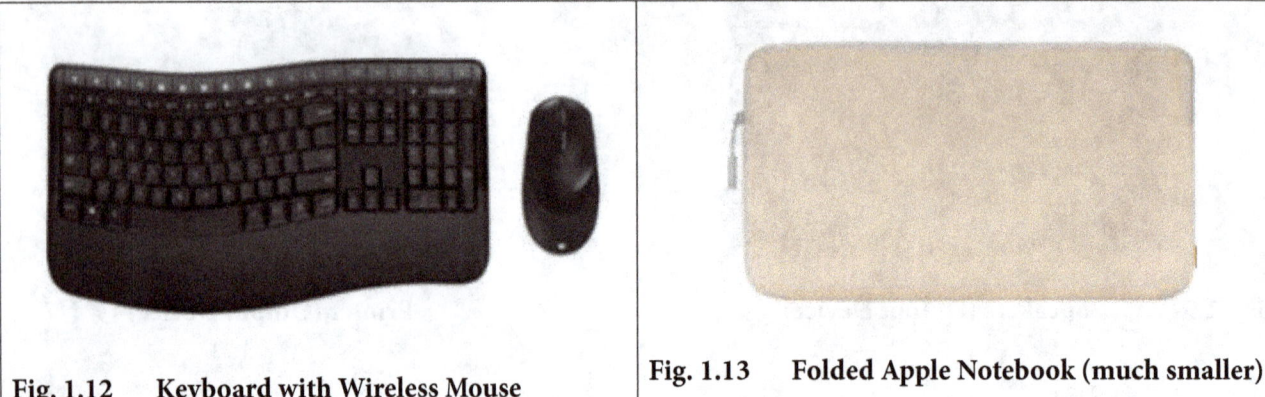

Fig. 1.12 Keyboard with Wireless Mouse   **Fig. 1.13** Folded Apple Notebook (much smaller)

Table 1.2

THE KEYBOARD – TERMS AND DEFINITIONS

Function Keys

These keys labeled **F1** to **F12** are located at the top of the keyboard. When pressed, they perform certain actions in the programs. For example, pressing **F1** will open the help window. Each program uses different function keys for different purposes. Other function keys include:

- **Page Up** — Located under the **Shift key**. Press **Page Up** key to move the cursor to the top of your document.
- **Page Down** — Located directly under the **Shift key**. Press **Page Down** key to move the cursor to the end of your document.
- **Home Key** — Located at top of the keyboard. Press the **Home Key** to move the cursor from right to the left of your document.
- **End Key** — Located at top of the keyboard. Press the **End Key** to move the cursor from left to the right of your document.
- **Insert Key** — Located at top of the keyboard next to the **Delete** key. Press the **Insert Key** to insert a word between words in your document. Press **Insert Key** again to release it from Insert mode.

- **Delete Key** – Located at top of the keyboard next to the **Insert** key and used to delete typed characters. Highlight the word or words to be deleted and press the **Delete** key to delete them.
- **Shift Key** – Located at both lower left and lower right and of the keyboard (5th row), below the **Cap Lock** and **Enter** keys. It is used to type a word in upper case and to highlight a group of typed texts. To type the first letter of your sentence in uppercase, hold down the **Shift Key** and type the word. To highlight a group of words in your document, hold down the **Shift Key** and use the arrow keys to highlight those words.

Navigation or Arrow Keys

These are arrow keys located at the lower right of the keyboard. Press these keys to move the cursor to the beginning of a line, to the end of a line, up the page, down the page, to the beginning of a document, or to the end of a document.

Numeric Keypad (Num Lock Key)

Located at top right of the keyboard, above the keyboard numbers. The **Num Lock** key allows you to type numbers only when it is pressed and turned on (indicated by a green light).

Status Indicators Keys

Included with the numeric keypads are two other keys that perform different functions when turned on, indicated by green lights.

Caps Lock key

Press this key to type in all uppercase letters. Green light indicates the caps lock is on. Press the key again to turn off caps lock and type in lowercase.

Scroll Lock

Located at the top right of the keyboard, the **Scroll Lock** controls the movement of the arrow. When the **Scroll Lock** is turned on, the arrow keys are locked; they can neither move up nor down nor right or left. Press the scroll lock again to release the lock and allow the arrow keys to function.

MOUSE & SKILL-BASED PRACTICE

If you are a beginner in computer technology, learning how to use the mouse can be quite a challenge. A **mouse** is a small device that controls the movement of the pointer or cursor on a computer monitor (computer screen). It is a small object you can roll along a hard, flat surface known as **mouse pad**. The name, mouse is derived from its shape, which looks like the small animal, mouse with its tail that serves as the connecting wire of the computer mouse. The mouse tail connects the mouse to the **PC** that helps the mouse move around on command. A computer mouse contains two buttons (left and right) and a scroll wheel, which can also act as a third button. As you move the mouse, the pointer on the display screen moves in the same direction of your movement across the screen. The primary purpose of the mouse pad is to allow the mouse to easily move across a surface. You can also move a mouse without a mouse pad, but it makes it hard on the surfaces and restricts the flow of movement causing it not to roll as well, which can slow down tasks. Some newer mice in the market today also include a scroll wheel for scrolling through long documents. Newer technologies have also produced wireless mouse without tails and do not need to be connected to the computer to work as shown in **table 1.2- fig. 1.12** above. The wireless mouse comes with a small wireless device that is plugged into the computer USB Port to propel the movement of mouse around the monitor. The two diagrams below illustrate the shape of a computer mouse to the likeness of an animal called mouse.

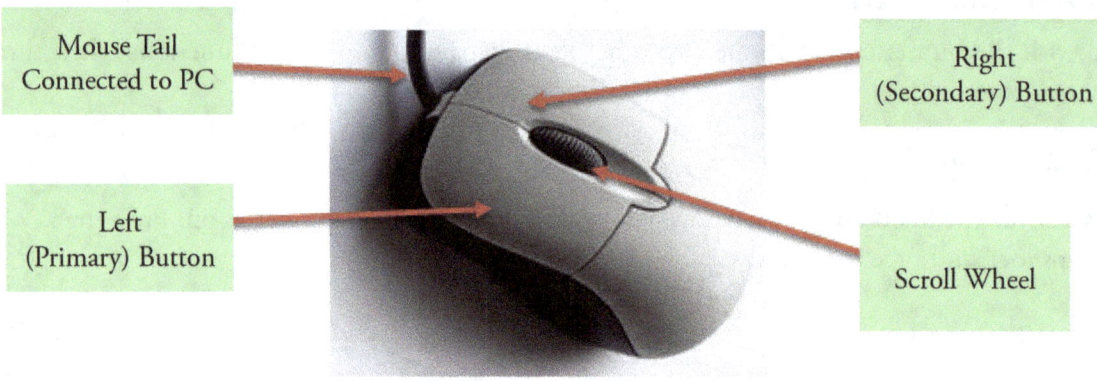

Fig. 1.14   **Computer Mouse**

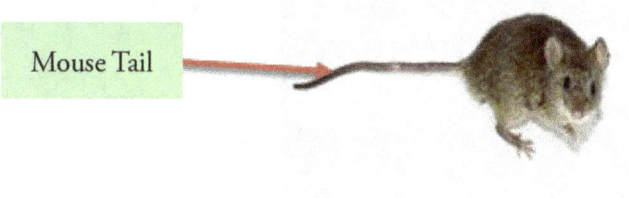

Fig. 1.15 Animal - Rat Fig.1.16 Mouse Pad

In the likeness of a computer mouse

How to Hold a Mouse

You use a mouse sitting in front of a computer with your right hand holding the mouse. If you are left-handed, you hold it with your left hand, which acts the same as it would for a right-handed person. Depending on what task you are performing on the computer, sometimes you do not need to keep holding the mouse unless you are surfing the Internet where you would move it around a lot to navigate your way through the websites or web pages and click where necessary. However, while on the computer, if you need to type text, release the mouse and type, then use the mouse to move around the computer screen to view and navigate through your document.

Rest the heel of your hand on the table of the mouse pad **(fig. 1.16)** above.

1. Hold the mouse loosely with your thumb on the left corner of the mouse with the index finger rested on the primary button and the rest of your fingers (middle, ring, and pinky) lightly covering the right corner of the mouse.
2. The mouse controls the cursor (also known as pointer) on your computer screen.
3. Whenever you move the mouse gently, the cursor will also move.
4. The cursor also changes form depending on how it is clicked. For example, look at these forms of mouse changes on **Table 1.3** below:

AS YOU MOVE THE MOUSE	CURSOR CHANGES FORMS TO
It may look like an arrow	↖
A hand	☝
A straight line	I
And sometimes a double arrow	↔

Table 1.3

Mouse Rules

In order to use the mouse and successfully accomplish simple tasks on the computer, you must follow these simple rules. **Figs. 1.17 – 1.19** in **Table 1.4** below shows how to hold the mouse whether you are left-handed or right-handed.

1. Always keep your index finger on the primary button.
2. To single click, gently press down the primary button and release.
3. To double click, quickly press the primary button twice in a row, then release.
4. Do not take your finger off while double clicking otherwise it is a single click and the task will not be done. For the double-clicking to work, you must leave your finger on the primary button and press down twice quickly.

5. A **click** or left click is done only once with the **index finger** on the **primary button**. For all mouse clicks, including right-click, drag, and drop, see **Table 1.5 (figs. 1.20 -1.23).**

6. A **double-click** is done twice quickly **(fig. 1.21)**, with the **index finger** on the **primary button.**

7. A **right-click** is done once with the middle finger on the secondary button. Right-click is often used to display a short menu list of program commands **(fig. 1.22).**

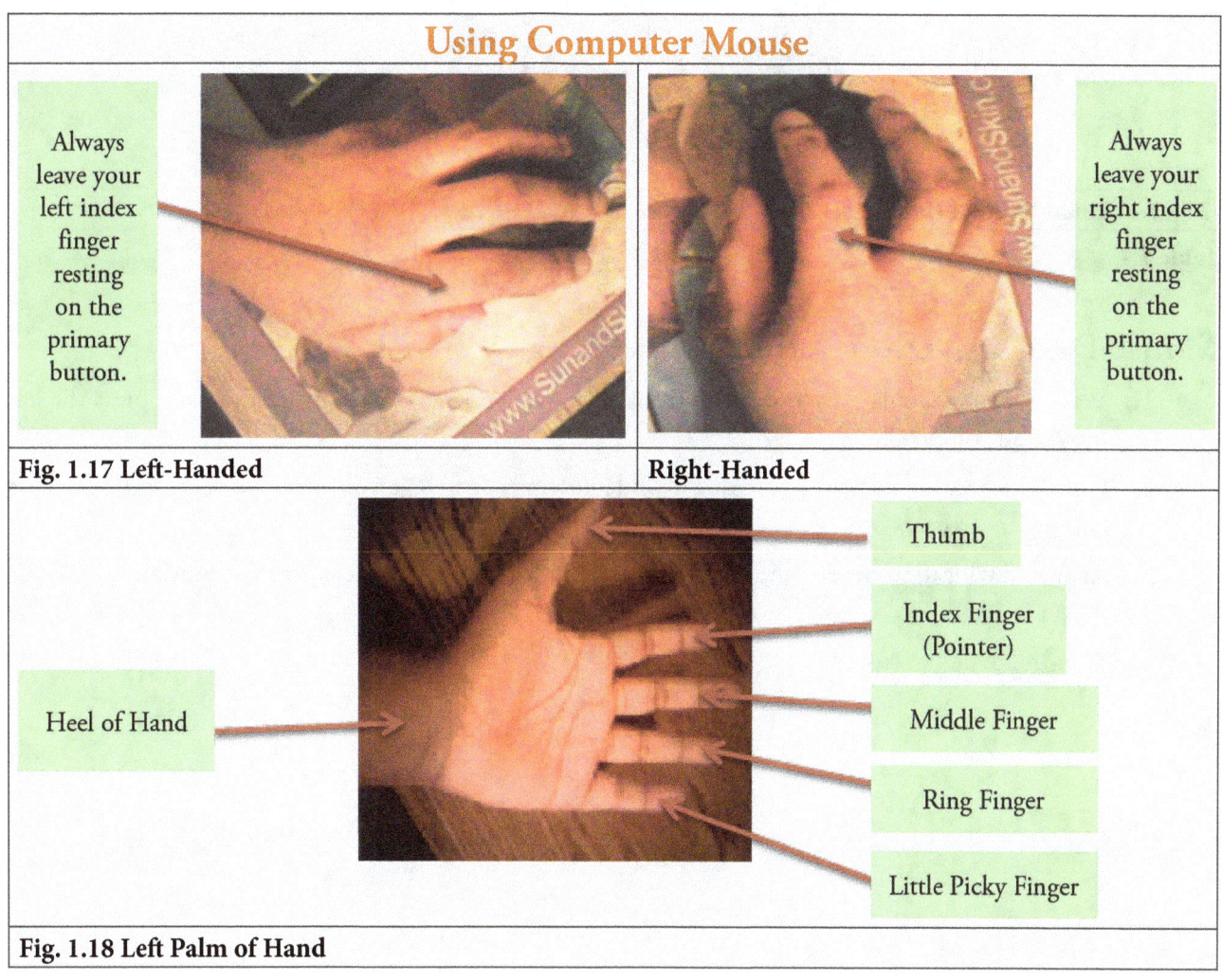

Fig. 1.17 Left-Handed   Right-Handed

Fig. 1.18 Left Palm of Hand

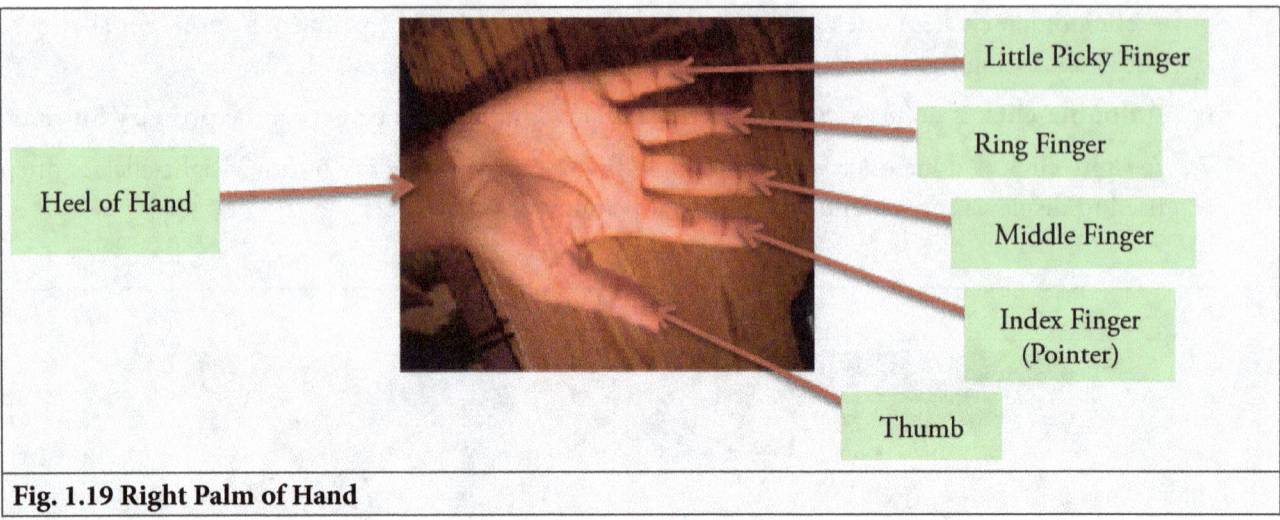

Fig. 1.19 Right Palm of Hand

Table 1.4

Mouse Drag and Drop Action (Table 5: fig. 1.20 – 1.23).

1. With your index finger on the left button, click on the object you want to drag and press the left mouse button down.
2. Continue holding the left mouse down while moving the dragged object to its new location on the computer screen.
3. At the new location, release the mouse button and the object is placed in that location.

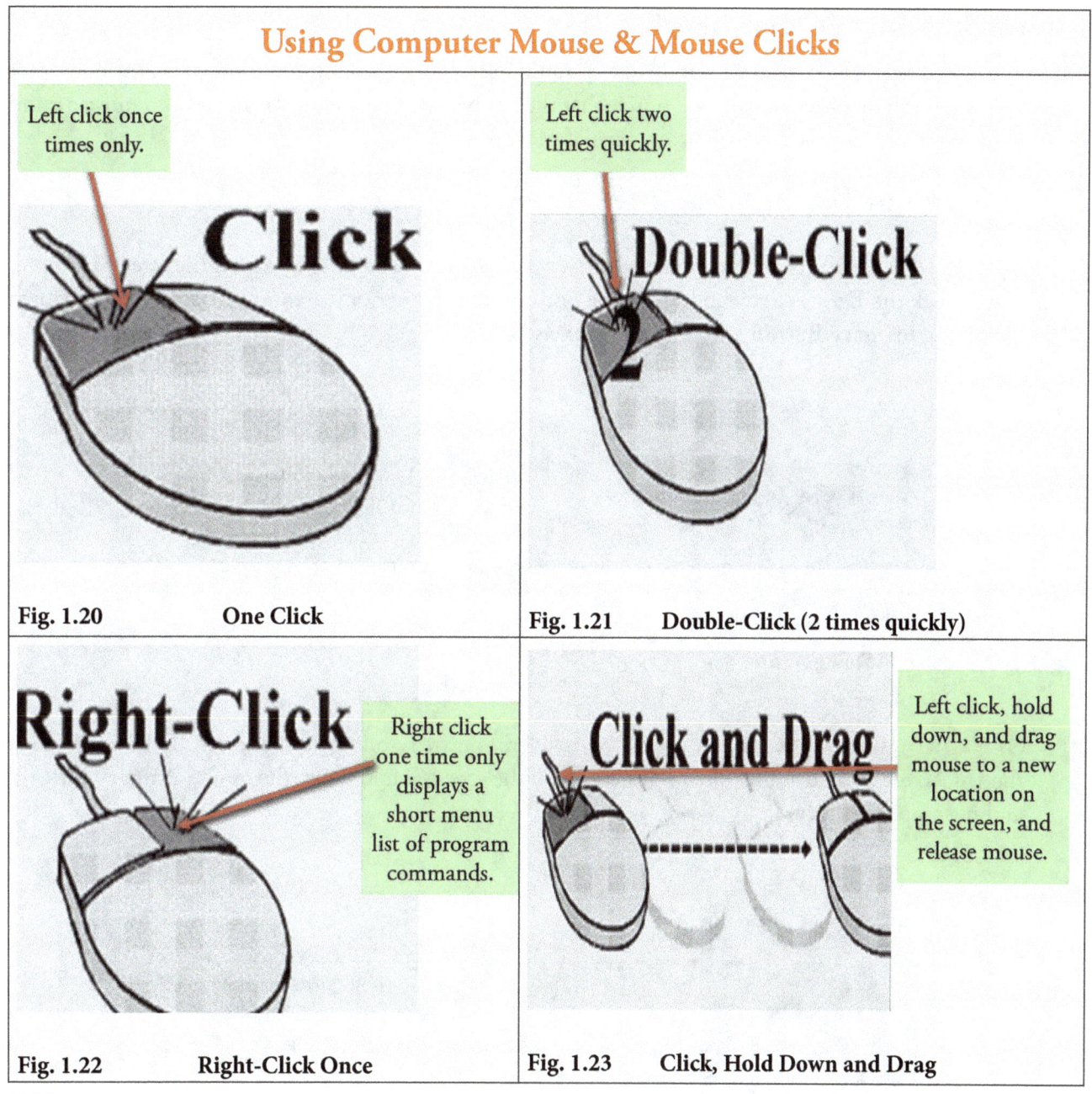

Table 1.5

Mouse Scrolling & Highlighting Text

You can use the mouse to navigate around your computer screen by scrolling up or down on the computer screen. As you scroll up or down, you will notice that the bar between up and down arrows also move up and down allowing you to see the top or bottom page of the screen.

Scroll Down or Up the Computer Screen

Scroll to the Lower Part of a Page: This involves scrolling down on the screen. To scroll down, click the **Down Arrow** located at the bottom right corner of the computer screen. Hold down the mouse **Primary Button** and push down the screen.

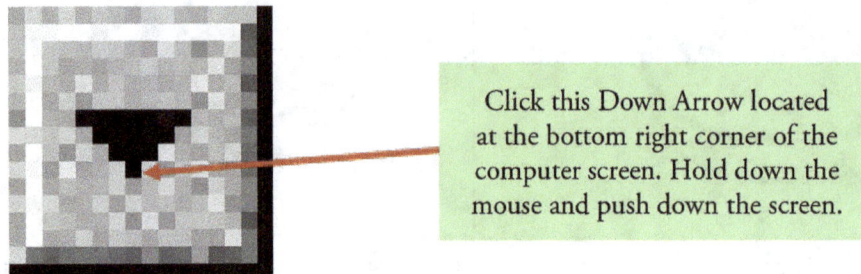

Click this Down Arrow located at the bottom right corner of the computer screen. Hold down the mouse and push down the screen.

Fig. 1.24   **Down Arrow**

Scroll to the Upper Part of a Page: Here you are scrolling up the screen. To scroll up, click the **Up Arrow** located at the upper right corner of the screen. Hold down the mouse **Primary Button**, and push up the screen.

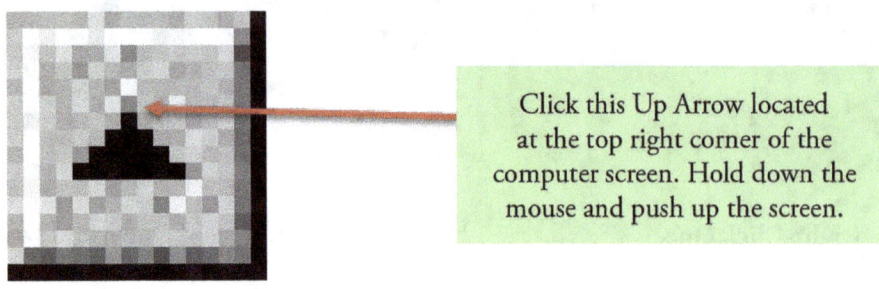

Click this Up Arrow located at the top right corner of the computer screen. Hold down the mouse and push up the screen.

Fig. 1.25   **Up Arrow**

36 | *Basic Computing Concepts*

Scroll Up or Down Simultaneously: This type of scrolling allows you to scroll up or down at the same time. To scroll, click the **Thick Bar** between the **Up** and **Down** arrows. Hold down the mouse **Primary Button**, and push it up or down as needed to see top page up or down page.

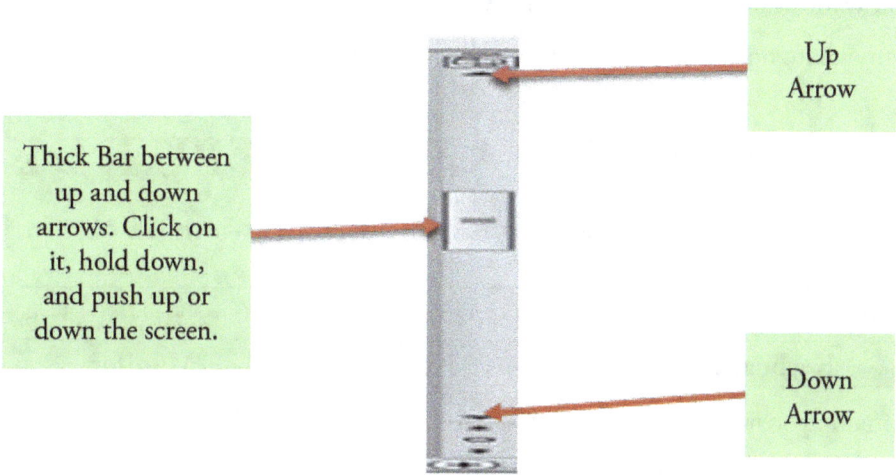

Fig. 1.26   Thick Bar between Up and Down Arrows

Highlight Text Using Mouse

Highlighting text is a way we tell the computer that we want it to copy, move, or format the group of text we have separated. The highlighted text will look different from other text in our document. When words are highlighted, the computer is looking to change only those words. We can then command the computer to change only the text highlighted, such as make corrections by retyping, enlarge, or reduce the type, delete words or move words. Highlighted text changes to sky blue like the diagram below until you click on it.

> You can use the mouse to navigate around your computer screen by scrolling up or down on the computer screen. As you scroll up or down, you will notice that the bar between up and down arrows also moves up and down allowing you the see the page at the top or page at the of screen.

Fig. 1.27   Highlighted Text

All-in-One Beginners Guide to Computer Proficiency | 37

Highlight a Group of Words

1. Place the tip of the mouse pointer at the beginning of the words to be highlighted.
2. Hold down the mouse **Primary Button,** highlight from left to your right, and down until all the text you want to highlight changes to sky blue color.
3. Click anywhere on the screen to remove the highlight.

COMPUTER INPUT AND OUTPUT DEVICES

A complete computer system is composed of two main categories

Input Devices	Output Devices
Keyboard	**Monitor**
<ul><li>Traditional keyboard (the old type)</li><li>Ergonomically correct models – New angled model that is currently replacing the traditional type. It is easy to use and conforms to human body, thereby reducing stress on the arms, wrist, and hand.</li></ul>	<ul><li>Primary output device</li><li>Two categories exist – **CRT** and **LCD**</li><li>Clarity of the monitor depends on the resolution. The higher the resolution, the sharper the image.</li><li>Common monitor sizes for desktop monitors are **17"** and **19"** diagonal.</li></ul>
Mouse	**Printer**
<ul><li>Cabled or cordless</li><li>Trackball – Upside-down mouse that requires little space than the regular mouse. If you have limited space on your desk, consider using a keyboard with trackball. It is designed to simulate a mouse that is turned upside down. As you use your fingers to rotate the ball, the cursor moves.</li></ul>	<ul><li>A printer is usually not included in a computer package; you have to buy it separately.</li><li>Two basic printer options are **Inkjet** and **Laser**</li></ul>

Trackball	Speakers
Keyboard with Built-in Trackball	- Usually included in a computer package when you buy a new computer. - Responsible for producing audio, sounds on the computer.

Table 1.6

DIFFERENCES BETWEEN CRT AND LCD MONITORS

CTR Monitor	LCD Monitor
1. Cathode ray tube – The old type	1. Liquid crystal display
2. Traditional monitor - Large - Bulky - Heavy - Requires a large space to sit on	2. Flat panel – Newer technology

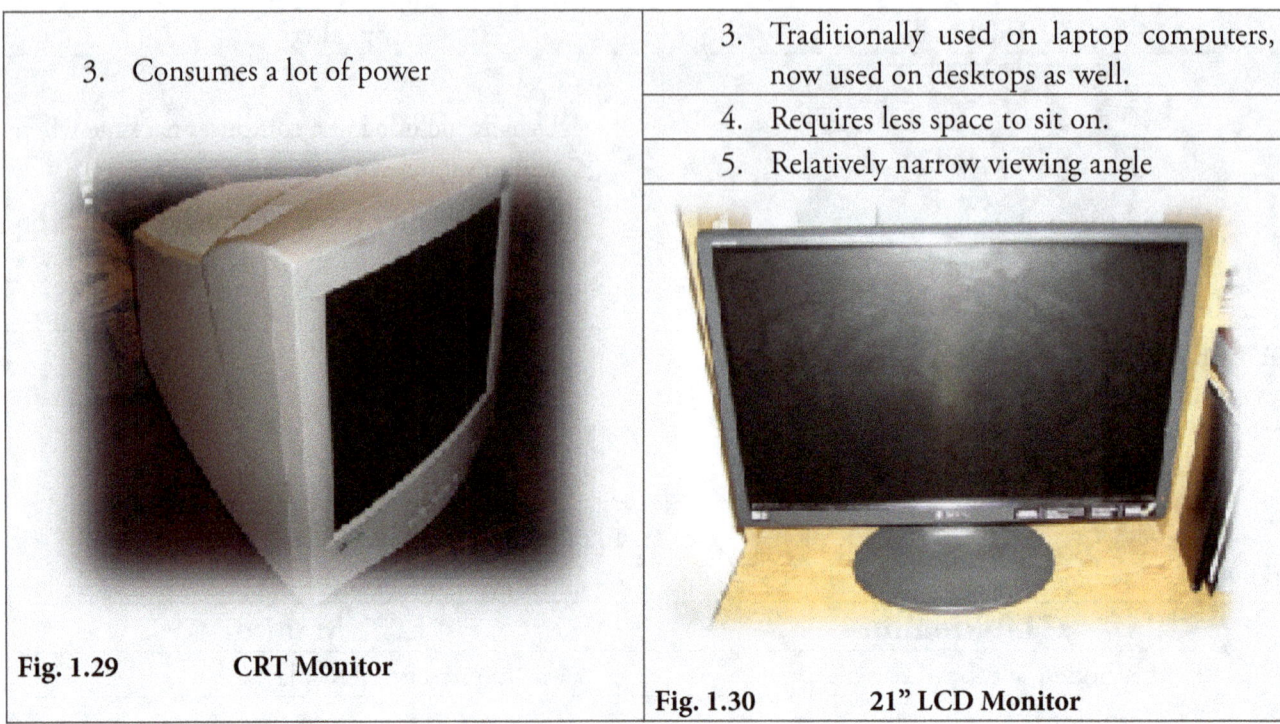

3. Consumes a lot of power	3. Traditionally used on laptop computers, now used on desktops as well.
	4. Requires less space to sit on.
	5. Relatively narrow viewing angle

Fig. 1.29   CRT Monitor

Fig. 1.30   21" LCD Monitor

Table 1.7

THE COMPUTER MEMORY

Memory is a very critical component of the computer located in the system unit. The computer memory plays two important roles; it holds information both temporarily and permanently. Data and programs are temporarily stored in the **memory** while they are being used. Computer memory requires a constant supply of electricity to retain its contents. The two basic types of memory that exist within the computer are **RAM** and **ROM**; both names are derived from their functions as described below:

RAM (Random Access Memory)

This memory acts as the computer's short-term memory and only stores data temporarily as it is being processed. RAM is considered to be **volatile** because this memory is erased when the computer is turned off. The more tasks you perform on your computer at the same time, the more memory is used up in your computer.

ROM (Read Only Memory)

This type of memory is prerecorded on a chip. As the name implies, ROM is a built-in memory that can be read from but not written to. Information on a ROM cannot be changed, removed, or rewritten, and is generally inaccessible to the computer user. Unlike RAM, ROM is considered to be a **nonvolatile** memory because it retains its contents even after the computer is turned off. ROM is used to store the most critical information, such as system startup program, or to boot the computer. The main purpose of ROM is to provide instructions that tell your computer how to boot up. As an operating system, Windows 10 is ROM because it provides instructions that tell the computer what to do. Since the size of the memory affects how fast or slow your computer works, the more space used up, the slower your computer runs. To find out available space in your computer, you have to evaluate the system.

Evaluate the System

1. Click the **Start** button, click **Settings**, and select **Systems**.
2. From the displayed system menu list, click **Storage** and view displayed storage window to see used and free (available) space on your computer.
3. To view all other details about your computer, in the **Storage** window, click **About;** under **Device Specification**, view computer details.

Byte, Kilobyte, Megabyte, and Gigabyte

The computer memory and storage capacities are measured in a unit called **byte**. It is a unit of measurement based on the binary system, representing one character at a time. The smallest binary component is the binary digit called a **bit** which can hold two possible values such as zero or one. A single character or number on the keyboard is made up of several bits called a **byte** which are organized into larger groups of **kilobytes, megabytes**, and **gigabytes.**

- Kilobytes – consists of 1,024 bytes.
- Megabytes – contains approximately one million bytes.
- Gigabytes (GB) – contains one billion bytes.

COMMON FACTS ABOUT COMPUTER VIRUSES, SPYWARE, AND ADWARE

It is a fact universally acknowledged that the Windows world of computers will always be threatened by viruses, adware, spyware, and other varieties of malware. Computer users should be aware that this threat is here to stay; it is not going to magically disappear; all computers would ever remain susceptible to viral attacks. The question should not be *"What can we do to stop them?"* because they will never stop; they are doing their job – attack computers, that's what viruses do. Instead, the question should be, *"What can we do to fight back?"* Regardless of how we choose to handle this fight, one thing remains clear; it would be foolish for anyone to operate a computer without some kind of protection. Protecting your computer from viral attack requires a proactive approach rather than reactive when the damage is already done. Before we plan how to care for our computers, it is important to understand what viruses means, how they get on computers, symptoms of virus, types of viruses that exist, the differences among them, and how to fight them.

What are Viruses?

These are malicious codes or programs that are installed in your computer, usually without your knowledge and against your wishes. Viruses infect a system, then attach themselves to a program or file from where they spread to other users. Some viruses cause certain files in your computer to be corrupted or erased, and others are capable of shutting down a computer and completely erasing the entire hard drive. These malicious programs earn their name (virus) by their ability to replicate themselves locally and often across networks.

How do Viruses Get on the Computer?

Viruses can be distributed to computers in several ways and spread to others. The most common ways are:

1. Sharing infected storage devices such as DVD, flash drive, CD, etc.
2. Sharing files over the Internet or downloading files from unknown authors, music, and other information from the Internet. Whenever you download anything from the Internet onto your computer, you take the risk of getting virus.
3. Sending or receiving email attachments that may contain viruses.

What are the Symptoms of a Virus Infected Computer?

Ordinarily when you first log onto your computer, you may not notice that anything is wrong or recognize the presence of virus. You should suspect viral activity when any or all of the following conditions exist:

- Programs take too long to load, longer than normal.
- Computer locks up often or stops responding to commands.
- Disk drives keep running even when you are not using them.
- Sometimes new files appear on the system; no idea where they came from.
- Strange sounds or beeping noises come from the computer or keyboard.
- Computer restarts automatically every few minutes.
- Computer hard drive constantly runs out of space.
- Files in your computer show strange names you don't recognize.
- Unusual error messages frequently appear and programs act erratically.

Types of Viruses

- **Trojan Horse:** A type of malware that do not duplicate itself or infect other files but can be very problematic in the computer. At first glance, a Trojan horse may appear to be a free, harmless, screen saver program downloaded from the Internet. Unfortunately, free software from the Internet often comes with an unwanted and hidden agenda of its own. After installation, the effects can be similar to those caused by viruses or worms.

- **Worms:** Similar to viruses because of their maliciousness and ability to spread into many computers as worms. Unlike viruses, worms can attack a computer without any human interaction, and are able to replicate themselves so that numerous copies can be sent to other computers. Worms can burrow into an e-mail address book or locate e-mail addresses on files saved to a hard drive, then send themselves out to many computers without help from anybody. When they get to one computer, they repeat the same process again and again, and so the process continues. Worms also have the ability to open a **"back door"** to your computer and allow hackers in with access to control your computer remotely. Some common examples of worms that have created serious problems for users in recent years are Sasser, Blaster, NetSky, and MyDoom.

Spyware and Adware

- **Spyware:** Software designed to capture personal and confidential information about you that resides on your computer system and send it elsewhere without your knowledge. Spyware is as much a problem to your personal life as virus is to your computer system because its primary threat is to your personal privacy and confidentiality. Although not intended to harm computer, it can sometime have such effect on it.

- **Adware:** This is a form of spyware that tracks your Internet browsing and can install malicious cookies on your computer. Adware software has an embedded advertising component--one that displays or downloads ads to your computer even when you don't need them. These ads automatically come along with information you intentionally download from the Internet. One symptom that indicates the presence of adware on your computer is an increased number of pop-up ads you receive, some of which might even address you by name. Adware can generate pop-up ads even when you are not online.

- **What is a Cookie?** This is a small text file that contains information capable of identifying you to a Web site. Cookies are data files stored on your computer that identify and keep track of your preferences. Companies use cookies to track consumer demographics, shopping and web-browsing habits for marketing and advertising purposes. Cookies are also useful for personalizing your Web browsing experience. For example, if you are a frequent shopper on an online store like OfficeMax, you have already created an online account that is password protected. Anytime you return to the site, you are asked to enter your password. Unless the site can identify you by the cookie on your system, you may not be allowed access to that online store. The same principle applies if you are enrolled in a distance education class, cookies might be necessary to verify your enrollment each time you log on to the school website. However, regardless of what good purposes cookies may serve, they can threaten your privacy if used to reveal too much information about you. If you don't want cookies installed on your computer, you can remove them by following these steps:

How to Remove Cookies from Computer in Windows 10

1. Open **Internet Explorer**, click **Tools** at top menu, and select **Internet Options**.
2. In the open options window, click **General** tab
3. Under **Browsing History**, click the **Delete** button.
4. In the open **Delete Browsing History** window, check the box **Cookies and website data**, and click **Delete** button **(fig. 1.31)**.

5. For additional cleanup on your computer, you may also check the boxes of all other listed items on the menu that you want to delete to improve the speed of your computer; then click **Delete** button.

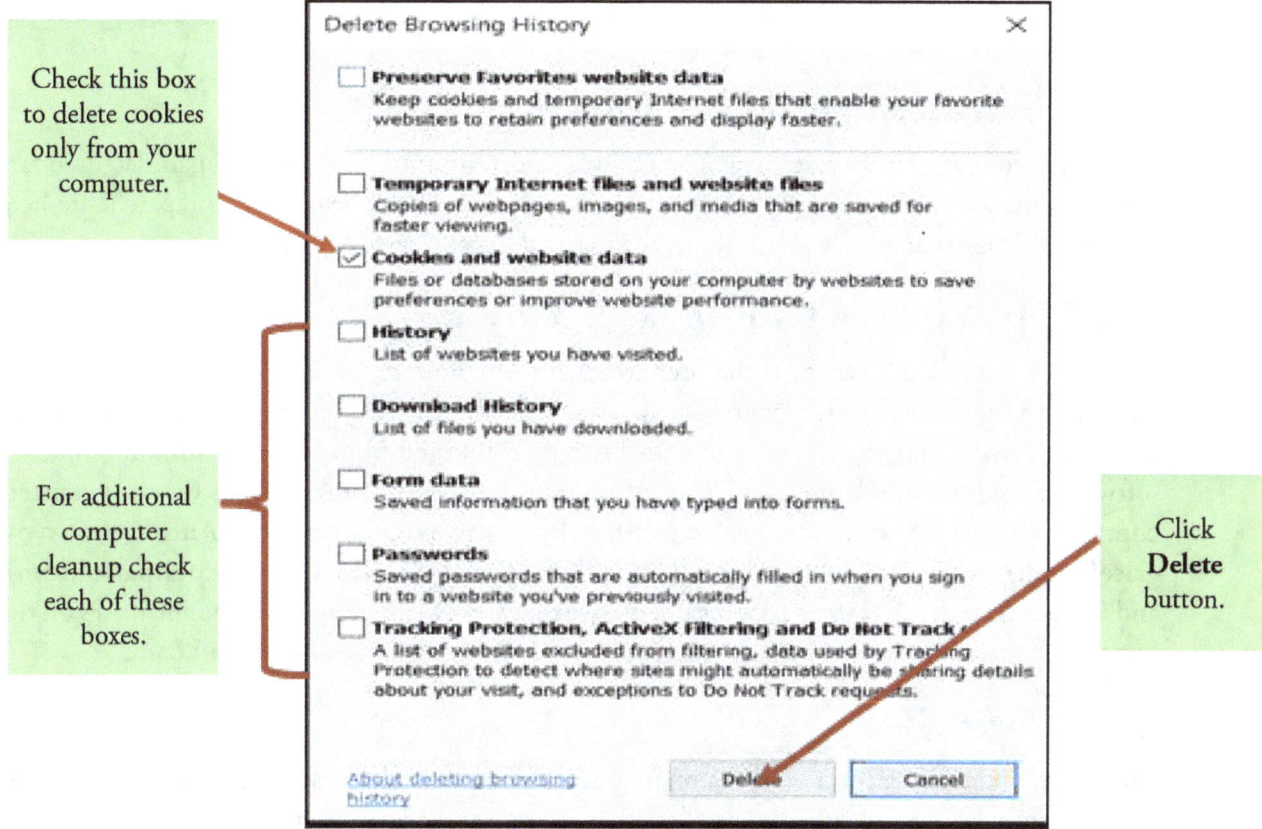

Fig. 1.31   Delete Cookies and Other Browsing History

- **Phishing:** Similar to Trojans, phishing are those schemes on the Internet that trick you into revealing personal and financial data, exploiting the weakness of the person sitting at the computer rather than the computer itself. They are usually fraudulent offers or warnings that arrive via email or instant message demanding that you provide credit card, social security number, password, or bank account information in order to win a certain prize. The personal information being requested is supposed to be used to secure your award and confirm the transaction. This is a scheme, do not fall for it. Once you provide the information requested, the crooks will clear your bank account.

All-in-One Beginners Guide to Computer Proficiency | 45

PROTECTING YOUR PRIVACY AND COMPUTER FROM VIRUSES, SPYWARE, AND ADWARE

1. **Install Software Updates and Patches**

   Protecting your operating system requires regular software update. Software manufacturers are always on the lookout for security threats to their products. They issue updates and patches to help you protect your system. Check for these updates and install them regularly.

2. **Install Antivirus and Antispyware Software**

   Antivirus software is a utility program used to search the computer hard drive and files for viruses, and remove them. Antispyware works in the same way as antivirus but only searches for spyware rather than virus. It is generally recommended that no computer should operate without protective software. Some commonly used antivirus software includes: **Norton AntiVirus (www.symantec.com) McAfee VirusScan (www.mcafee.com), Avira (www.Avira.com), AVG, Anti-Virus (www.grisoft.com).** Antispyware/adware products include **eTrust, PestPatrol (www.pestpatrol.com),** and **Spybot Search & Destroy (www.safer-networking.org).** There are other popular sites on the Internet to search for free computer protection software such as, **www.download.com.**

3. **Install Firewalls**

   These may come in the form of software programs or hardware devices installed to prevent access to your computer. When properly installed, firewalls can make your computer invisible to hackers and other invaders, prevent infections identity theft, and prevent hackers from accessing your computer and turning it into a **zombie.** A **zombie** computer is one that is entirely remotely controlled by hackers, and can be used to spread viruses, spyware, or junk-email known as spam to other computers. If your computer uses Windows 10 or Windows 7 operating systems, be rest assured that you already have firewall installed.

4. Use Caution when Opening Email

Because a great deal of the viruses that attack computers come from email, users should exercise extreme care when opening emails particularly if the sender is unknown. Here are some practical tips to help you decide whether or not to open an email attachment:

a. If you get an email with an attachment from someone you don't know, delete it. Just like you teach a child not to take candy from strangers, you should behave the same with email attachments. Opening such an email is like taking candy from a stranger (accepting an email from a stranger); don't do it, reject it by deleting the email.

b. If you get an email with an attachment from a friend, don't assume that it is harmless. Be watchful, many viruses especially worms spread by automatically sending themselves to the addresses found in the victim's address book. They often include something in the message body that looks like a personal message from your friend.

c. If you are unsure of where an email came from but suspect that it might be from a friend, call or email that friend and ask if he/she sent you an email, and if the friend meant to send an attachment. If the answer is "Yes," then you can open the email and attachment. It may also help if the friend can explain what the attachment is, such as photos of family picnic; it would be safe to open the attachment. If the friend says no, just delete it.

d. Do not make a habit of downloading everything you see on the Internet or entering every wacky sweepstakes to win a few bucks. Keep in mind that anytime you download information from the Internet, you run the risk of bringing in something else (virus) along with it whether you want to or not. Although from time to time people need legitimate information from a particular Web site, be selective about what you download and install on your computer.

Other Necessary Precautions

a. Scan all downloaded programs from the Internet before installing them in your computer.

b. Configure your antivirus software to download automatically at startup of your computer and to run at all times, scanning all downloaded materials, email attachments, and removable media.

c. Make backups of your most important files, such as financial information, family tree, photographs, and other files you can't do without.

CHAPTER SUMMARY & KEY TERMS

A computer is a programmable electronic device that can input, process, and store data. A computer processes data and converts it into information. The definition of a computer is derived from its four basic functions also known as the information processing cycle (IPC). The CPU is the brain of the computer that is responsible for controlling the commands and tasks performed by the computer. The CPU consists of two main parts – the control unit and the arithmetic logic unit (ALU). The control unit is responsible for obtaining instructions from the computer memory, interpreting the instructions, executing them, and coordinating the activities of all the other parts of the computer components.

The computer itself with its entire components is referred to as the system unit, also known as the tower, box, or console. The four basic functions of the computer – input, process, output, and storage, are performed within the system unit. One of the most essential components found within the system unit is the microprocessor chip, also known as the central processing unit (CPU). The CPU is housed in the microprocessor located on the motherboard – a large printed circuit board to which all other circuits within the computer are connected to. The speed of the CPU is measured in megahertz (MHz) or gigahertz (GHz**)**, with a speed in excess of 3 GHz. There are three important factors that determine how quickly a computer processes data: processor (CPU) speed, size of memory, video, and graphics cards. The operating system controls the entire operation of a computer and tells your computer how to act. It can change the way things appear on your screen or desktop. Microsoft Windows 10 and Windows 7 are the most common operating system for PCs. They are the software that control the hardware attached to your computer. They both use a graphical user interface (GUI), graphics or pictures to represent commands and actions. Hardware is the name for the physical parts of your computer. Hardware consists of CPU, Monitor, Keyboard, Mouse, Speakers, and Printer. Printers and speakers are often called peripheral devices attached to the computer. Speakers help you hear sounds from your computer, such as listening to music.

The two main input devices for the computer are the keyboard and mouse. The two main types of monitor for desktop computers are CTR Monitor and LCD Monitor. Output devices include Monitor, Speaker, and Printer. The three main types of printers available in the market are: Ink Jet Printers, Laser Printer**,** and Multifunction Printers. The two basic types of memory that exist within the computer are: RAM (Random Access Memory) which acts as the computer's short-term memory, very volatile, and holds information only temporarily until the computer is turned off. The other type is the ROM (Read Only Memory), which is nonvolatile and retains information in its memory even after the computer is turned off. The computer memory and storage capacities are measured in a unit called byte, a unit of measurement based on the binary system, representing one character at a time.

Protecting your operating system requires regular software update and installation of anti-virus protection. There are some popular sites on the Internet to search for free computer protection software such as, www.download.com. Because a great deal of the viruses that attack computers come from email, users should exercise extreme care when opening emails, particularly if the sender is unknown.

KEY TERMS

Adware
Back door
Browsing History
Cookie
Control Panel
CPU (Central Processing Unit), Volatile
CTR Monitor

kilobytes, megabytes, and gigabytes
Input Device
LCD Monitor
Mouse Pad
Navigation Keys
Nonvolatile
Output Device

Phishing
Primary Button
RAM (Random Access Memory)
ROM (Read Only Memory)
Secondary Button
Spyware
Viruses, Worms
Information Processing Cycle
Trojan Horse

Demonstrate Your Knowledge & Skill

CHAPTER 1 PRACTICE EXERCISES
BASIC COMPUTER CONCEPTS

1.1 – Match listed terms or names to the correct statements below:

1. Navigation or Arrow Keys
2. Numeric Keypad (Num Lock Key)
3. Status Indicators Keys
4. Caps Lock key
5. Scroll Lock
6. Page UP
7. Page Down
8. Home Key
9. End Key
10. Insert Key
11. Delete Key
12. Shift Key
13. Users
14. Peripheral Equipment
15. Computer
16. CPU
17. Speakers
18. Output
19. Software
20. Input Devices

Statements:

a. Located at top right next to Num Lock. Press the key to move cursor to the top of your document.

b. Located directly under Page Up. Press the key to move the cursor to the end of your document.

c. Located under the Home key. Press this Key to move the cursor from left to the right of your document.

d. These are arrow keys located at the lower right of the key-board. Press these keys to move the cursor to the beginning of a line, to the end of a line, up and down the page, and to beginning of a document, or to the end of a document.

e. Located between the Insert and Page Up keys. Press this key to move the cursor from right to the left of your document.

f. Located at top right of the keyboard, above the keyboard numbers. This key allows you to type numbers only when it is pressed or turned on (indicated by

g. a green light).

All-in-One Beginners Guide to Computer Proficiency

h. Included with the numeric keypads are two other keys that perform different functions when turned on, indicated by green lights.

i. Located under the Tab key. Press this key to type in all uppercase letters.

j. Green light indicates that the key is turned on. Press the key again to turn it off and type in lowercase.

k. Located at top right of the keyboard; this key controls the movement of the arrow keys. When the key is turned on, the arrow keys can either move up or down, right or left.

l. Located next to the Delete key and used to erase typed characters. Highlight the word or words to be erased and press this key to erase them.

m. Located at left of the keyboard, below the Cap Lock key. It is used to type a word in upper case and to highlight a group of typed items while holding it down.

n. Located at upper right of the keyboard next to the Home key. Press this key to add a word between words in your document.

o. Raw data processed into useful information

p. A machine used to process data into useful information

q. The brain of the computer system

r. All the input, output, and secondary devices attached to the computer

s. Data entered into the computer

t. Peripherals that allow you to hear sounds from your computer

u. Instructions or programs that run the computer

v. People who use computers

w. Two main peripheral (keyboard & mouse) used to enter text, data, and all other information into the computer

1.2 – Multiple Choices: Select the best answer to computer concepts described below:

1. A system that controls the entire operation of the computer and tells your computer how to act is called:
   a. Hardware
   b. Central Processing Unit (CPU)
   c. Computer Logical Unit
   d. Operating System

2. Which one of the following functions can you perform using the mouse?
   a. Click and drag
   b. Click on an icon
   c. Double-click and right-click
   d. All of the above

3. A part of the computer that looks like a TV screen where the document you type is displayed for your view is known as:
   a. The keyboard
   b. The monitor
   c. The mouse
   d. The speakers

4. A part of computer hardware that is responsible for processing information inside the computer and often considered the brain of the computer is called:
   a. System unit
   b. Function keys
   c. Central Processing Unit (CPU)
   d. Motherboard

5. The most common word processing software used for creating documents and letters is
   a. Microsoft Word
   b. Macintosh Word
   c. Corel WordPerfect
   d. Microsoft Works

6. All the physical parts of a computer such as CPU, monitor, keyboard, mouse, and speaker are collectively called:
   a. The main computer system
   b. Control unit and peripherals
   c. Hardware
   d. Software

7. The main difference between a word processor and a typewriter is that word processor allows you to do all of the following EXCEPT:
   a. Scan text
   b. Edit text
   c. Copy text
   d. Delete text

8. Programs that provide information and instructions for your computer are collectively called:
   a. Management information system
   b. Software
   c. Instructional system
   d. Operating system

9. The first screen you see when your computer first starts up is:
   a. Disk drive A
   b. Computer drives
   c. Desktop
   d. Network

10. The following items are external storage devices EXCEPT:
    a. DVD
    b. CD-RW
    c. Control Box
    d. Jump Drive

11. A place in the computer where you can organize the files you saved is called:
    a. Disk drives
    b. Folders
    c. Desktop
    d. File organizer

12. The main hard drive for your PC is:
    a. D Drive
    b. Desktop
    c. Drive D
    d. Drive C.

13. All of the following things are considered hardware attached to the computer EXCEPT:
    a. printers.
    b. programs
    c. mouse
    d. monitor

14. The primary input device for desktop and laptop computers is a:
    a. mouse.
    b. scanner.
    c. keyboard.
    d. microphone

15. The "mouse pointer" refers to the:
    a. little arrow that is on the bottom of most mice.
    b. connector on the back of the computer to which the mouse is attached.
    c. image on the screen (usually an arrow) that follows the mouse movements
    d. place on the screen where you must leave the cursor when you shut down the computer.

16. Common mouse interactions on the computer include all of the following EXCEPT:
    a. pressing both mouse buttons simultaneously.
    b. clicking.
    c. double-clicking.
    d. right-clicking.

17. Which of the following is NOT an input device?
    a. Keyboard
    b. Mouse
    c. Printer
    d. Track ball keyboard

18. To close a window,:
    a. turn off the computer.
    b. double-click the dark bar at the top of the window.
    c. click on the – in the upper right corner of the window.
    d. click on the X in the upper right corner of the window.

19. The amount of memory that a computer has is measured in:
    a. characters.
    b. inches.
    c. hertz.
    d. bytes.

20. The smallest unit of memory is called a:
    a. pixel.
    b. bit.
    c. byte.
    d. character.

21. CD-R, CD-RW, and DVD are all examples of:
    a. hard copy media.
    b. optical storage media.
    c. magnetic storage media.
    d. random access memory.

22. The hardware unit that houses the CPU is called a:
    a. system unit.
    b. motherboard.
    c. microprocessor.
    d. control unit.

23. A form of storage that is neither magnetic nor optical and has no moving parts is:
    a. DVD.
    b. Flash Drive
    c. CD-R.
    d. CD-RW.

24. A Flash drive is also known as all of the following EXCEPT a:
    a. thumb drive.
    b. USB drive.
    c. zip drive.
    d. pen drive.

25. Turning off the power to your computer system should only be done after:
    a. closing all open programs.
    b. performing a Shut Down.
    c. a POST has occurred.
    d. changing to DOS mode.

26. Although a computer virus may be transmitted in a variety of ways, the most common way to transmit a computer virus is through:
    a. hacking into a machine.
    b. a portable diskette.
    c. an e-mail attachment.
    d. a downloaded program.

27. Which of the following is NOT recommended if you install virus scan software?
    a. Scanning all downloaded files.
    b. Scanning all e-mail attachments.
    c. Having the software scan the computer for viruses every time it boots up.
    d. Setting the software to scan your computer every ten minutes.

28. An especially dangerous program that has the capability to recreate itself, travel across networks, and consume a great amount of system memory (or network bandwidth) is a(n):
    a. Trojan horse.
    b. worms
    c. macro virus.
    d. antivirus.

29. Which of the following statements about malware is FALSE?
    a. Malware is also known as a computer contaminant.
    b. It is a combination of the words malicious and software.
    c. It includes viruses, worms, Trojan horses, spyware, and adware.
    d. It is easily prevented and more a nuisance than destructive.

30. Which of the following statements is NOT a measure for avoiding computer viruses?
    a. Scan all downloaded files and attachments before they are opened.
    b. Realize there is no foolproof way to prevent a computer virus.
    c. Configure antivirus software to load automatically and run at all times.
    d. Keep your operating system current with the latest updates and patches.

31. The best defense against spyware is:
    a. investigate the developer.
    b. report the company responsible.
    c. install effective antivirus software.
    d. realize there is no protection.

32. Firewalls are used for all of the following EXCEPT:
    a. preventing theft of your data.
    b. preventing unauthorized access to your computer.
    c. shutting down your computer in case of lightning.
    d. acting as a barrier between your computer and the Internet.

33. Phishing is described by all of the following EXCEPT it:
    a. involves fraudulently claiming to be a legitimate enterprise (usually a financial institution).
    b. is a very serious crime that involves conning consumers into giving up personal financial information.
    c. is most commonly carried out through the distribution of e-mail messages.
    d. is a crime that is easily addressed through security software.

34. Which of the following statements about Cookies is FALSE?
    a. You have no control over cookies on your machine.
    b. Cookies pose some privacy issues.
    c. Cookies can be helpful in speeding up your access to Web sites.
    d. A cookie can accumulate information about your visits to a specific Web site

1.3 – Fill-in the blanks with correct words or terms for the statements and descriptions below:

1. Powering on your computer is called _____.
2. The _____ is the computer system's primary output device.
3. Computer monitors fall into two basic categories, LCDs and _____.
4. In computer monitors, the higher the _____, the sharper the image.

5. _____ printers are relatively inexpensive to purchase but are correspondingly expensive to operate due to the cost of ink cartridges.

6. _____ printers offer the highest resolution and speed of the various printer types.

7. The CPU's processing speed is measured in terms of megahertz or _____.

8. The system area where programs and data are temporarily kept while in use is called _____.

9. RAM is considered _____ meaning it will lose its contents if there is an interruption in the supply of electricity.

10. _____ is built-in memory that can be read from, but not written, and its purpose is to provide instructions that tell your computer how to boot up.

11. The most common computer storage device is the _____ folder, for example a hard disk or flash drive.

12. Digital cameras, digital cell phones, notebook computers, and other portable computer devices use _____ memory in the form of sticks, cards, or drives.

13. When setting up a new computer, it is important to keep all the _____, save all CDs, disks, and understand the warranty information.

14. Most software vendors provide their software on _____ media.

15. _____ memory is a form of portable storage that is neither magnetic nor optical.

16. To protect your computer from possible damage by a lightning storm you should plug your computer into the wall power via a(n) _____.

17. Most types of _____ software can be configured to update automatically for protection against known hazards.

18. Computer _____ don't occur naturally; they are maliciously written by individuals' intent on challenging networks and demonstrating their computer skills.

CHAPTER I SKILL-BASED PRACTICE PROJECTS BASIC COMPUTER CONCEPTS

1.1 Identify Computer Parts: The image below is a complete desktop package. Following the pointed arrows, enter the name of each part inside the boxes provided, 1-4. On the textbook, enter your name and date at top page of completed work; photocopy, and submit for instructor grading.

1.2 Description of Computer Parts: On the left column of the table below, enter the name of each computer part you identified in item 1.1 above; and provide a description of the item on the right column of the table. On the textbook, enter your name and date at top page of your completed work; photocopy, and submit for instructor grading.

Computer Parts	Description
1.	
2.	
3.	
4.	

1.3 Identify Types of Monitors: Provide the descriptive classification name for monitor types A and B. Enter your answers inside the boxes above the images. On the textbook, enter your name and date at top page of your completed work; photocopy, and submit for instructor grading.

A. [   ]   B. [   ]

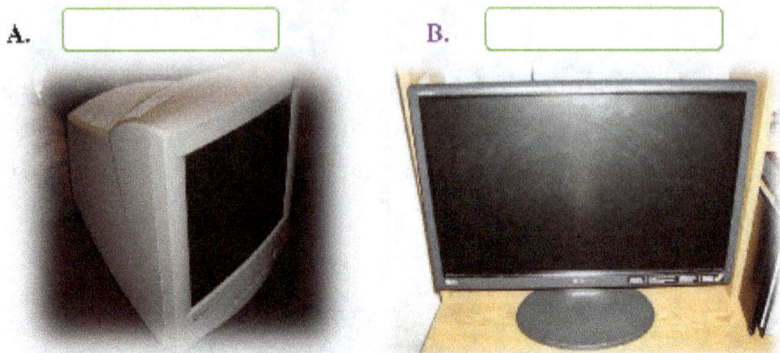

1.4 Input and Output Devices: Using the table below classify the five listed items either as input or output devices by places them in the correct column on the table. On the textbook, enter your name and date at top page of your completed work; photocopy and submit for instructor grading.

1. Keyboard
2. Monitor
3. Mouse
4. Printer
5. Speakers

Input Devices	Output Devices

CHAPTER 2

INTRODUCTION TO MICROSOFT WINDOWS 10

Windows 10 is Microsoft's most recent operating system packed with user-friendly features that allow people to enjoy the experience of computer technology. The newest version of Windows in the marketplace is Windows 11. Although many users are still skeptical about Windows 11, most newer computers some people purchase today come with Windows 11 already installed. Windows 10 PC contains RAM supported by the 32-bit version of Windows 10 with 4 GB. The file system uses a 32-bit numbering system to increase the number of data blocks that can be managed and organized as part of a single partition. This file system is known as FAT32. When you open Windows 10, at first glance, and from the Start button, you will notice many varieties of Apps that make it easier for users to quickly lunch programs at their fingertips. The familiar Start menu we know from Windows 7 is back, but with some improvements which includes a space for users to personalize their favorite apps, programs, people, and websites. To display the **Start** menu, click **Start** in the lower-left corner of the taskbar. Alternatively, press the **Windows logo** button on your computer keyboard to display the Start menu, and press it again to get off the Start menu.

Learning Objectives:

After completing this chapter, you will be able to:

- Explore and navigate Windows 10 desktop, and identify the unique features of Windows 10 apps for quick access to your programs.
- Know the difference between an operating system and application software.

- Manage programs and items by pinning them to the taskbar.
- Personalize and customize Windows 10 desktop background using color themes, display settings, screen resolutions, and date/time change.
- Create user accounts, modify accounts, and manage user accounts.
- Manage files by creating new folders and subfolders, copy files from one location to another within your computer.
- Rename folders, view, arrange folders, and create subfolders within main folders.
- Search for files in your computer using the Search Box.
- Improve the health of your computer with regular maintenance using MS Windows Updates.

What is Windows 10?

Windows 10 is software that runs the operating system of your computer which controls the hardware attached to your computer including its memory and **central processing unit (CPU)**. It is similar to other Windows versions because they are all designed to use a **graphical user interface (GUI),** graphics or pictures to represent commands and actions. A **GUI** is a component of the Windows that uses graphics or pictures to represent the commands and actions on your computer that allows you to see document formatting on the screen as it will look like when printed on paper.

What is the Difference Between Operating System and Application Software?

Operating System: An operating system is software that provides instructions that tell your computer what to do when prompted. For example, save a document, print, or copy/paste text in your document are all controlled by the operating system. Versions of operating systems in today's technology marketplace are MS Windows 10, MS Windows 7, and MS Windows 11 (the newest version). A common feature with all these Windows versions is that they all use a **graphical user interface (GUI)**, graphics or pictures to represent commands and actions. The operating system comes permanently installed on your new computer and its read-only memory. This means you do not have access to type, edit, or change anything on it. It can change the way things appear on your screen or desktop. The operating system provides commands that allow you to use Microsoft Office suites like MS Word, Excel, and PowerPoint. Operating system software also controls the hardware attached to your computer.

Application Software: This is software such as Microsoft Office suite, an application program used to create documents with Word, record accounting information with Excel; and create business presentations with PowerPoint. Without the operating system, application programs installed on your computer cannot work. You can work on a computer without application software, but you cannot work on a computer without an operating system because it is the brain of the computer that makes it work.

Unique features of Windows 10

- **Quick Links to frequently Used Apps:** Located at the left side of the Start menu, there are quick links to PC settings that allow you to personalize your computer desktop to your preference. To view a list of your apps, click **Start Windows** logo button and scroll through the alphabetically displayed list. Some apps are in folders within the app list, for example, the **Notepad** is located in the **Windows Accessories** folder.

- **Improved File Explorer Window:** Each file window contains a ribbon at top of the Explorer as shown in **fig. 2.1** below. This feature gives you the option to either **Save, Copy/Paste, Print,** create a new folder and organize your most frequently used files for quick access.

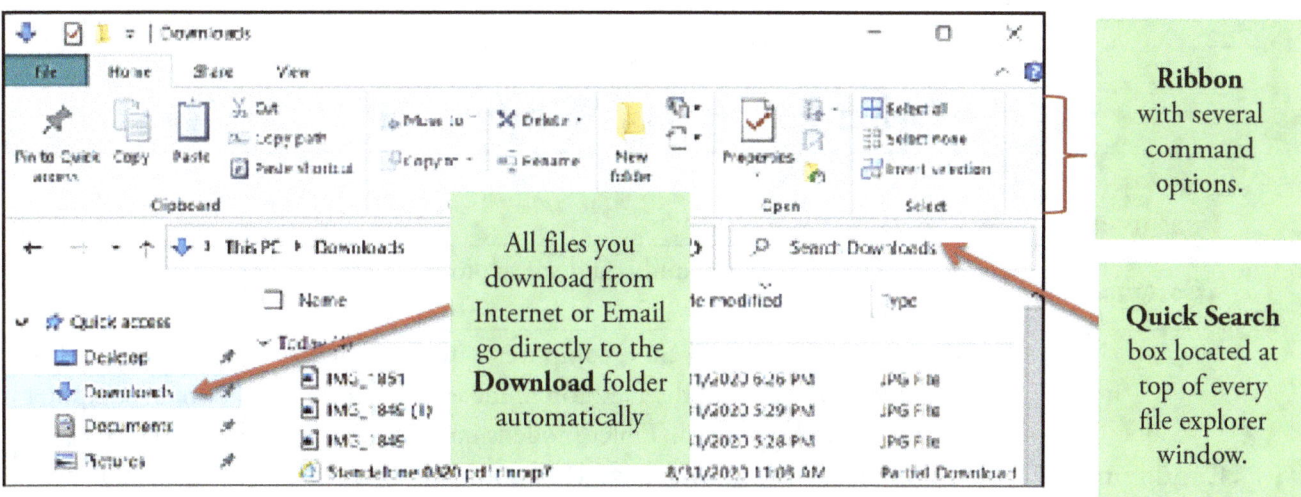

Fig. 2.1   File Explorer Window – Downloads Folder

- **Quick Search Box:** As in previous Windows versions, the search box also found at the taskbar of Windows 10 is now improved on each Explorer window and placed under the ribbons. In the **Search** box, type your key word and notice that once you start typing your search, all files you have previously created matching your description in the Search box or programs will automatically display. Click the **Search** button to complete your search.

- **Pinned Favorite Items:** You have the option to place your favorite or most frequently used apps where you want them for quick access. To pin your favorite apps or icons to the taskbar, follow these quick steps:

  1. Click **Start** button to display a list of Windows apps at left side of computer screen.

  2. Navigate the list to find your favorite app and right-click the app you want to pin.

  3. From the displayed menu, click **Pin to Start**. Your selected app or program will appear on the **Taskbar**.

Fig. 2.2   **Pinn Favorite Items to the Taskbar**

Other Features of Windows 10

Windows 10 Features	Description & Function
Cortana	Windows feature that uses audio and speech to interact with a user when searching for information.
Continuum	If Windows 10 is installed on a computer with a touch screen, it can be used in desktop mode or tablet mode. Desktop mode is designed for a traditional computer with a mouse and keyboard. Tablet mode is optimized to make touch screen easier by making icons larger. Windows 10 automatically adjusts the display and input methods depending on the form factor being used. When a keyboard is detached or folded away, the device automatically switches to tablet mode. This automatic switching between modes is called **Continuum**.

66 | *Basic Computing Concepts*

Virtual Desktop	A new feature in Windows 10 which allows the user to create multiple desktops that can host different open windows.
Modern Standby	A Windows 10 feature that allows a device to sleep but continue to perform basic tasks like downloading Windows updates.
Processor Affinity	The term used to describe a situation where a thread (series of system actions) is not finished running, perhaps because it had to wait or it was preempted, it is typically restarted on the same processor that previously ran it.
Hyperthreading	A type of CPU with built-in extra hardware to allow more than one thread to be processed at the same time on a single CPU.
Plug and Play Technology	Technology which assumes that hardware components can be connected or activated at any time while the operating system is running.
Virtual	A type of disk that can be stored in a single file on a physical disk.
Client Hyper-V	A Windows 10 feature you should use if you want to run an older application on an earlier version of Windows on the same computer you use to run Windows 10.
Domain	A collection of computers and users that are identified by a common security database.
Preemptive	A term used to describe system multitasking that allows a single process to be interrupted by another process, even if the first process has not completed.
Dynamic Link Library	A file that holds application code modules.
Remote Assistance	This is a stand-alone application that comes with all versions of Windows 10. A user can ask for help from a trusted professional over the network using email, file transfer, or the Easy Connect service which allows a computer to be discovered over the Internet using a generated password and the IPv6 network protocol. With the unique password your computer is identified on public servers configured to support this service. The professional service provider can connect to chat, transfer files, run diagnostics, reconnect across reboots, and help you with any troubleshooting issues.

Table 2.1

EXPLORE, NAVIGATE, AND UNDERSTAND WINDOWS 10 DESKTOP FEATURES

Windows 10 is Apps driven as you can see once you setup a new computer. From the Windows Store these apps now open in the familiar format that your desktop programs do. When you first open Windows 10, the desktop will appear as the image on **fig. 2.3** below. You can change the look of your desktop using the **Personalized** option to be covered later in this chapter. Windows 10 comes with several themes you can choose from to personalize your computer. A complete description of Windows 10 desktop features and their functions is presented on **Table 2.2** below.

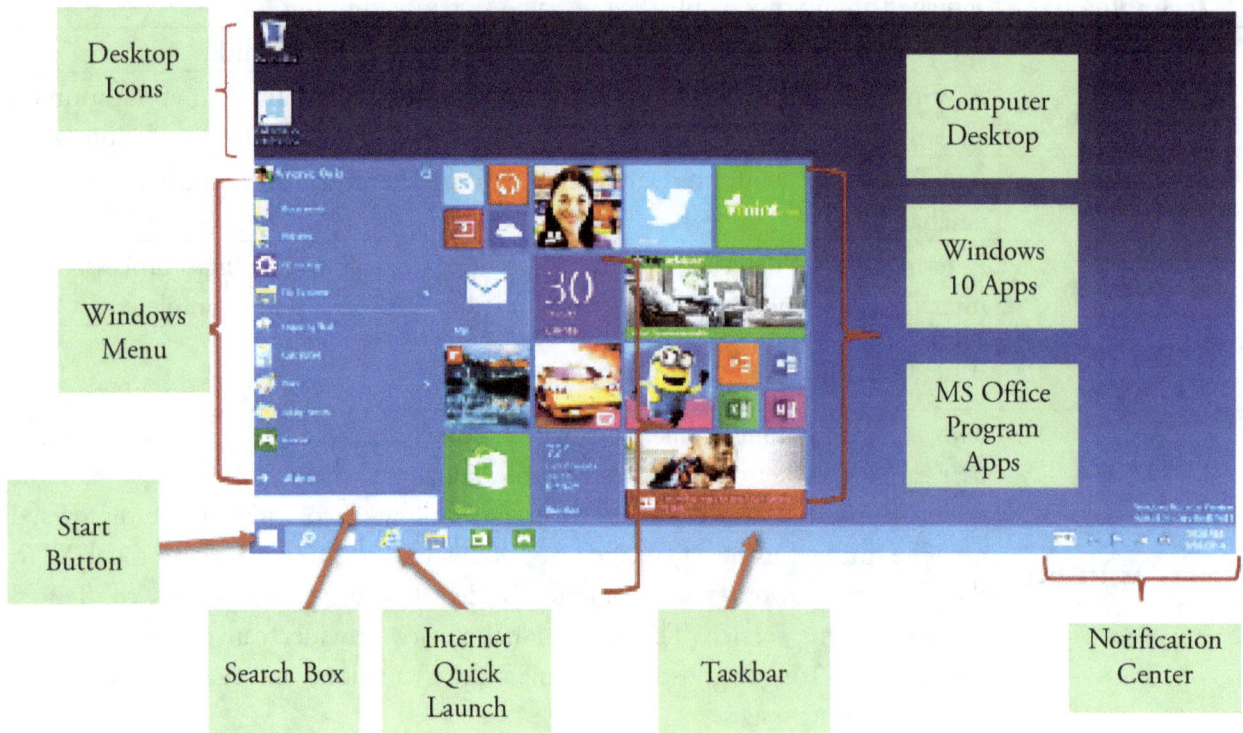

Fig. 2.3   **Windows 10 Desktop**

68 | *Basic Computing Concepts*

Parts of Windows 10

Parts	Description
Desktop Icons	These are some program icons that come with a new computer such as Internet Explorer icon and the Recycle Bin.
Computer Desktop	The computer home screen; it is the first screen that displays once you open your computer.
Windows Menu	Location of Windows accessories, programs, and PC settings.
Windows 10 Apps	Provides quick access to opening desktop apps when you click the app of your choice.
Start Button	Location of all Windows 10 settings options.
Search Box	Used for quick searches. Click inside the box, start typing the keyword of your search, and watch words matching the keyword begin to appear.
Internet Quick Launch	A quick way to open Internet Explorer by clicking the icon.
Taskbar	Located at the bottom of the desktop, opened programs that you are currently working on display on the taskbar.
Notification Center	Contains program icons that provide notifications, instructions, and important updates about your computer.
MS Office Program Apps	Provides quick access to opening MS Office programs when you click the Office program of your choice..

Table 2.2

Taskbar

The taskbar in Windows 10 has been completely redesigned and made larger to allow more space for the opened programs you are currently working on, including some Windows apps, and room for additional apps you may want to pin to the taskbar. An additional feature is also included on the taskbar to hide icons and apps that are not visible on the taskbar which can be viewed as needed by clicking on it. To help you easily manage and access your most important files and programs, the **Taskbar** buttons have been given a new look to do more than just show you which programs are running. In the default view, each program appears as a single, unlabeled button. If multiple items of a program are open, the taskbar remains clean and uncluttered. You can click on individual buttons for each open file to view it at any time while working on a different program. You can also rearrange and organize buttons on the taskbar, including pinned programs.

You can also run programs that are not pinned so they appear in the order you prefer. To rearrange the order of buttons on the taskbar, drag a button from its current position to a different location on the taskbar. You can rearrange buttons as often as you like.

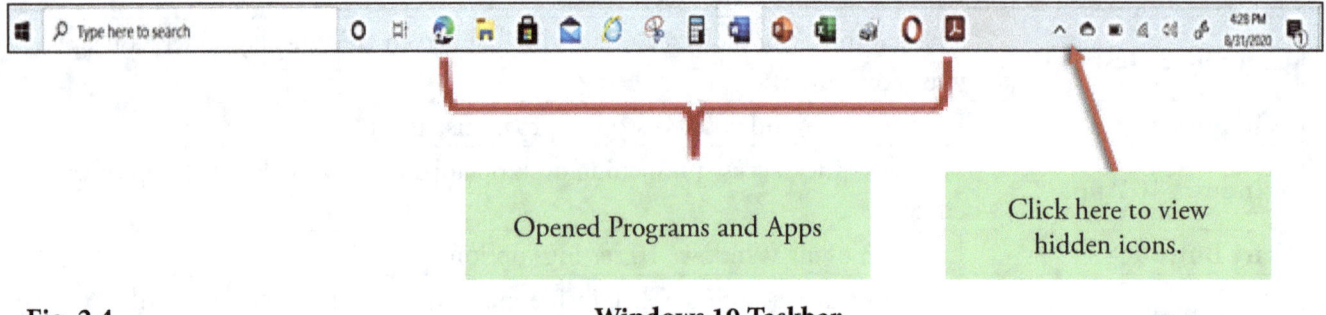

Fig. 2.4   **Windows 10 Taskbar**

Notification Center

By default, the notification area is located on the right side of the taskbar and contains program icons that provide status and notifications about things like incoming email, updates, and network connectivity. When you install a new program, you can sometimes add an icon for that program to the notification area. New computers often come with icons already in the notification area and some programs automatically add an icon to the notification area during installation. In Windows 10, you can see the number of notifications on your computer. The new way of managing notification area at the end of the taskbar means you have the option of clearing the notifications you don't need. In earlier Windows versions, the notification area could sometimes become cluttered with icons. With Windows 10, you can declutter the notification area by clearing the items you don't need to read. The last icon at bottom right of the taskbar is the notification icon which displays empty when there are no messages and brightens up with the number of notifications when it contains messages (**fig. 2.5**).

<u>Notification Icon when there is no message</u>   <u>Notification Icon when there is a message</u>

Fig. 2.5   **Notification Icons**

Managing Notifications: When you receive notifications on your computer, make sure to read them because they may contain important information about system and program updates that are necessary for the health of your computer. The message appears at top of the notification area. You can take one or more of the following actions in response to notifications:

1. Click the **Notification** icon to display the message (**fig. 2.6).**
2. Read the message and ensure it's from a trusted site, usually Microsoft Corporation.
3. Follow onscreen instructions and perform actions required to keep your computer safe.
4. Click **Learn More** for more details about the message or click **Dismiss** if you don't really want to know.
5. Click **Clear All Notifications** if you don't care.

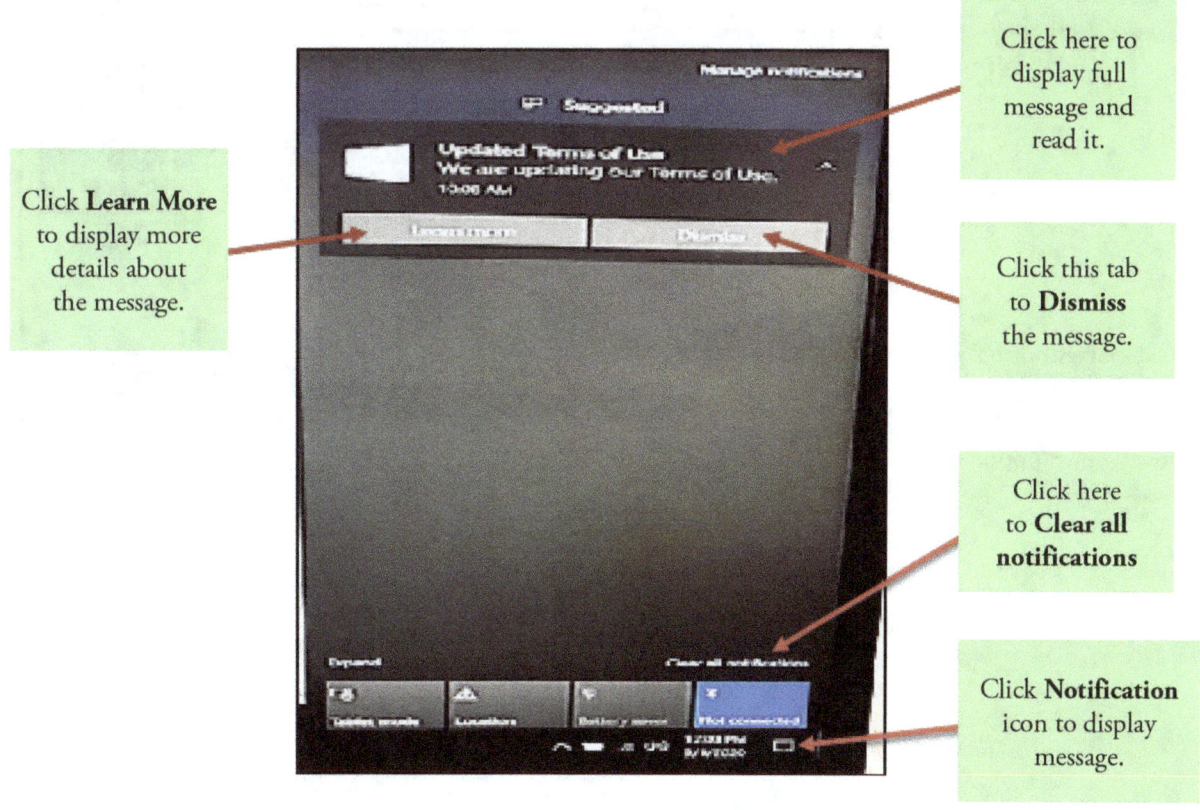

Fig. 2.6   Notification Center

Power Options

When you click the Power button, a list of options displays allowing you to choose what you want: sleep, shut down or restart your device. **Fig. 2.7** shows various power quick link options you can choose to power off your computer and how to use them.

Fig. 2.7   **Quick Links & Power Options**

72 | *Basic Computing Concepts*

Verify that Windows 10 is Installed on your Computer or to Find out what Version of Windows is Installed

1. Click **Start** button, place your mouse on **Settings,** and click **Documents** at left of your computer.
2. In the open **Document** window, at left pane, navigate down the list, and right-click on **This PC**.
3. From the displayed short menu, click on **Properties (fig. 2.8).**
4. The version of Windows on your computer will be displayed for your view **(fig. 2.9).**

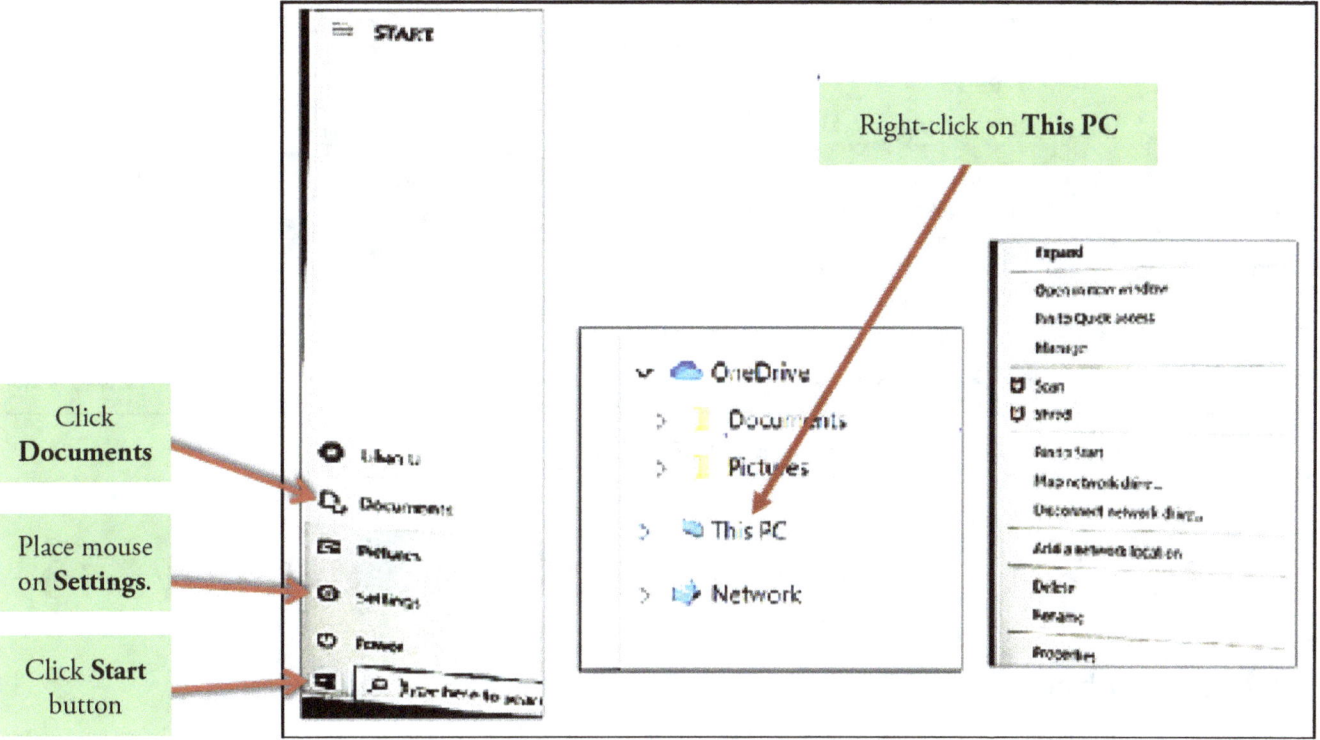

Fig. 2.8   **Verifying Installed Windows Version**

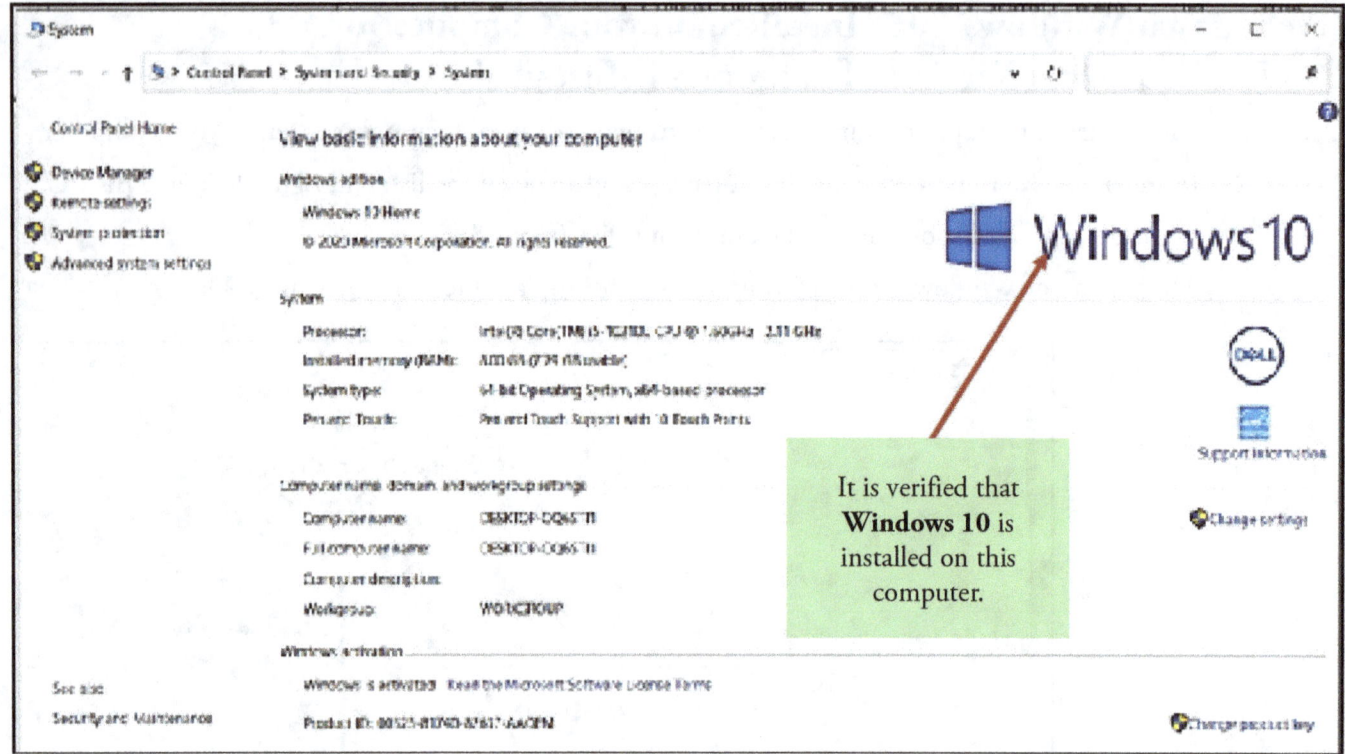

Fig. 2.9 Windows 10 Displayed

PERSONALIZE & CUSTOMIZE WINDOWS 10

What is a Theme?

A theme is a combination of pictures, colors, and sounds on your computer. It includes a desktop background, a screen saver, a window border color, and a sound scheme. Personalizing windows involves changing the overall theme and the way items appear on your computer desktop. Some themes may also include desktop icons and mouse pointers. Windows 10 comes with several themes you can choose from to personalize your computer. Windows 10 also contains other basic themes that allow you to customize your computer. For example, if your computer requires a **high-contrast** theme to make items on your screen easier to view, you can click that theme to select it and apply to your desktop. You can also change a theme's pictures, colors, and sounds individually to create a customized theme. You can change individual parts of a theme (the pictures, colors, and sounds), and then save the revised theme for your own use or to share with other people.

Personalize Your Desktop (fig. 2.10)
1. On your desktop, right-click anywhere to display Windows settings,
2. From the displayed short menu, select **Personalization** to display personalization options.
3. If you already have personal color or slideshow to use as your desktop background, click the down arrow of **Picture** box under **Background** and click on the color. The selected color or slideshow will appear on your desktop background. <u>**Note:**</u> To use this option, your selected color or slideshow must already be saved on your computer.
4. If you want to use system basic backgrounds, under **Choose your picture**, click on any of the basic themes provided.
5. If you have a specific background downloaded from Microsoft website and saved on your computer, click **Browse** to select that background.
6. Whatever option selected, when finished, your desktop background will change to your new selection.
7. To change **Contrast Settings**, repeat **step 1** above, from the displayed Windows settings **(fig. 2.10)**, under **Related Settings**, select either **High Contrast Settings** or **Sync Your Settings** link depending on the type of customization you want.
8. Follow simple onscreen instructions to achieve the customization you want.

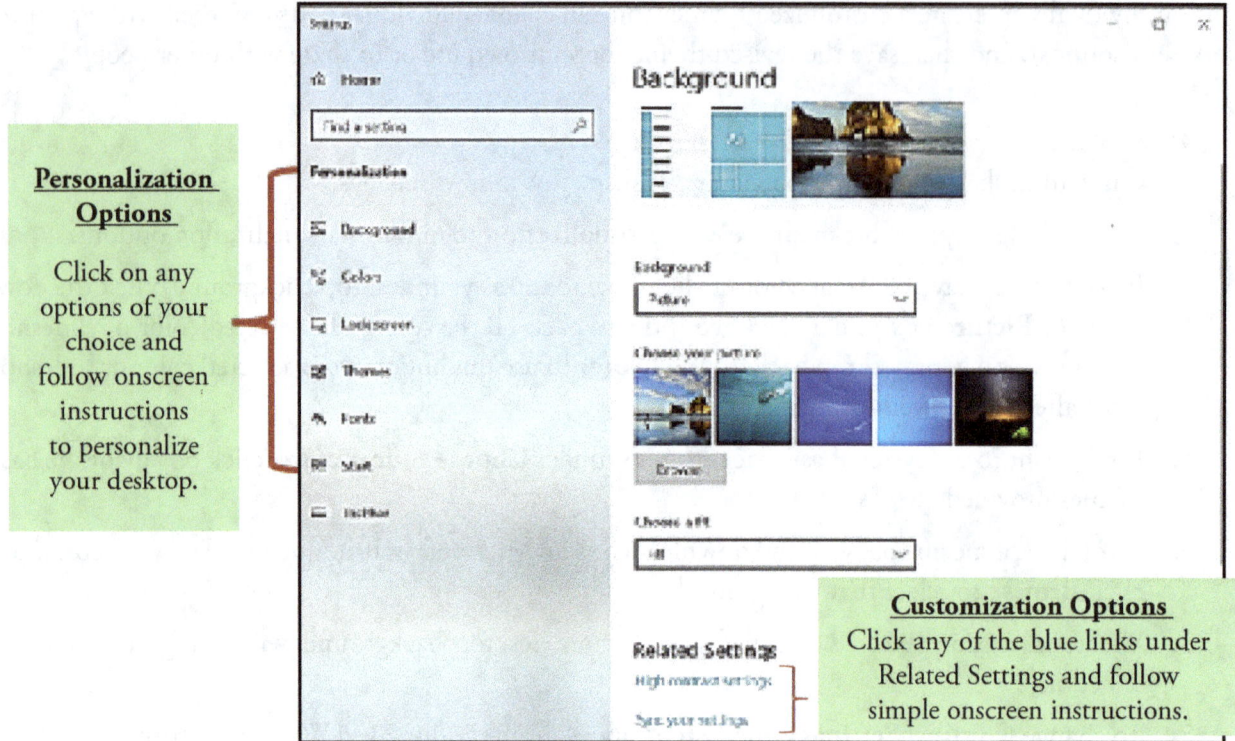

Fig. 2.10   **Windows Personalization Options**

Additional Desktop Customizations or Computer Settings

1. For additional customization, right-click anywhere on the desktop to display Windows settings, see **(fig. 2.11)** below. .

2. From the displayed short menu, select **Display Settings** to view a variety of customizations options at left pane of the **Settings** window.

3. Follow onscreen instructions to customize your computer. These are simple instructions ranging from **On** or **Off** to just moving a sliding scale while holding down your mouse.

More Customization Option

Select an option from the left pane menu and follow simple onscreen instructions to customize your computer or desktop.

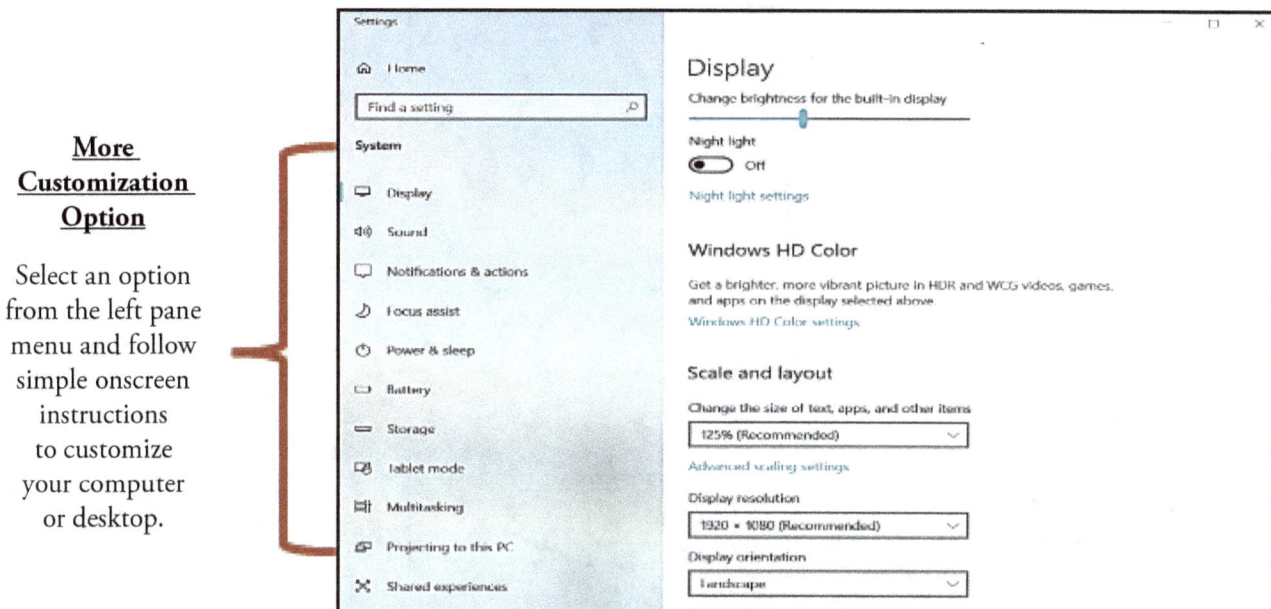

Fig. 2.11   **Additional Customization Options**

4. For all other settings you want to change or customize on your computer, click **Start** button.

5. From displayed icons on the left, select **Setting (fig. 2.12)** to open settings window which contains a gallery of all personalization and customization options for your computer.

6. From the open settings window, click the option you want and follow simple onscreen instructions **(fig. 2.13)**.

All-in-One Beginners Guide to Computer Proficiency | 77

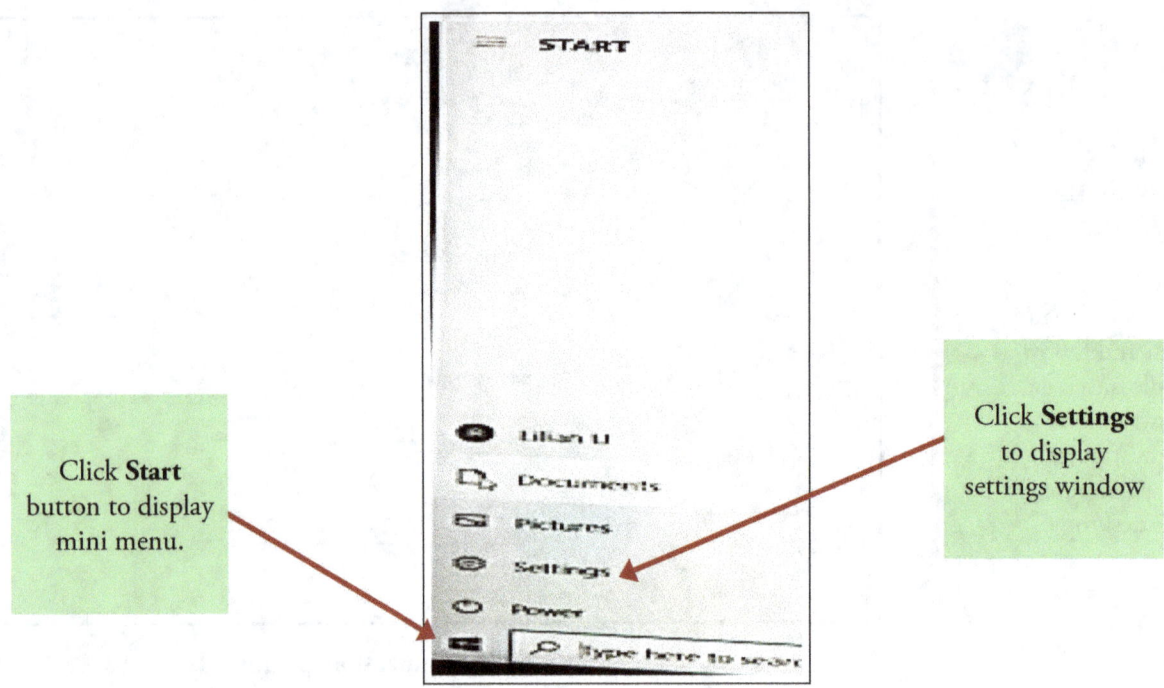

Fig. 2.12 Start Button Mini Menu

7. **Fig. 2.13** below is the **Settings** window, follow steps **4 & 5** above to display settings options and click on the option you want or use the **Search** box to find it.

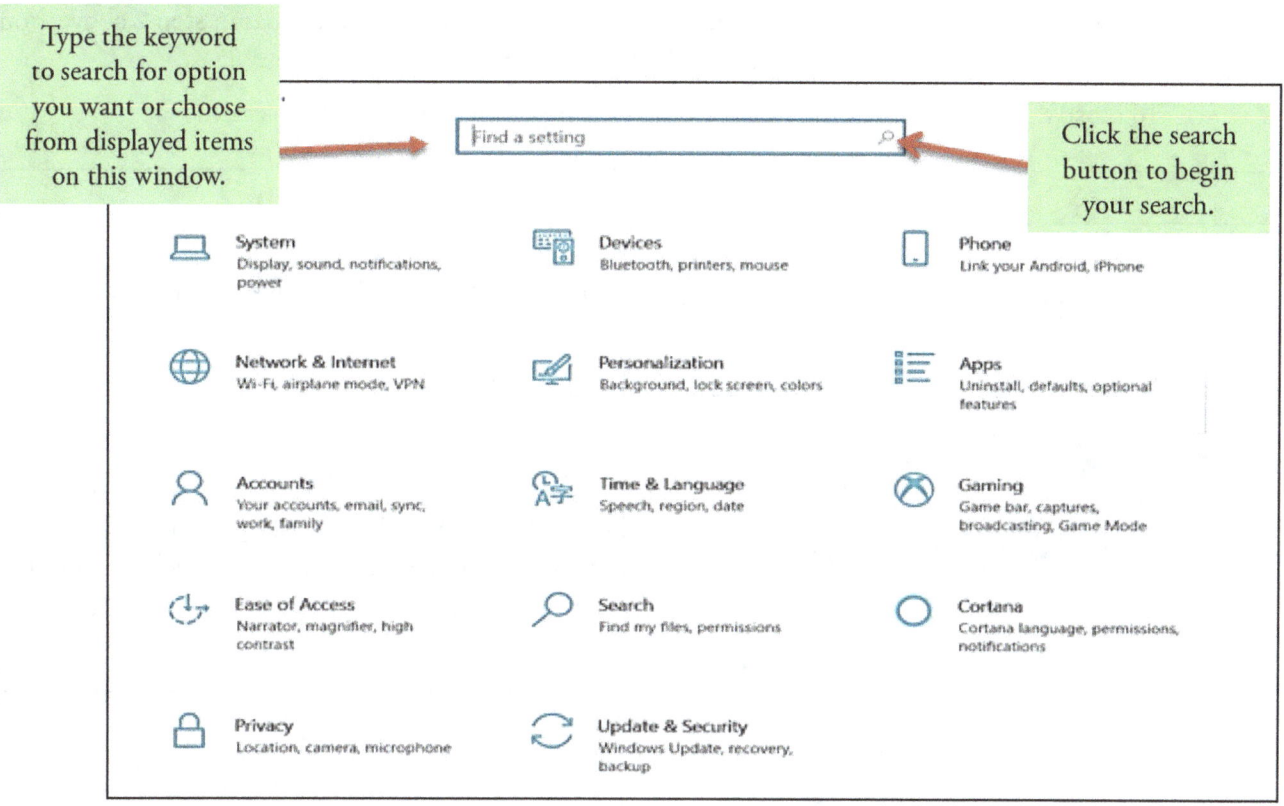

Fig. 2.13   **Windows 10 System Settings**

Change View of any Open Computer Window

When you **maximize** a window, it gets larger and occupies the entire screen. You can also **minimize** the window to reduce the size, **restore** it to its original maximized size, or simply **close** it. The buttons that control minimize, maximize, restore, and close actions are all located at the top right of the open window screen, see **Table 2.1** below.

Maximize, Minimize, Restore, and Close Windows

1. To minimize a maximized window, click the first left button at the top right of the window. Notice the entire window disappears from view and displays on the **Taskbar** at the bottom screens.
2. To **reduce** size of the window, click on the middle left button at top right of the window.

All-in-One Beginners Guide to Computer Proficiency | 79

3. To **restore** the window to its original maximized size, click the same button as in **step 2** above. You can also click the minimized window at the bottom of your screen to restore it.
4. To **close** the window, click the small **X** button at top right of the window screen.

Window Buttons	Action
Minimize Window Screen	To **minimize** a window, click this left line at the top right of the window.
Reduce, Maximize and Restore Windows Screen	To reduce the size of a window, click on this middle button at the top right of the window. To **maximize or restore** the window, click this middle button again.
Close Window Screen	To **close** the window, click this small **X** button, the last icon at top right of the window screen.

Table 2.3

MANAGE USER ACCOUNTS

What is a User Account?

A set of permissions associated with a user name. The account that come with your computer is created by Windows 10 at installation; it is set at the administrative level allowing you complete control of the system as the owner (Administrator). This means that you can install and remove software, delete files, and examine all system resources. If other people will be using your computer, you can create for them a standard user account. Each account contains its own desktop and system settings so that a user can completely personalize the account environment to a desired preference. Users of one account cannot modify or read files housed in another's account. Only the owner can make such changes.

Create Your User Account as Administrator/Owner (fig. 2.14)

1. Click **Start** button, select **Settings** to display the **Settings** window.
2. At left pane of the window, under **Accounts**, click **Your Info**, and enter your personal information.
3. Click **Email & Accounts** and enter your email address.
4. Click **Sign-in Option** to select how you would like to sign into your computer.
5. Several options will be displayed, two main options are **Password** or **Fingerprint.**
6. If you choose to log into your computer using password, enter your password, otherwise select another preference, and provide what is required.
7. If you want to add a new picture of yourself, click **Create a Picture**, and click **Camera.**
8. At right of the open camera window, click **Camera Icon** and take your photo. Your picture will appear on your sign-in window each time you log into your computer.
9. If you have a picture already saved on your computer, click **Browse for one.**
10. Navigate your folder to locate the picture, click on it, and click **Choose Picture** tab.

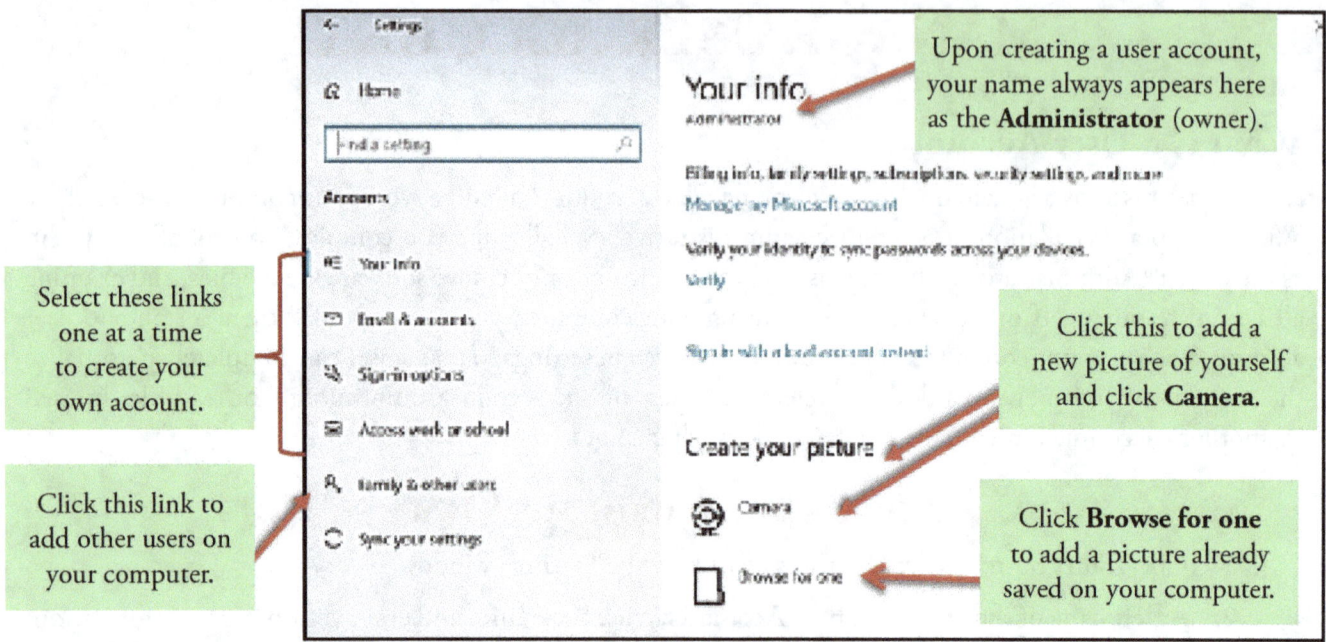

Fig. 2.14   Create Administrative User Account

Create Accounts for Other People on your Computer

As an Administrator (Owner), family members, friends, or other relatives must be authorized by you in order to use your computer. In families where there is only one computer available to all, the owner is usually the parents or head of household. Only the **Administrato**r (Owner) can create user accounts for other people. To create user account for any family member or friends, do these:

1. Click **Family & Other Users** as shown in **fig. 2.14**, above.

2. On the open family and other users window (**fig. 2.15**) below, click **Add a family member** and follow displayed onscreen instructions.

3. To add other people not family members, click **Add someone else to this PC**, answer some questions, and follow displayed onscreen instructions.

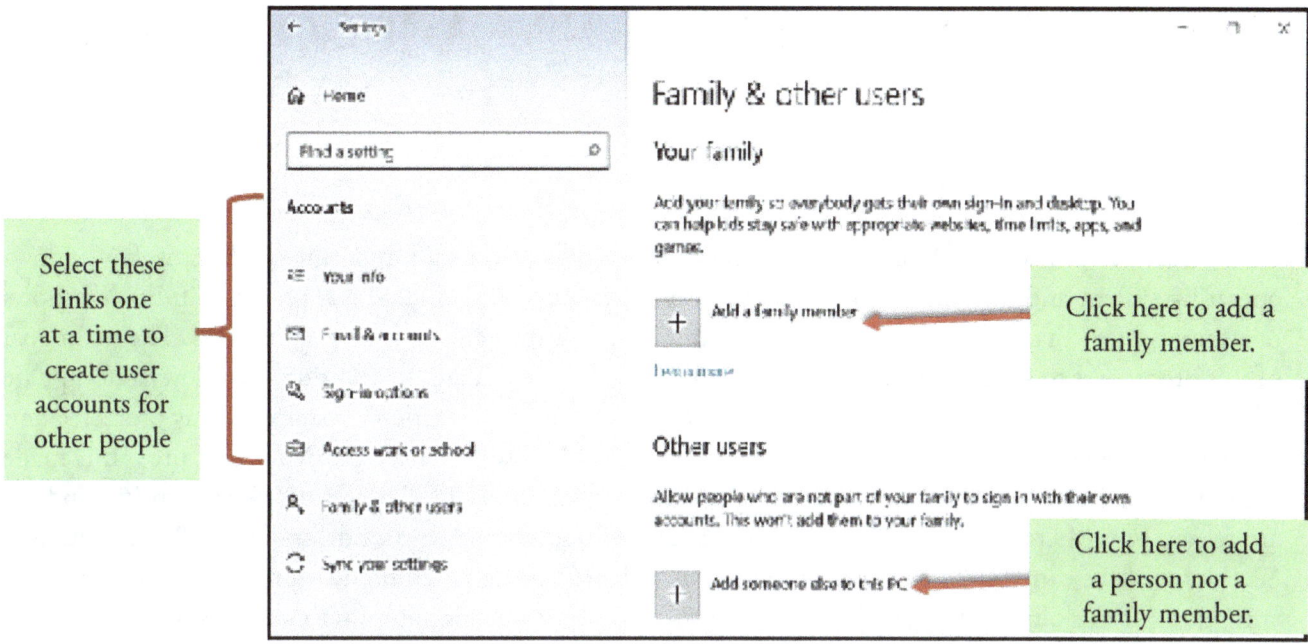

Fig. 2.15 Create User Account for Other People on Your Computer

Edit or Delete a User Account: You can make changes to a user account only if you are logged in as an Administrator. Some changes you could make include: change a password, choose a picture to associate a user account, change account name, change permission level, or even delete an account.

Edit a User Account

1. From the **Settings** window, under **Accounts**, click **Family & Other Users**.
2. Click the user account you want to edit.
3. Make the changes you want to make and click **Save**.

Delete a User Account

1. From the **Settings** window, under **Accounts**, click **Family & Other Users**.
2. Click the user account you want to delete.
3. Click the **Remove** button and click **Save**.

IMPROVE PROGRAMS IN YOUR COMPUTER USING MICROSOFT WINDOWS UPDATES

What is Windows Update?

This is a service provided by Microsoft Corporation to Windows users for updating the Microsoft Windows operating system and its installed components. Windows automatic update is a program in the Windows operating system that automatically downloads and installs important updates in Windows. The main goal of this program is to keep your computer system secured and up to date. In addition, Windows auto update allows you to receive security updates and the latest fixes so that your computer system can stay protected and run efficiently. The updates include Microsoft Windows, Microsoft Office, and Microsoft programs made available to users online as downloads. These updates, which are typically referred to as Security Updates are released by Microsoft and delivered on the second Tuesday of each month known as **Patch Tuesday**. Security updates can also be delivered whenever a software update is required to prevent hackers who use computer for exploiting and targeting Windows users to destroy their computer system. Windows Update contains features that allow users to choose how they want to update their computers. These features make it possible to configure and install updates automatically to ensure that the computer is always up-to-date and not vulnerable to computer worms, malware, and spyware. The process of setting up your computer to update itself is known as **Automatic Updates.** Microsoft operating system, Windows 10 provides a **Settings** button for use in configuring update settings and checking for updates.

Verify Automatic Updates Action in Your Computer

By default, Windows 10 is setup to automatically update your computer periodically. When you buy a new computer with Windows 10, don't take for granted that the automatic update is occurring. You have to verify that this process is actually taking place in your computer by following these simple rules below:

1. Click the **Start** button, click **Settings**, and select **Windows Update**.
2. If you want to check the updates manually, in the open **Update** window, click **Check for Updates**, and select **Advanced Option**, the last option on the list.
3. In the open **Advanced Option** window, ensure that the button under **Receive updates for other Microsoft products when you update Windows** is turned on **(fig. 2.16)**.
4. If the update button is turned off, click the button to turn it on.

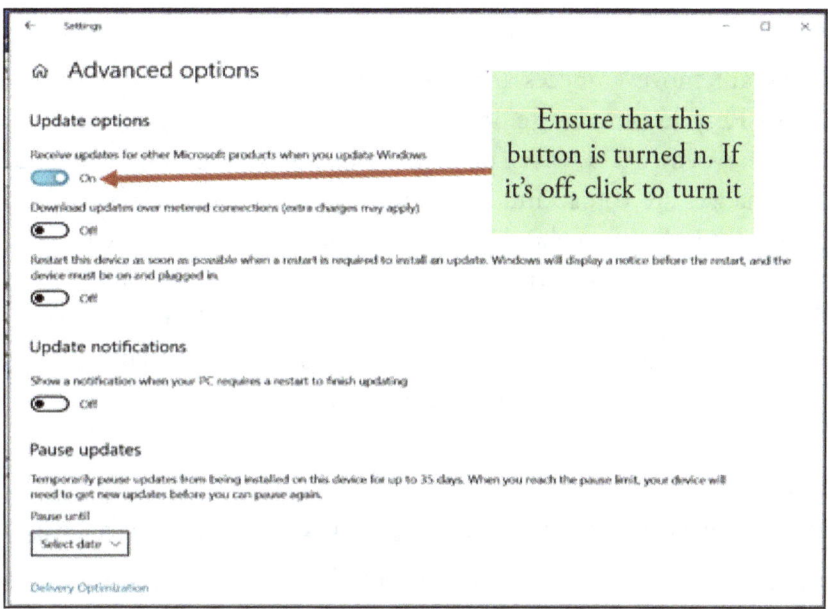

Fig. 2.16   **Verify Windows Automatic Update**

TAKE CARE OF YOUR COMPUTER WITH ROUTINE SYSTEM MAINTENANCE

Maintaining your computer and ensuring that it runs properly requires routine maintenance such as removing unused programs and files, and optimizing the hard drives in your computer by restructuring the system for better space utilization. The maintenance tasks should be carried out on a set schedule but the exact time depends on how often you access the hard drive. It is recommended that the more often you access your computer hard drive, such as creating documents or worksheets, saving, displaying, or copying files, the more often you should perform maintenance tasks. If possible, schedule some tasks to occur automatically so that you don't forget to do them. The two basic maintenance tasks required for proper computing are: **disk cleanup** and **disk defragmentation**.

Disk Cleanup

This is a utility activity that removes unnecessary files from your computer hard drive. These unwanted files may include items in the Recycle Bin, and temporary files (files containing data for every Internet site you visit and download items). As you access your computer, creating, saving, or copying files, and downloading files from the Internet, chances are you accumulate unnecessary files on your hard drive. Even if you're not struggling with storage space issues, you should make it a habit to clean out useless files on a regular basis. Your computer system gets bogged down with too many files that slows down its performance. Performing disk cleanup is similar to cleaning out your closet periodically (spring cleaning) to remove clothes you have outgrown that keep your closet crowded, and reorganize the closet for seasonal dressing (winter, spring, and summer). To run disk cleanup, follow these three simple steps:

Disk Cleanup in Windows 10 (fig. 2.17)

1. In the **Search** box next to the **Start** button type **Disk**, and select **Disk Cleanup** from list.
2. In the open cleanup window, check the boxes: **Downloaded Program Files** and **Temporary Internet Files** to be deleted.
3. Click the **OK** button to delete the selected files.

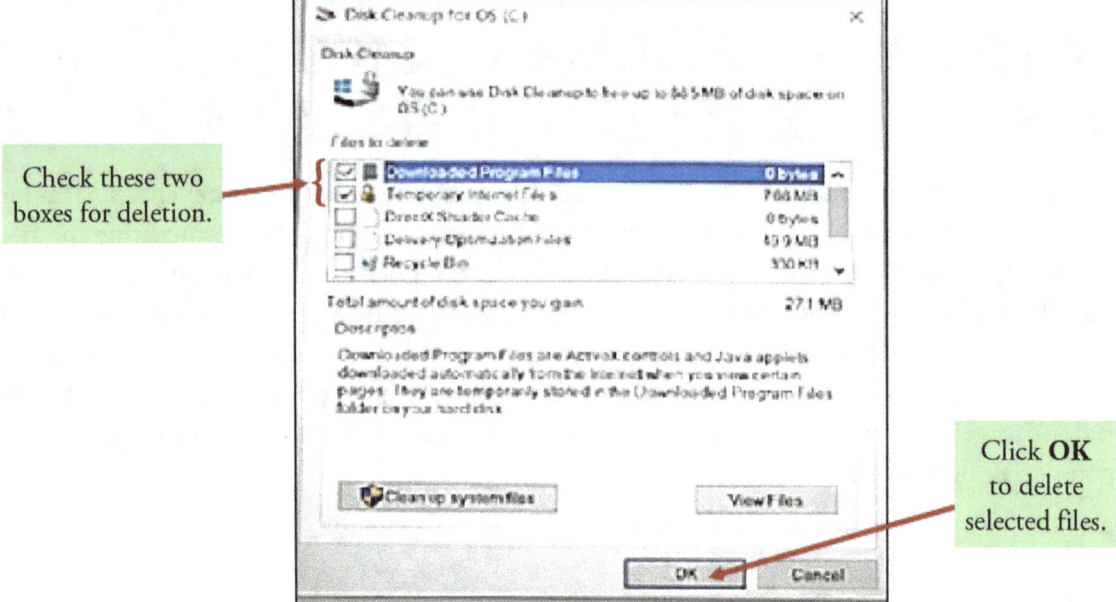

Fig. 2.17   **Run Disk Cleanup**

Disk Defragmentation

This is the process of consolidating fragmented data on a volume, such as a hard disk or a storage device so that it works more efficiently. Defragmentation is also referred to as optimizing your disk space. Fragmentation happens in volume over time as you save, change, or delete files. The changes you save to a file are often stored in a different place on the volume than the original file. This doesn't change where the file appears in Windows, only where the bits of information that make up the file are stored on the actual volume. Over time, both the file and the volume itself become fragmented, and your computer slows down as it has to look in different places to open a single file. Disk Defragmenter is a tool that rearranges the data on your volume and reunites fragmented data so your computer can run more efficiently. Defragmentation process compresses and arranges files on the hard drive in sequential order to improve file space in the computer. When you save a file in your computer, the operating system separates the file into small pieces called **sectors** as the system attempts to fill every available disk area, no matter how small. At this point, the file is said to be **fragmented**. When you retrieve the file later, the operating system automatically puts the pieces back together as a screen displays, but the actual file remains in pieces on the disk. Disk Defragmenter may take from several minutes to a few hours to finish depending on the size and degree of fragmentation of your hard drive. You can still use your computer during the defragmentation process.

Run Disk Defragmentation in Windows 10 (fig. 2.18)

1. In the **Search** box next to the **Start** button, type **Defragment**, and select **Defragment and Optimize Drives.**
2. In the open defragment window, select the drive you want to defragment from the displayed list.
3. If you want to view available disk spaces within the drive, click **Analyze** and allow time for the system to analyze the drive and provide result (optional).
4. To defragment the selected drive, click the **Optimize** tab.

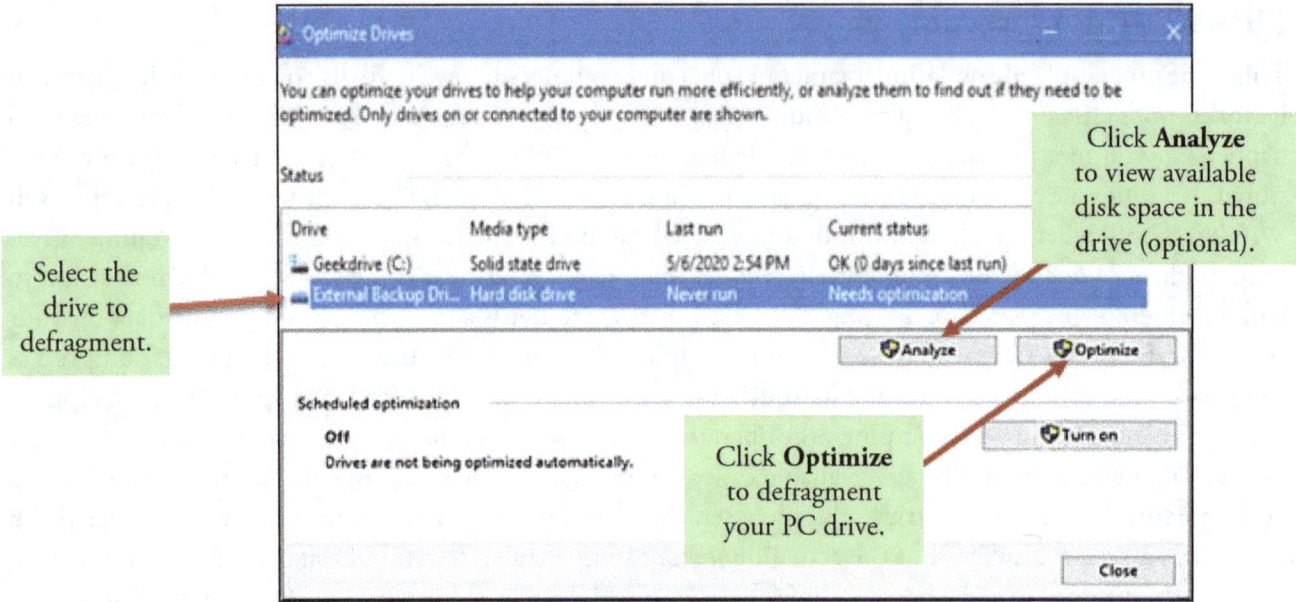

Fig. 2.18   **Run Disk Defragmentation**

Change Disk Defragmenter Automatic Schedule on your Computer

In Windows 10, **Disk Defragmenter** runs at regular intervals when your computer is turned on, so you don't have to remember to run it. It is scheduled to run once a week at an early hour in the morning. However, you can change how often you want disk defragmenter to run, and at what time of the day. Follow these simple steps and see **(fig. 2.19)**:

1. In the **Search** box next to the **Start** button type **Defragment**, and select **Defragment and Optimize Drives.**
2. In the open defragment window, click **Change Settings**.
3. Under **Optimization Schedule**, make sure that **Run on a schedule** box is checked, if not, check the box.
4. On **Frequency**, click **Weekly** down arrow, select preferred option, and click **Ok**.
5. Under **Frequency**, make sure that **Increase task priority, if three consecutive scheduled runs are missed** box is checked, if not, check the box.

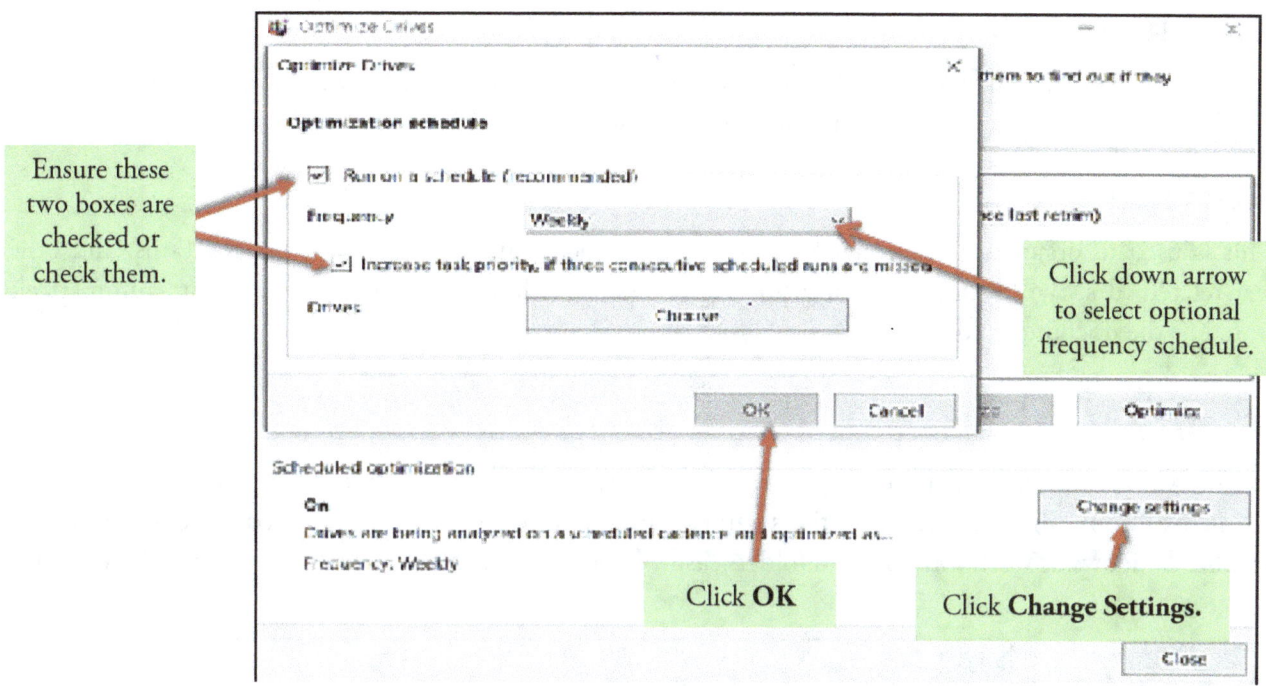

Fig. 2.19 Change Disk Defragmenter Automatic Schedule

MANAGING FILES IN WINDOWS 10

Windows 10 contains new features that make organizing files and folders very easy using functionalities at top ribbon Explorer folders. You do not need to start from scratch when managing files in Windows 10; you can use system folders under **Quick Access** to easily access your files and folders, and arrange them in any way you want. Here's a list of the four system default folders and what they are typically used for. To open any of these folders, click the folder.

Desktop

The first open screen on the monitor. All files and folders you create may be located on the desktop.

Downloads

Whenever you download files attached to an email you received or directly from a website, they are automatically saved in the download folder. You can move the file to another location of your choice on your computer.

Documents

This is used to organize and arrange word-processing documents, spreadsheets, presentations, and other text-related files. By default, files you move, copy, or save without specifying a location are automatically stored in the documents folder.

Pictures

Used to store, organize, and arrange your digital pictures, whether you get them from your camera, scanner, or in email from other people. The various parts of this Window10 folder are designed to help you navigate around Windows or work with files and folders easily. Here's a typical **Explorer** window with each of its parts:

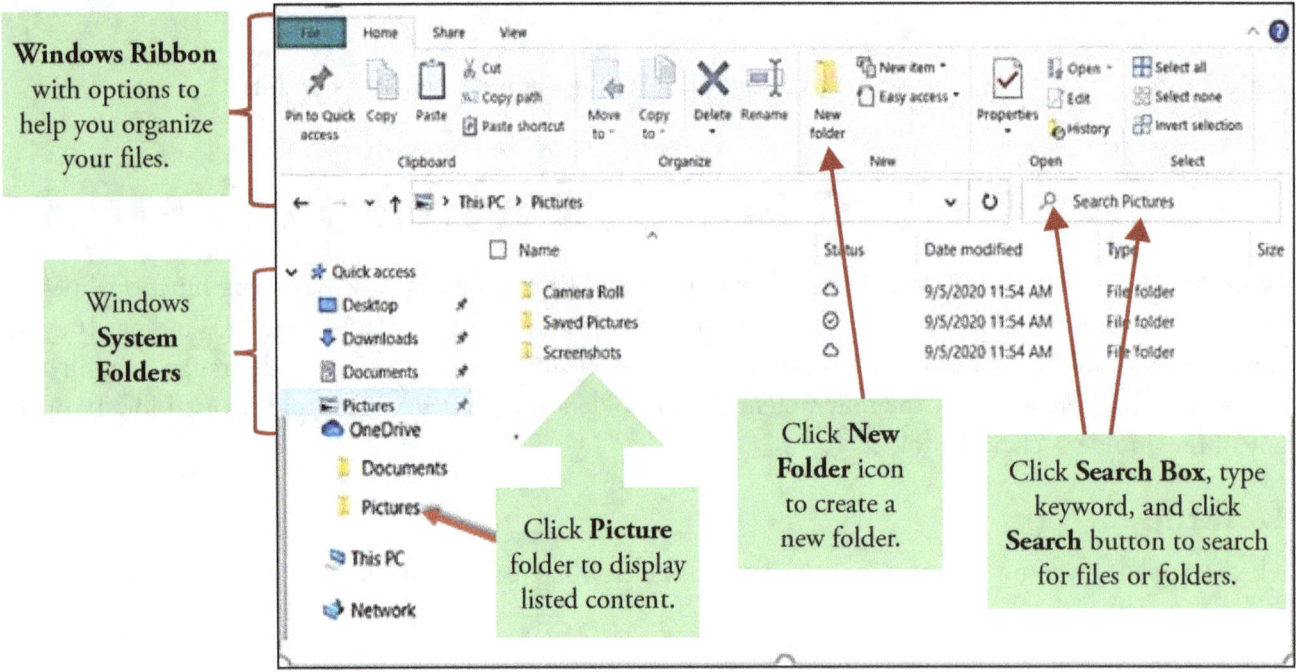

Fig. 2.20   **Windows 10 System Folders**

90 | *Basic Computing Concepts*

OneDrive

OneDrive is a cloud storage service from Microsoft where you can save your files offsite and access them from your computer, similar to Google Drive, Dropbox, etc. You can store any file in OneDrive and access them from Android, iPad, iPhone, Mac, Windows, and even on the web. In Windows 10 OneDrive is pre-installed on your computer; that's why you see OneDrive in File Explorer, Start menu, or the Taskbar. When you log into a Windows 10 computer using a Microsoft account, you are automatically signed in to OneDrive. Microsoft makes OneDrive your default saving place for your Desktop, Documents, and Pictures folder. You can save your files locally on the folders you create and still have them automatically saved (backed-up) by the system in OneDrive. This feature is optional, you can disable it if you choose to save locally. It's like a bonus folder installed for backing up all your files in case of accidental loss allowing you to recover your most important files from another location instead of relying on your computer alone. To store and secure your most sensitive files in this folder, you have to create a personal vault in your computer by following these steps **(fig. 2.21)**:

1. Click **Start** button and select **Settings** to display the window.
2. At the middle top of settings window, click **OneDrive Backup** to begin first-time
3. backup process.
4. When backup is complete, repeat **step 2** to open the backup folder.
5. On the open folder, click **Personal Vault** and follow onscreen instructions.
6. You will be required to enter a code for verification which Microsoft will send to your cell phone during this personal vault setup. Check your cell phone and enter the code.
7. When the process is completed, files you create and save in any drive of your computer are automatically backed up under **OneDrive** folder as shown in **fig. 2.21**.

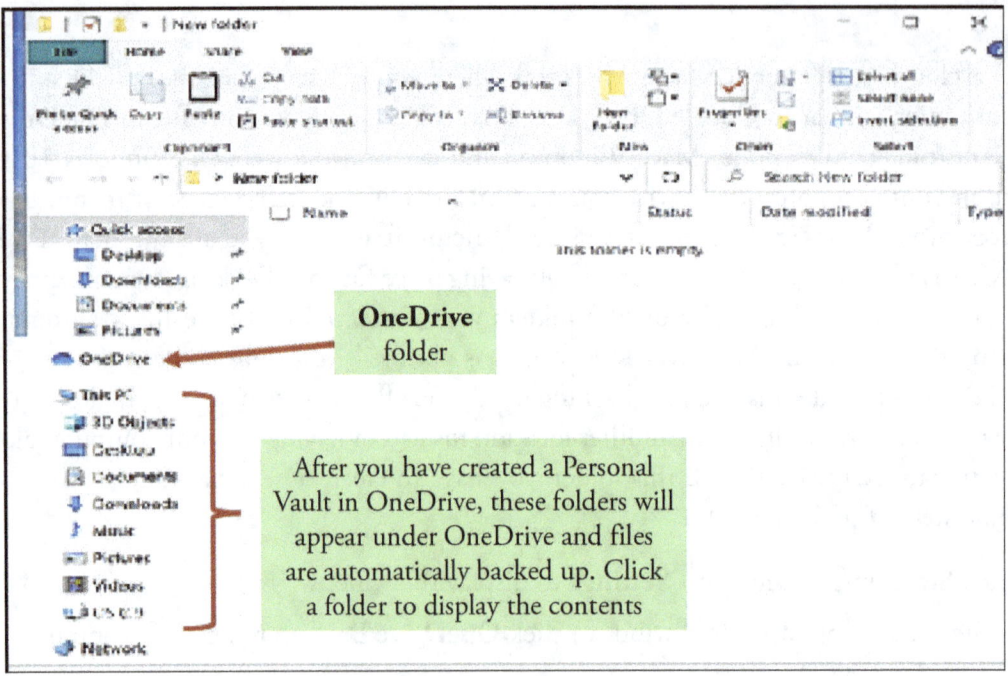

Fig. 2.21 OneDrive Window

What is a File?

A file is an item that contains information you create using application programs such as Microsoft Word, Excel, or PowerPoint. You can create documents, spreadsheets, presentations, and save them as files or download images and music from a Website and save them as files also. When opened, a file can look very much like a text document or a picture that you might find on someone's desk or in a filing cabinet. When you create information in a computer program, it is stored in the computer's memory, a temporary storage location. However, information stored in temporary memory location stands the risk of being lost if not saved in a more permanent location. To keep the information you create, you must save it as a file in one of the drives available on your computer, an external storage device, or both as a backup. The information you created becomes a **file** when saved, such as a research paper you typed in Microsoft Word. Files can be stored directly onto a drive, but quite often stored in a folder on a drive. On your computer, files are represented with icons which make it easy to recognize the type of file by looking at its icon. Here are some common file icons:

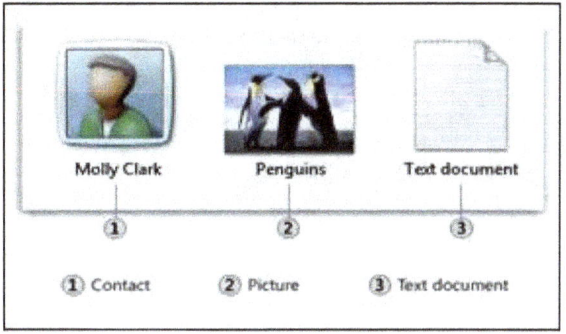

Fig. 2.22   File Icons

Save a File in a Removable Flash Drive: Recall the description of a removable flash drive from chapter one. It is a storage device that uses flash memory and gets connected to the computer by a USB port. Flash drives are often referred to as thumb drives, **universal serial bus (USB)** or simply jump drives. It is typically a device small enough to fit on a keychain or in a pocket. The flash drive is built with circuitry and contains no moving parts which makes it extremely durable. It is available in several storage sizes ranging from 16 MB to 64 GB and is the quickest way to save and transport files. Follow these simple steps to save a file in flash drive:

1. Insert the **Flash Drive** in the **USB** port at the back of your computer or on the side (right or left) of your laptop.

2. The flash drive **Explorer** window should automatically open. If it does not open, click the yellow folder on the **Task** bar to open it.

3. On your open document, click the **File** tab at top ribbon and click **Save As**.

4. On the left side of the open **Save As** window, navigate to locate the name of your **Flash Drive** and click to open it. **(fig. 2.23).**

5. In the open **Flash Drive** window, on **File Name** box, type the name of your file.

6. In the **Save As Type** box, ensure that the program name displays (for example: Word Document, Excel Workbook, PowerPoint Presentation, etc.)

7. Click the **Save** button at the bottom of **Save As** window to save the file in your **Flash Drive.**

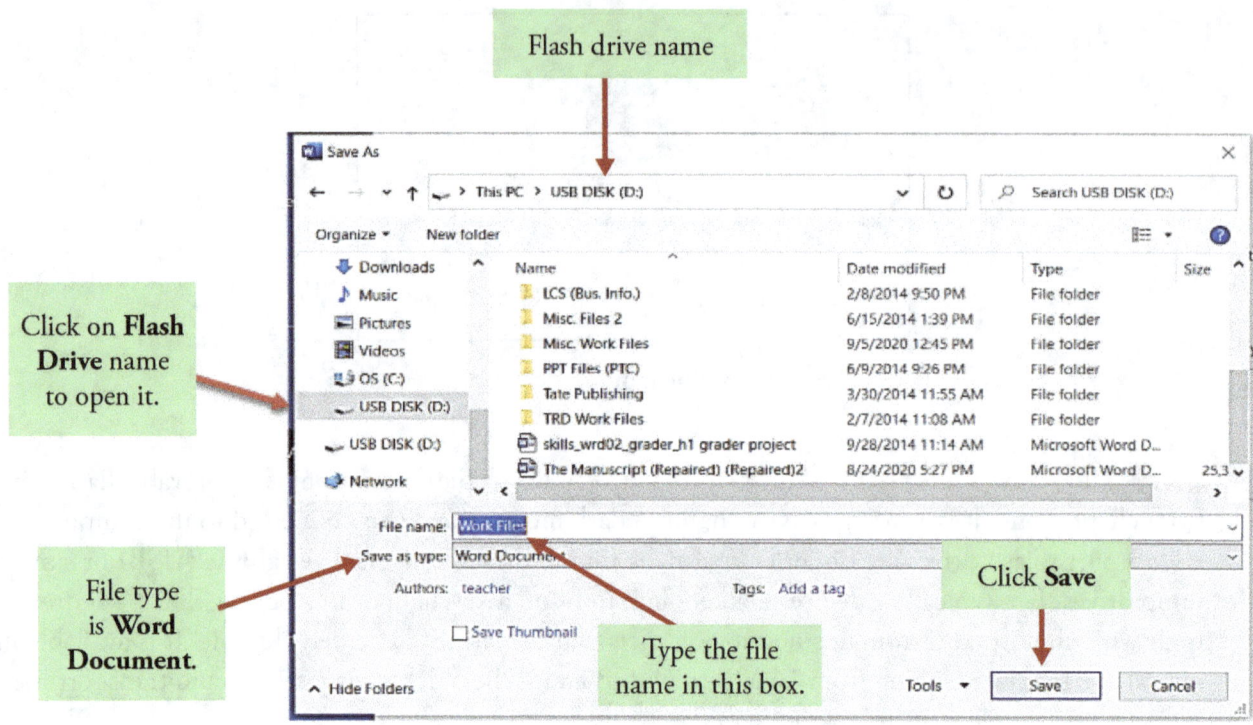

Fig. 2.23   **Save a File in a Removable Flash Drive**

What is a Folder?

A folder is a container used to store files. If you have thousands of paper files on your desk, it would be nearly impossible to find any particular file when you need it. That's why people often store paper files in folders inside a filing cabinet. On your computer, folders work the same way as filing cabinet. A folder is a container that holds programs and files represented on the screen by the picture of a light-yellow common manila paper. Folders are very important in file management and are the most commonly used tools in organizing files. For example, as a full-time student taking up to four courses; you can create folders for each course with the course name, such as Algebra 202, Computer 101, Management 150, and English 102. In each folder, you can save the related assignments, research paper, and study guides for each course. As you accumulate assignments and research projects during the semester, the files contained in each course folder get larger and larger. At some point, you may find that it becomes difficult to quickly locate files when you need them because they are now too many and all mixed up in one folder. You can solve this problem by further organizing your files in subfolders and placing the subfolders within the main course folders you created earlier. To do this, you will save all assignments for each course in one subfolder and another subfolder for research papers in each course, then save the subfolders in their respective main course folders. Here are some typical folder icons:

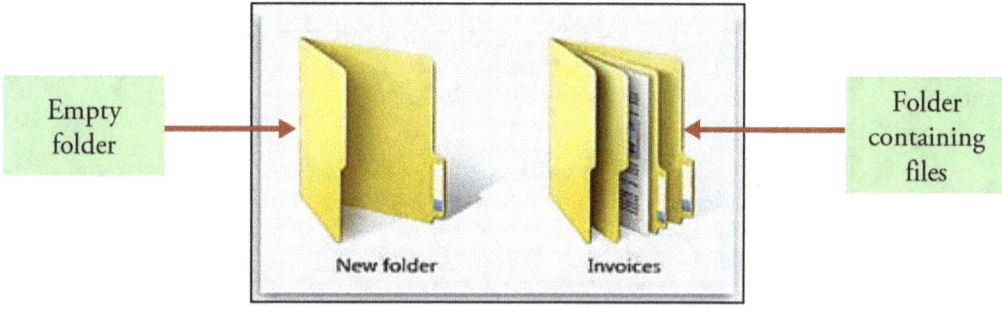

Fig. 2.24 New Empty Folder and Folder with Files

Create a New Folder and Save a File in the New Folder

1. Click the **File** tab of the program you are working on, and click **Save As** to open the **Save** window.
2. Click **Browse** to select a location for the new folder. Notice that the location, **Document** is automatically highlighted by default **(fig. 2.25)**.
3. At the top of **Explorer** window ribbon, click the **New Folder** icon and type a name **(ENG220)** for your new folder **(fig. 2.26)**.
4. In the open content area of the **Explorer** window, double-click the new folder name in which to save your document to open the folder.
5. Near the bottom of the **Save As** window, in the **File Name** box, type a name for your file. Ensure that **Save as type** shows **Word Document**, and click the **Save** button **(fig. 2.26)**.
6. Your document will be saved as a file inside the new folder you created. Documents become files when saved, and folders contain files.

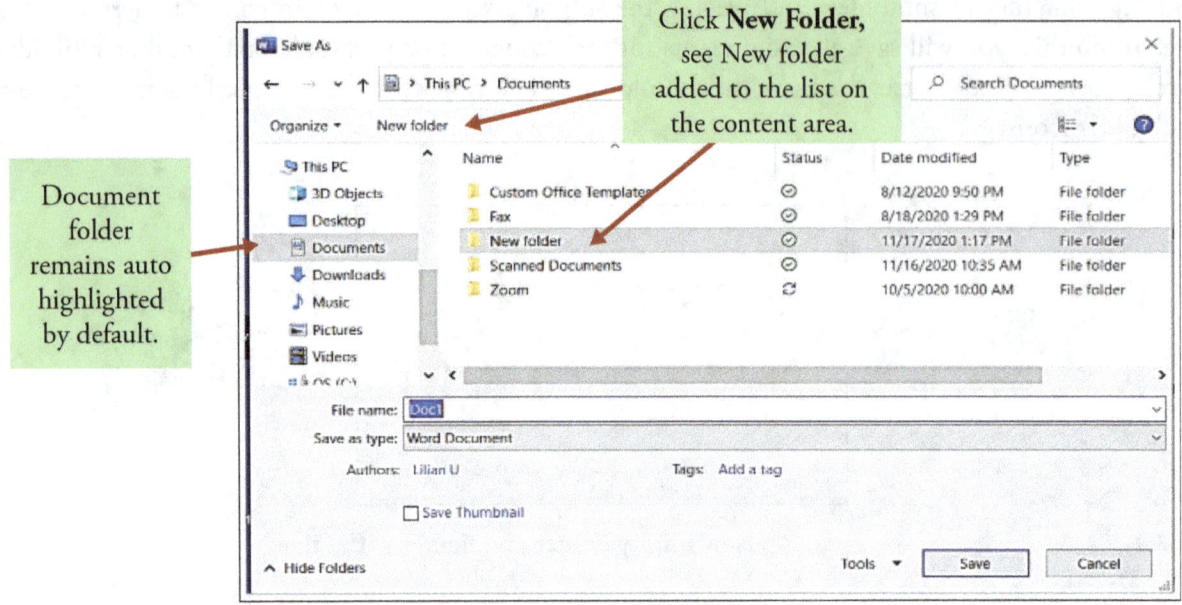

Fig. 2.25 Save As Window with New Folder

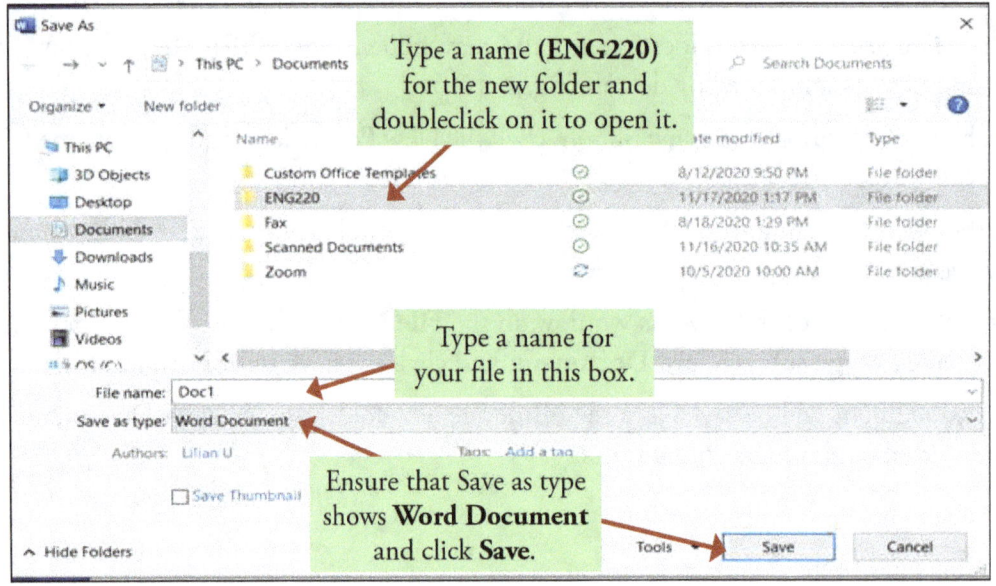

Fig. 2.26   Save File in New Folder

96 | *Basic Computing Concepts*

Quick Way to Create a New Folder on your Desktop

1. Right-click on any blank space on your desktop to display a short menu.
2. From the open short menu, place mouse on **New** arrow, and select **New Folder.**
3. Double-click the new folder and type a name for it.
4. To save a file in the new folder, follow saving instructions described in **steps 4 & 5** above under **Create a New Folder and Save a File in the New Folder**.

View and Arrange Files and Folders:
When you open a folder, it opens in default view, but you can change how the files look in the window, such as size of the icons. For example, you may prefer larger or smaller icons or a view that lets you see different kinds of information about each file. To make these kinds of changes, use the **Views** button at top ribbon of the file Explorer window. Each time you click a different option in the **Views** button, it changes the way your files and folders are displayed. There are several view options on the Explorer folder window but only six are visible: **Extra Large Icons**, **List view, Medium Icons**, **Large Icons**, **Small Icons**, and **Details** view which shows several columns of information about the file. **List view** displays only the file name. For additional view options, click **More** down arrow. The diagrams **(fig. 2.27 & 2.28)** below show different optional views of Windows 10 folder window. To change the view of your files in a folder follow these steps:

1. At the left pane of an open folder window, under **Quick Access**, click the folder name containing your saved files.
2. In the open folder window, at top of the window ribbon, click the **View** tab.
3. On the displayed view area, in the **Layout** group, click on the view option you want. The look of your saved files in the folder will change to the option you selected.
4. For additional view options, click **More** down arrow in the **Layout** group.

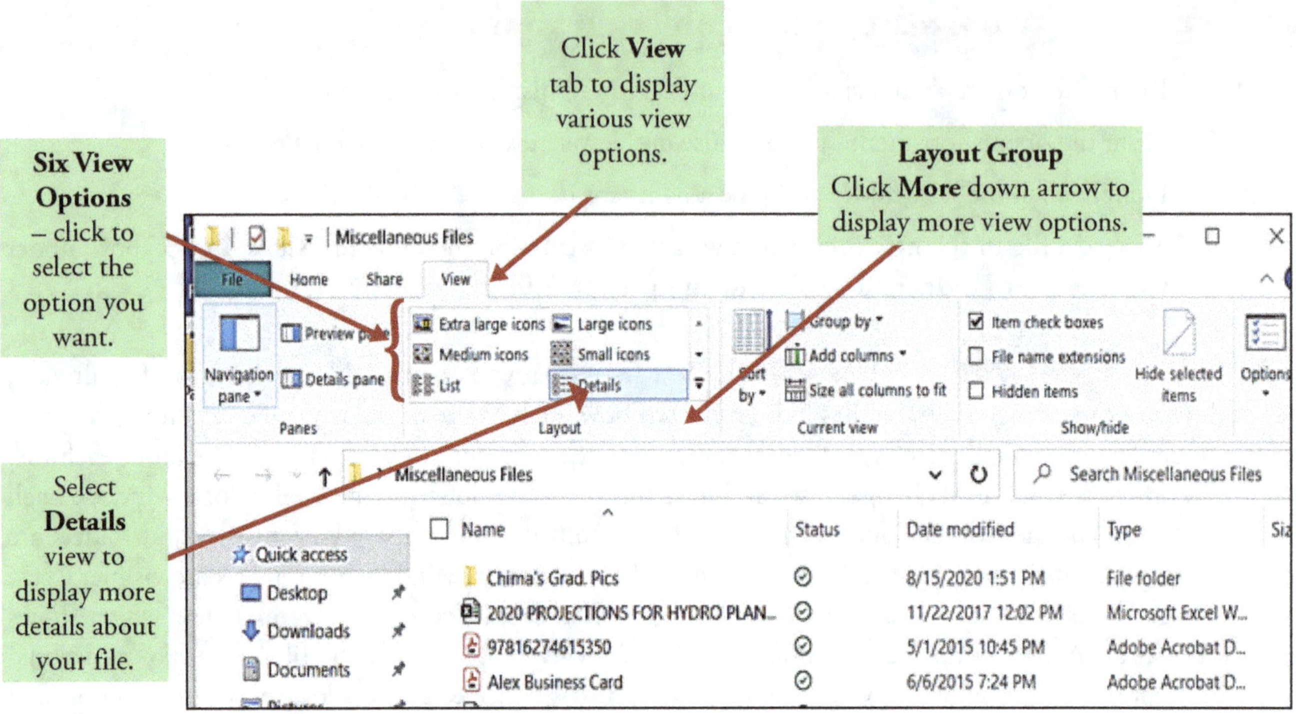

Fig. 2.27   **Files Displayed in Details View**

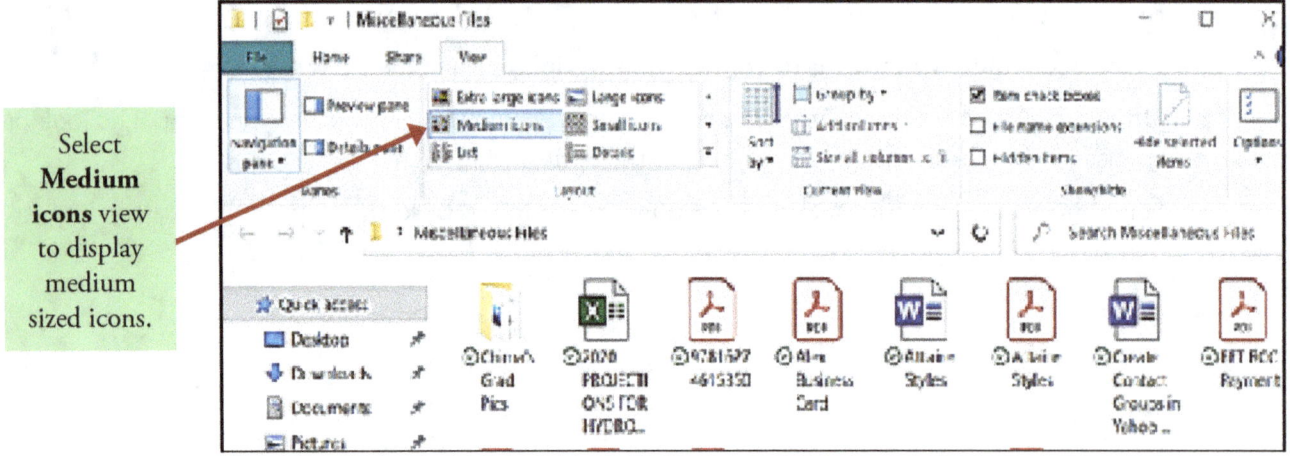

Fig. 2.28   **Files Displayed in Medium Icons View**

Search for Files and Folders: As you create information and store them on your computer, you accumulate a large number of files and folders that at some point, you forget where you stored a file or what you named the file. Very often you look for a file you know is stored somewhere in a particular folder in your computer, such as documents or pictures, but actually locating the file you want could mean browsing through hundreds of files and subfolders – not an easy task. Windows 10 provides a quick way to find files and folders using the **Search Box.** The search box is located next to the **Start** button and also at the top right of every folder Explorer window you open on your computer. To save time and effort, use the search box to find your file. Follow these steps **(fig. 2.29)**:

1. To search for a file from your computer desktop:
   a. Click on the **Search Box** next to **Start** button, and type the file name or keyword of your search. Notice that as you type, the system begins to display all files matching the first few letters you type.
   b. Click the **Search** button; navigate the list displayed to find the file you want and click on it.
2. To search for files from any folder Explorer window:
   a. Click the **Search Box** at top right of the open folder window and type the file name or keyword of your search. Notice that as you type, the system begins to display all files matching the first few letters you type.
   b. Click the **Search** button; navigate the list displayed to find the file you are looking for and click on it.

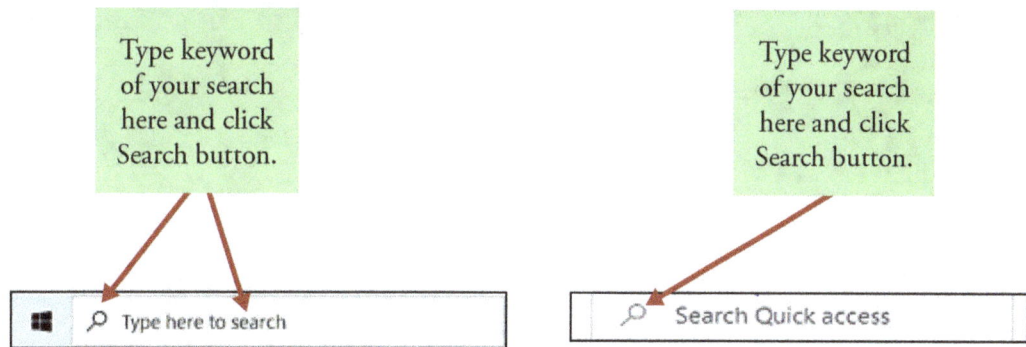

Fig. 2.29   **Desktop Search Box   Folder Window Search Box**

Move/Copy Files and Folders Using Drag & Drop Action:

As you accumulate files on your computer, sometimes you may want to change the location of the files by moving and storing them somewhere else within the computer or copy them to removable media (such as flash drive) as backups or to share with other people. The quickest and easiest way to copy and move files is through a method called **Drag and Drop**. When using the drag-and-drop method, you may notice that sometimes the file or folder is copied, and at other times it's moved. If you're dragging an item between two folders that are stored on the same hard drive, the item is moved so that two copies of the same file or folder aren't created in the same location. If you drag the item to a folder that's in a different location, such as a network location or to removable media like a CD, the item is copied not moved.

1. Start by opening the folder window that contains the file or folder you want to move.
2. In a new window, open the folder where you want to move the file **(receiving area)**.
3. Position the windows side by side on your computer screen so that you can see the contents of both windows **(fig. 2.30)**.
4. Holding down the **Primary Button** (left button), drag the file or folder from the first folder to the second folder, and release mouse.

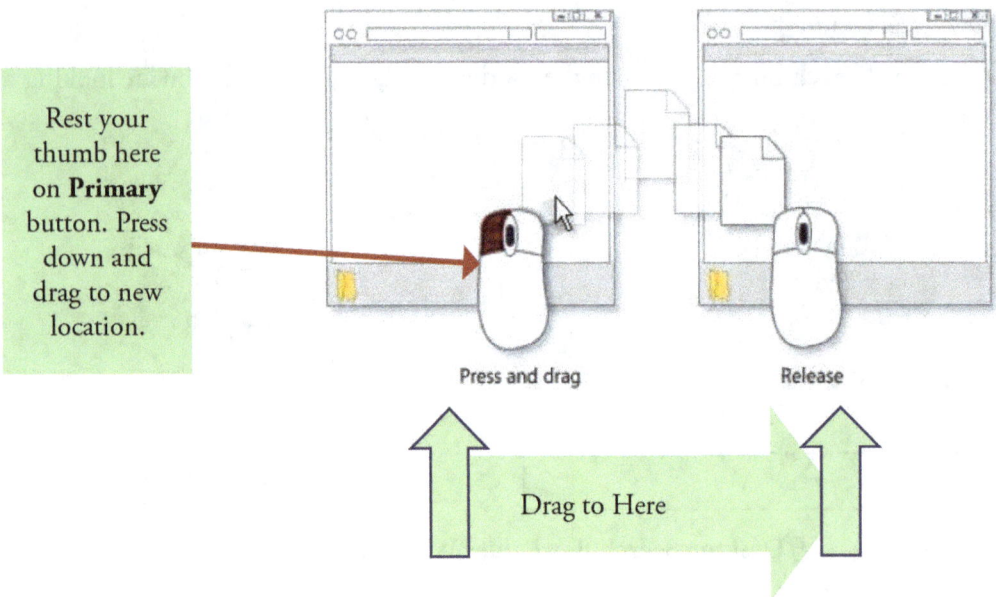

Fig. 2.30   **Copy from Here Move to Here and Release Mouse**

100 | *Basic Computing Concepts*

Copy Files or Folders from Computer to a Removable Drive:

1. Insert your **Flash Drive** in the **USB Port** which should automatically open **(receiving area)**.
2. If it does not open, right-click the flash drive name on the task bar, from the short menu, select **Open** to display **File Explorer** window.
3. Alternatively, click the yellow folder on the taskbar. In the open Explorer window, navigate the left pane to locate the **Flash Drive** name and click to display contents.
4. On the left pane of your computer Explorer window, navigate to locate the folder containing the file(s) you want to copy, click the folder to display its contents **(sending area)**.
5. Position the windows side by side on your computer screen so that you can see the contents of both windows (flash drive and computer).
6. On the sending area **(computer)**, click the file or folder you want to copy to flash drive.
7. Holding down the mouse, drag the file or folder to the flash drive **(receiving area)** and release the mouse. Notice the copied item placed in the new location on the flash drive.

Quick Way to Copy/Paste Files and Folders:

1. If copying a file, open the folder you are copying from to display contents.
2. Right-click the file you want to copy; from the displayed menu, select **Copy.**
3. Right-click anywhere on the location you want to place the copied file; from the displayed menu, select **Paste**. The copied file will appear on the new location.
4. If you want the copied file placed in a folder, open the folder first, then right-click anywhere on the open folder, and select **Paste**.
5. If copying a folder, right-click the folder name, from displayed menu, select **Copy.**
6. Right-click anywhere on the location you want to place the copied folder; from the displayed menu, select **Paste**.

Select Multiple Folders and Files at a Time: Selecting multiple files at once saves time and can be useful when moving, copying, or deleting many files or folders at one time.

1. If files or folders are displayed as a list consecutively:
   a. Click first file or folder.
   b. Hold down **Shift** key on your keyboard.
   c. Using the down arrow on the keyboard, highlight all the files or folders you want to move, copy, or delete.

2. If files or folders are not listed consecutively – non-adjacent to each other like icons appear on the desktop:
   a. Click any file or folder on the list.
   b. Hold down **Control (CTRL)** key.
   c. With the **Control** key still held down, continue clicking the files or folders until all files or folders are selected.

3. Once all items are highlighted or selected on the **sending area**, right-click, and select **Copy** from the displayed menu.

4. Right-click on the **receiving area**, and select **Paste** from the displayed menu. All highlighted or selected items will be copied onto the new location.

Rename a File or a Folder

1. Right-click on the file or folder you want to rename.
2. From the displayed menu list, click **Rename**.
3. Type the new name for your file or folder.

Delete a File or Folder

1. Right-click on the file or folder you want to delete.
2. From the open menu list, click **Delete**.
3. Alternatively, if the file or folder is located on the desktop, click on it, holding down the mouse, drag it to the **Recycle Bin**.

What is a Recycle Bin?

It is an icon located on the desktop that holds files and folders deleted from the hard drive, or from anywhere in the computer. You can clean-out the recycle bin periodically by emptying it or restore items you previously deleted by following these steps and see **(fig. 2.31)** below.

1. On the desktop, double-click **Recycled Bin** icon.

2. To delete all items on the recycled bin, click **Empty Recycled Bin** at the top of Explorer window ribbon.

3. A system message will appear to confirm that you want to permanently delete all items in the recycled bin, select **Yes**. All items you have previously deleted will disappear from sight.

4. Before you empty the recycled bin, if you want to keep certain files or folders you have previously deleted, click the item you want to keep, and click **Restore the selected items** at top window ribbon. Restored items are automatically placed in their original location.

5. The recycle bin does not hold files or folders deleted from **USB flash drive, CD,** and **DVD**.

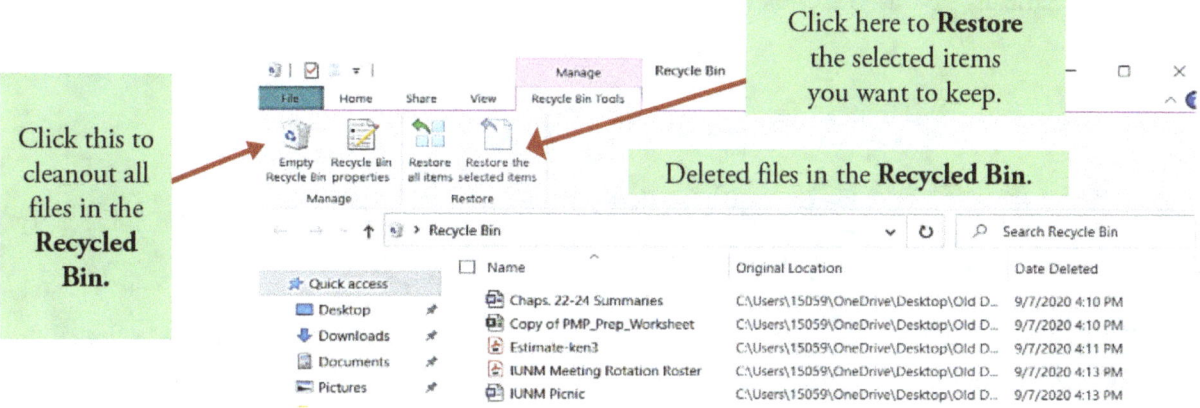

Fig. 2.31   **Recycled Bin Window**

All-in-One Beginners Guide to Computer Proficiency | 103

Capture an Image of a Screen

1. Click **Start** button, navigate the menu, and click **Windows Accessories** down arrow.
2. From displayed list, select **Snipping Tool** which opens into a small snipping tool window, see (fig. 2.32) below.

3. On the open snipping tool small window, click **New**.
4. Your entire computer screen will be grayed out. Holding down your mouse, highlight to block the image you want to capture, and release mouse.
5. Click anywhere on the captured image and press **Ctrl + C** on your keyboard.
6. Open any MS program you want to place the captured image. On the blank document, press
7. **Ctrl + V** to place the copied image on the open document.
8. Click on the captured image, drag, and resize as needed.
9. To save the image, on the captured image window, click **File** and select **Save As**. Screen shot images automatically save as **JPEG** files.

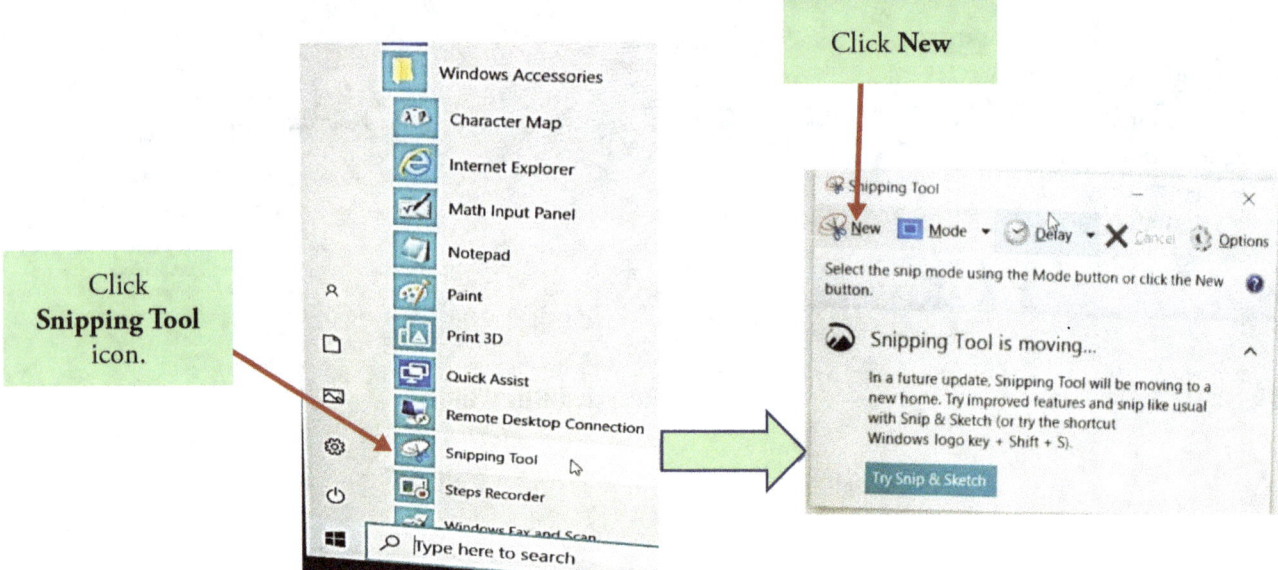

Fig. 2.32   **Snipping Tool Icon & Open Window**

104 | *Basic Computing Concepts*

Quick Way to Access the Snipping Tool: This feature is like a camera that allows you to take a quick picture of any image on your computer screen. To quickly capture an image of a computer screen without going through the Start button each time you want to perform this task, the quickest way is to pin the **Snipping Tool** icon to the Taskbar for quick access as needed. Follow these simple steps:

1. Click **Start** button, navigate the menu, and click **Windows Accessories** down arrow.

2. From the displayed list, right-click on **Snipping Tool**, and select **Pin to Start.** The snipping tool icon will appear on your computer taskbar.

3. Once pinned to the taskbar, anytime you want to capture an image of a screen, simply click the **Snipping Tool** icon on the **Taskbar** to open the snipping tool small window.

4. Repeat **steps 3-8** above under **Capture an Image of a Screen** and save image.

WINDOWS 10 BASIC SHORTCUT KEYS

Shortcut Keys	Function
Windows Key	Press **Windows Logo** key to activates the **Start** button that displays start menu.
Ctrl + C	Press **Ctrl + C** to copy highlighted text or image.
Ctrl + X	Press **Ctrl + X** to cut highlighted text or image.
Ctrl + V or (**Shift + Insert key**)	Press **Ctrl + V** to paste copied/cut highlighted text or image (content of clipboard).
Windows Key + Tab Key	Press **Windows key + Tab key** to display **Task View** of the computer.
Ctrl + Z	Press **Ctrl + Z** to undo an action, including undelete files.
Ctrl + Y	Press **Ctrl + Y** to redo an action.
Ctrl + Shift + N	Press **Ctrl + Shift + N** to create a new folder on desktop or in **File Explorer** window.
Alt + F4	Close active window. (If no active window present, then shutdown box appears.)
Ctrl + D (Del)	Press **Ctrl + D** to delete selected item to the **Recycle Bin**.
Shift + Delete	Press **Shift + Delete** to delete selected item permanently skipping Recycle Bin.
F2 key	Press **F2** to rename a file or folder.
Windows key + I	Press **Windows key + I** to open **Settings** app.
Windows key + E	Press **Windows key + E** to open **File Explorer**.
Windows key + A	Press **Windows key + A** to open **Action center**.
Windows key + D	Press **Windows key + D** to display and hide the desktop.
Windows key + L	Press **Windows key + L** to lock your computer.
Windows key + Shift + S	Press **Windows key + Shift key + S** to capture part of the screen with **Snip & Sketch**.

Table 2.4

CHAPTER SUMMARY & KEY TERMS

Windows 10 is similar to Windows 7 in many ways but contain faster functionality that allows you to get things done quicker than you would if you were using Windows 7. When you open Windows 10, at first glance, you will notice several new features that allow you to perform tasks faster. Windows 10 is software that runs the operating system of your computer, which controls the hardware attached to your computer including its memory and central processing unit (CPU). Windows 10 comes with several themes you can choose from to personalize your computer, such as the Windows 10 Basic theme. A theme is a combination of pictures, colors, and sounds on your computer. It includes a desktop background, a screen saver, a window border color, and a sound scheme. If your computer is performing slowly, you can select a high-contrast theme to make the items on your screen easier to view. You can click a theme to select it and apply to your desktop. You can customize windows settings by adjusting it to reflect your preferences more accurately. In addition, Windows 10 contains features that allow you to change the desktop background, select a screen saver, adjust mouse settings, change screen resolution, and adjust system settings such as the clock and volume.

Windows 10 also comes with features that automatically downloads and installs important updates in your computer. The main goal of the update process is to keep your computer system secured and up to date. Further, Windows auto update allows you to receive security updates and the latest fixes so that your computer system can stay protected and run efficiently. The updates include Microsoft Windows, Microsoft Office, and Microsoft programs made available to users online as downloads. Maintaining your computer and ensuring that it runs properly requires routine maintenance such as removing unused programs and files, and optimizing the hard drives in your computer by restructuring the system for better space utilization.

Windows 10 provides you various options to perform periodic system maintenance through disk cleanup and disk defragmentation. It is very easy to create files and folders, and organize them using folders window Explorer features in Windows 10. You do not need to start from scratch when managing files in Windows 10; you can use the Explorer window features to easily access your files and folders, and arrange them in any way you want. The search box is located next to the Start button of your computer, and also at the top of every folder Explorer window you open on your computer. Depending on how many files you have and how they are organized, finding a file may mean browsing through hundreds of files and subfolders, to save time and effort, use the search box to find your file quicker.

KEY TERMS

Action Center
Notification Area
Dialog Box
Display Settings
Disk Cleanup

File
Folder
Pinning
Search Box
Search Filter

Disk Defragmentation
Screen Saver
Drag and Drop
Resolution

Graphical User Interface
(GUI)
Recycle Bin

Screen
Spinning Tool
User Account

Demonstrate Your Knowledge & Skill

CHAPTER 2 PRACTICE EXERCISES
INTRODUCTION TO WINDOWS 10

2.1 – Select True or False answer to the following statements:

1. In Windows 10, the standard protocol for computers to format and exchange data across a network is Remote Assistance.
   a. True
   b. False

2. An alternatively to way to display the Start menu is to press the Windows logo button on your computer keyboard.
   a. True
   b. False

3. Windows 10 is similar to other Windows versions because they are all designed to use a graphical user interface (GUI), graphics or pictures to represent commands and actions.
   a. True
   b. False

4. You have the option to place your favorite or most frequently used apps where you want them for quick access using the Pin to Start option activated by clicking the Start button.
   a. True
   b. False

5. By default, the notification area is located on the left side of the taskbar, and contains program icons that provide information about the stock market on daily basis.
   a. True
   b. False

6. Windows 10 contain three power options Start button includes Sleep, Close, and Restart.
   a. True
   b. False

7. To verify that Windows 10 is installed on your computer or to find out what version of Windows is installed, click the Start button, and select Settings.
   a. True
   b. False

8. Computer routine maintenance involves removal of unused programs and files, and optimizing the disk by restructuring it for better space utilization on a regular basis.
   a. True
   b. False

9. Disk Cleanup allows you to delete the most-often used programs.
   a. True
   b. False

10. A good way to free up disk space on your computer is to run Disk Defragmentation.
    a. True
    b. False

11. When you delete a file, you store records of deleted files in the registry.
    a. True
    b. False

12. A file can be divided and recorded in disk areas called racks.
    a. True
    b. False

13. Defragmenting a disk is also called optimizing.
    a. True
    b. False

14. Defragmenting your disk goes faster if you are running application programs that speed up disk access.
    a. True
    b. False

15. A physical flaw in the disk is called a bad sector.
    a. True
    b. False

2.2 – Multiple Choices: Select the best answer to Windows 10 features and concepts described below:

1. How much RAM is supported by the 32-bit version of Windows 10.
   a. 4 GB
   b. 2048 GB
   c. 64 GB
   d. 16 GB

2. Which Windows feature uses audio and speech to interact with a user to search for information?
   a. Cortana
   b. Continuum
   c. Edge
   d. Start menu

3. Which Windows feature automatically adjusts the display and input methods depending on the form factor being used and whether a hardware keyboard is active?
   a. Cortana
   b. Continuum
   c. Edge
   d. Start menu

4. Where should you go on the Windows 10 desktop if you want to see important notification from the operating system?
   a. Taskbar
   b. Start menu
   c. Action Center
   d. Lock screen

5. Which Windows feature includes three columns with live tiles in the right-hand column?
   a. Lock screen
   b. Start menu
   c. Search interface
   d. Taskbar

6. What new feature in Windows 10 allows the user to create multiple desktops that can host different open windows?
   a. Open Desktop
   b. Virtual Desktop
   c. Window Manager
   d. Windows CardSpace

7. Which Windows 10 feature allows a device to sleep but continue to perform basic tasks like downloading Windows updates?
   a. Hiberboot
   b. Modern Standby
   c. Fast startup
   d. InstantGo

8. Which of the following terms represents a collection of data, files, and instructions with a specific purpose while it is running?
   a. command
   b. process
   c. thread
   d. order

9. If a thread is not finished running, perhaps because it had to wait or it was preempted, it is typically restarted on the same processor that previously ran it. What is this called?
   a. multitasking
   b. preemptive multitasking
   c. processor affinity
   d. cooperative multitasking

10. Which of the following systems have more than one physical CPU?
    a. Multiprocessor
    b. Multitasking
    c. Hyper-Threading
    d. Multi-Core

11. Which of the following types of CPUs have extra hardware built in to allow more than one thread to be processed at the same time on a single CPU?
    a. Multi-Core
    b. Multitasking
    c. Hyperthreading
    d. Preemptive

12. Which of the following assumes that hardware components can be connected or activated at any time while the operating system is running?
    a. Multitasking technology
    b. Plug and Play technology
    c. Multiprocessing technology
    d. Hyperthreading technology

13. Which of the following file systems uses a 32-bit numbering system to increase the number of data blocks that can be managed and organized as part of a single partition?
    a. FAT16
    b. FAT20
    c. FAT32
    d. NTFS32

14. What Windows 10 feature should you use if you need to run an older application on an earlier version of Windows using the same computer you are using to run Windows 10?
    a. Client Hyper-V
    b. Compatibility Troubleshooter
    c. Remote Desktop
    d. Remote Assistance

15. Which of the following terms is a collection of computers and users that are identified by a common security database?
    a. workgroup
    b. controller
    c. segment
    d. domain

16. In personalizing Windows 10, a theme is referred to as:
    a. a combination of programs that make a computer change colors when turned on.
    b. a combination of backgrounds with different screen savers and sounds on your computer.
    c. a combination of fonts, themes, and graphics that produce sounds on your computer.
    d. a combination of pictures, colors, and sounds on your computer.

17. Personalizing Windows involves:
    a. changing your desktop background, a screen saver, a window border color, and a sound scheme.
    b. changing the overall theme and the way items appear on your computer desktop.
    c. changing a theme's pictures, color, and sounds individually to create a customized theme.
    d. All of the above

18. Changing display settings to customize your computer involves all of the following EXCEPT:
    a. Selecting new system elements and adjusting existing settings
    b. Selecting a new background
    c. Selecting a new screen saver
    d. Adjusting screen resolution

19. All of the following statements about user account is true EXCEPT:
    a. User account is a set of permissions associated with a user name.
    b. The account that come with your computer is created by Windows 10 at installation is set at the administrative level allowing you complete control of the system as the owner.
    c. Any user with a password can install software in the computer and remove unwanted programs.
    d. Each account contains its own desktop and system settings, so that a user can completely personalize the account environment to a desired preference.

20. In Windows file management, a file is defined as:
    a. a program item contained on the Start menu of your computer.
    b. a list of things to do listed on the pinned items of your taskbar.
    c. an item that contains information you create using application programs.
    d. an item that holds all the documents you created in Microsoft Word.

21. Which of the following statements about a folder is true?
    a. A folder is a file used to store programs items on the computer.
    b. A folder is a drive used to store temporary files on the computer.
    c. A folder is a desktop item that helps to arrange icons.
    d. A folder is a container used to store files.

22. The best way to organize your files and keep them from getting clustered is to:
    a. create files and save them in a temporary place to be transferred into a temporary folder.
    b. save all your files in a document folder; then save them in a new folder.
    c. create new folders for related files and save them in that folder. You can also create subfolders inside main folders to save other related items.
    d. Save all your files on the desktop and arrange them in an orderly manner.

23. To rename a file or folder, perform one of the following steps:
    a. Right-click the file or folder to be renamed, type Rename, and select new folder name.
    b. Right-click the file or folder you want to rename, select Rename from displayed short menu, and type a new name for the file or folder.
    c. Click the file or folder you wish to rename, click new folder name, then type the new filename.
    d. Click on the file or folder you wish to rename, select Properties, type the new name for the file or folder.

24. A Recycled Bin is an:
    a. icon located on the desktop that holds files and folders deleted from the hard drive, or from anywhere in the computer.
    b. icon located on the computer window that holds files and folders deleted from the hard drive, or from anywhere in the computer.
    c. icon located on the C Drive that holds files and folders deleted from the hard drive, or from anywhere in the computer.
    d. icon located on the Start menu list that holds files and folders deleted from the hard drive, or from anywhere in the computer.

25. Which of the following statements about searching for files in Windows 10 is true?
    a. Searching for files in Windows 10 takes about 10 minutes.
    b. The search box is located next to the Start button and also at the top of every window Explorer you open on your computer.
    c. You can search for files or folders only in the hard drive.
    d. The search box is located on the desktop and the Navigation Area to provide quick access whenever you are ready to search for files.

2.3 – Fill-in the Blanks with correct words or terms for the statements and descriptions below:

1. Windows 10 includes a personalized virtual assistant application called _____.
2. Windows 10 is continuously improved as if it were a service the user has subscribed to. This operating system update strategy is commonly referred to as: _____.
3. _____ mode is designed for a traditional computer with a mouse and keyboard.
4. Programmers compile a list of instructions to build their applications. These instructions are typically grouped into units of code called _____.
5. _____ multitasking allows a single process to be interrupted by another process, even if the first process has not completed.
6. The _____ works much like the handheld physical device for adding numbers to obtain a total and is found by clicking the Start button and selecting the icon.
7. _____ does not correct software problems although it might eliminate some variables that could cause problems, such as a corrupted temporary file.
8. When you open a file after it has been saved, the operating system just puts the pieces back together as a screen display, although the file actually remains _____ (in pieces) on the disk.
9. An area of the hard disk that cannot be used due to a physical flaw is called a(n) _____.
10. The two basic maintenance tasks required for proper computing are: _____ and _____. disk defragmentation.

CHAPTER 2 SKILL-BASED PRACTICE PROJECTS INTRODUCTION TO WINDOWS 10

2.1 Identify Parts of Windows 10: Following the pointed arrows in the image below, enter the name of each part of Windows 10 inside the text boxes provided 1-10. On the textbook, enter your name and date at top page of your completed work; photocopy and submit for instructor grading

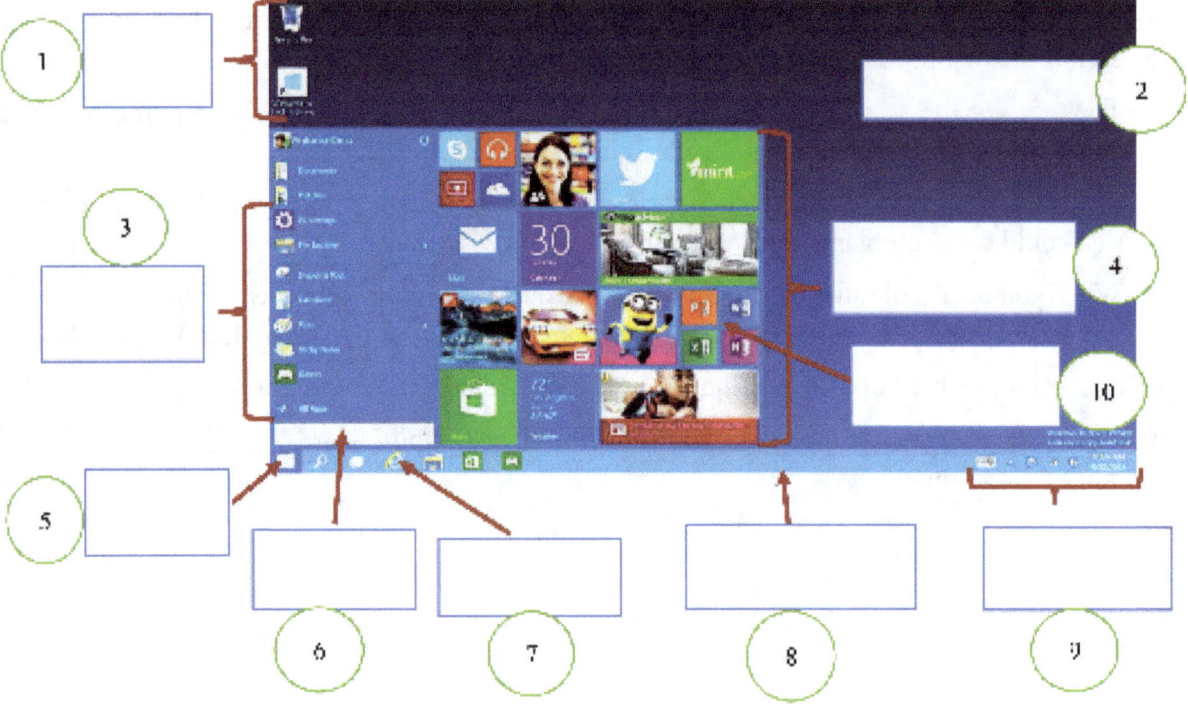

Basic Computing Concepts

2.2 Description of Windows 10 Parts: On the left column of the table below, enter the name of each Windows part you identified in item 2.1 above; and provide a description of the item on the right column of the table. On the textbook, enter your name and date at top page of your completed work; photo-copy and submit for instructor grading.

Windows 10 Parts	Description
1.	
2.	
3.	
4.	
5.	
6.	
7.	
8.	
9.	
10.	

2.3 Identify Windows Action Buttons: The three images on the left column of the table below are located at the top right side of any open Windows 10 screen.

Required:
1. In the middle column of the table, enter the name of the button.
2. On the right column, provide a description of the action the button performs when prompted.

Window Buttons	Button Name	Action Description

All-in-One Beginners Guide to Computer Proficiency

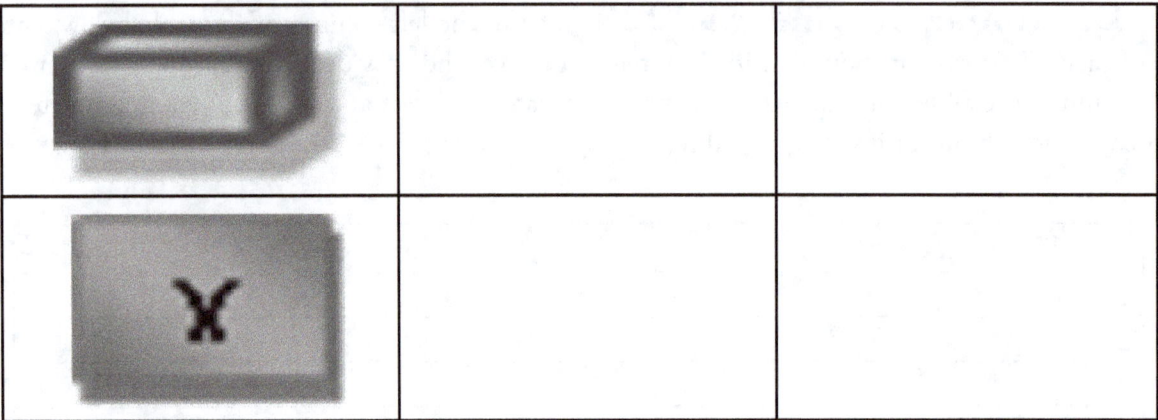

2.4 Manage Files and Folders in Windows 10:
A file is an item that contains information you create using application programs such as Microsoft Word, Excel, or PowerPoint. A folder is a container used to store files and helps you keep your stored files well organized in an orderly way to facilitate quick access to those files. The image below shows an empty folder and a folder containing files.

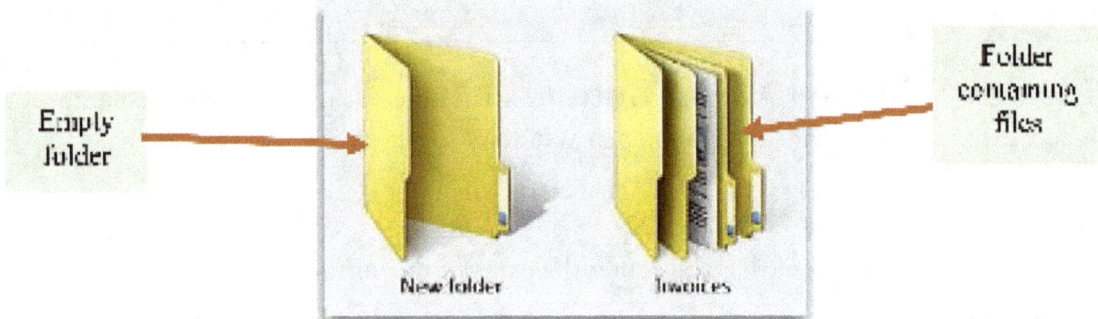

Required:
1. Open a MS Word document entitled **Files and Folders** at top page, and center title
2. Describe in detail the steps for creating a new folder in Windows 10, and saving a document (file) you created inside the new folder.
3. Save completed work as **2.4_FileFolders_Firstname_Lastname** in the preferred location on your computer using your first and last name. Submit your completed assignment following the instructor's preferred method – electronically or printed hardcopy for grading.

CHAPTER 3

OVERVIEW OF MICROSOFT OFFICE SOFTWARE

This chapter provides a summary and overview of MS Office programs and their functions, including software installation and general system maintenance. Software is information or instructions for your computer and must be installed on a computer usually from a CD or website download before it can work. In this chapter, we'll be discussing Microsoft Office products in general and the two specific versions of the product released between 2011 and 2018 – MS Office 365 and MS Office 2019. However, the focus of this beginner's manual is primarily on Office 2019 package. Most users find themselves confused in deciding which version of Office to purchase. Some make the decision based on how and what they plan to use the product for, such as affordability (cost), user friendly features, and availability of regular updates. Other users, particularly businesses make their purchase decisions based on the type of services or products they offer. In this case, cost is usually not an issue as long as the Microsoft Office product provides them the features they need to operate their businesses effectively. In general, individuals usually purchase Microsoft Office Home and Student which is more affordable for them while businesses go for a larger more expensive packages such as Microsoft Office 365 and Microsoft Office Professional.

Before we continue with our discussion of Microsoft Office in general, let's begin with a brief history of the two current products under review, Office 2019 and 365. Microsoft Corporation introduced Office 2019 on September 24, 2018 as a productivity suite succeeding Office 2016. It was released to general availability for Windows 10 and for macOS. Some features that had previously been restricted to Office 365 subscribers were made available in Office 2019 hence the similarity we see in the look and functionality of both. On

June 28, 2011, after series of research and beta testing, Microsoft Corporation launched Office 365. It was originally aimed at corporate users as a successor to Microsoft Business Productivity Online Suite (BPOS) because it comes with many of the features that most businesses need to operate effectively in today's business world. Then on April 21, 2020, Microsoft announced that most of the Office 365 products will be using the Microsoft 365 branding moving forward.

Consequently, many users now wonder what is the difference between Office 365 and Office 2019? Aren't they both the latest version of the Office applications we use every day? For many users, this can be very confusing. In this chapter, you will learn the differences between the two and understand which one suits you and/or your organization best. All Office 365 plans include up to 1TB (1terabyte) of cloud storage; Office Online (web-based versions of Outlook, Word, Excel, PowerPoint, Publisher), the full functionality of Office mobile apps; continuous updates to new features; security fixes as well as ongoing tech support. Microsoft 365 is designed to help people and businesses achieve more with innovative Office apps, intelligent cloud services, and world-class security needed to protect business intellectual property.

Learning Objectives:

After completing this chapter, you will be able to:

- Identify the most commonly used Microsoft Office application programs; know the difference between Office 219 and Office 365; and choose which one is best for you.
- Learn how to install and uninstall new software on your computer.
- Customize Microsoft Office programs for file auto-recovery settings; change automatic update settings; activate Microsoft Office programs; and learn privacy options.
- Find the contents you need in Microsoft Windows Help.
- Take care of your computer with regular maintenance using Microsoft Windows Update.

MS OFFICE 2019 VS. OFFICE 365 WHAT'S THE DIFFERENCE?

Technology industry is very dynamic; and the world we live in today is constantly changing with advancement in technology featuring Cloud-based and subscription-based offerings which have become mainstream and the new norm. This current business model puts new challenges on vendors as users can easily switch from one service to another if they are not satisfied with what they have. As a result, vendors have to continue innovating and making sure that their users know how to use the tools and benefit from using them. If you have invested in Microsoft 365 (previously known as Office 365) and want to make sure that users benefit from it, you have to make significant improvements and show them how to get most out of the product. To help users make a better purchase decision of what version of Microsoft Office product to use, we present here the similarities and differences between Office 365 and MS Office 2019. Like any purchasing decision you make, you need to look at your own situation – how you intend to use the product and what budget you have. The features and functionalities of Office 365 and MS Office 2019 are very similar; the differences are mostly external, method of updates, and affordability. Depending on your particular situation, **Table 3.1** provides a guide to help you make an informed buying decision of MS Office software that serves your specific need and also be affordable to you.

What is Office 2019?

It is currently the latest version of the "traditional" Office suite, following Office 2016. It's sold as a one-time purchase with a single up-front payment for one PC or Mac and when you purchase it, it's is yours to keep forever. Office 2019 includes Word, Excel, PowerPoint, and Outlook; it is most commonly used for home or business. There is no upgrade option when the next version comes out, you'll have to buy it at full price. While Office 2019 users will not receive any feature updates, they will receive frequent stability and maintenance updates. Although it is important to know the differences between Office 365 and MS Office 2019 to help users make informed buying decisions, our focus in this beginner's guide is on Microsoft Office 2019 package. This package contains the most commonly used application programs in business computing today such as: Internet Explorer, Microsoft Outlook, Microsoft Word, Microsoft Excel, Microsoft Access, Microsoft PowerPoint, and Microsoft Publisher. In general, Internet Explorer 11 comes already installed on your computer along with the operating system. Microsoft Office 2019 software comes in two different types of packages:

1. **Microsoft Office Professional:** This is the complete software package that contains Outlook, Word, Excel, Access, PowerPoint, and Publisher. It is are very expensive and most commonly used by business organizations and large corporations.
2. **Microsoft Office Home and Student:** This package contains only Word, Excel, and PowerPoint. It is less expensive than the professional package, and the most commonly used at homes and at schools because of its affordability. This affordability makes Office Home and Student the most commonly used MS Office programs in homes, schools, and colleges. Education leaders across United States and global consider these three essential programs to be very important learning tools that will prepare students for today's competing business world. For this reason, the beginner's guides to proficiency in Word, Excel, and PowerPoint application programs are covered in chapters 4 – 6 of this book.

Differences Between MS Office 2019 & Office 365

Microsoft Office 2019	Office 365
You purchase Office 2019 outrightly and own it just like buying a car and it's yours to keep. If a new version of Office comes out, your old version does not automatically update, you have to buy the new version.	You subscribe to Office 365 similar to renting a car without the worries of having the latest in technology and safety improvements because they are updated automatically with your package for a fee. If you rent regularly, the rented car automatically comes with the newest up-to-date technologies in the automobile industry.
Office 2019 is a one-time purchase that you can use for many years to come as long as you continue to maintain its functionality with Microsoft regular system updates.	You have to pay monthly subscription fee to receive and maintain the most updated technology. The monthly payment makes it more expensive than Office 2019.
Office 2019 comes in two packages – Microsoft Office Professional and Microsoft Office Home and Student giving users the option of buying whichever version they can afford. In general, Office 2019 is more affordable than Office 365.	With Office 365, you are getting monthly functionality updates more frequently than Office 2019 whether you like to or not. In addition, with Office 365 version of Excel, PowerPoint, Word, and Outlook, you also have additional functionality available. For example, PowerPoint in Office 365, you get a tool called "PowerPoint Designer."

If all you need is Word, Excel, PowerPoint, and Outlook, it will be much cheaper in the long run to own the license rather than to subscribe. You have the option of buying a package without Outlook and use free Email Client (Yahoo, Gmail, Hotmail, etc.) on the website to make the purchase more affordable for you.	In terms of total high subscription cost, currently Office Home & Business 2019 costs about **$249.99** (one-time purchase). If you commit to Office 365 with a monthly subscription cost of **$10.00**, this means that after two years, you have covered almost the cost of Office 2019 **$240.00**, and it's not even yours to keep forever.
If you are not using Microsoft's services for email, collaboration and communication, cloud storage, etc. and all you want is the "traditional" Office applications on your PCs or Macs, Office 2019 is a better option since it's not so tightly integrated with the rest of Microsoft's collaboration tools.	One advantage of buying Office 365 is that you don't have to pay "upfront"; you can spread out the cost over time. You have a much richer offering with numerous cloud-based tools that enable a new way of working – online, mobile Office apps, and continuous updates with new innovative functionality.
If you are a business owner, you don't have to worry about continuously training your employees on new functionality since no feature updates are provided except to refresh existing functionality through regular Microsoft updates.	As a business owner, you can align the cost of Office 365 to the actual number of employees you have at any point in time. If you have people joining, leaving, or working temporarily, you can provide them with Office 365 as needed.

Table 3.1

NEW FEATURES OF MS OFFICE 2019

The new Microsoft Office 2019 is packed with a lot of unique features that allow users to automatically backup their work in the case of unexpected loss due to connection or power failure. It contains automatic Auto-Recover information and provides users instructions on how to set their computers to perform auto-recovery periodically while they work. As you work in any MS Office program, if you are lucky enough to retrieve an unsaved document, then it is important to take steps to ensure that it never happens again.

Customize Microsoft Office 2019 Auto Recovery Settings

To set document recovery options in your computer so that you don't have to worry about losing unsaved document in the event of accidental loss due to a computer crash while you work, follow these steps:

1. Click **File** tab, click **Options**, and select **Save**
2. On the open save window, select the **Save AutoRecover information** checkbox.
3. Set how often you would like to back up your work. To be on the safe side, set a small number, so you never lose more than 5 or 10 minutes of work. If you want to make MS Office work faster, enter a larger number.
4. Select **Keep the last autosaved version if I close without saving** checkbox; click **OK**.

Search Windows for .asd or .wbk files

If you reopen the MS Office program you were working on before a computer crash and the default AutoRecover space is empty (no files are displayed) for some reason, you can always try to search your system for Microsoft Office draft file extensions. Microsoft Office autosaved files typically use the .asd or .wbk file extension. To search for extensions:

1. Press **Windows key + E** to open **File Explorer**.
2. In the **Search Quick Access** box at the top-right, type *.asd OR *.wbk without quotation marks. Please note that the **"or"** is part of the search function, that's why you include it in your search to make it work.
3. Click the **Search** button to search for your files.

OVERVIEW & SUMMARY OF OFFICE 2019 PACKAGE

This section provides a general overview, summary, and functions of MS Office 2019 full package (Outlook, Word, Excel, Access, PowerPoint, and Publisher). The purpose is to show beginners a preview of what each application looks like and what to expect if they wish to further their study of MS Office applications to intermediate and advance levels. The focus of this beginner's guide is on MS Office 2019 Home and Student which includes Word, Excel, and PowerPoint discussed in chapters 4-6.

Microsoft Outlook

Software used to send email messages and facilitates communication with other people electronically while connected to the Internet. This type of communication is called **emailing**, and the message being sent is referred to as **email.** Outlook is part of MS Professional package; it is not included in Microsoft Home Office and School. Because Microsoft Office Professional that contains Outlook is very expensive, most people buy the affordable Office Home and Student package without Outlook and utilize the free web-based email service known as **Email Client** on the Internet such as Yahoo, Hotmail, Gmail, MSN etc. They setup email accounts on these free email services for sending and receiving email communications. For this reason, the discussion of Outlook in this chapter will be limited to introduction and view of email message window. A full discussion on Internet free web-based email service is covered on chapter 7.

Before using Outlook 2019 to send and receive e-mail messages, you must add and configure an e-mail account in your computer. If you have used an earlier version of Microsoft Outlook on the same computer that you installed Outlook 2019, your account settings are automatically imported. Outlook supports Microsoft Exchange, **POP3** (A common protocol that is used to retrieve e-mail messages from an Internet e-mail server.), and **IMAP** (Internet Message Access Protocol): Unlike Internet e-mail protocols such as POP3, IMAP creates folders on a server to store/organize messages for retrieval by other computers. You can read message headers only and select which messages to download.) accounts. **POP3** is a common protocol that is used to retrieve e-mail messages from an Internet e-mail server, and IMAP is Internet Message Access Protocol. Unlike Internet e-mail protocols (POP3), IMAP create folders on a server to store/organize messages for retrieval by other computers. You can read message headers only and select which messages to download. Your Internet service provider (ISP) (ISP: A business that provides access to the Internet for such things as electronic mail, chat rooms, or use of the World Wide Web. Some ISPs are multinational, offering access in many locations, while others are limited to a specific region.) provides you access to the Internet for such things as electronic mail, chat rooms, or use of the World Wide Web. Some ISPs are multinational, offering access in many locations, while others are limited to a specific region. The ISP is your e-mail administrator who can give you the configuration information you must have to set up your e-mail account in Outlook. E-mail account information is contained in a profile. A profile is made up of accounts, data files, such as your name, email address, and password, including settings that specify where your e-mail messages are saved. A new profile is created automatically when you run Outlook for the first time. If you are new to Outlook or are installing Outlook 2019 on a new computer for the first time, the **Auto Account Setup** feature automatically starts and helps you configure account settings for your e-mail accounts. This setup requires only your name, e-mail address, and password. If your e-mail account cannot be automatically configured, you must enter the required additional information manually as needed to help you set up the account. Every e-mail message must have two parts: **Header** located at the top part of your e-mail window, and a **Message Body**, the bottom part of the window. The header contains the name and e-mail address of the recipient, the names and e-mail addresses of all other recipients the same message will be copied to, and the subject of your message. The message body contains your entire message. Free web-based email services found on the Internet work the same way as Outlook also containing two part: a header and message body. To use the free service online, you must create a profile, an email account in the **Email Client** website.

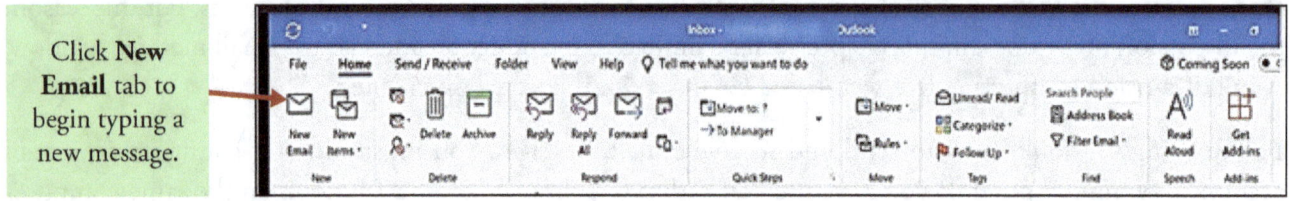

Fig. 3.1   **The New 2019 Outlook Ribbon**

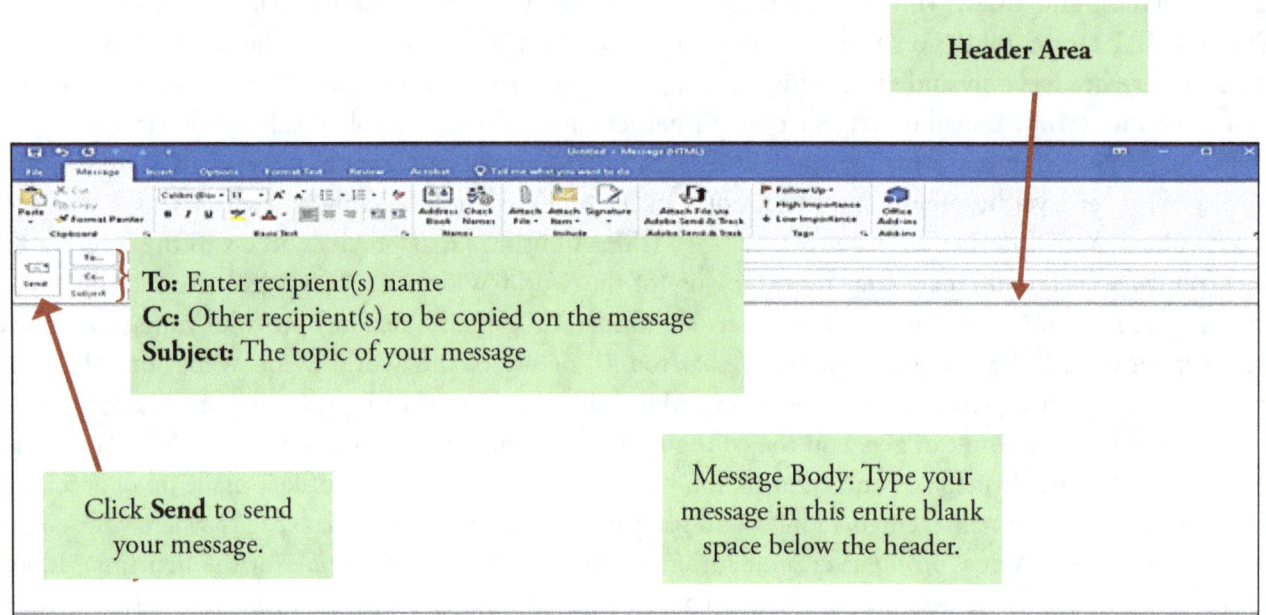

Fig. 3.2   **MS Office 2019 Outlook New Message Window**

Microsoft Word

MS Word is created by Microsoft Corporation and upgraded about every 3 years to release newer versions with new or modified features from the previous one. This program is Word Processor that works like a typewriter except that it contains features that allow you to edit typed document, copy, move, save, and delete text. Microsoft Word comes with a lot of features that allow users to make their documents look very professional. It is the most commonly used program in business organizations, schools, and homes to create documents, type letters, or resumes, check your spelling and grammar, mainly words because of its use-friendly format. Beginner's guide to proficiency on the use of this new version of Microsoft Word 2019 is covered in chapter 4.

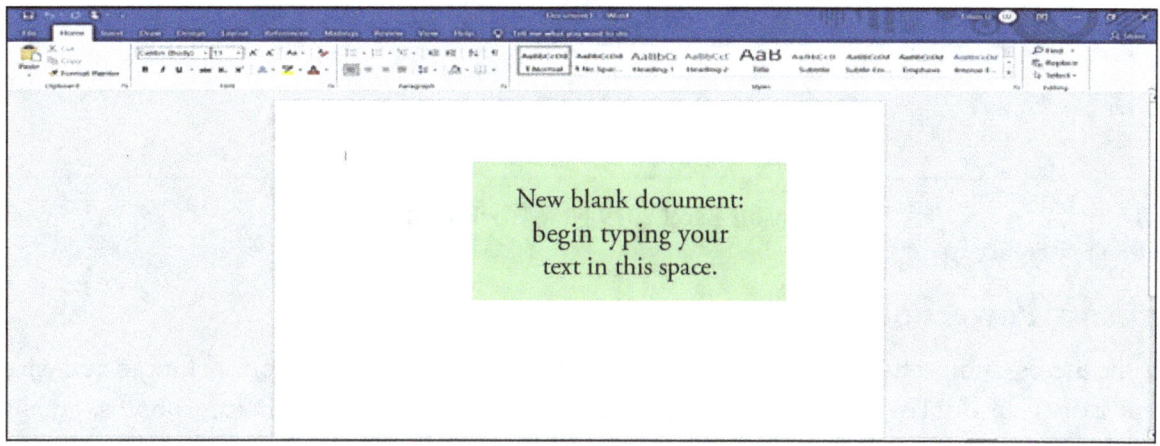

Fig. 3.3   **Microsoft Word 2019 New Document Window**

Microsoft Excel

This software is commonly used to enter accounting data (values) into worksheet cells. It contains a feature that performs arithmetic operations using the values in worksheet cells to produce new values (total) through addition, subtraction, multiplication, or division. It is often referred to as a spreadsheet and can also use numbers to produce graphs. Beginner's guide to proficiency in the use of Microsoft Excel 2019 is covered in chapter 5.

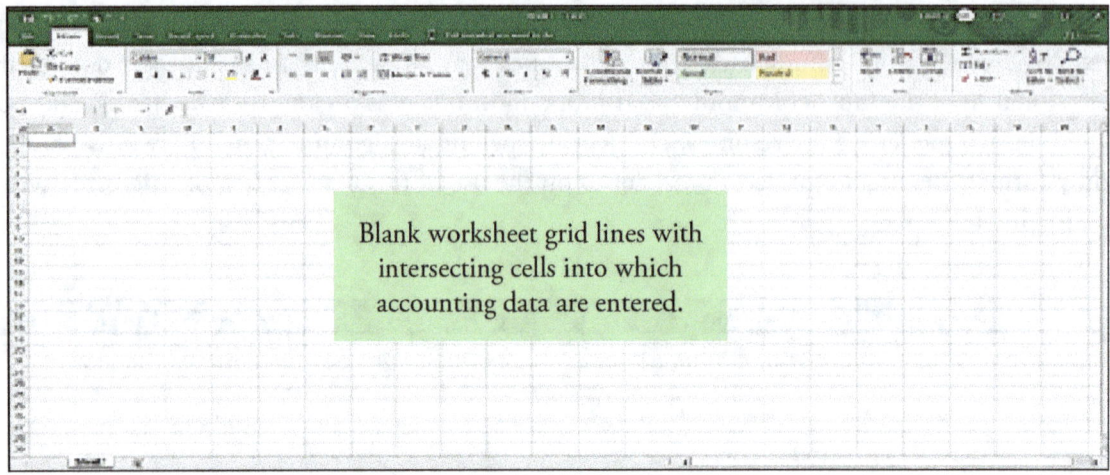

Fig. 3.4　　　　　　　　Microsoft Excel 2019 New Worksheet Window

Microsoft PowerPoint

This is the presentation software used for making visual and graphical presentations before an audience. The program is used to display slides containing presentation message, graphics, images, photos, graphs, and tables during presentations. It also produces professional looking documents, including handouts for the audience. Beginner's guide to proficiency in the use of MS PowerPoint is covered in chapter 6.

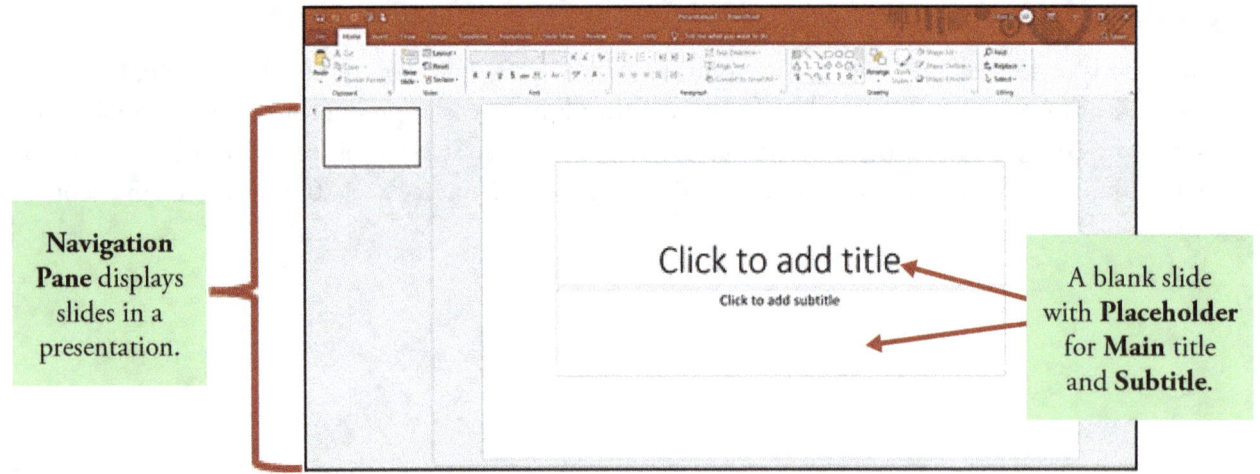

Fig. 3.5　　　　　　　　Microsoft PowerPoint 2019 New Slide View

Microsoft Access Database

A program that collects and organizes data such as facts about people, events, things, or ideas related to a particular topic or purpose and uses data collected to create a database of information. When the data has been organized in a useful manner, it provides useful information for business decision making. The grid lines layout of MS Access is similar to Excel worksheet that requires entering data into cells separated by intersection lines. Business organizations use **Access Database** program to track marketing information and create business reports. This book does not dedicate a chapter for discussion of MS Access because it is not part of the affordable MS Office Home and Student, the focus of this beginner's guide. The goal here is to introduce the program as part of MS Office Professional package for the benefit of people who wish to continue their computer training on MS Access beyond this beginner's guide to intermediate and advance levels. This introduction gives them an idea of what the program looks like and what to expect.

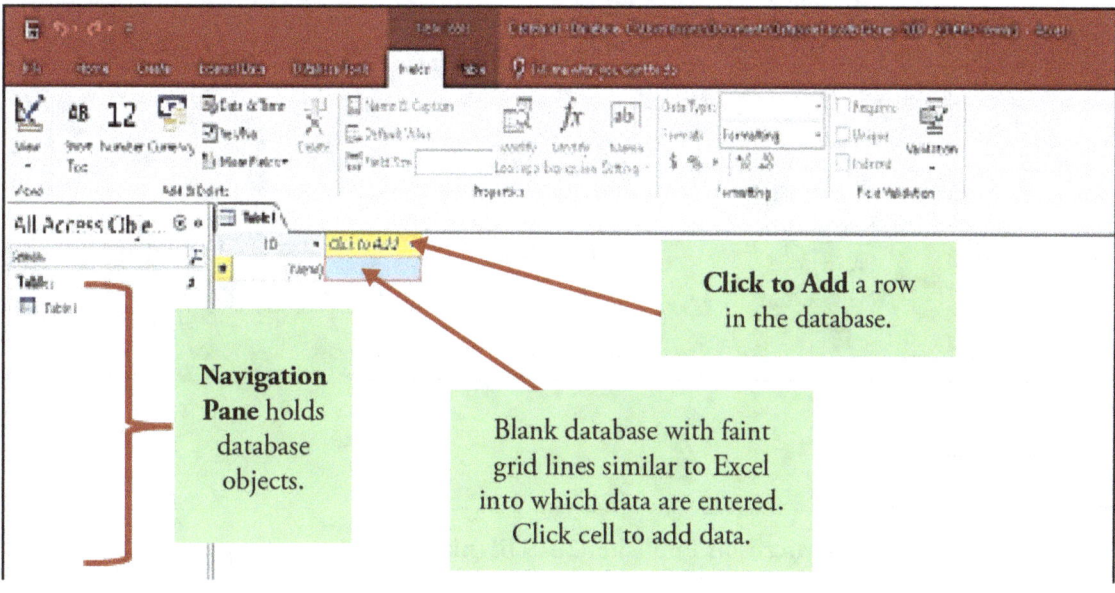

Fig. 3.6   Microsoft Access 2019 Blank Database View

Microsoft Publisher

Software that allows users to create a variety of professional looking documents such as newsletters, business cards, brochures, flyers, postcards, greeting cards, etc. Publisher can also be used to customize a publication by adding any pictures, graphics, or text you want. As in MS Access described above, Publisher also does not contain a chapter on how to use it in this book because it is not part of the affordable MS Office Home and Student, the focus of this beginner's guide. The goal here is to introduce the program as part of MS Office Professional package for the benefit of people who wish to continue their computer training on MS Publisher beyond this beginner's guide to intermediate and advance levels. This introduction gives them an idea of what the program looks like and what to expect.

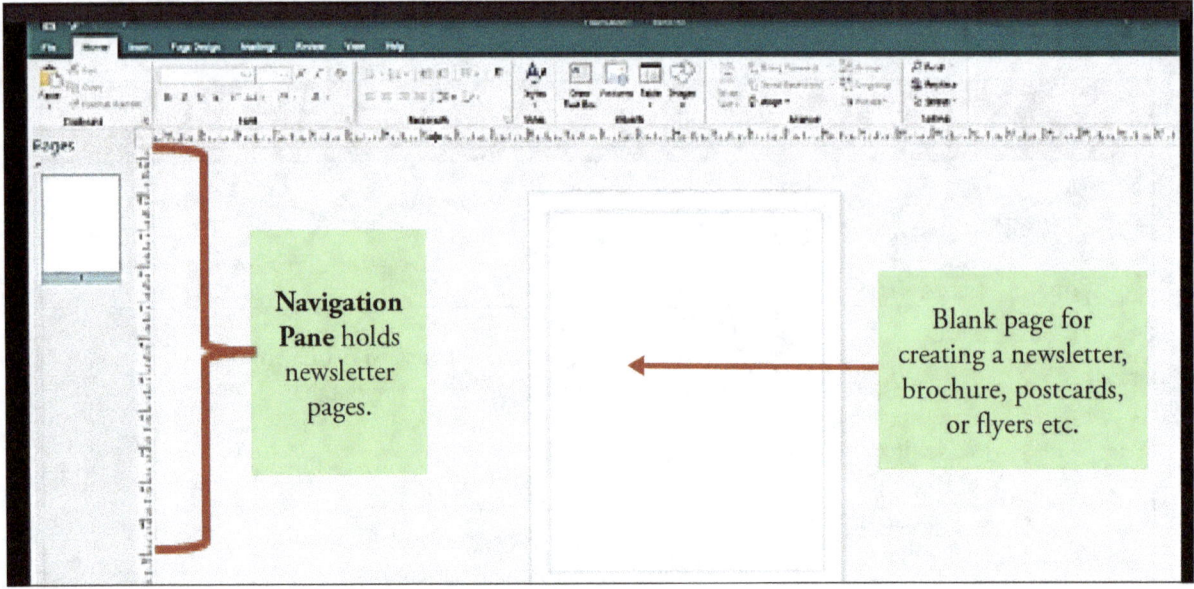

Fig. 3.7   Microsoft Publisher 2019 Blank Page

INSTALL, RUN, AND UNINSTALL SOFTWARE

Your computer system does not automatically come with all the software you need. With the exception of the operating system and Internet Explorer, you must purchase and install or download from website any additional software you may need before you can use it on your computer.

Install Software

This process copies and configures the software program to your computer hard drive and makes it run properly on your computer. Software applications packed and delivered in boxes often come with a list of required computer specifications. The software comes in a CD, packed with some paperwork, along with instructional manual or quick tips sheet. Depending on the computer design, your new computer may not have a CD drive in which case you have to purchase and download the software from Microsoft website by following simple onscreen download instructions. If your computer comes with a CD drive, most of the commercial software available in the market today are configured to begin installation automatically when you place the CD in the CD drive. To install software on a computer with CD drive, follow these steps:

1. On the upper side of your PC, press the button to open the **CD** drive.
2. Place the **CD** on the open drive drawer with the shiny side faced down, and press the button again to close the drive.
3. You do not need to do anything else for a few seconds as the auto-install process begins.
4. The installation process begins with the appearance of a dialog box called a **wizard** on your screen with a question asking whether you want to proceed with the installation.
5. Follow the onscreen guided instructions provided by the **installation wizard** to install the software.
6. Answer questions asked, and follow instructions to modify settings as needed for your computer.
7. During the installation process you may be asked to register or activate your software. Registering and activating newly installed software is discussed in the next section.

Run Software

Also known as executing or launching a software program, this process involves locating a newly installed program title on your computer double-clicking on it to launch it on your computer. Very often, some programs are installed simply as a title in a program list. To run the program:

1. Click the **Start** button.
2. From the displayed program list at left of your computer screen, navigate through up or down to locate the program title you want to launch, run, or open.
3. Double-click on the program title to run or open it.

What is the Difference between Operating System & Application or Program Software?

This is a question that most new beginners in computer technology find very confusing, including some college students. Operating system is software with instructions and commands that tell your computer what to do when you click to prompt a system action such as save, print, or delete. **Windows 10** is an example of operating system and it comes already installed on your computer. An application program is software used to create files saved on your computer, such as **MS Word**. Operating system allows application programs to function the way they are supposed to when you click to prompt actions like copy/paste, create a new folder, print, save, etc. Example of application software program is Microsoft Office packages summerized in previous paragraph that you use to create documents, accounting reports, presentations, etc, that are saved as files in your computer. You can work on a computer without application software, but you cannot work on a computer without an operating system because it is the brain of the computer that makes it work. Application programs do not come already installed in your computer. You have to purchase and install them in your computer in order to use them.

Uninstall Software

Unisntalling involves removing a program from your computer. Your hard drive may be large enough to hold all your programs and files, but sometimes you want to make more spaces available. This may require you to remove some unwanted programs that are just sitting there taking up space. Uninstalling is not the same thing as deleting a program icon; it involves removing all program components from a computer system. Be careful when manually removing files from your computer because you can mistakenly remove files that are necessary for other software applications to run properly. To remove an unwanted program and all its components, you must do a complete uninstallation which ensures that the removal does not adversley affect other software applications you need. To uninstall a program, do these **(fig. 3.8)**:

1. Click the **Start** button, in the **Search** box next to the start button, type **Programs**.
2. On the displayed menu, click **Add or Remove Programs**.

3. Navigate the displayed program list and click to select the program you want to uninstall.
4. Click **Uninstall** tab at bottom of the window to begin the uninstall process.
5. Follow onscreen prompts and instructions to remove the program from your computer.

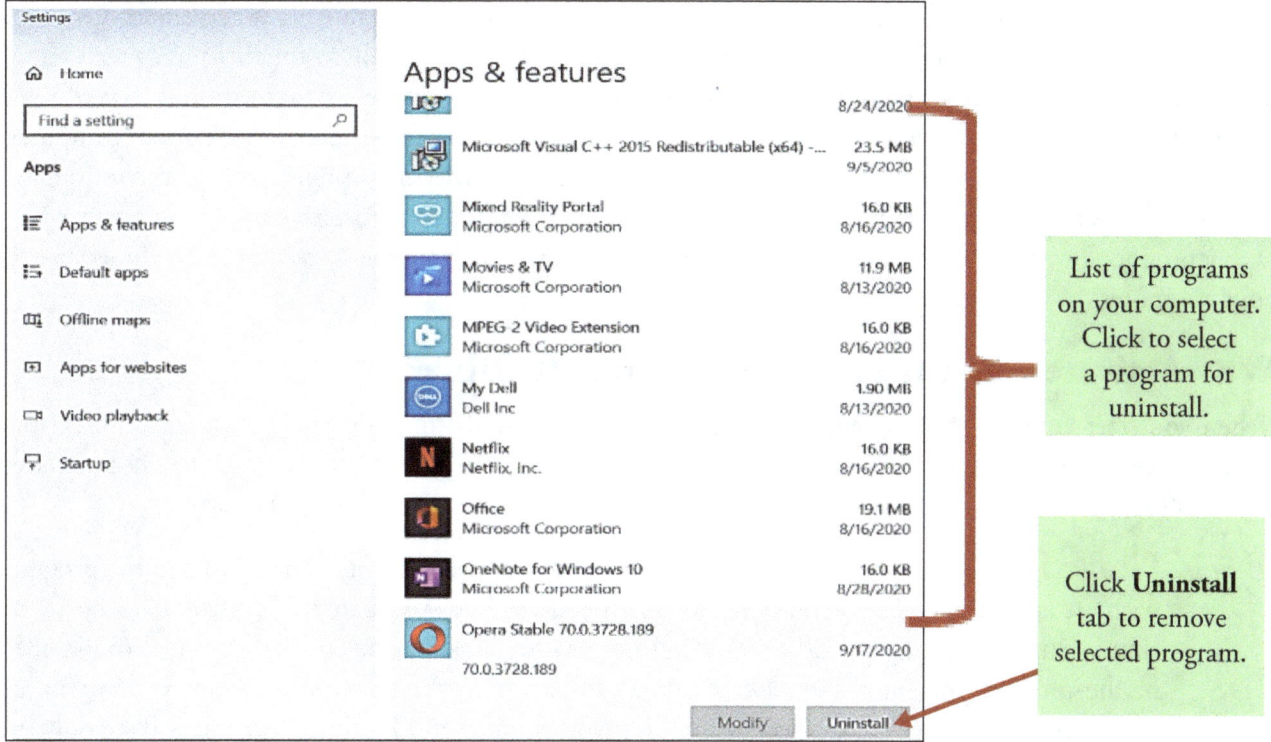

Fig. 3.8   **Settings Window for Add or Remove Programs**

ACTIVATE MICROSOFT OFFICE PROGRAMS

What is Activation?

To continue using all of the features of your product on your computer, you must first activate the product. **Microsoft Product Activation**, also referred to as product registration, is a Microsoft anti-piracy technology designed to verify that software products are legitimately licensed. The purpose of activation is to verify that the **Product Key,** which you must supply to install the product, is not in use on more personal computers than are permitted by the software license. Activation also ensures that the installed program continues to function as expected. If you purchase and download the software from Microsoft website, you are provided with a product key that you must enter in the product key box to activate the software for continued use on your computer.

Why Activate Current Edition of Microsoft Office?

When you start your Office program for the first time after installation, you are prompted to enter your **Product Key,** if you have not already done so during setup. If you do not activate your newly purchased Microsoft Office software right away, you may encounter the following two problems:

1. **Grace Period Expiration:** This is the period of time you are allowed to run the program without activation. Before you enter a valid **Product Key**, you can run the software up to **25** times. During the grace period, certain features or programs may be enabled that are not included in the product you purchased. Don't take it for granted; these features are not yours; you are simply running them on borrowed time. After you enter a valid Product Key, you will see only the programs and features you have purchased.

2. **Reduced Functionality Mode:** At the end of the grace period, if you have not entered a valid **Product Key** through registration, the software goes into **Reduced Functionality** mode. In this mode, your software behaves similarly to a viewer. You cannot save modifications to documents or create new documents, and functionality may be reduced. No existing files or documents are harmed in Reduced Functionality mode but you cannot create a new one either. After you enter your Product Key and activate your software, you will have full functionality for the programs and features you purchased.

Activate Newly Installed Software

After installation, a wizard window opens up with a question asking if you want to activate your program now or later. If you click **"Yes"** follow onscreen instructions to activate or register the program. When you enter your valid Product Key, the Activation Wizard automatically runs and displays the current edition of the MS Office release that is available to you. When you click **Next**, the **Activation Wizard** lists the programs that are in your current edition. Full version programs are indicated with a check mark. Trial version programs are indicated with the word **"Trial."** The Activation Wizard gives you three choices on how to proceed and register your product:

Automatic Activation Using the Internet: This type of activation may occur automatically while you install Microsoft Office software or soon after installation. Before you begin installation, make sure you are connected to the Internet. The **Activation Wizard** automatically contacts the Microsoft licensing servers through your Internet connection. If you are using a valid **Product Key** that has not already been used for the allowed number of installations, your product is activated immediately. When you activate through the Internet, your **Product ID** (derived from the installation Product Key) is sent to Microsoft through an encrypted transfer. A response **(the confirmation ID)** is sent back to your computer to activate your product. If you choose to activate your product through the Internet and you are not already connected, the wizard alerts you that there is no connection. To activate follow these steps:

1. In the **Activation Wizard**, from the down arrow, select the country/region where you reside and where you plan to use the product, and enter the **Product Key** in the space provided.
2. Type the **Confirmation ID** in the spaces provided at the bottom of the screen, and presses **ENTER.**
3. Follow onscreen instructions in **Activation Wizard** and click **Finish** when done.

Activate Using the Telephone: You can telephone an **Activation Center** and activate your product with the help of a customer service representative. Telephone activation may take longer than activation through the Internet. You should be at your computer when you call, and you should have your software **Product Key** available. Telephone numbers for **Activation Centers** vary by product license and country/region.

1. Use the telephone number provided on your **Activation Wizard** screen to call the **Microsoft Activation Center**.

2. The customer service representative will ask you for your **Installation ID** (displayed on your screen) and other relevant information.
3. Give the **Product Key** to customer service over the phone.
4. After your installation ID is verified, you receive a **Confirmation ID;** your product is now activated.

Activate Manually at a Later Time: If you choose to activate your copy of the software at a later time, you will have to do a manual activation on your computer. To do this, make sure you are connected to the Internet. If you have a problem with your activation, contact a customer service representative by using the telephone number provided in the wizard.

1. Open any Microsoft Office program (Word) and click the **File** tab.
2. From the displayed menu, click **Account**.
3. Under **Product Information**, click **Activate**, and follow simple onscreen instructions in the **Activation Wizard**, including entering your **Product Key** when prompted.
4. When activation is complete, exit the **Office** program, and restart your computer.
5. When you activate an Office edition such as Microsoft Word 2019 from an Office program, the entire Office edition (package) on your computer becomes activated.

What is a Trial Version?

When you purchase a new computer, you will notice that a few software is already installed in your computer. The computer manufacturers have installed a specific edition of the Microsoft Office programs on your hard drive which may include a mixture of full version and trial version programs. This is the manufacturer's way of marketing the product by letting consumers use the trial version for free to see if they like it. A Trial version allows you to evaluate the Office release for a limited amount of time, typically 30 or 60 days.

Software Purchase

Purchase means you are done evaluating the Trial version and want to purchase the full product. At the end of the trial period, when you open the program again, a message window opens asking if you want to purchase the product. If you click **"Yes"** you will be automatically directed to the manufacturer's website where you will be prompted to enter your credit card information to pay for the software. Once the purchase is complete, you will be provided with a **Product Key** which you will be prompted to enter during product activation.

View Privacy Options and Protect your Privacy

Some privacy options affect what information and files are downloaded from or sent to Microsoft. Depending on which Microsoft Office program you are using, some of these privacy options may not be available. To protect your privacy on your computer, follow these steps:

1. Open **Microsoft Word**, and click the **File** tab.
2. Click **Options,** at the bottom of the displayed list, click **Trust Center**, and click **Trust Center Settings** button **(fig. 3.9)**.
3. At the left pane of the open **Trust Center** window **(fig. 3.10)** click **Privacy Options,** then click the link**: Read our Privacy Statement.** You will be directed to Microsoft Office website where you can read Microsoft entire privacy statement including information about how to protect your privacy on your computer.
4. To perform this function, make sure your computer is connected to the Internet.

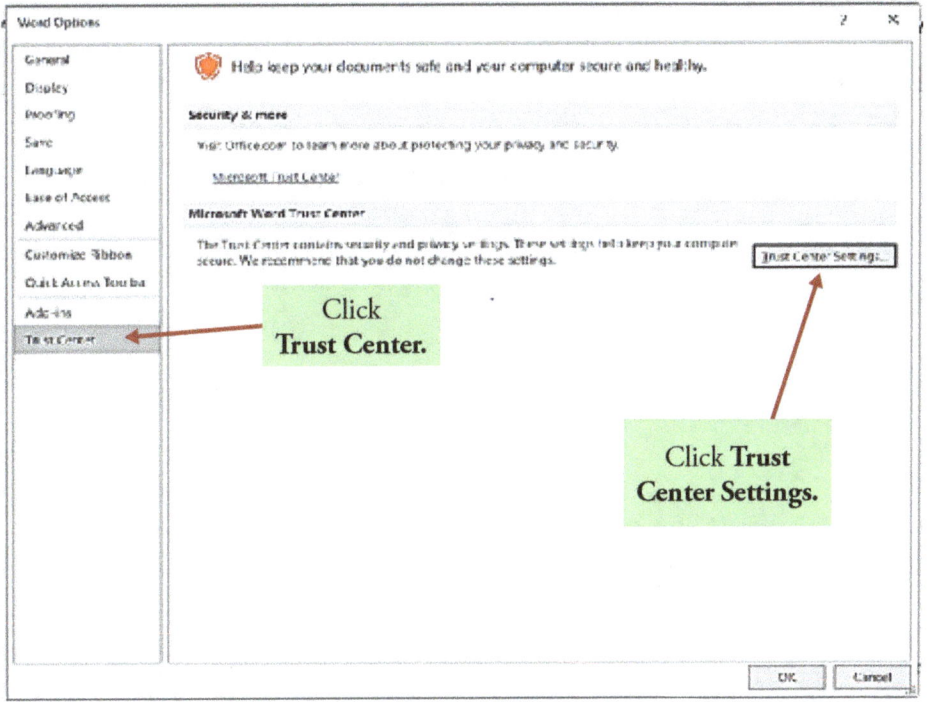

Fig. 3.9   **Trust Center Window**

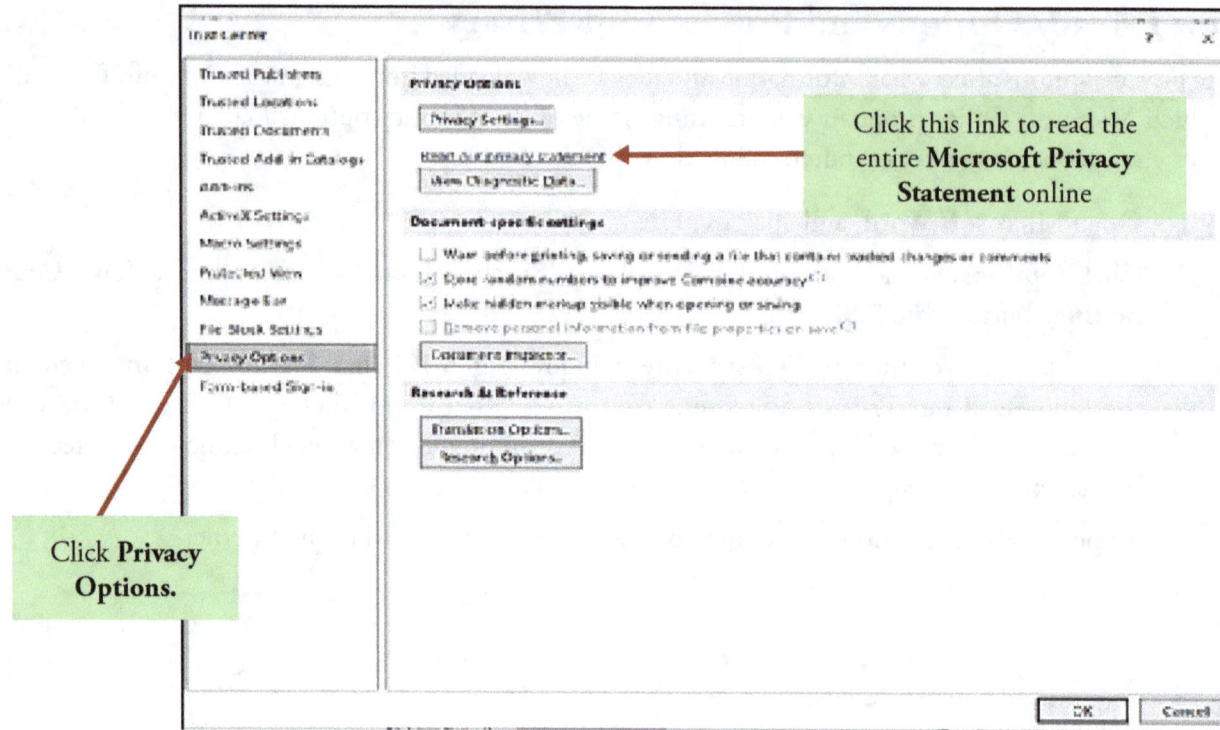

Fig. 3.10　　　　　　　　　View or Read Microsoft Privacy Statement

140 | *Basic Computing Concepts*

FIND CONTENTS YOU NEED IN MICROSOFT OFFICE HELP WINDOW

Navigating the **Help** window is similar to the way you navigate the Web in a Web browser such as Windows Internet Explorer. The difference is that the Help window has additional features that are lacking in a Web browser. **Help** is automatically installed on your computer when you install an Office program. You can also get additional Help content from **Microsoft Office Online** by specifying where you want to search for Help, or restrict the scope of your search to online or offline or to a specific category within a program. Listed below are various options available to you on searching for Help both online and offline:

1. When you open a **Microsoft Office** program while connected to the Internet, **Help** tap appears in the uppermost ribbon of your window screen.
2. Click the **Help** tap to open the **Help** window which may take you to Microsoft Office Online to get the information you need.
3. While in an Office program, **Help** window also opens up on the right side of your computer screen up when you press the **F1** key on your keyboard.
4. If Offline, **Help** window appears in the right corner of your computer where you can search and get **Help** from the files stored on your computer.

Search Microsoft from Office Program

1. Before searching for help online, make sure you are connected to the Internet.
2. Open the Microsoft Office program you need the help from, such as Word, Excel, PowerPoint, or any other Office program.
3. Click the **Help** button at top ribbon and click the **(?)** sign to display the help window, or press **F1** on the keyboard to open the **Help** window (**fig. 3.11**).
4. From the **Help** window, in the **Search** list, type your question, keyword, title or topic of your search, and click **Search** button to begin the search
5. Navigate through the list to locate the topic or category related to what you are searching for, and click on the content link for more detailed information on the topic (**fig. 3.12**).

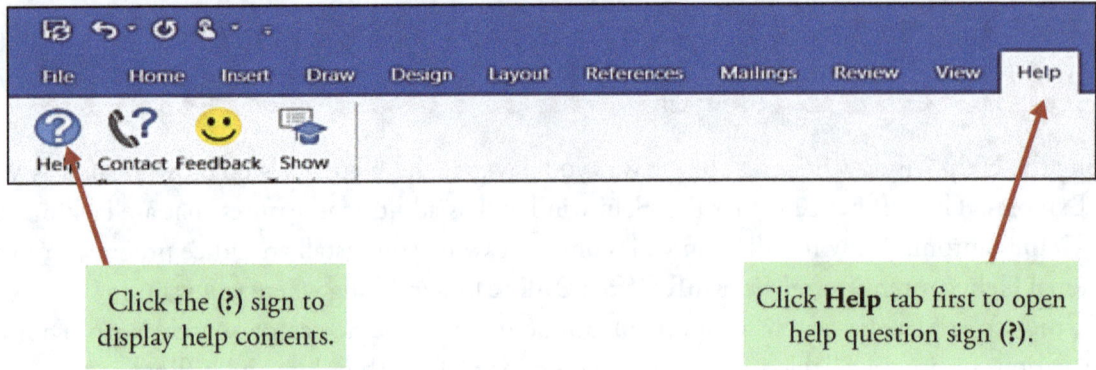

Fig. 3.11   **Find Microsoft Word Contents Using Help Tab**

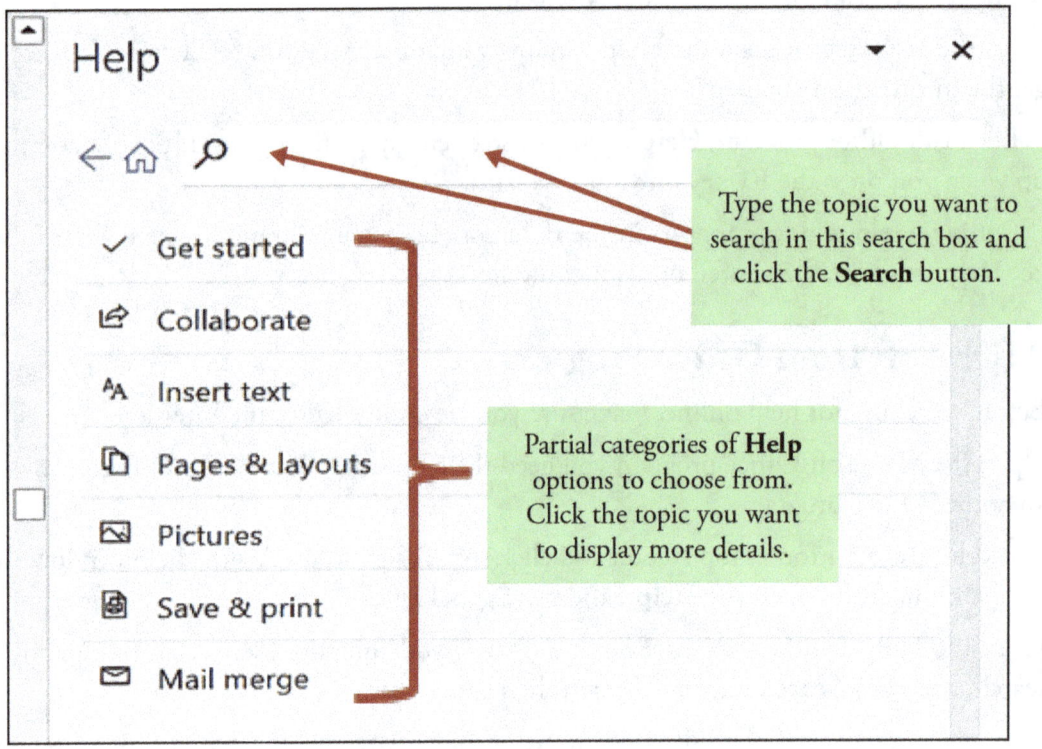

Fig. 3.12   **Help Window with Content Categories**

Basic Computing Concepts

CHAPTER SUMMARY & KEY TERMS

Software is an instruction program that tells your computer what to do. The software comes in a CD, packed with some paperwork along with instructional manual or quick tips sheet on how to install it on your computer. You may also download software from a website and install on your computer. Software installation is the process of coping and configuring the software program to your computer hard drive and makes it run properly on your computer. To continue using all of the features of your product, you must first activate the product. Microsoft Product Activation, also referred to as product registration is a Microsoft anti-piracy technology designed to verify that software products are legitimately licensed. Grace Period is the period of time you are allowed to run the program without activation. Before you enter a valid Product Key, you can run the software up to 25 times. During the grace period, certain features or programs may be enabled that are not included in the product you have purchased. Reduced functionality in a computer is a situation that occurs at the end of the grace period, if you have not entered a valid Product Key through registration to activate the product causing the software to go into Reduced Functionality mode on your computer. In this mode, your software behaves similarly to a viewer. You cannot save modifications to documents or create new documents, and functionality may be reduced. The trial version of a software already installed in a new computer when you purchase it is the manufacturer's way of marketing the product by letting consumers use the trial version for free to see if they like it.

KEY TERMS

Activate	Fragmented	Security Updates
Bad sector	Patch Tuesday	Software Sectors
Compatibility Diagnostics	Product Key	Windows Update
Defragmentation	Reduced functionality	

Demonstrate Your Knowledge & Skill

CHAPTER 3 PRACTICE EXERCISES
OVERVIEW OF MICROSOFT OFFICE SOFTWARE

3.1 – Select True or False answer to the following statements:

1. Microsoft Office Professional is the complete software package that contains Outlook, Word, Excel, Access, PowerPoint, and Publisher.
   a. True   b. False

2. Microsoft Office Home and Student is the most expensive software package in the market and most commonly used by business corporations.
   a. True   b. False

3. Individuals can setup MS Outlook online using free emailing services found on the Internet.
   a. True   b. False

4. The main difference between Microsoft Office 2019 and Office 365 is that MS Office 2019 can be purchased outrightly while Office 365 requires payment of monthly subscription fee.
   a. True   b. False

5. The most commonly used MS Office software by schools, colleges, and private individuals are Word, Excel, and PowerPoint.
   a. True   b. False

6. 6Microsoft Product Activation, also referred to as product registration, is a Microsoft anti-piracy technology designed to verify that software products are legitimately licensed.
   a. True   b. False

7. Microsoft Office Home and Student package may also contain Database software, including Outlook, and Publisher.
   a. True   b. False

8. Registration of all MS Office software on your computer either online, manually, or through telephone requires a Product Key
   a. True
   b. False

9. When you install MS Office software on your computer, you are allowed to run the program up to 50 times without activation.
   a. True
   b. False

10. Reduced Functionality Mode describes a situation where the software on your computer behaves similarly to a viewer. In this mode, you cannot save modifications to documents or create new documents.
    a. True
    b. False

3.2 – Multiple Choice: Select the best answer to Microsoft software features described below:

1. Which of the following statement does NOT describe the process of installing software:
   a. Software is copied to your computer's hard drive and makes it available for use.
   b. During installation, the program is configured so that it runs properly on your system.
   c. Software applications are packaged in boxes that list the required computer specifications.
   d. Installation of software on a hard drive is not required to run it on a regular basis.

2. A series of guided screens that simplify a task by asking questions and allowing you to modify some settings is a(n):
   a. installation program
   b. installation wizard.
   c. application program.
   d. commercial software program.

3. The first thing you should do once you install new MS Office in your computer to maintain program functionality and also enables you to receive information on software upgrades and discount product purchase opportunities.
   a. registration
   b. purchasing
   c. wizard
   d. processing

4. The Windows Registry is a:
   a. way of registering your copy of Windows.
   b. special file that holds only network settings.
   c. program that allows you to register other Windows users on your computer.
   d. special file that keeps track of Windows and program settings.

5. The Windows Registry is a:
   a. way of registering your copy of Windows.
   b. special file that holds only network settings.
   c. program that allows you to register other Windows users on your computer.
   d. special file that keeps track of Windows and program settings.

6. The only way to remove a program and all of its components is through:
   a. a complete uninstall.
   b. deleting the program's executable file.
   c. deleting the folder with the program and the executable file in it.
   d. copying the program back to the original CD.

7. Running a program is called:
   a. installing or uninstalling.
   b. administering or managing.
   c. executing or launching.
   d. executing or coordinating.

8. Most programs, when installed, appear as:
   a. icons in the Control Panel.
   b. a title on the program list of the Start menu.
   c. a title on the desktop.
   d. icons on the taskbar.

9. Which of the following statements regarding Startup programs is FALSE?
   a. Some of the listed programs may not be necessary.
   b. They may slow the boot process.
   c. They will not impact the performance of scheduled tasks.
   d. They may lessen the amount of memory.

10. Microsoft makes corrections available in the form of downloads (Windows Updates) to do all of the following EXCEPT:
    a. correct bugs.
    b. distribute development of minor improvements.
    c. keep your software updated with version changes.
    d. advise you of when your system has been attacked.

11. Patches are a type of update distributed by Microsoft to:
    a. solve security problems or to enhance the operating system.
    b. fix holes in the operating system.
    c. temporarily stop security weaknesses until the next version release.
    d. prevent malicious attacks on your computer.

12. The type of updates required to prevent your computer from being vulnerable to hackers or other serious security threats is known as:
    a. serious
    b. critical
    c. essential
    d. necessary

13. Service packs are:
    a. much larger updates that address large-scale security problems.
    b. much smaller updates that address small-scale security problems.
    c. optional updates that address a variety of security problems.
    d. optional updates that address only specific security problems.

14. A free online service provided by Microsoft available in both Windows 10 and Windows 7 that automatically provides updates and patches is:

    a. Microsoft Windows Utilities.
    b. Microsoft Windows Update.
    c. Microsoft Windows Auto-Update.
    d. Vista and XP Update.

15. A software suite that includes Word, Excel, and PowerPoint is:
    a. Windows Utilities.
    b. Windows Productivity Suite.
    c. Microsoft BackOffice.
    d. Microsoft Office – Home & Office

16. To access the Privacy option in any MS Office program, you start by clicking one of the following tabs at top menu of the open program:
    a. Save tab
    b. Review tab
    c. File tab
    d. Layout tab

3.3 – Fill-in the Blanks with the correct words or terms for the statements and descriptions below:

1. Most _____ software is configured to begin installation automatically when you place the CD in the CD drive.
2. The series of screens that guides you through the installation process is known as a(n) _____.
3. Only _____ a program will remove the program and all its components from a computer system.
4. A special file that keeps track of Windows and program settings is the _____.
5. The process of initially running a software program is referred to as executing or _____.
6. _____ does not correct software problems although it might eliminate some variables that could cause problems, such as a corrupted temporary file.
7. Microsoft provides patches or _____ to solve security problems or to enhance the operating system.
8. If _____ are not applied, your computer could be vulnerable to hackers or other serious security threats.
9. Updates that address large-scale security problems are called _____.
10. Microsoft Windows Update is a free _____ that provides updates and patches.

CHAPTER 3 SKILL-BASED PRACTICE PROJECTS OVERVIEW OF MICROSOFT OFFICE SOFTWARE

3.1 – Identify MS Office Window: Six (6) window images of a complete MS Office package are presented below. In the middle of each window, a text box is provided. Inside the text box, enter the program name, including what version (year) of MS Office program it is.

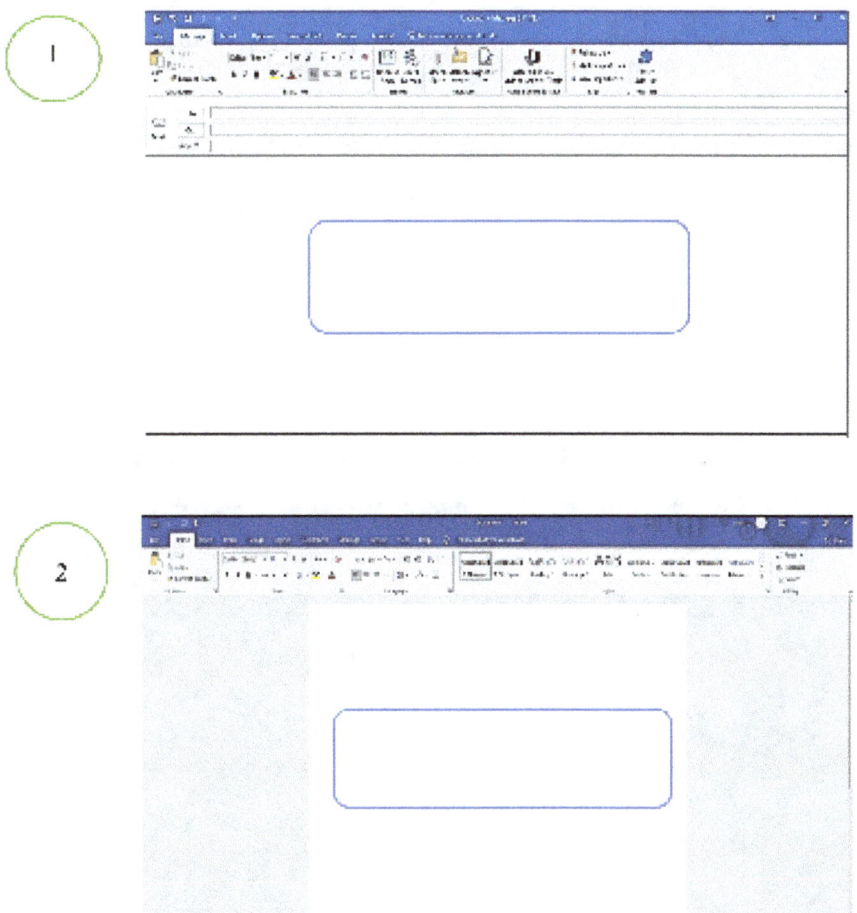

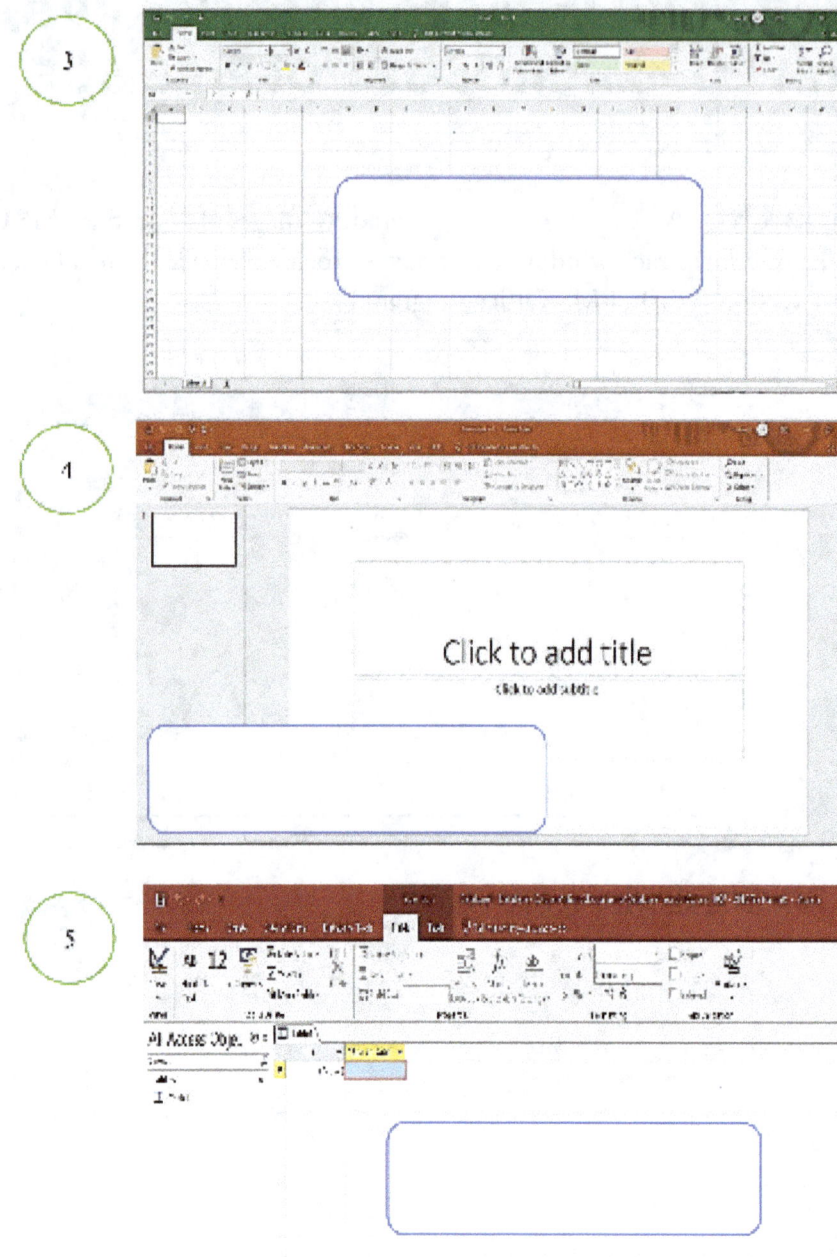

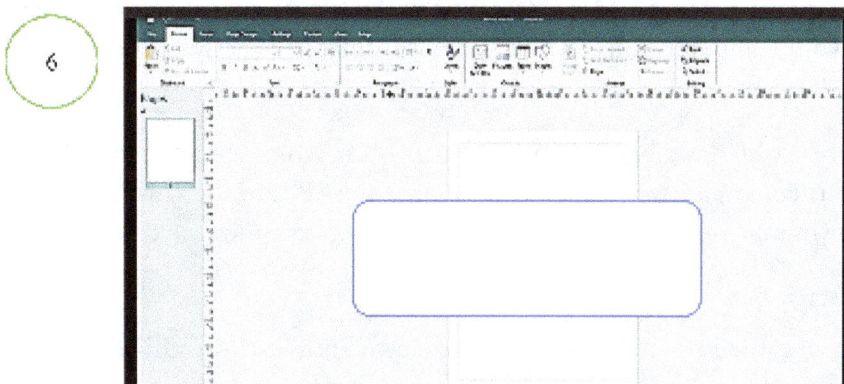

3.2 – Uses of Microsoft Office Programs: On the left column of the table below, enter names of the six MS Office programs you identified in item 3.1 above; and on the right column describe what the program is used for. On the textbook, enter your name and date at top page of your completed work; photocopy and submit for instructor grading.

Program Name	Program Use
1.	
2.	
3.	
4.	
5.	
6.	

All-in-One Beginners Guide to Computer Proficiency

3.3 – Activate Newly Installed Software:
As discussed in chapter 3, whenever you install MS Office software on your computer, you are immediately prompted to activate the software and provided with activation onscreen instructions and options.

Required: Based on the facts described in item 3.3, open a new Word document entitled **Software Activation** at top page, center title, and answer the following questions. Please use correct Standard English in your responses and keep your answers brief, concise, and straight to the point.

1. What is Activation?
2. Why is it important to always activate your newly installed MS Office program?
3. What happens to the installed program on your computer if not activated within the time period allowed? What is the term used to describe the program in this mode?
4. What is the term used to describe the allowable period for activation?
5. List the three methods of software activation.
6. Save your document as **3.3_Activation_Firstname_Lastname** using your first name and last name in the preferred location on your computer using your first and last name. Submit your completed assignment following the instructor's preferred method – electronically or printed hardcopy for grading.

CHAPTER 4

INTRODUCTION TO MICROSOFT OFFICE WORD 2019

If you think Microsoft Word 2016 is great, wait till you see the awesome features packed in Microsoft Word 2019. In the exciting world of information technology, creating and formatting a document has never been easier. Microsoft Word 2019 makes it easier to collaborate and to navigate through long documents allowing a user to create more professional looking documents with a simple click of the mouse. As word processing software, Microsoft Word 2019 combines the familiar features you know in 2016 with some new easy-to-use features designed to help you create professional-quality documents. With the finest document-formatting tools, Word helps you organize and write your documents more efficiently. You can create or update your documents using many of the same formatting tools that you already know from 2013 but now improved to help you do more in your document such as: using **AutoCorrect** to correct typos and misspelled words, using improved selection mode to select content more precisely, count number of words and characters in a document, format text with font styles, and format lists with bullets or numbers.

Learning Objectives:

After completing this chapter, you will be able to:

- Work with all the new features in Microsoft Word 2019.
- Navigate the new Word 2019 window, create, and format a new document.

- View several pages in Word navigation pane, search for a specific document with many pages on the navigation pane, and delete pages.
- Organize documents in files, create a new folder, and save files in the folder.
- Format a document, change page margins, orientation, and text size.
- Copy, move, and paste text within a document or to another location on the computer.
- Insert table, header, footer, and page number in a Word document
- Use spell and grammar checker, and save a new, unnamed document
- Preview a page, print a document, and print selected pages or range of pages from a Word document.
- Use various Microsoft shortcuts and function keys to perform tasks in Word 2019.

NEW FEATURES OF MICROSOFT WORD 2019

In the new Word 2019 version you can easily recover unsaved work, find, and apply a template or start a document from a template, save and reuse templates, select and read only the page you want to read without scrolling through large documents on your computer screen; copy and paste only text and exclude items you do not want to be pasted; view Word program in backstage view; and move the **Quick Access Toolbar** to a new location on the ribbon. When you first open a Word 2019 window you will quickly notice that the familiar **Microsoft Office** button is now replaced with a **File** tab, placed to the left of the **Home** tab as shown in the diagram **fig.4.1** below:

Quick Access Toolbar

This feature is very common with all MS Office products. As an ardent user of Office products, you may already be familiar with this handy tool. Quick Access is the toolbar at the very top left of MS Office programs – Word, Excel, and PowerPoint window. As the name implies, this feature allows you to perform quick actions. The Quick Access Toolbar is made up of three main icons – Save, Undo, Redo, including a down arrow that allows you to Customize the toolbar by relocating to a more convenient location while you work.

Save Icon: Allows you to quickly save the file you are working on with the current file name, instead of going through the file tab.

Undo Icon: While working on a document, if you make a mistake and want to undo it, just click the **Undo** button. When you click it once, it will undo the last action you took. However, as you keep clicking the undo icon, it will continue to undo each previous action you've taken by moving backward. Alternatively, you can click the arrow next to the Undo icon and highlight all actions you want to undo and undo them at once.

Redo Icon: The **Redo** icon changes in shape only when you click the **Undo**. The new shape is the same as Undo icon except that it points to the right allowing you to redo what you have just undone. Like the Undo icon, you can redo your last action with one click or use the arrow next to the Redo button to Redo multiple actions.

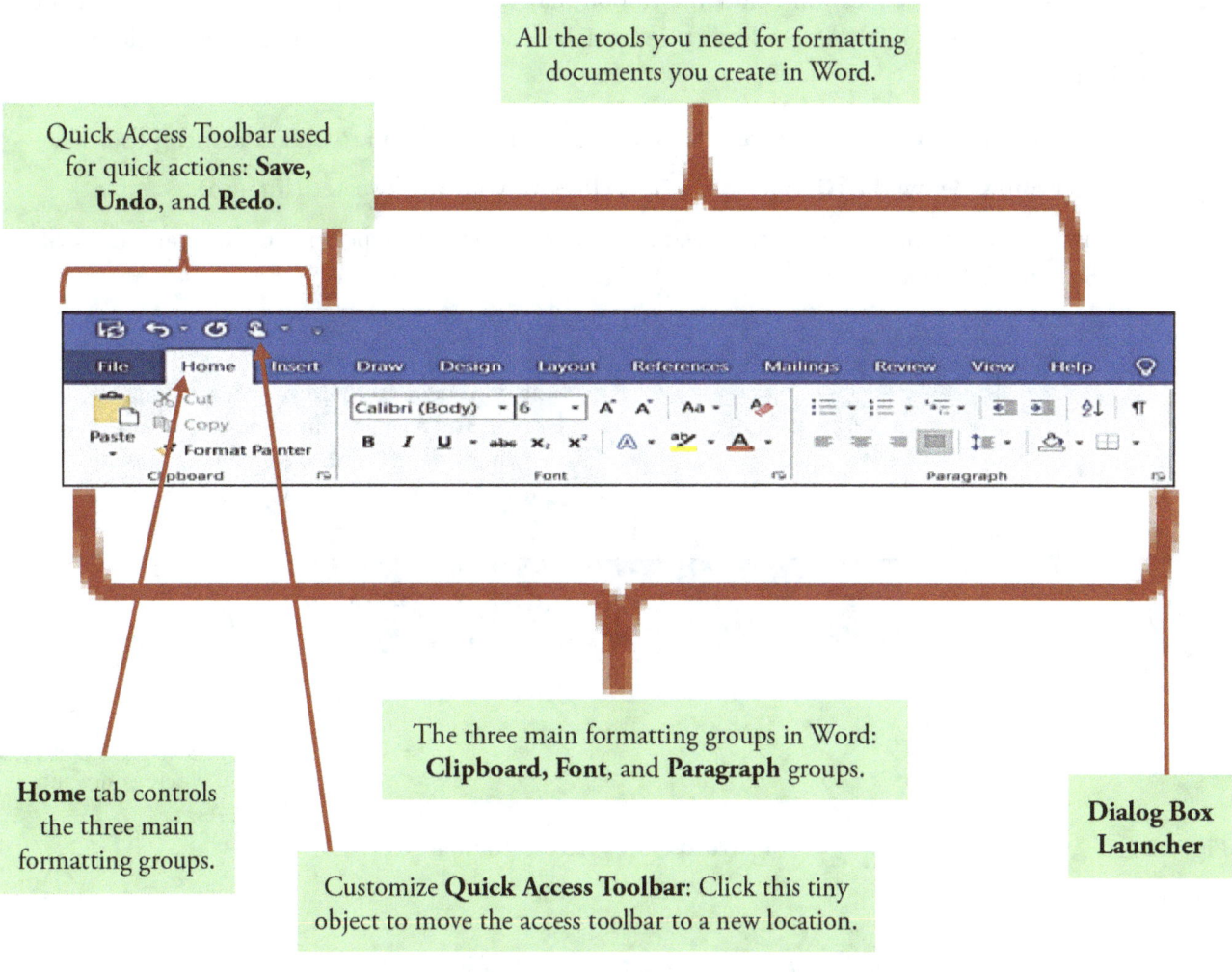

Fig. 4.1   **Microsoft Word 2019 Ribbon with Formatting Tools**

All-in-One Beginners Guide to Computer Proficiency | 157

Move Quick Access Toolbar to a New Location on the Ribbon

By default, the **Quick Access Toolbar** is always located at the top left corner of the ribbon. This is not a permanent location; you have the option to move to a more convenient location of your choice. There are only two places on a Word screen where you can place the quick access toolbar – on its current place and below the ribbon. If you don't want the Quick Access Toolbar to be displayed in its default location, you can move it to the next alternate location. For example, if you find that the default location is too far from your work area to be convenient, you have the option to move below the ribbon below, closer to your work area. On the other hand, the location below the ribbon may interfere with your work area, in which case you may want to keep the Quick Access Toolbar in its default location. Follow these steps to relocate quick access toolbar:

1. Click on **Customize Quick Access Toolbar** icon ⬄ at top ribbon to open the menu list.
2. Select **Show Below the Ribbon** so that it is closer to your work space. **(fig. 4.3)**.
3. This is a toggle option, to move it back to its default location, repeat steps **1 & 2** and click **Show Above the Ribbon**.

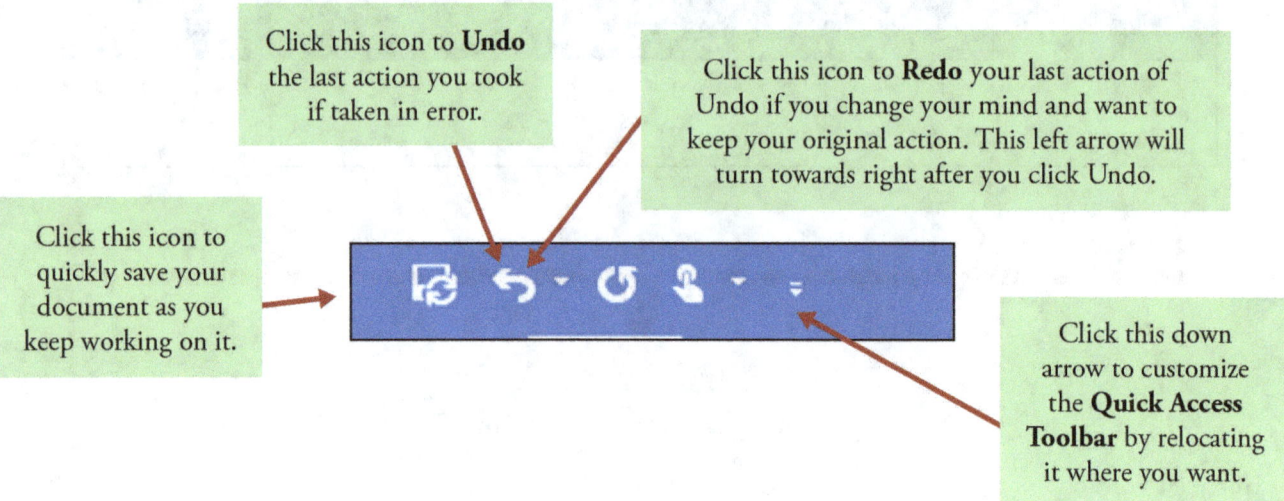

Fig. 4.2   MS Word Quick Access Toolbar

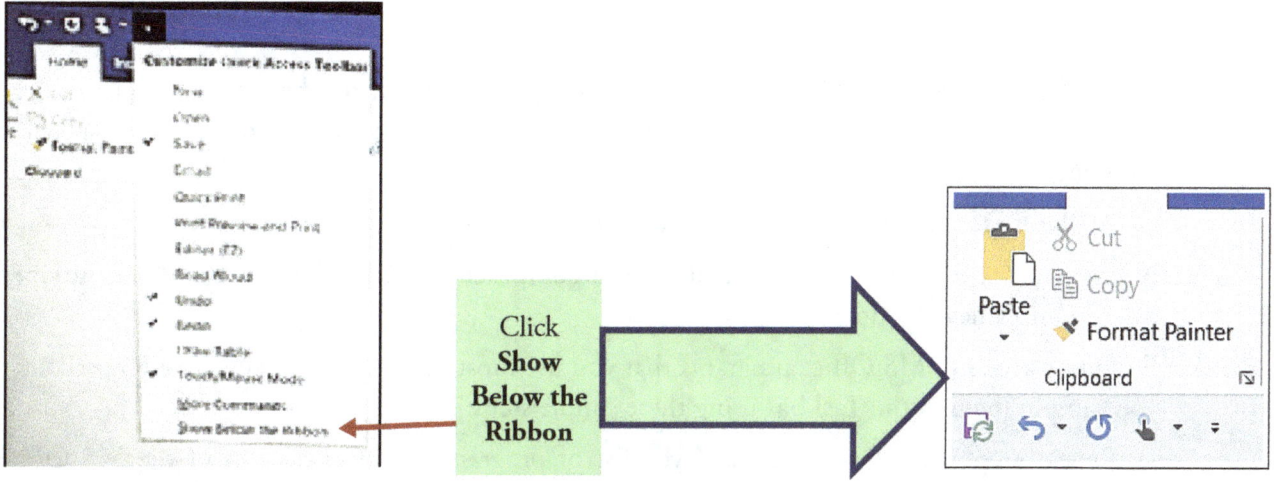

Fig. 4.3   **Relocating the Quick Access Toolbar**

Creating New Documents

When you first open MS Word, the window always defaults to normal as highlighted by the **Normal** button at the toolbar. This default normal automatically puts everything you type in double spaced format. To type in single space, click the **No Spacing** button. The **AutoComplete** feature in Word provides commonly used words and phrases, such as salutations and dates. **Word-wrap** determines if the next word in line will fit and moves it to the next line if necessary.

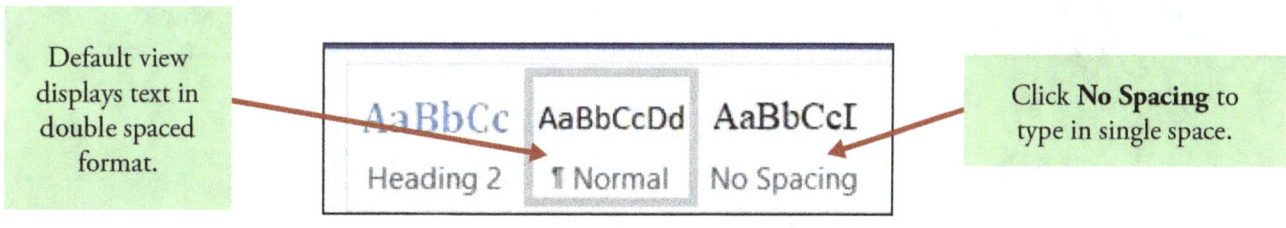

Fig. 4.4   **Default (Normal) View of Typed Words**

All-in-One Beginners Guide to Computer Proficiency | 159

Create a New Word Document

1. With Microsoft **Word 2019** already installed on your computer, on the search box next to the **Start** button, type **Microsoft Office**, navigate the displayed list, and select **Word** to open the program.
2. Click **Blank Document** to display a blank page, and begin typing text **(fig. 4.6)**.
3. Alternatively, if you have **Word** pinned to your computer **Taskbar**, click on **Word** icon to open directly into a new document and start typing.
4. For quick access to MS Office programs that you use most often (Word, Excel, and PowerPoint), you can pin them to the **Taskbar** using these simple steps:

    a. Repeat **step 1** above, on the displayed list of programs, right-click each of the MS Office program you want to pin, and select **Pin to Start**.

    b. You will notice that all the program icons you selected now appear on the taskbar. Once the program icons are pinned to the taskbar, each time you want to open a program, simply click the icon on the taskbar without going through the start button as in step I above.

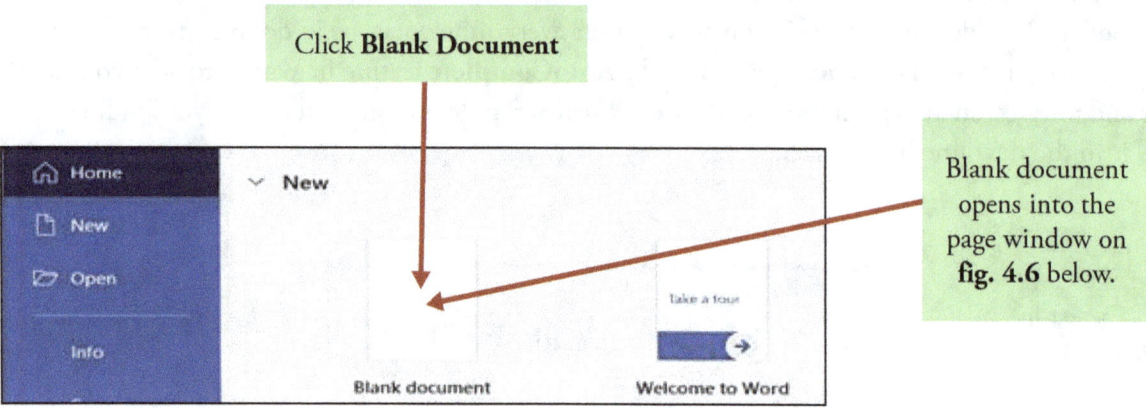

Fig. 4. 5   **New Blank Document**

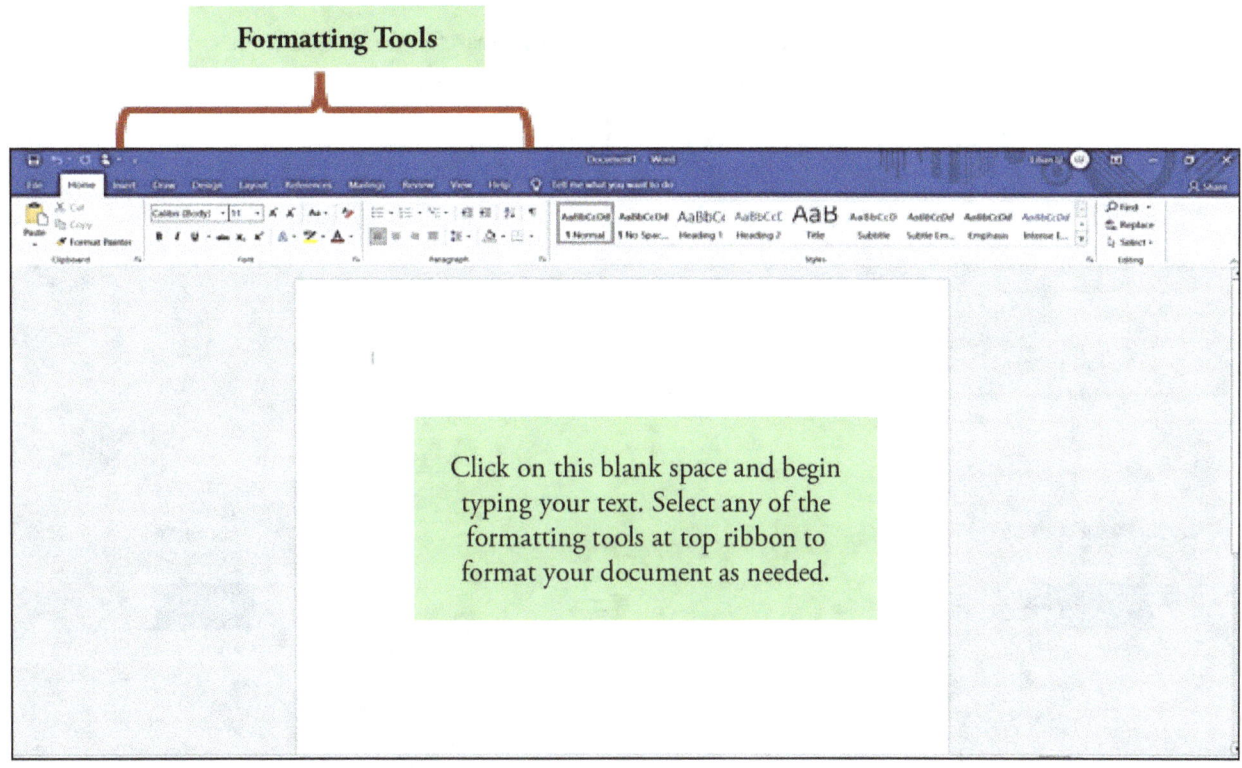

Fig. 4.6   Create a New Document

Start a Document from a Template

1. Click the **File** tab, at the left pane of the open **File** window, select **New** from the list.
2. Templates available on your computer will display, select the template you want and start typing your document.
3. If you want to use a template from **Microsoft Online**, type your keyword in the **Search for Online Template** box and click the **Search** button. You must be connected to the Internet to download the template.
4. From the downloaded templates, double-click to select the template you want, start typing your text and format as needed. Formatting documents will be discussed in the proceeding sections.

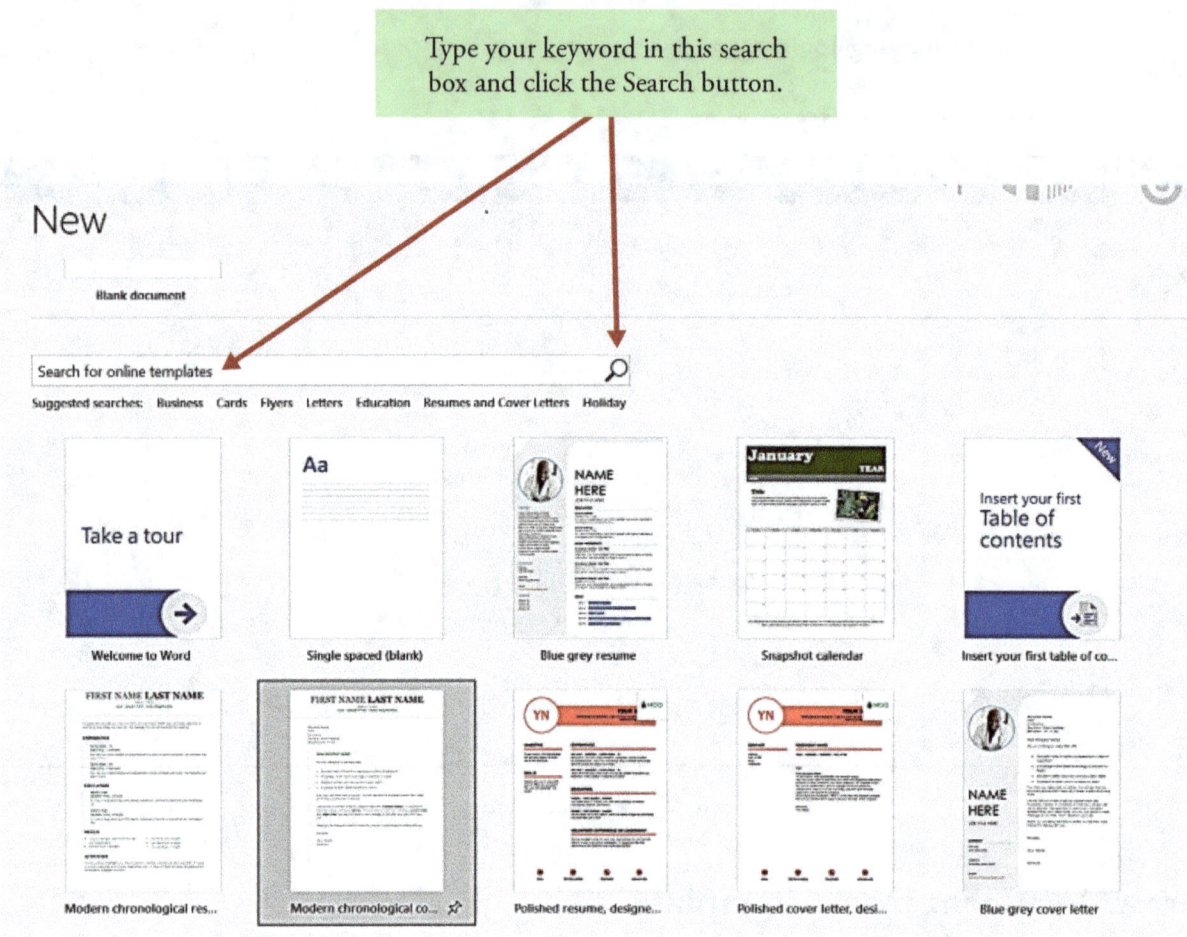

Fig. 4.7   **Partial List of Word Available Templates on Your Computer**

View Documents in the Navigation Pane or a Selected Page

The new Word 2019 allows you to quickly find your way and navigate through long documents using the new document navigation pane to view only the page you want to view without going through all pages.

1. Click the **View** tab at the top ribbon.
2. In the **Show** group, click to check the **Navigation** box.

3. Under **Navigation** box, click **Pages**; your multiple documents will be displayed page by page on the left side of the screen **(fig. 4.8)**.

4. Scroll up or down the navigation pane, click on any page you want to view.

5. To view a particular page by number, on the **Navigation Pane**, click the **Search Document** box down arrow and click **Go To**.

6. In the open **Find and Replace** dialog box, in the **Enter Page Number** box, type the page number you want to view and click the **Go To** tab at top of the dialog box. You will be directed straight to the page you want to view **(fig. 4.9)**.

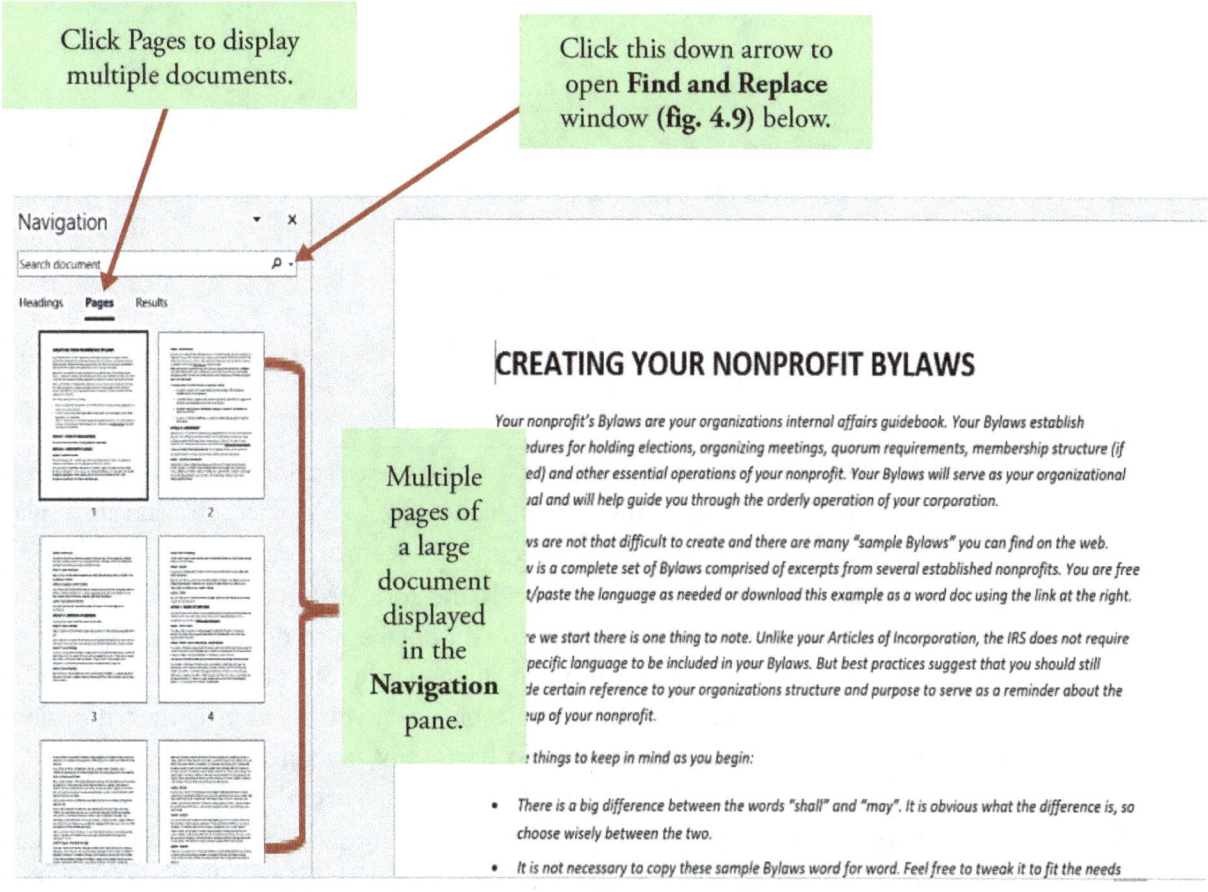

Fig. 4.8   View Partial List of Multiple Word Documents in the Navigation Pane

All-in-One Beginners Guide to Computer Proficiency

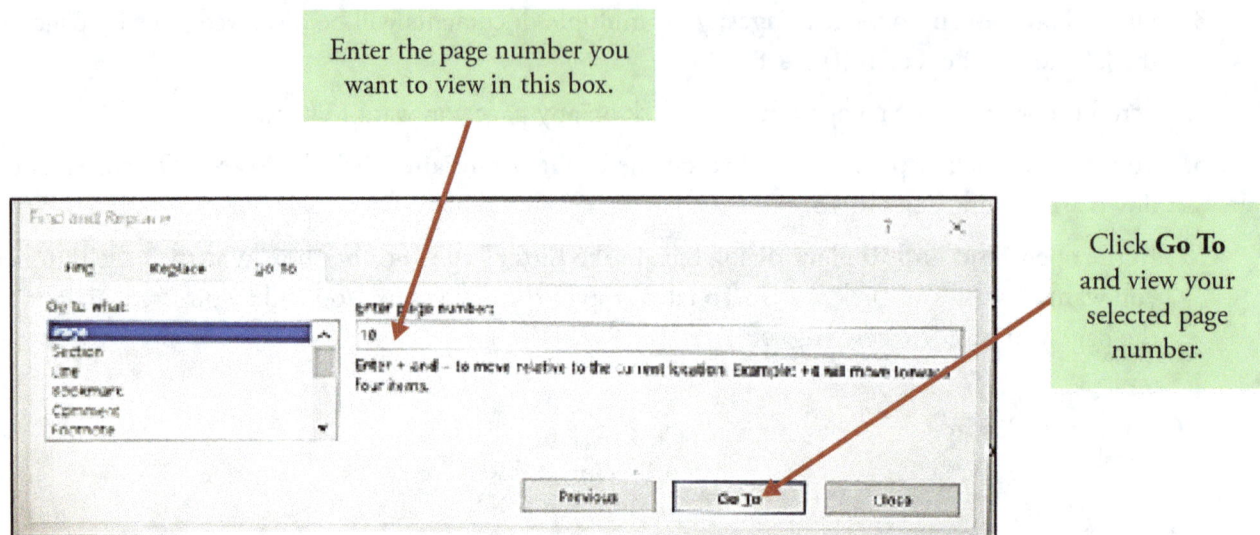

Fig. 4.9   View a Page in Multiple Documents

Word 2019 Basic Formatting Tools & Groups

Formatting Tools & Groups	Description & Uses
File	The **File** tab contains actions that allow you to save, print, export or share files you create in Word. These are just a few of file actions; several others exist and are displayed when you click the file tab. To save or print a document begin by clicking the **File** tab.
Home	The **Home** tab houses and controls the formatting groups that you click to begin document formatting. When you open a new document, it opens to the eight main tools at the ribbon and three main groups below the ribbon. Other groups exist within the formatting tools when you click on a selected option to display more tools and groups. To begin any type of formatting, click on the **Home** tab first to display all formatting tools. Select the option you want.
Insert	Contains a list of items that can be inserted into a document or report such as tables, pictures, clip arts, shapes, page numbers, footers, headers, and several other items a user wants to insert into documents. Selection of the **Insert** tab opens up a variety of items you can choose from.

Draw	Used for drawing or sketching on a document. The **Draw** tab is not used very often as a formatting tool. Click the Draw tab to sketch an image.
Design	Provides a list of styles, colors, and fonts for creating professional looking documents, business reports, and research papers.
Layout	The **Layout** tab provides you with all the formatting tools you need to change margins, page orientation, select page sizes, and apply columns to text in your document. To set page margins, change page orientation and other document formatting, click the Layout tab, and select the option you want.
References	The **References** tab contains report writing tools that allow you to give credit to sources used in your report. It provides a variety of options from table of contents, footnotes to research, report format, including citations and bibliography. Refences is a very important tool for writing school papers where you may be required to use information from other sources but give credit to the source. Click the References tab, select the option you want, and apply the required format to your report or school paper.
Mailings	Provides tools for large mailings; frequently used by business organizations in offices that mail correspondences in bulk. Click **Mailings** tab to start mail merge.
Review	Used for doing spell and grammar check and correcting errors on completed documents. Click Review tab and select **Spelling & Grammar**.
View	Allows you to view your document in several different layout formats, and sizes. Click **Vie**w tab and select an option.
Clipboard Group	The group that provides you with copy/paste options, including **Format Painter** tools. The dialog box launcher when clicked contains additional formatting tools. Click **Copy** on highlighted text, click **Paste** on blank space on a document. Each group comes with a dialog box launcher.
Font Group	Contains options that allow you to change font types and font sizes on the document you create. The dialog box launcher when clicked contains additional formatting tools. Click down arrow of font type and size boxes to select an option.
Paragraph Group	Provides line-spacing, indent, and page justification options. The dialog box launcher when clicked contains additional formatting tools. Click dialog box launcher and select an option.

Table 4.1   **Word Basic Formatting Tools**

FORMATTING DOCUMENTS – CHANGE PAGE MARGINS, TEXT SIZE, PAGE ORIENTATION & LINE SPACING

This section covers basic formatting tools a beginner in MS Word needs to know for creating and formatting documents. These basic tools include: editing text; setting page margins; changing page orientation and text size; changing line spacing; applying fonts to text; including copy/pate; saving, printing, spellchecking, and deleting a saved document. In MS Word, the formatting features located at the top ribbon and within the tabs come organized in groups. Each group has its own dialog box launcher that opens into additional windows when prompted. These windows display detailed formatting options a user can choose from. Some formatting tools related to such as **Draw, Design, References, and Mailings** listed in **Table 4.1** above are beyond the scope of this beginner's guide. These topics are usually covered in most MS Word instructional books designed for intermediate users. They are included in the table because they are part of the formatting tools at the ribbon. Our focus in this section is on basic formatting for new beginners in MS Word. Keep in mind that before you apply formatting to text, a group of texts/words, or paragraph, you must first highlight what you want to format.

Editing Text

Editing simply involves changing words, sentences, or formatting text in a document as you type to create a complete document. Making corrections as you type reduces the number of errors you have to correct using the spellcheck feature. You can edit text in your document using these three main keys on your computer keyboard:

1. **Delete Key**: This key removes one character at a time to the right of where you want to insert a word (insertion point). To use the delete key, position the cursor to the **Left** of the word(s) you want to delete and press the delete key until all the words are deleted, then type the new word(s).

2. **Backspace key:** Removes text from the screen one character at a time to the left of where you want to insert a word (insertion point). To use backspace key, position the cursor to the **Right** of the word(s) you want to delete and press the backspace key until all the words are deleted, then type the new word(s).

3. **Insert Key:** Inserts a word or sentences in the middle of text. When an insertion point is in the middle of a word or sentence, existing text moves to the right to make room for the new words.

It is the default setting in MS Word. To use the insert key, position the cursor where you want to insert a new word(s) and press the insert key, then type the new word(s). As you type, notice that the words to the right of your text delete automatically and replaced by the new words you type. When finished inserting words, press the insert key again to turn it off.

Select and Highlight Text

This refers to highlighting and dragging with your mouse over text. Selected text can be edited, formatted, copied, or moved. Formatting text sets the overall appearance of the text. You can change the layout, color, shading, emphasis, or font characteristics of your text.

1. To highlight an entire document page, place cursor at top page, and press **CTRL+ A**.
2. To highlight a block of text, place the cursor at the first word in the block of text.
3. Holding down the mouse, highlight your selected text from left to right and edit as needed.

Format Text and Change Fonts

When you right-click as you type your document in MS Word, notice that the **Mini** toolbar appears to the right of your text. The **Mini** toolbar helps you work with fonts, font styles, font sizing, font types, alignment, text color, indent levels, and bullet features.

1. **Font Styles:** Font styles are used to emphasize text and visualize cues within text in a document. They include: **Bold,** *Italics,* and Underline.
2. **Font Sizes:** Font sizes range from **8" to 72"** and help to make words appear larger in a text. Larger words also help to show emphasis.
3. **Font Types:** The most commonly used font types in creating documents in **MS Word** are **Times New Roman, Arial, Calibri,** and **Arial Narrow**. There are several others in font type list. The following diagram shows the full **Mini Toolbar** at top ribbon. To use the toolbar, click on the commands you want to use.

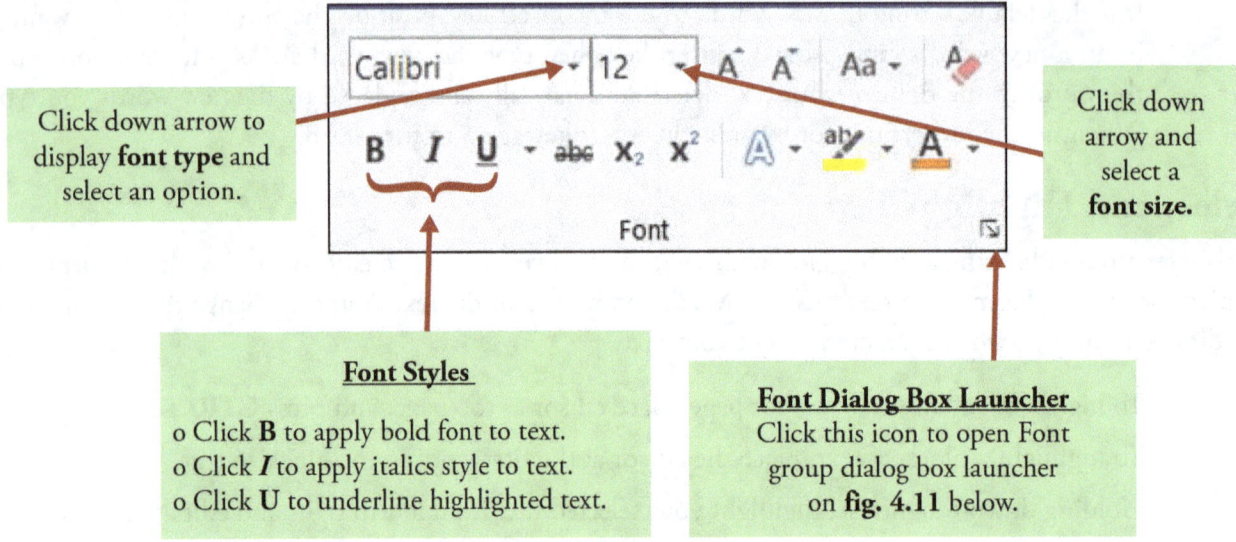

Fig. 4.10   Font Group

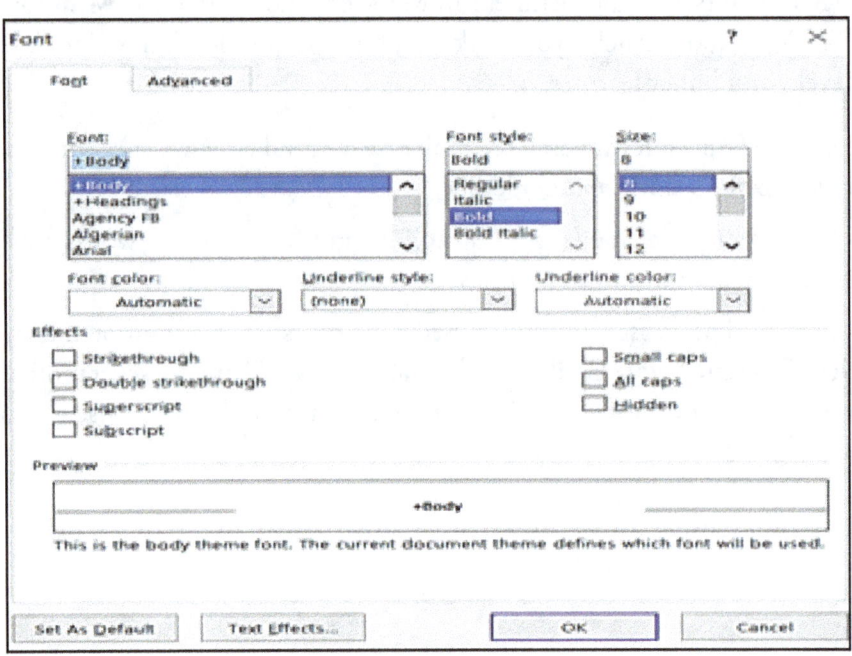

Fig. 4.11   Font Group Dialog Box

Paragraph Group

Majority of the document formatting you do while typing your document are contained in the paragraph group which provides tools that allow you to change line spacing; apply numbers and bullets to listed items; and indent texts in your document. Text you type in your document always aligns to the left by default. **Fig. 4.12** displays various formatting icons that you can use as needed when creating a new document in Word. Follow instructions in the boxes of the image below to apply the formatting of your choice to your document.

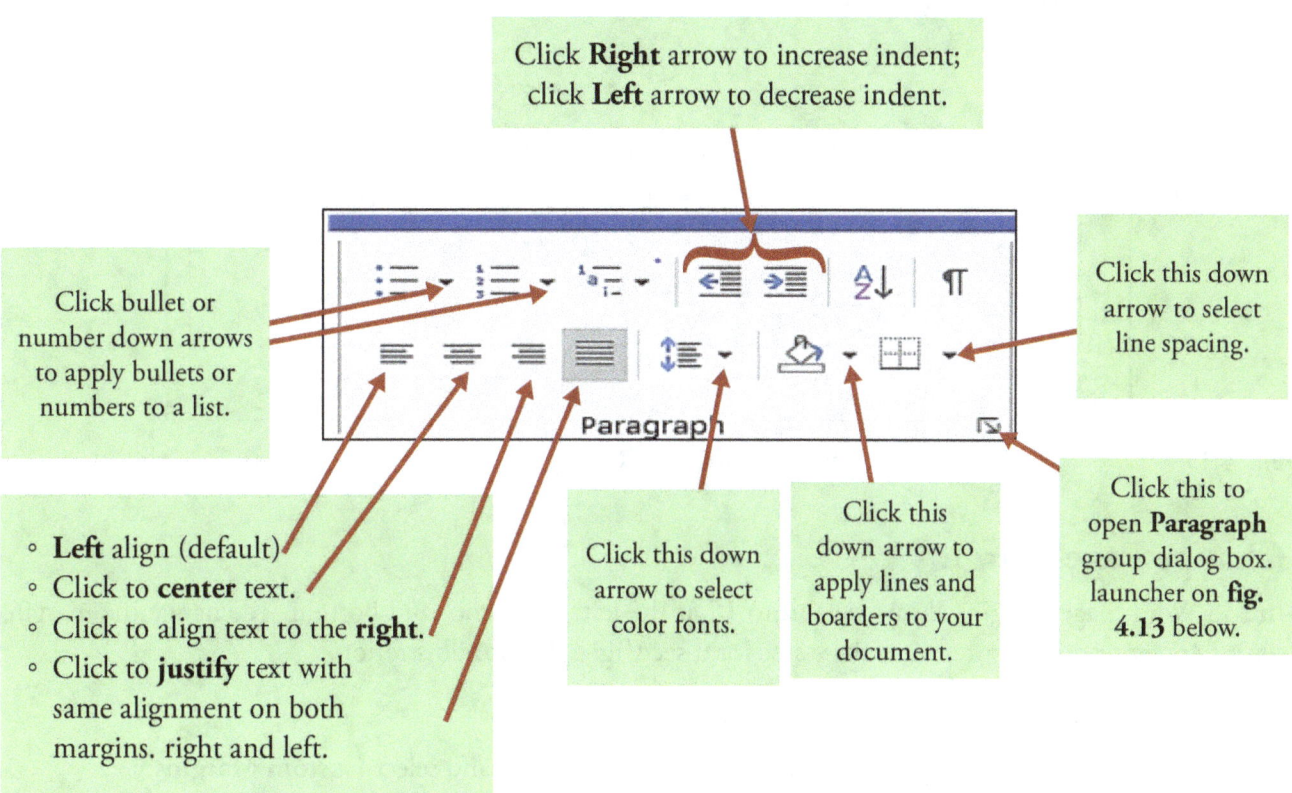

Fig. 4.12   Paragraph Group

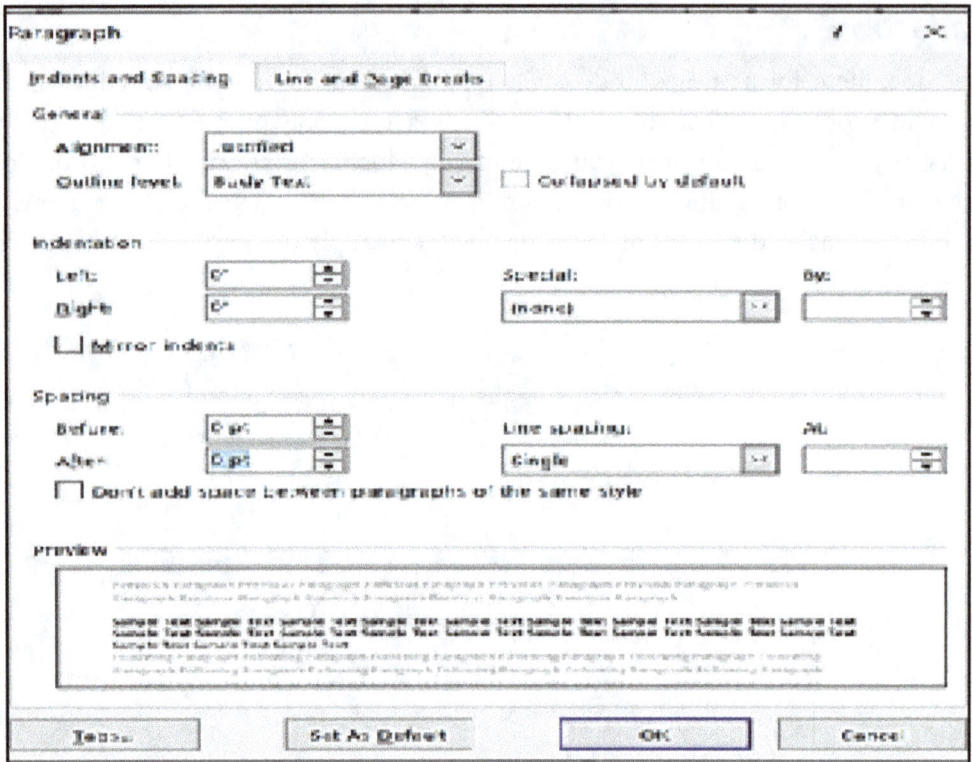

Fig. 4.13   **Paragraph Group Dialog Box**

Change Page Margins

In MS Word, page margins always default to **1"** at the left, right, top, and bottom. To change the margin settings on your document, follow these steps and see **(fig. 4.14)** for illustration.

1. Click **Layout** at top ribbon on the Word window.
2. From the **Page Setup** group, click **Margins** down arrow, and select **Custom Margins**.
3. On the open **Page Setup** dialog box, using the up and down arrows, increase or decrease left, right, top, or bottom margins as needed for your document, and click **OK**.

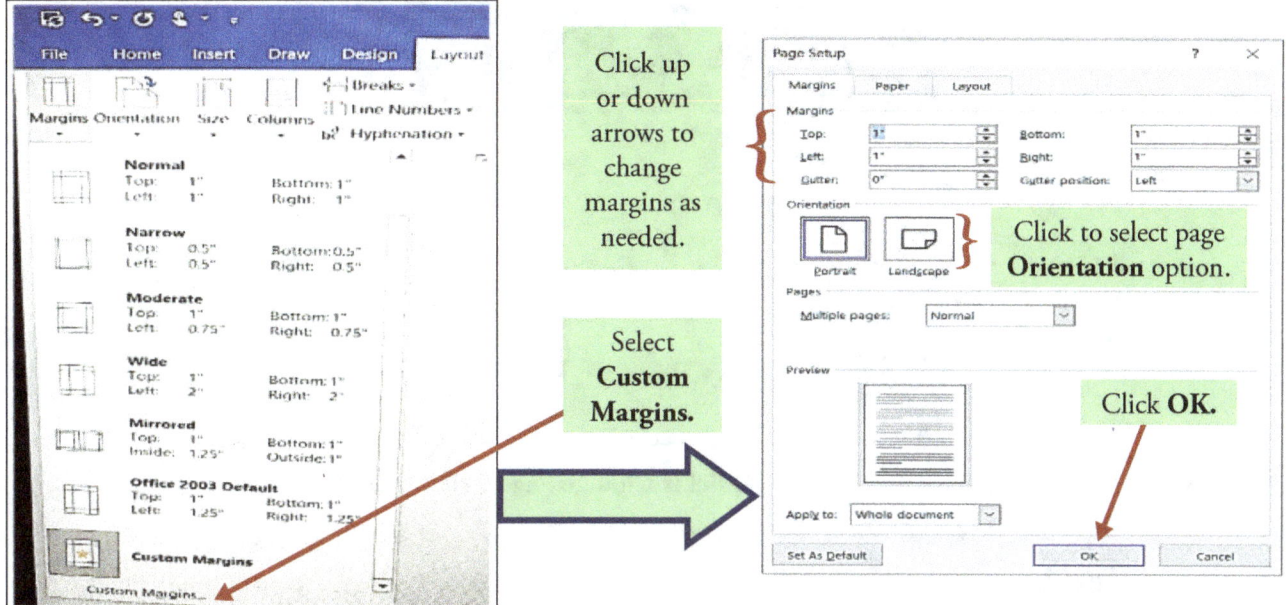

Fig. 4.14   Change Page Margins & Orientation

Quick Way to Change Page Orientation

1. Click **Layout** at top ribbon of the Word window.
2. In the **Page Setup** group, click **Orientation** down arrow **(fig. 4.15)**
3. From the displayed options, click to select **Portrait** or **Landscape** option.

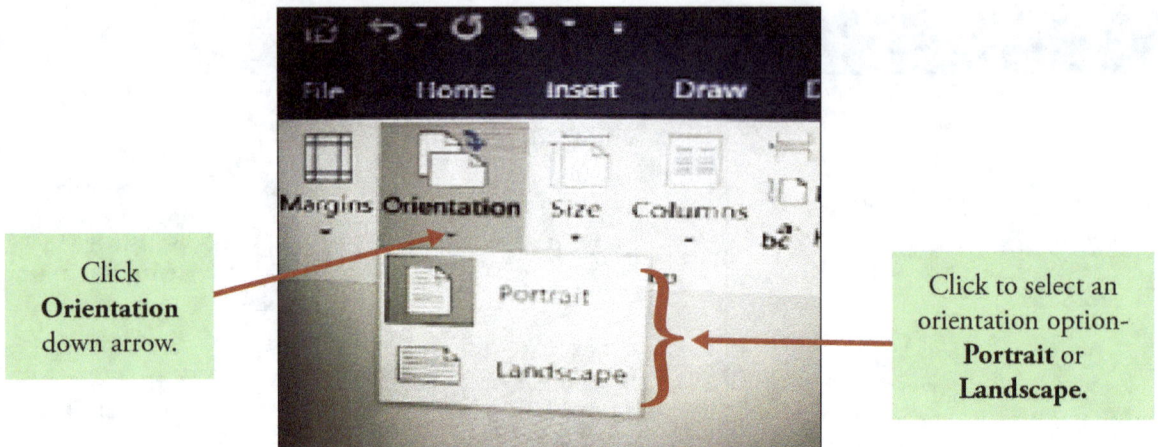

Fig. 4.15   **Quickly Change Page Orientation**

Change Line Spacing

1. Highlight to select the paragraph for which you want to change the linespacing.
2. On the **Home** tab, in the **Paragraph** group, click the **Line Spacing** down arrow
3. On the open menu, select the line spacing you want. For example, if you click **1.0**, the selected text is single-spaced; **1.5**, the selected text is a single and half spaced; and **2.0**, the text is double spaced.
4. Alternatively, in the **Paragraph** group, click the **Dialog Launcher**
5. In the open **Paragraph** dialog box, click the **Indent and Spacing** tab **(fig. 4.16)**.
6. Under **Spacing**, click **Line Spacing** down arrow, select the spacing you want; click **Ok.**

Line Spacing Options: Clicking line spacing down arrow displays these options:

- **Single** – This option accommodates the largest font in that line, plus a small amount of extra space. Amount of extra space varies depending on font size used.
- **1.5 lines** – This option is one-and-one-half times the size of single-line spacing.
- **Double** – This option is twice the size of single line spacing.
- **At least** – This option sets the minimum line spacing that is needed to fit the largest font or graphic on the line.

- **Exactly** – This option sets fixed line spacing that Word does not adjust.
- **Multiple** – This option sets line spacing that is increased or decreased from single spacing by a percentage that you specify. For example, setting line spacing to **1.2** will increase the space by **20** percent.

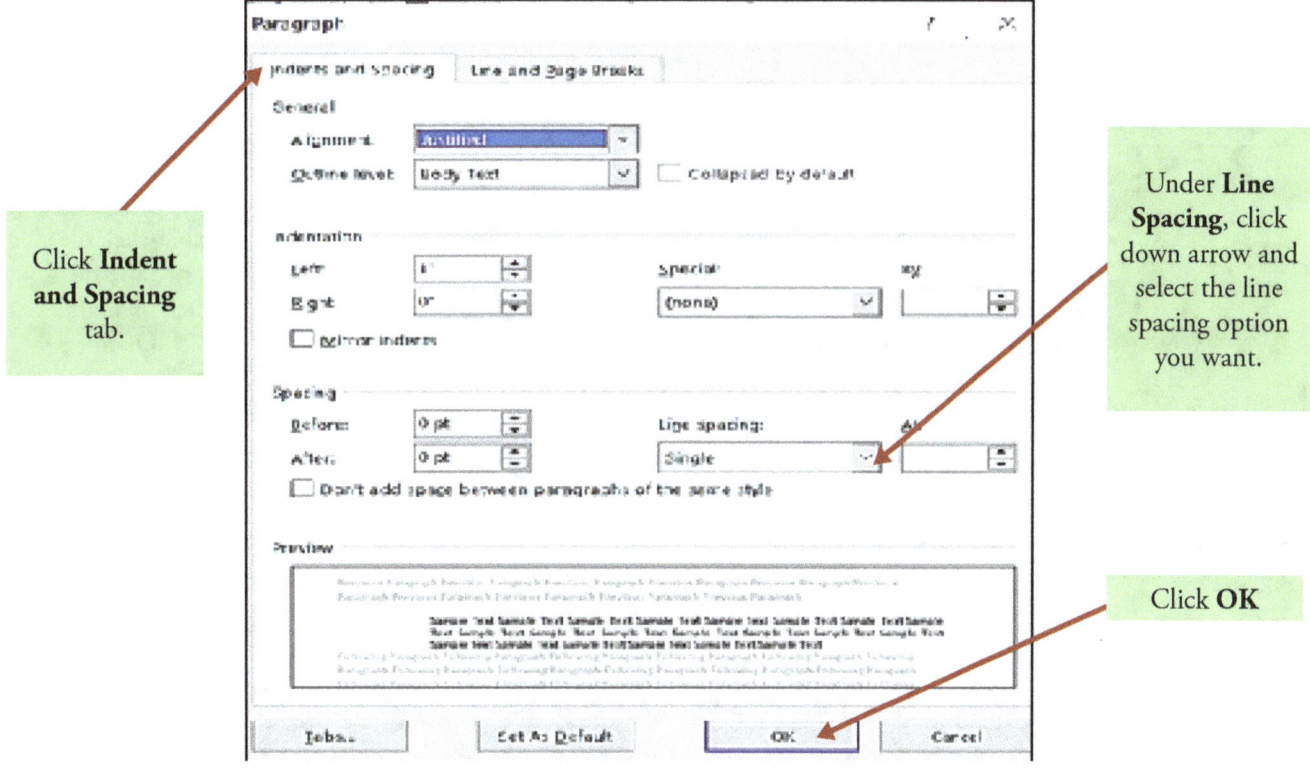

Fig. 4.16   **Paragraph Dialog Box**

Open an Existing Document

1. Click the **File** tab, and click **Open**.
2. At left side of the **Open** window, click **Browse** to display **Explorer** window **(fig. 4.17)**.
3. On the left pane of the of the **Explorer** window, under **Organize**, navigate to find the drive where the document is located, and double-click on that drive to display the contents.

All-in-One Beginners Guide to Computer Proficiency

4. If the document is located in a folder, double-click the folder, then double-click the document to open it. Alternatively click the document and click the **Open** tab at bottom of the window.

5. If the document is not saved in a folder, once the content of the drive is displayed as in item **#2** above, locate the document you want and double-click to open it or click the document and click the **Open** tab.

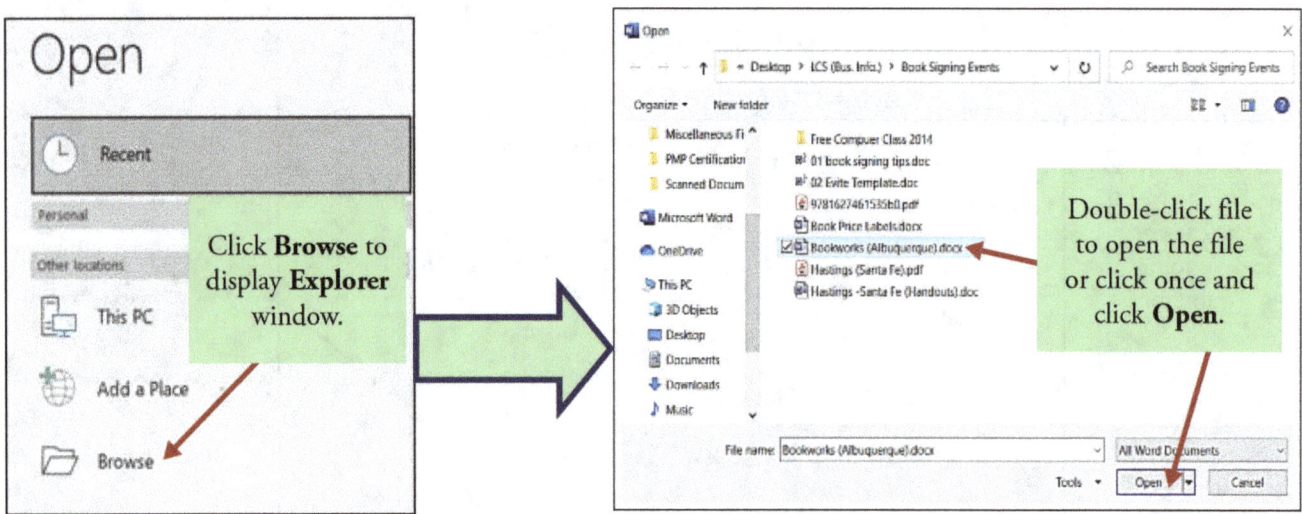

Fig. 4.17   Open an Existing Document & Display of Explorer Window

MOVE, CUT, OR COPY TEXT TO A NEW LOCATION IN A DOCUMENT

MS Word has features that allow you to copy, cut, and paste text in a new location. With the clip-board feature which serves as a temporary storage area for your text, you can copy text and move it to the clipboard while your original text remains in place. You can also cut/paste the text, which removes it from its original location and places it in a new location. The paste feature allows you to insert the contents of the clipboard into a new location. Three ways to change the location of text in your document are:

Move, Copy, or Cut & Paste Text Using the Keyboard

1. Click, hold down the mouse, highlight to select the text you want to move or copy; then do one or more of the following:
   a. To move the item, press **CTRL+X.**
   b. To copy the item, press **CTRL+C.**
2. If you want to move or copy the text to another document, switch to that document.
3. Click where you want the text to appear and press **CTRL+V.**
4. Another quick way to move, copy or cut and paste is to follow these steps:
5. Click on the document, holding down the mouse, highlight to select the text you want to move or copy.
6. Right-click the mouse to open the formatting option menu, and select **Copy.**
7. Right-click on blank space of the document where you want to place text and select **Paste** from the displayed short menu.

   - **Copy & Paste:** When you copy, the text remains in the original location and another copy is pasted in the new location.
   - **Cut & Paste:** When you cut the text, it is removed from the original location and appears in the new location where it is pasted.
   - **Move:** This involves highlighting the text or block of text, holding down the mouse while dragging the highlighted text to the desired location. Once you drag the text, it is removed from its original location and appears in the new location as you release the mouse.

Quick Way to Copy/Paste Texts Using the Mouse

1. If copying texts within a document, highlight the group of text you want to copy
2. Right-click the highlighted area, from the displayed menu, select **Copy.**
3. Click on a blank area of the document where to place copied text and right-click.
4. From the displayed menu, under **Paste Options**, select a **Paste Icon**. Your copied text will be placed in the new location.

SPELLING AND GRAMMAR CHECK

As you work on projects and the deadline approaches, often there is not enough time to check a document for spelling and grammar mistakes before you print and deliver your document. MS Office program provides you with tools for correcting your mistakes faster. It is up to you to decide how you want to handle the error corrections. You can set up the MS Office program so that you can easily see potential mistakes while you work or if you find the wavy red and green lines distracting, you can just check your document and correct them as you type. The spell-check function can be performed by turning the automatic spell-check on or off. When you check spelling automatically while you type, you have more confidence that you won't have to correct a lot of spelling mistakes when you are ready to deliver your document. MS Office program can flag misspelled words while you work allowing you to easily spot them. When MS Word flags a misspelled word, simply right-click the misspelled word to see suggested corrections, and select the correct one. Depending on the MS Office program you are using, right-clicking a word can provide you with other options, such as adding the word to your custom dictionary. If automatic grammar checking is enabled, Word flags the potential grammar and style mistakes while you work in Word documents. You can also choose to ignore the error, especially if it's a name or click the suggested correct word to change the word.

How Spelling and Grammar Checker Works

As you type, MS Word compares the words in your document to the Word dictionary and compares your phrases and punctuation to a list of grammar rules. Words not in the Word dictionary are marked with a **wavy red underline** showing that a word is spelt incorrectly. Phrases and punctuation that differ from the grammar rules are marked with a **double blue underline**. In using MS Word grammar and spell checker, certain rules apply, such as:

1. Computer applied grammar rules can never be exact.
2. MS Word does not check for usage.
3. MS Word will not flag the word "**sign**" as misspelled, even though you intended to type "**sing**".
4. MS Word will almost always flag names with a **wavy red underline** because they are not in the Word dictionary. It does not mean the spelling of the name is wrong, if spelled correctly as typed. You do not have to change the word during spell check. Simply click **Ignore.**
5. You do not have to change the names of people, place, or object, if spelt correctly even though Word flags them as incorrect.
6. Make sure you check words flagged by MS Word always.

Use Grammar and Spellchecker

1. Click the **Review** tab at top menu toolbar.
2. In the **Proofing** group, click on **ABC Spelling & Grammar** button to open the **Proofing** window at the right side of your screen **(fig. 4.18)**.
3. The misspelled word will be displayed under **Spelling Not in Dictionary**; the flagged words will be highlighted in the window.
4. On the list of **Suggestions,** select the correct word to change and replace the incorrect word on your document.
5. If the flagged word is the name of a person, place, or an object, at the bottom of the window, select **Ignore All.** This will automatically accept all instances of that particular word in your document as being correct.
6. When finished, click the **X** at top of the dialog box to close the window.
7. To spell check using shortcut as you type:
    a. Right-click on the word with a **wavy red** or **double blue underline**.
    b. Click to select correct word from the list of suggested words to change your word or click **Ignore** to keep your words.

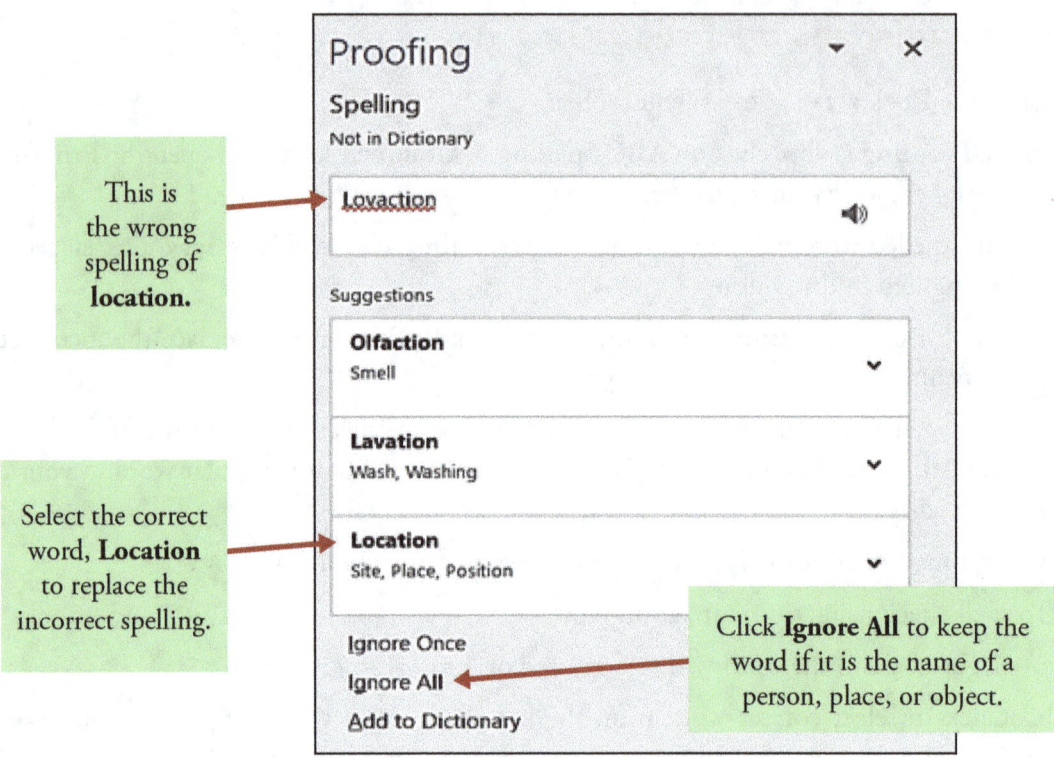

Fig. 4.18   **Proofing Window for Spelling and Grammar Check**

INSERT & FORMAT A TABLE IN A WORD DOCUMENT

As you create documents in MS Word, Table is a very effective way to organize your information so that they make sense to your readers. The table helps make your data stand out to your readers, and adding a table in Word is very simple. Tables are particularly useful in presenting statistical data because it makes the data easier to read and interpret. You have a variety of options for customizing your table and you can even choose from existing templates to make inserting tables completely painless. For this beginner's guide, we'll illustrate the simplest way to insert and format a table in a Word document using the sample project below.

Sample Word Project

CREATE AND FORMAT A REGISTRATION TABLE FOR GIRL'S VALLEY BALL TEAM.

To illustrate solution to this project, we'll insert and format a table listing the names and other contact information of students registered in **Girl's Valley Ball Team** at a **New York High School** for competition with another high school. Registration deadline is **March 17, 2020** and competition date is set for **April 30, 2020**. We have **10** students who have registered within the deadline. Registration is open only to students in grade levels **08 – 12**. For this table we'll insert **5 columns** and **11 rows**, then enter student's data provided in the box below.

Insert a Table

1. Click location of the document where you want to insert the table, type these texts: **Students Registered for Valley Ball Competition;** this is the title of your table.

2. Highlight the title, change font size to **16**; apply **Red,** and **Bold** font to title.

3. Below the title heading, click **Insert** tab at top ribbon, and click **Table** down arrow.

4. In the displayed boxes, click the first box, highlight the first **5 columns** from top row, then continue highlighting down to the default **8**th **row** of the displayed boxes.

5. Although we only need **10 rows** for the registered students, we'll highlight the entire default **8 rows** and add **3 more rows** making it a total of **11 rows.** This is because we need the top tow to enter our column headings.

6. Notice that as you highlight the rows and columns, the table is already being inserted in the location of the document you want it inserted.

7. To insert 3 additional rows, do these:
    a. Click the last row of the table you've already inserted.
    b. Click **Layout** tab at top ribbon.
    c. In the **Rows & Column** group, click **Insert Rows Below** 3 times.

Format a Table

1. Click the first row of each of the **5 columns** cells and type the following column headings to describe table data for your readers:
   - Date Registered
   - Student Name
   - Grade Level
   - Phone Number
   - Home Room Teacher
2. To increase or decrease the width of table columns, click the intersection line, holding down the mouse, drag the line to the right or to the left as needed.
3. On this table, increase the columns for **Student Name**, **Home Toom Teacher**, and slightly for **Phone Number** so they can contain the text. Decrease the columns for **Date Registered** and **Grade Level.**
4. Highlight the enter first row, and click **Layout** tab at top ribbon.
5. In the **Alignment** group, click **Align Center** icon to center the column headings within table cells (**fig. 4.18**).
6. Highlight the first row, in the **Font** group, click **B** to apply **Bold** font to column headings to make it standout and look professional.
7. In the cells of the table you inserted, type students' contact information contained in the blue box below.
8. When finished entering all data, highlight one at a time all texts in columns: **1, 3, & 4**, in the paragraph group, click **Center** icon to center text in the three columns. See completed student registration table on (**fig.4.19**).

Students Contact Information

Date Registered:
01/06/20, 01/19/20, 01/22/20, 02/05/20, 02/07/20, 02/19/20, 02/27/20, 03/03/20, 03/11/20, 03/16/20.

Student Name:
Kayla Owen, Maria Dumez, Loretta Rice, Shanaya Prescot, Emily Lerner, Dorothy Ameshi, Cindy Waters, Jamine Laffeta, Victoria Kent, Alice Udoh

Grade Level: 10, 12, 10, 09, 08, 08, 11, 09, 11, 12

Phone Number:
212-243-1170, 212-476-9166, 212-330-7345, 212-440-8130, 212-960-1100
212-863-5214, 212-146-7961, 212-920-5526, 212-232-4738, 212-118-1964

Home Room Teacher:
Joseph Smith, Anabel Walker, Brianna Kinsley, Franklin Bowman, Andy Lowe Christina Baker, Alicia Kunle, Emmanuel Uttah, Lovette Amos, Anna Odeh

Fig. 4.19   The Alignment Group in the Layout Tab

Students Registered for Valley Ball Competition

Date Registered	Student Name	Grade Level	Phone Number	Home Room Teacher
01/06/20	Kayla Owen	10	212-243-1170	Joseph Smith
01/19/20	Maria Dumez	12	212-476-9166	Anabel Walker
01/22/20	Loretta Rice	10	212-330-7345	Brianna Kinsley
02/05/20	Shanaya Prescot	09	212-440-8130	Franklin Bowman
02/07/20	Emily Lerner	08	212-960-1100	Andy Lowe
02/19/20	Dorothy Ameshi	08	212-863-5214	Christina Baker
02/27/20	Cindy Waters	11	212-146-7961	Alicia Kunle
03/03/20	Jamine Laffeta	09	212-920-5526	Emmanuel Uttah
03/11/20	Victoria Kent	11	212-232-4738	Lovette Amos
03/16/20	Alice Udoh	12	212-118-1964	Anna Odeh

Fig. 4.20   **Completed Registration Table**

Insert and Delete Table Rows and Columns

Sometimes after creating a table, you find that you may need more rows or columns based on the type of data you want to enter into the table. You may also find that you have more columns than you need and want to remove some.

Insert a Row or Rows:

1. Click on the row of the table where you want to add a row or rows.
2. Click the **Layout** tab at top ribbon.
3. If you want to add row(s) above or below the row you clicked, in the **Row & Columns** group, select either **Insert Above** or **Insert Below**.
4. If you need more than one row continue clicking your selected option for the number of rows you need.

Delete a Row or Rows:

1. Click on the row of the table where you want to delete or highlight the number of rows you want to delete.
2. Click the **Layout** tab at top ribbon.
3. In the **Row & Columns** group, click **Delete** down arrow, and select **Delete Rows**.

Insert a Column or Columns:

1. Click on the column of the table where you want to add a column or columns.
2. Click the **Layout** tab at top ribbon.
3. If you want to add column(s) to the right or left of the column you clicked, in the **Row & Columns** group, select either **Insert Left** or **Insert Right.**
4. If you need more than one column, continue clicking your selected option for the number of columns you need.

Delete a Column or Columns:

1. Click on the column of the table you want to delete or highlight the number of columns you want to delete.
2. Click the **Layout** tab at top ribbon.
3. In the **Row & Columns** group, click **Delete** down arrow, and select **Delete Columns**.

Delete an Entire Table

1. Click the table edge to display a **+** sign; and click the **+** sign to highlight the table.
2. With the table highlighted, click the **Layout** tab at top ribbon.
3. In the **Row & Columns** group, click **Delete** down arrow, and select **Delete Table**.

INSERT HEADER, FOOTER, & PAGE NUMBER IN A DOCUMENT

Headers and footers in a Microsoft Word document refer to tiny pieces of information such as page numbers, date, and author's name that appear at the top and/or bottom of the page that serves as an identifier on a document. They can be very useful when multiple people in an organization are working on one large project where other people contribute their own writtem materials. Headers and footers help to identify contributed topics towards the prpoject and who wrote them. Headers and footers may also include book titles, chapter titles, and the name of the author. A header appears at the top of a Word document while a footer appears at the bottom of a document. See **figs. 4.21a/4.21b** and **4.22a/4.22b** below on various options for inserting or removing headers, footers, and page numbers.

INSERT OR REMOVE HEADER

1. On your open document, click **Insert** tab at the ribbon.
2. In the **Header & Footer** group, click **Header** down arrow, and select **Edit Header** at bottom of the displayed menu **(fig. 4.22a)**.
3. At top of the document, above the dotted grayed line, type text (title, date, name, etc.).
4. Whatever you type at the header will appear at the top left on every page of your document.
5. Click the red **X** at top right: **Close Header & Footer** in the **Close** group.
6. To remove header, repeat **step 2** above and select **Remove Header**; the header will be removed from all pages of your document **(fig. 4.22a)**.

INSERT OR REMOVE FOOTER

1. On your open document, click **Insert** tab at the ribbon.
2. In the **Header & Footer** group, click **Footer** down arrow, and select **Edit Footer** at bottom of the displayed menu **(fig. 4.22b)**.
3. At the bottom of our document, above the dotted grayed line, type your text (title, date, name, etc.).
4. Whatever you type at the footer will appear at the bottom of every page of your document.
5. Click the red **X** at top right: **Close Header & Footer**.

6. To remove footer, repeat **step 2** above and select **Remove Footer**; the footer will be removed from all pages of your document **(fig. 4.22b)**.

INSERT OR REMOVE PAGE NUMBERS

1. On your open document, click **Insert** tab at the ribbon.
2. In the **Header & Footer** group, click **Page Number** down arrow **(fig. 4.21b)**.
3. Depending on your preference, from the displayed short menu, select any of two options (top or bottom page). More options exists on the displayed menu such as top left, top right, top middle, and bottom left, right, and center. Two options are described below:

   <u>*Option 1 – Top of Page*</u> – Click **Top of Page** right arrow to display location options menu on the left side of your computer screen. Select the location of your page numbers, either at **top left**, **top middle**, or **top right** of your document.

   <u>*Option 2 – Bottom of Page*</u> – Click **Bottom of Page** right arrow to display location options menu on the left side of your computer screen. Select the location of your page numbers, either at **bottom left**, **bottom right** or **bottom center** of your document.

4. If you have multiple pages of documents, whatever option you select, page numbers will appear on every page of the document.
5. To remove page nuumbers, repeat **step 2** above and select **Remove Page Numbers;** page numbers will be removed from all pages of your documents. See **fig. 4.23** below for a document formatted with header, footer, and page number.

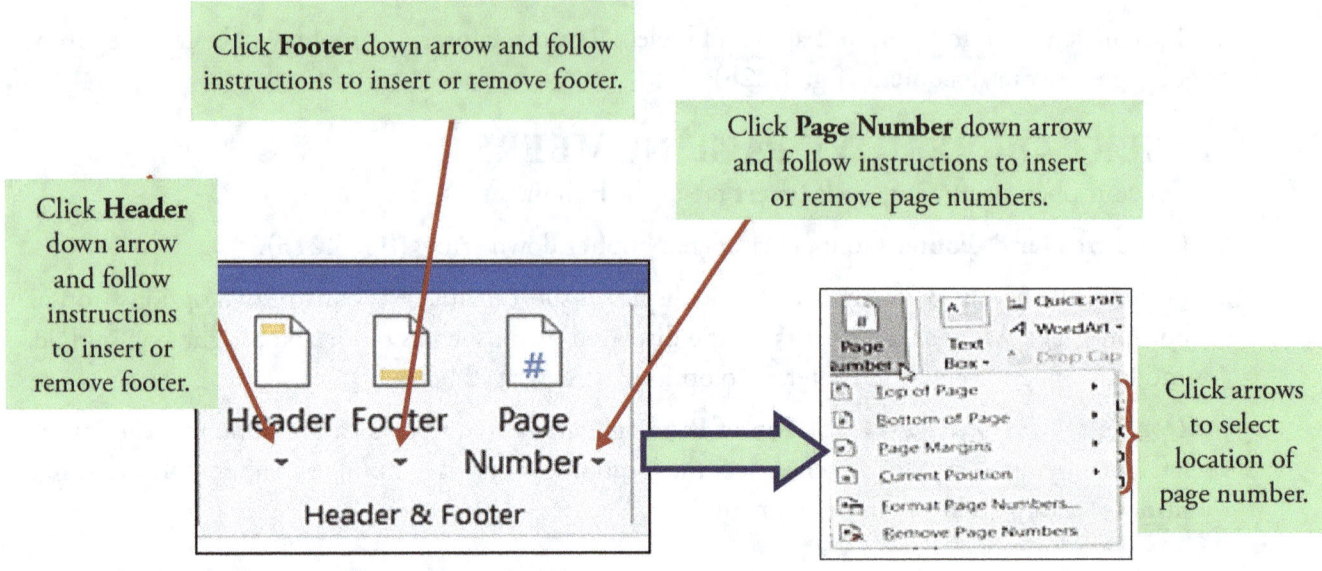

Fig. 4.21a   **Header & Footer Group**   **Fig. 4.21b**   **Page Number Menu**

When you click **Header** down arrow, When you click **Footer** down arrow, this window opens up. this window opens up.

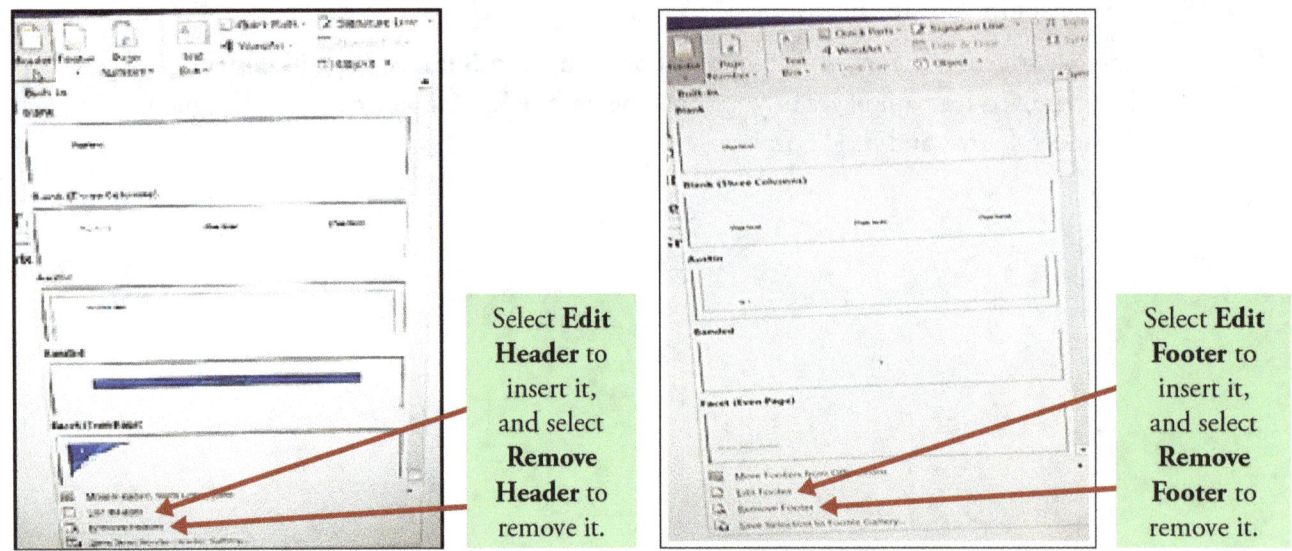

Fig. 4.22a   **Displayed Header & Footer Windows Fig.4.22b**

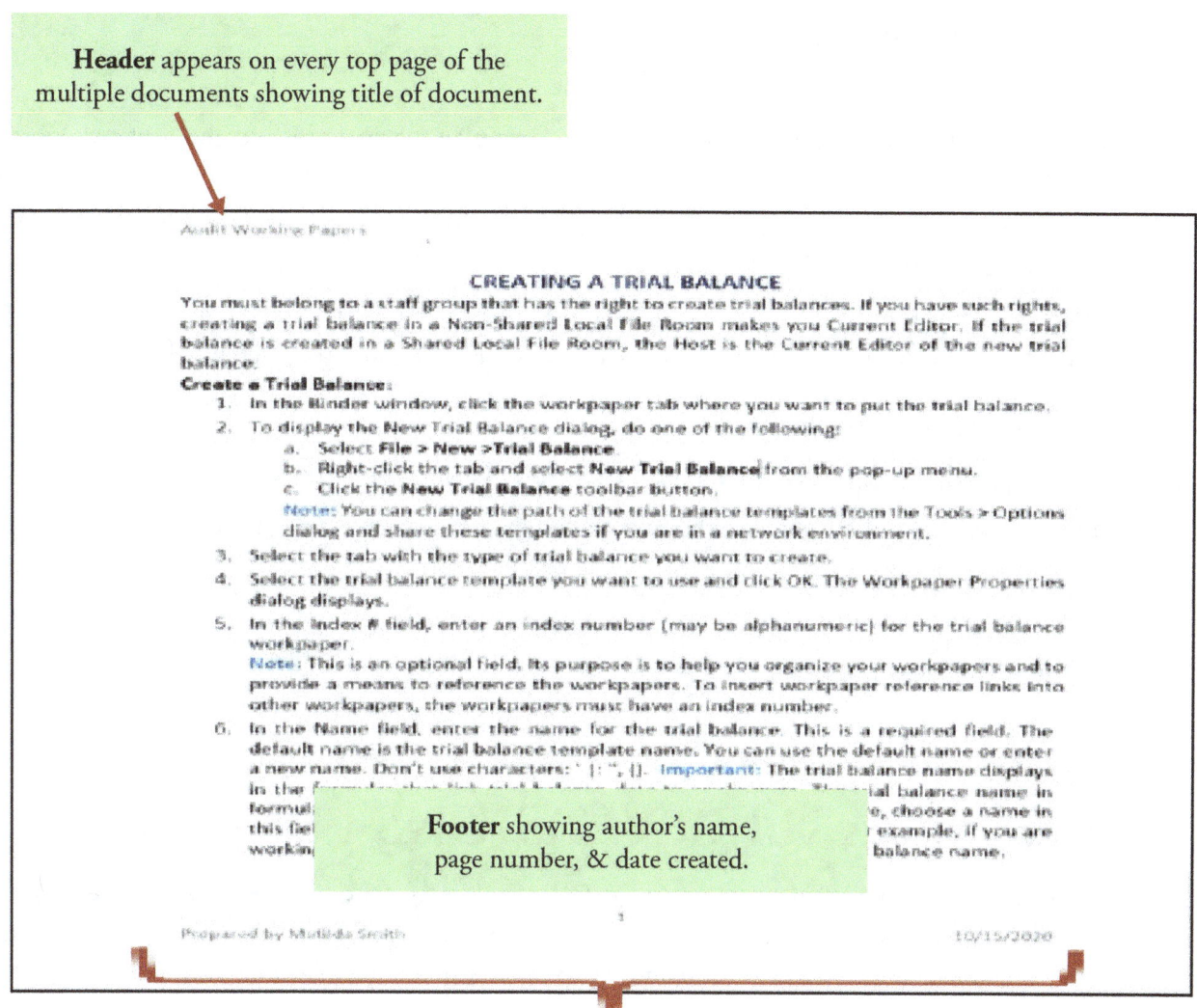

Fig. 4.23   Page 1 of Multiple Documents Showing Header, Footer, & Page Number

Delete a Document or a File

1. Click the **File** tab, click **Open**, and select **Browse**.
2. In the left pane of the **Open** dialog box, under **Organize**, navigate to find the drive where the document is located, and double-click on that drive to display the contents.
3. If the document is located in a folder, double-click the folder, then right-click the document, from the displayed shortcut menu, click **Delete**.
4. If the document is not saved in a folder, once the content of the drive is displayed as in item **#2** above, locate the document you want to delete, right-click on it and select **Delete** from the menu.

Save a Document in Word 2019

1. On the open document, click the **File** tab, click **Save As**, and select **Browse**.
2. In the open **Save As** dialog box, in the **File name** box, type a name for your document.
3. Click the **Save** button at the bottom of the window. When a document is saved it becomes a file.
4. If saving the document in a folder, double-click the folder first to open it, then click the **Save** button. The document will be saved as a file inside the folder.

SAVE A WORD 2019 DOCUMENT IN WORD EARLIER VERSIONS (97-2003)

You can type document in Word 2019 and save it as Word earlier versions. This is usually the case with students or individuals who have older versions on their home computers and can't afford the newer version. If you save your document in new 2019 version and try to open it in an older version, your document may not open because the older version does not have enough strength to open 2019 version on your computer. However, any older version (97-2003) of MS Word document can always open in a newer version (2019) because it has enough strength to do so. Therefore, regardless of what new version of Word you created your document, make sure you save it with the older version on your home computer so that you can open it later. If you have the same new version (2019) on your home computer, you do not have to save your document as the earlier version. All you have to do is type a file name for your document and click **Save** button (**fig. 4.24**).

1. With the document open, click the **File** tab.

2. Click **Save As** and type a name for your file in the **File name** box at the bottom of the **Save As** explorer window.
3. In the **Save as Type** box, click the down arrow to display a list of file types.
4. From the displayed list, **(fig. 4.25)** select **Word 97-2003 Document** and click **Save**.

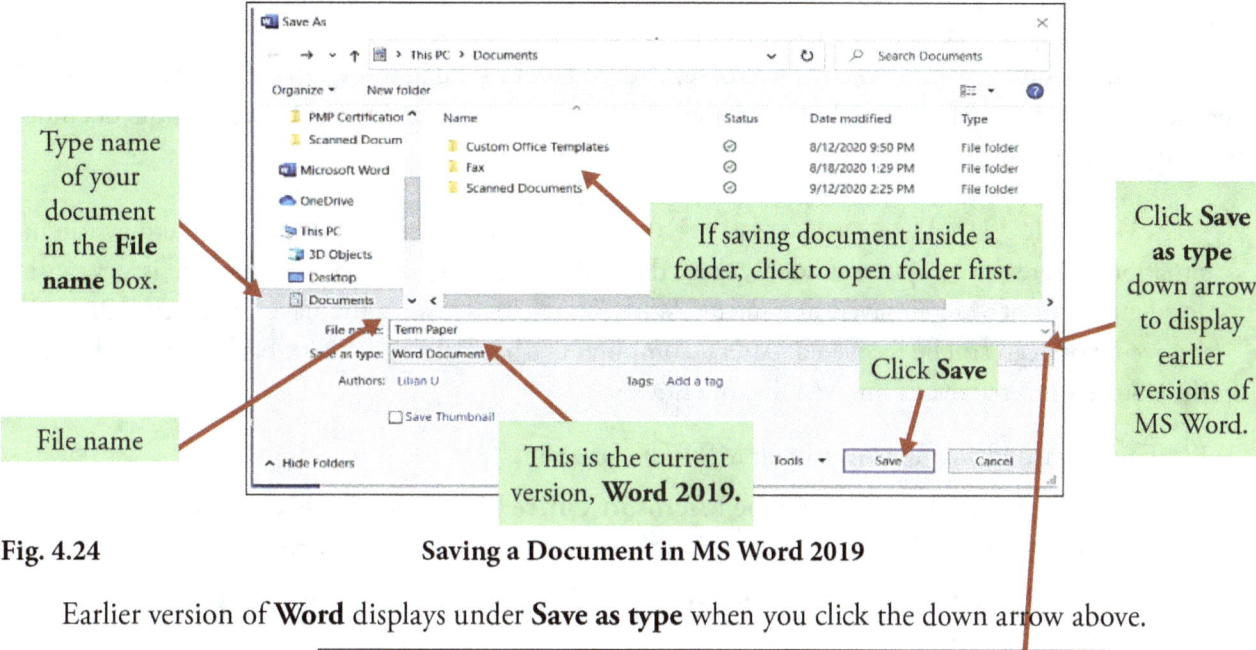

Fig. 4.24   Saving a Document in MS Word 2019

Earlier version of **Word** displays under **Save as type** when you click the down arrow above.

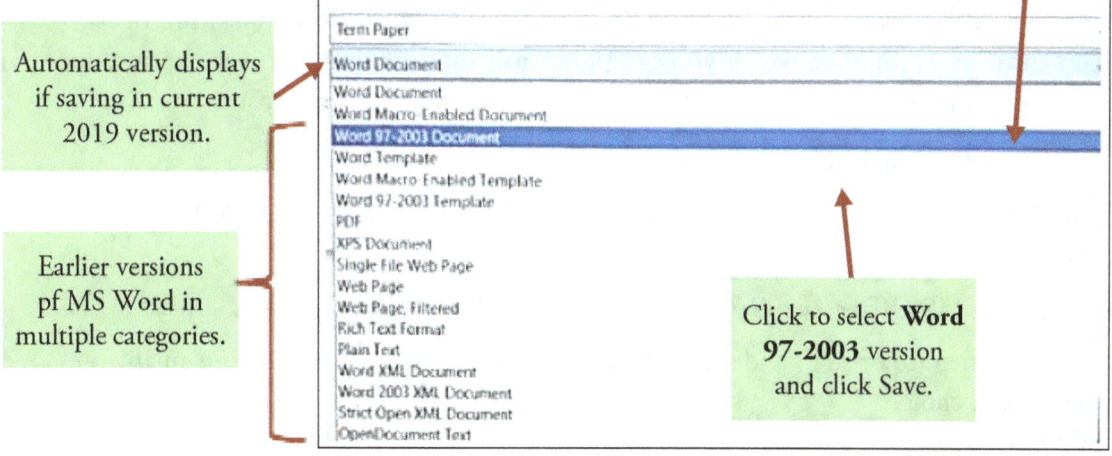

Fig. 4.25   Save a Document in New (2019) or Earlier Versions of Microsoft Word

All-in-One Beginners Guide to Computer Proficiency | 189

Recover Unsaved Work

With the new Word 2019, it is easier to recover a Word document if you happen to close your file without saving it. In the earlier versions of Word, enabling **AutoRecovery** will save your file while you work on it at the interval you select. Now, you can keep the last auto saved version of a file in case you accidentally close that file without saving it, so that you can easily restore it the next time you open the file. Even with the good MS Office file saving habits, many times, documents disappear from the screen before you can hit the save button. If your window screen suddenly turns blue, or even if your local power is cut off, your document will disappear from the screen. Fortunately, the modern versions of Microsoft Office do most of the document recovery legwork for you.

MS Word 2019 Automatic File Recovery:
As you create documents, you may run into situations where the computer suddenly shuts down due to power failure or other system issues causing accidental loss of your unsaved document. With Word 2019, you don't have to worry because the unsaved work can still be recovered. After a computer crash, it's time to return back to normal. Follow these steps to recover your unsaved document:

1. The first thing you do is to reopen MS Word program.
2. Upon opening it, you will meet the **Microsoft Office Document Recovery Panel** at left side of your document window with a list of files that are not in use before a system crash.
3. Select file(s) you want to recover from the list and save document to keep it/them.

MS Word 2019 Manual Document Recovery:
Another new feature of MS 2019 is the document retrieval method which you can perform if the automatic recovery option does not work, you can try to recover your work manually by following these simple steps:

1. Open **MS Word** and open a new document.
2. Click the **File** tab, click **Info**, click **Manage Documents** down arrow, and select **Recover Unsaved Documents.**
3. Browse through **MS Office AutoSave** files listed and find your lost document.
4. Click the document to open it; and save the recovered document with a file name in any preferred location of your choice.

Print a Document

The new MS Word 2019 displays both **Print Preview** and **Print** options when prompted, all in one window with **Print** options at left and document preview at the right side of your computer screen. Print preview shows what the printed document will look like. You can also select all your printing options in the print window, such as printing a selected page or a range of pages or even modify page margins as needed.

1. On the **Home** tab, click the **File** tab, and select **Print**.
2. In the open **Print** window **(fig. 4.26)**, on the **Copies** box, using the up and down arrow select the number of copies you want to print, and click the **Print** tab.
3. To print a selected page in a file of several pages, under **Settings**, in the **Pages** box, enter the page number or page range you want to print, for example **5-10**, and click **Print** tab to print the document.
4. If you want to change paper size or page orientation, follow instructions described inside boxes on **fig. 4.26** below.

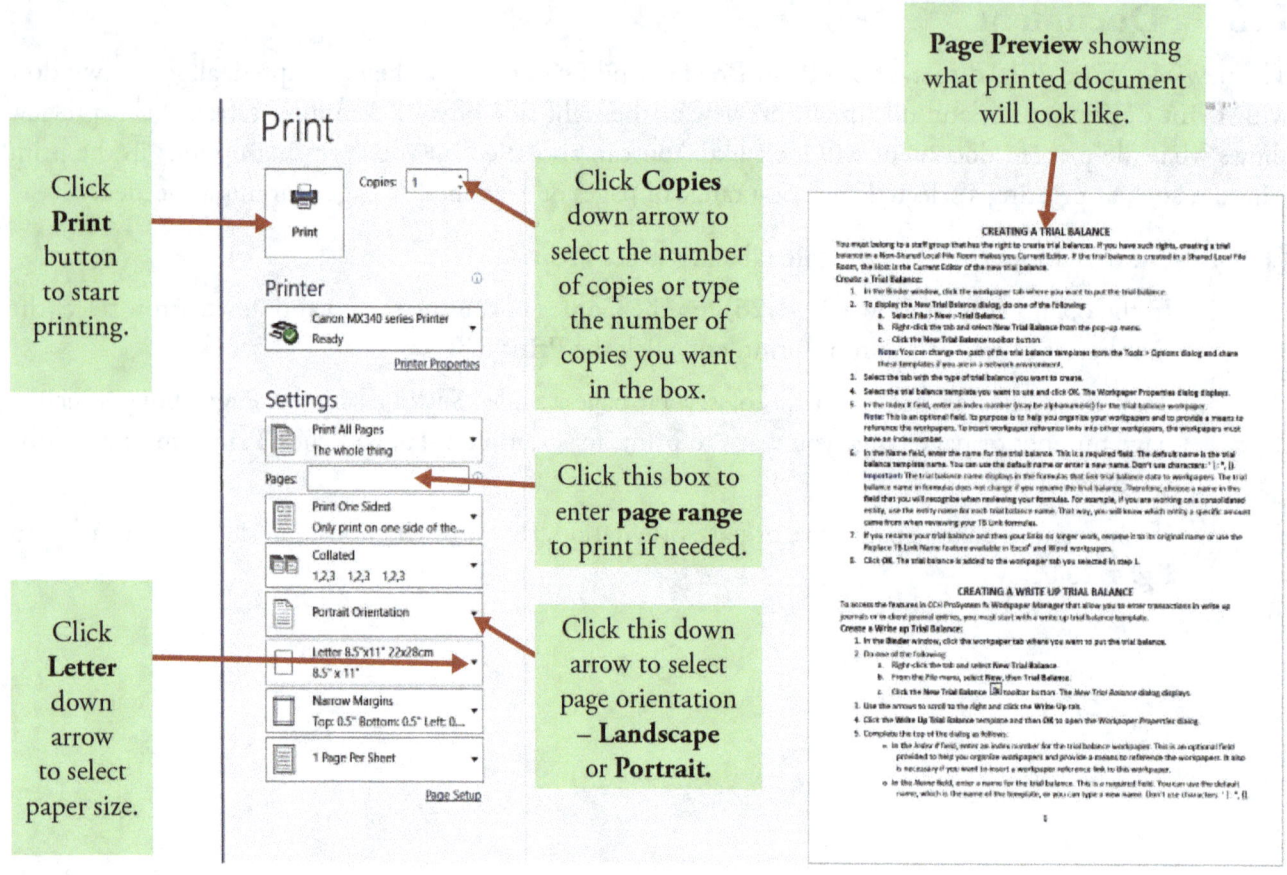

Fig. 4.26   Print Dialog Box All in One – Preview & Print

CHAPTER SUMMARY & KEY TERMS

Word processing is the function of creating a document using a word processing program known as Microsoft Word. Word processing is similar to using a typewriter to type a document except that you can edit text, copy, move and delete text. The word processing program comes in the form of software that is installed on a computer and used to create documents. Quick Access Toolbar allows you to place your frequently used command icons within view at the top of the toolbar or below the toolbar. You can add icons at the toolbar for quick access without first clicking the Microsoft Office button. When you first open MS Word, the window always defaults to normal as highlighted by the Normal button at the toolbar. This default normal automatically puts everything you type in double spaced. To type in single space, click the No Spacing button. The AutoComplete feature in Word provides commonly used words and phrases, such as salutations and dates. Word-wrap determines if the next word in line will fit and moves it to the next line if necessary.

As word processing software, Microsoft Word 2019 combines the familiar features you know in 2013 with some new easy-to-use features designed to help you create professional-quality documents. With the finest document-formatting tools, Word helps you organize and write your documents more efficiently. Editing text involves changing words, sentences, or formatting the text in a document. Three ways to edit text in Microsoft Word are by using backspace key, delete key, and insert key. Font styles are used to emphasize text and visualize cues with text in a document. They include Bold, *Italics,* and Underline. Font sizes range from 8" to 72" and help to make words appear larger in a text. Font types refers to the text character used in creating documents in Word, such as Times New Roman, Arial, and Arial Narrow, Cambria, etc. Microsoft Word contains a feature known as Spell checker that allows you to check your spelling and grammar in your typed document and make corrections. The best way to organize files on your computer is to create folders and save your documents as files inside the folders. Word 2019 also contains user-friendly features that allow you to insert tables, headers, and footers into your documents to make them look very professional.

KEY TERMS

AutoRecovery	Quick	Word Processor Recovery
Access Toolbar	Formatting Tools Page Margins	Word-wrap Zoom View
File Landscape Orientation	Navigation Pane Paste Option	
	Spell checker Portrait	

Demonstrate Your Knowledge & Skill

CHAPTER 4 PRACTICE EXERCISES
INTRODUCTION TO MICROSOFT WORD 2019

4.1 – Select True or False answer to the following statements:

1. One of the new features of MS Word 2019 that allows you to correct typos or misspelled words is called AutoCorrect.
   a. True
   b. False

2. The Quick Access Toolbar is always located permanently at the top left corner of the ribbon and cannot never be moved from that location.
   a. True
   b. False

3. When you first open MS Word, the window always defaults to Normal spacing, but you can change this default setting to a spacing of your choice.
   a. True
   b. False

4. You cannot start a document from a template because there are no templates available on your computer.
   a. True
   b. False

5. The File tab contains features that allow you to save, print, export or share files you create in Word.
   a. True
   b. False

6. The Home tab does not contain the formatting groups, you must go through the File tab to find them to begin your document formatting.
   a. True
   b. False

7. To insert a table in your document, click the Insert tab at top ribbon, click Table down arrow, and highlight the number of rows and columns you want in your table.

   a. True
   b. False

8. The Font group contains font size, font color, and font type.
   a. True   b. False

9. The Page Setup group is located in the Insert tab and contains Orientation down arrow.
   a. True   b. False

10. To change margins, click the Layout tab, and select Margins down arrow, select Custom Margins, and proceed to changing the default margin to the number you want.
    a. True   b. False

11. To tab that controls the placing of header, footer, page number, and table in a document is the Insert tab.
    a. True   b. False

12. You cannot save a document created in Word 2019 in any other earlier version; the system does not allow such actions.
    a. True   b. False

4.2 – Fill-in the blanks with correct terms or words for the statements of descriptions below:

1. The most striking difference between Word 2019 and earlier versions is the _____, which replaces the menu toolbar.
2. To see how a page will look when it is printed, click the _____ tab, select _____, then view the document on the right side of the print window.
3. _____ are displayed when you hover the mouse pointer over a menu toolbar icon.
4. When text automatically wraps to the next line it is called a(n) _____ return.
5. Press the _____ key to remove characters to the right of the insertion point.
6. To delete a character to the left of the insertion point, press _____.
7. If you accidentally delete a paragraph in your document, you can restore it by clicking the _____. Undo icon at top menu.
8. Questionable _____ is indicated by a double wavy blue lines.

9. If you have made changes and have not saved a document, when you close the document, you will be prompted by a small dialog box asking if you want the document _____.

10. When you finish typing your document and want to save it in a specific folder, in the open Save As window, under Organize, double-click the _____ you want to save your document in.

4.3 – Multiple Choice: Select the best answer to Microsoft Word features and actions described below:

1. The most commonly used word processing program by many people is:
   a. WordStar.
   b. Microsoft Word.
   c. 123Write.
   d. WordPerfect.

2. All of the following are TRUE statements about Microsoft Word 2019 EXCEPT:
   a. It enables you to type, edit, format (change text appearance), print, and save text.
   b. It corrects spelling and grammatical errors.
   c. It is a word processing system that can be purchased as an individual software item or included in Microsoft Office package.
   d. Windows 2010 is a new version of Windows XP operating system.

3. The most striking feature of Microsoft Word 2019 which differentiates it from earlier versions is the:
   a. Ribbon, which replaces the former menu bar.
   b. Ribbon, which replaces the former title bar.
   c. Tab feature, which replaces the former menu bar.
   d. Tab feature, which replaces the former title bar.

4. Which tab offers access to font changes, styles, and the clipboard?
   a. Insert
   b. Home
   c. Page Layout
   d. Review

5. Word 2019 can be customized by clicking on the File button and selecting:
   a. Customize.
   b. Edit.
   c. Options.
   d. Configure Office.

6. Groups can be displayed on the screen by selecting a tab from the:
   a. Title bar.
   b. Ribbon.
   c. File menu.
   d. View menu.

7. A tab that is active on the Ribbon is:
   a. highlighted.
   b. dimmed in gray highlighting.
   c. capitalized and bold.
   d. italicized.

8. What are the steps to start Microsoft Word 2019?
   a. Click Start, Microsoft Office, Microsoft Office Word.
   b. Click Programs, Start, Microsoft Office, Microsoft Office Word.
   c. Click Start, navigate the displayed menu, and select Word.
   d. Click Start, Accessories, Microsoft Word.

9. In addition to the Normal view, Microsoft Word provides all of following views EXCEPT:
   a. Web Layout view.
   b. Figures view.
   c. Print Layout view.
   d. Outline view.

10. In Word 2019, the default view is the:
    a. Print Layout
    b. Web Layout
    c. Outline
    d. Draft

11. The button located at the extreme right side of the Title bar is the:
    a. Minimize button.
    b. Maximize button.
    c. Resize button.
    d. Close button.

12. What happens if you click the Close button in the Word window?
    a. The Word application and all documents are closed after you are prompted to save the documents.
    b. Only the current Word document is closed.
    c. All open Word documents are closed without being saved.
    d. An error message displays.

13. What down arrow button appears on the left side of the top ribbon bar and contains commands that are used frequently, such as Save, Undo, and Redo?
    a. Status Bar
    b. Quick Access toolbar
    c. Quick Function toolbar
    d. Office Button

14. To the left of the Quick Access toolbar is the button which contains:
    a. common tasks such as creating tables and graphics.
    b. common tasks such as save, undo, and redo.
    c. a hyperlink to the Microsoft Help and Support Web site.
    d. a hyperlink to the Microsoft ClipArt online Web page.

15. A helpful description that appears by hovering the mouse pointer over an icon is called:
    a. Help Wizard
    b. Help Pointer
    c. Screen Tip
    d. Icon View

16. The Zoom option can be found on the:
    a. Home tab.
    b. Page Layout tab.
    c. Home tab.
    d. View tab.

17. When you click the File tab, the displayed Word document in the content area is entitled:
    a. New Tasks.
    b. Blank Document.
    c. Document1.
    d. Task1.

18. A red wavy line under a word indicates that the:
    a. usage may be grammatically incorrect.
    b. word needs a comma preceding it.
    c. word may need a comma following it.
    d. word may be misspelled.

19. To bold text within a document, what should you do?
    a. Highlight the text and click the B icon, in the font group of the menu bar.
    b. Highlight the text and type the word bold in the font group of the menu bar.
    c. Highlight the text and press <Ctrl>B.
    d. All of the above.

20. A quick way to copy text is to do one of the following:
    a. Highlight the text, choose Edit, and then choose Copy.
    b. Highlight the text, click the right mouse button, and then choose Copy.
    c. Highlight the text, right-click, and select Copy.
    d. Highlight the text and press <Ctrl>C.

21. What is the correct way for spell-checking of your document?
    a. Click Tools and then Spell checker.
    b. Click the right mouse button on the word and select Spell checker.
    c. Click View tab, click Spelling & Grammar tab, and select the correct displayed word at right menu.
    d. Click Review tab, click Spelling & Grammar tab, and select the correct displayed word at right menu.

22. To open an existing document, perform one of the following group of steps:
    a. Click File tab, then click Open to display the document.
    b. Click on the file folder icon on the toolbar and select Open.
    c. Click File tab, click Open, click Browse, then navigate the list to find the document and double-click on it to open it.
    d. Click File tab, click Open, then double-click folder to display file.

23. How do you save a new document?
    a. Click File tab, click Save As, click Browse, under Organize, select a location to save the document, name the document, and click Save.
    b. Click File tab, click Save As, click Folder, under Organize, select a location to save the document, name the document, and click Save.
    c. Click File tab, click Save As, click File name, under Organize, select a location to save the document, name the document, and click Save.
    d. Click File tab, click Save As, click File name, under Folder, click Organize, select a location to save the document, name the document, and click Save.

24. How do you align text to the right margin of a document?
    a. Click Format tab at top menu, then click Align Right.
    b. Highlight text, in the Paragraph group, click Align Right icon.
    c. Click on the text and select Align Right icon at top menu.
    d. Right-click on the text you want to align, and select Align Right.

25. Editing text involves pressing one the following items on the computer keyboard:
    a. Delete Key
    b. Backspace key
    c. Insert Key
    d. All of the above

26. To change default page margins settings of "1" on all sides to the margin setting you want. Select one item listed below that describes the complete and correct steps:
    a. Click Layout tab; on the Page Setup group; click Margins down arrow; click Normal, select Custom Margins, and click Ok.
    b. Click Layout at top ribbon on the Page Setup group; click the Margins down arrow; click Custom Margins, on the Page Setup group, using the up and down arrows, increase or decrease left, right, top, or bottom margins as needed for your document, and click OK.
    c. Click Layout tab, on the Page Setup group, click Normal, click Margins down arrow, click Normal, select Custom Margins, and click Ok.
    d. Click Layout tab; on the open Page Setup dialog box, click Margins down arrow, select Settings, enter the margin number you want, and click Ok.

27. A double blue wavy line under a word indicates that the:
    a. word needs a comma preceding it.
    b. usage may be grammatically incorrect.
    c. word may be misspelled.
    d. word needs a comma following it.

28. The file name of the default document that appears on the Title bar when you first start a new Microsoft Word document is:
    a. Document1.
    b. Default 1.
    c. Default Document.
    d. New Document.

29. The Print window allows you to select all of the following EXCEPT:
    a. which pages to print.
    b. which font to use.
    c. which section of a document to print.
    d. the number of copies to print.

30. The Print window allows you to change all of the following EXCEPT:
    a. orientation.
    b. margins.
    c. paper size.
    d. print schedule.

31. In Word 2019, text may be highlighted to perform all of the following actions EXCEPT:
    a. Bold.
    b. Italics.
    c. Underlined.
    d. Animation.

32. A quick way to set emphasis of a word using bold and italics is to double-click the word to select it, then do any one of these:
    a. click the Bold/Italicize button on the toolbar.
    b. click the Bold button and the Italicize button.
    c. select Bold and Italicized on the Format menu.
    d. press the CTRL-B combination followed by the CTRL-I combination.

CHAPTER 4 SKILL-BASED PRACTICE PROJECTS INTRODUCTION TO MICROSOFT WORD 2019

4.1 – Create and Format a New Document in MS Word: As the most commonly used word processing software in the market today, MS Office Word 2019 comes with new and exciting features that makes creating and formatting a document easier than ever before. In this project, you will create a new document and apply some formatting to the document that will give it a professional look. The short paragraph below provides a brief review of motion pictures and silent films in the entertainment industry.

Literature Review
Motion Picture and Silent Films
By Wikipedia-The Free Encyclopedia
February 03, 2009

"The idea of combining motion pictures with recorded sound is nearly as old as film itself, but because of the technical challenges involved, synchronized dialogue was only made possible in the late 1920s with the introduction of the Vita phone system. After The Jazz Singer in 1927, "talkies" became more and more commonplace and within a decade silent films essentially disappeared. The silent film era is sometimes referred to as the "Age of the Silver Screen". The first film was created by Louis Le Prince in 1888. It was a two second film of people walking around in Oakwood Grange garden, titled "Roundhay Garden Scene." The art of motion pictures grew into full maturity in the "silent era" before silent films were replaced by "Talking Pictures" in the late 1920s. Many film scholars and buffs argue that the aesthetic quality of cinema decreased for several years until directors, actors, and production staff adapted to the new "talkies". The visual quality of silent movies, especially those produced during the 1920s, was often extremely high. However, there is a widely held misconception that these films were primitive and barely watchable by modern standards."

Required:

1. Open a new MS Word document, click **No Spacing** tab in the **Styles** group at top ribbon, and type the title heading and the entire paragraph.
2. Press **Enter** key twice after title heading to allow two spaces between title and body of the paragraph.
3. Highlight all text, in the **Font** group, change font style to **Times New Roman** and change font size to **12**.
4. Highlight title heading, **Center** text, change font size to **14** and apply **Bold** font.
5. In the middle of the paragraph, underline the text "**Age of the Silver Screen**".
6. Highlight the body of all texts except the title, in the **Paragraph** group, apply **Double line Spacing** to the texts.
7. Click the **Layout** tab at top ribbon, in the **Page Setup** group, using the **Custom Margin** feature, change the default margin settings of the Word document from "**1**" on all sides to "**2**" at **left** and **right** margins only.
8. Click the **Insert** tab at top ribbon, in the **Header & Footer** group, insert **footer** at bottom of the document.
9. Type your **name** at bottom left of the document, and **today's date** at bottom right.
10. Save the formatted document as **4.1_MoviesReview_Firstname_Lastname** using your first name and last name in any preferred location on your computer using your first and last name. Submit your completed assignment following the instructor's preferred method – electronically or printed hardcopy for grading.

4.2 – Review, Format, and Spellcheck a Letter:

A local high school teacher has just returned from a visit to a movie studio with her students and has written the partially completed thank you letter presented below to show appreciation for the warm welcome and hospitality she and her student received during their visit with Andrew Pitt, the studio owner. She has not proofread and formatted the letter before she was called into a quick staff meeting. Assume you are the teacher's secretary, your job is to complete, proofread, and have this letter ready for the teacher's signature after her meeting.

Andrew Pitt
110 Vista Studios
Hollywood, California 90028
Today's Date

We enjoyed the tickets you provided for the students at hollywood High to atend the studio premiere. They prarticularly enjoyed the Pirates ride along with the King kong exhibit. We were all very entertained and everyone had a good time. Since we returned from the show, the students have written reports about their exeperiences on the trip as their term paper for the current school term. I was amazed by the positive things they all had to say about the trip to Hollywood.

Thank you for giving us the opportunity to attend the show.

Sincerely,
Annie Jolie
Art/Drama Teacher

Required:

1. Open a new MS Word document, click **No Spacing** tab in the **Styles** group at top ribbon, and begin typing the address left justified.
2. Change the font type of text to **Cambria**, and change font size to **12**.
3. Enter **today's date** below the address, and press **Enter** key twice.
4. Type **Dear Mr. Pitt,** press **Enter** key once and begin typing the entire body of the letter in single space; all text left justified.
5. Click **Review** tab at top ribbon, using the **Proofing** group feature, correct the misspelled words with red wavy underline. Ensure that the name of a place or a movie title begins with uppercase letter.
6. After the one-line thank-you closing paragraph, press **Enter** key twice.
7. Type **Sincerely,** and press **Enter** key twice to allow room for the teacher's signature above the name and designation.
8. Save the formatted letter as **4.2_ ThanksLetter_Firstname_Lastname** in the preferred location on your computer using your first and last name. Submit your completed assignment following the instructor's preferred method – electronically or printed hardcopy for grading.

4.3 – Insert and Format a Table: You have been designated as a group leader for an upcoming one-week *Boy's Summer Camp Team* sponsored by a local community center in Santa Fe, New Mexico. Your team consists of 7 teenage boys, ages 12 – 16. In planning the trip, you need to obtain some basic personal and contact information about the boys in your team. The **5** categories of the required data are: **Name, Address, Age, Parent Name, and Parent Cell Phone #.** Data obtain from the boys and their parents are listed below:

Name – **Daniel Morris**
- Address – 191 Calhoun Road, Santa Fe, NM, 87505
- Age – 16
- Parent Name – Michael Morris
- Parent's Cell Phone #: 505-212-4677

Name – **Patrick Rodriguez**
- Address – 1400 Saint Michaels Drive, Santa Fe, NM, 87505
- Age – 12
- Parent Name – Monica Rodriguez
- Parent's Cell Phone #: 505-660-9542

Name – **Christopher Martinez**
- Address – 2110 Cerrillos Road, Santa Fe, NM, 87507
- Age – 15
- Parent Name – Timothy Martinez
- Parent's Cell Phone #: 505-432-1200

Name – **Emmanuel Gomez**
- Address – 1113 Rufina Road, Santa Fe, NM, 87507
- Age – 13
- Parent Name – Sophia Gomez
- Parent's Cell Phone #: 505-330-9145

Name – **Maxwell Darren**
- Address – 3716 Old Zion Hwy, Santa Fe, NM, 87508
- Age – 14
- Parent Name – Sharon Darren
- Parent's Cell Phone #: 505-993-2183

Name – **Mathew Shaw**
- Address – 435 Hospital Drive, Santa Fe, NM, 87505
- Age – 16
- Parent Name – Peter Shaw
- Parent's Cell Phone #: 505-770-8140

Name – **Richard Hunt**
- Address – 1200 Old Santa Fe Trail, Santa Fe, NM, 87502
- Age – 15
- Parent Name – Nathan Hunt
- Parent's Cell Phone #: 505-313-4010

Required:

1. Open a new MS Word document, click **No Spacing** tab in the **Styles** group at top ribbon, and change font type for all text to **Arial Narrow**.

2. Enter a name for the title of your table: **Boys Summer Camp Team – June 2021**; highlight title, change font size to **16**, and apply **Bold** font.

3. Press **Enter** key twice; click **Insert** tab at top ribbon, using the **Tables** group feature, highlight the first **5 columns** and down **8 rows.**

4. Click on table column intersections; drag as needed to resize and fit texts.

5. Enter the **5** listed categories of data in the first row of your table as column titles. Highlight column titles, change font size to **14**, apply **Bold** font, and **Center** texts.

6. Use font type **Times New Roman**, and font size **12** for all text typed inside the table cells.

7. Begin entering contact information listed above inside the table rows and columns for each member of the summer camp team.

8. Save the completed table document as **4.3_BSCT_Contact_Firstname_Lastname** in the preferred location on your computer using your first and last name. Submit your completed assignment following the instructor's preferred method – electronically or printed hardcopy for grading.

CHAPTER 5

WELCOME TO MICROSOFT EXCEL 2019

Microsoft Excel is a program used for recording and detailing accounting information. Microsoft Excel is the most popular spreadsheet software that is developed by Microsoft for various operating systems like Windows, macOS, Android and iOS calculation, used for graphing tools, creating pivot tables, and with a macro programming language called Visual Basic for Applications. Most businesses with a dedicated accounting software still use Excel to record, process, and manage accounting data using information from their primary accounting software. The new Microsoft Excel 2019 contains all the features you're used to from earlier versions, but you'll notice a few new ones as well. Excel makes it easy to calculate numbers using its formula feature. With Excel, businesses can streamline their data entry with AutoFill, get chart recommendations based on the data, and create charts with one click. The charts easily help them plot trends and patterns with data bars, color coding, and icons.

Learning Objectives:

After completing this chapter, you will be able to:

- Create Excel worksheet from scratch, and add accounting data into worksheet cells.
- Create an Excel workbook from a template, format a worksheet with borders, and create/format column headings.
- Insert rows and columns to a worksheet and delete rows and columns from a worksheet.
- Merge/center rows/columns and format column headings.
- Create Excel formulas to add, subtract, multiply, and divide data in a worksheet cell.

- Copy formulas to other worksheet cells; create a formula that refers to values in other cells.
- Link formulas between worksheets within a workbook.
- Understand the description and functions of Excel formulas in calculating accounting data.
- Insert headers & footers, and charts & graphs into a worksheet.

WHAT'S NEW IN MS EXCEL 2019

Excel is a software used to create spreadsheets, documents in which data is laid out in rows and columns similar to a big table. Due to its extreme versatility and power, Excel has become one of the most-used software programs in the business world since its launch in 1985. The personal computing renaissance of the 1980s and 1990s was primarily driven by the many uses of Excel and other spreadsheet software. Businesses also use Excel to perform the following functions:

- Keep track of sales by customer from month to month.
- Monitor customer payments to ensure timely payments.
- Keep track of expenses and assign them to particular employees.
- Calculate hours worked per employee for monthly payroll.
- Calculate monthly payments on the office mortgage.
- Create graphs or charts to explain company performance over time.
- Estimate monthly sales for the next three years based on historical data.
- Assign projects and tasks to employees in a centralized location.

The new Microsoft Excel 2019 is loaded with new features and some familiar features from earlier versions have been modified to be more user friendly. There are so many new or improved features for all Excel users: beginners, intermediate, and advance users. Our discussion in this chapter is limited to basic features for beginners in Microsoft Excel, including the following:

Improved Autocomplete

Excel autocomplete now functions differently from the way it used to be. For example, if you type "Book Review" into a worksheet cell and try to type it again in another cell, all you have to do is type B into that cell. Excel autocomplete feature will complete the rest of the phrase for you to read "Book Review." Also, as you continue working in that worksheet, anywhere else you want to type the same word, when you type the first letter, Excel will autocomplete it for you.

New Themes

Excel now provides three Office background themes that you can apply to your screen: Dark Gray, Black, and White. To access these themes, follow these steps:

1. Click **File** and click **Options** to display the **General** window.
2. In the open options window, under **Personalize your copy of MS Excel**, click the down arrow of **Office Theme** box, select the theme you want and click **OK**.

Black Theme

This feature allows you to change your **Office** theme. Simply click **File**, click **Account**, click the **Office Theme** drop-down arrow, and select the theme you want. The theme you choose will be applied across all your Office apps.

No Warnings when Saving a CSV File

Recall the familiar warning: *"This file may contain features that are not compatible with CSV..."* that you always see whenever you download and save a CSV file from other applications? In response to popular demand, Microsoft Corporation has removed that warning from Excel 2019 and you will longer get that warning when saving a CSV file. A CSV (comma-separated values) file is a text file that has a specific format which allows data to be saved in a table structured format. The new Excel 2019 contains **CSV (UTF-8)** support that allows you to open and save CSV files that use **UTF-8-character** encoding. **CSV UTF-8** is a commonly used file format that supports more characters than Excel's existing CSV option. This means better support for working with non-English data, and ease of moving data to other applications. To save CSV file in Excel format, follow these steps:

1. Click **File**, click **Save As**, and select **Browse**.
2. At the bottom of the open **Save As** window, click the **Save as type** down arrow to display Excel saving menu options **(fig. 5.1)**.
3. Navigate menu to find the new option for **CSV UTF-8 (Comma delimited)**. Click on it to select the option and click **Save** button at bottom of the **Sav**e window. Your file will be saved in Excel format.

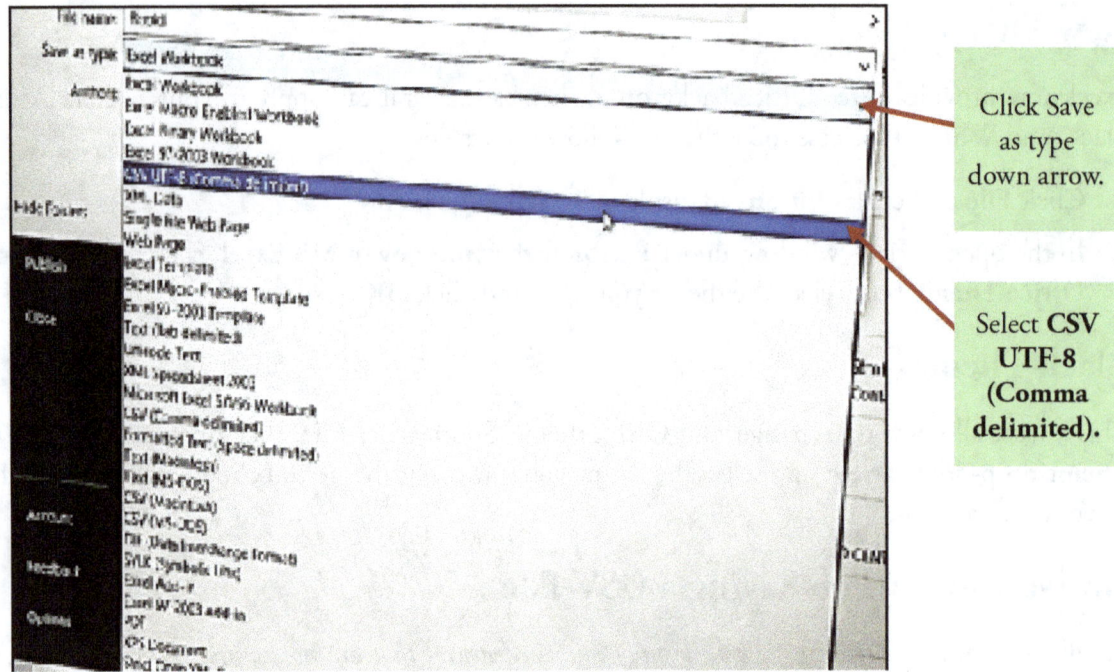

Fig. 5.1　　　　　Save a CSV File in Excel 2019

CREATE A WORKBOOK & FORMAT A WORKSHEET WITHIN THE WORKBOOK

Before we begin the discussion of creating Excel workbook and formatting a worksheet within the workbook, we must differentiate a workbook from a worksheet. The main difference between Excel Workbook and Worksheet is that Excel Workbook contains a number of worksheets while worksheet is a single sheet in Excel workbook. It is like a complete book and a single page. Excel Workbook is the complete book and Excel Worksheet is like a single page in a book. To add worksheets within a workbook, simply click the plus sign (+) at the bottom of the workbook.

Spreadsheet vs Worksheet

Users often use the word Worksheet and Spreadsheet interchangeably, but there is a difference. The main difference between Spreadsheet and Worksheet is that spreadsheet is software that allows users to organize data in rows/columns and perform calculations on the data, while the rows and columns in a spreadsheet collectively are called a worksheet. A major accounting benefit of using spreadsheets is that you can link worksheets within a workbook together. Spreadsheets are extraordinarily powerful tools, and are used frequently in the business world to store and manipulate data.

What is a Worksheet?

It is a document contained in a workbook comprising of columns (the vertical sets of boxes labeled A, B, C, etc. at the top of the screen), and rows (the horizontal sets of boxes labeled 1, 2, 3, etc. across the screen). At the intersection of each row and column is a cell into which a user can enter either numbers or text. The address of any given cell is generated by combining the letter of the cell's column with the number of the cell's row. For example, the cell highlighted in the diagram below, **fig. 5.2** is at address B4, because it lies at the intersection of column **B** and row **4**. When we refer to this cell verbally, we call it, **Cell B4**. The image below represents a very simple spreadsheet, more complex spreadsheets can contain hundreds or even thousands of rows and columns, the combination of which can represent millions of cells. Cells in a worksheet can easily be linked together with calculations and formulas to perform complex mathematical logic.

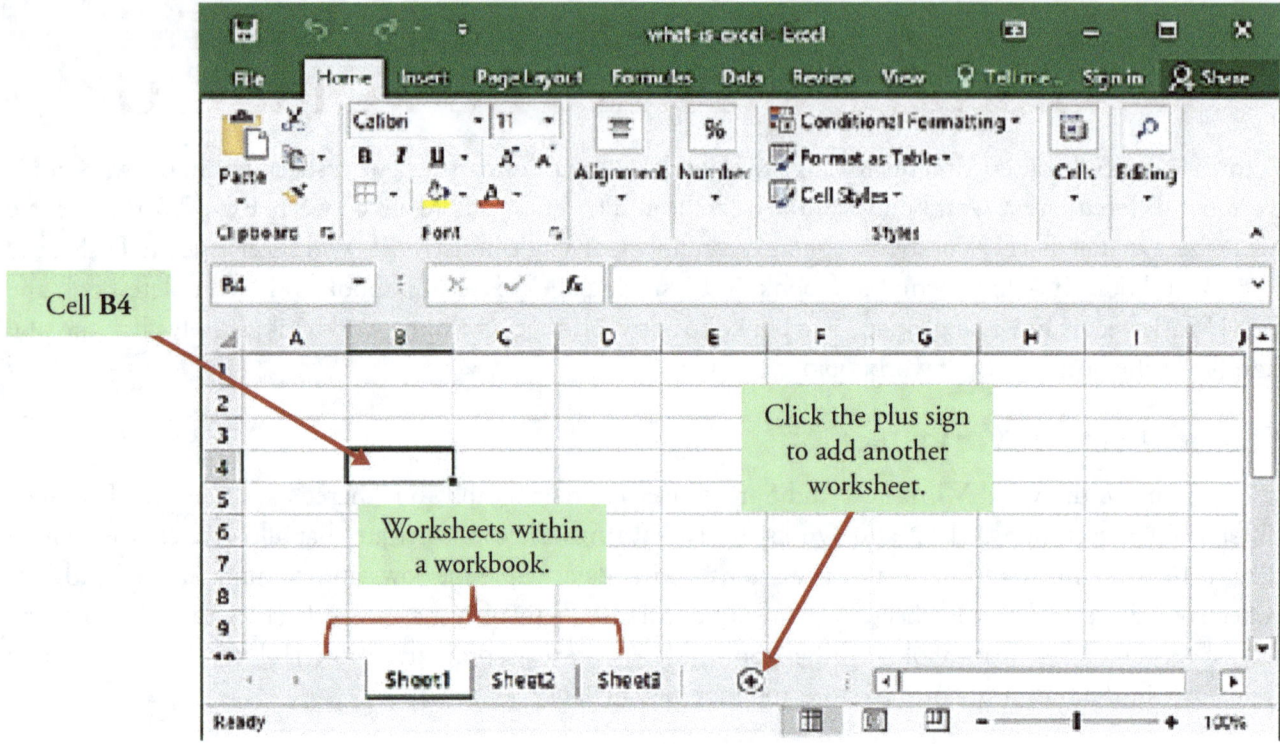

Fig. 5.2 Excel Workbook with Worksheets

Open a Workbook & Create a Worksheet

When you first click on Excel program it opens into a workbook that displays an active worksheet. To create a workbook:

1. Click the **Start** button, navigate the start menu, and click **Excel** icon to open the program.
2. In the open blank worksheet, click on a cell and enter data.
3. Press the **Tab** key on your keyboard to advance to the next cell in a row and enter more data as needed.
4. To type data below the row, press **Enter** key to move one row below and enter data into worksheet cells.

Manually Enter Data into Excel Worksheet Cells

Several options exist for manually entering data into worksheet cells. You can enter data in one cell, in several cells at the same time, or in more than one worksheet at once. The data you enter may be numbers, text, dates, or times. You can also format the entered data in many ways, and also adjust several settings to make the data entry easier for you. To manually enter data in worksheet cells, follow these steps:

1. Click on an empty cell to select it, such as **A1**, and type text or a number into the cell.
2. Press **Enter** tab, or use **keyboard forward** arrow to move to the next cell.
3. To fill data in a series, for example 1 to 10 or January to October **(fig. 5.3)**:
    a. Enter beginning of the series in the first two cells such as **1** and **2** or **January** and **February.**
    b. Click on **2** or **February**, click the intersection to form a **+** sign.
    c. Holding down your mouse, drag the fill handle down the column until all cells are filled with the series you want, and release mouse. Excel will auto fill the series as you drag from one cell to another.
    d. If the series do not change as you drag, click the **Autofill Options,** and check the **Fill Series** button, and continue to drag down the mouse to fill the rest of the cells.

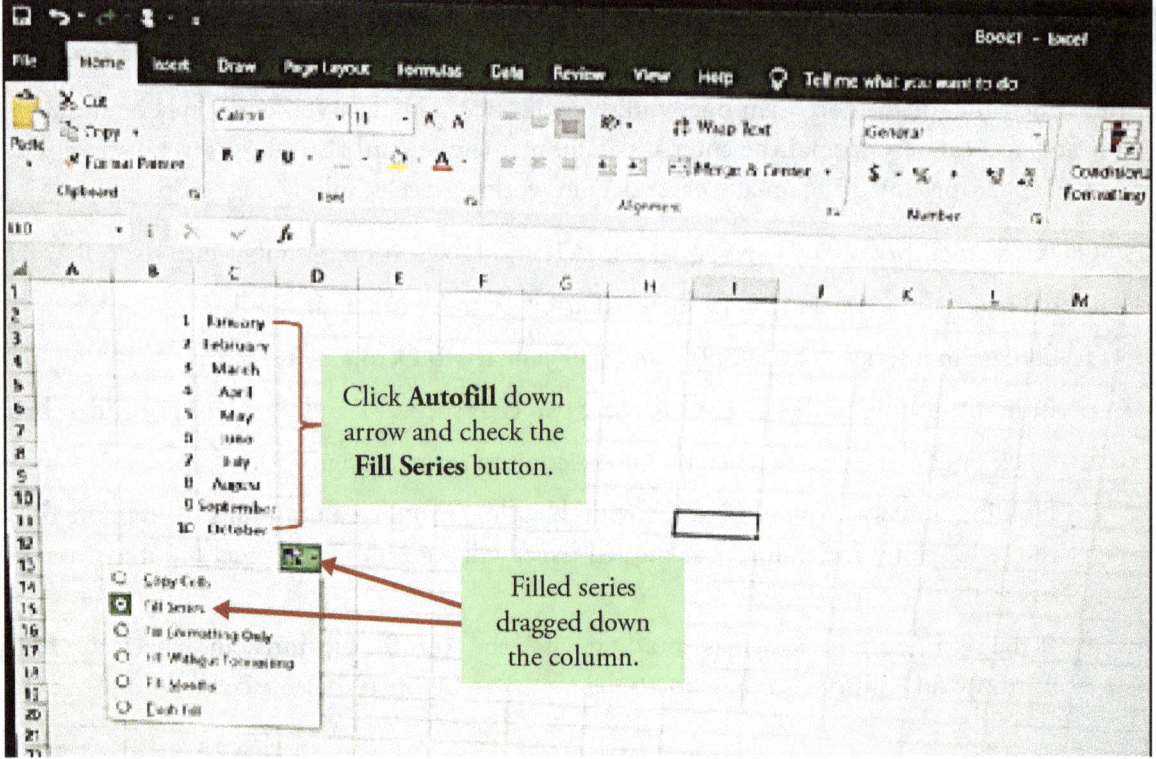

Fig. 5.3   **Fill Data Series**

Create a Workbook from a Template

1. Open Excel workbook and click the **File** tab, from the displayed menu, select **New**.
2. In the open **New** window, view several types of Excel templates installed on your computer, and click to select the template of your choice.
3. To find more templates online, in the search box above the templates, type the name of the template you want, and click the **Search** button. To perform this task, make sure you are connected to the Internet **(fig. 5.4)**.
4. Click the selected template to open it, and begin entering data into worksheet cells.

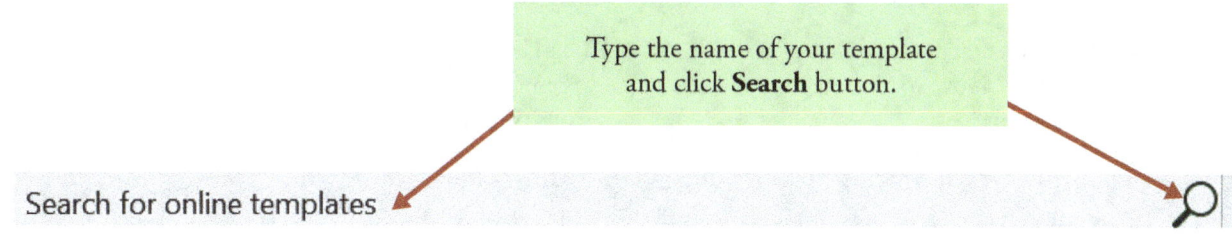

Fig. 5.4　　　　　　　　　　Search for Excel Templates Online

Can you Always Enter Data into a Worksheet Cell?

The answer is No. Sometimes you cannot enter or edit data in a worksheet, this is because the worksheet may have been protected by you or someone else to prevent data from being changed accidentally or by an unauthorized person especially if it's a worksheet containing confidential information. On a protected (locked) worksheet, you can select cells to view the data, but you will not be able to type information in cells that are locked. In most cases, you cannot remove the protection from a worksheet unless you have permission to do so from the person who created and protected the worksheet.

Protect a Worksheet (fig. 5.5a):

1. At the top ribbon, click the **Review** tab.
2. In the open **Protect Sheet** dialog box, make sure that **Protect worksheet and content of locked cells** box is checked, if not check the box.
3. Under **Allow all users of this worksheet to**, check the boxes of items you want users to be able to do on the worksheet **(fig. 5.6)**.
4. Type a password in the box and click **OK**.
5. In the open **Confirm Password** dialog box, retype the password, and click **OK**.

Unprotect a Worksheet: When you protect a worksheet, the **Protect Sheet** tab changes to Unprotect Sheet (fig. 5.5b):

1. At the top ribbon, click the **Review** tab.
2. In the **Protect** group, click **Unprotect Sheet**.
3. Enter the password used to protect the worksheet and click **Ok.**

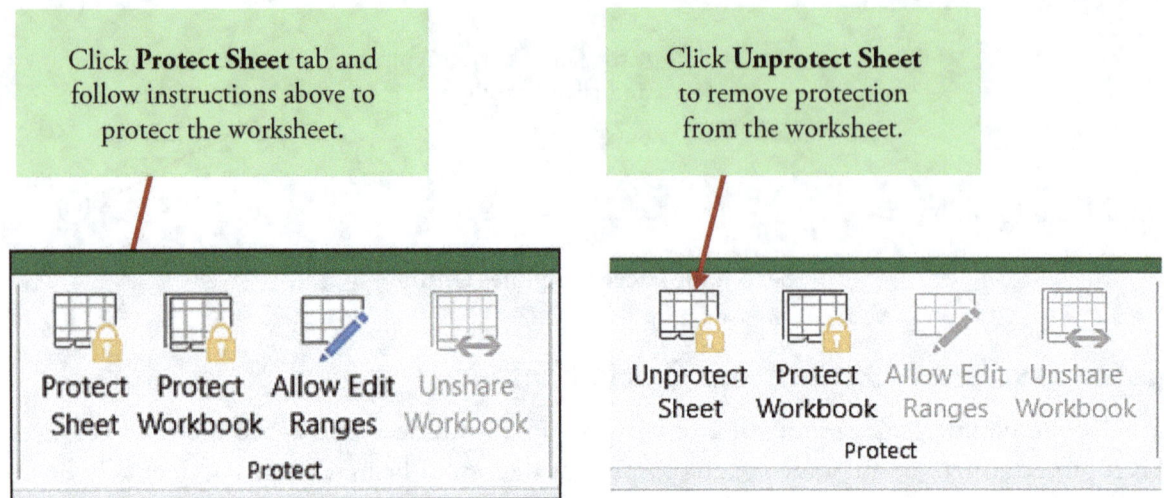

Fig. 5.5a Protect Worksheet **Fig. 5.5b** Unprotect Worksheet

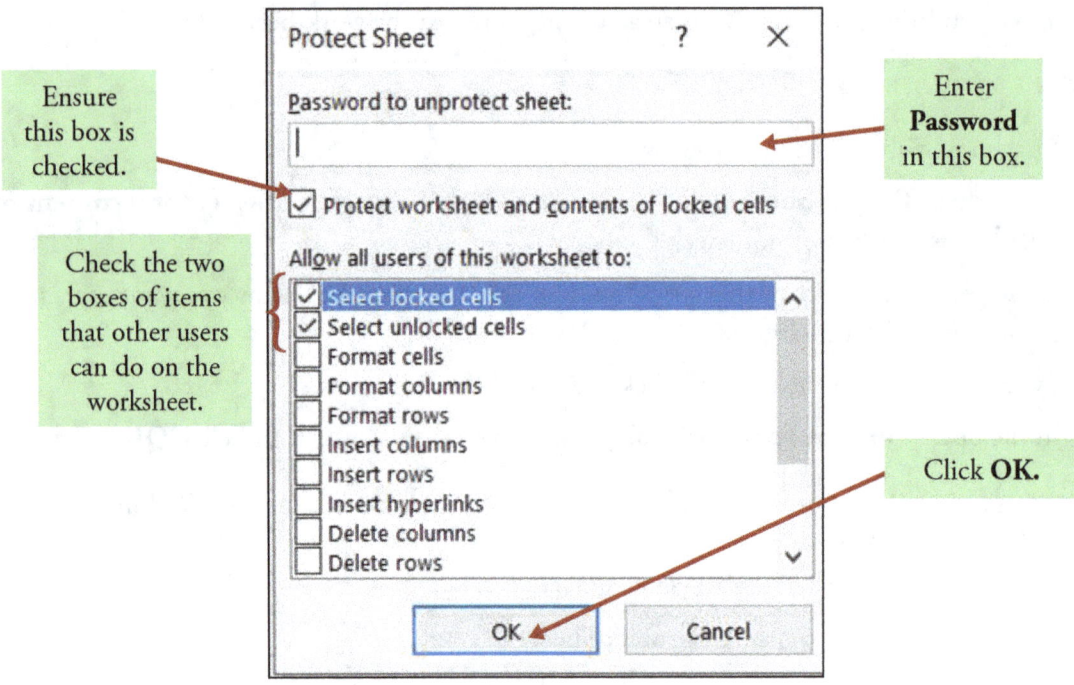

Fig. 5.6   **Protect Sheet Dialog Box**

INSERT/DELETE ROWS/COLUMNS & ADJUST ROW HEIGHT & COLUMN WIDTH

As you work in a worksheet, sometimes you may need to add more rows or columns to the worksheet you created or even remove some rows or columns depending on how much data you want in the worksheet. Inserting, deleting rows/columns, and formatting worksheets begin from the **Cells** group **(fig. 5.7)** below. There are two ways you can do this – the formal way from the top ribbon and the quick way using mouse **Right-click**.

Insert or Delete a Row or Rows (fig. 5.8):

1. Click on the cell where you want to add a row.
2. From the **Home** tab, in the **Cell** group, select **Insert** down arrow.
3. Select **Insert Sheet Rows**; one row is added below the cell you clicked in **step 1**.
4. To add multiple rows, click on one cell, holding down the mouse, highlight the number of rows below the cell that you want to add.
5. Repeat steps **2 & 3** to add the number of rows highlighted. The highlighted rows will be added below the cell you clicked in **step 1**.

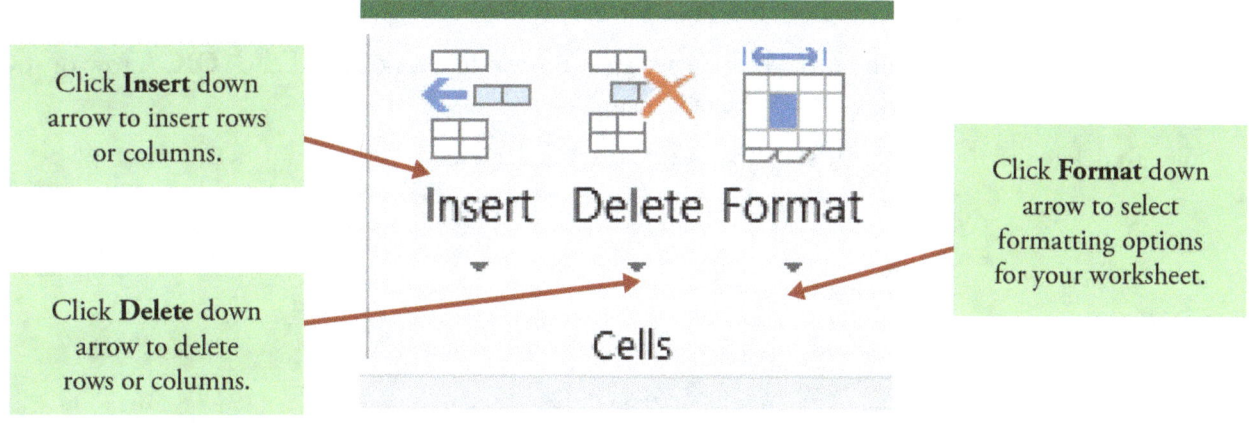

Fig. 5.7   Cell Group at Top Ribbon

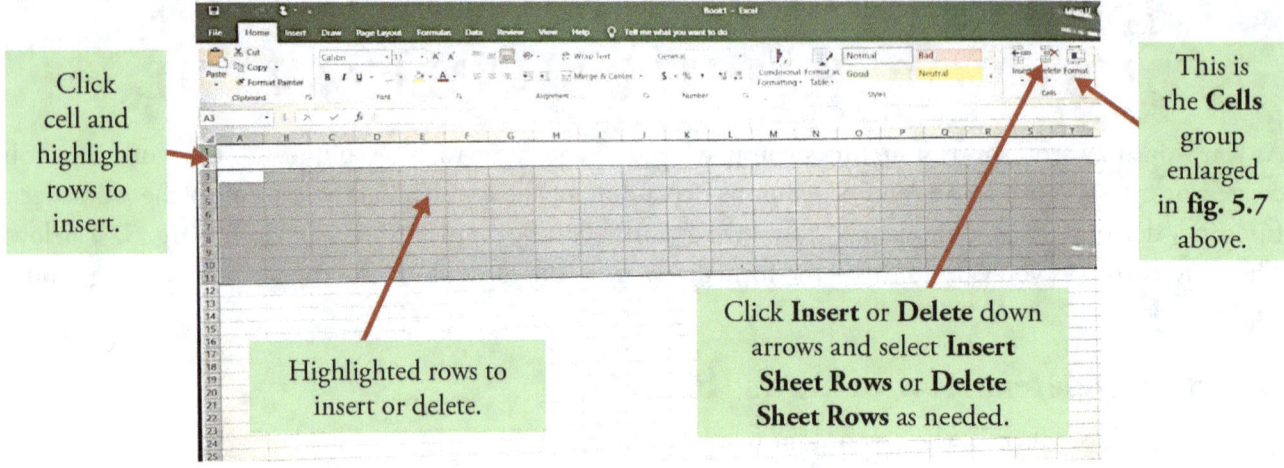

Fig. 5.8   Insert or Delete Multiple Rows in a Worksheet

Quick Way to Insert or Delete a Row or Rows (fig. 5.9):

1. Right-click on the cell where you want to add a row.
2. If adding multiple rows, holding down the mouse, highlight the number of rows you want to add or delete.
3. From the displayed menu, click **Insert** or **Delete** as needed.
4. In the open **Inser**t dialog box, click **Entire Row** button to check it, and click **OK**. A row or rows will be added below the cell you clicked in **step 1**.
5. To delete the row(s), repeat **step 1** above, and select **Delete**.

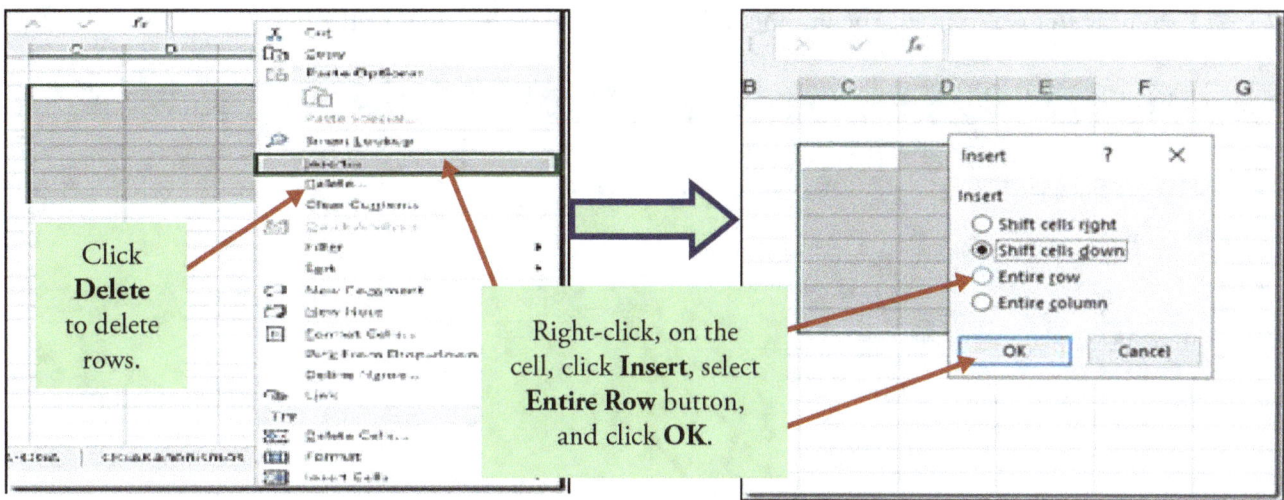

Fig. 5.9   Quick Way to Insert or Delete a Row or Rows

Insert or Delete a Column or Columns

Excel top columns usually contain the heading or title of data entered into the worksheet cells intersected with rows and columns. Each column heading describes the type of data contained in that column such as transaction date, customer name, account number, amount due, etc. You can insert a column to the left or to the right of your selected cell.

1. To add a column to **right** of column **B (fig. 5.10),** place mouse on column **B**.
2. From the **Home** tab, in the **Cell** group, select **Insert** down arrow.
3. Select **Insert Sheet Columns**; column **C** is added **(right of B)**.
4. To add a column to the **left** of column **F (fig. 5.10),** place mouse on column **F**.
5. From the **Home** tab, in the **Cell** group, select **Insert** down arrow.
6. Select **Insert Sheet Columns**; column **E** is added **(left of F)**.
7. To add multiple columns to right or left:
8. Click the cell and highlight toward **right** of the number of columns to insert.
9. Repeat **step 3** to insert the number of columns you highlighted to the **right**.
10. Click the cell and highlight toward the **left** the number of columns to insert.

11. Repeat **steps 6** to insert the number of columns you highlighted to the **left**.

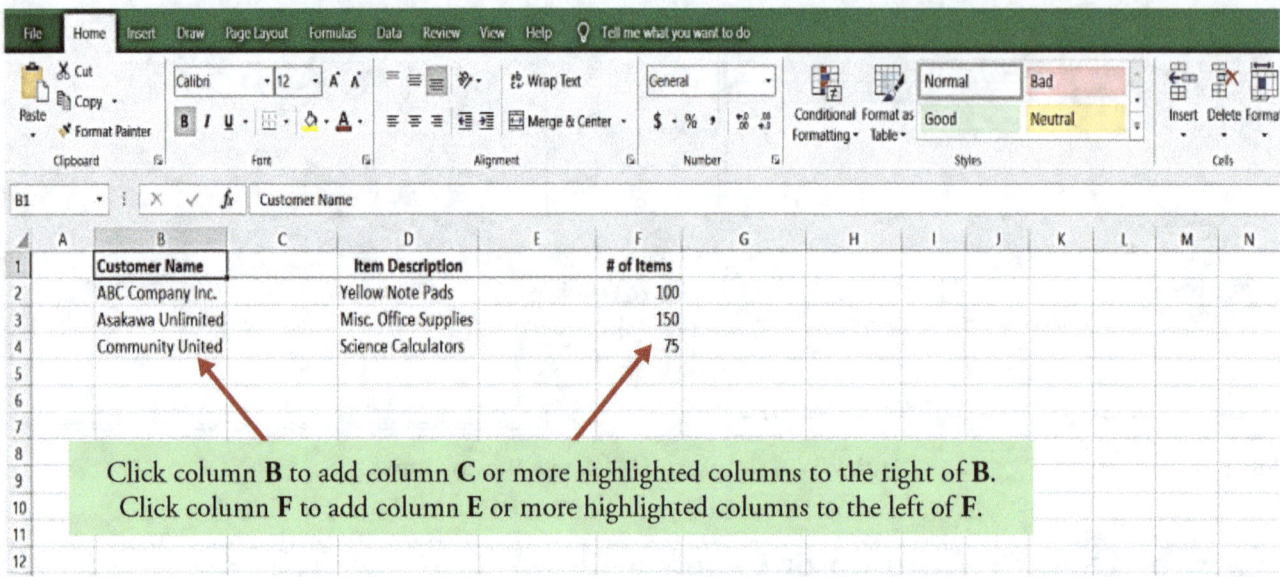

Fig. 5.10   **Insert a Column or Columns**

Quick Way to Insert or Delete a Column or Columns (fig. 5.11):

1. Right-click on column **B** to add column **C** or more highlighted columns to the right of **B**.
2. Right-click on column **F** to add column **E** or more highlighted columns to the left of **F**.
3. From the displayed menu, click **Insert (fig. 5.11).**
4. In the open **Insert** dialog box, click **Entire Column** button to check it, and click **OK.** A column or multiple columns will be added to the **right or left** as highlighted.

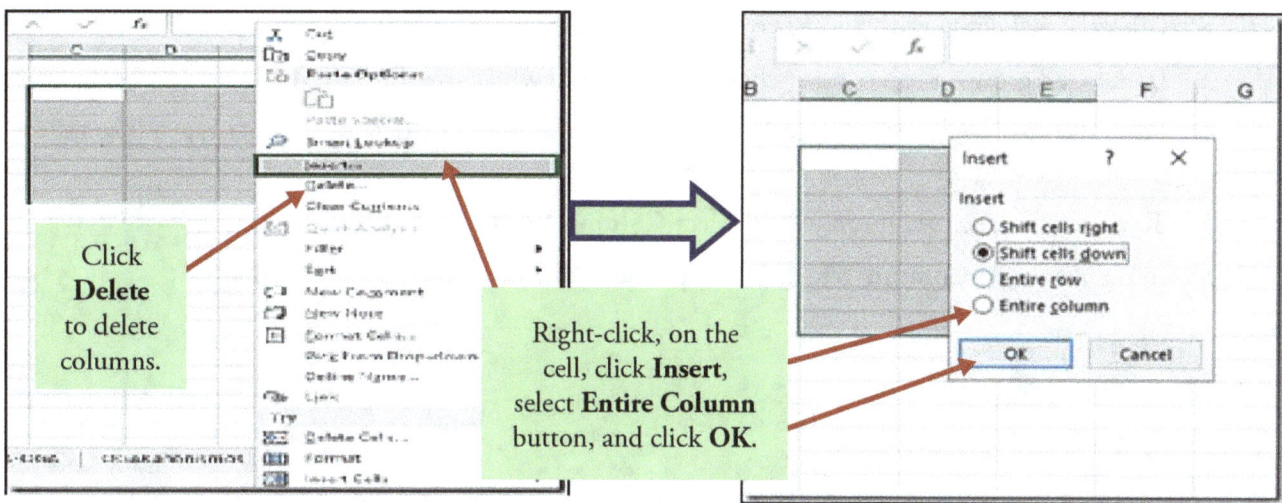

Fig. 5.11   Quick Way to Insert a Column or Columns

Change the Width of a Column

As you enter data into worksheet cells, a cell may display data as ##### **(fig. 5.12)**. This can occur when a number is too long to fit into the column or the column is too small to contain the number or a date. For example, suppose a cell with date format "mm/dd/yyyy" contains 10/30/2020 but the column is only wide enough to display six characters. The cell will display this: ##### in the column. To see the entire contents of the cell in its current format, you must increase the width of the column or height of the row. Follow instructions below to widen the column.

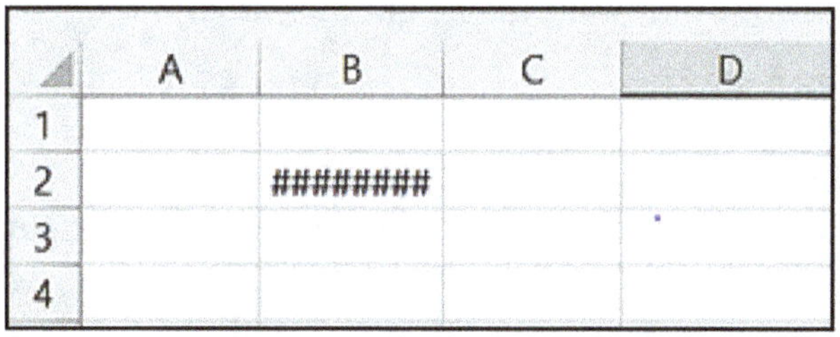

Fig. 5.12   Narrow Column Width 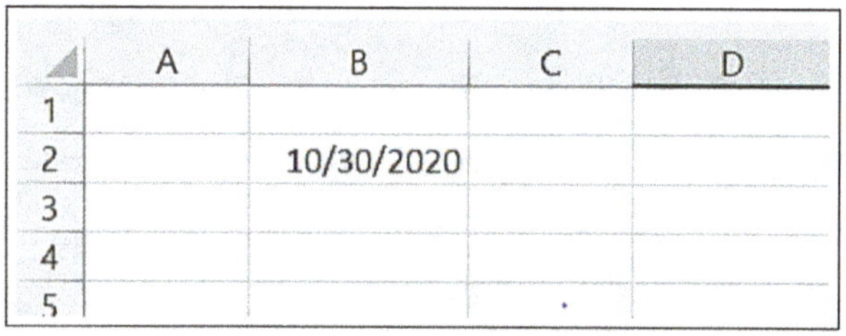   Wider Column Displays Cell Content

1. Click the cell containing number or date you entered.
2. In the **Cell** group at top ribbon, click the **Format** down arrow **(fig. 5.13)**.
3. From the displayed menu, select **AutoFit Column Width**. The date or number typed into the cell can now be viewed.
4. To manually specify column width, select **Column Width**.
5. In the displayed **Column Width** box, type the width you want and click **Ok**.

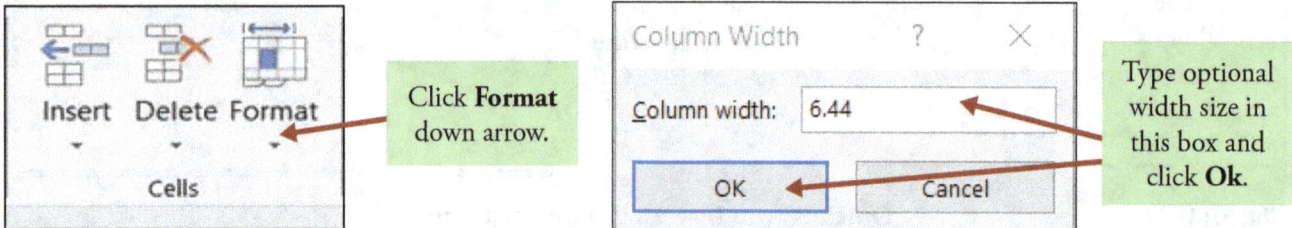

Fig. 5.13   **Increasing Worksheet Column With**

Increase the Height of a Row

The default height of Excel 2019 worksheet is **14.4."** Sometimes when you enter text into worksheet cells, this default height is not high enough to fit your text. The text may also be too long and crossover to another cell. To make the text fit into one cell, you have to increase the height of the row and wrap text so that they appear on two lines in one cell. This is particularly useful when formatting column headings that describe what data in the worksheet are about.

1. Click the worksheet cell or click and highlight the rows you want the height increased.
2. In the **Cell** group at top ribbon, click **Format** down arrow.
3. In the displayed **Cell Size** menu, select **Row Height**.
4. On the open **Row Height** box, **(fig. 5.14)** type the optional size needed to increase the row height and click **Ok**.

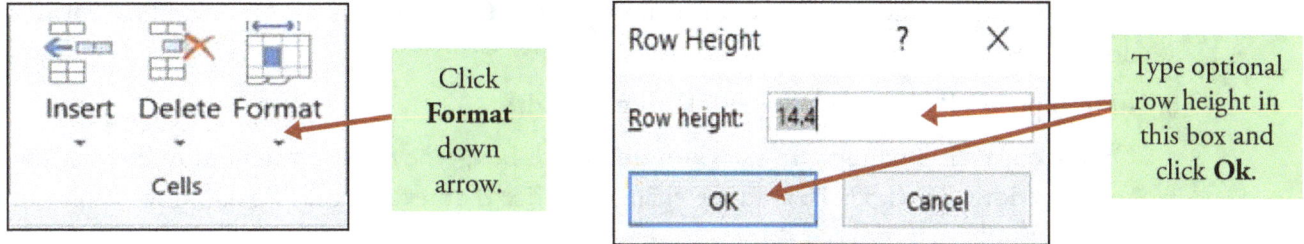

Fig. 5.14   Increasing Worksheet Row Height

To illustrate when text entered into a cell is too long for the row height, notice that in **fig. 5.15**, cell **A3** contains the texts **Daily Allowance** and cell **B3** contains **High School Students**. Notice that the texts do not fit into their respective cells. Cell **B3** crossed over into cells **C3** and **D3.** To increase worksheet row height to contain long texts, we can do one of two things or both.

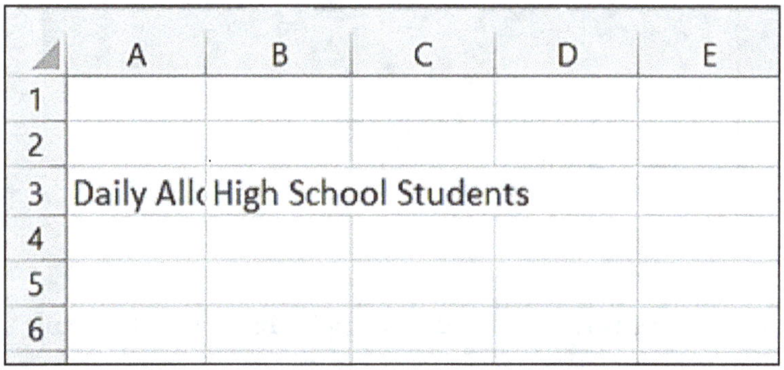

Fig. 5.15   Text in Worksheet Cells Overlap

1. **Wrap Text:** Wrap the text to automatically increase the row height and adjust the column to fit the texts (**fig. 5.16**).
   a. Using the example on **fig. 5.15**, click cell **A3** and highligt up to cell **B3**.
   b. In the **Alignment** group, click **Wrap Text** at top ribbon. Notice that the row automatically increases in height and the texts now display on two lines all fitted in cells **A3** and **B3**.
2. **Adjust Column Width:** If the columns appear too narrow after text wrap, increase the column width.

All-in-One Beginners Guide to Computer Proficiency | 225

a. Click the cell that appears to be too narrow; in the **Cell** group at top ribbon, click **Format** down arrow.

b. In the open **Cell Size** window, select **Column Width**.

c. On the open small window, in the **Column Width** box, type the size you need to increase the column width. See **fig. 5.16** after the changes; notice that texts in cells **B3-D3** now display in three lines all fitted into cell **B3**.

d. Alternatively, to increase column with, click at top of the column intersection you want to increase to form a + sign. The **Pixels** size displays at top of the column with + sign, for example (**width: 15.22 (144 pixels)**).

e. Holding down the mouse, drag the plus sign to the right. You will notice the **Pixels** number increaseing as you drag to increase the column width.

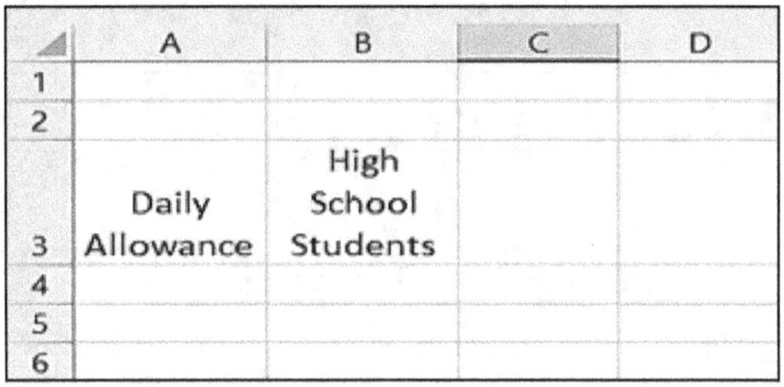

Fig. 5.16   **Text in Worksheet Cells Adjusted to Fit in Rows & Columns**

BASIC EXCEL WORKSHEET FORMATTING OPTIONS

Formatting Excel worksheet is important to maintain consistency in the way that Microsoft Excel stores numbers, texts, and graphics. With this in mind, it is important to format the fields in your spreadsheet accordingly using various formatting options available in Excel 2019. The ultimate goal of a formatted worksheet is to present information in a way that it makes sense to other people and enables users of the worksheet to make informed business decisions. To accomplish this goal, you have to give readers a head start by titling your worksheet correctly and clearly. A good title lets readers know immediately what the content of the worksheet is all about and eliminates the problem of readers having to work so hard to understand your information. For example, if you are presenting 2020 Revenue Projections, format your worksheet in a way that the reader can quickly tell whether the projection shows that revenue is expected to be high or low this year. The revenue amounts should be formatted with dollar signs and commas instead of general numbers. In Excel 2019, formatting worksheet data is easier than ever. You can use several fast and simple ways to create professional-looking worksheets that display your data effectively. For example, you can use document themes for a uniform look throughout all of your Excel spreadsheets styles to apply predefined formats, and other manual formatting features to highlight important data. Here are some suggestions for formatting your worksheet:

- Give your worksheet a good title.
- Let the format lead the eye by using good descriptive column headings.
- Apply a theme to make it look more professional.
- If you use charts to describe data, don't cram your charts.
- Use diagrams to clarify worksheet data if need be (intermediate users).
- Take advantage of conditional formatting to differentiate descriptive data (intermediate users).
- When in doubt, spell it out by adding a short comment about data in a particular cell(s).
- Apply boarders: double or thick boarders where necessary.
- Invite feedback from other people to test how your worksheet comes across to the readers.

Remove Worksheet Formatting

When you select a formatted row or column, that formatting will be transferred to a new row or column that you insert. However, if you do not want the formatting to be applied, you can remove it by selecting the **Editing Options** button after you insert the row or column, and choosing **Clear Formats.** To remove formatting from rows and columns, follow these steps:

1. Click the worksheet cell or highlight the row or column you want to remove formatting.
2. In the **Editing** group, click the **Clear** down arrow.
3. In the displayed short menu, select **Clear Formats** to remove formatting from the selected cells (**fig. 5.17**).

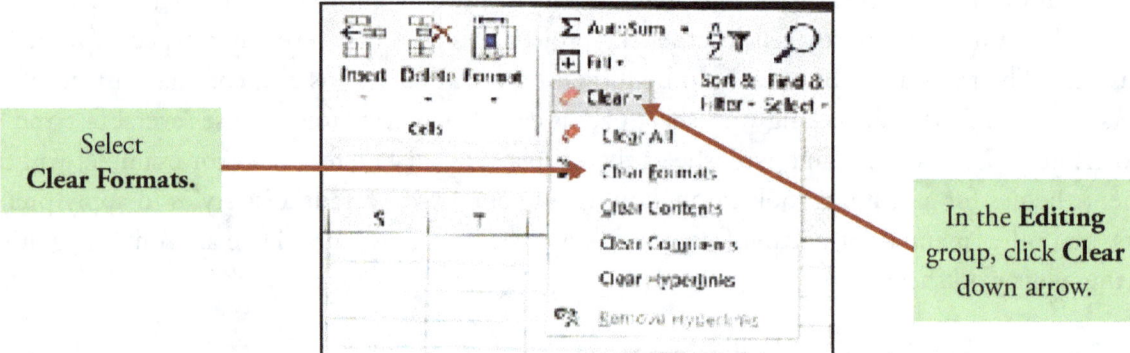

Fig. 5.17   **Remove Formatting from Worksheet Cells**

Sample Excel Project 1

In our discussion of basic worksheet formatting for beginners in Excel, we illustrate how to format a worksheet using a partially populated worksheet containing sales data from *Zazuma Office Supplies, Inc.,* (**fig.5.18**). We will continue to use this unformatted worksheet throughout our discussion of basic worksheet formatting and show how the worksheet changes as we apply various Excel formatting options. As we proceed in this section, please pay particular attention to the same unformatted worksheet in **fig. 5.18** to notice changes in the same worksheet after we apply all appropriate formatting in each step.

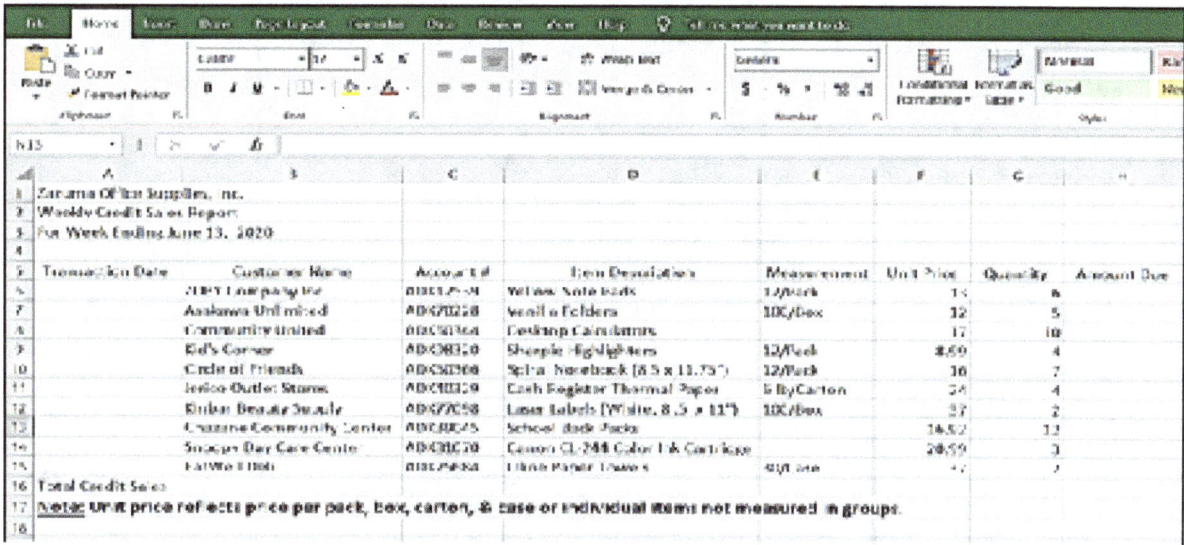

Fig. 5.18 Unformatted Worksheet Containing Data

Format Worksheet with Boarders

When you open an Excel worksheet, you will notice grid lines. Those lines are not boarders; and when you print the worksheet, the grid lines do not appear on a printed Excel worksheet. However, if the worksheet is formatted with boarders, custom lines will appear on the printed worksheet. Gride lines that displayed on an opened worksheet define the perimeter of cell locations. Adding custom lines to a worksheet is known as adding borders which are different from the grid lines. The **Borders** command allows you to add a variety of line styles to a worksheet to make reading the worksheet much easier. Boarders also help to keep columns separate from each other, make data stand out, make data easier to read, and give your worksheet an overall good professional look. To apply boarders to the unformatted worksheet in **fig. 5.18** above follow these steps:

1. Click on cell **A5**, holding down the mouse, highlight cells **A5 – H15**.
2. In the **Font** group at top ribbon, click the **Boarders** down arrow **(fig. 5.19)**.
3. From the displayed **Boarders** menu, select **All Boarders** to apply the selected formatting. Custom lines are applied to highlighted range of the worksheet, see **fig.5.20** below.

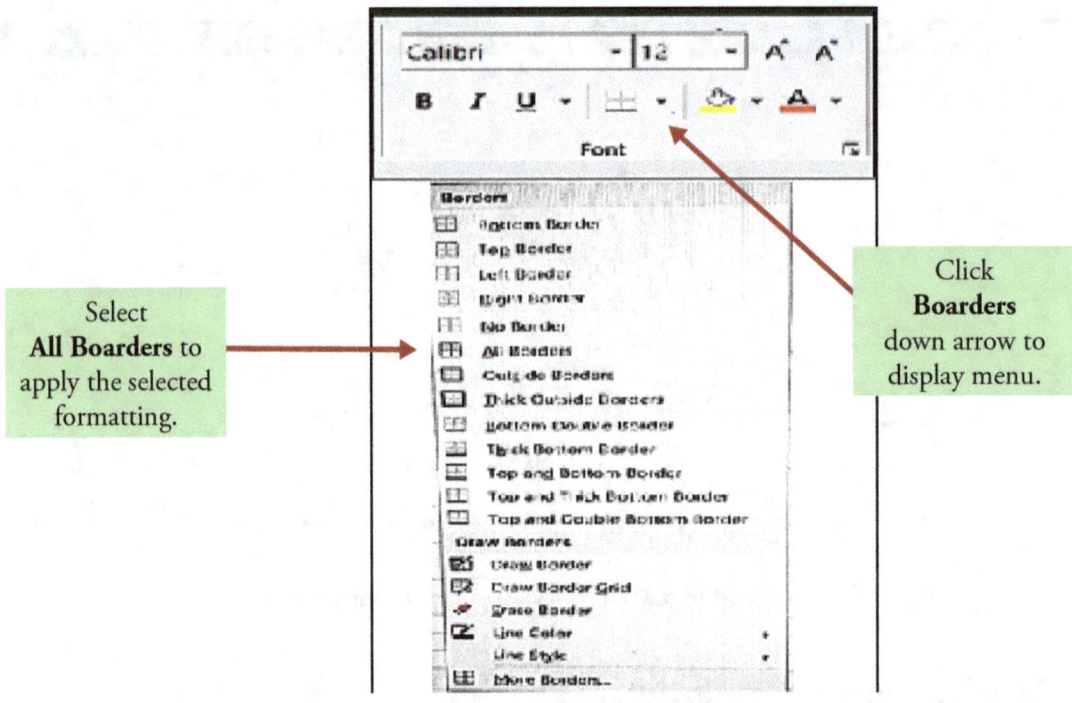

Fig. 5.19   **Apply Worksheet Boarders**

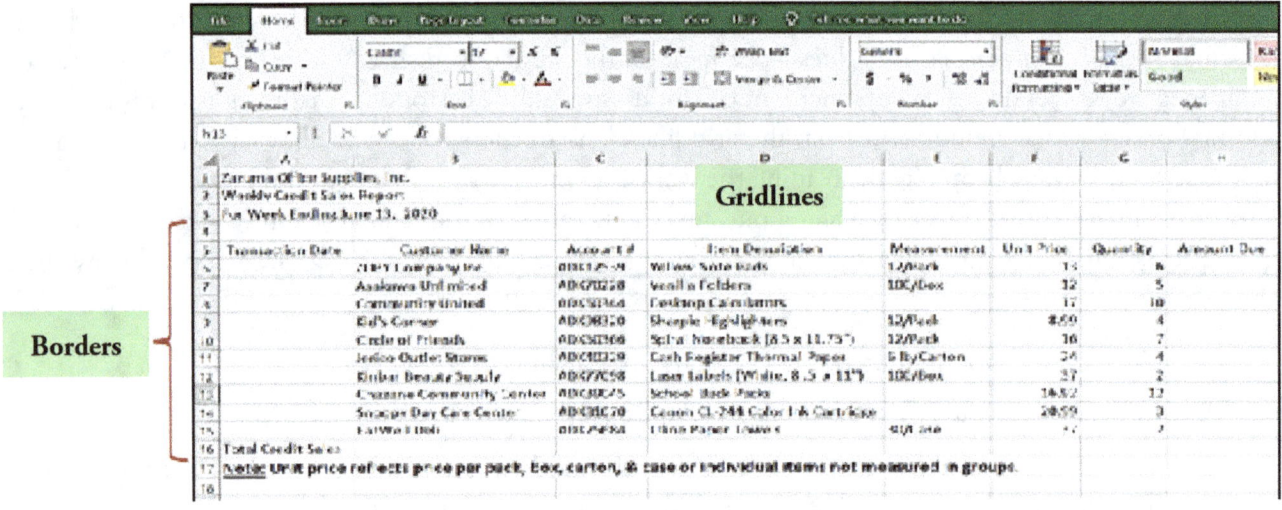

Fig. 5.20   **Worksheet Formatted with Boarders (cells A5 – H15)**

230 | *Basic Computing Concepts*

Merge & Center Worksheet Cells

Merge and center function is a feature that allows you to merge several rows and columns into one worksheet cell. It is most commonly used for centering the title of a worksheet to clearly describe what the data on the worksheet are about. For example, notice on **fig. 5.20** that the title of the worksheet from **A1 – A3** contains the company name, *Zazuma Office Supply Inc.* along with what the data on the worksheet is telling us, including the specific date of the report. This type of information should be placed across the center of the worksheet it describes. We can center this title using Excel **Merge and Center** feature. In this illustration, we'll also format the worksheet column headings on rows **A5 – H5** to make then stand out in describing the data they contain. See **fig. 5.21** for the newly formatted worksheet.

Merge & Center Cells

1. On the same worksheet **(fig. 5.20)**, click cell **A1** and highlight through cell **H1**.
2. In the **Alignment** group at top ribbon, click **Merge & Center**.
3. Click cell **A2**, highlight through cell **H2**, and click **Merge & Center.**
4. Click cell **A3**, highlight through cell **H3**, and repeat steps **2 & 3**. Notice the entire cells in each row highlighted are merged into one cell per row thereby centering the title at top of the worksheet.
5. Click and highlight the three merged rows, in the **Fonts** group, click **B** to apply bold font to the texts to make the heading stand out.

Format Worksheet Columns Headings

1. Click cell **A5**, highlight through cell **H5**.
2. In the **Fonts** group, click **B** to apply bold font to texts in the highlighted cells.
3. Repeat **step 1**, in the **Fonts** group, click the **Boarder** down arrow.
4. From the displayed **Boarders** menu, select **Top and Double Bottom Boarder** to apply formatting to the highlighted cells. Column heading in row **A5 – H5** show double lines **(fig. 5.21)**.

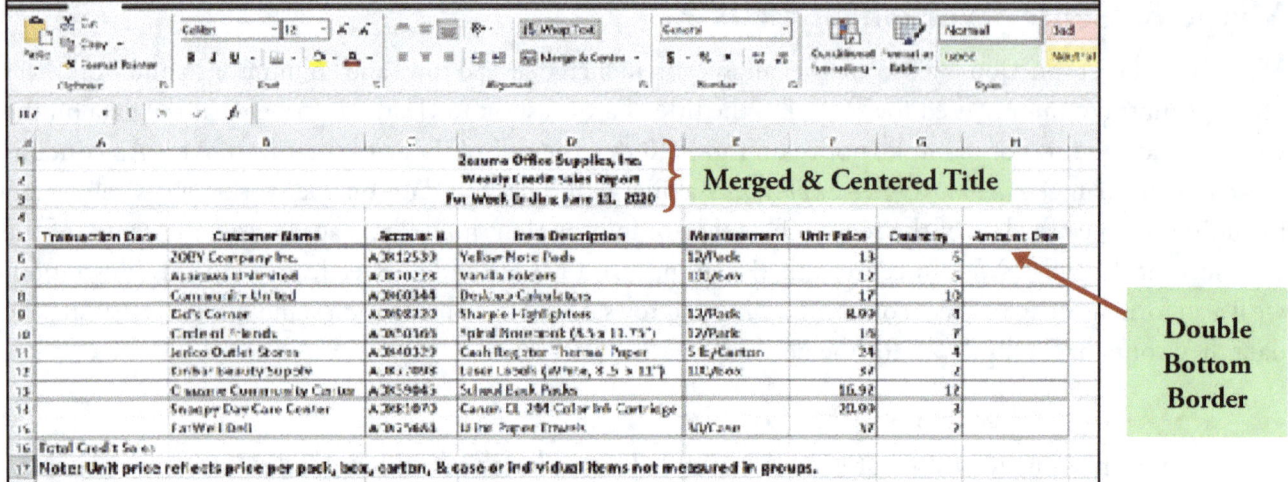

Fig. 5.21   Worksheet with Centered Title, Bold font & Double-Lined Column Headings

Insert & Format Date

Excel comes with quite a few types of date format but contains features that allow you to choose the date option you want. When you enter date into a worksheet such as **5/16/20,** Excel assumes this to be a general number and displays it as a number unrelated to date such as **43967** according to the default date settings which is often set to General. If you mean your entry to be a date, you have to change the formats to make it appear as a date. In this section, we will learn how to enter the correct transaction date format in *Zazuma Office Supply Inc.* Sales Report **(fig. 5.21)**. Before we enter dates, let's format the **Transaction Date** column **A** first. It is always a good idea to change cell format first before entering dates.

1. Click on cell **A6** and highlight through **A15**.
2. In the **Number** group at top ribbon, click the down arrow under **General** box **(fig. 5.22)**.
3. From the displayed number menu **(fig. 5.23)**, select **Short Date**.
4. Alternatively, click the **Number** group **Dialog Box Launcher** to display number format options, select **Date**, and click **Ok (fig. 5.24)**.
5. On the worksheet cell **A6 – A15**, enter the transaction dates. The dates will appear as dates the way you want them to look.

6. If you have entered dates already and the dates look like general numbers, highlight all your entries, and repeat steps **2 & 3**. The numbers will change to real dates.

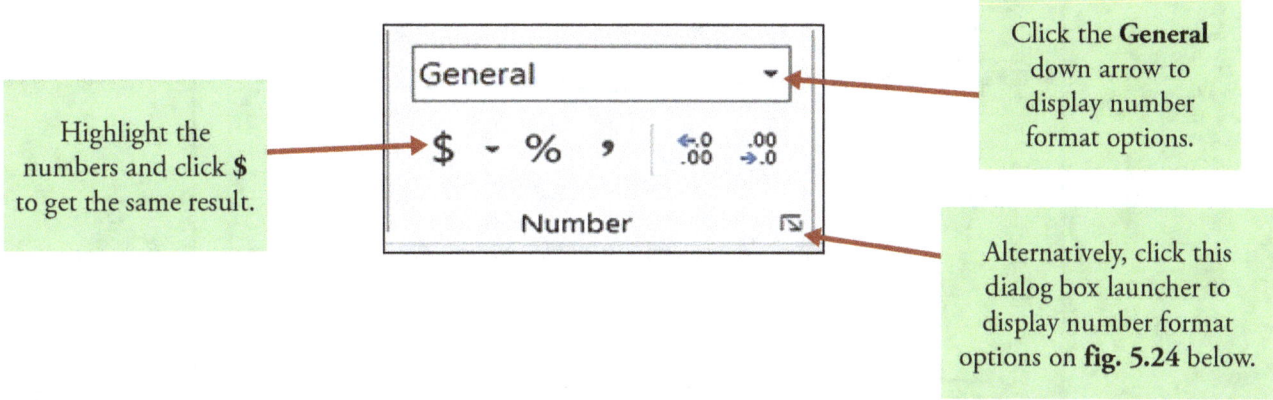

Highlight the numbers and click **$** to get the same result.

Click the **General** down arrow to display number format options.

Alternatively, click this dialog box launcher to display number format options on **fig. 5.24** below.

Fig. 5.22   **Number Group**

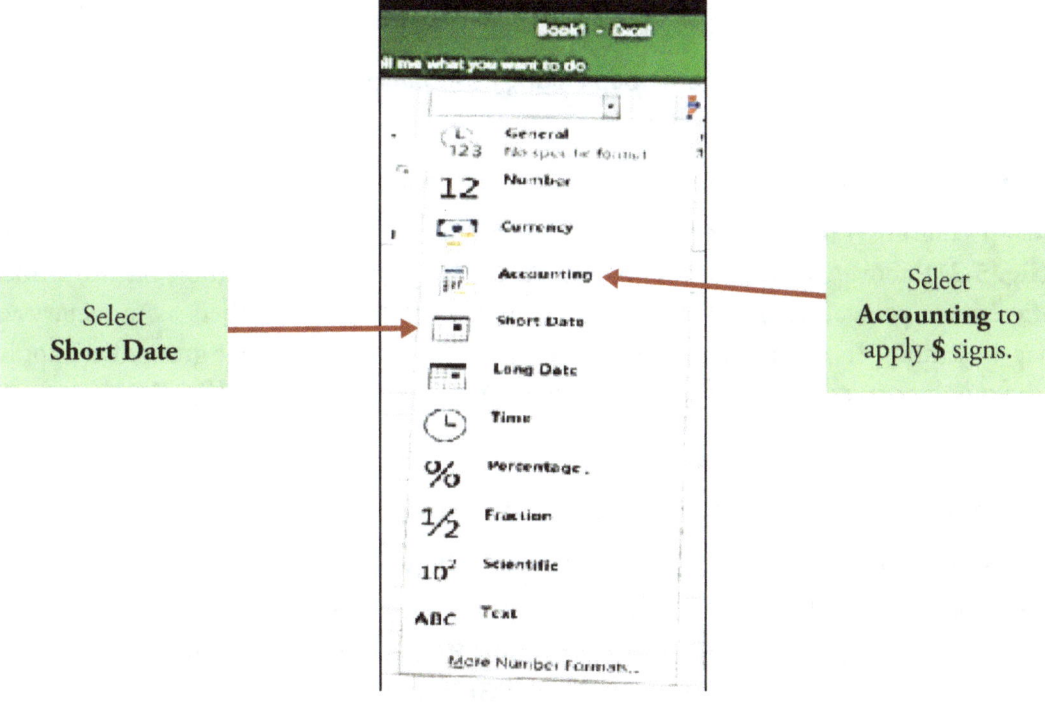

Select **Short Date**

Select **Accounting** to apply $ signs.

Fig. 5.23   **Number Menu Options**

All-in-One Beginners Guide to Computer Proficiency | 233

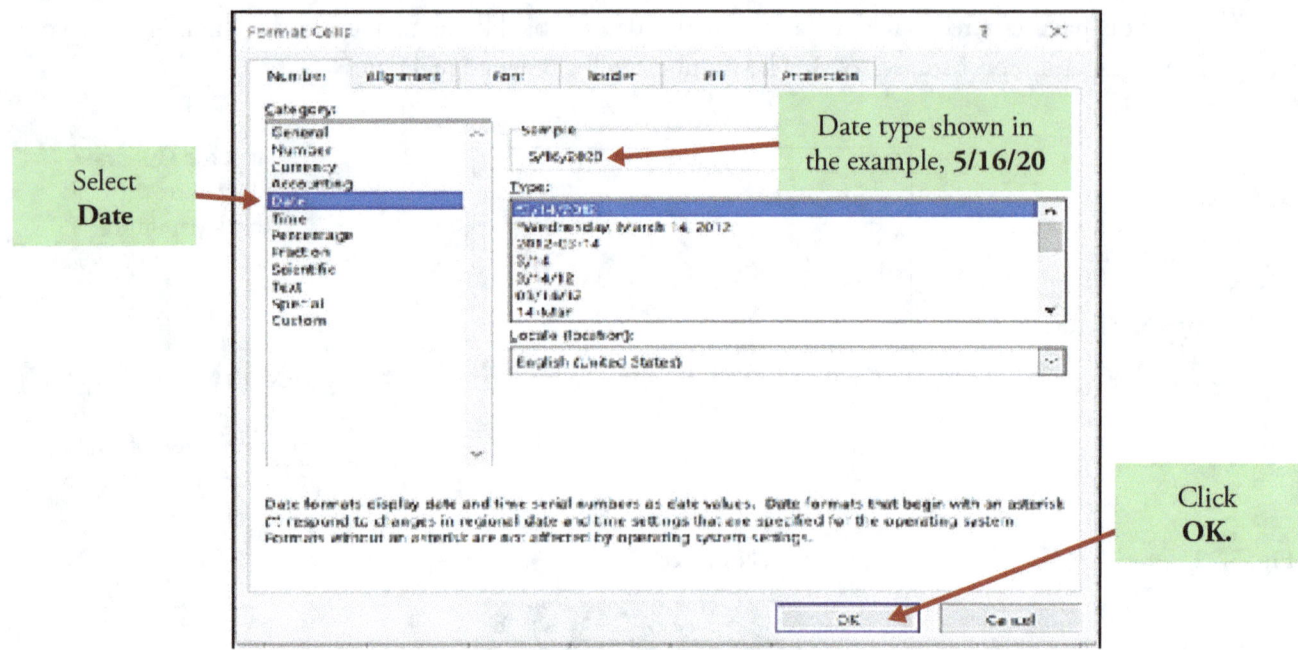

Fig. 5.24   Number Group Dialog Box Launcher

Apply Currency Format to Amounts

Notice that on columns **F & G** of *Zazuma Office Supply Inc.* Sales Report data in the cells are general numbers **(fig. 5.21)** above. To help readers of this report understand information on the worksheet, you have to differentiate general numbers from dollar amounts. To display numbers as monetary values, you must format those numbers as currency. This process takes place in the **Number** group. Let's apply currency format to the numbers in column **F** of *Zazuma Office Supply Inc.* Sales Report **(fig. 5.21)**.

1. On the sales report worksheet, click on cell **F6** and highlight through **F15**.
2. In the **Number** group at top ribbon, click the down arrow under **General** box.
3. From the displayed number menu, select **Accounting** to apply dollar format, see **fig. 5.23** above. The highlighted numbers on cell **F6 – F15** will be displayed with dollar signs **($)**.
4. Alternatively, click the **Number** group **Dialog Box Launcher** as shown in **fig. 5.22** above to display number format options, select **Accounting**, and click **Ok (fig. 5.25)**.

234 | *Basic Computing Concepts*

5. If you highlight the numbers and simply click the dollar sign in the **Numbers** group, you will get the same **$** signs result **(fig. 5.22)**.

6. See **fig. 5.26** below for *Zazuma Office Supply Inc.* Sales Report with formatted date and dollar **($)** signs.

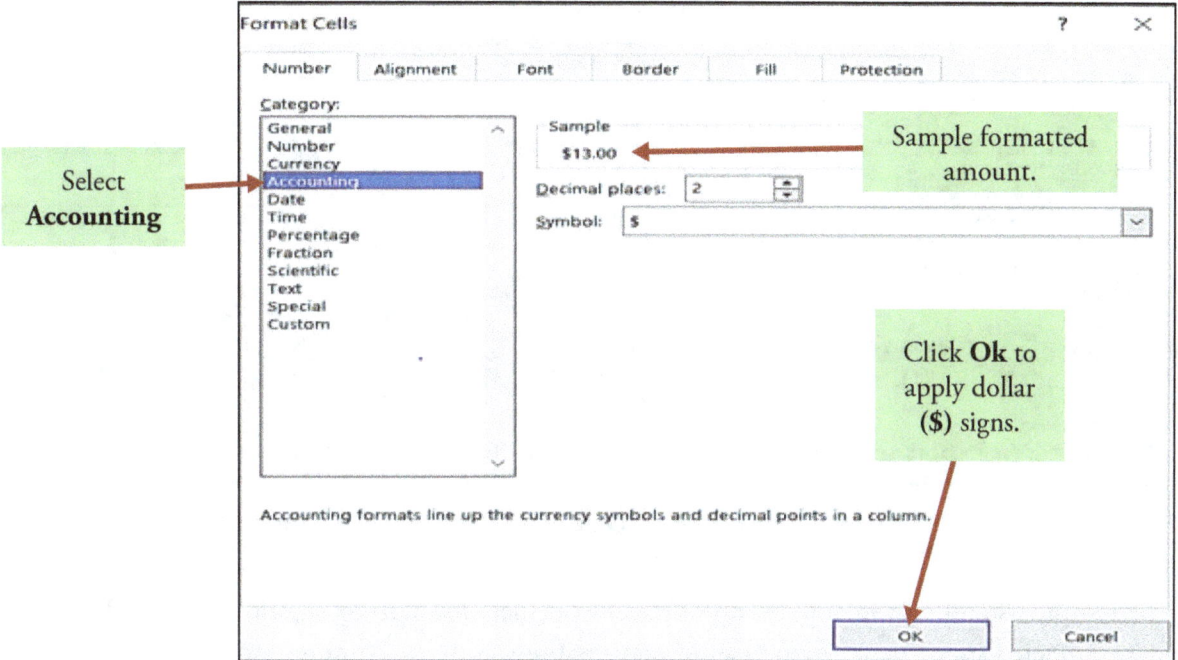

Fig. 5.25   **Number Group Dialog Box Launcher**

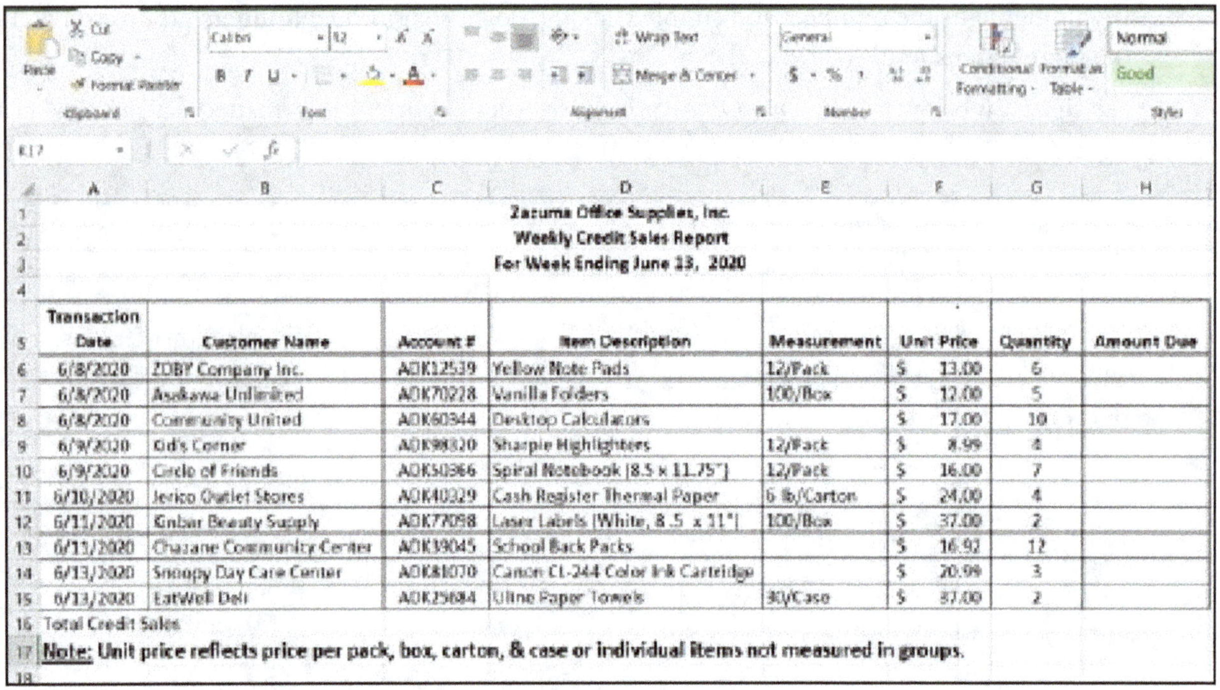

Fig. 5.26   Worksheet with Formatted Date and Dollar Signs (Columns A & F)

For a better understanding and application of Excel worksheet formatting functionalities, **Table 5.1** below provides complete list and description of all formatting options in the **Number** group.

Format	Description
General	The default number format that Excel applies when you type a number. For the most part, numbers that are formatted with the **General** format are displayed just the way you type them. However, if the cell is not wide enough to show the entire number, the **General** format rounds the numbers with decimals. The **General** number format also uses scientific (exponential) notation for large numbers (12 or more digits).
Number	Used for the general display of numbers. You can specify the number of decimal places you want to use, whether you want to use a thousand separator, and how you want to display negative numbers.

Format	Description
Currency	Used for general monetary values and displays the default currency symbol with numbers. You can specify the number of decimal places you want to use, whether you want to use a thousand separator, and how you want to display negative numbers.
Accounting	Also used for monetary values, but it aligns the currency symbols and decimal points of numbers in a column.
Date	Displays date and time serial numbers as date values, according to the type and locale (location) that you specify. Date formats that begin with an asterisk (*) respond to changes in regional date and time settings that are specified in Control Panel. Formats without an asterisk are not affected by Control Panel settings.
Time	Displays date and time serial numbers as time values according to the type and locale (location) you specify. Time formats that begin with an asterisk (*) respond to changes in regional date and time settings that are specified in Control Panel. Formats without an asterisk are not affected by Control Panel settings.
Percentage	Multiplies the cell value by 100 and displays the result with a percent (%) symbol. You can specify the number of decimal places you want to use.
Fraction	Displays a number as a fraction, according to the type of fraction you specify.
Scientific	Displays a number in exponential notation, replacing part of the number with **E+n**, where E (which stands for Exponent) multiplies the preceding number by 10 to the **nth** power. For example, a 2-decimal **Scientific** format displays 12345678901 as **1.23E+10**, which is **1.23** times **10** to the 10th power. You can specify the number of decimal places you want to use.
Text	Treats the content of a cell as text and displays the content exactly as you type it, even when you type numbers.
Special	Displays a number as a postal code (ZIP Code), phone number, or Social Security number.
Custom	Allows you to modify a copy of an existing number format code. Use this format to create a custom number format that is added to the list of number format codes. You can add between 200 and 250 custom number formats, depending on the language version of Excel that is installed on your computer.

Table 5.1   **Description and Use of Excel Formatting Options**

EXCEL REFERENCES, CONSTANTS, & OPERATORS

Before we continue our discussion of various Excel features used for creating formulas to calculate data that we enter into worksheet cells, let's spend some time understanding the basic terms that make up formulas in worksheet cells.

References

A reference identifies a cell or a range of cells on a worksheet, and tells Excel where to look for the values or data you want to use in a formula. References to the use of data are contained in different parts of a worksheet in one formula or the value from one cell in several formulas. You can also refer to cells on other sheets in the same workbook, and to other workbooks. References to cells in other workbooks are called **links** or external references. For example, **A2** refers to value in cell **A2; B2** refers to cells at intersection of column **B** and row **2**.

Relative Cell Reference

In Excel, relative reference is the type of reference which changes to another cell number when the same formula is copied to any other cells or in any other worksheet. For example, in cell **D1** we have the formula, **=B1+C1**; when we copy this formula to cell **C2**, the formula becomes **=B2+C2.** This is because in the first formula the cells were referred to the two right cells of cell **B1** while in the second formula the two cells on the right are **B2** and **C2**. You will notice more of this relative cell reference as we begin to create and copy formulas in the next section.

Constants

A constant is a value that is not calculated; it always stays the same. For example, the date **08/9/2010**, the number **325**, and the text "**Quarterly Earnings**" are all constants. An expression or a value resulting from an expression is not a constant. If you use constants in a formula instead of references to cells (for example, **=40+60+115**) where cell **A5** contains **40**; cell **B5** contains **60**; and **C5** contains **115**, by Excel standard this is not a valid formula because it made no reference to any column letter or row number. To enter a formula that calculates the total of these three numbers, we will enter in cell **C6** this formula: **=A5+B5+C5** to obtain a total of **210** . In general, it's best to place constants in individual cells where they can be easily changed if needed, then reference those cells in formulas.

Operators

Operators define the type of result that you obtain from the formula you create. The Excel operators perform actions on numeric values, text, or cell references. There are five different types of Excel Operators. These are: **Arithmetic Operators, Text Operator, Comparison Operators** and **Reference Operators**. Each of these types of operator are listed below along with their symbols on **fig. 5.27**. In this section, we'll be discussing only basic Excel formula for beginners, all other operators you come across in this chapter are beyond the scope of this beginners guide; they are presented here for information purposes.

- Arithmetic operators
- Comparison operators
- Text operators
- Operators reference
- **Excel Arithmetic Operators**:
    - \+ Plus (addition)
    - \- Minus (subtraction and negation)
    - * An asterisk (multiplication)
    - / Slash (division)
    - % Percent
    - ^ Caret (exponentiation)

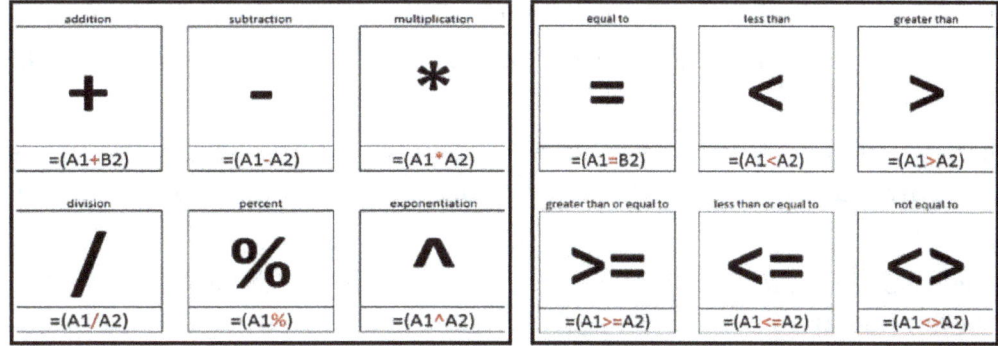

Fig. 5.27   **Excel Arithmetic Operators**

CREATE EXCEL FORMULAS INTO CELLS & COPY TO OTHER WORKSHEET

An Excel spreadsheet is a useful tool for displaying accounting information in an organized way by entering data into cells defined by column headings. Excel accounting feature gives users the ability to create formulas that calculate, manipulate, and analyze numbers contained in the cells. Creating formulas in Excel is different from writing an equation in a math class. The most notable difference is that Excel formulas start with the equal sign (=) instead of ending with it. For example, while Excel formulas reads as = 7 + 3, math equation reads as 7 + 3 =. In Excel, the equal sign indicates that what follows is part of a formula and not just a word or number that is expected to appear in the cell. After you type the formula and press **Enter** on your keyboard, the result of the formula appears in the cell. Using the same example above, if you type the formula above, =7 + 3 into a cell and press **Enter**, the result, **10** appears in the cell. The formula is still there but it doesn't appear in your spreadsheet. You can see this formula in the **Formula Bar** at top screen.

Formulas & Cell References

Excel formulas are entered into cells according to the **Cell References**. Continuing with our example, when entering the formula for that calculation, you would not enter the numbers **7** and **3**, instead would name cells where these numbers have been entered (reference the cell not the number). When you write a formula this way, the formula cell always shows the sum of the numbers in those cells, even if the numbers change.

Using Cell References:
An Excel worksheet is built with intersections and as such each cell is part of a row and a column. Rows are designated with numbers (**1, 2, 3**, etc.) displayed at the left side of the spreadsheet while columns are designated with letters (**A, B, C**, etc.) at the top. Refer to **Table 5.2** below for correct use of cell references in creating formulas.

1. To refer to a cell, use the column letter and row number together, such as **A5** or **H10** (the column letter always comes first).

2. When you select a cell, you can see its reference at the top of the screen in the **Name Box** next to the **Formula Bar** which displays the formula contained in the cell with the calculated total **(fig. 5.28)**.

3. In the image below, notice the selected cell references, **D3** which displays in the **Name Box** next to the **Formula Bar** shows the formula.

4. The cell with the calculated total shows only the total amount not the formula which only displays in the **Formula Bar** at top of your screen.

5. Notice that in the image below, the formula **(=SUM(A3-C3)** contained in cell **D3** is displayed in the **Formula Bar** while only total of **(A3:C3)** is displayed in **D3**.

6. If you update the numbers in one or more of those cells, Excel will recalculate and the result will still be the sum of the numbers in the referred cells.

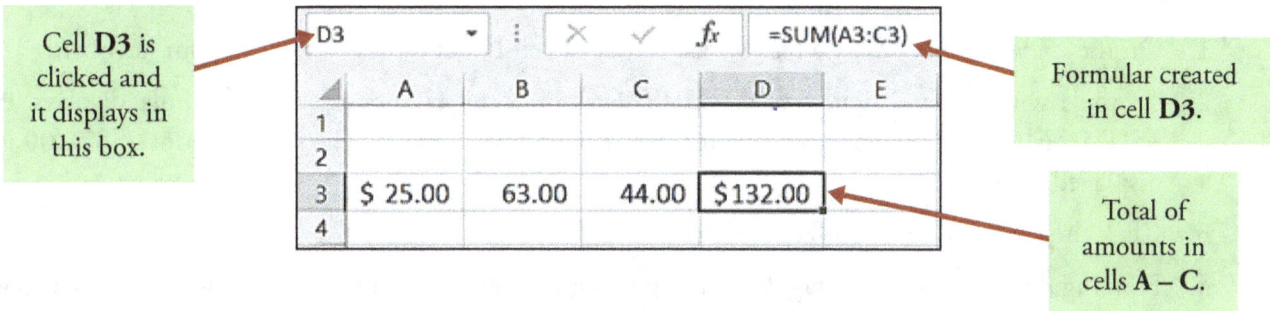

Fig. 5.28   Excel Formulas & Cell Reference

To Refer to	Use
The cell in column A and row 10	A10
The range of cells in column A and rows 10 through 20	A10:A20
The range of cells in row 15 and columns B through E	B15:E15
All cells in row 5	5:5
All cells in rows 5 through 10	5:10
All cells in column H	H:H
All cells in columns H through J	H:J
The range of cells in columns A through E and rows 10 through 20	A10:E20

Table 5.2   Correct Use of Excel Cell References

Create Formula in a Worksheet Cell & Copy to Other Worksheet Cells

In this section, we are going to create formulas to calculate total price of each item recorded in *Zazuma Office Supply Inc.* Sales Report. Notice that the office supplies come in packs, cartons, boxes, cases or individual units with specific unit prices and quantity sold on credit. The goal here is to multiply quantity sold by the unit price to obtain total sold for each supply item. At the bottom of the worksheet, we will add a formula that calculates total supplies sold on credit for the week ending **June 30, 2020** as shown on the worksheet title and copy the same formular to other cells on this worksheet **(fig. 5.26)** above.

1. On the *Zazuma Office Supply Inc.* worksheet, click cell **H6** and press = sign on your keyboard.
2. To the right of the = sign, type **SUM(F6*G6)** into cell **H6**, so that the formula displays as =SUM(F6*G6) on the **Formula Bar** at top screen and press **Enter**. The total amount of **$78.00** is displayed in cell **H6**.
3. Click the intersection of cell **H6** to form a **+** sign on the intersection.
4. Holding down the mouse, drag down the plus sign to cell **H15** and release mouse. All cells below **H6** now contain their individual totals.
5. Click on each cell on column **H** and notice that the formula you copied automatically adjusts to the column and row number of each item. This is the relative cell reference feature of Excel.
6. To obtain a grand total amount of all items on the worksheet, do these:
   a. Click cell **H16** and press = sign on your keyboard.
   b. Type **SUM(H6:H15)** into cell **H16** so that the formula displays as =SUM(H6:H15) and press **Enter**. The grand total amount of **$965.97** is displayed in cell **H16.**

Format the Total Row: Now let's format the row containing grand total amount of all credit sales for the week of **June 13, 2020** to make it stand out. See the completed professional looking worksheet with totals showing *Zazuma Office Supply Inc.* Sales Report on **fig. 5.29**.

1. Click cell **A16**, holding down the mouse, highlight up to **F16**.
2. In the **Alignment** group at top ribbon, click **Merge & Center**. Notice that the phrase, **Total Credit Sales** is centered.
3. In the **Fonts** group at top ribbon, click **B** at top ribbon to apply bold font to the text.
4. Click cell **H16** and click **B** at top ribbon to apply bold font to the grand total.

5. Click **A15**, holding down the mouse, highlight up to **H15**.
6. In the **Fonts** group, click **Boarder** down arrow, and select **Thick Bottom Boarder**.
7. Click the merged cell, row **16** and highlight up to the grand total in **H16**.
8. In the **Fonts** group, click **Boarders** down arrow, and select **Double Bottom Boarder**.

	A	B	C	D	E	F	G	H
1				Zazuma Office Supplies, Inc.				
2				Weekly Credit Sales Report				
3				For Week Ending June 13, 2020				
4								
5	Transaction Date	Customer Name	Account #	Item Description	Measurement	Unit Price	Quantity	Amount Due
6	6/8/2020	ZOBY Company Inc.	ADC12539	Yellow Note Pads	12/Pack	$ 13.00	6	$ 78.00
7	6/8/2020	Asakawa Unlimited	ADC70228	Vanilla Folders	100/Box	$ 12.00	5	$ 60.00
8	6/8/2020	Community United	ADC60344	Desktop Calculators		$ 17.00	10	$ 170.00
9	6/9/2020	Kid's Corner	ADC98320	Sharpie Highlighters	12/Pack	$ 8.99	4	$ 35.96
10	6/9/2020	Circle of Friends	ADC50366	Spiral Notebook (8.5 x 11.75")	12/Pack	$ 16.00	7	$ 112.00
11	6/10/2020	Jerico Outlet Stores	ADC40329	Cash Register Thermal Paper	6 lb/Carton	$ 24.00	4	$ 96.00
12	6/11/2020	Kimbar Beauty Supply	ADC77098	Laser Labels (White, 8.5 x 11")	100/Box	$ 37.00	2	$ 74.00
13	6/11/2020	Charane Community Center	ADC39045	School Back Packs		$ 16.92	12	$ 203.04
14	6/13/2020	Snoopy Day Care Center	ADC81070	Canon CL-244 Color Ink Cartridge		$ 20.99	3	$ 62.97
15	6/13/2020	EatWell Deli	ADC25684	Uline Paper Towels	30/Case	$ 37.00	2	$ 74.00
16				Total Credit Sales			55	$ 965.97
17	**Note:** Unit price reflects price per pack, box, carton, & case or individual items not measured in groups.							

Fig. 5.29   Completed Zazuma Office Supply Inc. Credit Sales Report

Copy, Cut, & Paste Contents of a Cell or Cells

1. Click the cell from where you want to begin copying, holding down the mouse, highlight to select all other cells you want to copy or highlight an entire worksheet, and do one or more of these:
   a. To cut contents of the worksheet, press **CTRL+X** on the keyboard.
   b. To copy contents of the worksheet, press **CTRL+C** on the keyboard.

2. If you want to copy the contents to another worksheet, switch to that worksheet.
3. Click where you want the contents to appear and press **CTRL+V** on the keyboard.
4. Another quick way to copy or cut and paste is to follow these steps:
   a. Click the cell, holding down the mouse, highlight to select the contents of the worksheet you want to move or copy.
   b. Right-click the mouse to open the formatting options menu.
   c. On the open short menu, click on **Copy.**
   d. Right-click any cell on a blank worksheet where you want to place the contents of the copied worksheet, and select **Paste** from the displayed short menu.

- **Copy & Paste:** When you copy, the contents of the worksheet remains in the original location and another copy is pasted in the new location.
- **Cut & Paste:** When you cut, the entire content is removed from the original location and appears in the new location of the worksheet where it is pasted.

LINK A WORKSHEET FORMULA TO ANOTHER WORSHEET

Microsoft Excel 20129 provides users the ability to link cells in one worksheet to cells in other worksheets in the same or different workbook. In this section, you'll learn how to link worksheet data to other worksheets. Creating links or external cell references eliminates the need to have the same data maintained in multiple sheets thereby saving time, reducing errors, and improving data integrity. For example, continuing with our sales report from *Zazuma Office Supply Inc.*, the Sales Manager can have a detailed sheet to record credit sales per week and a summary worksheet to record credit sales per day. We can use the worksheet in **fig. 5.29** above as our detailed sheet tab and link it to the summary sheet tab **(fig. 5.30)** that shows total credit sales each day of the week, **June 13, 2020**. Note that credit sales were made on only **5 days** of week ending **06/13/20** namely**: 06/08/20, 06/09/20, 06/10/20, 06/11/20 & 06/13/20.**

Rename Worksheets within a Workbook & Enter Data

1. Open the completed *Zazuma Office Supply Inc.* worksheet.
2. At the bottom of the worksheet, right-click on the active **Sheet 1**, select **Rename,** and type **Detail.**

3. Alternatively, double-click on the active **Sheet 1** and type **Details**.
4. Click on **Sheet 2,** repeat steps **2 or 3** above, and type **Summary**.
5. On **Sheet 2**, click cell **A1** and type the heading, **Daily Credit Sales Summary – 06/13/2020.**
6. Highlight cells **A1 – C1**, apply bold font to text, and click **Merge & Center** at top ribbon**.**
7. Click on cell **A3**, type **Transaction Date**; advance to cell **B3**, type **Quantity Sold Per Day**; advance to cell **C3**, and type **Credit Sales Total Per Day**.
8. Highlight cells **A3 – C 3**, in the **Alignment** group at top ribbon, click **Wrap Text**. Notice that the row automatically increases in height and the texts on row 3 now display on two lines all fitted in each cell **A3 – C3.**
9. Highlight cells **A3 – C3**, in the **Font** group, click **B** to apply bold font to the texts.
10. On cell **A4** of **Sheet 2**, type date **06/08/20**; on cell **A5**, type date **06/09/20**; on cell **A6**, type date **06/10/20;** on cell **A7,** type **06/11/20;** and on cell **A8,** type **06/13/20.**

Create a Formula in One Worksheet & Link it to Another Worksheet

Continuing with the *Zazuma Office Supply* worksheet, we have determined that credit sales were made on **5 days** of the week ending **06/13/20** and have identified those days. The dates obtained from the **Detailed** worksheet are entered in the **Summary** worksheet. Our next step is to add together the total amount of each of those **5 days** on the summary worksheet.

Summarize Quantity Sold Per Day

1. Click **Summary** worksheet tab, click **B4** and press the = sign on your keyboard.
2. Click **Detail** worksheet tab, (refer to **fig. 5.59** above) click cell **G6** and press **Enter**.
3. Click **Summary** worksheet tab, double-click cell **B4,** hold down **Shift** key, and press + sign on your keyboard.
4. Click **Detail** worksheet tab, click cell **G7** and press **Enter**.
5. Click **Summary** worksheet tab, double-click cell **B4,** hold down **Shift** key, and press + sign on your keyboard.
6. Click **Detail** worksheet tab, click cell **G8** and press **Enter**.

7. Notice that on cell **B4**, total quantity sold on **06/08/20**, is **21**. The **Formula Bar** at top screen displays the formula as **=Detail!G6+Detail!G7+Detail!G8.**

8. Repeat steps **1-6** above to summarize quantities sold for **06/09/20, 06/10/20, 06/11/20,** and **06/13/20.**

9. If done correctly, the formulas for the remaining days will display in the **Formula Bar** at top screen as follows:

   a. 06/09/20 **=Detail!G9+Detail!G10**

   b. 06/10/20 **=Detail!G11**

   c. 06/11/20 **=Detail!G12+Detail!G13**

   d. 06/13/20 **=Detail!G14+Detail!G15**

Summarize Credit Sales Total Per Day

1. Click **Summary** worksheet tab, click **C4** and press the **=** sign on your keyboard.

2. Click **Detail** (refer to **fig. 5.29** above) worksheet tab, click cell **H6** and press **Enter**.

3. Click **Summary** worksheet tab, double-click cell **C4,** hold down **Shift** key, and press **+** sign on your keyboard.

4. Click **Detail** worksheet tab, click cell **H7** and press **Enter**.

5. Click **Summary** worksheet tab, double-click cell **C4,** hold down **Shift** key, and press **+** sign on your keyboard.

6. Click **Detail** worksheet tab, click cell **H8** and press **Enter**.

7. Notice that on cell **C4**, total amount of credit sales on **06/08/20**, is **$308.00**. The **Formula Bar** at top screen displays the formula as **=Detail!H6+Detail!H7+Detail!H8.**

8. Repeat steps **1-6** above to summarize total amount of credit sales for **06/09/20, 06/10/20, 06/11/20,** and **06/13/20.**

9. If done correctly, the formulas for the remaining days will display in the **Formula Bar** at top screen as follows:

   a. 06/09/20 **=Detail!H9+Detail!H10**

   b. 06/10/20 **=Detail!H11**

c. 06/11/20 **=Detail!H12+Detail!H13**

   d. 06/13/20 **=Detail!H14+Detail!H15**

Calculate Grand Total on the Summary Worksheet:
We have summarized the Detail worksheet into Summary worksheet, calculated total quantity sold per day, and total amount of credit sales per day during the week of **06/13/20**. At this point, let's sum up all quantities sold and amount of credit sales for the entire week.

1. Click the **Summary** worksheet; on cell **A9** type **Grand Total**.

2. Click cell **B9**, and press the = sign on the keyboard.

3. To the right of the = sign, type **SUM(B4:B8)** into cell **B9** so that the formula appears on the **Formula Bar** at top screen as **=SUM(B4:B8)** and press **Enter** key. For the week of **06/13/20**, grand total quantity sold is **55.**

4. Click cell **C9,** and press the = sign on the keyboard.

5. To the right of the = sign, type **SUM(C4:C8)** into cell **C9** so that the formula appears on the **Formula Bar** at top screen as **=SUM(C4:C9)** and press **Enter** key. The grand total amount of credit sales for the week is **$965.97** as shown on cell **C9 (fig. 5.30)**.

Format Summary Worksheet:
Finally, let's format the **Summary** worksheet with boarders as we did on the **Detail** worksheet. Formatting the summary worksheet makes it look more professional.

1. Click cell **A1**, highlight through cell **C1**, and in the **Alignment** group at top ribbon, select **Merge & Center** to format the worksheet title.

2. Click on cell **A3**, highlight through cell **C9**; and in the **Font** group at top ribbon, click the **Boarder** down arrow, and select **All Boarders**.

3. To format column headings, click cell **A3**; highlight through **C3**; in the **Font** group at top ribbon, click the **Boarder** down arrow, and select **Top and Double Bottom Boarder.**

4. To format the **Grand Total** row, click cell **A8**; highlight through cell **C8**; in the **Font** group at the ribbon, click the **Boarder** down arrow, and select **Thick Bottom Boarder**.

5. Click cell **A9**, highlight through **C9**, in the **Font** group at the ribbon, click the **Boarder** down arrow, and select **Double Bottom Boarder**.

6. Click cell **A9**, highlight through **C9**, in the **Font** group at the ribbon, click **B** to apply bold font to all text and data on row **9**.

7. **Fig. 5.30** below shows the completed **Summary** worksheet of *Zazuma Office Supply Inc.*, for the week ending **06/13/2020**.

8. If you click the **Detail** tab, the completed *Zazuma Office Supply Inc.* Credit Sales Report in **Fig. 5.29** now displays in **Fig. 5.30** with Summary sheet tab.

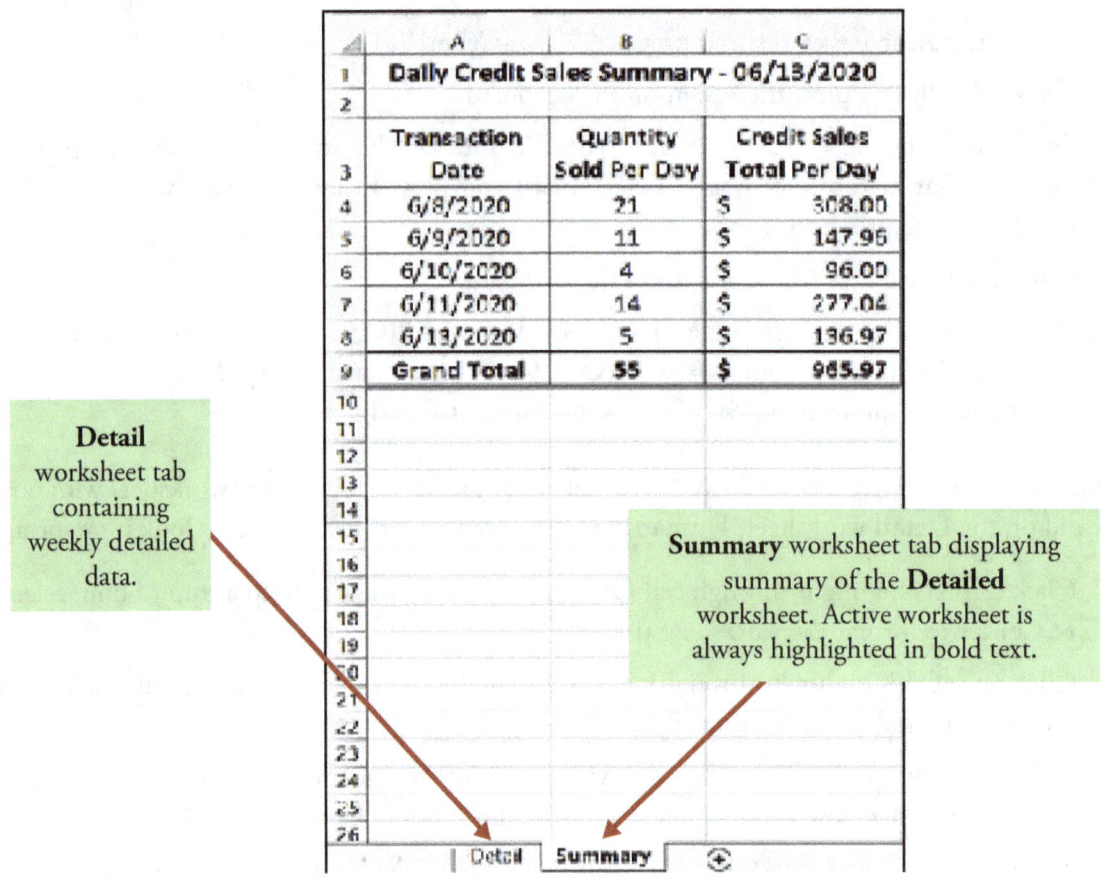

Fig. 5.30   Zazuma Office Supply Inc. Summary Credit Sales Report

Change Worksheet Margins

Unlike MS Word margins which defaults to **"1"** on the left, right, top, and bottom, MS Excel default margin setting is "0.75". In Excel, this setting is referred to as **Normal**. When printing your worksheet, you may want to align it better on a printed page by changing the default margins. You can also choose to center the worksheet—either horizontally or vertically on the page simply by checking the appropriate box. Page margins are the blank spaces between your data and the edges of the printed page. Top and bottom page margins may be used for inserting headers, footers, and page numbers. To change worksheet page margins, follow these steps:

1. At top ribbon of the worksheet, click **Layout tab**.
2. On the displayed **Page Setup** group, click **Margins** down arrow, and select **Custom Margins.**
3. In the open **Page Setup** window, click **Margins** tab at top **(fig.5.31)**.
4. Using only the **Top**, **Bottom**, **Lef**t, and **Right** up or down arrows as needed, select the margin number you want.
5. To center the worksheet **Horizontally** or **Vertically** on the page, check the appropriate box.
6. Click **Print Preview** tab to see how the worksheet will look when printed and click **Ok**.

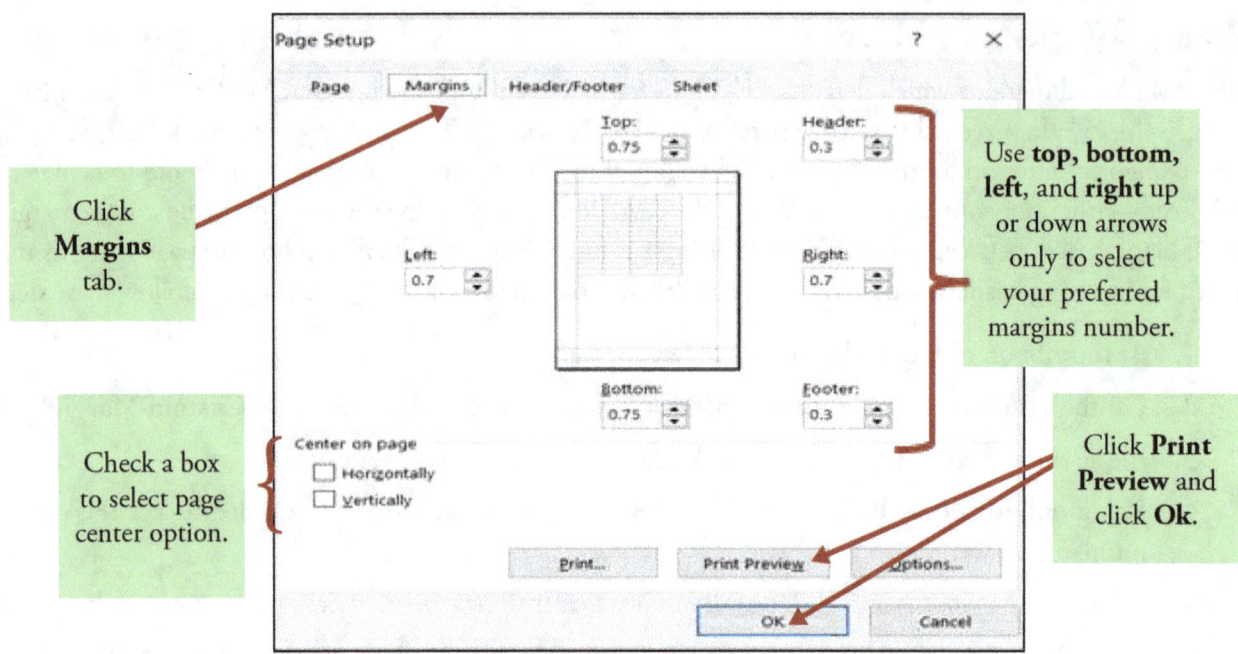

Fig. 5.31   Page Setup Window for Changing Page Margins

INSERT HEADERS & FOOTER IN A WORKSHEET

The primary benefit of inserting headers and footers in an Excel worksheet is to help you identify the report you created, especially where your worksheet is included as part of a large project report involving many other people in an organization. In Excel, the header and footer feature allows you to place your name, date report was created or updated, and page number. If you work in an organization where data in a certain worksheet are required to be updated daily or regularly because other people use the same report to do their jobs, it is necessary to always include date the worksheet was last updated at the footer. This gives users confident that they are using the most updated information. In this section, we will apply footer to *Zazuma Office Supply Inc.* detail worksheet, see the final version on **fig. 5.35** below. Follow these steps to insert custom header to the worksheet:

Insert Header

For this worksheet header, we'll insert only name of the report; page number and date will come at the footer of the worksheet.

1. Open *Zazuma Office Supply Inc.* credit sales report, and click **Detail** worksheet tab.
2. Click **Page Layout** tab at top ribbon, in the **Page Setup** group at top ribbon, click **Margins** down arrow, and select **Custom Margins**.
3. On the displayed **Page Setup** window, click **Header/Footer** tab, and click **Custom Header** in the middle of the window (**fig. 5.32**).
4. On the open **Header** window, click **Custom Header**.
5. Click on the left section box of the window, and type **Zazuma Weekly Credit Sakes**, click **Ok**.
6. If multiple pages of this worksheet were created, this name will appear at top of every worksheet (**fig. 5.33**).

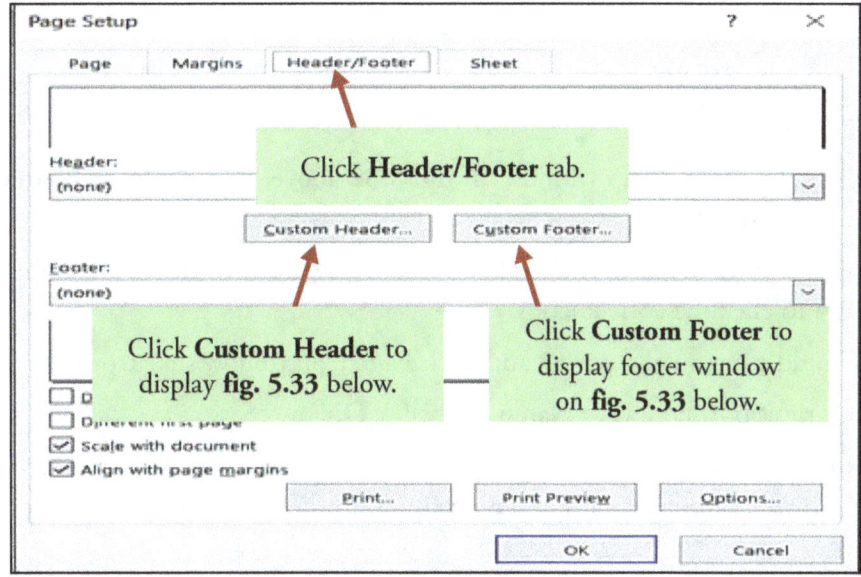

Fig. 5.32   **Page Setup Window**

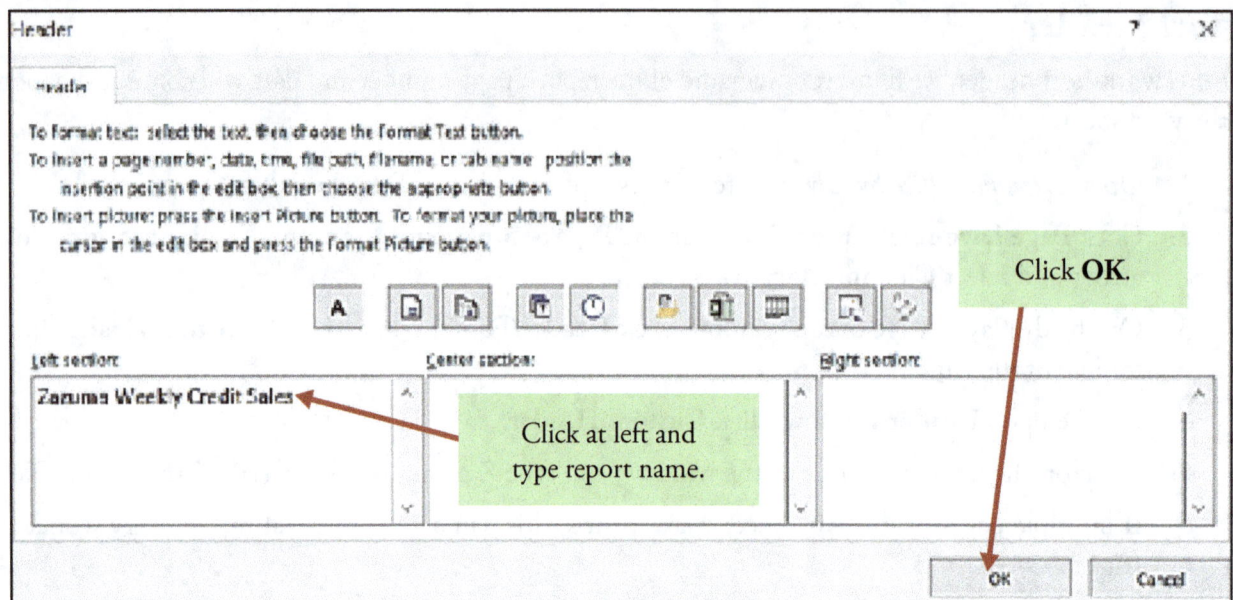

Fig. 5.33 **Custom Header Window**

Insert Footer

1. On the displayed **Page Setup** window on **fig. 5.32** above, click **Custom Footer** to display footer window on **fig. 5.34** below.

2. On the open **Footer** window, click at left box to add date and click **Date** icon. Follow the arrows on **fig. 5.34** to click the correct icons.

3. Click the middle box to add page # and click **Page** icon (follow the arrows).

4. Click at far right box, type your **Name**, and click **Ok.**

5. Click **Print Preview** to view how the footer appears on your worksheet when printed, and click **Ok.** The printed worksheet is displayed on **fig. 5.36** showing header and footer.

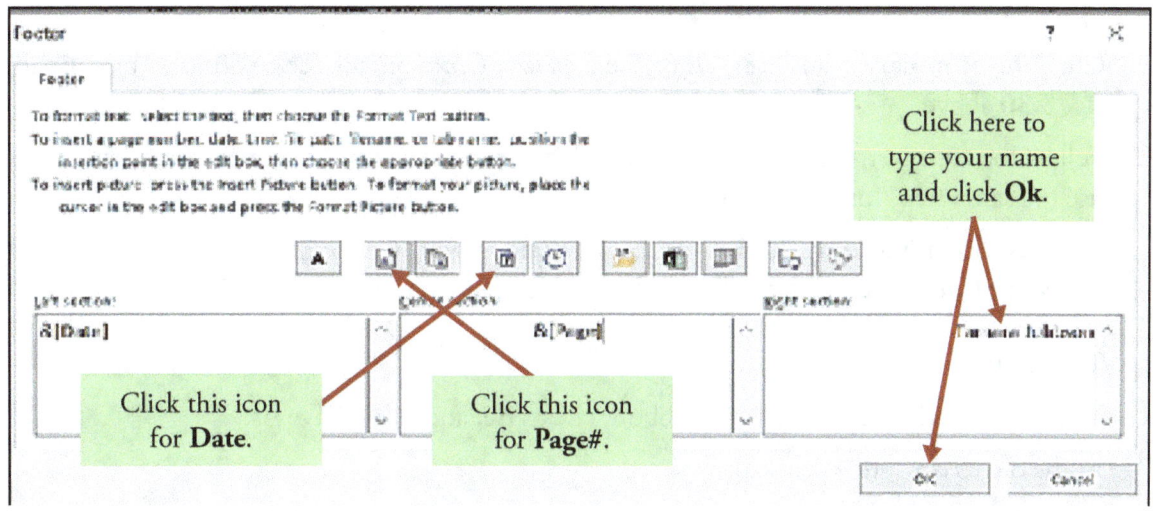

Fig. 5.34   **Custom Footer Window**

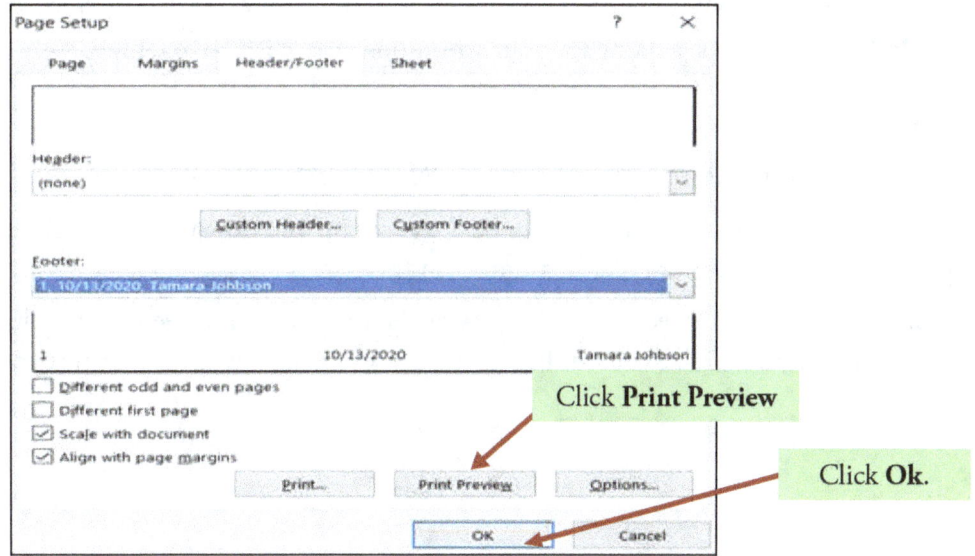

Fig. 5.35   **Page Setup – Header/Footer Window**

Add Header & Footer On The Summary Worksheet:

1. Click the **Summary** worksheet tab of the *Zazuma Office Supply Inc* credit sales report shown on **fig. 5.30** above.

2. Follow the same instructions provided above for inserting header and footer on the detail worksheet; use the same steps for the summary worksheet.

3. Pay close attention to **figs. 5.32 – 5.35** above along with detailed instructions on each step. See **fig. 5.36** the completed detailed worksheet with header and footer.

Save Worksheet

1. With your worksheet open, at top ribbon, click **File**, and select **Save As**.

2. In the **Save As** window, click **Browse**.

3. In the **File Name** box, type a name for your Excel workbook and click **Save** tab.

4. If you want to save your workbook in a folder, on the open **Save As Explorer** window, under **Organize**, navigate to find the folder in which to save your file, and click to open the folder.

5. In the **File Name** box, type a name for your workbook, and click **Save** tab.

Print Worksheet

1. With your worksheet open, at top ribbon, click **File**, and select **Print.**

2. On the open **Print** window, in the **Copies** box, use the up and down arrows to select the number of copies you want to print or type the number in the box.

3. View your worksheet displayed in the **Preview** at the right of your screen to see what the printed copy will look like; and click the **Print** button at top of the print window to print your worksheet.

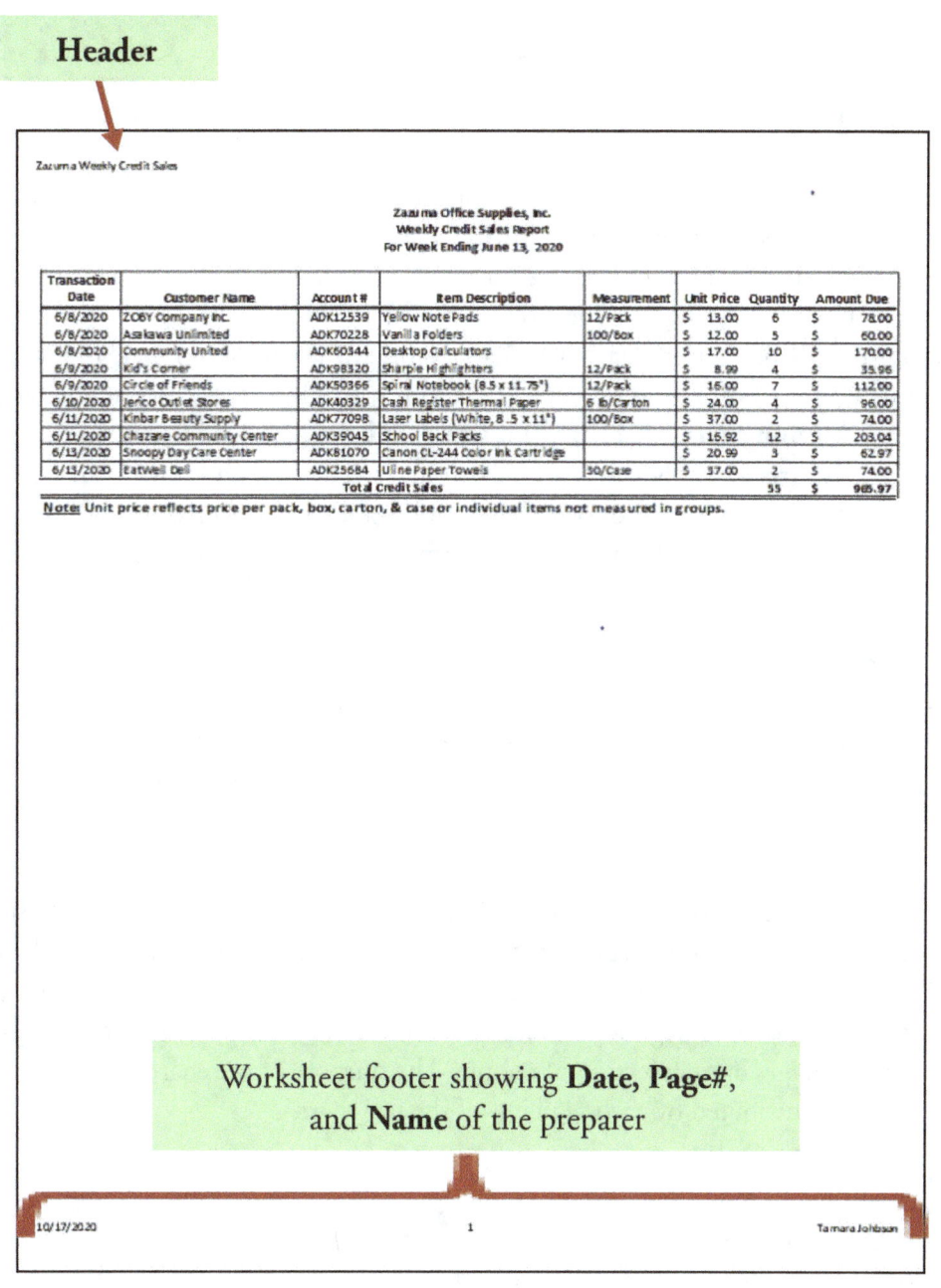

Fig. 5.36 Zazuma Office Supply Inc. Detail Credit Sales Report with Header & Footer

WORKING WITH CHARTS & GRAPHS

We often hear the statement: *"a good picture says a thousand words."* This is so true when it comes to charts and graphs in Excel worksheets. From the standpoint of data clarity in Excel, we'll say: *"a good picture is worth thousands and millions of numbers."* Charts and graphs are important because they make financial **information clearer and easier to understand for the user who needs them to make important business decisions.** They are most suitable in presenting financial information to senior management or corporate officials for investment and spending decisions to ensure a stable financial health of their companies. A chart can create a clearer picture of a set of data values than a table with rows of numbers in it allowing managers to incorporate this understanding into analysis and future planning. The three main types of charts for beginners in Excel – **column chart**, **pie chart**, and **line graph** are described below. In this section, you will learn what these three charts mean; how to create them in a worksheet; and how to analyze them for better business decision making. Our discussion on charts and graphs will focus only on the basic things new beginners need to build a solid foundation toward intermediate and advanced users if they so desire.

Column Chart

Also known as vertical bar charts, it is a data visualization method where each category is represented by a rectangle, with the height of the rectangle being proportional to the values being plotted. The purpose of a column chart is to compare the values of each chart category to identify the highest or lowest values.

Pie Chart

This is a type of data representation that contains different segments and sectors in which each segment and sectors of a pie chart forms a certain portion of the total (percentage). The total of each data segment must always equal **100%** of the pie taken as whole. To work with the percentage for a pie chart, the data must be categorized, total calculated, categories divided, and converted into percentages. The pie chart created displays the final percentages of each section of the pie. The purpose of pie chart is to show what percentage of the total **(100%)** is contributed by each segment of the pie chart.

Line Graph

A line graph is a type of chart used to show data that changes over time identifying the trends (movement) of data over a period of time. Line graphs are plotted using several points connected by straight lines. The line graph comprises of two axes known as '**x**' axis and '**y**' axis. The **horizontal** axis is **x-axis** while the **vertical** axis is known as the **y-axis** parts of a line graph. Line graphs can include a single line for one data set, or multiple lines comparing two or more data sets.

Sample Excel Practical Project 2

To better understand the usefulness of charts and graphs in Excel and how to work with them, you are provided with some worksheets from *Tamona Furniture Industries (TFI)*, a family-owned business operated by Fred Tamona and his two sons. The company manufactures 4 types of furniture sets namely: **(1)** 3 Sofas & Center Table Set, **(2)** Beddings & Headboards, **(3)** Dinning Table Set, and **(4)** Kitchen Cabinets. The business operates on a calendar year basis: January – December and evaluates its overall sales performance semi-annually (January – June) and (July – December). The Tamonas believe that because the business has been performing well year-after-year, there was no need for the time-consuming quarterly evaluation. To illustrate working with charts and graphs in Excel, the company's two Semi-annual Sales Reports and one Annual Sales Report are presented below. Using these Sales Reports, you will be taken through the process of inserting charts and graphs into a worksheet; changing the chart designs & formatting; analyzing them; and show you how to use charts and graphs to make informed business decisions.

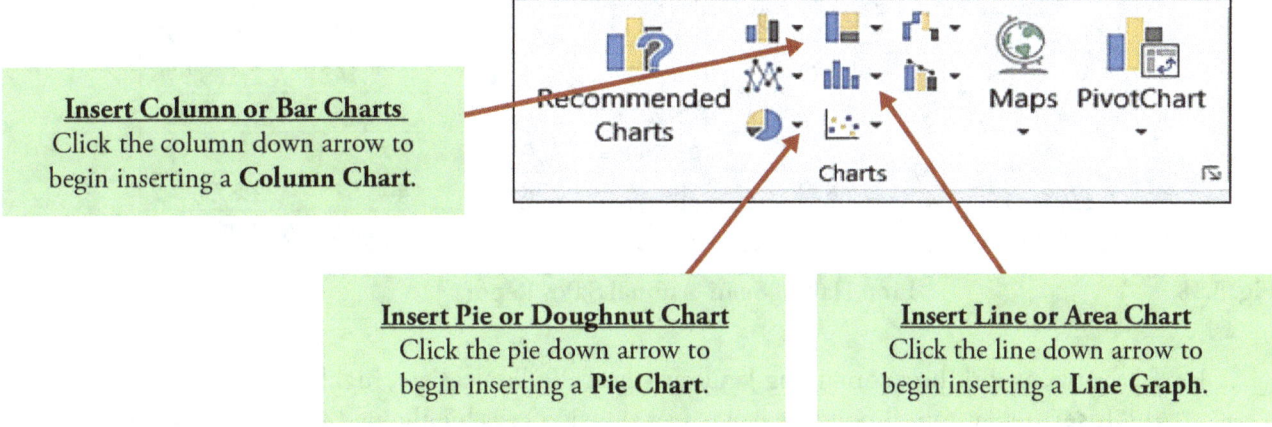

Fig. 5.37   **The Charts Group at Top Ribbon**

Insert a Column Chart, Format, and Change Chart Design: This chart is intended to compare sales of each of TFI's 4 product types to one another to identify the biggest seller from January to June 2019 using height of the vertical chart bars. Throughout this project, you will be using the **Charts** group, **fig. 5.37** above. Clicking the identified down arrows will open various chart and graph options you would need to complete the project. Simply follow the step-by-step instructions described in the proceeding sections below. The worksheet on **fig. 5.38** contains TFI's sales data for the first 6 months of the year 2019. A completed column chart with proper design and formatting options is displayed on **fig. 5.40**. The months listed at right of the column chart are called **Legends**.

	A	B	C	D	E	F
1			Tamona Furniture Industries (TFI)			
2			Semi-Annual Sales Report			
3			January - June 2019			
4						
5	Accounting Periods	3 Sofas & Center Table Set	Beddings & Headbords	Dining Table Set	Kitchen Cabinets	Total Monthly Sales
6	January	$ 202,247	$ 511,502	$ 139,490	$ 229,935	$ 1,083,174
7	February	159,942	489,409	170,159	153,415	972,925
8	March	187,388	481,271	245,167	212,148	1,125,975
9	April	284,676	475,220	268,452	314,849	1,343,197
10	May	389,273	443,859	339,755	378,290	1,551,177
11	June	275,839	618,636	538,391	446,575	1,879,441
12	Total	$ 1,499,365	$ 3,019,897	$1,701,415	$1,735,213	$ 7,955,891

Fig. 5.38   First Half of Semi-Annual Sales Report

1. In the open worksheet containing January – June 2019 sales data, highlight cells **A5:E11** and click the **Insert tab** at top ribbon. See worksheet showing cells highlighted for **column chart (fig. 5.39)**.
2. On the displayed **Charts** group, click **Insert Column or Bar Charts** down arrow, and select **2-D Column**.

3. Click the chart, holding down the mouse, drag chart, place below the worksheet, and resize as needed to fit chart contents.
4. Click the chart, click **Design** tab at top ribbon, in the **Data** group, select **Switch Rows/ Columns.**
5. Click the chart, click **Design** tab, in the **Chart Style** group, select **Style 7**.
6. Click the chart, click **Design** tab, in the **Charts Layout** group, click **Quick Layout** down arrow and select **Layout 1**.
7. Right-click on **Chart Title** at top of the chart, select **Edit Text** from the displayed menu, and type **TFI Monthly Comparative Sales Report January - June 2019.**
8. Highlight the chart title, in the **Font** group at top ribbon, click font type down arrow, select **Arial Black and** change font size to **10**.
9. Highlight the chart title, click **Format** at top ribbon in the **Shape Styles** group, click **Shape Fill** down arrow, and select **Light Gray, Background 2.**
10. Click the chart vertical bars, click **Format** at top ribbon, in the **Shape Styles** group**,** click **Shape Fill** down arrow, and select **Light Gray, Background 2.**
11. Click the chart, click **Format** at top ribbon in the **Shape Styles** group, click **Shape Fill** down arrow, and select **Gold, Accent 4, lighter 80%** (8th color on 2nd row).
12. Click the **$** amount placeholder at left of chart and change text to font size **10.**
13. Click products placeholder at bottom of the chart and months at right of the chart, change texts font sizes to **10** and apply **Bold** font to text in the products placeholder.

	A	B	C	D	E	F
1			Tamona Furniture Industries (TFI)			
2			Semi-Annual Sales Report			
3			January - June 2019			
4						
5	Accounting Periods	3 Sofas & Center Table Set	Beddings & Headbords	Dining Table Set	Kitchen Cabinets	Total Monthly Sales
6	January	$ 202,247	$ 511,502	$ 139,490	$ 229,935	$ 1,083,174
7	February	159,942	489,409	170,159	153,415	972,925
8	March	187,388	481,271	245,167	212,148	1,125,975
9	April	284,676	475,220	268,452	314,849	1,343,197
10	May	389,273	443,859	339,755	378,290	1,551,177
11	June	275,839	618,636	538,391	446,575	1,879,441
12	Total	$ 1,499,365	$ 3,019,897	$1,701,415	$1,735,213	$ 7,955,891

Fig. 5.39   Worksheet Showing Cells Highlighted for Column Chart

(Clicking the chart displays highlighted cells on the worksheet above)

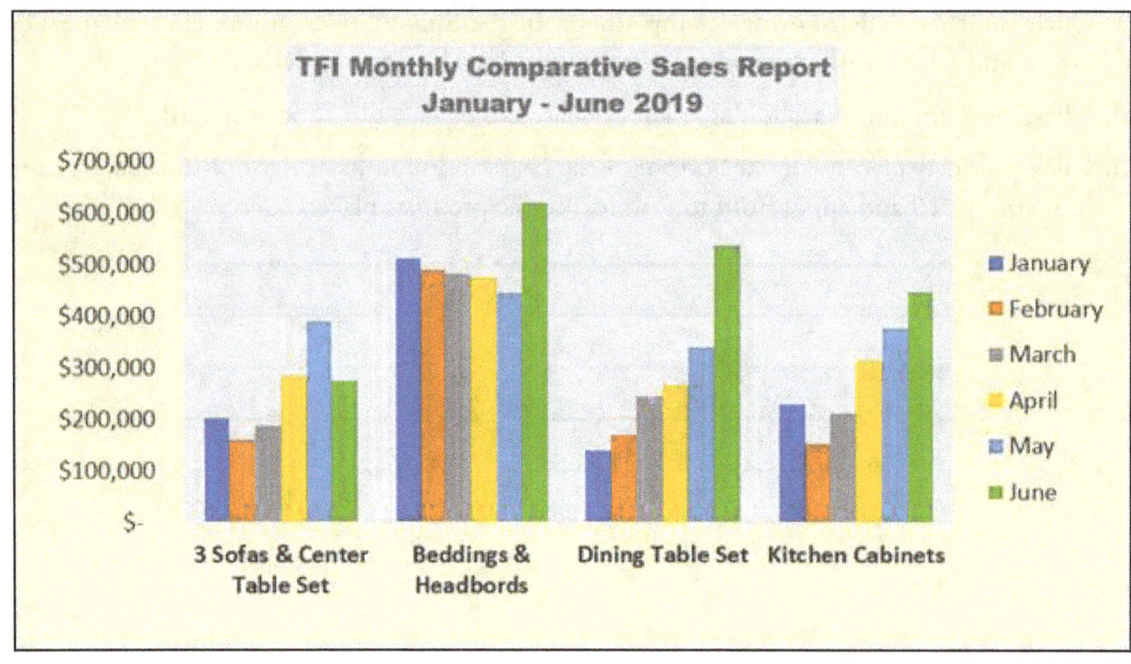

Fig. 5.40   Column Chart Comparing Month-by-Month Sales Activity Per Product

Analyze the Column Chart: Based on the color-coded bar heights of the chart, we can draw the following conclusions:

1. **Bedding & Headboards** are the biggest sellers of all *TFI's* products because they show the tallest vertical bars **(green bars)** on the chart.
2. The best month of sales for all products was **June (green vertical bars)**.
3. **Dining Table Set** made good sales in June almost close to **Beddings & Headboards**.
4. Sales of **Kitchen Cabinets** was the second lowest in June.
5. **3 Sofas & Center Tables Set** had the lowest sales in June with shortest vertical green bar.

Conclusion & Business Decision: The overall look of the column chart may help the *Tamonas (TFI)* adopt a stronger marketing strategy that increases advertising and promotional activities on Sofas Set, Diner Set, and Kitchen Cabinets to increase their sales so that these 3 products can meet up with Bedding & Headboard sales.

Insert and Format a Line Graph:
Line graph is used to identify changes (trends) in the sales of TFI's 4 products over a period of time. The focus here is on which month between July to December 2019 shows the biggest change in total sales using line makers (dots). The second half of TFI's semi-annual sales report is presented in **fig. 5.41** and the completed line graph is displayed on **fig. 5.43** below.

	A	B	C	D	E	F
16		Tamona Furniture Industries (TFI)				
17		Semi-Annual Sales Report				
18		July - December 2019				
19						
20	Accounting Periods	3 Sofas & Center Table Set	Beddings & Headbords	Dining Table Set	Kitchen Cabinets	Total Monthly Sales
21	July	$ 373,295	$ 563,712	$ 150,318	$ 252,637	$ 1,339,962
22	August	262,164	677,007	362,527	219,567	1,521,264
23	September	258,226	409,104	261,365	430,976	1,359,671
24	October	345,209	443,763	327,564	323,308	1,439,845
25	November	520,152	783,887	416,296	515,963	2,236,297
26	December	732,993	836,461	648,579	712,865	2,930,897
27	Total	$ 2,492,039	$ 3,713,934	$2,166,648	$2,455,316	$10,827,937

Fig. 5.41   **Second Half of Semi-Annual Sales Report**

1. In the open worksheet containing July – December 2019 data, highlight data cells **A20:A26.**

2. Press **CTRL** key on your keyboard, holding down this key, highlight cells **F20:F26,** and release key.

3. With cells still highlighted, click the **Insert** tab at top ribbon. See **fig. 5.42** for worksheet showing cells highlighted for line graph.

4. On the displayed **Charts** group, click **Insert Line or Area Chart** down arrow, and select **Stacked Line with Markers** (5th on the 1st row).

5. Click the graph, holding down the mouse, drag graph, place below the worksheet, and resize as needed to fit graph contents.

6. Right-click on **Chart Title**, select **Edit Text** from the displayed menu, and type **TFI Monthly Sales Trends July - December 2019.**

7. Highlight the chart title, in the **Font** group at top ribbon, click font type down arrow, select **Arial Black**, change font size **12.**

8. Click the graph, click **Design** tab at top ribbon, in the **Charts Style** group, select **Style 14** (6th style on the 2nd row).

9. Click middle of the graph (line markers), click **Format** tab at top ribbon, in the **Shape Style** group, click **Shape Fill** down arrow, and select **Light Gray, Background 2** (3rd color on the 1st row). This action changes the original background theme of the inside graph with line markers.

10. Click the graph, click **Format** tab at top ribbon, in the click **Shape Style** group, **Shape Fill** down arrow, and select **Orange, Accent 2, Lighter 80%.** This action changes the original background theme of the entire graph.

11. Right-click the **Axis** placeholder along the dollar amounts at left of the graph, select **Edit Text** from the displayed menu, and type **Sales in Millions**. Change font size to **14** and apply **Bold** font to the text.

12. Click the placeholder containing months at bottom of graph, change font size to **10**, and apply **Bold** font to text. Click total monthly sales placeholder right below the months and change font size to **10**.

	A	B	C	D	E	F
16		Tamona Furniture Industries (TFI)				
17		Semi-Annual Sales Report				
18		July - December 2019				
19						
20	Accounting Periods	3 Sofas & Center Table Set	Beddings & Headbords	Dining Table Set	Kitchen Cabinets	Total Monthly Sales
21	July	$ 373,295	$ 563,712	$ 150,318	$ 252,637	$ 1,339,962
22	August	262,164	677,007	362,527	219,567	1,521,264
23	September	258,226	409,104	261,365	430,976	1,359,671
24	October	345,209	443,763	327,564	323,308	1,439,845
25	November	520,152	783,887	416,296	515,963	2,236,297
26	December	732,993	836,461	648,579	712,865	2,930,897
27	Total	$ 2,492,039	$ 3,713,934	$2,166,648	$2,455,316	$10,827,937

Fig. 5.42   **Worksheet Showing Cells Highlighted for Line Graph**

(Clicking the graph displays highlighted cells on the worksheet above)

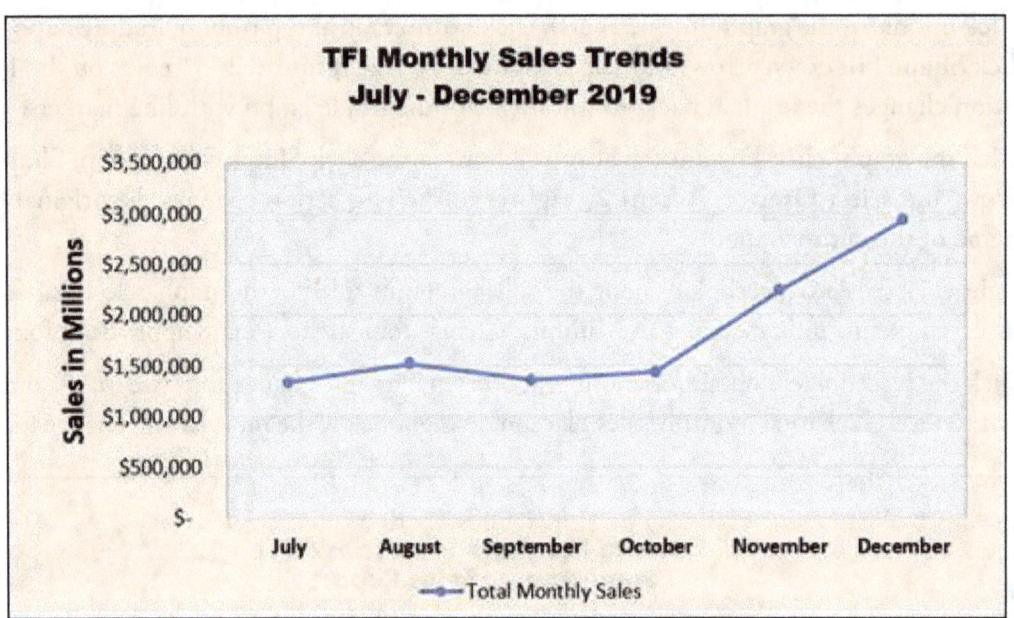

Fig. 5.43 Line Chart Showing Sales Trends Per Month - All Products

Analyze the Line Graph: Looking at the markers (dots) on the line graph, it is clear that December showed the highest amount of total sale, **$2,930,897**, almost $3 million. This is followed by November, the second highest with **$2,236,297**, close to $2.5 million.

Conclusion & Business Decision: In general, during November, particularly after Thanksgiving, people shop more which is essentially the beginning of Christmas sales season. Christmas shopping continues and reaches the highest peak weeks before December 25th (Christmas Day). Based on the structure of the line graph in **fig. 5.43** above, the *Tamonas (TFI)* may consider ramping up production of their 4 products during November/December months (Thanksgiving & Christmas) seasons to meet the higher demands and take advantage of the seasonal increase in sales.

Insert and Format a Pie Chart: This is the chart that identifies exactly what percentage each of *TFI's* 4 products contributed towards the total annual sales of **$18,783,828** January – December 2019. All percentages contributed by each product added together must equal **100%**. The worksheet on **fig. 5.44** contains sales data for the entire year and the completed pie chart is shown on **fig. 5.46** below.

	A	B	C	D	E	F
35		Tamona Furniture Industries (TFI)				
36		Annual Sales Report				
37		For the Year Ended December 2019				
38						
39	Accounting Periods	3 Sofas & Center Table Set	Beddings & Headbords	Dining Table Set	Kitchen Cabinets	Total Annual Sales
40	January	$ 202,247	$ 511,502	$ 139,490	$ 229,935	$ 1,083,174
41	February	159,942	489,409	170,159	153,415	972,925
42	March	187,388	481,271	245,167	212,148	1,125,975
43	April	284,676	475,220	268,452	314,849	1,343,197
44	May	389,273	443,859	339,755	378,290	1,551,177
45	June	275,839	618,636	538,391	446,575	1,879,441
46	July	373,295	563,712	150,318	252,637	1,339,962
47	August	262,164	677,007	362,527	219,567	1,521,264
48	September	258,226	409,104	261,365	430,976	1,359,671
49	October	345,209	443,763	327,564	323,308	1,439,845
50	November	520,152	783,887	416,296	515,963	2,236,297
51	December	732,993	836,461	648,579	712,865	2,930,897
52	Total	$ 3,991,404	$ 6,733,832	$3,868,063	$4,190,529	$18,783,828

Fig. 5.44   Full Year Annual Sales Report

1. In the open worksheet containing **Annual Sales Report December 2019** sales data, highlight cells **B39:E39**.

2. Press **CTRL** key on your keyboard, holding down this key, highlight cells **B52:E52,** and release key. See **fig.545** worksheet showing cells highlighted for pie chart.

3. With cells still highlighted, click the **Insert** tab at top ribbon, click **Insert Pie or Doughnut Chart** down arrow, and select **3-D Pie**.

4. Click the chart, holding down the mouse, drag chart, place below the worksheet, and resize as needed to fit chart contents.

5. Right-click on **Chart Title**, select **Edit Text** from the displayed menu, and type **TFI Total Annual % Sales Per Product – 2019.**

6. Click the chart, click **Design** tab at top ribbon; in the **Charts Style** group, select **Style 3** (3rd style on the row).

7. Highlight the chart title, in the **Font** group at top ribbon, click font type down arrow, select **Arial Black,** and change font size to **12.**

8. Click the chart, click **Format** tab at top ribbon; in the **Shape Styles** group, click the **Shape Fill** down arrow, and select **Green Accent 6, Lighter 80%** (last color on the 2nd row). This action changes the original background theme of the entire pie chart.

9. Click the placeholder containing product names at right of the pie chart; change text size to **10**, and apply **Bold** font to text.

10. Sum up percentages from each piece of the pie chart **(21%+22%+21%+36%)** to obtain **100%** of total annual sales, **$18,783,828** calculated on the worksheet.

	A	B	C	D	E	F
35		Tamona Furniture Industries (TFI)				
36		Annual Sales Report				
37		For the Year Ended December 2019				
38						
39	Accounting Periods	3 Sofas & Center Table Set	Beddings & Headbords	Dining Table Set	Kitchen Cabinets	Total Annual Sales
40	January	$ 202,247	$ 511,502	$ 139,490	$ 229,935	$ 1,083,174
41	February	159,942	489,409	170,159	153,415	972,925
42	March	187,388	481,271	245,167	212,148	1,125,975
43	April	284,676	475,220	268,452	314,849	1,343,197
44	May	389,273	443,859	339,755	378,290	1,551,177
45	June	275,839	618,636	538,391	446,575	1,879,441
46	July	373,295	563,712	150,318	252,637	1,339,962
47	August	262,164	677,007	362,527	219,567	1,521,264
48	September	258,226	409,104	261,365	430,976	1,359,671
49	October	345,209	443,763	327,564	323,308	1,439,845
50	November	520,152	783,887	416,296	515,963	2,236,297
51	December	732,993	836,461	648,579	712,865	2,930,897
52	Total	$ 3,991,404	$ 6,733,832	$3,868,063	$4,190,529	$18,783,828

Fig. 5.45   Worksheet Showing Cells Highlighted for Pie Chart

(Clicking the chart displays highlighted cells on the worksheet above)

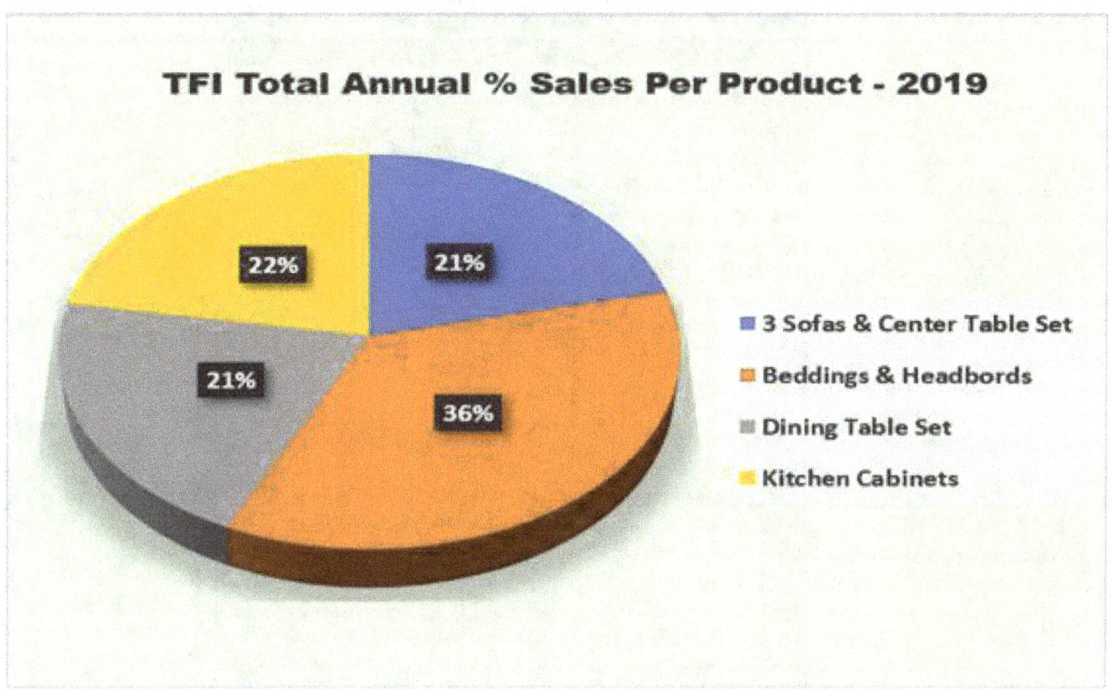

Fig. 5.46   Pie Chart Showing % of Product Sales Contribution Towards Total Annual Sales

Location of Pie Piece %: In the completed pie chart on **fig. 5.46**, notice that for each piece of the pie, the percentage is located inside the piece. However, Excel feature provides various location options for inserting a pie chart allowing you to select the location of your choice. The chart location feature is also available for all chart or graph types (column chart and line graph) discussed in previous sections of this chapter. In this sample project, the percentages are placed inside pieces of the pie. To select an optional location, follow these steps. The steps are the same for all chart and graph types but the menu options may differ.

1. Click the chart, in the **Chart Layout** group at top ribbon, click **Add Chart Element** down arrow **(fig. 5.47)**.
2. On the displayed short menu, click **Data Labels** forward arrow to display location options.

All-in-One Beginners Guide to Computer Proficiency | 267

3. From the open menu option list, select the location option you want.

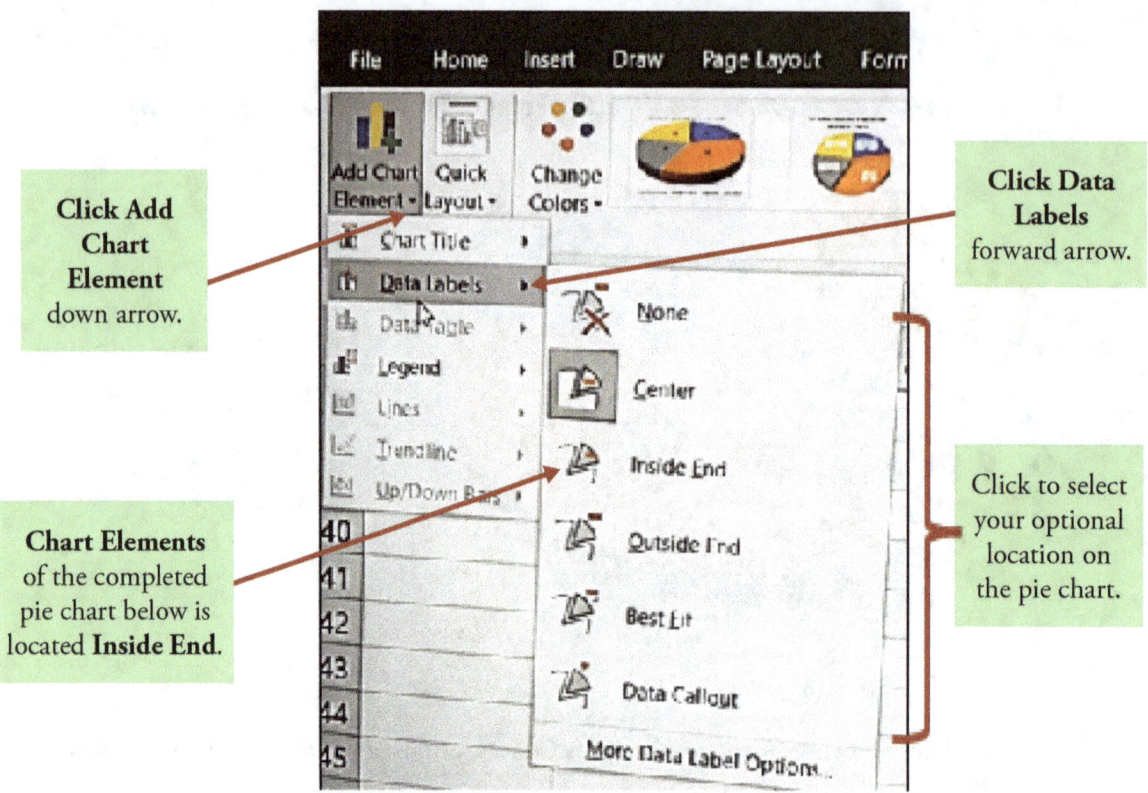

Fig. 5.47 Selecting Location of Pie Chart Elements

Analyze the Pie Graph: Based on the percentages shown in each piece of the pie chart on **fig. 5.46**, and the color-coded legend (product names at right of the chart), it is clear that **Beddings & Headboard** contributed the highest percentage, **36%** towards total *TFI's* total annual sales from January to December 2019. The second highest contributor was **Kitchen Cabinets** showing a **22%** contribution. **3 Sofa Sets with Side Tables** and **Dining Table Set** contributed about the same, **21%** each**,** just one point less than Sofa Set (percentages are rounded to whole numbers).

Conclusion & Business Decision: As in the same decision under column chart above, the *Tamonas* (*TFI)* should adopt the same marketing strategy that increases advertising and promotional activities on Sofas Set,

Dining Table Set, and Kitchen Cabinets to increase their sales so that these 3 products can meet up with Bedding & Headboard sales.

CHAPTER SUMMARY & KEY TERMS

Microsoft Excel is a program used for recording and detailing accounting information. It is the most popular spreadsheet software that is developed by Microsoft for various Operating Systems like Windows, macOS, Android and iOS calculation. The new Microsoft Excel 2019 comes with new features and some familiar features from earlier versions have been modified to be more user friendly. There are so many new or improved features for all Excel users – beginners, intermediate, and advance users such as Improved Autocomplete, New Themes, Black Theme, and No Warnings when Saving a CSV File. The main difference between Excel Workbook and Worksheet is that workbook contains a number of worksheets while worksheet is a single sheet within a workbook. Users often use the word Worksheet and Spreadsheet interchangeably, but there is a difference. The main difference between spreadsheet and worksheet is that spreadsheet is software that allows users to organize data in rows and columns and perform calculations on the data, while the rows and columns in a spreadsheet collectively are called a worksheet.

A worksheet is a document contained in an Excel workbook comprising of columns and rows. At the intersection of each row and column is a cell into which a user can enter either numbers or text. The address of any given cell is generated by combining the letter of the cell's column with the number of the cell's row. Sometimes you cannot enter or edit data in a worksheet, this is because the worksheet may have been protected by you or someone else to prevent data from being changed accidentally or by an unauthorized persons especially if it's a worksheet containing confidential information. On a protected (locked) worksheet, you can select cells to view the data, but you will not be able to type information in cells that are locked. In most cases, you cannot remove the protection from a worksheet unless you have permission to do so from the person who created and protected the worksheet.

Formatting Excel worksheet is important to maintain consistency in the way that Microsoft Excel stores numbers, texts, and graphics. With this in mind, it is important to format the fields in your spreadsheet accordingly using various formatting options available in Excel 2019. The ultimate goal of a formatted worksheet is to present information in a way that it makes sense to other people and enable users of the worksheet to make informed business decisions. To accomplish this goal, you have to give readers a head start by titling your worksheet correctly and clearly. A good title lets readers know immediately what the content of the worksheet is all about and eliminates the problem of readers having to work so hard to understand your information. By following specific instructions detailed in this chapter, you can create a worksheet and format the worksheet in a variety of ways such as applying boarders to the worksheet; insert rows/columns; delete rows/columns; adjust rows/columns to fit data or text; and format date and numbers, including formatting amounts with dollar signs. This chapter also provides you instructions on how to create formular in Excel worksheet cells to calculate numbers or amounts you enter into the cells, including copying the formula to other cells and linking a worksheet to other worksheets. Charts and graphs are important because they make financial information clearer and easier to understand for the user who needs them to make important business decisions. They are most suitable in presenting financial information to senior management or corporate officials for investment and spending decisions to ensure a stable financial health of their companies. A chart can create a clearer picture of a set of data values than a table with rows of numbers in it allowing managers to incorporate this understanding into analysis and future planning. The three main types of charts for beginners in Excel at column chart, pie chart, and line graph.

KEY TERMS

All Boarders	Custom Margins	Row Height
Alignment Group	CSV UTF-8 (Comma delimited)	Summary Worksheet Tab
Arithmetic operators	Detail Worksheet tab	Text operators
Cell Reference	Excel Arithmetic Operators	Worksheet Cell
Clear Formats	Formula Bar	Spreadsheet
Constants	Headers & Footer	Unprotect
Columns Headings	Intersection	Worksheet
Column Width	Merge & Center	Worksheet
Comparison operators	Operators	Wrap Text
Custom Footer	Operators Reference	
Custom Header	Protect Worksheet	

Demonstrate Your Knowledge & Skill

CHAPTER 5 PRACTICE EXERCISES
INTRODUCTION TO MS EXCEL 2019

5.1 – Select True or False answer to the following statements:

1. An Excel file is called a workbook?
   a. True
   b. False

2. If you press the "Tab" key it moves one cell to the left.
   a. True
   c. False

3. You can format text in a cell in Excel.
   d. True
   a. False

4. Excel automatically adjusts row height to accommodate the size of data in a row.
   a. True
   b. False

5. You can create mixed references by placing a dollar sign in front of only the column letter or only the row number.
   a. True
   b. False

6. You can insert a row by right clicking a column heading.
   a. True
   b. False

7. Values can include numbers, formulas, and functions.
   a. True
   b. False

8. The "Fill handle" is a small square in the lower-left corner of a selected cell or range of cells.
   a. True
   b. False

9. Will the formula =A7+A9 subtract the two cells?
   a. True
   b. False

10. When you have selected a range of cells and then you press CTRL+P. Excel will automatically print the selected range.
    a. True
    b. False

11. One method you can use to change a worksheet name is to go to the cells group on the Format tab, click Format and choose Rename Sheet.
    a. True
    b. False

12. To delete a worksheet, close the current workbook and it's automatically deleted.
    a. True
    b. False

13. You cannot copy a formula using "AutoFill".
    a. True
    b. False

14. When editing the "Margins" you can only edit the left and right side of the Worksheet.
    a. True
    b. False

15. You can rename the "sheet" tabs on the bottom left corner.
    a. True
    b. False

5.2 – Multiple Choice: Select the best answer to Microsoft Excel features and actions described below:

1. What one of the following combination of keyboards is used to correctly copy and paste data in an Excel worksheet cell?
   a. CTRL+X and CTRL+V
   b. CTRL+C and CTRL+V
   c. CTRL+A and CTRL+V
   d. CTRL+V and CTRL+X

2. Which function can you use to capture the contents of an open window?
    a. Icon Set
    b. Clip Art
    c. SmartArt
    d. Screenshot

3. What is the default file extension when you save a workbook for Excel 2019?
    a. .xls
    b. .xlsx
    c. .excel
    d. .xlav

4. Excel provides the following functions to be used except:
    a. AVERAGE
    b. MIN
    c. MAX
    d. HIGH

5. When you copy a formula that contains an absolute reference to a new location, the cell reference:
    a. is updated automatically
    b. does not change
    c. becomes bold
    d. has a dotted outline in its cell

6. Which of the following is a logical function?
    a. AVERAGE
    b. IF
    c. SUMPRODUCT
    d. VLOOKUP

7. On the Sort & Filter group of Data tab, worksheet cells can be arranged content in reverse alphabetical order, from Z to A.
   a. Reverse
   b. Major
   c. Ascending
   d. Descending

8. What Excel tool can quickly group, summarize, and rearrange larger datasets?
   a. Cell references
   b. Functions
   c. Pivot tables
   d. Ranges

9. The range of cells in column A and rows 10 through 20 should be stated as:
   a. A10 – A20
   b. 10A:20A
   c. A10:A20
   d. 10A – 20A

10. The range of cells in row 15 and columns B through E should be stated as:
    a. B15 – E15
    b. B15:E15
    c. 15B:15E
    d. 15B – 15E

11. All of the following items are types of Excel operators EXCEPT:
    a. Arithmetic operators
    b. Comparison operators
    c. Financial operators
    d. Operators reference

12. In Excel, an asterisk represents one of the following arithmetic operators:
    a. Multiplication
    b. Addition
    c. Division
    d. Subtraction

13. References to cells in other workbooks are called.
    a. Mixed cells
    b. Reference cells
    c. Relative sells
    d. Links

14. A2 refers to the value in cell A2; B2 refers to cells at intersection of column:
    a. A2 and B2
    b. B and row 2
    c. column A and row B
    d. B2 and A2

15. Which of the following statements correctly describes a constant in Excel?
    a. A constant is a value that is not calculated; it always changes depending on the cell.
    b. A constant is a value that is calculated; it returns the sum total calculated.
    c. A constant is a value that is not calculated; it always stays the same.
    d. A constant is a value that is not calculated; it always stays the same row and column.

16. By Excel standard, the correct formula for cells with these numbers: A5 contains 40; cell B5 contains 60; and C5 contains 115 is one of the following:
    a. =40+60+115
    b. 40+60+115=210
    c. +40A5+60B5+115C5
    d. =A5+B5+C5

17. Which of the following statements about Excel relative cell reference is correct?
    a. In Excel, relative reference is the type of reference which changes to another cell number when the same formula is copied to any other cells or in any other worksheet.
    b. In Excel, relative reference is the type of reference which does not change when a value is copied to another cell number or in any other worksheet.
    c. In Excel, relative reference is the type of reference which changes to another cell row number at the intersection point.
    d. In Excel, relative reference is the type of reference which does not change if another cell number at the intersection is added to it.

18. Formatting cell, rows, and columns in a worksheet involves any of these tasks:
    a. Insert rows and columns
    b. Delete rows and columns
    c. Wrap texts in column, including merge and center
    d. All of the above

19. The keyboard shortcut to copy, cut, and paste the contents of a worksheet cell include all of the following keyboard mixed letters EXCEPT:
    a. CTRL+C
    b. CTRL+X
    c. CTRL+P
    d. CTRL+V

20. To insert header and footer in a worksheet, you have to start by clicking one of the following tabs at the top menu:
    a. Insert tab, clicking Custom Margin, and selecting header/footer tab
    b. Margin down arrow, clicking Custom Margin, and selecting header/footer tab
    c. Page Layout tab, clicking Custom Margin, and selecting header/footer tab
    d. All of the Above

5.3 – Fill in the Blanks with the correct terms or words.

1. As a general rule, Excel will _____-align numbers.
2. On the Sort & Filter group in the Data tab, _____ order arranges content in alphabetical order from A to Z.
3. You can use Excel_____ feature to restrict other user's access to your worksheet.
4. In Excel, the _____ command doesn't affect the text font.
5. To change the page orientation to landscape, you start by clicking on the _____ tab.
6. When entering data in Excel worksheet cells, you can press _____ key to move from one cell to another.
7. To specify that the number in a worksheet cell is an amount, you have to format the number by clicking the _____ symbol.
8. You can activate a worksheet cell simply by _____ the cell.
9. Inserting rows and column in a worksheet is very simple; just right-click the row or column heading and select _____ or _____ from the shortcut menu.
10. An Excel workbook can contain many _____ tabs.
11. To create a formula, you begin first by typing the _____ into the cell that contains the formula.
12. Centering a worksheet title across a range of cells requires clicking the _____ tab, in the _____ group at top ribbon.
13. When a text or data is too long to fit within a worksheet cell, you typically must _____ the size of the column or _____ the height of the row.
14. The primary purpose of inserting a column chart in Excel if for _____.
15. Pie chart displays what_____ each segment of the pie contributes toward the whole total of the pie chart.
16. A line graph is a type of chart used to identify data _____ over a period of time.

CHAPTER 5 SKILL-BASED PRACTICE PROJECTS INTRODUCTION TO MS MICROSOFT EXCEL 2019

5.1 – Create and Format a Worksheet: *Grandma Lynn Bakery* (GLB) located in a small Milwaukee town of Wisconsin state is a family business pass down three generations from 1980 to present day. The bakery makes about 20 lines of popular bakery products, and business has been very successful in the past years (millions of dollars annually) until in 2020 when coronavirus (COVID-19) pandemic spread across United States. Consequently, sales of all products began to fall as states, local and federal government lockdowns took a major toll on the bakery's operation. During the pandemic lockdowns, customers where not coming out to the bakery for purchases. The bakery also suffered a significant reduction in sale orders from restaurants, and other small retailers causing sales of all products to fall even lower. In early April 2020, adhering to CDC social distancing guidelines, the bakery decided to start making deliveries of phone orders to people in their homes, and were able to see some revenues coming in. The Excel worksheet presented below shows the sales of their 5 products tracked for the first 6 months of 2020 (January – June). They chose to track only these 5 products because they have always been their lowest sellers even during normal times. The bakery hopes to use the result of this six-month evaluation to decide which product(s) to discontinue from their product lines permanently.

	A	B	C	D	E	F	G
1	Grandma Lynn Bakery						
2	Semi-Annual Sales Report						
3	January - June 2020						
4							
5	Accounting Periods	Bacon & Egg Pie	Sweet Cup Cakes	Fresh Cinnamon Rolls	Pineapple Upside Down Cake	French Bread	Monthly Totals
6	January	12,774	8,639	16,490	20,851	5,688	
7	February	14,998	7,958	15,115	19,468	6,733	
8	March	7,946	4,635	10,643	10,573	2,995	
9	April	11,866	2,536	8,396	8,664	3,876	
10	May	15,734	9,447	12,973	18,675	10,323	
11	June	20,313	10,864	16,414	23,932	12,459	
12							

Required:

1. Open an Excel workbook, type worksheet title in cells **A1 – A3**.
2. Click cell **A1 – G1**, in the **Alignment** group at top ribbon, click **Merge & Center**.
3. Repeat step 2 for rows **A2 – G2**, and **A3 – G3** to make the worksheet title standout.
4. Highlight the entire cells **A1 – G3**, change font size to **14,** and apply **Bold** font to the title. Use font size **12** for all text and data within worksheet cells.
5. Begin entering **Grandma Lynn Bakery** sales data presented above into worksheets cells using **Tab** key to navigate through rows and columns. Enter all text and data to appear as the worksheet above.
6. Highlight cells **A5 – G12**, in the **Font** group, click **Boarders** down arrow, and select **All Boarders.**
7. Highlight cells **A5 – G5**, in the **Font** group, click **Boarders** down arrow, and select **Double Bottom Boarder.** Center texts in this row, and apply **Bold** font.
8. Click cell **A11**, highlight through **G11**, in the **Font** group click **Boarders** down arrow, and select **Thick Bottom Boarder.**
9. Click cell **A12**, type **Total**, highlight cells **A12 – G12**, in the **Font** group, click **Boarders** down arrow, and select **Double Bottom Boarder.**
10. Save the *Grandma Lynn Bakery* formatted worksheet a **5.1_GLB_Formatting_Firstname_Lastname** in the preferred location on your computer using your first and last name. Submit your completed assignment following the instructor's preferred method – electronically or printed hardcopy for grading.

5.2 – Create Formula and Copy to Other Worksheet Cells:

The worksheet you created in item 5.1 above is only formatted at this point. To help *Grandma Lynn Bakery* complete their 6-months sales evaluation, they need to see the total sales per product. In this section, your job is to calculate the data you entered in the worksheet.

Required:

1. Open the Excel file you saved as **5.1_GLB_Formatting_Firstname_Lastname** on your computer.
2. Click cell **B6**, highlight through **G6**, in the **Number** group at top ribbon, click the **$** sign to display amounts in USD currency.

3. To show amounts in whole dollars by removing the **.00,** highlight **B6 - F6,** in the **Number** group at top ribbon, click **Decrease Decimal** tab twice (last tab in the number group).

4. Click cell **G6**, enter a formula that calculates the values in cells **B6 – F6** to obtain total sales of all products in January.

5. Click the intersection of cell **G6** to form a + sign; then holding down the mouse, drag formula down to column **G11**, and release mouse. This action copies the same formula for total January sales into February – June cells.

6. Click cell **B12**, enter a formula that calculates values in cells **B6 - B11** to obtain total sales per product (January – June 2020).

7. Click the intersection of cell **B12** to form a + sign; then holding down the mouse, drag formula straight across to **G12**, and release mouse. This action copies the same formula in cell **B12** to all cells in the **Total** row.

8. Click cell **B12**, highlight through cell **G12**, and repeat steps **2 &3** above to add **$** signs and display totals in whole numbers.

9. Click cells **G7**, highlight through **G11**, in the **Numbers** group, click the comma (,) sign to remove **$** signs, then repeat **step 3** above to display amounts in whole numbers.

10. Save the completed worksheet as **5.2_GLB_SalesTotals_Firstname_Lastname** in the preferred location on your computer using your first and last name. Submit your completed assignment following the instructor's preferred method – electronically or printed hardcopy for grading.

5.3 – Insert Column Chart, Format, & Change Chart, Design:

Recall our discussion of charts and graphs in chapter 5. A column also known as vertical bar charts is a data visualization method where each category is represented by a rectangle, with the height of the rectangle being proportional to the values being plotted. For the bakery to get a clearer view of the 5 product sales under evaluation, they need a visual view of the sales total for each product of the 5 products (January – June 2020). Remember, despite what the totals show, *"a picture says a thousand words."* For this project you will create a column chart to compare the total sales figures among the 5 products to identify the highest and lowest sellers.

Required:

1. Open the Excel file you saved as **5.2_GLB_SalesTotals_Firstname_Lastname** on your computer.
2. Highlight worksheet cells **A5 – F11**, and click the **Insert** tab at top ribbon.
3. On the displayed **Charts** group, click **Insert Column or Bar Charts** down arrow, and select **2-D Column**.
4. Click the chart, holding down the mouse, drag it below the worksheet, and resize as needed to fit contents of chart.
5. Click the chart, click **Design** tab at top ribbon, in the **Data** group, select **Switch Rows/ Columns**.
6. Click the chart, click **Design** tab, in the **Chart Style** group, select **Style 6**.
7. Click the chart, click **Design** tab, in the **Charts Layout** group, click **Quick** Layout down arrow, and select **Layout 1**.
8. Right-click on **Chart Title** at top of the chart, select **Edit Text** from the displayed menu, and type **Grandma Lynn Bakery Monthly Comparative Sales Report January – June 2020**.
9. Highlight the chart title, in the **Font** group at top ribbon, click font type down arrow, select **Arial Black**, and change font size to **10**.
10. Click the chart, click **Format** at top ribbon, in the **Shape Styles** group, click **Shape Fill** down arrow, and select **Blue, Accent 1, Lighter 80%**.
11. Click the chart vertical bars, click **Format** at top ribbon, in the **Shape Styles** group, down arrow, and select **Colored Outline-Gold, Accent 4**.
12. Click the chart vertical bars, click **Format** at top ribbon, in the **Shape Styles** group, click **Shape Fill** down arrow, and select **Light Gray, Background 2**.
13. Click the **$** amount placeholder at left of chart and change text to font size **10**.
14. Repeat **step 13** for months and food placeholders (left & bottom of chart); then apply **Bold** font to text in food placeholders.
15. Save the completed worksheet as **5.2_GLB_SalesTotals_Firstname_Lastname** in the preferred location on your computer using your first and last name. Submit your completed assignment following the instructor's preferred method – electronically or printed hardcopy for grading

5.4 – Analyze Column Chart:
Review the column chart you created in item 5.3 above to analyze various heights of the vertical bars. This analysis will help *Grandma Lynn Bakery* to make an important business decision by identifying which of the 5 products to discontinue. Please use correct Standard English in your responses and keep your answers brief, concise, and straight to the point.

Required:

Based on the structure of the column chart, you reviewed, open a Word document titled **Analyze Chart** at top page; center title, and apply bold font to the title and answer the following questions:

1. What is the purpose of a Column Chart?
2. Which product shows the highest sales with the tallest vertical bars?
3. Which month shows the highest sales with tallest vertical bars?
4. Which of the 5 products are the lowest sellers with shortest vertical bars?
5. What is the total amount of all product sales for the entire 6 months?
6. Which two of the 5 products would you advise *Grandma Lynn Bakery* to discontinue and why?
7. Save your completed responses to the questions as **5.4_Analyze Chart_ GLB_Firstname_ Lastname** in the preferred location on your computer using your first and last name. Submit the Word document following the instructor's preferred method – electronically or printed hardcopy for grading.

CHAPTER 6

WELCOME TO MICROSOFT POWERPOINT 2019

Microsoft PowerPoint is a presentation program, created by Robert Gaskins and Dennis Austin at a software company named **Forethought, Inc**. It was released on April 20, 1987 initially for Macintosh System Operating system-based computers only. Microsoft Corporation acquired PowerPoint for about $14 million three months after it was released. PowerPoint presentation is software used for making visual and graphical presentations before an audience and provides professional looking documents, including handouts for the audience. It is basically a presentation creation tool that produces slideshows with text, images, shapes, animations, audio, and much more. You can create your presentation onto a big screen to display it to others or save it as a visual document for yourself. MS PowerPoint has been the most widely used program for presentations and the leading tool for creating professional presentation documents ever since its inception in 1987. It gives creators and speakers a chance to present important facts, instructions, and notes with visually pleasing, professional-looking slides.

Learning Objectives:

After completing this chapter, you will be able to:

- Know what PowerPoint is, how to use the program in creating a presentation, and learn how the program is used in business, schools, and professional training.
- Learn the new features of PowerPoint 2019, terms, and definitions, and know their functions.

- Create a PowerPoint presentation from scratch, insert new slides, format slides, and display your presentation in slide show to your audience.
- Learn how to choose the main points of your presentation and apply bullet points to the main ideas of your message.
- Insert new slides to your PowerPoint presentation; display it in slideshow, rearrange slides, duplicate slides, delete slides, and display slides in Slide Sorter View.
- Insert graphics and photos into a PPT slide, add notes to slides, and print PowerPoint handouts from Slide Master.

General Uses of PowerPoint

- In businesses, it is used for presentation of new products, proposed improvements of old products, including introduction of new and innovative ideas for products and services.
- Used as an effective educational tool in delivering slideshows for classrooms lectures, and other types of professional trainings.
- Used as slideshows to display and preserve personal family photos.
- A very effective tool for displaying sales plans, marketing materials, project activities, marketing budgets, and financial presentations.
- For planning event presentations such as weddings, anniversaries, or family reunions.
- For creating certificates, calendars, reports, diagrams, and charts for any business.

NEW FEATURES OF POWERPOINT 2019

What is PowerPoint?

It is a comprehensive slideshow software from the **MS Office Suite** that assists presenters by handling digital data and displaying it in a user-friendly format that audience can easily understand. During a presentation, PowerPoint has the capabilities of going forward and backward, slide-to-slide, at the click of a button. If you want people to buy into a new idea you may have, PowerPoint will make it easy for you to create, collaborate, and present your ideas in dynamic, visually compelling ways to achieve your goal. In business, educational, and personal situations, PowerPoint offers users the flexibility to make the simplest presentations stand out with its multiple interesting features. In this chapter, we will be covering basic guide to PowerPoint;

everything a beginner needs to know in creating a presentation independently and becoming proficient with PowerPoint presentation.

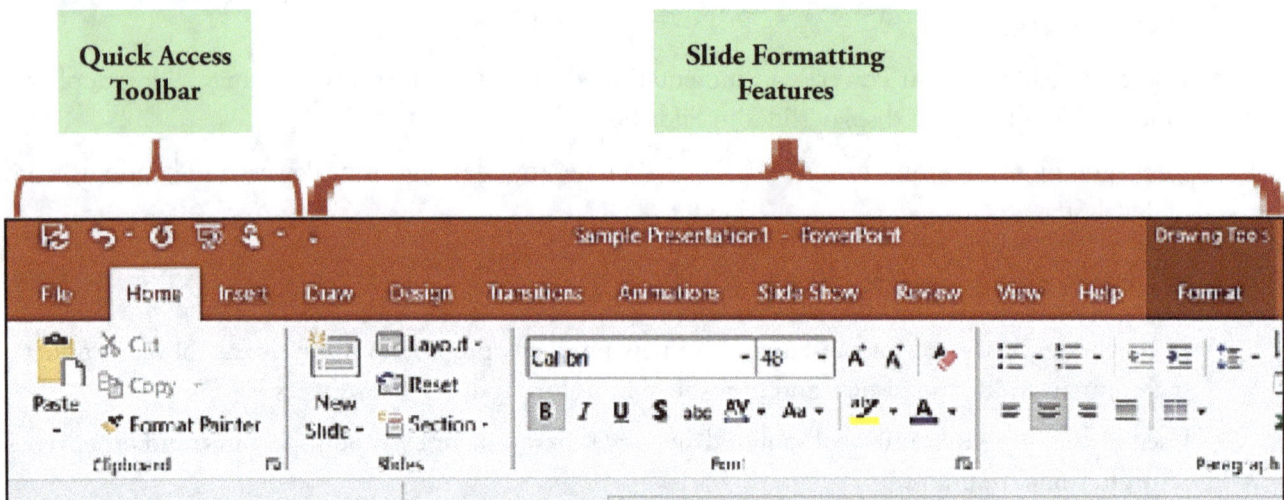

Fig. 6.1   PowerPoint 2019 New Ribbon Features

PowerPoint Basic Terms

If you are new to PowerPoint, it is important that you understand the basic terms that will guide you in creating a professional looking presentation and keep your audience well engaged as you deliver your message. As you begin your study of PowerPoint presentation, you will come across many words and terms used frequently throughout this guide. The terms listed and described below will help you understand what each term means and what role they play in the PPT presentation you may be creating.

Slide Show & Presentation
: In a PPT presentation, these two terms are used interchangeably because they each represent the overall document you create in the application. **Slide Show** view occupies the full computer screen exactly the way your presentation will look on a big screen.

Slides
: A slide layout contains formatting, positioning, and serves as a placeholder for the contents of your presentation. Placeholders are displayed as dotted line containers of presentation texts. Each slideshow in a PPT represents a page in a book. For example, if you are writing a school term paper that will contain multiple pages, each page you fill with words is a slide from PPT standpoint. Just like

your term paper, think of slides as pages that you can add to your presentation and then move through them one at a time.

Animations: Animations are visual effects that give your PPT slide a unique appearance. They are features that allow you to add movement and eye-catching elements on your slide to draw attention from your audience.

Transitions: These are animation-like movements that occur when you move from one slide to the next during a PPT presentation. It is added to a presentation to bring it to life. Using a transition in your presentation makes it stand out to your audience and gives it a dramatic effect.

Slide Master: The **Slide Master** is located in the **View** tab at the ribbon. In the **View** tab, the **Slide Master** is a feature that allows you to choose the option you want for printing your presentation handouts.

PowerPoint Ribbons & Tabs: As with all other Microsoft Office applications, PPT ribbon comes with tabs located at top ribbon containing features that allow you to create a presentation from scratch, modify, and customize it the way you want. **Table 6.1** below provides brief summaries of how to use PPT tabs. Detail instructions on how to use these listed tabs in creating a PPT presentation are covered in several sections of this chapter.

PPT Tabs	Quick Way to Use PPT Tabs
File	Create a new presentation, open an existing one, save, print, and share slideshows.
Home	Control the clipboard, slides, font, paragraph, drawing, and editing.
Insert	Insert slides, tables, images, illustrations, links, comments, text, and media.
Design	Select a theme, pick a variant, customize slides, and get design ideas
Transitions	Choose a transition, preview it, adjust the effects, and add timing.
Animations	Pick an animation, preview it, adjust the effects, use advanced features, and add timing.
Slide Show	Start a slideshow, set one up, pick a monitor, and use presentation view.
Review	Use tools for proofreading, accessibility, language, comments, and comparisons.
View	Change the presentation view, adjust the master views, zoom in or out, select colors, and work with windows and macros.

Table 6.1　　　　　　　　　　**PowerPoint Ribbon & Tabs**

Quick Access Toolbar

This feature is very common with all MS Office products. As an ardent user of Office products, you may already be familiar with this handy tool which was also discussed in MS Word (chapter 4). Quick Access is the toolbar at the very top left of MS Office programs – Word, Excel, and PowerPoint windows. As the name implies, this feature allows you to perform quick actions. The **Quick Access Toolbar** is made up of four main icons – **Save, Undo, Redo**, including a **Down Arrow** icon that allows you to customize the toolbar by relocating it to a more convenient location while you work.

> **Save Icon:** Allows you to quickly save the file you are working on with the current file name, instead of going through the file tab.
>
> **Undo Icon:** While working on your PPT presentation, if you make a mistake and want to undo it, just click the Undo icon. When you click it once, it will undo the last action you took. However, as you keep clicking this icon, it will continue to undo each previous action you've taken by moving backward.
>
> **Redo Icon:** The **Redo** icon changes in shape only when you click the **Undo**. The new shape is the same as Undo icon except that it points to the right allowing you to redo what you have just undone. Like the Undo button, you can redo your last action with one click or use the arrow next to the **Redo** icon to redo multiple actions.
>
> **Presentation Icon:** The fourth item to the right of **Undo** arrow. This feature allows you to start your presentation slideshow as a test drive for you to view what it will look like to your audience or for the actual presentation. It should take up your entire screen for a nice view of the presentation. At any time during this "test drive" you can make any necessary change, and editing needed to create a good professional looking PowerPoint presentation.

Move Quick Access Toolbar to a New Location on the Ribbon

As with all MS Office applications, by default, the Quick Access Toolbar is always located at the top left corner of the ribbon. This is not a permanent location; you have the option to move it to a more convenient location of your choice. Like in MS Word (chapter 4) discussion, there are also only two places on a PowerPoint screen where you can place the quick access toolbar – on its current place or below the ribbon. If you do not want the **Quick Access Toolbar** to be displayed in its default location, you can move it to the next alternate location. For example, if you find that the default location is too far from your work area to be convenient, you have the option to move it and place it below the ribbon, closer to your work area. On the other hand, the location below the ribbon may interfere with your work area, in which case you may want to keep the Quick Access Toolbar in its default location. Follow these steps to relocate the quick access toolbar:

1. Click on **Customize Quick Access** Toolbar **(fig. 6.2a)**.
2. In the open menu list, click **Show Below the Ribbon** to place it closer to your work space.
3. This is a toggle option, to move it back to its default location, repeat **steps 1 & 2** and click **Show Above the Ribbon (fig. 6.2b)**.

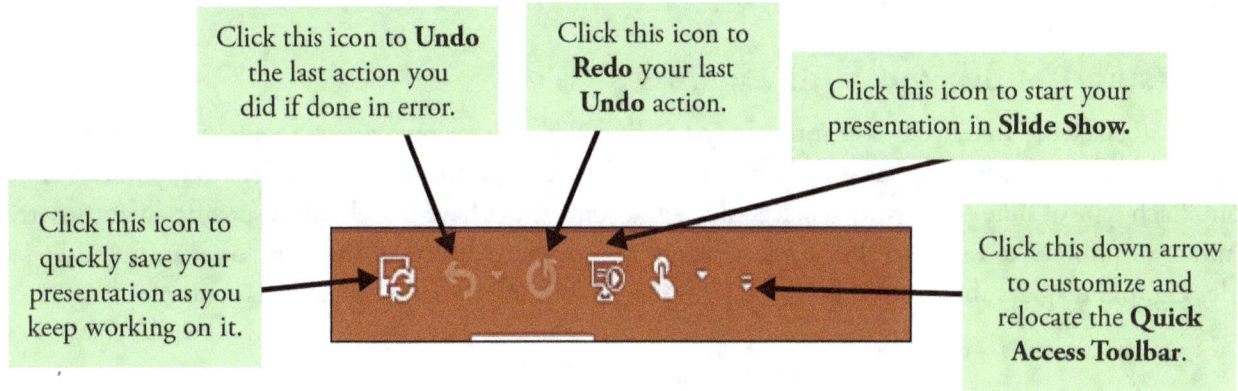

Fig. 6.2a   PowerPoint Quick Access Toolbar

Fig. 6.2b   Quick Access Toolbar Relocated Below the Ribbon

WORK WITH POWERPOINT SLIDES & CREATE A NEW PPT PRESENTATION

Before we begin our discussion of how to create a PowerPoint presentation, let's take a moment to understand the basic role of slides in PPT presentation in general. Every PPT presentation is composed of a series of slides. To begin creating your presentation, you must have slides into which you will type your texts, insert graphics, create a slide show, apply optional formatting to your overall presentation, then make the presentation to your audience. In this section, we'll describe slide layouts, placeholders within slides, and how to work with slides in a presentation.

Understand Slides and Slide Layouts

When you click the **Insert** tab at top ribbon, and click **New Slide** down arrow to add a new slide to your presentation, you will notice that slides have different layouts options for placeholders that you can choose from. Each type of slide comes with a placeholder, and some slides have placeholders specifically for inserting graphics or photos. You select a slide option depending on the type of information you want to add to the slide. **Fig. 6.3** displays the composition of different types of PPT presentation slide layouts.

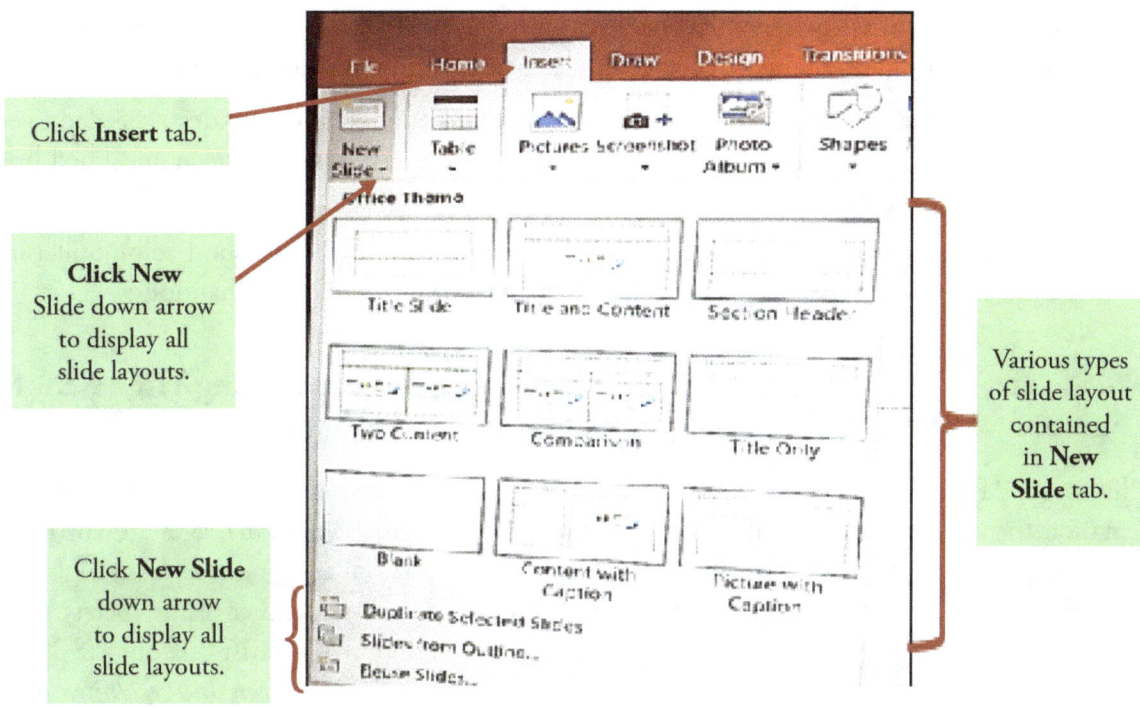

Fig. 6.3   **PPT Slide Layouts**

Create a New PowerPoint Presentation

When you first open a PowerPoint program, notice that it opens into a default slide with two placeholders – one for title of your slide and the other placeholder for the subtitle. Depending on the size of your presentation, you must manually add more slides as you need them. To create a PPT presentation from scratch, we will be illustrating the process using a PPT project in which you are required to "CONVINCE HIGH SCHOOL STUDENTS TO STAY IN SCHOOL". Using this project, you will be taken through each step from start to completion. Here are the main steps which will be described in detail as we work on this project.

1. Click the **Start** button, navigate the start menu, and select **PowerPoint**.
2. Click on the **Placeholder to Add Title,** click the line edges of the placeholder, drag to adjust the size and position it at top of the slide, then type the title of your presentation.

3. Click on the **Subtitle** placeholder, click the line edges, drag to adjust the size, position it to your preferred location below the main title, and type the subtitle of your presentation.

4. As you continue working on your presentation, you will be adding more slides as needed to contain your message. Notice that as you add slides, they are displayed in full screen and lined up at left pane of your presentation as well.

5. Format your presentations slide with font size, color fonts, slide background color, bullet list, add notes to slides where necessary, apply slide show, and print presentation handouts.

Sample PPT Project: **Create a PPT Presentation to Persuade Young High Schoolers in Louisiana to Stay in School and graduate from high school.**

To illustrate PPT presentation steps, you have been assigned a project to create a new PowerPoint presentation to convince a group of young high school students from Louisiana, ages **14-18** (the state with the highest dropout rate) of how important it is to stay in school and graduate from high school, get a good education, live a good decent life, and become a productive member of the society. To help you prepare for this project, you have been provided with the following statistics from US National Center for Education Statistics (NCES) and it states: "*The status of dropout rate in the United States—the percentage of 16- to 24-year-olds who are not enrolled in school and do not have a high school diploma or alternative credential—was 5.4% in 2017*". The NCES report went further by stating that: "*Trends in High School Dropout and Completion Rates in the United States: 2019," found that Louisiana had the highest average dropout rate from 2013-17: 9.6%. The lowest average status dropout rate over those years was 3.8% in Massachusetts.*" Finally, NCES provided the following list of 10 states with the highest average status dropout rate from 2013-17:

States	Dropout Rates (%)
1. Louisiana	9.6%
2. Nevada	9.0%
3. New Mexico	8.6%
4. Arizona	8.5%
5. Oklahoma	8.1%
6. Mississippi	7.5%
7. Indiana	7.5%
8. Alabama	7.4%
9. Georgia	7.3%
10. Texas	7.1%

Source: National Center for Education Statistics (2013-2017) Last Updated January 14, 2020

Do the Research & Plan Your Presentation:

This planning stage involves researching your presentation topic, data collection, organizing materials, and arranging facts in sequential order for delivery to your audience. When inserting slides and naming title slides, and subtitles, you will follow the plan of presentation to enable your audience gain a good understanding of your message. For this project, let's assume that you live in Louisiana where the high school dropout rate is the highest. Although you have been provided with the facts of this project, you still need to do some research to find out why these Louisiana high school students are dropping out of school and come up with some possible solutions to this ongoing problem. Through your research, you can identify the benefits of staying in school and what the students stand to gain if they complete their high school education. Then finally organize all materials from your research in such a way that you can keep your audience engaged and persuade them to stay in school because completing high school is the beginning of a brighter future for them. Your planning, research, and actual presentation process will include but not limited to the following:

1. Prior to the actual PPT presentation, write a report on your research findings on a MS Word document; it is from this detailed report that you will create your presentation.

2. Although the presentation comes from the detailed report, but in your PPT slides, you will be highlighting only the main points of your message in bullet points or numbered items format.

3. Summarize the main points of your message in a short, concise, and straight-to-the point format while using your MS Word notes to explain details as you make the presentation to your audience.

4. Know your audience (high school students) and adjust the language of your speech to suit your audience; use simple words that are easy to understand. If you have to use any big word, be sure to explain the meaning first before speaking about it.

5. State the purpose of the presentation and what it is intended to accomplish – To reduce high school dropout rate in the State of Louisiana.

6. Identify suggested primary reasons why some high school students drop out of school. You can do this by conducting personal interviews with at least two high schools in your area. You can interview some teachers and students to get facts from both sides to make your presentation argument stronger and more convincing.

7. Suggest some possible solutions that can help them resist the urge to drop out of school providing some examples of real-life situations (if any) where the solutions you suggest have worked.

8. Identify and list the benefits of staying in school to complete high school education and how it will improve their lives in the future.

9. Wrap up the presentation by summarizing in a list, the main points of your message, and allow time for your audience to ask questions before ending the presentation.

10. Print presentation handouts prior to the event and make available to your audience in case they need copies. A full discussion on printing handouts is coming up later in this chapter.

Begin Creating the PowerPoint Presentation: Default slide is displayed (fig.6.4).

1. Open **PowerPoint** program; click the top **Placeholder** line edges; drag it to the top of the slide, and type the title of your message which could be: **"Stay in School for a Better Future."**

2. Click the **Subtitle Placeholder**, type the purpose of your presentation, and what you intend to accomplish. Type the subheading: **To Reduce High School Dropout Rate in the State of Louisiana.**

3. Click the line edges of the **Subtitle Placeholder** and drag to enlarge it for entering text.

Format Presentation Slides:
This process involves changing text fonts size, color overall color background and appearance of the slides. All formatting tools are located at top ribbon of the open PPT window.

Refer to fig. 6.1 above to view all PPT formatting tools.

1. Format main title and subtitle for a more professional look as follows:

   a. To change text font size of slide main title, highlight the **Main Title**; in the **Fonts** group, select font size **60**, apply **Bold,** with **Red** color font and **Center** the title.

   b. Increase the font size of **Purpose of Presentation** to **50**; apply **bold** and **Purple** color font.

   c. On the **remaining** text: **To Reduce……….,** increase text size to **48** and apply **Bold** font; no color font on the text.

2. Format **Title Placeholder** – Highlight the **Main Title**; click **Format** tab, in the **Shape Style** group, click the down arrow, and select **Subtle Effect-Blue, Accent 5** (located on the 5th row).

3. Apply color font to slide background – The selected background color used on **slide 1** will be the same background displayed on all slides in this project. Let's change the selected background by following these steps:

   a. Click the **Placeholder** containing text, click **Format** tab at top ribbon.

   b. Click **Fill Shape** down arrow, and select **Light Gray, Background 2** (3rd color on the first row).

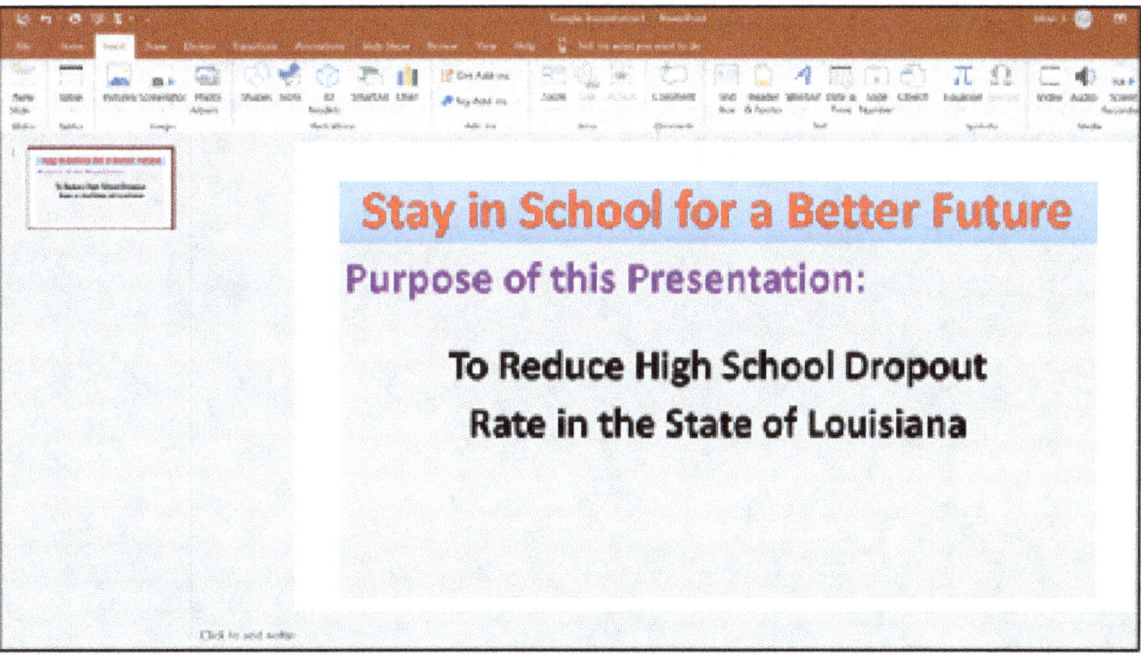

Fig. 6.4   MPPT Presentation Slide 1

Insert & Format Slide 2: On this second slide, show why dropping out of high school is a social problem by listing the statistics from National Center for Education Statistics (NCES) **highlighting Louisiana as a state with highest dropout rate (fig. 6.5).**

1. Click **I**n**sert** tab at top ribbon, click **New Slide** down arrow and select **Title Slide**.
2. Repeat your actions on steps **2 & 3** as on **slide 1** above.
3. Repeat steps **3a & 3b** above to change the color background of the main slide.
4. On the **Title Placeholder**, type **National Center for Education Statistics (NCES): 2013 -2017 States with the Highest High School Dropout Rates.** Use font size **32**.
5. Apply the same formatting on **slide 2** main heading as in **step 2** of **slide I** above: **Subtle Effect-Blue, Accent 5** (located on the 5th row) and **Center** the title.
6. Adjust and expand the **Subtitle** placeholder to contain the **10 states** listed by **NCES.**
7. Type the entire **10** states on NCES list and the dropout rate for each state on the list.
8. Click to **Add Notes** at bottom of **slide 2** and type these – **Source: National Center for Education Statistics (2013-2017) Last Updated January 14, 2020** to give credit to the source of statistics used in your presentation. After correctly applying all formatting described in **Formatting Presentation Slides** above and inserting **slide 2,** slides **1 & 2** of your presentation will appear as shown in **fig. 6.4** above and **fig. 6.5** below :

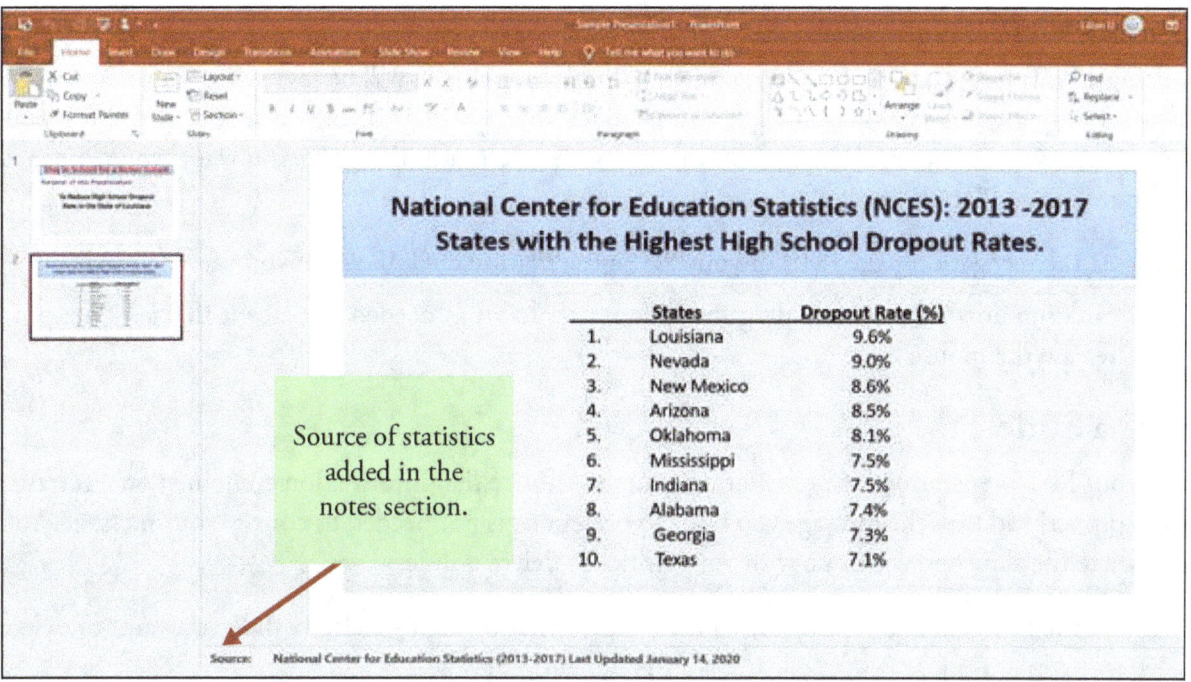

Fig. 6.5   PPT Presentation Slide 2- Slides Display at Left Pane

Duplicate a Slide

As you work on your PPT presentation, you may have the need to duplicate a slide instead of inserting a new one. This is usually the case when you have a long bullet point list or text paragraph that extends into more than one slide but with the same title heading. Instead of adding a new slide and retyping the same title heading, and applying the same formatting, simply duplicate the original slide with the same title heading, then delete all text on the duplicated slide except the title heading. To duplicate a slide, follow these steps:

1. At the navigation pane (left) of your PPT presentation right-click the slide to be duplicated.
2. From the displayed short menu, select **Duplicate Slide**. The duplicated slide will appear below the original slide with the same title heading.
3. Click the placeholder of the duplicated slide, highlight the entire text in the placeholder below the title, press **Delete** on your keyboard.
4. Begin typing your new texts in bullet point list or paragraphs in the blank placeholder .

Rearrange a Slide

In creating a PPT presentation, depending on your chosen topic, you will be reviewing your notes, checking slide title headings, and making sure that your slides follow a logical or sequential order for effective presentation to your audience. If you notice that the slides are not in the order you want, you can rearrange them. To rearrange PPT slides:

1. At the navigation pane (left) of your PPT presentation click the slide you want to move.
2. Holding down the mouse, drag the slide up or down as needed to place it in the right spot, and release the mouse.

Delete a Slide

During your PPT preparation for presentation, you may notice that information contained on a certain slide does not properly address the message you want to present or is not needed to convey your message. You can simply delete the slide and continue with your work. To delete a slide:

1. At the navigation pane (left) of your PPT presentation right-click the slide you want to delete.
2. From the displayed short menu, select **Delete Slide**.

Moving Forward with Body of the Presentation

You can see that the NCES statistics presented on slide 2 speaks for itself – Louisiana holds the highest dropout rate in high school education and that's why it is the focus of this presentation. In this section, we will insert more slides to begin presenting information obtained from your research in the planning stage. In addition to the responses, you obtained from your research interviews, keep in mind that the reasons for high dropout rate of Louisiana State high schools may not necessarily apply to all students from the families described on your summary list. You have to keep an open mind to the fact that some students may have the worst family upbringing, and live at "Housing Project" neighborhood, yet they stay in school, graduate, and go on to college.

On the other hand, students with the best family upbringing, raised in upscale nice neighborhood with educated parents still drop out of high school. To explain this phenomenon will require extensive research, statistics, creating hypothesis, and developing theories. This process is the function of expert psychologist, which is beyond the scope of this beginner's guide. For this project, we shall focus only on the responses obtained from the people you interviewed. Recall that prior to the actual PPT presentation, you had to plan your presentation which is a detailed MS Word document containing your research findings. The high school dropout reasons listed below are in detail format. For the PPT presentation, you need to summarize each item in bullet points. Your summary bullet points should contain enough main points to clearly convey your message to the audience. Then using the notes from your Word document, you can explain details of each listed bullet point during your presentation. In order to make the presentation more persuasive to your audience, it will be more effective to ask questions at the title heading of each slide instead of making a statement. This means that for each slide title heading, we'll ask a question about the subject matter, then answer the question with bullet point list. Let's assume that you interviewed **4 teachers** and **4 students** from each of the **2 high schools** you selected in your community and obtained a total of **16** responses which are summarized below:

Suggested Reasons for High Dropout Rate in the State of Louisianan High Schools

- ✓ High divorce rate in our society today creates many single-parent homes with emotional distress on the children resulting to anger, rebelliousness, and lack of interest in school work.
- ✓ Single-parent home where a woman is the only bread winner, working two jobs to make ends meet; too busy to spend quality time with the children and help them with their homework. In addition, there is no father figure to instill strong discipline in the children. This may mean that the children are practically raising themselves.
- ✓ Lack of strong family discipline even in two-parent homes where children are given a free pass (liberal family tradition) for disobedience without any consequences for their actions. In these types of homes, there may not be strong emphasis from the parents about the importance of education. With the believe that they can do whatever they want and get away with it, these high school students may drop out of school just because they are tired of it.
- ✓ Children raised in poor neighborhood commonly referred to as "The Project Housing," primarily characterized by drug use/sales, and gun violence have the propensity to drop out of high school. According to experts on social issues, these children (The At-Risk Group) face significant pressure from their peers who show no interest in school. As the peer pressure intensifies, the students decide to drop out of school in order to fit in and be accepted by their hang-out groups.
- ✓ Students from low income families cannot afford to hire private tutors to help them with courses they are struggling with (homework). As the feelings of not being good enough creates low self-esteem continues, out of frustration, the student drops out of school thinking it's a waste of time. "I'm not smart enough to do this anyway" as some of them say.

> ✓ Some high school students working part-time jobs may have opportunities to work full-time and make more money. With the option to make more money, the students sometimes feel that they don't need school, in essence: "Why continue with school when I can make good money without completing school?" The student drops out of school, and may never have the courage to return to graduate from high school. The longer some students stay out of school while working, the harder it is to return and complete their high school education.
>
> ✓ Emergence of street gangs across many communities in Louisiana state and peer pressure from this group attract students struggling with school work because they believe the gang is their new family that really understands them and praises their toughness for committing street crimes.

Insert & Format Slide 3:

1. Click **Insert** tab at top ribbon, click **New Slide** down arrow and select **Title Only**.
2. On **Click to Add Title**, click and type: **Why do Youths in Our Community Drop Out of High School?** On this slide, you will enter responses from the teachers and students you interviewed from two high schools in your area during your research. Change the title font size to **40**.
3. Notice that this new slide has no placeholder below the title placeholder; you have to manually add a placeholder to be able to type texts in the slide. To manually add placeholder, do these:
   a. Click **Insert** tab, in the **illustrations** group, click **Shapes** down arrow, and select the first **Text Box** at top left (top row).
   b. Right-click in the **Text Box** and select **Edit Text**; then begin typing the main points of your research.
   c. In bullet points, summarize the list of detailed responses from your research interviews provided in the blue box above. Let's assume that you interviewed **4 teachers** and **4 students** from each of the **2 high schools** you selected obtaining a total of **16** responses summarized in **8** bullet points in the blue box above.
4. To display lists in bullet points, highlight the entire text; in the **Paragraph** group, click ▭ bullet down arrow, and select any bullet style of your choice.
5. Change the font size of the bullet point texts you listed on **slide 3** to **22.**
6. Highlight the entire bullet list; in the **Paragraph** group, click the **Dialog Box Launcher**.

7. In the open **Paragraph** dialog box, under **Spacing**, click the **After** up arrow to **6 pt.** and click **Ok** (**fig. 6.6**). Ensure that the **Line Spacing** box displays **Single**; if not, click down arrow and select **Single**. The purpose of this step is to put enough space between the bulleted point list so that your audience can clearly identify each item on your list.

8. Format **slide 3** main **Title** the same as **slide 2**, apply **Bold** font, and **Center Title**.

9. Click the **Placeholder** containing bulleted list, and click **Format** tab.

10. In **Style Shape** group, click **Fill Shape** down arrow, and select **Light Gray, Background 2** to change slide **3** background. If you have correctly followed all the steps listed under **Insert Slide 3**, see below (**fig. 6.7**) for the completed **slide 3**.

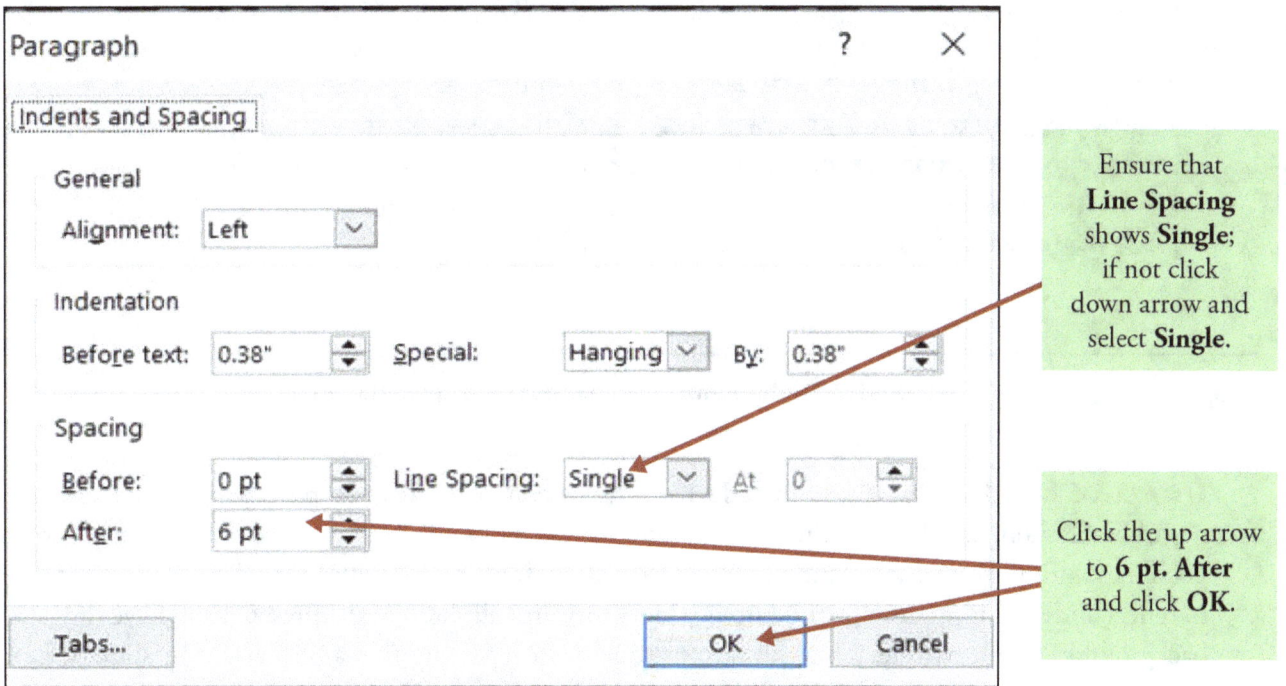

Fig. 6.6   **Paragraph Dialog Box to Add Spaces between Bullet Point List**

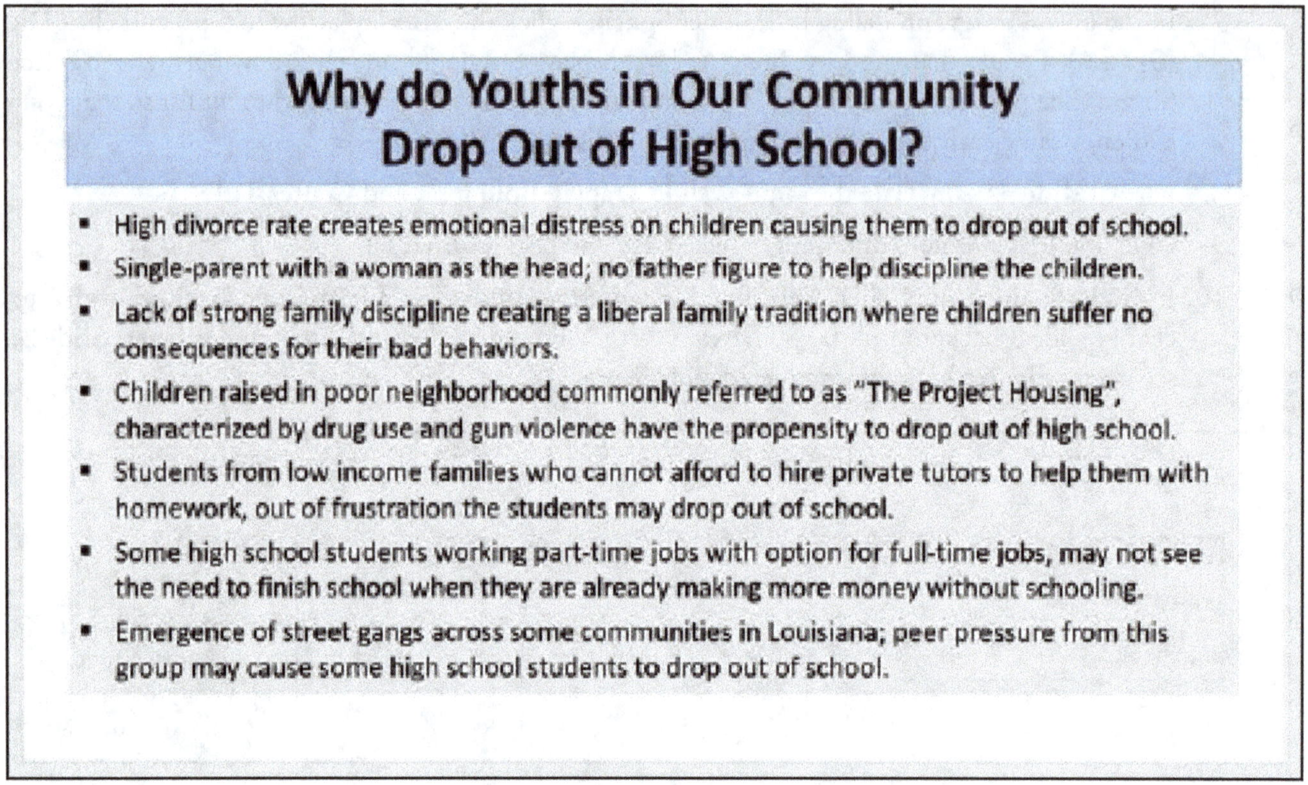

> **Why do Youths in Our Community Drop Out of High School?**
>
> - High divorce rate creates emotional distress on children causing them to drop out of school.
> - Single-parent with a woman as the head; no father figure to help discipline the children.
> - Lack of strong family discipline creating a liberal family tradition where children suffer no consequences for their bad behaviors.
> - Children raised in poor neighborhood commonly referred to as "The Project Housing", characterized by drug use and gun violence have the propensity to drop out of high school.
> - Students from low income families who cannot afford to hire private tutors to help them with homework, out of frustration the students may drop out of school.
> - Some high school students working part-time jobs with option for full-time jobs, may not see the need to finish school when they are already making more money without schooling.
> - Emergence of street gangs across some communities in Louisiana; peer pressure from this group may cause some high school students to drop out of school.

Fig. 6.7   Slide 3 Bullet Point List – Summary of Detailed List

Insert & Format Slide 4: In **slide 3**, we discussed the reasons why people think students drop out of high school based on your research interviews. On this **slide 4**, it's time to brainstorm for some possible solutions to this social problem. To insert **slide 4**, we have to duplicate **slide 3** and modify it to reflect **slide 4** information because from **slide 3** forward, all slides in the presentation have the same background and formatting. This will save us time from repeating the same steps as in **slide 3**. Let's assume that for this project, based on your research interviews, you brainstormed and came up with the following solutions:

Suggested Solutions for Preventing High School Dropout in Louisiana State

- ✓ High school Counselors should collaborate with some mentorship support groups (Big Brother/Big Sister) in the community and encourage troubled high school students to sign up for mentorship provided by these groups. According to experts on social issues, members of these mentorship programs serve as role models for troubled youth, and have helped to turn around some students with poor course grades from F to A – C students. Students enrolled in the mentorship program get help with their homework; learn the importance of education; learn how to work hard and stay in school; take responsibility for their future; and learn proper behaviors as young adults. Expert studies have shown that the mentorship programs have reported high success rates in many communities.

- ✓ The Counselors should also encourage students to utilize the school tutoring lab as often as necessary to get help with their homework if they are experiencing difficulties grasping the subject matter. Some students have the tendency to drop out of high school due to frustration from not understanding the subject matter; it makes them feel not smart enough to continue schooling. Some go as far as thinking that they are stupid and can never learn anything. At this point, without proper guidance, these students simply drop out of school.

- ✓ Provide behavioral counselling for children of divorced parents to help them deal with any emotional issues that may interfere with school work or push them to the point of dropping out of school.

- ✓ Community leaders in Louisiana state should collaborate with nonprofit organizations to establish a program initiative such as "After-School Program" designed to help the "At Risk High Schoolers." This type of initiative is operated primarily by volunteer qualified teachers who are on hand at the center to help the students with homework. They teach students good study habits and good behaviors as young adults. Students also learn how to stay out of trouble; to stay in school and graduate from high school. Social issues experts have reported high success rates on communities operating this type of program.

- ✓ Divorced parents should make proper arrangements as specified in the divorce decree to spend as much time as possible with their children and let them know they are still very much loved regardless of the divorce. Most importantly, divorced parents should explain clearly to their children that they are not the cause of the divorce to eliminate the children's feelings of guilt. The guilt of a child knowing that he or she may be the reason mom and dad are now divorced is too much of an emotional baggage for any young person to bear.

- ✓ All parents should maintain strong family discipline at homes, and endeavor to support their children's education by helping them with homework. Talk to them very often; and continue to "sing" the same message: "Stay in school, no matter how though things get, we are always here to help because we love you and want the best for you." Even if you think they are not listening, keep on talking to them; at some point, they begin to hear you.

1. To insert **slide 4**, at the navigation pane (left) of your PPT presentation right-click the **3rd slide**.
2. From the displayed short menu, select **Duplicate Slide**. The duplicated slide will appear below the original slide with the same title heading.
3. Delete the title heading and type **What Can We Do to Keep Our High Schoolers in School and See them Graduate from High School?** Change the title font size to **28** and **Center** title.
4. Click the placeholder of the duplicated slide, highlight the entire text in the placeholder below the title press **Delete** on your keyboard and begin typing text.
5. To display text in bullet list, repeat **step 4** of **slide 3** above. In bullet points, summarize the list of detailed suggested solutions for preventing high school dropout in Louisiana State contained in the blue box above.
6. Change font size of bulleted points texts to **22**.

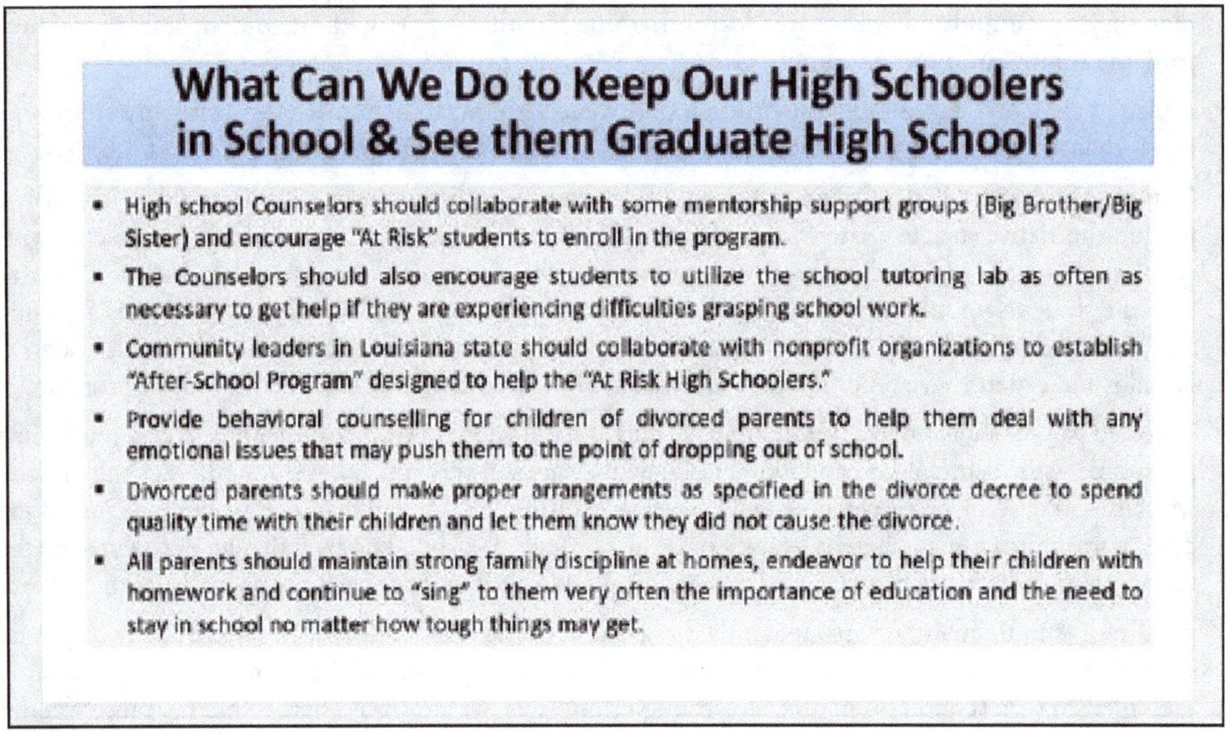

Fig. 6.8   Slide 4 Bullet Point List – Summary of Detailed List

304 | Basic Computing Concepts

Insert & Format Slide 5: While educators, school counselors, and community leaders collaborate to find solutions to the high dropout rate in Louisiana state high schools, the students themselves bear some responsibility to solving this social problem. In this section, we take a look at what the high school students (the audience of your presentation) can do to help themselves and improve their lives. On this project, the focus of their responsibility is to take advantage of the resources provided by their schools and program initiatives established by the community.

Students' Responsibilities to the Solution of High Dropout Rate in Louisiana State High Schools

- ✓ Students, stay in school, listen to/respect your parents and teachers; study very hard and always do your homework.
- ✓ Get help with homework from your school tutoring lab if you need it.
- ✓ Enroll in a mentorship program to have a good role model in your life that you can look up to.
- ✓ Enroll in your community After School Program for help with homework.
- ✓ This is your life; this is your future; take charge of it and become a productive member of our society.

1. To insert **slide 5**, repeat the same steps as in **slide 4** to duplicate and insert **slide 5**
2. Click the placeholder of the duplicated slide, highlight the entire text in the title placeholder, press **Delete** on your keyboard and type: **What Can the High Schoolers in Our Community Do to Reduce High Dropout Rate?** Change the title heading to font size **28**.
3. Click the placeholder of the duplicated slide, highlight the entire text in the placeholder below the title, press **Delete** on your keyboard and begin typing text.
4. To display text in bullet list, repeat **step 4** of **slide 3** above. In bullet points, summarize the list of students' responsibilities to reducing high school dropout rate detailed blue box above.
5. Change font size of bulleted points texts to **22.**

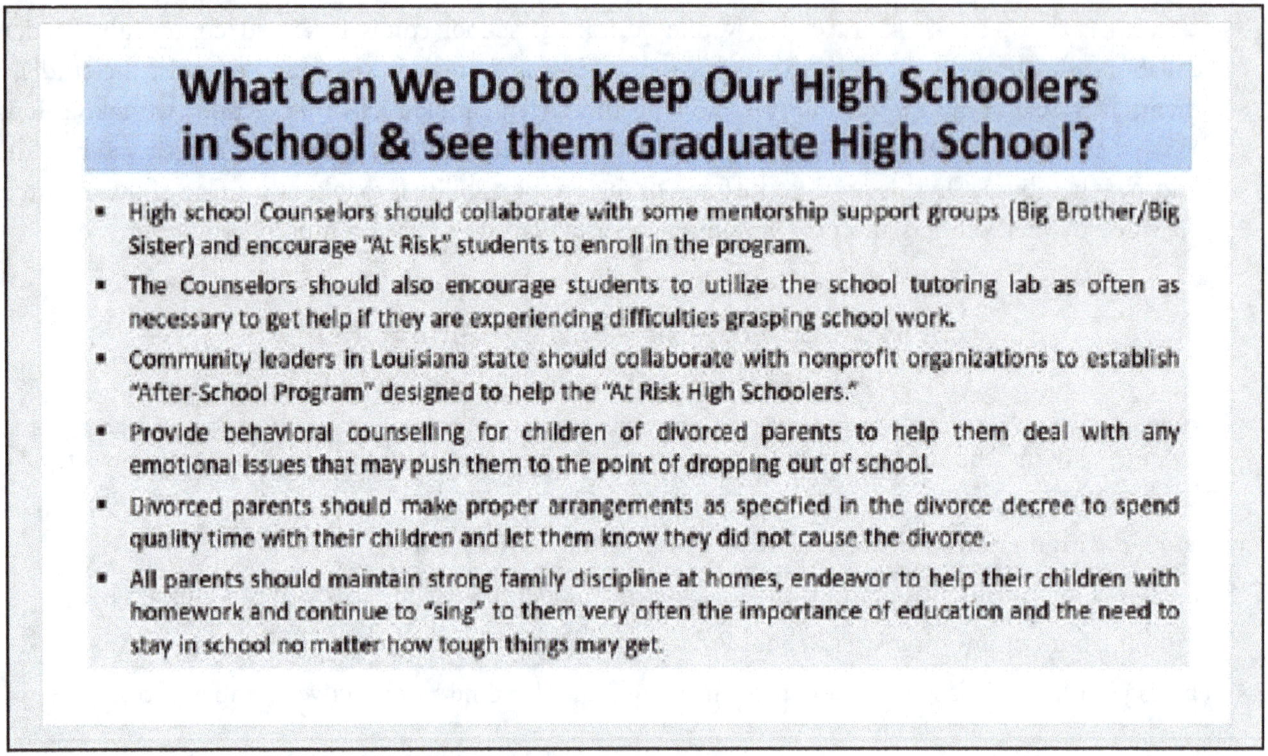

> ### What Can We Do to Keep Our High Schoolers in School & See them Graduate High School?
>
> - High school Counselors should collaborate with some mentorship support groups (Big Brother/Big Sister) and encourage "At Risk" students to enroll in the program.
> - The Counselors should also encourage students to utilize the school tutoring lab as often as necessary to get help if they are experiencing difficulties grasping school work.
> - Community leaders in Louisiana state should collaborate with nonprofit organizations to establish "After-School Program" designed to help the "At Risk High Schoolers."
> - Provide behavioral counselling for children of divorced parents to help them deal with any emotional issues that may push them to the point of dropping out of school.
> - Divorced parents should make proper arrangements as specified in the divorce decree to spend quality time with their children and let them know they did not cause the divorce.
> - All parents should maintain strong family discipline at homes, endeavor to help their children with homework and continue to "sing" to them very often the importance of education and the need to stay in school no matter how tough things may get.

Fig. 6.9   Slide 5 Bullet Point List

Insert & Format Slide 6: Continuing with the assigned project, based on the responses from your research interviews, and brainstorming, you were able to obtain some solutions to the problem. In this section you will tell your audience the benefits of staying in school to graduate from high school, such as go to college, acquire good knowledge and skill, get a good job, with the chance of a better future. You have to brainstorm again to come up with some benefits of staying in school to graduate from high school. Listed below is a detailed list of a few benefits:

Benefits of Graduating from High School

- ✓ Staying in school to graduate with a High School Diploma gives you the opportunity to study for and take the SAT Exam, the passing score of which is the basis of your admission into a good college or university.
- ✓ Obtaining a High School Diploma provides you the strong knowledge and foundation you need to further you education by going to college. It is the starting point of your lifetime educational journey to higher endeavors up to graduate school and beyond.
- ✓ Knowledge is Power – Good college education arms you with varieties of knowledge that empowers you to analyze life situations, make informed decisions about your life, accept challenges with successful outcomes, and function as a productive member of our society.
- ✓ Obtaining a college degree opens many doors to better job opportunities, higher paying jobs, with good careers of a lifetime which makes you a decent and well respectable person by your peers.
- ✓ Generally, here in United States, you must have at least a High School Diploma to be employed at any minimum wage job except under some extenuating circumstances depending on the employer and type of job involved.

1. To insert **slide 6**, repeat the same steps as in **slide 5** to duplicate and insert **slide 6**.
2. Click the placeholder of the duplicated slide, highlight the entire text in the title placeholder, press **Delete** on your keyboard and type: **What are the Benefits of Graduating from High School?** Change the title heading to font size **28**.
3. Click the placeholder of the duplicated slide, highlight the entire text in the placeholder below the title, press Delete on your keyboard and begin typing text.
4. To display text in bullet list, repeat step 4 of slide 3 above. In bullet points, summarize the list of benefits of graduating from high school detailed blue box above.
5. Change font size of bulleted points texts to **22**.
6. Click the notes section of **slide 6** and type the paragraph in the blue text box below:

A Note of Caution: Potential employers view someone who dropped out of high school as an irresponsible person who fails to finish what he/she started. They may use this behavior to evaluate someone's job performance and see the person as a poor performer who never completes assigned tasks.

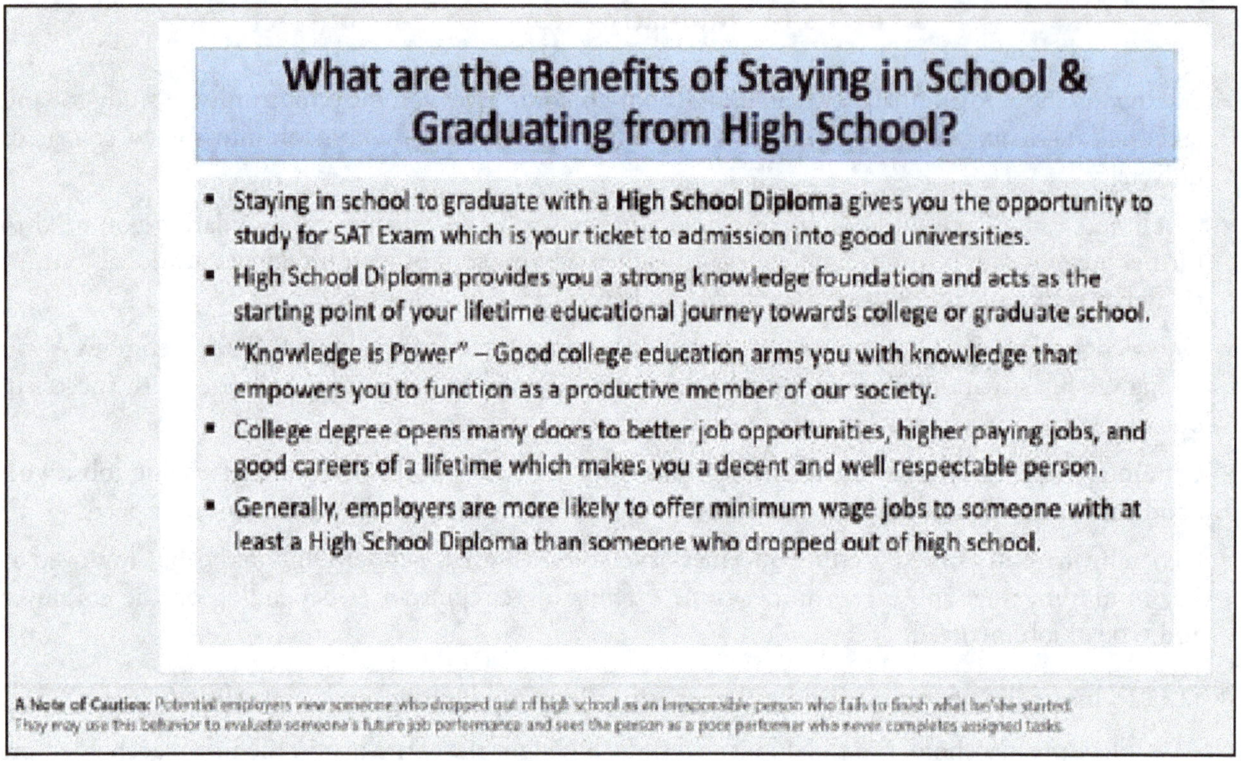

> **What are the Benefits of Staying in School & Graduating from High School?**
>
> - Staying in school to graduate with a **High School Diploma** gives you the opportunity to study for SAT Exam which is your ticket to admission into good universities.
> - High School Diploma provides you a strong knowledge foundation and acts as the starting point of your lifetime educational journey towards college or graduate school.
> - "Knowledge is Power" – Good college education arms you with knowledge that empowers you to function as a productive member of our society.
> - College degree opens many doors to better job opportunities, higher paying jobs, and good careers of a lifetime which makes you a decent and well respectable person.
> - Generally, employers are more likely to offer minimum wage jobs to someone with at least a High School Diploma than someone who dropped out of high school.
>
> *A Note of Caution:* Potential employers view someone who dropped out of high school as an irresponsible person who fails to finish what he/she started. They may use this behavior to evaluate someone's future job performance and sees the person as a poor performer who never completes assigned tasks.

Fig. 6.10   Slide 6 Bullet Point List – Summary of Detailed List with Additional Notes

Insert Slide 7, Insert Graphics & Format Slide: As we approach the end of this presentation, let's make **slide 7** a little more interesting by adding some graduation graphics to show your high school audience that hard work really does pay off when they are crowned with graduation outfit on that very special day.

1. Click **Insert** tab at the ribbon, click **New Slide** down arrow and select **Two Content.**

2. At the top placeholder, **Click to add title**, and type this title: **The Hard-Work Paid Off – It's Graduation Day!** Center the title and change the font size to **40.**

3. Format **Title Placeholder** – Highlight the **Main Title**, click **Format** tab, in the **Shape Style** group, click the down arrow, and select **Subtle Effect-Blue, Accent 5** (on the 5th row).

4. **Click to add text** on the first box subtitle, and type **"Homework is Over"**.

5. Backspace to delete the bullet point on the subtitle; center the text, change font size to **36,** apply **Bold** and **Red** color fonts to both subtitles.
6. **Click to add text** on the second box **subtitle**, and type "**Let's Celebrate!**"
7. Repeat **step 5** to format the second box **subtitle**.

Insert & Format Graphics:

1. Click anywhere below first box **subtitle**, and click **Insert** tab at top ribbon.
2. In the **Images** group, click **Pictures** down arrow, and select **Online Pictures.** You must be connected to the Internet to perform this step.
3. If you already have a picture save on your computer that you want to insert in this slide, click **Pictures** down arrow, click **This Device**.
4. In the open Explorer widow click the picture you saved. If the picture is saved in a folder, in the open Explorer window, double-click the folder to open the it, then click on the picture to insert it into the slide.
5. For this project, we are using online, pictures. Click the first box under subtitle **Homework is Over** in the open window, under **Online Pictures**, type **Books** in the search box and press **Enter** key.
6. From the varieties of book pictures displayed, click on any stack of books of your choice, and click **Insert (1)** tab at bottom of the window.
7. Click the inserted picture, holding down the mouse, drag to resize and adjust the picture to place it under the subtitle **Homework is Over**.
8. Click the second box subtitle, **Let's Celebrate!**, repeat **steps 5 & 6**, type **Graduation** in the search box, and press **Enter.**
9. From the varieties of graduation cap pictures displayed, click on any picture of of your choice, and click **Insert (1)** tab at bottom of the window.
10. When you download and insert your chosen picture, it comes with this link:

    This Photo by Unknown Author is licensed under CC BY-NC

11. Double-click the link, in the **Clipboard** group at top ribbon, click **Cut** to remove the link.

12. Click each of the pictures one at a time, click **Picture Boarder** down arrow at top ribbon, click **Weight**, and select **¼ pt**. to block and separate each picture on the slides of the box.
13. If you have properly followed all steps to insert slide 7, insert graphics, and format slide outlined above, your completed **slide 7** will look like **fig. 6.11** displayed below.

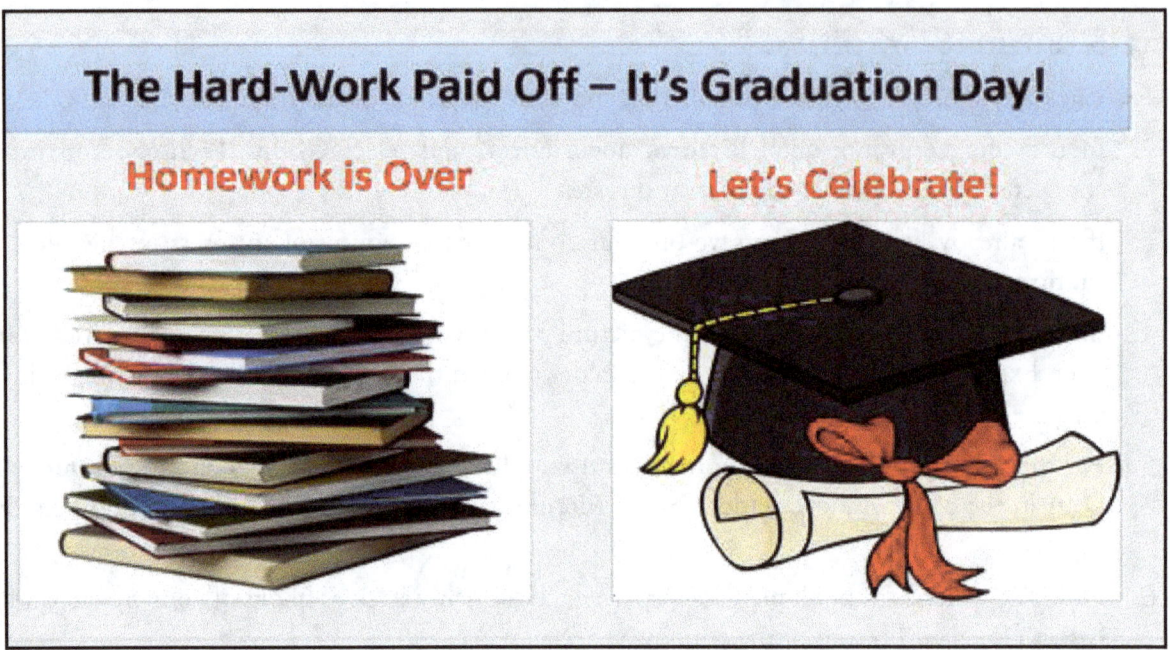

Fig. 6.11　　　　　　　　　　Slide 7 with Graduation Graphics

Insert & Format Slide 8: We'll use **slide 8** as a summary slide outlining in bullet list items discussed in your presentation. This summary slide is optional, but recommended as a way of remining your audience once again what has been discussed. Sometimes seeing the topics again may jug the memory of someone or people in the audience who may have a question about the presentation. This slide provides opportunity for your audience to ask any questions they may have about your speech.

1. Click **Insert** tab at the ribbon, click **New Slide** down arrow and select **Title Only.**
2. At the top placeholder, **Click to add title**, and type this title: **Presentation Summary.** Change the title font size to **60**, apply **Bold** font and **Center** the title.

3. Apply the same formatting on **slide 2** main heading as in **step 2** of **slide 1** above: **Subtle Effect-Blue, Accent 5** (located on the 5th row) and **Center** the title.

4. Repeat the same steps as in **slides 3 – 6** above to manually add placeholder below the main title to enable you type your text.

5. In the **Style Shape** group at top ribbon, click **Fill Shape** down arrow, and select **Light Gray, Background 2** to change **slide 8** background.

6. On **slide 8**, in bullet points, type the summary of main headings of **slides 1 – 7** as listed in the blue box below.

7. Change text font size of the bullet list to **24**; change the font size of **Any Questions?** to **54,** apply **Red** color font to the text and **Bold** font to make it stand out.

Presentation Summary

✓ Stay in School for a Better Future

✓ National Center for Education Statistics (NCES): 2013 -2017 High School Dropout Rates.

✓ Why do Youths in Our Community Drop Out of High School?

✓ What Can We Do to Keep Our High Schoolers in School & See them Graduate High School?

✓ What Can the High Schoolers in Our Community Do to Reduce High Dropout Rate?

✓ What are the Benefits of Staying in School & Graduating from High School?

✓ The Hard-Work Paid Off – It's Graduation Day!

Any Questions?

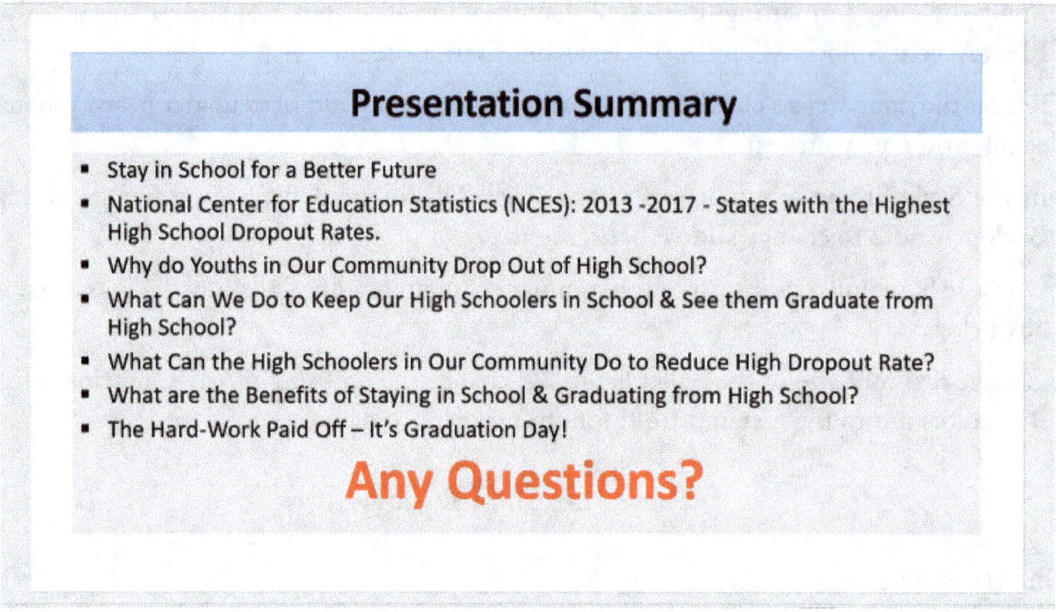

Presentation Summary

- Stay in School for a Better Future
- National Center for Education Statistics (NCES): 2013 -2017 - States with the Highest High School Dropout Rates.
- Why do Youths in Our Community Drop Out of High School?
- What Can We Do to Keep Our High Schoolers in School & See them Graduate from High School?
- What Can the High Schoolers in Our Community Do to Reduce High Dropout Rate?
- What are the Benefits of Staying in School & Graduating from High School?
- The Hard-Work Paid Off – It's Graduation Day!

Any Questions?

Fig. 6.12   Slide 8 – Summary of Presentation

CHANGE SLIDE BACKGROUND THEMES

Throughout this project, we have used **Light Gray, Background 2** on all slides for consistency and to keep things simple for beginners in PowerPoint presentation. As you continue your study into intermediate and advance levels, you will become familiar with more features of PPT and use them to make presentation look more attractive. The **Design** tab provides you with varieties of background themes and color fonts you can use on your slides. The selected theme applies outside the placeholder and does not change the color of the placeholder containing texts, but the title placeholder color font will change.

Apply Themes to Presentation Slides

1. On the left pane, click **slide 1** of your presentation. When you change themes from **slide 1,** the same theme will apply to all slides in your presentation. In future presentations, choice of theme is optional.
2. Click **Design** tab at top ribbon to display all themes in the row **(fig. 6.13)**.
3. For this project, select **Organic** (8th theme on the row) and notice all slides in this presentation change to the same theme. After applying the organic theme, your slides will assume the same theme as **slide 1** and look like **fig.6.14** below.

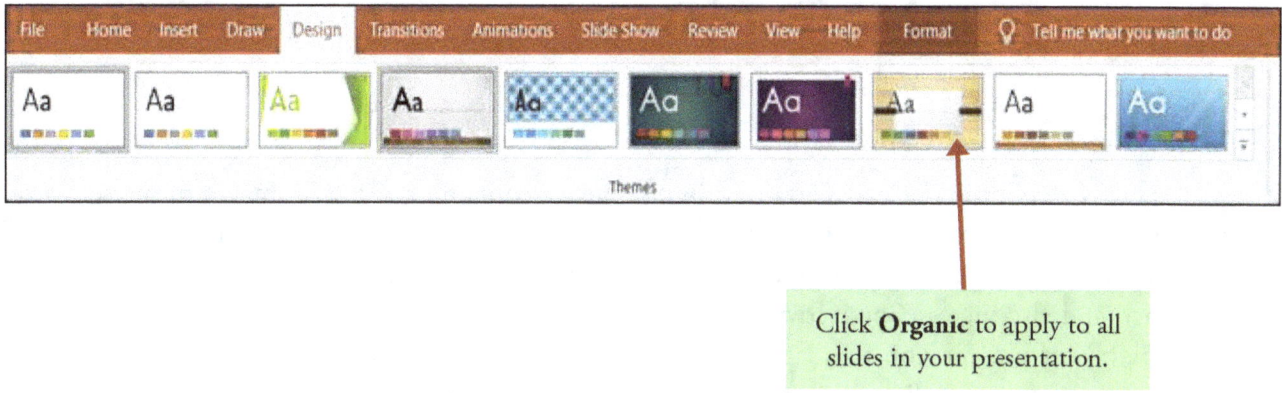

Click **Organic** to apply to all slides in your presentation.

Fig. 6.13   PPT Design Themes

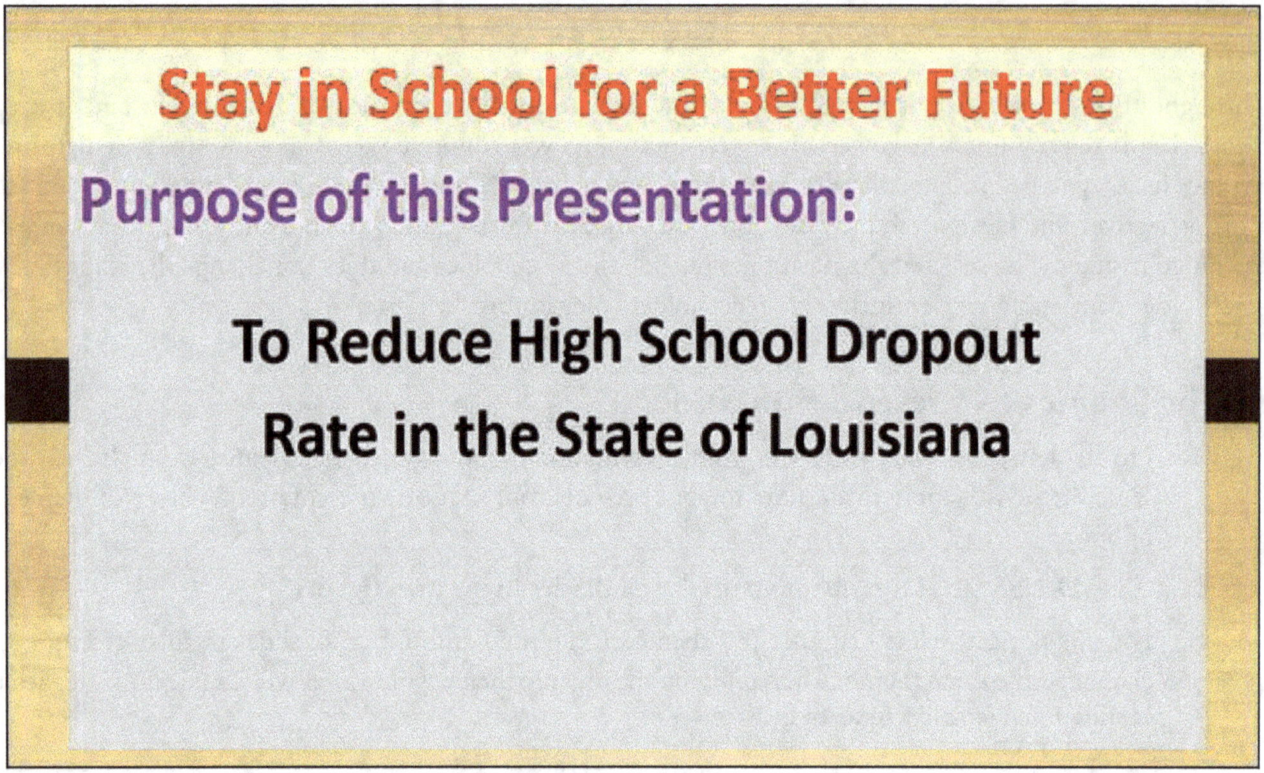

> **Stay in School for a Better Future**
>
> **Purpose of this Presentation:**
>
> **To Reduce High School Dropout Rate in the State of Louisiana**

Fig. 6.14   **Slide 1 with Organic Theme**

Display Presentation in Slide Show

The slideshow is a collection of pages arranged in a sequence containing text and images for presentation to an audience. PowerPoint slideshows are flexible and allows you, the presenter to customize the slides according to how you want to present them. For presenters, it helps to improve audience focus, increase visual impact, and also increase interactivity and spontaneity during a presentation. Slide show also allows you to display your presentation in a larger format to occupy the entire screen making the texts appear bigger and easier for your audience to read. For beginners in PPT presentation, at this level during your presentation, you have two options for displaying your slides. You can slide show your presentation from the beginning slide or from current slide of your choice.

1. Click **Slide Show** tab at top ribbon, in the **Start Slide Show** group, select **From Beginning**. This displays your presentation from **slide 1,** one at a time till the end.
2. When finished discussing **slide 1**, click the slide to display **slide 2**.
3. Continue clicking on one slide at a time to move through all your presentation slides.
4. Click **From Current Slide** to display from any slide you select.
5. If you want to go back to a slide already shown, right-click on the current slide to display selection options.
6. From the displayed menu, click either **Previous** or **Last Viewed**.
7. When finished with slide show presentation, right-click the current slide and select **End Show**.

Display Slides In Slide Sorter View

Slide sorter is a good feature that allows you to get an overall view of your entire presentation slides. This helps you to ensure that your topics are organized in a way that makes them connect very well to one another and for effective presentation delivery. If your materials are not arranged the way you want them to be, you can rearrange them in the **Slide Sorter** view. To display slides in slide sorter view, follow these steps.

1. Click the **View** tab at the ribbon.
2. In the **Presenters View** group, click **Slide Sorter**. Notice that the overall slide background theme outside the placeholders have changed from white to **Organic** design we selected but the light gray color font of the placeholders remains the same.
3. To rearrange slides, click the slide in slide sorter view, holding down the mouse, drag the slide to the location of your choice.
4. To return to normal view, click **Normal** tab at top ribbon.

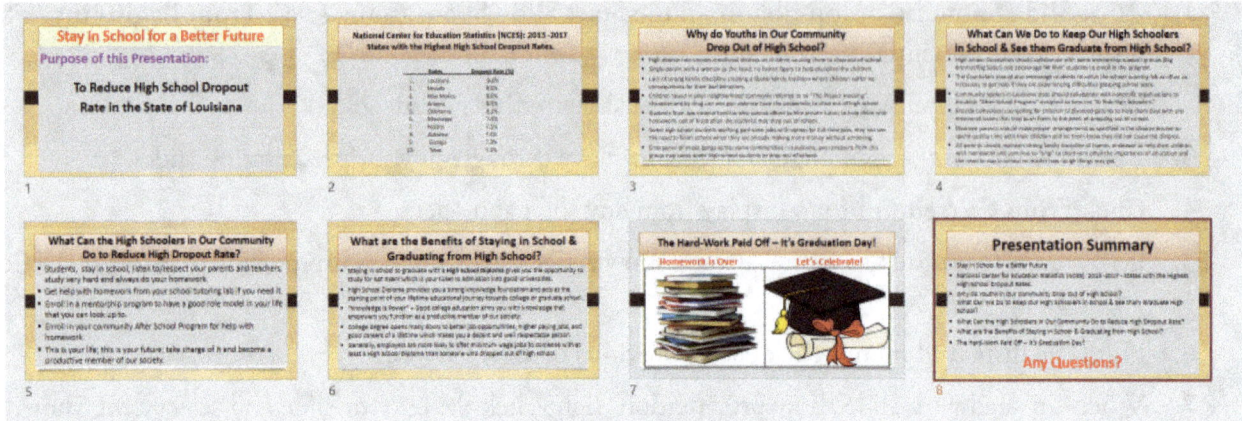

Fig. 6.15   **Presentation Slides in Slide Sorter View**

Outline View

In PowerPoint the outline view displays your presentation as an outline made up of all the titles and main text from each slide. The **Outline View** is located in the **Presentation Views** group. Click the **View** tab at top ribbon to display the **Presentation Views** group, and click **Outline View**. In this view, each title of your presentation slide appears on the left side of the pane along with a slide icon and slide number. The main text is indented under the slide title. You can print the outline view and use it as a guide during your presentation to help you remember the order of topics in your presentation.

INSERT HEADER & FOOTER IN PRESENTATION HANDOUTS

Headers and footers in a PowerPoint handout refer to tiny pieces of information such as date, page numbers, and author's name at bottom of the page that serves as an identifier on a PPT document. The date on a PPT handout appears at top right while the author's name appears a bottom left. Header and footer information can be very useful when multiple people in an organization are working on one large project where other people contribute their own written materials. They help to identify individual who contributed topics towards the project and who wrote them. Headers and footers may also include book titles, chapter titles, and name of the author.

Insert Header and Footer

1. Click **Insert** tab at top ribbon, in the **Text** group, click **Header & Footer**.
2. In the open window that follows, click **Notes and Handouts** tab so that the header and footer will only appear on the handouts not on the slides **(fig. 6.16)**.
3. Ensure that **Date and Time** box is checked, if not check the box. Notice that once this box is checked, the button below it, **Update Automatically** is also highlighted. This means that each time you open the PPT file or make any changes to the presentation, the date on the handout will change.
4. If you want to add your name as the creator, check the **Footer** box and type **Prepared by Your Name** in the space provided.
5. Click the **Apply to All** tab, the header and footer information will appear on all your printed handout.

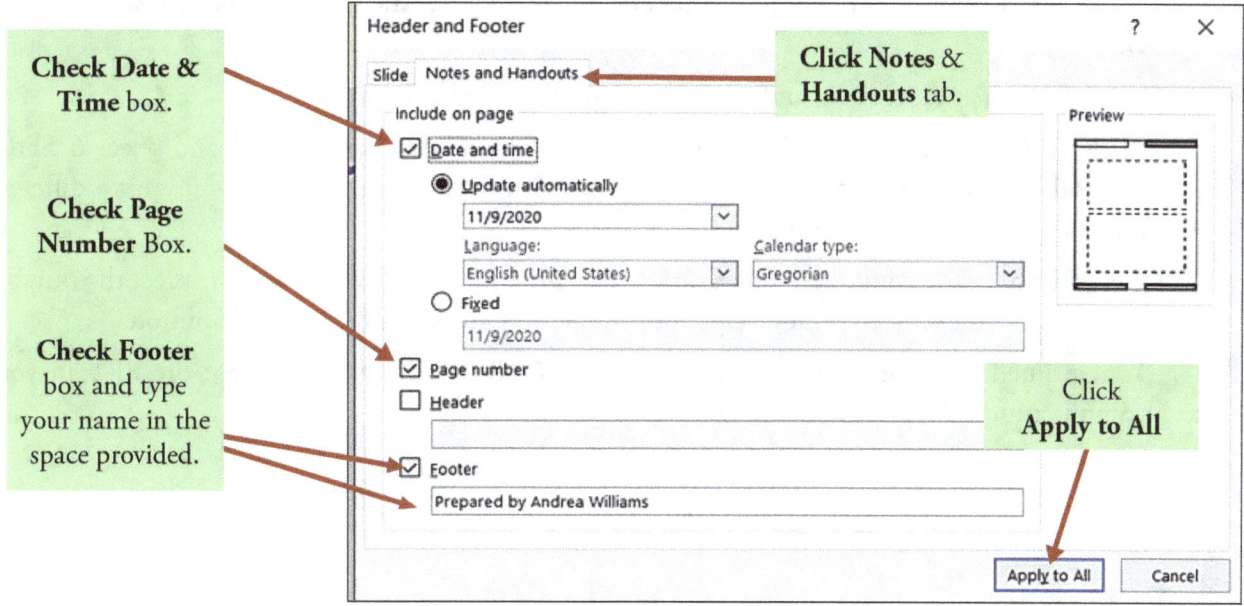

Fig. 6.16   **Handout Header & Footer Window**

Print Presentation Handouts

Printing your presentation handouts is a good way to provide your audience more detailed information about your presentation that they can read on their own at a later time. This means you may have two sets of PPT presentation – the summary PPT and the detailed PPT. To provide your audience with more detailed information, print the handouts from the detailed PPT presentation. For long and complex presentations, the handouts may contain more details too long to put on your slides. Handouts are especially useful for highly technical or complex presentations. For example, they may contain supporting data not included in the detailed PPT presentation, such as contact information, case studies, references, marketing literature, or other materials for the audience. They give your audience something to take away from your presentation, for later review. They are one more way for your audience to be reminded of the key points in your messages. There are **8** slides in this presentation, handouts defaults to **6** slides or less per page. To print the handouts, follow these steps:

1. Click **View** tab at top ribbon, in the **Master Views** group, click **Handout Master** to view the footer and date you inserted into the handouts. Click **Close Master View**, the red **X** to close the view.

2. Click **File** tab at the ribbon, and select **Print** from the displayed left menu.

3. In the **Print** window, under **Settings**, click **Full Page Slides** down arrow, and select **6 Slides Vertical**. This is always the default number of slides per page **(fig. 6.17)**. If you want a different number per page, select that number.

4. Under **Print** at top window, on the **Copies** box, using the up and down arrows, select the number of handouts you want to print or type the number in that box and click **Print** button.

5. Your printed handouts display as shown on **fig. 6.18** below. **Save** and close the PPT in your computer until the presentation day.

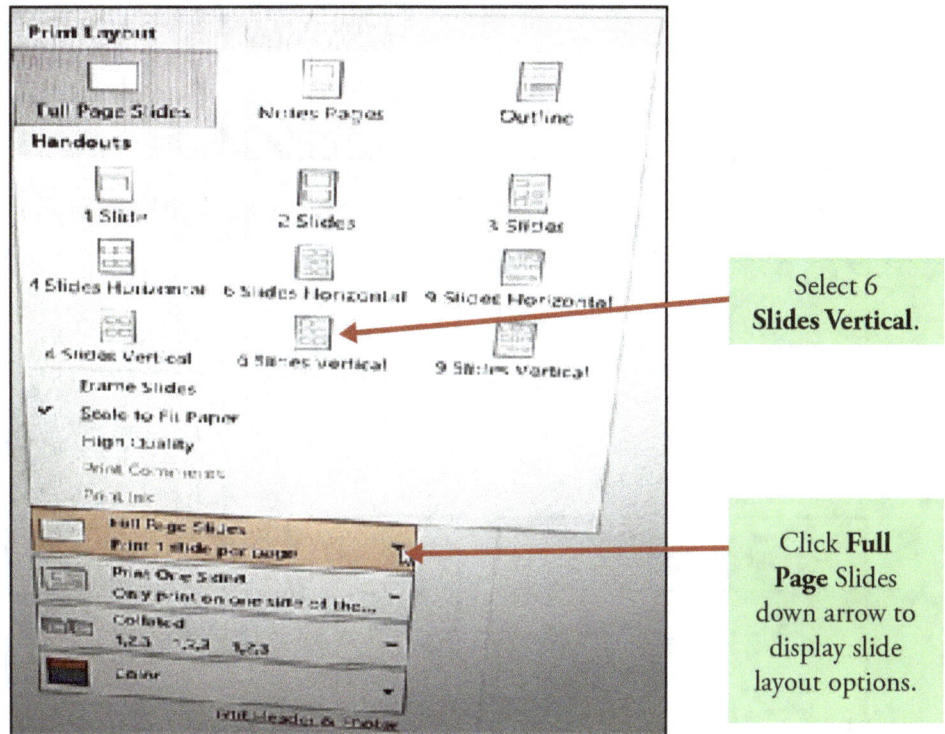

Fig. 6.17 **Slides Print Layout**

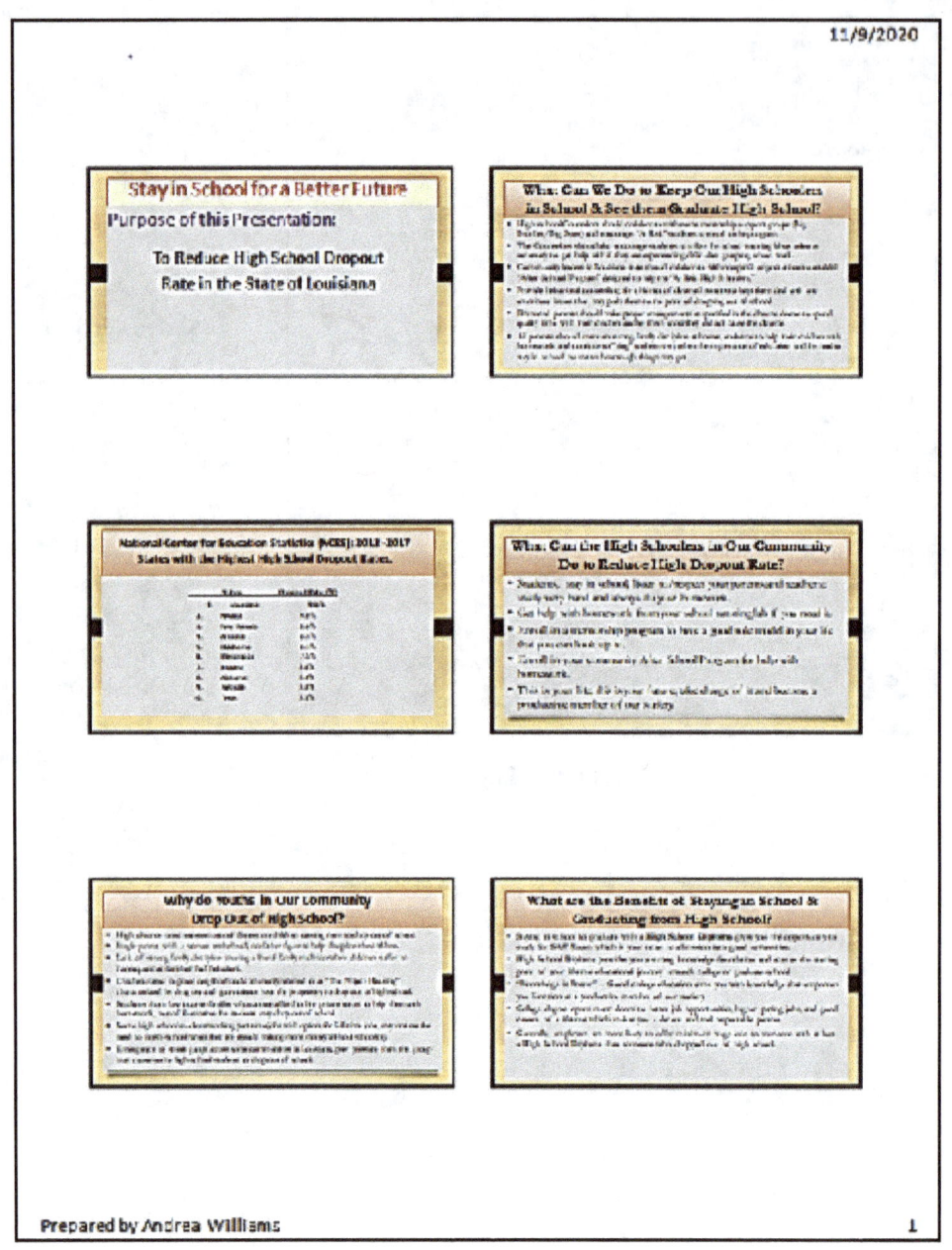

Fig. 6.18   Preview – First Page of Printed Handout. Next 2 Sides will Appear on Page 2

CHAPTER SUMMARY & KEY TERMS

PowerPoint presentation is software used for making visual and graphical presentations before an audience and provides professional looking documents, including handouts for the audience. It is basically a presentation creation tool that produces slideshows with text, images, shapes, animations, audio, and much more. You can create your presentation onto a big screen to display it to others or save it as a visual document for yourself. MS PowerPoint has been the most widely used program for presentations and the leading tool for creating professional presentation documents ever since its introduction in 1987. It gives creators and speakers a chance to present important facts, instructions, and notes with visually pleasing, professional-looking slides. The Quick Access Toolbar is a feature very common with all MS Office products. As an ardent user of Office products, you may already be familiar with this handy tool which was also discussed in MS Word (chapter 4). Quick Access is the toolbar at the very top left of MS Office programs: Word, Excel, and PowerPoint windows. As the name implies, this feature allows you to perform quick actions. The Quick Access Toolbar is made up of four main icons —Save, Undo, Redo, including a down arrow that allows you to customize the toolbar by relocating it where it is more convenient to you while you work. When you first open a PowerPoint program, notice that it opens with a default slide with two placeholders – one for title of your slide and the other placeholder for the subtitle. Depending on the size of your presentation, you have to manually add more slides as you need them.

Before you begin work on your presentation, you must plan the presentation. This planning stage involves researching your presentation topic, data collection, organizing materials , and arranging facts in sequential order for delivery to your audience. When inserting slides and naming title slides, and subtitles, you will follow the plan of presentation to enable your audience gain a good understanding of your message. The top ribbon of a PowerPoint window consists of multiple slides formatting tools, including design tab that provide you with varieties of background themes and color fonts you can use on your slides. The selected theme applies outside the placeholder and does not change the color of the placeholder containing texts, but the title placeholder color font will change. The slideshow is a collection of pages arranged in a sequence containing text and images for presentation to an audience. PowerPoint slideshows are flexible, and allow you to customize the slides according to how you want to present them. For presenters, it helps to improve audience focus, increase visual impact, and also increase interactivity and spontaneity during a presentation. Slide show also allows you to display your presentation in a larger format to occupy the entire screen making the texts appear bigger and easier for your audience to read.

PowerPoint contains feature that allow you to insert slides layout of your choice, display slides in slide sorter view, rearrange slides, duplicate slides, and delete slides as needed. Headers and footers in a PowerPoint handout refer to tiny pieces of information such as date, page numbers, and author's name at bottom of the page that serves as an identifier on a PPT document. The date on a PPT handout appears at top right while the author's name appears at bottom left. Header and footer information can be very useful when multiple people in an organization are working on one large project where other people contribute their own written materials. They help to identify individual who contributed topics towards the project or who wrote them. Headers and footers may also include book titles, chapter titles, and the name of the author. Printing your presentation handouts is a good way to provide your audience more detailed information about your presentation that they can read on their own at a later time. For long and complex presentations, the handouts may contain more details too long to put on your slides. Handouts are especially useful for highly technical or complex presentations.

KEY TERMS

Animations	Handout Master	Slide Show
Background Themes	illustrations Group	Slide Master
Dialog Box Launcher	Master Views Group	Slide Sorter View
Delete Slide	New Slide	Transitions
Design	Picture Boarder	Title Only
Duplicate Slide	Presenters View	Text Box
End Show	Paragraph Group	Title
From Beginning	Placeholder	Subtitle
From Current Slide	Rearrange Slide	
Handouts	Slides	

Demonstrate Your Knowledge & Skill

CHAPTER 6 PRACTICE EXERCISES
INTRODUCTION TO MS POWERPOINT

6.1 – Select True or False answer to the following statements:

1. In a PPT presentation, Slide Show view occupies the full computer screen exactly the way your presentation will look on a big screen.
   a. True
   b. False

2. A slide layout contains formatting and positioning, but does NOT serve as a placeholder for the contents of your presentation.
   a. True
   b. False

3. Each slideshow in a PPT presentation represents a bookmark on the formatting options.
   a. True
   b. False

4. Animations are visual effects that give your PPT slide a unique appearance; and the features allow you to add movement and eye-catching elements on your slide to draw attention from your audience.
   a. True
   b. False

5. The Slide Master is located in the Design tab at the ribbon and allows you to choose the design option you want for your printed handouts.
   a. True
   b. False

6. When you click the Insert tab at top ribbon, and click New Slide down arrow to add a new slide to your presentation, you will see that slides have different layouts options for placeholders that you can choose from.
   a. True
   b. False

7. To type the title of your presentation on a slide, click on the Placeholder to Add title.
   a. True
   b. False

8. The default slide that displays at the left pane of the window when you first open PowerPoint is a blank slide and does not contain any placeholder.
   a. True
   b. False

9. To add a new slide to your presentation, click Insert tab at top ribbon, click New Slide down arrow and select Title Slide.
   a. True
   b. False

10. You can insert graphics into your PPT presentation only from online pictures, and NOT from your computer.
    a. True
    b. False

6.2 – Multiple Choices: Select the best answer to MS PowerPoint concepts, features, and actions described below:

1. PowerPoint presentations are widely used as
   a. Note outlines for teachers
   b. Project presentations by students
   c. Communication of planning
   d. All of above

2. Objects on the slide that hold text are called
   a. Auto layouts
   b. Object holders
   c. Placeholders
   d. Text holders

3. Which PowerPoint view works best for adding slide transition?
   a. Slide sorter view
   b. Slide show view
   c. Slide view
   d. Notes

4. In planning your presentation before you actually write and present it, you should first perform all of the following tasks EXCEPT:
   a. Prior to the actual PPT presentation, write a report on your research findings on a MSWord document; it is from this detailed report that you will create your presentation.
   b. Determine the total number of slides you would need and bookmark them first before you begin typing your main points in the placeholder.
   c. Although the presentation comes from the detailed report, but in your PPT slides, you will be highlighting only the main points of your message in bullet points or numbered items format.
   d. Summarize the main points of your message in a short, concise, and straight-to-the point format while using your MS Word notes to explain details as you make the presentation to your audience.

5. You can edit an embedded organization chart object by ?
   a. Double clicking the organization chart object.
   b. Clicking edit object
   c. Right clicking the chart object, then clicking edit MS-Organization Chart object.
   d. A and C both

6. Special effects used to introduce slides in a presentation are known as?
   a. transitions
   b. effects
   c. Custom animations
   d. Annotations

7. MS PowerPoint contains a feature that allows you to do one of the following on a slide:
   a. Change a slide into a box
   b. Place a slide in the notes area
   c. Duplicate a slide
   d. Attach a slide to an Excel file

8. Slide sorter can be accessed from which tab at the top ribbon?
    a. View
    b. Edit
    c. File
    d. Insert

9. This planning stage of a PPT presentation involves which of the following tasks:
    a. Researching your presentation topic
    b. Collecting data related to your presentation topic
    c. Organizing the materials by arranging facts in sequential order for delivery to your audience
    d. All of the above

10. To reformat a pre-formatted style in PPT, what ribbon tab would you click first?
    a. Slide sorter view
    b. Slide layout
    c. Format
    d. None of above

11. To resize the placeholder in a PPT slide, which one of these should you do?
    a. Right-click the placeholder, and select Resize from displayed menu
    b. Click the edge of the placeholder, holding down the mouse drag and resize
    c. Triple click the placeholder and resize it
    d. Click the placeholder, right-click, then drag and resize

12. Which tab is not available on the left panel when you open a presentation?
    a. Outline
    b. Slides
    c. Notes
    d. All of above are available

13. All of the following statements about PowerPoint are true EXCEPT
    a. You can type text directly into a PowerPoint slide but typing in text box is more convenient.
    b. To add a picture saved on your computer into a slide, click Insert tab, click Picture down arrow, and select This Device.
    c. You can view PowerPoint presentation in Normal, Slide Sorter or Slide Show view.
    d. All types of views are located in the Presentation View group

14. To start Microsoft PowerPoint 2019 application, you should do one of the following:
    a. Click on Start button, click Programs, and select Microsoft PowerPoint
    b. Click on Start button, type Programs, click Windows, and select Microsoft PowerPoint
    c. Click on Start button, click Microsoft package, and select Microsoft PowerPoint
    d. Click on Start button, from the displayed menu, navigate the list and select Microsoft PowerPoint

15. Which of the following section does not exist in a slide layout?
    a. Titles
    b. Lists
    c. Charts
    d. Animations

16. In PowerPoint View tab, all of the following are found in the Master View EXCEPT
    a. Slide Master
    b. Presentation View
    c. Handout Master
    d. Notes Mater

17. Which of the following views is the best way to see your slides all at once and rearrange them in a specific order for your presentation?
    a. Slide sorter view
    b. Notes pages view
    c. Slide view
    d. Outline view

18. Which of the following provides a means of printing out hard copy information about your presentation for your audience?
    a. Slide with animation
    b. Outline view
    c. Notes page
    d. Handout

19. The Microsoft PowerPoint clip gallery allows you to
    a. Add word art images to a slide
    b. Spell check your presentation
    c. Add clip art images to a slide or slides
    d. Add slides to a presentation

20. The part of a displayed slide that allows you to add additional notes to your presentation is located in what area of the slide?
    a. Left area of the slide
    b. Bottom area of the slide
    c. Middle area of the slide
    d. Right area of the slide

21. When working on a PPT presentation, the slides always display in what default view?
    a. Normal view
    b. Special view
    c. Slide show view
    d. Slide sorter view

22. Which is the best view for getting your thoughts for a presentation out on the computer?
    a. Slide view
    b. Notes page view
    c. Slide sorter view
    d. Outline view

23. A second title placeholder that displays on a PPT presentation slide is known as the:
    a. Second title
    b. Placeholder title
    c. Subtitle
    d. Main title

24. Select the correct steps for adding a picture into a PPT presentation slide:
    a. Click the Insert tab at top menu; in the Pictures group, click Images down arrow, and select This Device or Online Pictures
    b. Click the Insert tab at top menu; in the Images group, click Pictures down arrow, and select This Device or Online Pictures.
    c. Click the Format tab at top menu; in the Insert group, click Pictures down arrow, and select This Device or Online Pictures
    d. Click the Design tab at top menu; in the Format group, click Pictures down arrow, and select This Device or Online Pictures

25. In which tab on an open PowerPoint window is the illustrations group located?
    a. Insert tab
    b. View tab
    c. Design tab
    d. File tab

6.3 – Fill in the Blanks with correct terms or words for the statements or descriptions below:

1. To rearrange a slide in your PPT presentation, click the slide and simply _____ it to the location you want.

2. To remove a slide from your PPT presentation, _____ the slide and select Delete slide from the displayed short menu.

3. A quick way to copy a slide at the PPT navigation pane is to right-click the slide and select _____ from the displayed short menu.

4. To display the Format tab at top ribbon of a PPT window, you must first click the _____

5. The first slide you see when you open a PPT window always contains two commands which are _____ and _____

6. If you want to insert a slide in which you plan to add text and picture, your best slide layout option to select is _____.

7. Two main options to display slide show of your PPT presentation is to start either from _____ or from _____.

8. In displaying the main points of your presentation message to the audience, listing the items in _____ is highly recommended.

9. Formatting presentation slides involves changing text fonts, size, color, overall color _____ and appearance of the slides.

10. The _____ tab at the top ribbon of a PPT windows allows you to select the best theme for your presentation slides.

CHAPTER 6 SKILL-BASED PRACTICE PROJECTS INTRODUCTION TO MS POWERPOINT 2019

6.1 – Create a New PowerPoint Presentation and Insert Slides: As we transitioned from 2020 into 2021, the COVID-19 pandemic continued to affect nearly every aspect of our lives. For many families, this health crisis has created a range of unique and individual impacts—including food access issues, income disruptions, and emotional distress. People need some guidelines that will help them manage their health better and stay healthy. Information presented below is taken from ***My Food & My Family***, an organization that specializes in promoting healthy leaving in America. The article below was published on https://www.myfoodandfamily.com/, updated 02/25/2021. **NOTE**: Your summarized bullet point lists are expected to be shorter than all the details in the article and the format of the article will change in your presentation slides because the message is intended to be an instructional guide to healthy living.

Cut back on foods that are high in added sugars, sodium and solid fats

When you are at the grocery store, use the Nutrition Facts Panel to help you compare products in the same category. Look for reduced fat, reduced sodium, and no added sugar options whenever possible. Choose fresh fruit, vegetables or unsalted nuts as snacks more often. Here are some tips to help you:

a. **Choose foods and drinks with little or no added sugars.** Drink water instead of sugary drinks. Try replacing at least one sugar sweetened beverage per day with water. Select fruit for dessert. If whole fruit is not an option, choose 100% fruit juice instead of fruit-flavored drinks. Eat sugary desserts like cake, candy and cookies less often.

b. **Check the Nutrition Facts Panel to compare the sodium levels in foods you buy.** Compare sodium in foods like soup, bread, and frozen meals—and choose the foods with lower numbers. Also consider lower-sodium versions of favorite foods. Add spices or herbs to season food without adding salt.

c. **Eat less foods that are high in solid fats.** Make major sources of dietary saturated fats—such as pizza, sausages, hot dogs, ice cream, cakes, cookies occasional foods, *not* everyday foods. Select leaner cuts of meats or poultry and remove the skin and all visible fat. Choose fat-free or low-fat milk, yogurt, and cheese. Switch from solid fats, like butter or shortening, to oils when cooking or preparing food.

Eat the right amount of calories for you
Everyone has unique caloric needs based on age, activity level and gender. Staying within your caloric needs can help you achieve or maintain a healthy weight.

a. **Enjoy your food, but eat less.** Avoid oversized portions and don't be a member of the "clean plate" club. Leave a few bites from each meal as a simple tool to help you eat less calories at each meal. You can also try using smaller plates, bowls, and glasses at home as a way to control your caloric intake. Most importantly, stop eating when you are satisfied, not full. Eat slowly so your body has a chance to recognize the feeling of fullness.

b. **Try to cook more often at home and bring a brown bag lunch.** When dining out, check posted calorie amounts and choose the lower calorie option. Opt for dishes that are baked, grilled or roasted instead of fried, breaded or sautéed. Choose dishes that include vegetables, fruits, and/or whole grains. Go easy on the bread basket, and be sure to order sauces and salad dressings on the side. If possible, order an appetizer portion or share a meal with a friend. Otherwise, after the order comes to the table, put half your meal in a to-go bag and save it for the next day.

c. Write down what you eat to keep track of how much you eat. For a few days, try journaling to track how much food you're eating. Pay attention to the quantity as well. Try measuring your food out for a few days until you can estimate what the recommended servings of food looks like. Most people tend to underestimate how much they eat so you might be surprised to see how your typical portions compare.

d. Adults who choose to drink alcoholic beverages should do so in moderation. Limit to 1 drink a day for women or to 2 drinks a day for men *(1 drink = 5fl. oz. of wine, 1.5 oz. of spirits, or 12 oz. of beer)*. There are some instances when adults should not consume alcoholic beverages.

Be physically active your way
Start slowly with activities you enjoy – every little bit helps. Try to fit at least 10 minute bouts of activity at a time and work up to at least 30 minutes of activity most days of the week. If you are trying to maintain your weight, the goal is 60 minutes of activity most days of the week. If you are trying to lose weight, shoot for 90 minutes of activity on most days of the week.

a. **Physical Activity Recommendations** The Physical Activity Guidelines for Americans recommend adults to have at least 150 minutes of moderate-intensity physical activity and should perform muscle – strengthening exercises on 2 or more days each week. Youth ages 6-17 years need at least 60 minutes of physical activity per day, including aerobic, muscle-strengthening, and bone strengthening activities.

b. **Note to parents** Make smart living a family affair. Work as a team on activities such as meal planning, grocery shopping, cooking, housecleaning, and yard work. These activities teach kids valuable life skills and give you an opportunity to shine as a role model. Have fun, too, by taking walks, going swimming and playing active games together.

Required:

1. Open MS PowerPoint program to display the default slide with title and subtitle placeholders.

2. On the main title placeholder, type the title of your message: "**Living Healthy in America**" and type the subtitle "**How to Get it Done.**" Highlight title texts, apply bold font and change text color to **Dark Red**.

3. Click the main title placeholders, holding down the mouse, drag to top of slide and resize as needed. Click the subtitled placeholder, drag to the middle of the slide, and resize as needed.

4. Highlight the main title, in the Font group, change font type to **Comic Sans MS**, and change font size to **66**. Repeat the same action on the subtitle placeholder, and change font size to **60**. Use upper case on the first letter of each title word on all slides in the presentation, and **Center** all titles.

5. Use font type **Comic Sans MS** for all title of inserted slides with font size **48**; use font type **Cambria** with font size **28** for all text within inserted slides.

6. Highlight title text, in the **Font** group at top ribbon, click the **Font** color down arrow, and select **Turquoise, Accent 1, Darker 25%** (5th color on the 5th row). Use this font color for all title slides you insert throughout the presentation.

7. Click **Insert** tab at top ribbon, click **New Slide** down arrow, and select **Title Only** layout.

8. Click title placeholder of the new slide and type the first title of the article above highlighted in orange. Title is too long, shorten it to "**Cut Back on Foods with High Sugars, Sodium & Solid Fats.**" Highlight title, apply **Bold** font.

9. Click the **Insert** tab at top ribbon, in the **illustrations** group, click the **Shapes** down arrow, and select the first **Text box** on the top row to create a placeholder for texts.

10. Click and drag the placeholder wide enough to contain texts; right-click, and select **Edit Text** to begin typing.

11. In bullet points, summarize items **a – c** with the main idea of the message making it brief, short, concise, straight to the point, reducing too much detail without losing the main facts of the message.

12. Insert another slide **Title Only** layout, if you need more room for your bullet point summarizes with the same title, but include **(Cont.)** at the end of the title to show it's a continuation of the same slide.

13. Save the PPT presentation file as **6.1-4_HealthyLiving_Firstname_Lastname** in the preferred location on your computer using your first and last name. Submit your completed assignment following the instructor's preferred method – electronically or printed hardcopy for grading.

6.2 – Insert Additional Slides to the Presentation:

More blank slides are required to contain the entire message of the article from *My Food & My Family* presented above. Insert more slides to your presentation and continue summarizing in bullet points, the main ideas of the article about healthy living in America.

Required:

1. Open the PPT file you save in **6.1** above.

2. Repeat steps **6 – 11** of item **6.1** above for the two remaining title headings of the article **highlighted in orange** (for items **a – d** and **a – b**).

3. Insert a new slide with **Title Only** layout if needed to contain summary bullet points for items **a – d**.

4. Use font type **Comic Sans MS** for all title headings of inserted slides with font size **48**; and use font type **Cambria** with font size **28** for all text within inserted slides.

5. At this point you should have about **7 – 8** slides in your presentation. Click the **Save** icon at top ribbon (the 1st icon at upper left of the ribbon) to update your presentation.

6.3 – Insert Graphics, Format Presentation Slides, & Change Slide Background Theme:

The graphics you add to a presentation helps to drive your message home. It must be the type of image that supports the message you are presenting to your audience. In this section, you will be inserting the image of healthy foods to help promote the importance of healthy living. In addition, you will also be formatting all slides and changing the overall slide background theme in your presentation to give it a more professional look.

Required:

1. In the open PPT presentation, click the **Insert** tab at top ribbon, click New Slide down arrow and select **Two Content** slide layout.
2. Click on left placeholder of the slide, in the **Images** group of the **Insert** tab, click **Pictures** down arrow, and select **Online Pictures**. Make sure you are connected to the internet to perform this action.
3. In the long **Search** bar below **Online Pictures**, type **Healthy Foods**, and press **Enter key.**
4. From the displayed food images, select the image named **Diary** and click **Insert (1)** tab at bottom of the picture screen.
5. Click on right placeholder of the slide, in the **Images** group click of the **Insert** tab, click **Pictures** down arrow, select **Online Pictures**, and repeat **step 3** above.
6. From the displayed food images, select the image named **My Healthy Checklist** and click **Insert (1)** at bottom of the picture screen. Close the picture screen.
7. Click on each graphic, click **Format** tab at top ribbon, in the **Picture Style** group, click **Picture Boarder** down arrow, click **Weight** forward arrow, and select **¼ pt.**
8. Click above each picture, click the **Insert** tab at top ribbon, in the **illustrations** group, click the **Shapes** down arrow, and select the first **Text box** on the top row to create a placeholder for texts.
9. Inside the placeholder picture at left, type **Food Class**, on the right picture placeholder, type **Healthy Foods**. Highlight text, change font type to **Cambria**, font size to **28**, and apply **Bold** font to texts.
10. Below each of the pictures, there are links that came along when you downloaded them from online, double-click the links, and click **Cut** in the **Clipboard** group at the **Home** tab.
11. Click **slide 1** of your presentation at left pane, click the **Design** tab at top ribbon, click **Themes** group down arrow, and select **Savon** (6th theme on the last row). This will change the entire background theme of all slides in your presentation.
12. Review all slides and resize any placeholder that shifted when theme background was added to place them in their proper position. Click the **Save** icon at top ribbon to update your presentation.

6.4 – Insert Header & Footer in Presentation Handouts, and Print Slide Handouts:
Printing your presentation handouts is a good way to provide your audience more detailed information about your presentation that they can read on their own at a later time. As a final step in this project, it's time to prepare and print presentation handouts for your audience. First add header and footer to handouts; then print the handouts.

Required:

A. Insert Header & Footer to Slide Handouts

1. Click **Insert** tab at top ribbon; in the **Text** group, click **Header & Footer**.
2. In the open window that follows, click **Notes and Handouts** tab so that the header and footer will only appear on the handouts not on the slides.
3. Ensure that **Date and Time** box is checked, if not check the box. Notice that once this box is checked, the button below it, **Update Automatically** is also highlighted.
4. Add your name as the creator, check the **Footer** box and type **Prepared by Your Name** in the space provided.
5. Click the **Apply to All** tab, the header and footer information will appear on all your printed handouts.
6. Click the **View** tab, in the **Masters View** tab, click **Handout Master** to see the date and footer you added, and click **Close Master View**, red **X**.

B. Print Slide Handouts

1. Click View tab at top ribbon, in the Master Views group, click Handout Master
2. Click File tab at the ribbon, and select Print from the displayed left menu
3. Under Settings, click Full Page Slides down arrow, and select 4 Slides Vertical. You have 8 slides in this presentation which will appear as 4 slides per handout page.
4. Under Print at top window, on the Copies box, using the up and down arrows, select the number of handouts you want to print or type the number in that box and click Print button to print your presentation handouts.
5. Click the **Save** icon at top ribbon to update your presentation file named **6.1-4_HealthyLiving_Firstname_Lastname.**

CHAPTER 7

INTRODUCTION TO INTERNET EXPLORER 11 & ELECTRONIC COMMUNICATION

Internet Explorer 11 (E11) is the eleventh and final version of the Internet Explorer web browser by Microsoft. It was officially released on October 17, 2013 for Windows 8.1 and on November 7, 2013 for Windows 7. It is a software that allows you to use the internet to search for information or use the internet to send/receive e-mail, and view contents of the World Wide Web (WWW). The Internet is a global group of interconnected networks that originated in 1969 as part of Department of Defense ARPANet project. It started initially with only text; graphics began to appear on the World Wide Web (WWW) in 1989. The World Wide Web became a subset of the Internet that displays graphics. Hyperlinks are connections to other Web pages and viewed with a graphical browser. The advent of the WWW drew commercial interest in the Internet all over the world and has continued to this present day. It connects you to the Internet to display Web pages that allow you to search for information. The Internet receives e-mail, assists with downloading and transferring files from one location to another, displays Web site graphics, and plays audio and video files associated with a Web site. Windows Internet Explorer web browser was developed by Microsoft and released on March 19, 2009 for Windows XP, Windows Vista, and Windows 7 operating systems, including Windows Server 2003 and Windows Server 2008. It is available in both 32-bit and 64-bit. Within the last decade, Internet Explorer browser and the top menu bar has gone through updates to provide users varieties of options when surfing the Internet. E11 is the latest version of Internet Explorer that comes with Windows 10 packed with new features that make web browsing faster, easier, and safer than ever. MS Internet Explorer window has several buttons and icons located just below the browser at the toolbar, each serving specific purposes in searching for information and performing specific settings from **Tools** tab.

The Internet also plays a major role in electronic communications around the world using free emailing services offered by such companies as Yahoo, Hotmail, Gmail, MSN Network, etc. Internet serves as the main vehicle through which free web-based email services can work by providing the platform upon which emailing is facilitated. We live in a fast-paced world where everything is done in a hurry. People need information as soon as possible to make decisions about their finances, jobs, education, and other issues in their personal lives. Organizations typically require information to make business decisions; the information is needed very quickly because waiting till tomorrow or even the next minute may be too late and could cost some business organizations millions of dollars. The new world of information technology provides us online access to the most efficient and fastest means to send and receive information electronically within seconds. This method of communication is typically referred to as **Emailing**. Emailing and instant messaging have become by far the quickest means of communication in our society as we strive to stay in touch with other people. These two forms of communication can only take place with a computer or cell phone while connected to the Internet.

Learning Objectives: After completing this chapter, you will be able to:

- Login to the Internet, navigate Internet Explorer window, and identify various parts.
- Describe the Internet Explorer address bar, and use the web browser.
- Change Internet default home page, save a web page on your computers and print it.
- Create, use the Favorite center, and learn common internet explorer terms.
- Set the default browser on new computers or change an existing one.
- Connect to the internet and understand types of internet connection.
- Disable Add-ons, Pop-ups, and delete unwanted webpages to improve computer speed.
- Perform Internet searches effectively, and share files and printers on the Internet.
- Define emailing, email account, email client, and learn how emailing works.
- Create an e-mail account online and describe parts of an email window.
- Create a message; send an email; reply or forward a message to someone else or multiple recipients, and add an attachment to an email message.
- Create an email contact list or address book, and insert electronic signature to outgoing email messages.

LOGIN TO INTERNET EXPLORER AND NAVIGATE THE WINDOW

When you open **Internet Explorer 11**, at first glance, you will notice the new features added just below the top menu that allow users to enjoy surfing the Internet. Online functionalities now work faster because the icons people use most often are placed at their fingertips. Other features of the address bar include support for pasting multi-line URLs, an improved model for inserting the selection caret, and selecting words, or entire URLs in the Address bar. As an added feature of the Explorer, if a website or add-on causes a tab to crash, only that tab is affected. The browser itself remains stable and other tabs remain unaffected, thereby minimizing any disruption to your browsing experience. This feature is known as **Automatic Tab Crash Recovery.** To successfully log into the Internet, you must enter the Internet address in the browser using correct address format as shown in **Table 7.1** below. The new features of Internet Explorer 11 are described in **fig. 7.1** below.

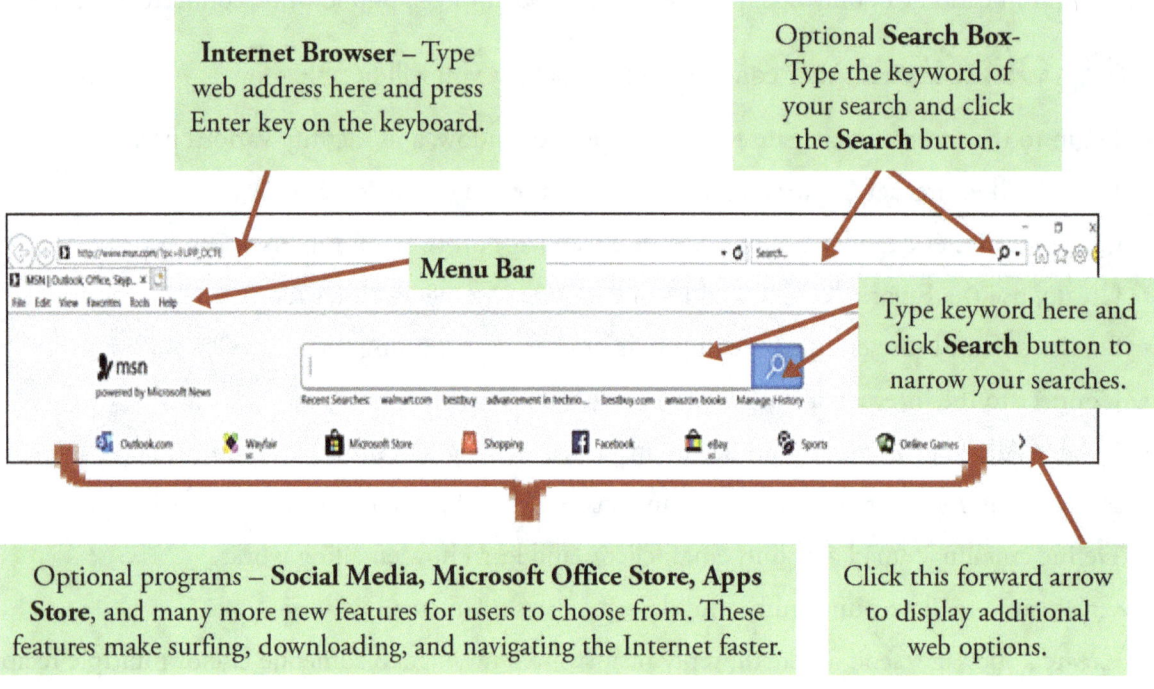

Fig. 7.1   **Internet Explorer 11 with New Features**

The Internet Explorer Address Bar

Part of Web Address	Description
http	The abbreviation of **Hypertext Transfer Protocol**—the standard **protocol** for retrieving Web sites. Another protocol is **ftp**, or **File Transfer Protocol.** A protocol is a set of rules for transferring data over the Internet.
://	Three characters identified by Internet creators for separating the protocol from the rest of the Web address. These particular three characters were identified because they had never appeared together in computer programs and other computer-related contexts.
www.firstgov.gov	This is the domain name. The domain name includes the abbreviation for World Wide Web (www), the name of the organization, and the domain type—**.gov** stands for government. Not all domain names start with www, but many do. Other domain types include **.com** (commercial), **.edu** (education), **.org** (organization), **.net** (network), **.mil** (military), and **.mus** (music). Most countries have their own domain types such as **.ca** for Canada and **.fr** for France.

Table 7.1

Inline Search within Pages

Every Internet Explorer web page you open contains a **Search** box located at the top right corner of the webpage. This makes it easier for users to perform instant searches while surfing the Internet. This feature **(fig.7.2)** is known as **In-line Find Toolbar**, which can also be activated to appear at top left of the screen by pressing **CTRL+F**. Internet Explorer displays the number of items matching your search word and highlights in yellow, **fig. 7.3** below shows all instances of found words while allowing the user to continue the navigation normally.

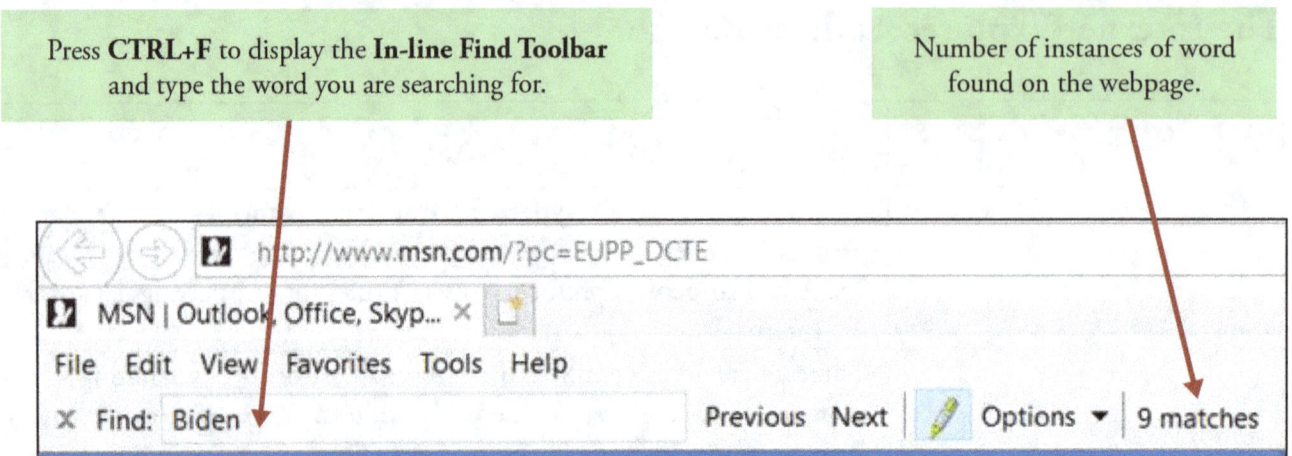

Fig. 7.2   **Internet Find Feature for Instant Searches**

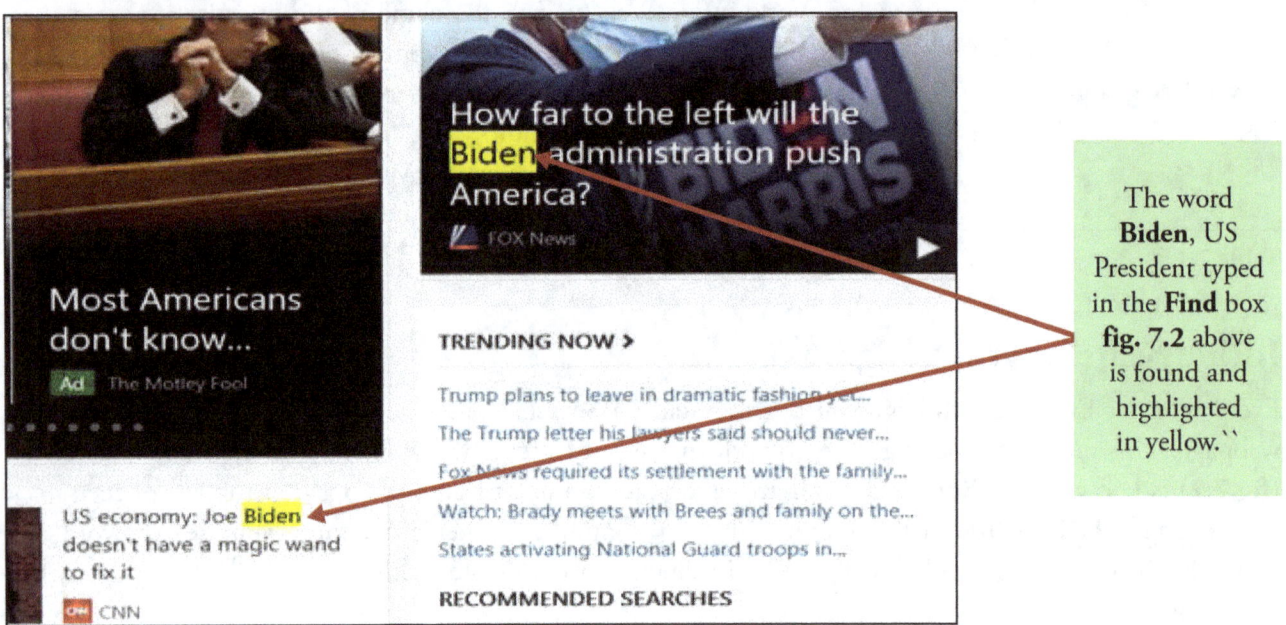

Fig. 7.3   **Internet Find Feature Highlighted 2 Searches Found**

(Total of 9 searches were found see **fig**, **7.2** above, 2 of the found word shown in this image)

342 | *Basic Computing Concepts*

CONNECTING TO THE INTERNET & TYPES OF INTERNET CONNECTIONS

The three important factors to consider before connecting to the Internet are: your computer equipment, the type of connection you want, and your Internet service provider. In order to make the right choice of connection equipment and service provider, it is important to consider what you expect from your Internet connection in terms of speed, reliability, and cost. Majority of the computers in the market today are configured for Internet access, which means they come already equipped with all the necessary hardware to enable them connect to the Internet. The minimum speed requirement for Internet connection on a computer is at least **512 MB** of RAM (random access memory) and a processor speed of **600 MHz** or faster. Although a faster processor and more RAM enables you to travel the Internet quickly, the travel speed is often determined by three important factors such as the speed of your computer equipment connected to the Internet and the speed of the equipment utilized by your Internet service provider (ISP). The speed of your ISP equipment can slow you down. For example, when accessing the Internet at any time of the day while others are doing the same thing, you may experience a significant reduction in speed.

The two main categories of Internet connection are **dial-up** and **broadband**. Dial-up is a type of connection in which your computer is connected directly to a phone jack. With a dial-up connection, you can only be either on the phone or on the Internet at a time but not both at the same time because each action ties up the phone line for the other. Dial-up connection is rarely used these days because of its relatively slow speed when compared to broadband connection types. Broadband consists of various types of Internet connection such as: **Cable, DSL, Wireless, Satellite**, and in most cases **Internet TV**, which includes **WebTV** or **MSN® TV**. These types of Internet connections are all referred to as **broadband** Internet communication characterized by "always on" connections. This means that your computer is always connected to the Internet, even when you are not actively working online. With broadband connection, you can be on the phone and on the Internet at the same time without losing speed.

- ### Cable
  This is a modem that transmits at more than **1 Mbps** (million bits per second). With a cable Internet connection, several users can be online at the same time without any loss of speed. Many home computers can be networked with a cable connection so that each computer can be online at the same time with users visiting different websites.

- **Digital Subscriber Line (DSL)**

A high-speed telephone connection that connects a subscriber's computer through a router to the ISP's communication network. Most telephone companies that offer DSL to their customers can install the service on the customer's computer. However, the person must be within **18,000** feet (5,460 meters) of the telephone company's central office to be eligible for a DSL connection. As part of the installation process, the telephone company usually provides you a DSL modem, which is connected to your computer. The telephone company charges a monthly subscription fee for the service including an account activation fee. Depending on the side of the town you live, not everyone can get a DSL connection. To determine if you are eligible for DSL service, call your local telephone company. All Internet connections involve uploading and downloading. Uploading is the process of sending a file from your computer to another computer through the Internet. Downloading refers to copying a file or program from the Internet or from another computer to yours or viewing a web page. There is a type of DSL called **Asymmetric DSL (ADSL)** which transmits through existing phone lines with upload speed of **400 kbps** (kilobits per second) allowing you to download files at up to **1.4 Mbps**. All connection technologies show a disparity between upload and download speed; typically downloading takes place with greater speed than uploading.

- **Wireless Connection**

A wireless access is the most appropriate option for connecting a laptop to the Internet allowing mobile users to be online while on the go. Most Windows 10 laptops in the market today already come equipped with wireless connection. Even if you are not mobile, you can still set up a home wireless network to connect all computers in your household so that they can all be online at the same time. For the wireless connection to work, a wireless company must be equipped with a network card that will communicate through a wireless access point. This allows mobile users to connect to the Internet while sitting in locations that have wireless access connections such as public libraries, hotel lobbies, Internet cafes, coffee shops, airports free of charge.

Set Up a Wireless Connection on your Computer

1. Click the **Start button**, and click on **Settings.**
2. From the open **Settings** window, click **Network & Internet.**
3. Click **Properties,** follow onscreen instructions, and enter your wireless **Password** when prompted. A message will appear at top of the **Network Status** window: *"You're Connected."*

- **Satellite**

  This is appropriate for people who live outside the service area of DSL or cable. Satellite Internet does not use telephone or cable connections, instead, it uses a two-way dish for communication. Compared to DSL and cable, the cost of satellite can be quite high sometimes double that of DSL and cable. The most common users of satellite service are colleges and universities with multiple campuses at several locations where the instructor can teach from one location and see classrooms in other locations; students in those locations can see the instructor also. Sometimes businesses with multiple locations use satellite for the same purposes as schools.

- **Internet TV**

  Also known as Web TV or MSN TV is a service that displays the Internet on your television screen instead of a computer screen allowing you to visit web sites and send emails through the television. For Internet TV connection to work, you must have a setup appliance, then from the convenience of your couch, you can navigate the web using a remote control and a wireless keyboard.

FACTORS AFFECTING INTERNET CONNECTION SPEED

As described earlier in previous paragraphs, there are three important factors that affect internet speed namely – your computer equipment, the type of connection you have, and your Internet service provider. These factors are divided into two distinct categories – internal and external factors.

Internal Factors

1. **Spyware and Viruses:** Two of the most frequent causes of poor Internet performance are spyware and viruses. Spyware can slow your system by interfering with your browser and monopolizing your Internet connection. When a virus infects a computer, it installs computer code which will attempt to propagate itself usually by sending copies of itself through email.

    a. **Reduced Bandwidth:** Some viruses can multiply at the rate of hundreds of email messages per minute, which leaves little computing power and Internet connection bandwidth for anything else. Viruses often don't give any obvious indication that they are running; so, it's best to run antivirus software at all times.

b. **Multiple Spyware Programs:** Spyware monitors your Internet use and keystrokes, which causes delays in connection. This problem is further compounded if you have multiple spyware programs on your computer running at the same time which can cause you to lose connectivity altogether. To get your Internet performance back, you should regularly run an antispyware program to clean out any spyware infestation.

2. **Low Memory and Limited Disk Space:** Your Internet connection speed can also be affected by add-on programs, the amount of computer memory, hard disk space and condition, and the programs that are currently running. Just like the programs on your computer, Internet Explorer also requires a certain amount of computing power, memory, and disk space to run efficiently. Whenever you view an Internet webpage, it is first downloaded to memory and then saved to temporary disk files before you can view it. If you are running another program that is using lots of memory while downloading a webpage from the Internet, the computing power begins to compete with Internet Explorer and cause delays in system performance. To solve this problem, try closing any open program before surfing the web. However, if you have a computer with large memory, this is not a problem. Low disk space can also cause performance problems. You can increase your disk space by deleting Internet Explorer's temporary files or webpage history. Anytime you browse the web, Internet Explorer stores information about the websites you visit, including information the websites you visit frequently ask you to provide (such as your name and address). The Internet stores the following items on your computer:

- Temporary Internet files
- A history of the websites you've visited
- Information that you've entered into websites or the Address bar
- Saved web passwords and cookies – Having this information stored on your computer is considered helpful because it can improve your web browsing speed and also save you from having to type the same information over and over. However, if you are using a public computer, it is advisable to delete that information because you don't want any of your personal information to be left behind after you log out.

Common Rules about Browsing History

a. When you are done surfing the web, close Internet Explorer to clear cookies that are still in memory from your current browsing session. This is especially important when using a public computer.

b. Be aware that deleting your browsing history does not delete your list of favorites or subscribed feeds.

c. You can delete all settings that have changed since you first installed Internet Explorer on your computer, including browsing history, and then reset the settings.

Delete all or Some Browsing History (Webpage History)

1. Open Internet Explorer, click **Tools** at top menu, and select **Internet Options**.

2. In the open **Internet Options** window, click the **Delete** button to display items to be deleted (**fig. 7.4**).

3. From the open **Delete** window, if not already checked click to select and mark these: **Preserve Favorite website data, Temporary Internet Files, History,** and **Cookies** for deleting, and click **Delete** tab at bottom of window (**fig.7.5**).

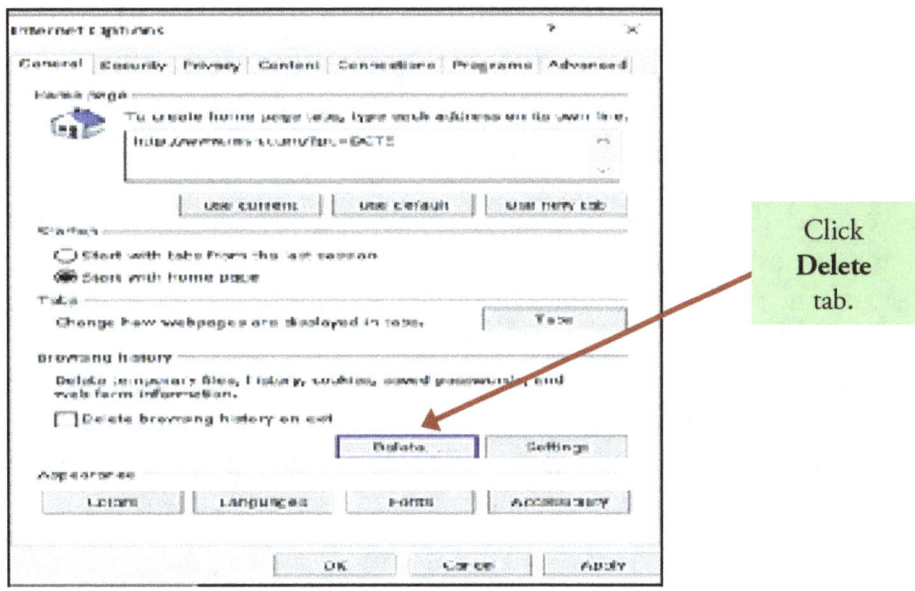

Fig. 7.4   Internet Options Window

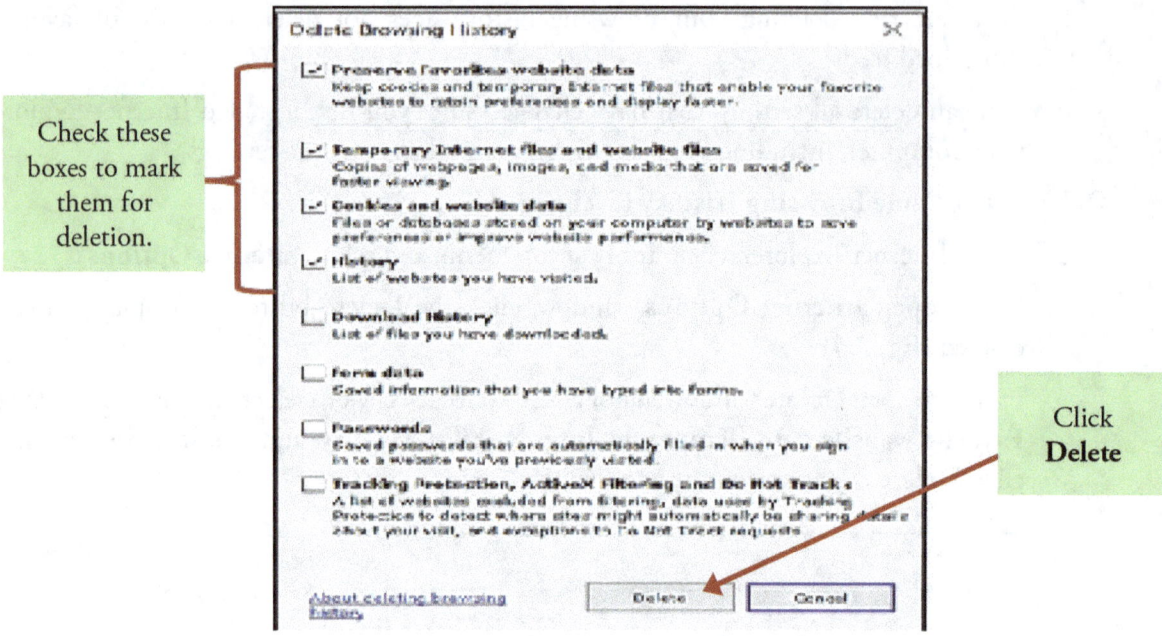

Fig. 7.5   **Deleting Browsing History**

3. **Browser Add-Ons:** Browser add-ons, such as multimedia add-ons, search bars, or other programs that usually appear on your browser's toolbar can also cause slow performance problems. Browser add-ons are not necessarily a bad thing; many of them can add to a rich browsing experience, offering multimedia or specialized document viewing. On the other hand, some add-ons can slow your Internet connection. If you suspect that add-ons are causing your connection to be very slow, your best solution is to start Internet Explorer in Add-ons disabled mode. Add-ons are disabled only for the session you are running, but if you find that your Internet performance is improving, you can use the Add-on Manager to turn them off permanently.

Disable Add-Ons

1. Open **Internet Explorer** and click on the **Tools** button.
2. On the open **Tools** window, click **Manage Add-ons.**
3. On the displayed items in the open **Manage Add-ons** window, click the file you want to disable and click **Disable** tab **(fig. 7.6).**

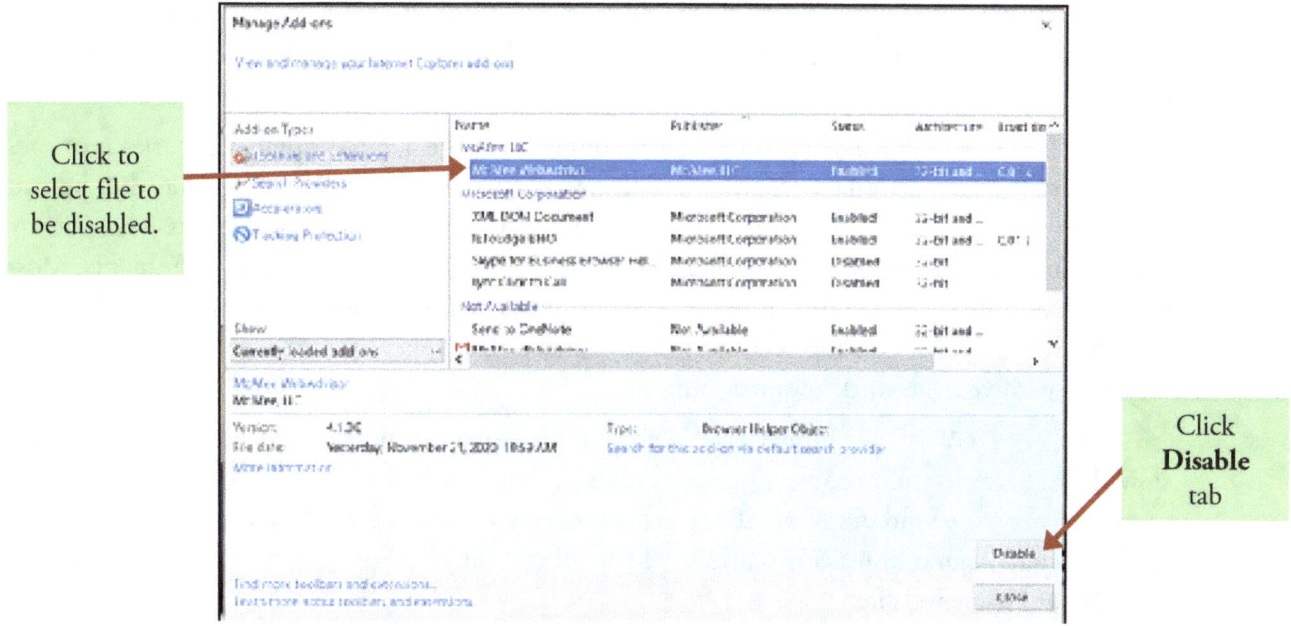

Fig. 7.6   Disabling Ad-Ons

4. **Pop-Up:** This is a small web browser window that appears at top of the website you're viewing. Pop-up windows often open as soon as you visit a website and are usually created by advertisers. Most web browsers include a way to block pop-ups from appearing. To turn off Pop-up blocker, do these:

1. Open Internet Explorer and click on the **Tools** button.
2. In the open **Tools** menu, place mouse on **Pop-up Blocker**, and select **Turn off Pop-Up Blocker**.

External Factors

Unlike internal factors, certain external factors that slow down your connection speed may be outside your environment with conditions that are beyond your control. In these cases, you may just have to wait it out and pray that things will eventually return to normal. Even with a fast connection, the following external factors can negatively impact your Internet connection speed:

1. **Website Traffic:** Busy or popular websites can get overwhelmed with users. For example, when a business advertises their product on a television commercial and mentions a website where

All-in-One Beginners Guide to Computer Proficiency | 349

people can go to check out the product and print discount coupons, many people try to visit the site at the same time. If the website is not equipped to handle the traffic, you may encounter delays.

2. **Local (Intranet) Congestion:** Users connected to the same corporate network sometimes experience slow connection especially at peak times when people are trying to download or upload files at the same time. This is also the case with computers on a college campus where many students are on the computer at the same time downloading files or submitting assignments. Most network administrators monitor Internet use, and will try to keep people from doing things like downloading large files during peak hours. If you find that your Internet access is slow at times, discuss it with your network administrator.

3. **Virus Outbreak:** Sometimes people experience heavy computer virus outbreaks which can slow down Internet connection. During periods of virus outbreak, many viruses spread as they cause computers to send out hundreds or thousands of copies of the virus to several computers. To find out what major outbreaks are currently happening, visit your antivirus vendor's website, or the <u>Security at Home</u> website.

How to Increase Internet Connection Speed

In addition to resetting your Internet browser, disabling browser add-ons, deleting webpage history, and cookies from your computer as discussed in the previous paragraphs, you can increase your Internet connection speed by taking the following actions:

1. If you use a dial-up connection, you can optimize your Internet speed by investing in the fastest modem possible which can send and receive information at a rate of **56** kilobits per second (Kbps).

2. If you don't get the full **56 Kbps** speed you want most of the time, it could be that the telephone wiring in your home is old or deteriorating, which may cause you to be picking up stray signals or cross talk from other phone lines. This will slow your Internet connection because the modem will have to send the same information over and over until it's transmitted without interruption. To solve this problem, get a good phone line that can improve your speed to at least **45-50 Kbps.**

3. If the problem persists, check your telephone wires to be sure they aren't damaged, frayed, or twisted around power or other telephone cables.

4. If you notice crackling noise in your phones, contact your telephone provider to have them check the lines inside and outside your home to make sure they are in good condition.

Useful Tips for Wireless Network Users

After setting up your wireless connection, your Internet connection speed to a wireless network **(WiFi),** may be affected by the following factors:

1. Location of the computer or laptop in your home, and whether or not other wireless devices in the same area can affect how Wireless networks operate on frequencies that are similar to those used by other devices in the same vicinity, such as microwave ovens or cordless phones.

2. If you are operating a **2.4 gigahertz** (GHz) cordless phone next to your **2.4 GHz** wireless laptop, this can cause interference, or completely block the wireless network connection.

Solutions:

a. If making phone calls while surfing the web, either use a wired telephone or a cordless phone operating at a frequency different from the wireless network.

b. Proximity to the wireless access point or router as well as physical obstructions can affect the quality of your Internet connection. To improve your connection speed, move closer to the access point and make sure that there are no physical obstructions between the access point and your computer.

PERFORM BASIC TASKS ON THE INTERNET

Create and Use the Favorite Center

Favorite center is a very important part of surfing the web especially if you visit certain websites more frequently than others. A home page favorite center contains a list of web addresses of the websites or webpages you visit most often and provides quick access to those sites. With a favorite list you do not have to type the web address in the address bar each time you visit the website. Favorites, also known as bookmarks, are a convenient way to organize and find webpages that you visit frequently. If you use Internet Explorer on several computers, you can save your favorites from one computer and import that list to another computer. To create a list of your favorite websites, follow these steps

1. In the **Internet Explorer** toolbar, click the **Favorites** tab.
2. In the displayed menu, click **Add to Favorites**.

3. In the open **Add a Favorite** dialog box, ensure that the website name or webpage is displayed in the name box **(fig. 7.7)**.

4. Click the **Add** button to add the name to the **Favorite Center**.

5. At top right of the Internet Explorer window click the middle yellow star button to display the **Favorite Center** list. The new web name added will display on the list **(fig. 7.8)**.

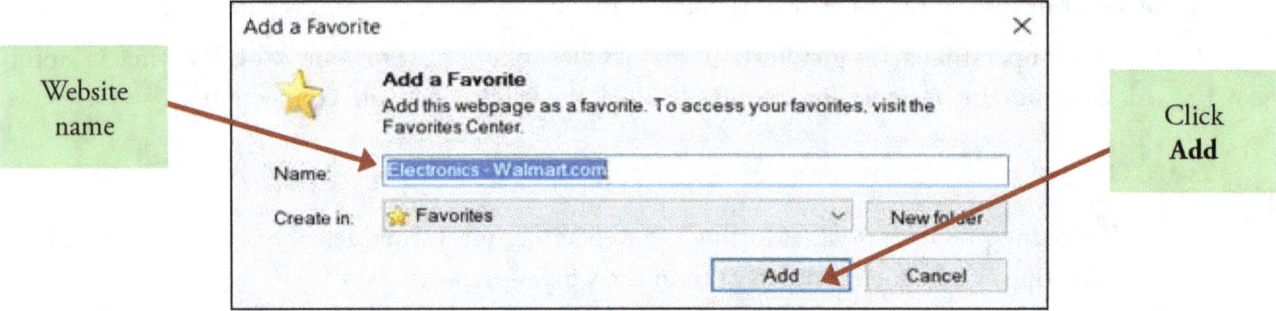

Fig. 7.7   **Add a Website to the Favorite Center**

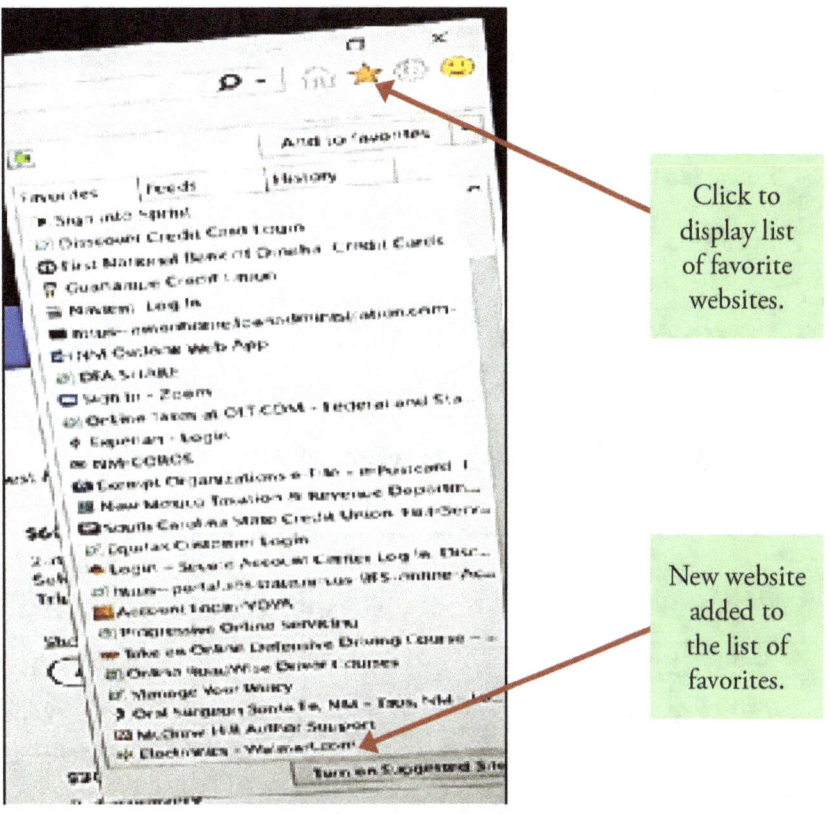

Fig. 7.8   Favorite Center List

Create a Folder to Organize Websites on the Favorite Center

1. In the **Add a Favorite** dialog box, click **New Folder**.
2. In the **Create a Folder** dialog box, type a name for the new folder.
3. Click the **Create In** down arrow, select **Favorites**, and click **Create (fig. 7.9)**.
4. See new folder created (**fig. 7.10**). You can now categorize your favorite websites in folders.

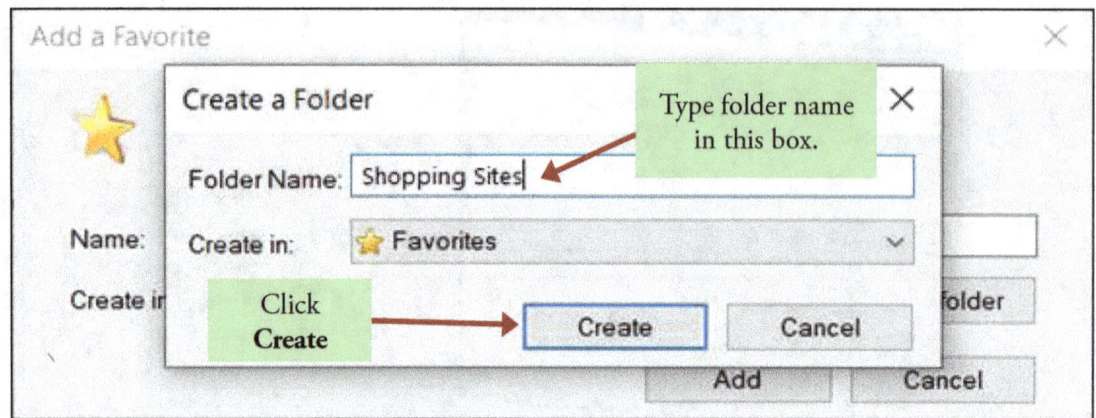

Fig. 7.9   Create a Folder in the Favorite Center

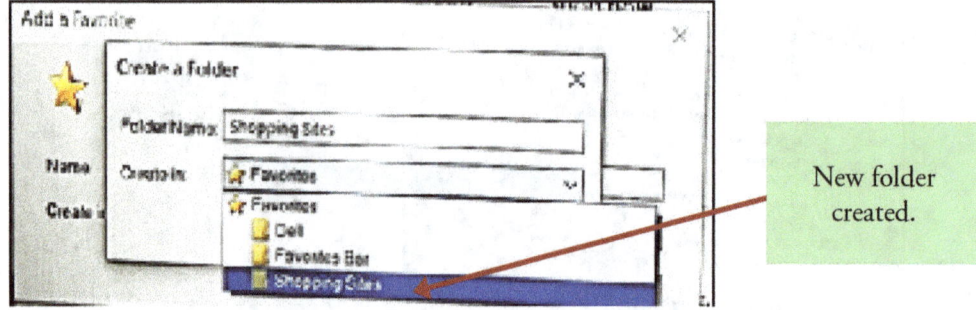

Fig. 7.10   New Folder Displayed in the Favorite Center

Delete a Web Address from Favorite Center

1. On the toolbar, click the **Add to Favorites** button, and click **Organize Favorites**.
2. In the **Organize Favorites** dialog box, click the web address, and click **Delete** button.
3. To delete a web address using shortcut:
   a. Click on the **Favorite** button to open the list of web addresses.
   b. Scroll down the list to select web address to be deleted.
   c. Right-click on the web address, from the displayed shortcut menu list select **Delete**.

Change Your Default Web Browser

Your current default browser is the application that Windows use to manage web and html pages. When you buy a new computer, it is not uncommon to have more than one Internet browser installed on your computer but you have to decide which one you plan to use. The most commonly used Internet browsers include: Google Chrome, Yahoo, Apple, Bing, Fox Fire, and Microsoft Edge (the newest web browser). If you choose to use Internet Explorer for most of your Internet browsing needs, you can make it the default browser on your computer. When you set Internet Explorer as your default browser, you eliminate the problem of having to select from a list of browsers whenever you want to go online. You can simply click the Internet Explorer icon and Internet Explorer will automatically open.

Set Internet Explorer as Default Browser on a New Computer

1. Click the **Internet Explorer** icon on your computer to open it.
2. On the toolbar menu, click on **Tools** tab.
3. From the displayed menu, select **Internet Options,** and click on **Programs** tab **(fig. 7.11).**
4. Make sure the box **Open Internet Explorer titles on the desktop** is checked; if not check the box and click **Ok**.
5. Your default browser is now Internet Explorer. Any web link you click from your computer should automatically open Internet Explorer. For instance, if you click a link someone sent to you via email, the Web site should automatically load in a new Internet Explorer window.

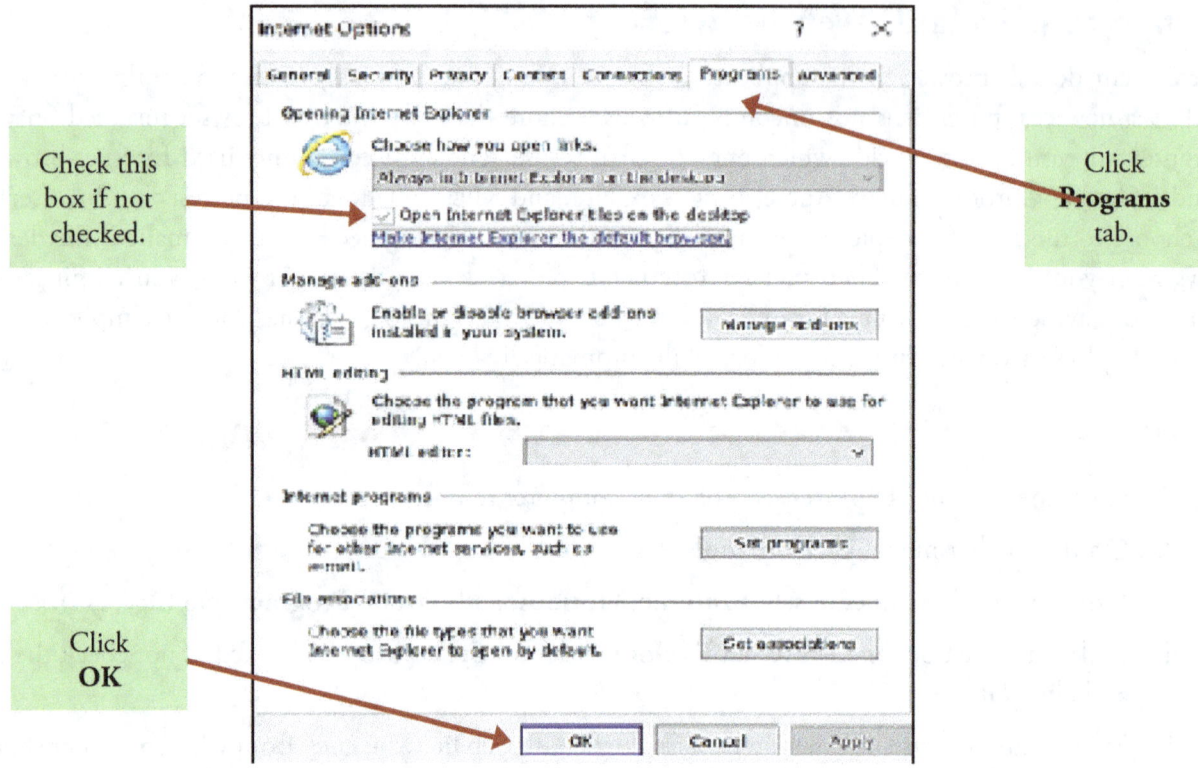

Fig. 7.11 Internet Explorer Options Window

Change Internet Explorer Settings

When you reset Internet Explorer settings, all add-ons and customizations are deleted, and you basically start with a fresh version of Internet Explorer just like starting on a new slate. There are several reasons to change the settings on your Internet Explorer; a few of them are listed below:

1. Browsing is always slow on the Internet Explorer.
2. The Internet frequently stops responding (hangs up) or stops working (crash).
3. You receive error messages indicating that Internet Explorer has "encountered a problem and needs to close."
4. A **Visual C++ "runtime error"** has occurred in Explore.exe.

Reset Internet Explorer Settings

1. Click the **Internet Explorer** icon on your computer to open it.
2. Click the **Tools** button, and click **Internet Options**.
3. Click the **Advanced** tab, and click **Reset** button and click **OK (fig. 7.12)**.
4. If you would like to remove browsing history, search providers, Accelerators, home pages, and InPrivate Filtering data, select the **Delete personal settings** check box **(fig. 7.13).**
5. In the **Reset Internet Explorer Settings** dialog box, click **Reset,** and click **OK**
6. The system will automatically restore original settings of the Internet Explorer like new. Your changes will take effect the next time you open Internet Explorer.

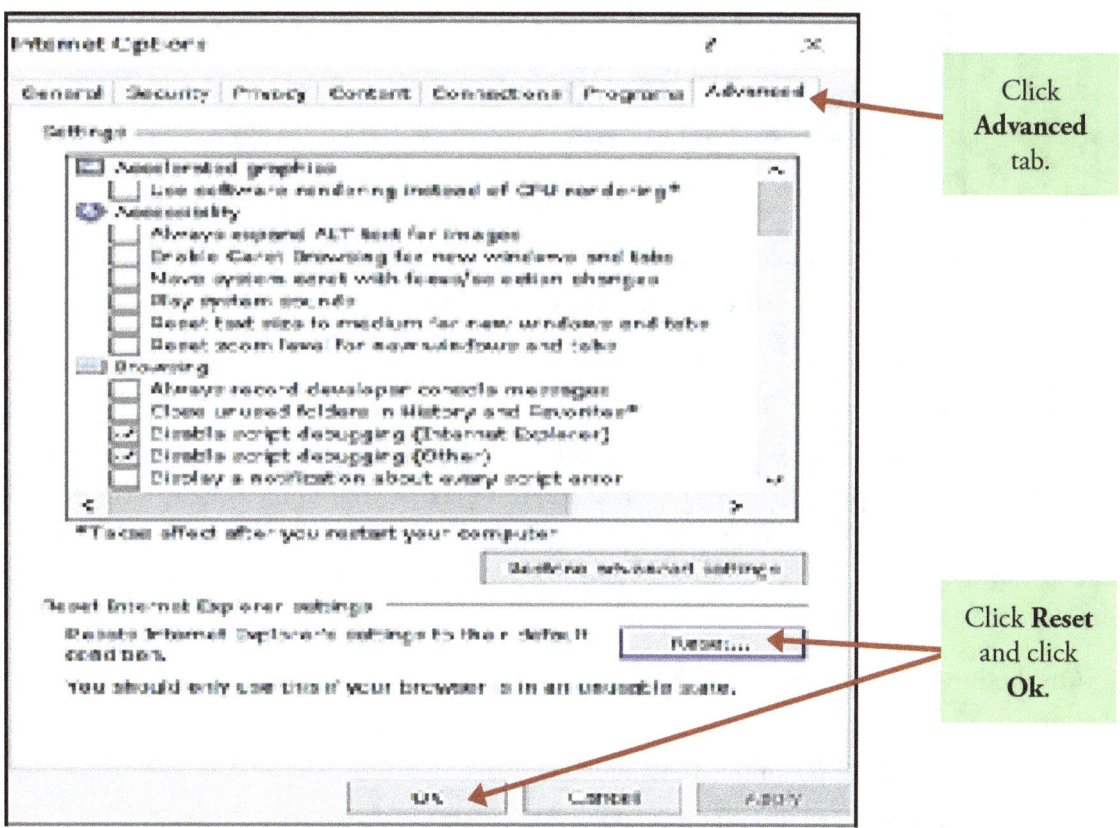

Fig. 7.12   Settings Reset Window

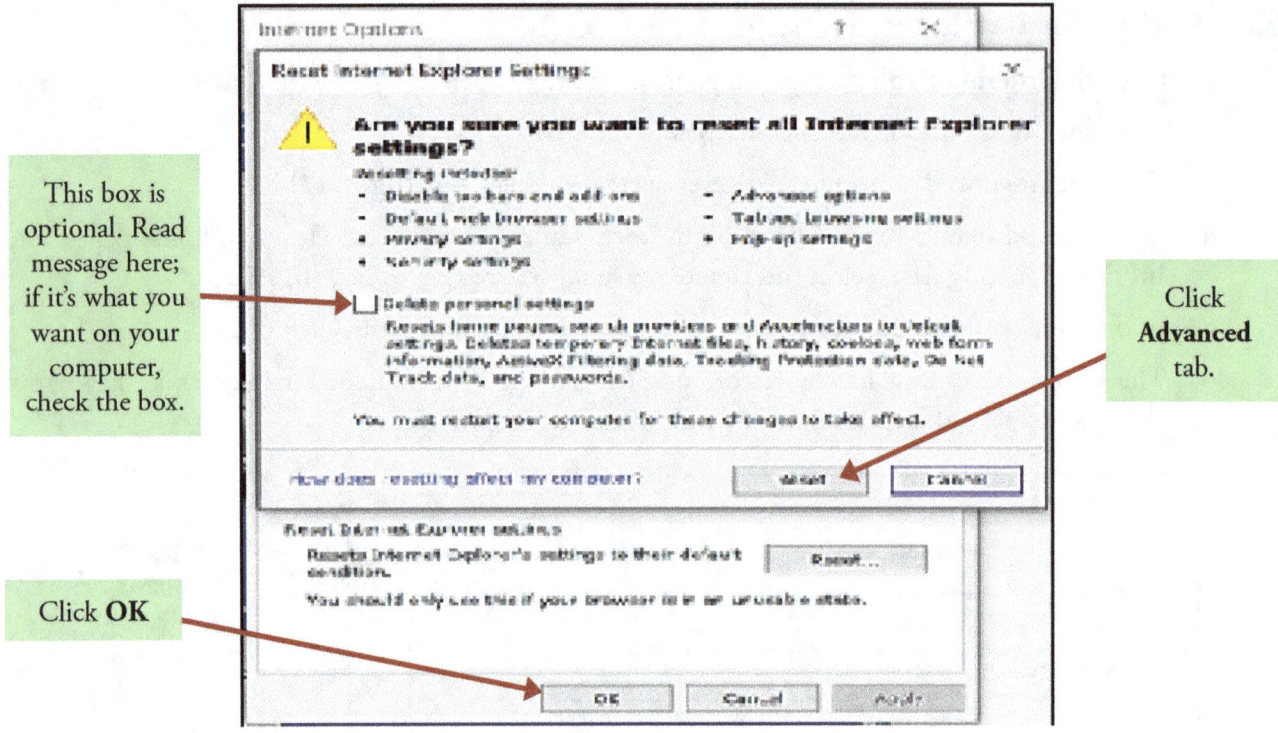

Fig. 7.13 Reset Internet Explorer Settings

Change Default Home Page

Your home page also known as the default page is the webpage that appears every time you open Internet Explorer. If there is one webpage you visit the most, you can make it your home page so that every time you start Internet Explorer or click the **Home** button that page will automatically appear. Select a page that you would like to view frequently, and customize it for quick access to all the information you want, such as the **msn.com** Home Page.

1. On the Internet browser, enter Web address to open the web page you want to appear when you start.
2. Click **Internet Options** on the **Tools** menu.
3. On the open **Internet Options** dialog box, click the **General** tab **(fig. 7.14)**.

358 | *Basic Computing Concepts*

4. Under **Home page**, the web address you chose is highlighted in blue which is the current page you are on. Click **Use Current** and click **Ok**.
5. To make this website your home page, click **Use Default** and click **Ok.**

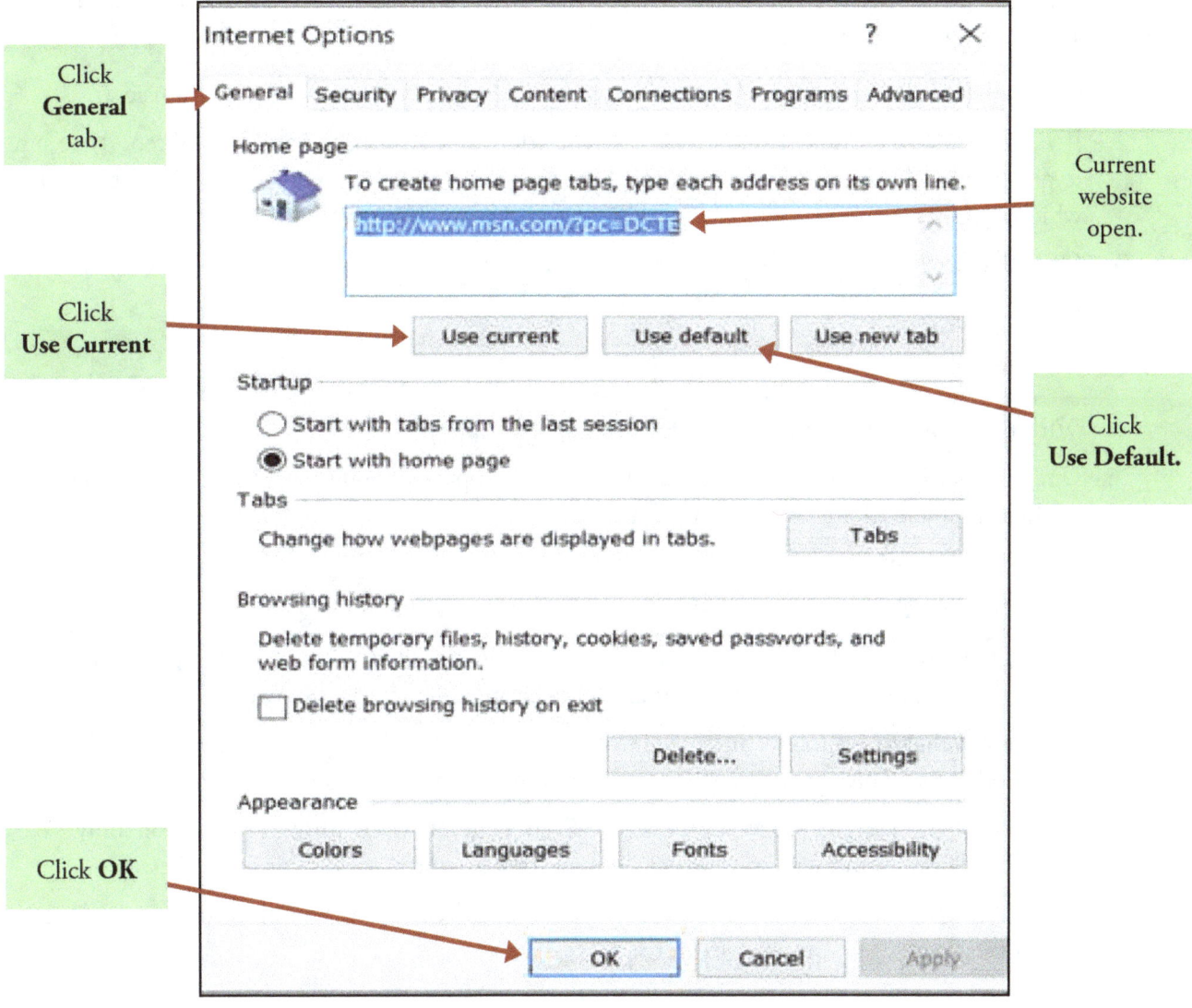

Fig. 7.14   **Change Default Home Page**

All-in-One Beginners Guide to Computer Proficiency | 359

Download, Save, and Print a Web Page

Downloading is the process of saving a copy of a Web page on your computer or storage device. When downloading a Webpage be aware of widespread threat of computer viruses. In addition, ensure that you are not violating copyright-protected Web materials if you are using the materials to write research paper. Here are some basic copyright rules to keep in mind:

1. Copyright laws protect original works of authors like text, art, photographs, and music.
2. If you use copyright protected materials to write your research paper or any type of report, be sure to give credit to the source of your information otherwise your action will be considered plagiarism which is against the law.
3. One of the exceptions to this law is the use of small amounts of information for educational purposes, which falls under **Fair Use** guidelines.

Save a Web Page on Your Computer

1. With the webpage displayed, on the **File** menu, click **Save As**.
2. Under **Organize**, select a location or folder for your webpage. If you want to save the webpage into a folder double-click the folder to open it first.
3. In the **File Name** box, type a name for the page.
4. In the **Save As Type** box, select a file type. Choose one of the following options as file type:
    a. Click **Web Page, Complete** to save all of the files needed to display this page, including graphics, frames, and style sheets. It allows each file to be saved in its original format.
    b. Click **Web Archive** to save all of the information needed to display this page in a single MIME-encoded file. This option saves a snapshot of the current Web page.
    c. To save the current **HTML** page, click **Web Page, HTML only**. This option only saves information on the Web page; it does not save the graphics, sounds, or other files.
    d. To save only the text from the current Web page, click **Text Only.** This option saves information on the Web page in straight text format.

Print a Web Page: The Internet Explorer Print dialog box is the same as those seen in the Print dialog box for other programs, and contain options that enable you to print pages or a table of pages that are linked to the active Web page.

1. Open the Web page you want to print
2. Go to the **File** menu, and click **Print.**
3. Set the printing options you want by doing these:
4. To print a frame or item on a Web page, right-click on the frame or item, holding down the mouse drag to highlight the frame or item.
5. When the **Print** window opens up, click on **Selection** button, click **Ok.**
6. To preview what the Webpage will look like when printed or to see how many pages will be printed, click the **File** menu, and select **Print Preview.**

Copy and Paste a Web Page on a Word Document

1. Open **Internet Explorer**, and enter the web address in the **Address Bar**.
2. Place your mouse at the beginning of the word or text you want to copy.
3. Hold down the **Primary Button** of the mouse and drag from left to right and down the **Web Page** until all text and pictures are highlighted.
4. Right-click the mouse; from the displayed menu list, select **Copy.**
5. Open a blank Word document, right-click at top of the document, from the displayed menu select **Paste.**
6. Alternatively, on the open Word document, click at top of the document, and click the **Paste** button at top left of the ribbon.

Summary of Some Internet Quick Tasks

To Do These	Try These
Save a page or picture without opening it.	Right-click the link containing the item you want to save, and click **Save as Target**.
Copy information from a Web page onto an MS document.	**Highlight** the information you want to copy, **right click** the highlighted block, and select **copy,** click on a blank Word document, **right click** again, and select **paste**.
Create an icon of the current page on the desktop.	Click on **file** at the menu toolbar and select **save as**. From the drop-down arrow of the save window, select **desktop**, type the file name, and click **save**.
Use a Web page image as desktop wallpaper (or background).	Right-click the image on the Web page you want to use, and click **Set as Wallpaper** or **Set as Background**.
Send a Web page via Email	Click on **File** at the menu toolbar, point the mouse to **Send**, and click **Page by E-mail** or **link by E-mail**. Type your message in the open window, and click **send** the message. (**Note:** To do this, you must have an e-mail account and an e-mail program set up on your computer).

Table 7.2

BASIC INTERNET EXPLORER TERMS & DEFINITIONS

- **History:** A feature of Internet Explorer that tracks recently visited Web pages and sites. The History list can be displayed using the **Favorites Center** button and then selecting a site that was recently visited. By default, Internet Explorer tracks sites visited within the last 20 days.
- **Address Bar:** Also known as the web browser into which the web address is typed.
- **Performing Commands Using the Toolbar:**
  - **Back Button:** A backward arrow used to return the user to the home page or webpage previously viewed.

- **Forward Button:** Becomes available once the **Back** button has been used. This button is a forward arrow that takes the user to the next Webpage that has been previously been viewed before going backward.

- **The Home Page:** The Webpage that displays every time Internet Explorer is started. The default home page is installed when Windows is set as a Microsoft site because Internet Explorer is a Microsoft program. Home pages, including MSN, act as portals or launching sites to other Web pages. The default home page can be changed to any webpage of your choice.

- **Webpage:** A document on the World Wide Web that displays as a screen with associated links, frames, pictures, texts, and other features of interest.

- **Website:** A group of related Webpages published to a specific, unique location or **Uniform Resource Locator** (URL).

- **A ScreenTip:** A small note activated by holding the pointer over a button or other screen object which displays information about a screen element. It identifies the Webpage that will display when you click the button.

- **Favorite Center:** Located at the toolbar, the **favorite center** displays a list of the websites visited most frequently. Using the **Tools** command, you can add your favorite sites to this list to make it easier to access them. To access a website on the list only requires clicking the **Favorites** button, and selecting the web address listed rather than typing the web address on the address bar.

- **Search Engines:** Several Web sites have search capabilities known as **search engines**–a database of Internet files collected over time by a computer program. The Internet Explorer contains an **Instant Search** box that connects to a default search engine referred to as **Windows Live** and easily enables additional engines to be added. Other search engines found on the Internet are **Google, Yahoo,** and **Bing.** Yahoo serves as a search engine, but it is actually an example of a subject directory – databases or lists of selected web resources arranged by topic.

- **Hyperlinks:** These include text, buttons, pictures, or other objects displayed on Web pages that when clicked, access other Webpages or display other sections of the active page. Linked Webpages may also be pages within the same Website or Webpages on sites of other companies, schools, or organizations.

- **Internet Service Provider (ISP):** A company that provides Internet connection through a telephone line, a special high-speed telephone line, or a cable line.

- **Animated Banners:** A series of rotating or changing text and images embedded within the Web page – colorful images used to attract attention and stimulate interest to a Website.
- **Pop-Ups:** Distracting and annoying windows that display on the Internet screen without being requested. Many Web users use a **Pop-Up Blocker** to stop these windows from displaying.
- **Web Authoring:** This is software that simplifies Webpage programming by allowing Web developers to specify the design of a Webpage without actually writing the supporting code.
- **Cyber Squatting:** Refers to the act of registering or licensing a domain name in bad faith with the intent of profiting from the name at the expense of another person. People that carry out these unethical acts are often referred to as **Dot.Com Grabbers**.
- **World Wide Web Consortium (W3C):** The leading organization that creates Web standards, and develops specifications, guidelines, and tools allowable on the Internet.

TIPS FOR PERFORMING SEARCHES ON THE INTERNET

The Internet is the home of a vast collection of information we need in our daily lives, but sometimes finding exactly what you're looking for can be a challenge. However, using the new features of Internet Explorer 11, you can perform searches in many ways to find what you want. Here are a few tips to help you search the web more effectively.

Use the Browser & Search Box

1. In the **Internet Explorer Browser**, type the keyword or phrase for your search and press **Enter** on your keyboard.
2. A list of the websites matching the similar descriptions will display, click on the website you want to display the page and begin your navigation.
3. If you know the website name, type it in the address bar or browser and press **Enter.**
4. For a specific search, on the far right of the **Internet Explorer** window, in the **Search Box**, type a keyword or phrase for your search and press **Enter.**

Perform Search More Effectively

Performing searches more effectively involves applying some search techniques that enable you to improve your search results. Here are a few ideas for improving the results of searches:

1. Use specific words for the information you seek instead of generic categories. For example, instead of searching for "cats," in general, search for a specific breed of cat, such as **Persian Cat.**

2. Avoid using common words such as "**a**," "**my**," or "**the**," unless you're looking for a specific title that must have those words in order to be complete. If the word is part of the information you seek, for example, a poem title, it is okay to include the common word and surround the phrase with quotation marks (i.e., "the").

3. Use quotation marks to search for specific phrases; use colon to surround your terms. Quotation marks limit the search results to only those webpages that contain the exact phrase you have specified. This means that your search results will not include any page containing words without quotation marks regardless of what order those words are in.

4. Use the minus (-) sign before a keyword to tell search providers what terms and webpages to exclude from your search. Using a minus sign will retrieve webpages that don't include those words you specified in your search. When using minus sign make sure there are no spaces between the signs and search terms (for example, **-Chill**, not - Chill).

5. Narrow your search by searching only a specific website or domain. Type the search term you are looking for followed by **site** and the address of the website you want to search. For example, to search the Microsoft website for information, type windows updates **site:www.microsoft.com** (with no spaces between site: and the URL).

6. Be creative in your search by using synonyms or alternative search terms. You can also use a thesaurus for more search ideas. To do this, simply type **thesaurus** in the search box to find an online thesaurus.

7. When searching for specific items, use a specialty search engine or provider, such as MSN Image search to look for pictures. Many websites offer their own special searches for anything from recreation, shopping to hobbies. Internet Explorer contains features that can detect specialty search providers on some websites, and you can add them to your list of search providers.

Find Words or Phrases on a Webpage

Very often the searches you perform on the Internet are mostly general information on a particular webpage either by category or by type. Internet Explorer has features that allow you to find specific words or phrases on a webpage and can help you find them on a webpage. Here's how:

1. On your keyboard, press **Ctrl+F** to open the **Find** box below the toolbar.
2. Type a word or phrase you wish to find, and press **Enter** to locate the first match.
3. Sometimes as you type the words or phrases, they are automatically highlighted in yellow and the number of matches display at the top of your screen.
4. To filter the matches, click **Options** down arrow, and select one or both of these: **(fig. 7.15)**.
   a. Match Whole Word Only
   b. Match Case
5. Click **Next or Previous** to move from one matched word or phrase to another.

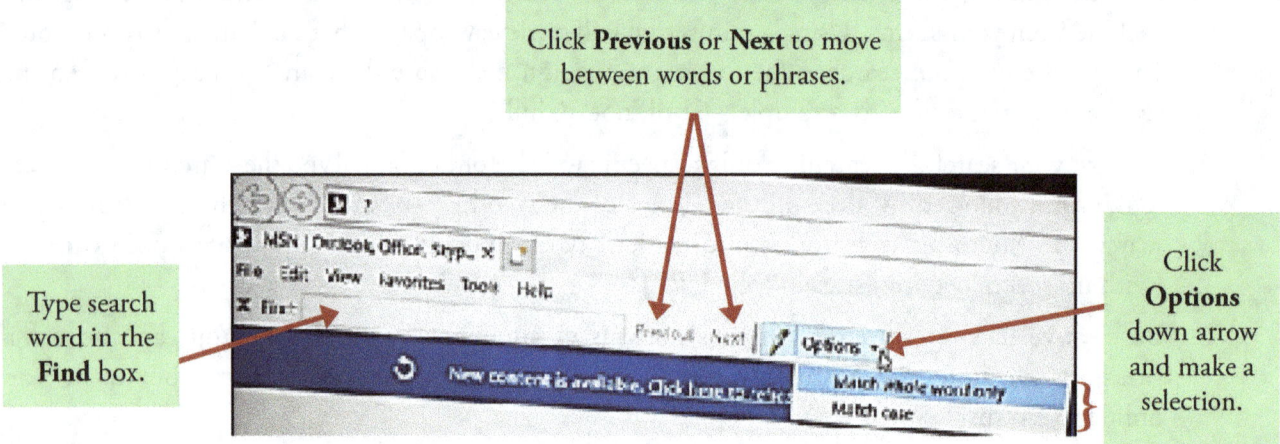

Fig. 7.15   **Activated Find Box**

OTHER INTERNET FEATURES & HOW TO USE THEM TO PERFORM BASIC ONLINE TASKS

RSS Features (Rich Site Summary)

This is a format for delivering regularly changing web content. It allows people who regularly use the web to easily stay informed by retrieving the latest content from their favorite web sites without visiting each site individually. Most business organizations with news-related sites, such as weblogs and other online publishers syndicate their content as **RSS Feeds** to whoever wants it. **RSS** now contains the following improved features:

- **Authenticated Feeds**: The new RSS Windows Platform can now perform authentication without user interaction. Username and password can be set in **Properties** dialog box of the feed.
- **Effective ID**: A hash algorithm is used to produce a unique ID for feed items. You can use this value to synchronize an item's read and unread states between computers, or to compare items in the **Common Feed List** with items stored by other programs.

Multilingual User Interface (MUI)

This is the name used to describe Microsoft technology for Microsoft Windows, Microsoft Office and other applications that allow users to install multiple interface languages on a single system. With this installation, each user would be able to select a preferred display language. **MUI** technology which was originally introduced with Windows 2000 is covered by an international patent titled "**MULTILINGUAL USER INTERFACE FOR AN OPERATING SYSTEM.**" Since the last decade to the current day, Internet Explorer has grown to more than 100 languages.

Web Zoom Enhancements

Internet Explorer 11 comes with a significant improvement over the previous versions by providing users with a higher-quality, more predictable and persistent zooming experience. In addition to introducing more persistent zoom states, it eliminates horizontal scroll bars for the majority of mainstream scenarios. New windows, dialogs, and pop-up windows automatically inherit the zoom level of their parent. An improved zooming and image scaling experience comes in the form of a full-page zoom which now allows text to reflow thereby removing the appearance of horizontal scrollbars on zooming. Image scaling is done using **Bicubic Interpolation** resulting in sharper looking images when scaled. **Bicubic Interpolation** is a mathematical term used to describe the extension of cubic interpolation for interpolating data points on a two dimensional regular grid. In image processing on a webpage, bicubic interpolation allows images to be sampled with bicubic interpolation and are smoother and appear sharper when viewed.

Zoom in on a Webpage
: While on a webpage, IE11 allows you to Zoom in or out, enlarge or reduce the view of a webpage. Unlike changing font size, zoom enlarges or reduces everything on the page, including text and images. You can zoom from 10% to more than 100%. To perform the zoom function, follow these steps:

1. On the top menu of **Internet Explorer** screen, click the **View** tab.
2. In the open **View** short menu, place mouse of **Zoom**, and select the percentage level you want; observe the screen zoom enlarge or decrease as needed.
3. You can also increase or decrease the zoom value using these keyboard shortcuts:
    a. To zoom in, press **Ctrl+(+).**
    b. To zoom out, press **Ctrl+(-).**
    c. To restore the zoom to 100%, press **Ctrl+0.**

Enable or Remove Cookies

There are several ways you can control the cookies stored on your computer. You can block or allow all cookies or you can choose the specific sites that you'll accept cookies from. The changes you make to accept or block cookies do not affect the cookies that are already stored on your computer. For this reason, before making changes, delete the cookies already stored on your computer, and follow these steps to proceed with your changes:

Allow Cookies from Specific Websites

1. Open Internet Explorer browser, and click on the **Tools** tab.
2. From the displayed menu, select **Internet Options**.
3. In the open window that follows, click on the **Privacy** tab, and click on **Sites** tab.
4. Enter names of websites for which you'd like to enable cookies; click **Allow**, and click **OK**.

Remove Cookies from Your Computer

1. Open **Internet Explorer**, click **Tools** at top menu, and select **Internet Options**.
2. In the open options window, click **General** tab
3. Under **Browsing History**, click **Delete** button.
4. In the open **Delete Browsing History** window, check the box **Cookies and website data**, and click **Delete** button **(fig.7.16)**.
3. For additional cleanup on your computer, you may also check the boxes of all other listed items on the menu that you want to delete to improve the speed of your computer; then click **Delete** button.

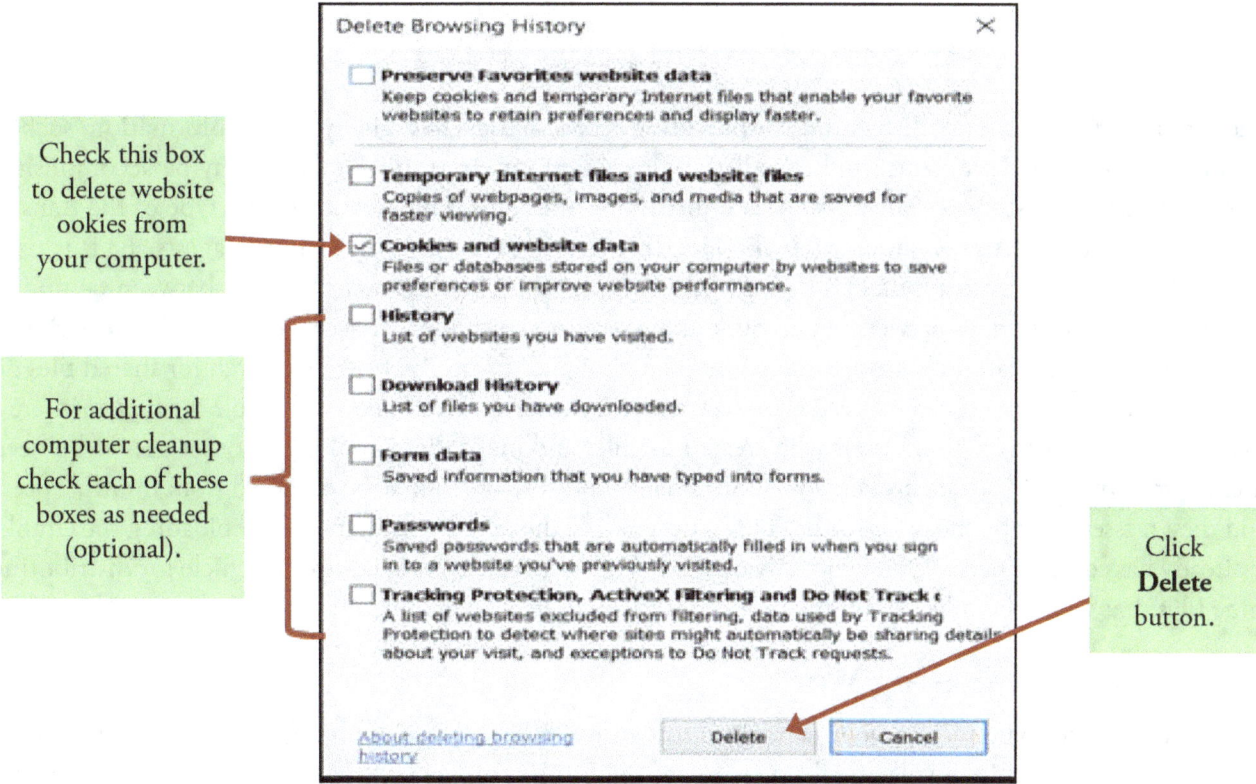

Fig. 7.16   **Delete Cookies and Other Browsing History**

What is a Blog?

Also referred to as **Weblog,** a blog is a type of website where people make entries in the form of a diary or journal fashion. It can be described as an electronic diary where millions of people record their thoughts and opinions on every issue from political, controversial, down to what's for dinner. Some blog provide commentary on particular subjects such as social issues, economy, politics, the environment, national security, etc. Political consultants, news services, and political candidates often use blogs for outreach and opinion surveys. Blogs primarily contain all text but some may also contain photos, videos, and other graphics relating to a message being posted. Some examples of blog websites include **www.blogger.com/start** for *blogger*, and **www.livejournal.com** for *LiveJournal*.

SHARING FILES & PRINTERS ON THE INTERNET

File sharing is the practice of distributing or providing access to users to digitally stored information, such as documents, computer programs, multi-media (audio, video), or electronic books. It may be accomplished through a variety of storage, transmission, and distribution models. The most common type of file transfer method many people use is known as **FTP (File Transfer Protocol).** As the name suggests, FTP is used to transfer files between computers on a network. It can also be used to exchange files between computer accounts, and transfer files between an account and a desktop computer, or access online software archives. In this process, users can use software that connects in to a peer-to-peer network to search for shared files on the computers of other users (i.e., peers) connected to the network. This makes it possible for files of interest to be downloaded directly from users who created the files and make them available to other users who need them. Typically, large files are broken down into smaller chunks, which may be obtained from multiple peers and then reassembled by the downloader. This is done while the peer is simultaneously uploading the chunks it already has to other peers. One major advantage of FTP is that it serves as a strong vehicle for distributing large files that would be otherwise difficult to transmit to users via email because of size.

How Does File Sharing Work?

The easiest way to share files on your network is to set up a sharing home-group. In the absence of a home-group, you can share files by placing them in one of the **Public folders** on your network. Any file or folder placed in a Public folder is automatically shared with the people connected to that network. Each type of library has its own Public folder for (Documents, Pictures Music, and Videos). To access the Public Folders, everyone connected to that network must have a user account to log in and get the files. Before you can share your files on the network, you must first save them or copy them to a Public folder on your computer. If you want to upload files, delete files, or rearrange the folder structure on an FTP site, you need to open the site in Windows Explorer. If you just want to open FTP sites and download files from them, you can use Internet Explorer or create a short cut. When you create a short cut to an FTP site, the site will automatically open in Windows Explorer when prompted. Internet Explorer 11 that's already installed on Windows 10 operating system on your new computer is already equipped with FTP setup.

Verify that FTP is Setup on Your Computer:

1. Open **Internet Explorer**, click on **Tools** tab, and select **Internet Options.**
2. In the open **Internet Properties** window, click **Advanced** tab **(fig. 7.17)**.
3. On the displayed listed options, make sure the box **Enable FTP folder view (outside of Internet Explorer)** is checked. If not checked, check this box, and click **Ok**.

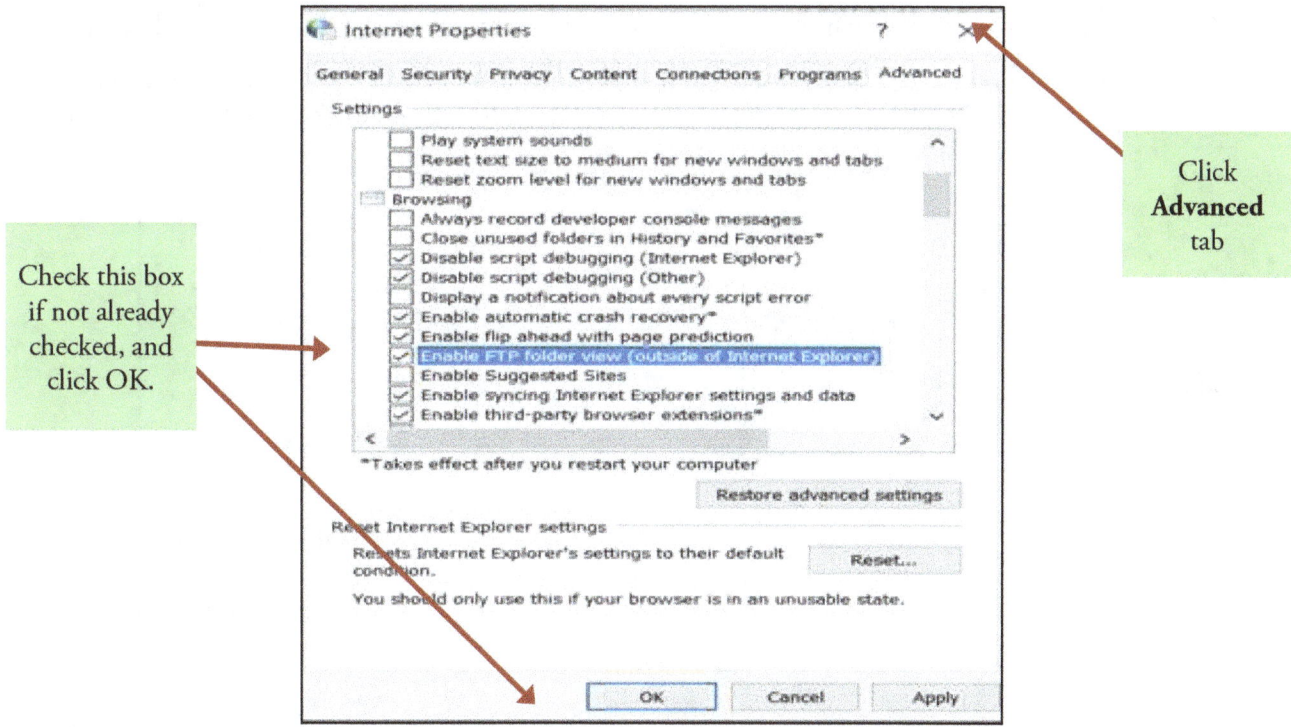

Fig. 7.17   **Advanced Tab View to Verify FTP Setup**

Create a Shortcut to Open an FTP Site in Windows Explorer:

To create an FTP folder on your computer, you have to use the FTP address provided by the owner of the FTP site outside your computer (**Site Administrator**). The owner will also provide you a login ID. Using password created during setup, and login ID, you can log into the FTP as needed to upload or download files.

1. In the **Search** box next to **Start** button on your computer, type **This PC** and click on the phrase at top window screen.
2. On the displayed Explorer window, right-click anywhere on the blank space, and click **Add a Network Location.**
3. In the open **Add Network Location** window, click **Next. (fig. 7.18)**.
4. Click **Choose a Custom Network Location**, and click **Next.**
5. Enter the **FTP site name**, with the full format, **FTP://** in front of the name and click **Next.**
6. If you already have the location on your computer, click **Browse** and select the location address or name.
7. Follow simple onscreen **Wizard** instructions – provide password when prompted by the **Wizard** to complete setup. When finished, a shortcut to the FTP site will appear under **This PC** on your computer.

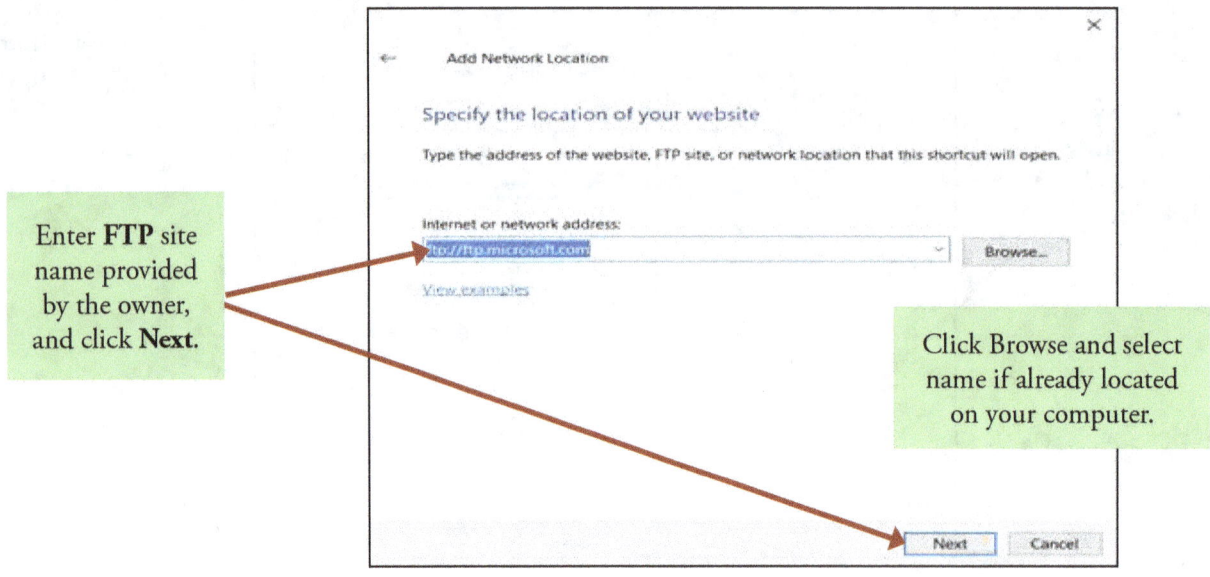

Fig. 7.18   **Wizard Window for Setting Up FTP Folder**

372 | *Basic Computing Concepts*

NOTE: *When you first connect to the FTP site, you'll be prompted for a password. Select the Save password check box if you want Windows to remember that password and connect you directly to the site in the future. You can open FTP sites in Windows Explorer even if Internet Explorer isn't your default browser. Many FTP sites are heavily used and require several attempts before connecting. You need to use a client that supports secure FTP to transfer files to and from your network.*

Upload Files to the FTP Site: Instructions on how to upload files to an FTP site may differ from site to site depending on the remote administrator's protocol. Follow instructions provided by your FTP site administrator to upload your files. You may be required to enter an ID and log-in password. However, if the Webmaster of the remote site has set permissions for **"Anonymous FTP,"** you will be able to upload without an ID. Generally, the following steps apply to uploading files to an FTP site:

1. Enter the remote **FTP site** address in your browser window (**fig. 7.19**) and press **Enter** or click **Go**. Your web browser will open the remote site.

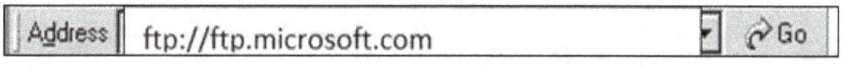

Fig. 7.19   **Web Browser (Internet Explorer Address Bar)**

2. On the open **Login** window, either check the box **Login Anonymously** or enter your **Username** and **Password**, then click **Login (fig.7.20).**

3. Navigate the site to locate the area that invites you to upload file or files.

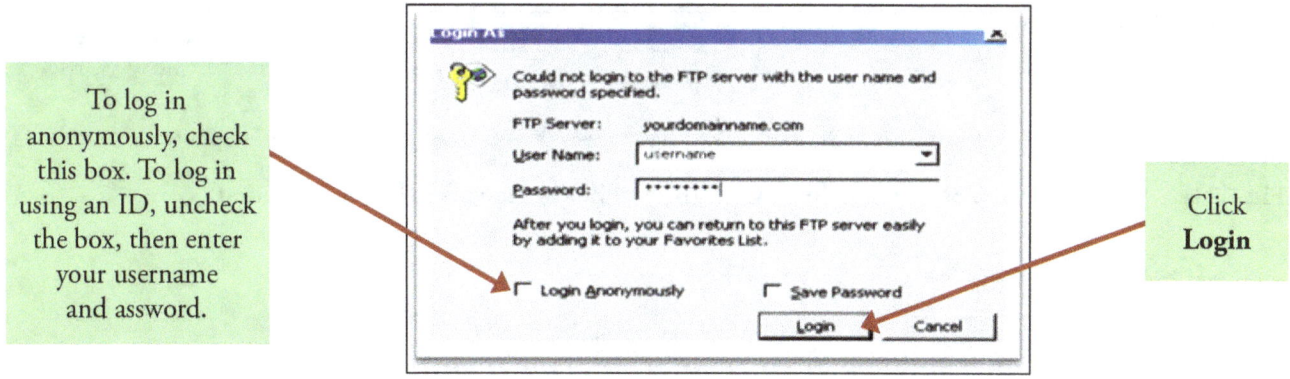

Fig. 7.20   **Site Log in Window**

All-in-One Beginners Guide to Computer Proficiency | 373

4. In your computer, CD, or flash drive, locate the file(s) you want to upload and click to select the file(s) according to the site's directions. Once you successfully login, you will see a listing of the files on the **FTP** server.

5. You can also drag files from your local computer into this folder to upload files to your server or drag files from this folder to your local computer to download files off the **FTP** website.

6. Follow onscreen instructions provided by the **FTP sites** to upload files as needed.

Download Files from the FTP Site:

1. Repeat **steps 1 – 3** above under upload files to access the **FTP** site.

2. Once on the site, follow onscreen instructions provided by the **FTP** site administrator to download files as needed **(fig. 7.21)**.

3. You can also drag files from the **FTP** site folder to your local computer.

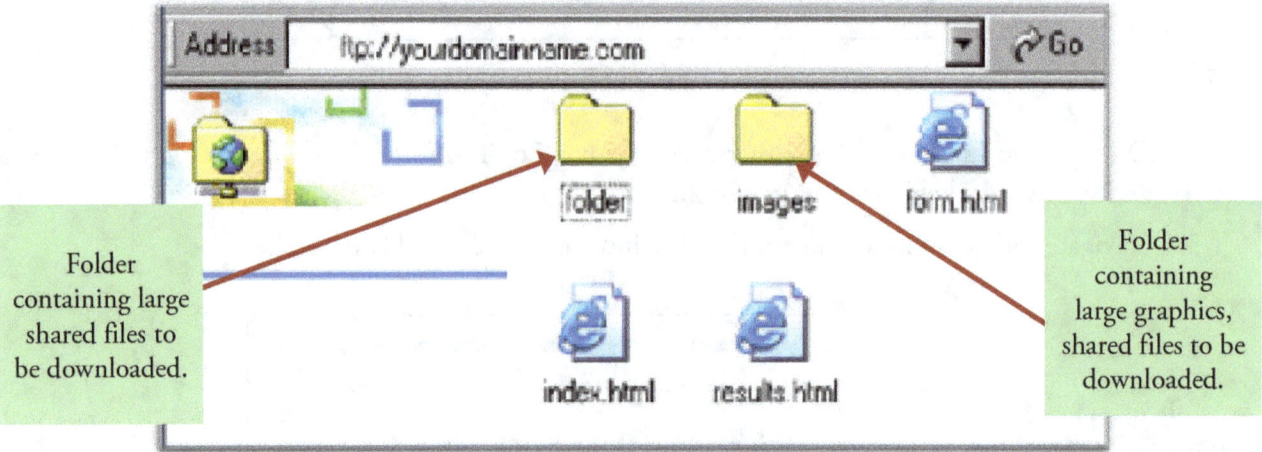

Fig.7.21   **FTP Site Showing Folders Containing Files or Images to be Downloaded**

Tips & Warnings

- In all FTP cases, the permissions for uploading must be set by the remote administrator before you can transfer a file to another site.
- If your remote administrator allows you permission for **"Anonymous FTP"**, it means permissions are set so that anyone on your network can log in using a password such as **"guest"** or **"justme"**.
- If permissions are not set to **Anonymous FTP**, you must log on using passwords and ID that is pre-determined by the site administrator.
- Run a virus scan on any file(s) that you intend to upload to another computer.
- Make sure that the materials you are uploading is rightfully yours. It is illegal to distribute software, music, graphics, or other material unless you own the copyright or are otherwise licensed to do so.

Share a Printer

If you have more than one computer at home and a printer is attached to only one of them, you can print from any computer connected to your wireless network. Follow these steps:

1. On the computer with attached printer, click the **Start** button and click **Settings**.
2. From the open **Settings** window, click **Devices**, and select **Printers & Scanners.**
3. Click **Add a Printer or Scanner;** select the printer name from the displayed list, and click **Manage** tab **(fig. 7.22)**.
4. On the open **Settings** window, click **Printer Properties**, **(fig. 7.23)**.
5. On the open printer window, click the **Sharing** tab, and click **Share this printer** checkbox to check the box **(fig. 7.24)**.
6. In the **Share name** box, type **Name** of the shared printer, click **Apply,** and click **OK**.
7. To print from the shared printer, click **File** at top ribbon of your document, click **Print**, under **Printer** box down arrow, select the printer name, and click the **Print** tab.

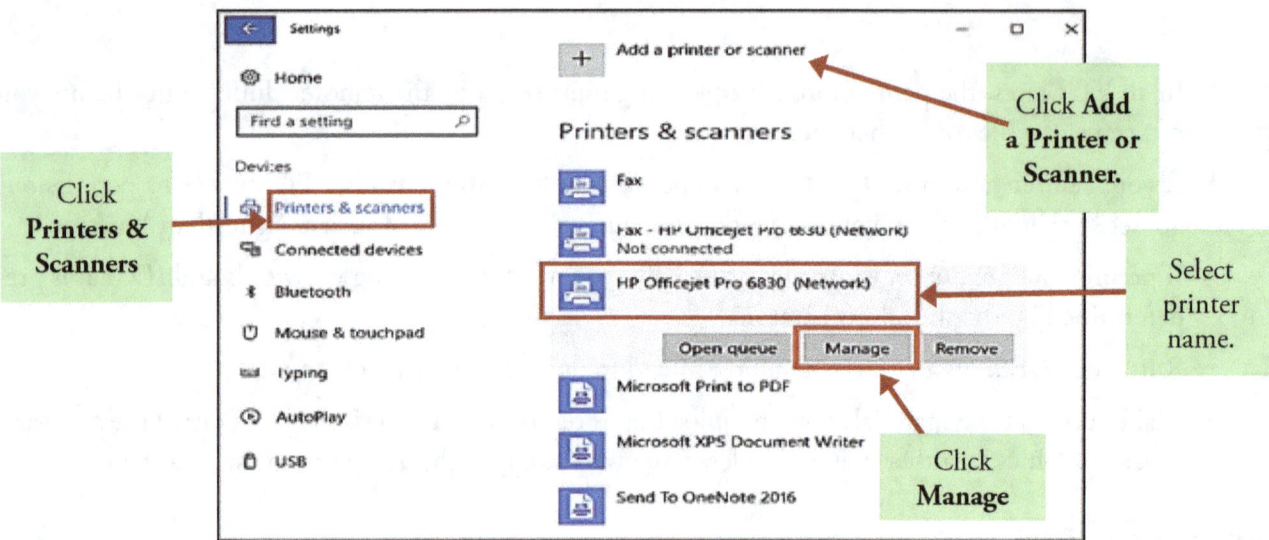

Fig.7.22   **Printers & Scanners View**

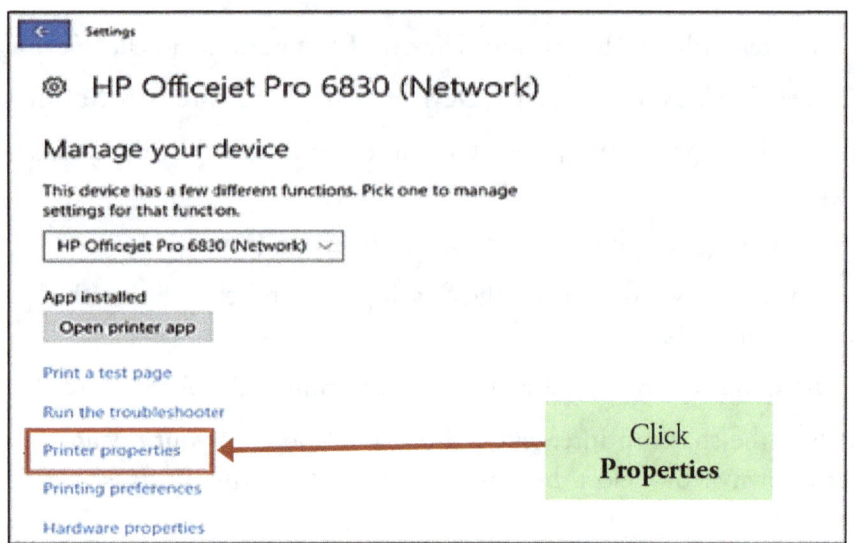

Fig.7.23   **Printers Setting View**

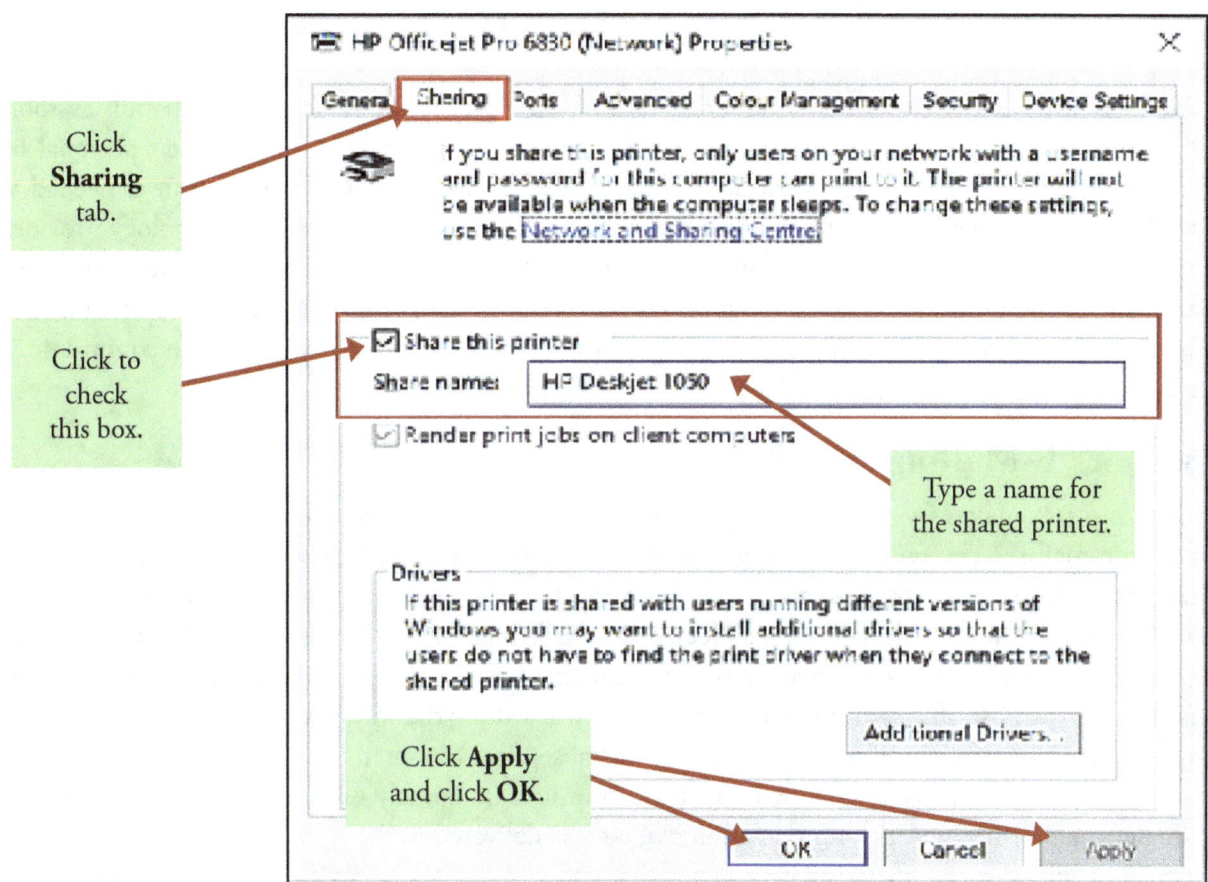

Fig.7.24   **Printers Properties View**

THE EMAILING PROCESS

We live in a fast-paced world where everything is done in a hurry. People need information as soon as possible to make decisions about their finances, jobs, education, and other issues in their personal lives. Organizations typically require information to make business decisions; the information is needed very quickly because any delays may be too costly to bear. The new world of information technology provides us online access to the most efficient and fastest means to send and receive information electronically within seconds. This method of communication is typically referred to as **Emailing.** It is the process of transmitting messages electronically to other people around the world using Internet connection as the communication vehicle.

How Does E-Mailing Work?

An e-mail message makes several stops along the way before getting to its final destination called the **e-mail server**. An e-mail server, commonly referred to as a **computer dedicated server**, is dedicated to the task of managing and passing along e-mail messages on the Internet. When an e-mail message arrives at the destination mail sever, it is held safely in an **electronic mailbox** until you connect to the Internet and access your **e-mail account** to receive the mail. This electronic mail process is similar to the way you receive your letters through the post office. Your letter makes several stops along the way at various postal stations before finally making its way to you. However, unlike the postal service, an e-mail travels in a matter of seconds to pass messages from coast to coast, allowing you to communicate quickly with people all over the world at any time of the day or night. For your email message to be delivered to the rightful recipient, you must use the correct email address. Otherwise, it will come back to you, a term referred to as **bounce back** just like an incorrect mailing address on a letter will be returned to you by the post office with the message, **"return to sender."**

What is an E-mail Account?

An e-mail account is a profile that contains basic personal information about you, data files, and account settings where your e-mail is stored. E-mail accounts usually come in **profiles**, and a new profile is created automatically when you run the **email client** such as Outlook, or Yahoo for the first time. After the first run, the profile runs each time you start the program because it is setup for sending and receiving e-mail. When you create the profile and start using it, it becomes an E-mail account containing your profile information. Most people need only one e-mail account; others need more than one, and sometimes you may find it useful to have multiple e-mail accounts. For example, you may need one account for work, one for school, and another for home. Also, if other people use the same computer as you do, their e-mail accounts and settings can be kept in a separate profile under a different profile name. Depending on your needs, you can add several email accounts as needed.

The Email Client

This is an application program installed on your computer that allows you to send, receive, and organize your e-mail. The most commonly used type of e-mail client is **Microsoft Outlook**. Other examples of Email Clients are found on the Internet free web-based email service such as **Yahoo, Hotmail,** and **Gmail.** The email clients for these free web-based services are the companies that placed the application programs on the website for you to use.

FREE WEB-BASED E-MAIL SERVICE

Free Web-based e-mail service is an e-mail client that is made available free on the Internet by some companies that offer free Web-based messaging services. For example, **Yahoo** offers Web-based e-mail service called **Yahoo Mail**, and so does **Hotmail** and **Messenger** by **Windows Live,** and **Gmail** by **Google.** The service is free, easy to setup and work with, and includes similar features commonly found in **MS Outlook**, and other e-mail services, such as an address book, attachment facility, and filtering, etc. These companies provide **IMAP** (Internet Messaging Access Protocol) servers on which people can create an e-mail account, and can access the account from any Internet-connected computer. Before you can send or receive an email on a free web-based email service you must have an existing email account. For your email message to be delivered to the rightful recipient, you must use the correct email address. Otherwise, it will come back to you **(bounce back)** just like an incorrect mailing address on a letter will be returned to you by the post office with the message, **"return to sender."** In this chapter, you will learn how to create messages and deliver them electronically through email. Setting up an email account online using the free web-based email service is very easy by following simple onscreen instructions. You can choose any email client you want such as Yahoo, Hotmail, Gmail, etc. They are all free of charge. To create a Yahoo email account or any other e-mail client, follow these steps:

Create or Setup a Yahoo Email Account

1. Open **Internet Explorer**, and type **www.yahoo.com** in the browser to display **Yahoo** website, click **Mail**, and click the **Create A New Account** button.
2. Complete the registration form, read the **Licensing Agreement**, click **Continue**, and follow instructions to create your Yahoo email account **(fig.7.25)**.
3. During signup, if you select an email address that is unavailable (being used by someone else), Yahoo notifies you and gives you a chance to select another email address .
4. Whatever email address you select must always end with **@yahoo.com**. For example, **smith.10@yahoo.com**
5. For security reasons, choose a **Password** that is unique; it should be something you can easily remember, a word or phrase that only you would know.
6. As a security measure, Yahoo opens a window with option for you to select method of receiving your **Verification Code**, select the option that appears with your cell phone #.
7. Check your phone immediately, and enter the **5-digit** code (e.g., 83019) in the box provided, and click **Verify**.
8. Yahoo will notify you when your registration is complete; click **Done** on the next window that appears to open your email account.
9. Your new email account opens with a welcome message from Yahoo **(fig. 7.26)**.

Fig.7.25   **Create Yahoo Email Account**

Fig.7.26   **New Yahoo Email Account with 2 Welcome Message**

All-in-One Beginners Guide to Computer Proficiency | 381

CREATE AND SEND MESSAGES ONLINE

Every e-mail message must have two parts – a **header** located at the top part of your e-mail window, and a **message body**, the bottom part of the window. The header contains the name and e-mail address of the recipient, the names and e-mail addresses of all other recipients the same message will be copied to, and the subject of your message. The message body contains your entire message. To send an e-mail message, you must have an email address, and know the correct e-mail address of the recipient or recipients. It is important that you use the correct address otherwise your message will either come back to you **(bounce back)** undelivered or be sent to the wrong person. The consequences of using wrong e-mail address is similar to what happens when you use the wrong address to mail a letter through the postal service; the letter will come back to you undelivered with a stamp across the face **"Return to Sender."** With an active Yahoo email account, you can perform the following functions:

- Send an email to a recipient,
- Send an e-mail to multiple recipients,
- Reply to the same recipients,
- Forward the same message to someone else,
- send the same message again,
- Save the message as a file,
- Send a message with an attachment, and
- Send an email with electronic signature.

Send an E-mail in Yahoo Mail

1. Open **Internet Explorer**, and type **www.yahoo.com** in the browser (address box) to display **Yahoo** website.

2. Click **Mail**, enter your **Yahoo ID** (your e-mail address) in the **ID** area.

3. You may be required to go through a verification process, check the box "**I'm not a Robot**" and identify some pictures. This is part of Yahoo's security measure to help protect you against identity theft.

4. Enter **Password** in the white box, and click **Sign In** or press **Enter.** This is the same **ID** (email address) and password you created in account setup above.

5. Click the **Compose** button, click **To** box, type the recipient's e-mail address; click **Subject** box and type the subject of your message **(fig. 7.27)**.

6. If you are sending the same message to more than one recipient, at top right of your mailbox, click **CC/BCC** to enter multiple recipients email addresses **(fig. 7.28)**.

7. In the **CC/BCC** boxes, type the e-mail address of each recipient followed by a colon **(;)** after each address for all recipients you want to receive the same message.

8. In the **Message body**, type your entire message, and click the **Send** button at bottom of the mailbox.

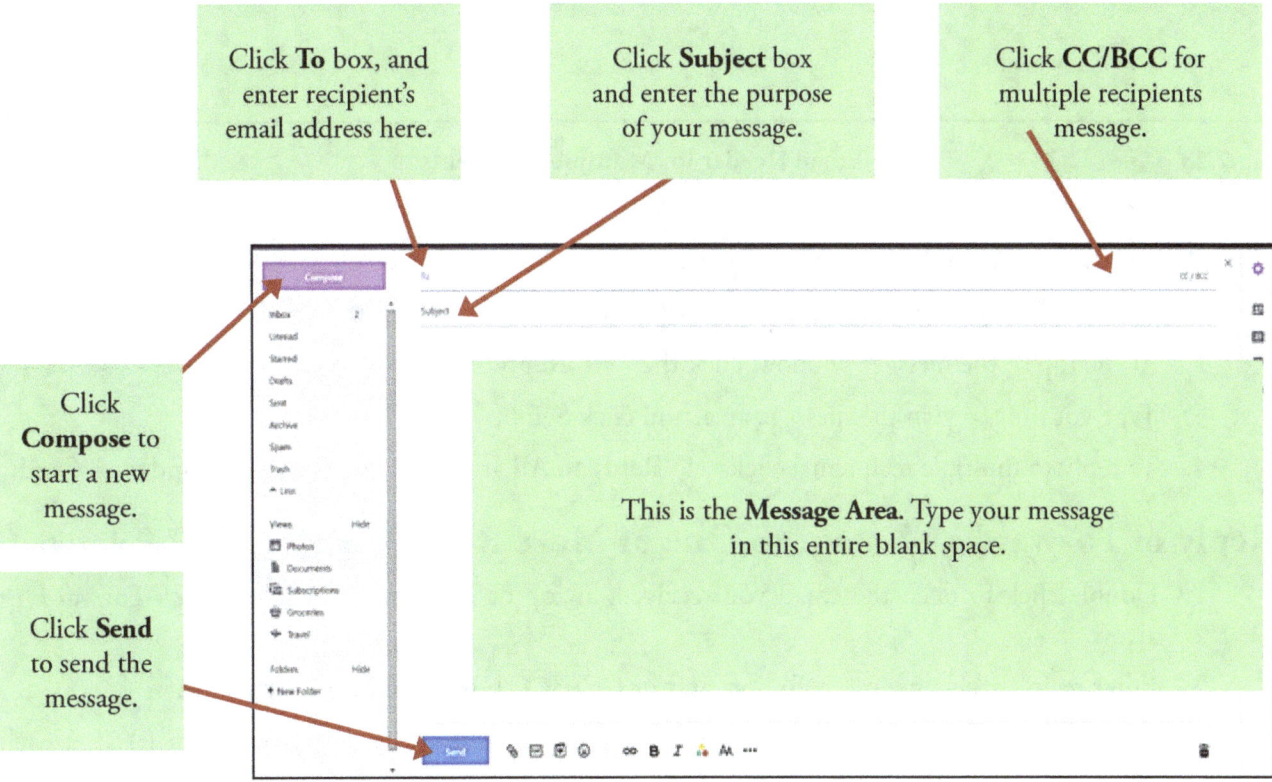

Fig.7.27   **Email Message Window (Mailbox)**

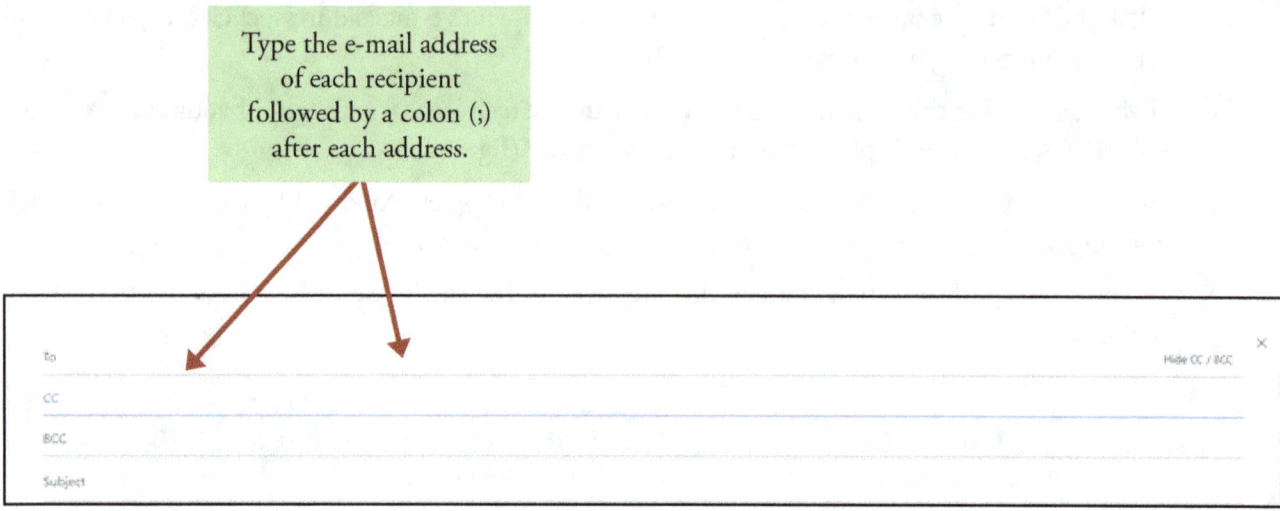

Fig.7.28   **Email Header for Multiple Recipients**

Reply to an Email Message Only to the Sender

1. Double-click the message you received to open it.
2. At the top of the message window, click the **Reply** arrow.
3. Type your message in the message area, and click **Send**.
4. To reply to multiple recipients, click **Reply to All** arrow type your message, and click **Send.**

Reply or Forward a Message to One or More Recipient(s) – Fig.7.29

1. Double-click to open the email you received, at top of the message window, click **Forward** ➡ arrow.
2. Enter recipient's name in the **To** box, and/or **CC/BCC** box for multiple recipients.
3. If you are forwarding to more than one recipient, be sure to include **Semicolon (;)** after each address or select from a contact list.
4. If you are forwarding your message with a different subject matter, type the new subject matter (i.e., the purpose of your message) in the **Subject** box. Click **Send.**

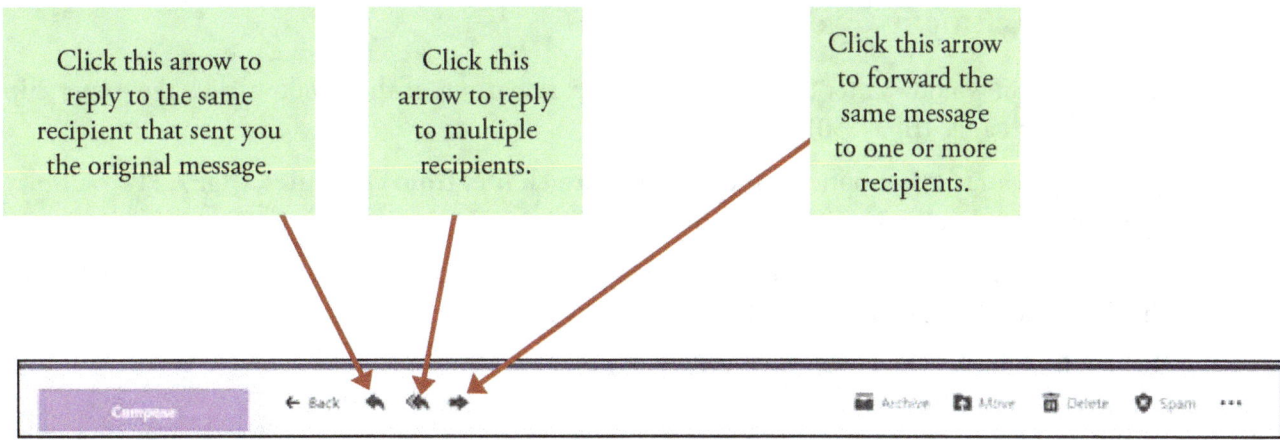

Fig.7.29   Message Sending Options

Save a Message as a File

1. Double-click on the message you want to save as a file.
2. Right-click anywhere on the message body, from the displayed short menu select **Save As**.
3. On the open **Explorer** window, under **Organize** at left pane, navigate to find a location to save the email.
4. In the **File Name** box at bottom of the **Explorer** window type a name for the file.
5. In the **Save As Type** box, select **Webpage Complete**.
6. Click on the **Save** button to save the email message as a file

Email Attachment

This is an electronic file created in a Microsoft Office program or other applications, saved on your computer, and included in an e-mail message. Before you can attach a file to your message, you must have already created the file or have the item such as a picture saved on your computer or other storage devices. In Yahoo mail, the attachment icon is located at the bottom of message window. Also included at the bottom are text formatting options; highlight the text you want to format and select the appropriate option. Recall that we covered text and document formatting in Microsoft Word chapter 4, the same process applies here.

Add an Attachment to a Yahoo E-mail

1. In Yahoo Mail window, after typing your message, at bottom of the window, click the **paper clip** icon to attach a file **(fig. 7.30)**.

2. On the open attachment option window, select **Attach files from computer, (fig. 7.31)** to display your computer **Explorer** window.

3. In the open **Explorer** window, under **Organize**, navigate to locate the file you want to attach, click the file name, click **Open**, and click **Send**.

4. To attach multiple files, repeat steps **2 & 3** above.

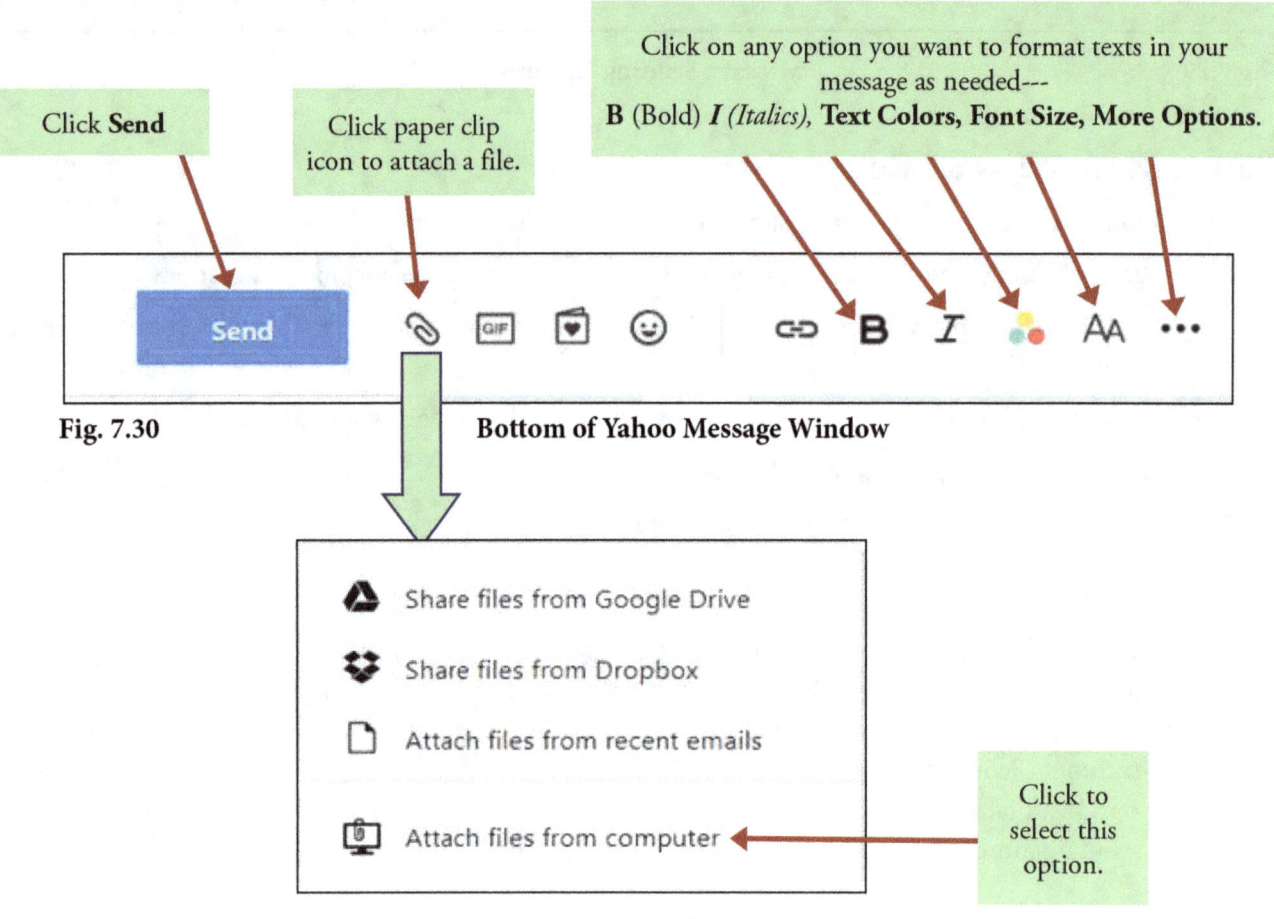

Fig. 7.30   **Bottom of Yahoo Message Window**

Fig. 7.31   **Attachment Option Window**

Contact List

A contact list also referred to as an address book contains a list of your contacts; the people you maintain email communication with on regular basis. If there are people you send messages to very often, it will save you time to have their contact information on your contact list so that you do not have to type their email addresses in the recipient box again each time you want to send them a message. You can also send an email to a contact from the contact list.

Create a New Contact & Contact List in Yahoo E-Mail Account

1. Click the email you want to add to your contact list.
2. At top toolbar, click on **More** icon down arrow to display settings options.
3. On the open menu list, select **Add Sender to Contacts** to display contact form, **(fig. 7.32)**.
4. Enter sender's contact information on the open contact form and click **Save**.
5. To add more contacts to the list, click **Contact** icon at top right of the message window, click **All** tab **(fig. 7.33)**.
6. At the bottom of the displayed **Contact List**, click **Add a new contact**, complete the displayed form with the contact's information, and click **Save** to add your contact to the list.
7. If you have a long list of contacts, it can be quite time consuming to go through the list and find a contact. Use the **Search Contacts** box to find a contact.
8. To search for a contact on the list, type keyword in the **Search** box, and click **Search** button.
9. To organize your contacts by **first** or **last** names, click **More Contact Options** icon and follow on screen instructions to organize your contact list **(fig. 7.33)**.

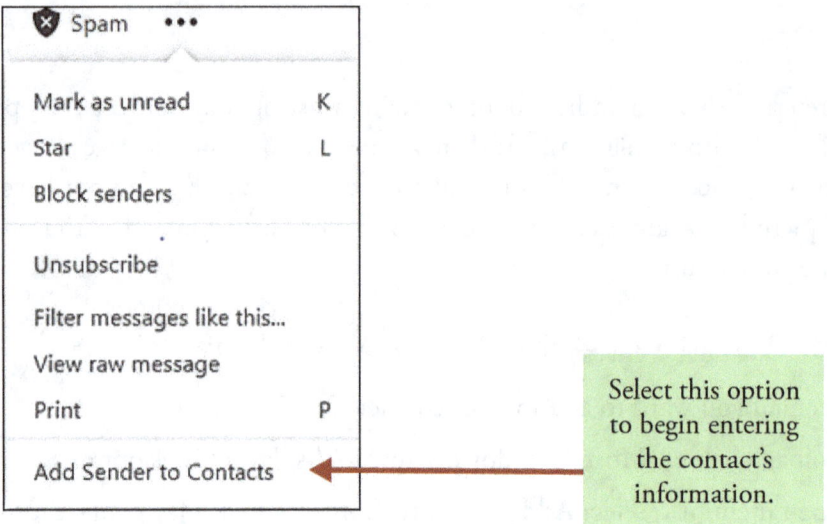

Fig. 7.32   **Create a New Contact**

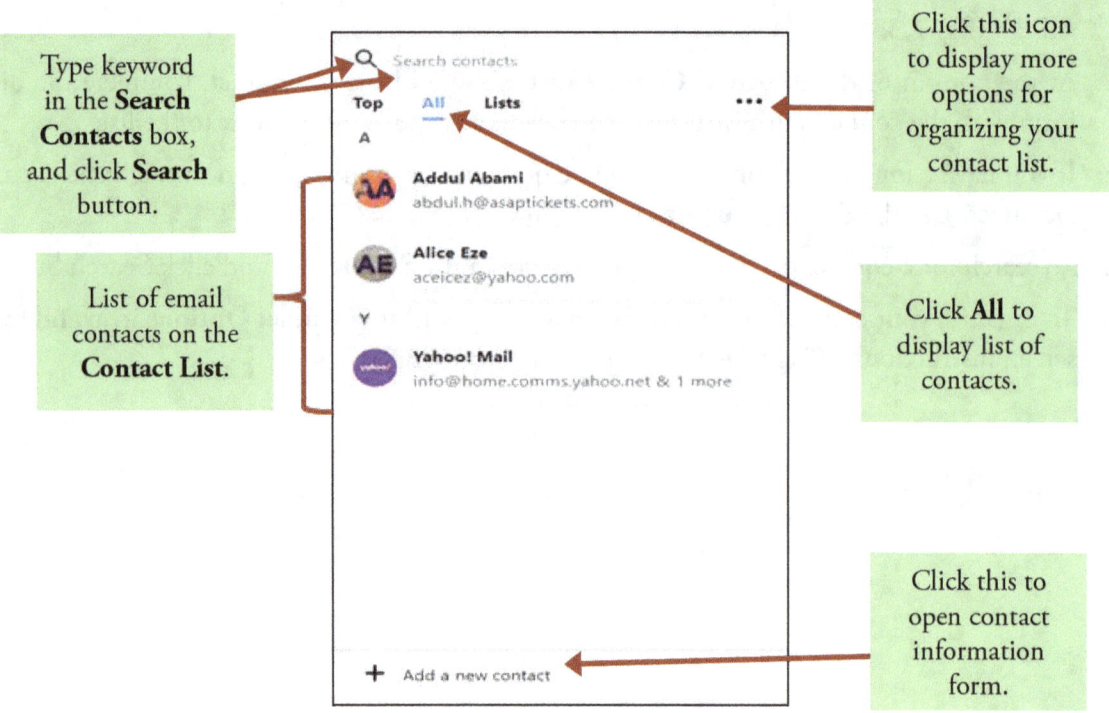

Fig. 7.33   **Add More Contacts to the Contact List**

388 | *Basic Computing Concepts*

Create an Email from the Contact List

1. Click the **Contact** icon at top right of the message window, click **All** tab.
2. From the displayed **Contact List**, click the contact's email address to open message window.
3. Type your message and click **Send** button.

Electronic Signature

The free web-based email service also contains features that allow you to create personalized signatures, composed of text, images, and your electronic business cards. Electronic business card (EBC) is a view of specific information about a contact in a format similar to a paper-based business card, and can be inserted into messages. You may also include a logo in e-mail messages. The signature may be updated as needed or be used as templates on which a new signature is based or to produce multiple signatures for a variety of purposes, such as business and family communications. An electronic signature when created will appear at the bottom of all your outgoing messages. An e-mail signature may include all or some of the following items:

- Your name and job title (if employed)
- Your place of work
- Location of your workplace (address)
- Home address (if unemployed)
- Phone, mobile, and fax number
- Your email address
- Your company website address

Insert Electronic Signature to all Outgoing Email Messages

1. Click the **Settings** icon at top right of the message window.
2. On the displayed menu, select **More Settings**, and click **Writing email**.
3. Under **Signature**, click the grayed-out **Toggle button** to enable a signature for your outgoing email messages. Once enabled, a text box opens up **(fig. 7.34)**.

4. In the open text box below your email address, type your name, and all contact information you want on your signature.

5. At top left of your email window, click **Back to Inbox.** All your outgoing messages will contain the signature information you entered in this box.

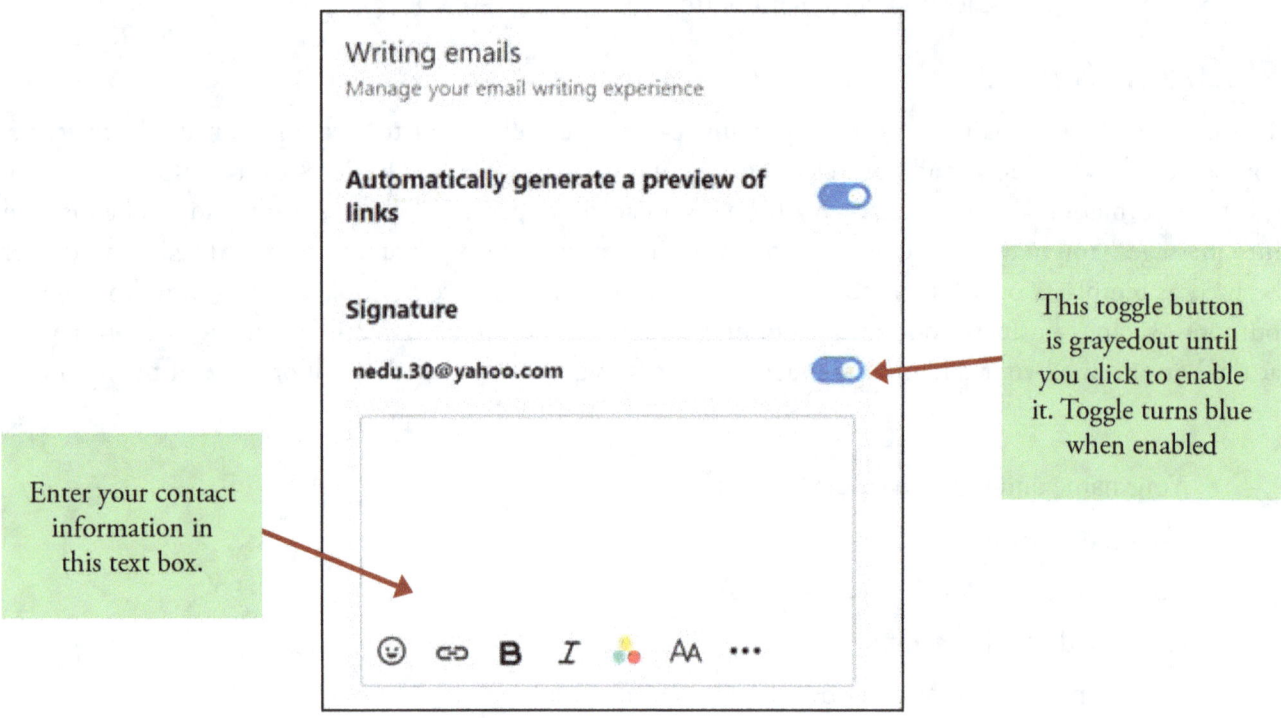

Fig. 7.34   **Yahoo Signature Window**

Spam or Junk Mail

These are unsolicited, unwanted, and annoying e-mail that often comes with offensive languages including pornographic materials. Spam and junk mails are sent out by advertisers who hope to convince you to purchase their products. Advertisers know that most spam go unanswered, so they must send them out in very large volumes hoping to attract a few buyers. As a result, your inbox may contain just a few personal messages and monopolized by unwanted junk mail. One sure way to remove spam or junk mail from your inbox is to select and delete them without opening them. However, this is just a temporary solution to an ongoing problem because similar mail will come in the same or next day. If the same spam comes into your inbox daily, a more permanent solution will be needed. You can set up filters to automatically delete or block them from your inbox. Check with your Internet service provider (ISP) for directions on filtering. Antispam software products that attempt to control spam are available in the market and some are included in Internet security packages that come with your new computer, such as Norton Internet Security and McAfee Internet Security software. One thing you should never do is to respond to unwanted e-mail or send a message asking to be removed from their mailing list. This action may compound the problem because it confirms that your email address is a valid one, possibly adding you to even more spam mailing lists. Although it is not possible to completely stop spam once it has started, there are a few things you can do to minimize them. Follow these simple rules:

- When subscribing to anything on the Internet, if asked, always indicate that you do not want your e-mail address or personal information be shared with anyone else.
- Never reply to any junk e-mail or click on a link contained in the junk mail that will take you to another web site.
- Never reply to a request to let a mailer know you want to be removed from the mailing list.
- Listen to your ISP's suggestions for dealing with unwanted e-mail and make sure you follow recommendations. Some ISPs may want you to forward unwanted e-mail to a special account to enable them help you filter future e-mails from the same sender.
- Install an Internet security software package or anti-spam software.

CHAPTER SUMMARY & KEY TERMS

Internet Explorer is software that enables you to view the contents of the World Wide Web (WWW). It connects you to the Internet to display Web pages that allow you to search for information. The Internet also serves as a communication vehicle that facilitates sending and receiving e-mail messages. It assists with downloading and transferring files from one location to another, displays website graphics, and plays audio and video files associated with a website. The latest version of Internet Explorer 11 is packed with new features that make web browsing faster, easier, and safer than ever. The three important factors to consider before connecting to the Internet are your computer equipment, the type of connection you want, and your Internet service provider. The two main categories of Internet connection are dial-up and broadband. Dial-up is a type of connection in which your computer is connected directly to a phone jack but you can only be either on the phone or the Internet at a time but not both at the same time because each action ties up the phone line for the other. Broadband consists of various types of Internet connection such as: Cable, DSL, Wireless, Satellite, and in most cases Internet TV, which includes WebTV or MSN® TV. These types of Internet connection are all referred to as broadband Internet communication characterized by "always on" connections, which essentially implies that your computer is always connected to the Internet even when you are not actively working online. With broadband connection, you can be on the phone and on the Internet at the same time without losing speed.

Internet Explorer 11 comes with the following new features such as In-line Search within Pages, SmartScreen Filter, Search Suggestions, Authenticated Feeds, Multilingual User Interface (MUI), Security and Privacy, RSS Features, Zoom Enhancements, and much more. Of these features, the two most time-saving noticeable ones are AutoComplete Changes and Automatic Tab Crash Recovery. If there is one page you visit most, you can make it your home page so that every time you start Internet Explorer or click the Home button that page will automatically appear. Your home page is the page that appears every time you open Internet Explorer. Making a webpage available offline by saving the page on your desktop allows you to read its content even when your computer is not connected to the Internet. This includes viewing web- pages on your laptop or computer when you don't have a network or Internet connection.

An email client for free web-based service is an online application program provided free by companies such as Yahoo, Hotmail, and Gmail. These services are easy to setup, does not cost the user anything, and very easy to use. An e-mail server is a computer dedicated to the task of managing and passing along e-mail messages on the Internet. Every e-mail message must have two parts: a header located at the top part of your e-mail window, and a message body, the bottom part of the window. The header contains the name, e-mail address of the recipient, e-mail addresses of all other recipients the same message will be copied to, and the subject of your message. The message body contains your entire message. You can follow simple online instructions to create an online email account, send messages, add attachments to your messages, create a contact list, and add electronic signature to all your outgoing messages. An electronic business card is a view of specific information about a contact in a format similar to a paper-based business card that can be inserted into messages. Spam or junk mail are unsolicited, unwanted, and annoying e-mail that often comes with offensive languages including pornographic materials. Spam and junk mails are sent out by advertisers who hope to convince you to purchase their products. Advertisers know that most spam go unanswered, so they must send them out in very large volumes hoping to attract a few buyers. As a result, your inbox may contain just a few personal messages and monopolized by unwanted junk mail. Check with your Internet service provider (ISP) for directions on filtering or how to minimize junk mail in your mailbox.

KEY TERMS

Address Bar
Pop-Up Blocker Pop-Up
Profile
Junk Mail
Navigation Pane
Web-based e-mail
Anonymous FTP
Animated Banners
Attachment
Asymmetric DSL (ADSL)
Authenticated Feeds
Blog
Bounce Back

Contact List
Favorite Center
FPT (File Transfer Protocol)
Hyperlinks
Search Bar
Multilingual User
Interface (MUI)
RSS Features (Rich
Site Summary)
Email Server
Emailing
Email Client
Header

Electronic Mailbox
File compression
Software Profile
IMAP
Pop-Up Blocker
Pop-Up
(Internet Message
Access Protocol)
Junk Mail
Navigation Pane
Web-based e-mail

Demonstrate Your Knowledge & Skill

CHAPTER 7 PRACTICE EXERCISES
INTRODUCTION TO INTERNET EXPLORER
& ELECTRONIC COMMUNICATION

7.1 – Match listed terms to correct statements & questions below:

a. Keyword
b. Address Bar Down Arrow
c. Search Box
d. Protocols
e. Favorite Center
f. World Wide Web (WWW)
g. Hyperlinks
h. Hotspots
i. Two
j. Connection
k. Animated Banners
l. Web Authoring
m. Dial-Up
n. wireless or Wi-Fi
o. Not regulated by any particular agency
p. URL
q. Cyber Squatting
r. Autocomplete
s. Browser
t. Search Engine
u. Surfing
v. Address Bar
w. Internet Explorer
x. Google
y. Pop-Ups

Statements & Questions

1. A feature located at top right of a webpage used for performing searches on the websites.
2. What is the term used to describe a word or phrase typed to begin web search?
3. An Internet feature that allows you to browse through a list of Web pages you recently when you click on it.
4. The subset of the Internet that displays pages of information in a way that is easy to navigate and understand.
5. The variety of formats or languages through which communication can occur on the Internet.
6. What areas on the screen that can be clicked to open other websites or webpages?

7. Why is it that information you find on certain websites may not be in good taste?
8. Something you must have on your computer in order to access the Internet.
9. A situation where internet connection is directly to a phone jack.
10. Public locations where mobile users can access the Internet free of charge with a wireless connection.
11. The public connection place cannot work if it does have a specific type of access feature.
12. At least how many parts must a domain name have separated by a dot?
13. The Internet feature that specifies a web address with a string of characters.
14. Software that simplifies webpage programming by allowing developers to specify the design of a webpage without actually writing the supporting code.
15. A term that refers to registering or using a domain name in bad faith with the intent to profit from the name at the expense of another person or company.
16. The software that locates and displays webpages.
17. Software that comes already installed on your computer.
18. A key element of a browser interface where a URL is entered.
19. What feature of Internet browser suggests recently accessed sites similar to text typed?
20. Another name used to describe browsing or navigating the Internet.
21. A database of Internet files collected by a computer program.
22. The preferred search engine for many people and has won numerous awards.
23. Located at the toolbar, an Internet feature you can create that displays a list of the websites visited most frequently.
24. A series of rotating or changing text and images embedded within the webpage; colorful images used to attract attention and stimulate interest to a website.
25. Distracting and annoying windows that display on the screen without being requested.

7.2 – Multiple Choices: Select the best answer to Internet Explorer and Electronic Communication concepts, features, and actions described below:

1. Adding a page to your list of favorite pages requires one of the following steps:
   a. Drag a link from a Web Page to your Links Bar.
   b. On the toolbar menu, click on Favorites, click Add to Favorites, and click the Add button.
   c. Drag the link to the Links Folder in your Favorites List.
   d. Click on Create In button, and click Ok; the page will be added to your list.

2. If your Internet window does not show the Links bar on the toolbar, do one of these:
   a. On the Tool Bar menu, click on View menu, click on Toolbars, and select Links.
   b. Click Internet Options on the Tools menu.
   c. Check the box: Make Available Offline.
   d. Go to the File menu, and click Print.

3. Which one of the following is NOT a step for changing your home page on the Internet?
   a. Click Internet Options on the Tools menu.
   b. Click the Back arrow on the toolbar to return to the last page you viewed.
   c. When the Options dialog box opens, click the General tab.
   d. Go under Home Page, and click Use Current.

4. The Internet is a:
   a. broadband connection that utilizes existing telephone lines.
   b. secure high-speed transmission media.
   c. group of interconnected networks that span around the world.
   d. network subset, which is the most accessible of Internet services.

5. The Internet first originated and was originally sponsored by the:
   a. National Science Foundation.
   b. Department of State.
   c. Department of Defense.
   d. Department of Treasury.

6. To create, and send email message, the next thing you do after opening Yahoo Mail is:
   a. Click the Start button, click Programs, and select MS Outlook from the list.
   b. Enter recipient's email address in the To: box
   c. On the Inbox window at the Toolbar, click the Compose button.
   d. Click the Outlook icon on the desktop (if the icon's shortcut is on the desktop).

7. Before you can select a recipient name from an email address book, you must first:
   a. Call the recipient and get his/her email address.
   b. Setup a contact list so that the names will be on the list already when you click to select the contact.
   c. Type your message in the message box.
   d. Copy another recipient in the Cc: box.

8. One of the three main components needed for connecting to the Internet is:
   a. A dialup modem
   b. Cable service
   c. Cellular phone service
   d. Computer equipment

9. Which of the following can inhibit wireless Internet service?
   a. Night time
   b. Cloud cover
   c. Thunderstorms
   d. Cable outages

10. Which one of the entity is the leading organization that creates Web standards and develops
    a. specifications, guidelines, software, and tools.
    b. Advanced Research Project Agency (ARPA)
    c. NSFNet Academic Enterprise
    d. World Wide Web Consortium (W3C)
    e. Department of Defense (DOD)

11. When replying to an email to only the sender, do one of these:
    a. Click on Email, select Reply to Only sender, and click Send.
    b. Click on the toolbar menu and select Reply to Sender, and click Send.
    c. Click on Subject box and type Reply to Sender
    d. Click Reply on the toolbar menu, type your message, and click Send.

12. To include an attachment to your email message, do one of these:
    a. Double-click to open the email you received, and press CTRL+V.
    b. In the Subject box, type the subject matter of your message, and click Send.
    c. Click on the Attach button, double-click on the file you want to attach, and click Send.
    d. Click on the Insert button, select Attachment, and click Send.

13. To forward an email to more than one recipient, you must include one of the following after each recipient in the To box:
    a. Equal sign (=)
    b. Semicolon (;)
    c. Plus (+)
    d. Colon (:)

14. To connect to the Internet, you must consider three main components that include:
    a. software, hardware, and connection type.
    b. computer equipment, connection type, and the WWW.
    c. software, hardware, and a wireless connection type.
    d. computer equipment, connection type, and Internet service provider.

15. Which of the following is NOT a choice of an Internet access provider?
    a. Ground Wave distribution
    b. Wireless Internet
    c. Cable network
    d. DSL

16. A dial-up modem connects your computer to:
    a. an electrical outlet.
    b. the cable television network.
    c. the telephone system.
    d. a wireless Internet provider.

17. Which of the following is NOT a way to minimize spam?
    a. Install an Internet security software package or anti-spam software.
    b. Never reply to any junk e-mail or visit any web site suggested in the mail.
    c. Sign up for subscriptions and always accept further e-mail from that subscription.
    d. Never reply to a request to let a mailer know if you want to be removed from a mailing list.

18. A popular free Web-based e-mail service that includes features common to other e mail services, such as an address book, an attachment facility, and filtering is offered by:
    a. Yahoo.
    b. ICQ.
    c. Symantec.
    d. McAfee.

19. The two areas in an e-mail message are:
    a. Title area and text area
    b. Header area and text area
    c. Header area and message area
    d. Title area and message area

20. One of the following is NOT a reason an e-mail message might be returned as undeliverable?
    a. The recipient cancelled e-mail account.
    b. There were too many misspellings in the body of the message for the server to interpret the message.
    c. The server is too busy with high traffic at the time.
    d. The recipient's e-mail address is incorrect.

21. When a message comes back to you as undeliverable, the process is described as:
    a. Sending
    b. Returning
    c. Bouncing Back
    d. Cycling

22. Which of the following is NOT included in the header of an e-mail message?
    a. The subject of the message as well as the time and date of the message
    b. The name and e-mail address of the recipient and the sender, and the subject of the message
    c. The e-mail addresses of the sender and receiver
    d. The body of the message

23. The following statements about an e-mail address book are true EXCEPT:
    a. It is the equivalent to writing addresses down on a piece of paper for later use.
    b. It allows e-mail addresses to be grouped in a specific order for quick access.
    c. It makes it easier to determine if the email has virus.
    d. It prevents you from having to remember or type multiple e-mail addresses.

24. Why would you want to preview e-mail before opening it?
    a. The e-mail may contain a virus.
    b. The e-mail may include a stationery pattern.
    c. The e-mail may contain an attachment.
    d. There is no good reason to preview e-mail.

25. Passing along e-mail you've received to others is known as:
    a. spamming.
    b. flaming.
    c. forwarding.
    d. sharing.

26. A type of DSL that uses existing phone lines is:
    a. SDSL.
    b. ADSL.
    c. ISDN.
    d. broadband.

27. In DSL, typical download speeds are:
    a. the same as upload speeds.
    b. faster than upload speeds.
    c. slower than upload speeds.
    d. always changing.

28. The following statements about broadband are true EXCEPT:
    a. types include cable and DSL.
    b. it has stronger capability.
    c. it provides high speed access.
    d. it requires a telephone company connection.

29. Which of the following is specifically configured so that even if you lose phone service, you may still have the Internet?
    a. DSL
    b. Dial-up
    c. Satellite
    d. Cable modem

30. Wireless connectivity is described by all of the following statements EXCEPT:
    a. it allows mobility and multiple users to be online at the same time.
    b. computers require a network card that will communicate through a wireless access point.
    c. you can take advantage of hotspots for public use.
    d. it is not a form of broadband technology.

31. All of the following are TRUE about an Internet Service Provider (ISP) EXCEPT:
    a. it is a company that allows you to connect to the Internet through its host server.
    b. it can include local phone companies, long-distance carriers, national online services, and locally owned firms.
    c. the cost varies and is dependent upon the level of service provided and the number of hours contracted per month.
    d. the cost is stable and independent of the level of service provided and the number of hours contracted per month.

32. Hypertext transfer protocol (HTTP) is:
    a. the Internet itself.
    b. the language that web pages are written in.
    c. the authority that decides who gets what domain name.
    d. a set of rules that determine how Web pages get from the Internet to you.

33. Which one of these is NOT a way to get an e-mail account?
    a. Work for a business that gives their employees e-mail accounts.
    b. Create your own e-mail service.
    c. Receive an e-mail account when signing up for America Online.
    d. Sign up for a free Web-based e-mail service.

34. What is a benefit of e-mail over telephone messages?
    a. You can attach a file to the e-mail message.
    b. An e-mail message can be brief.
    c. An e-mail message reaches its destination quickly.
    d. An e-mail message can be retrieved at the recipient's convenience.

35. What is an e-mail server?
    a. A program that will allow you to write an e-mail
    b. A Web site that gives you an e-mail account
    c. A messaging program that allows you to send e-mail
    d. A computer dedicated to the task of managing and passing along e-mail on the Internet

36. Transmitted effectively through e-mail, a computer virus is:
    a. an invitation to visit a web site that appears reputable but requests that you update your personal information.
    b. a program specifically written to damage or annoy computer users.
    c. more annoying than destructive.
    d. a form of junk mail.

37. Spam is the electronic equivalent of:
    a. telemarketing calls.
    b. highway billboards.
    c. television commercials.
    d. junk mail.

38. Viruses can be transmitted through a file accompanying an e-mail message known as a(n):
    a. script.
    b. attachment.
    c. junk mail message.
    d. spam mail message.

39. The "http://" in "http://www.google.com" is known as the:
    a. top-level domain name.
    b. domain name.
    c. protocol.
    d. URL.

40. Which of these is handy if you want to revisit a page, but can't remember the URL?
    a. The history list
    b. The homepage
    c. Bookmarks
    d. Subject directories

41. To attach a file to an e-mail message, you must first:
    a. type the file name in the body of the message.
    b. click the File button on the message area.
    c. click on the Attach or Add File icon.
    d. Click on the Forward icon.

42. Which of the following statements about an e-mail attachment is false?
    a. Needs to be checked for viruses.
    b. Must be downloaded and opened before it can be viewed.
    c. File size may be too large for transmission.
    d. Cannot be printed.

43. On the e-mail window, what icon is typically used to graphically represent an attachment?
    a. A paper clip
    b. A paper clip or a disk
    c. A smiley face or a disk
    d. A disk or a computer

44. What type of software is normally used to make a file take up less space and speed up the
    a. file transfer process?
    b. Decompression
    c. Zip compression
    d. File reducer
    e. File compression

45. An Internet connection that is NOT commonly used these days because of its relatively slow speed compared to broadband connection types.
    a. DSL
    b. ISDN
    c. dial-up
    d. cable

7.3 – Fill in the Blanks with the correct terms or words.

1. _____ is a profile that contains basic personal information about you, data files, and account settings where your e-mail is stored.
2. An application program that allows you to send, receive, and organize your e-mail is called an _____.
3. A type of web site where people make entries in the form of a diary or journal fashion is known as a _____.
4. _____ is a subset of the Internet that displays pages of information in a way that is easy to navigate, understand, and view graphics.
5. The _____ made information and resources available to everyone and introduced the use of graphical browsers for easy navigation of information.
6. An address book contains a list of your _____.
7. An email attachment is referred to as _____ file created in any computer software program.
8. Most free e-mail services simply require an e-mail address and a(n) _____ and _____ to open an account.
9. _____ refers to a transmission type that carries several data channels over a single cable.
10. The _____ is the top-level page from which you can access other pages on the same site.
11. _____ is technology used by business websites to secure a monetary transactions.
12. The two parts that exist in e-mail are the header area and the _____ area.
13. _____ is a communication system that works the same way as a private chat room between two people.
14. In many e-mail software applications, to create a new message, you must first click the _____ button.
15. When an email you sent returns back to you is equivalent to undeliverable US mail with the phrase _____ captioned on the mail.

Basic Computing Concepts

CHAPTER 7 SKILL-BASED PRACTICE PROJECTS INTRODUCTION TO INTERNET EXPLORER 11 & ELECTRONIC COMMUNICATION

7.1 – Internet Search Engine (Web Analysis): Internet search engine allows you to find the information you need on the Web anywhere around the world, including finding the materials you need for your school term paper. In this project, you will use a search engine to find a government website and answer some questions about the website in the form of website analysis. Please use correct Standard English in your responses and keep your answers brief, concise, and straight to the point.

Required:

1. Open **Internet Explorer**, click the **Address Bar**, type **U.S Department of Labor**, and press **Enter**. Click on **Home | U.S. Department of Labor** to open Web page.
2. Open MS Word document entitled **Website Analysis** at top page, center title, and answer the following questions:
    a. How many color combinations are used on the web page?
    b. List the names of the buttons at top of the web page.
    c. If the web page contain a search engine, where is the search engine located on the web page?
    d. List the number of title headings containing links to other web pages.
    e. What do you like about the web page in terms of organization, simplicity, and style?
3. In the **Search** box at top right, type **2020 Census**, and click the **Search** button.
4. Describe what you see on the open webpage. How many **Hyperlinks** are listed on this webpage?
5. **Save** your **Word** file as **7-1_SearchEngine_Firstname_Lastname** in the preferred location on your computer using your first and last name. Submit your completed assignment following the instructor's preferred method – electronically or printed hardcopy for grading.

7.2 – Create a Favorite Center:
A home page favorite center contains a list of web addresses of the websites you visit most often and provides quick access to those websites. With a favorite list you do not have to type the web address in the address bar each time you visit the website. In this project, you will create a favorite center for a few new media websites:

Required:

1. Open **Internet Explorer**, using the long **Search** box at top of the window screen, type each of these news media websites and click the **Search** button to display their webpages **Good Morning America, NBC Nightly News,** and **CBS Evening News.**

2. Open a new Word document entitled **Favorite Center** at top page, and center title. Describe in detail the steps for creating a **Favorite Center** to add these news media websites on the Internet window.

3. Save your Word file as **7-2_FavoriteCenter_Firstname_Lastname** in the preferred location on your computer using your first and last name. Submit your completed assignment following the instructor's preferred method – electronically or printed hardcopy for grading.

7.3 – Internet Explorer Knowledge Capture:
Demonstrate your knowledge of Internet Explorer by correctly answering the questions listed below. Please use correct Standard English in your responses and keep your answers brief, concise, and straight to the point.

Required:

1. Open a Word document, type title name **Internet Explorer Knowledge Capture** at top page, center title and answer the following questions.

2. List and describe the three main types of Internet broadband connections commonly used in business and homes today.

3. What is a **Home Page**? Describe the steps you would use to change the default home page of your Internet window.

4. Who are Internet **Service Providers (ISPs)** and what is their role in internet connectivity?

5. Define the following Internet Explorer terms:

    a. **History Button**

    b. **ScreenTip**

c. **Hyper Links**
   d. **Pop Up Blocker**
6. Save your Word file as **7-3_InternetKnowledge_Firstname_Lastname** in the preferred location on your computer using your first and last name. Submit your completed assignment following the instructor's preferred method – electronically or printed hardcopy for grading.

7.4 – Free Web-Based Email Service:
As discussed in chapter 7, this is a free online communication service that is easy to setup, work with, and includes similar features commonly found in other e-mail services, such as an address book, an attachment facility, and electronic signatures. Email message for this assignment is presented in the text box below:

Dear Mr. or Ms. (your instructor's name here),

Welcome to (the name of your school here) and we hope that your stay at our school will be a very positive one. We are all beginners in computer technology and are very eager to learn all we can to become proficient with using the computer. We look forward to learning a lot from your wealth of experience in technology. See you in class next week.

Sincerely,
Your Name

Required:

1. Open a new Word document entitled **Create Yahoo Email Account** at top page; center title, and describe the detailed steps for creating a new email account on **Yahoo** website (www.yahoo.com).
2. Save your Word file in the preferred location on your computer as **7-4_Yahoomail_Firstname_Lastname** using your first and last name, print document, and submit for grading.
3. Create a new email message and send to your computer instructor. Make sure you have the correct email address to prevent your message from bouncing back to you.
4. In the **Subject** box of your email header, type **Welcome Message** as the topic of your message.
5. In the **Message** area of the email, type the message provided in the text box above.

6. After sending the message, click the **Sent** tab at left pane of your email window to display the message you sent.

7. Right-click anywhere on the displayed message, and select **Save as** from the menu list to save message in the preferred location on your computer.

8. On the open **Save As** window, in the preferred location on your computer, on the **File name** box, type **7-4_WelcomeMessage_ Firstname_Lastname** using your first and last name.

9. Ensure that **Save as type** box under the **File** name box displays **Webpage, Complete**, and click the **Save** button.

10. Print the sent message as a hard copy document, and submit for grading or follow the instructor's preferred method –submitted electronically or printed hardcopy for grading.

7.5 – Emailing:

Open a Word document entitled **The Emailing Process** at top page, and center title. Apply the knowledge you have gained from the study of electronic communication by answering the following questions. Please use correct Standard English in your responses and keep your answers brief, concise, and straight to the point.

Required:

1. Define **Email Client** and give an example of email client.
2. What is an **Email Account** and why do you need one?
3. Describe how emailing works in terms of sending and receiving messages.
4. Describes the two main parts of an email window: **Header** and **Message Body** and state what each part is used for in sending a message.
5. Describe how you would **Forward** an email you just received in your mailbox to someone else.
6. Save your Word file in the preferred location on your computer as **7-5_Emailing_Firstname_ Lastname** using your first and last name. Submit completed assignment (the Word document) following the instructor's preferred method – electronically or printed hardcopy for grading.

CHAPTER 8

INTRODUCTION TO REMOTE ONLINE LEARNING

The history of distance learning dates back to the mid-1800s during the agrarian era born out of the need for educational opportunities to reach a geographically dispersed population. The first distance learning started in the form of correspondence courses. By the onset of the industrial revolution in the 1920s, other more advanced form of distant learning began to emerge. New developments in technology between late 1920s and 1970s led to a tremendous growth in distant learning opportunities through the use of radio and television. By the mid-1970s, the power of technology with computer gradually moved distant learning into its virtual age. The widespread improvement of the internet digital technology in the 1990s, including the changing demographics of the distance learning, students began yet another chapter in the history of technology in education and online learning. Today, advancements in computer technology, instructional technologies, and curriculum development along with learning assessment have made distant education through remote online learning a desirable and efficient way of learning worldwide.

The idea of online learning often referred to as "**computer-mediated distance education**" is relatively new and many students have not quite grasped it yet because the whole idea is now just beginning to catch on. However, as the more technologically adept students are embracing the idea of legitimizing the "virtual classroom," traditional resistance to the brave new world of online learning seems to be limited to a few. However, as a result of the coronavirus (COVID-19) 2020 global pandemic, it does not appear that students have much of a choice than to school remotely online as they were forced to do so on lockdowns. The pandemic has made remote online education a new normal for students around the world. According to educational researchers, several millions of courses are now being offered on the Internet by almost all academic institutions worldwide. This number is growing as more assessment, study and research continue to make their way into online learning environment.

The purpose of this chapter is to help such students navigate their way through remote online learning and ensure that they have all the tools they need to become successful. With the 2020 coronavirus pandemic, it appears that remote online learning is here to stay for many years to come as students worldwide learn to adapt to a new way of schooling. Knowledge gained from this chapter would provide students planning to enroll in distant online learning a strong platform on which to build their strengths and develop the necessary computing skills required for a successful online education. Depending on which learning management system in use at any school, such as Blackboard, Illuminate, D2L (Desire to Learn), Brightspace, etc. beginners in online learning will learn what they need to know in order to successfully participate in remote online education. They will learn how to use the discussion board, download assignment files, submit completed assignments, conduct online research effectively, take online exams, and all other learning activities required in an online classroom.

Learning Objectives: After completing this chapter, you will be able to:

- Understand what virtual online education means, its advantages, disadvantages, how it works in real life, and how to prepare you for online learning.
- Determine if online learning is for you and ask yourself: "Do I have what it takes to pursue my education online?"
- Identify the requirements for a successful online education, and learn how to meet those requirements by following some simple guidelines.
- Navigate the online learning management system (LMS); and apply the five netiquette rules of online communication when sending messages to other people.
- Understand the importance of course management tools in an online learning environment post or respond to posted topics on the discussion board; and send email to fellow online students and your instructor.
- Conduct online research effectively; and learn how to apply effective test-taking tips in taking online exams/quizzes.
- Manage your study time effectively to become a successful online student.

WHAT IS VIRTUAL ONLINE EDUCATION & HOW DOES IT WORK?

Today online education is often referred to as **"E-Learning."** Educational experts define **"virtual education"** as the study of credit and non-credit courses from worldwide remote sites that are neither bound by time nor physical location. It is a form of learning environment that allows a student to hook up with other students and an instructor in both real and virtual time. Whether at home, in the office, or even in an air plane, at any given moment a student can log into a virtual classroom. Assignments can be sent or received from a computer desktop or laptop, e-mail and study materials, research, and discovery of new knowledge are right there at the student's fingertips. Some examples of virtual classrooms are Blackboard, Illuminate, D2L (Desire to Learn), Brightspace, etc. These online learning environments are often referred to as artificial intelligence applications that serve as a virtual learning environment designed to support teaching and learning in an educational setting to create a distinct managed learning environment. The systems allow faculty to add resources for students to access online, such as assignments, links to websites containing materials for research, bulletin notices, and discussion boards. They also allow students to submit their completed work. These types of learning environment typically take place through the Internet and provide a collection of tools such as assessment, communication, discussion boards, uploading of content, return of students' work, peer assessment, administration of student groups, collecting and organizing student grades, questionnaires, tracking tools, etc. They contain features that automatically grade exams, quizzes, or tests in the form of multiple-choice questions, and add students' grades to their grade books.

Unique Features of Online Learning

Virtual online education is a learning environment that provides a single experience that incorporates the three distinct learning styles such as auditory, visual, and kinesthetic. In these ways, learning is inclusive of a maximum number of participants with a maximum range of learning styles, preferences, and needs. It facilitates efficient learning opportunities of a globally dispersed audience; and reduced publishing and distribution costs as Web-based training becomes standardized. Despite its unique form, virtual online education does not conform to the collaborative learning theory which contends that human interaction is a vital ingredient to learning. This is a very important factor affecting the design of e-learning because it has the potential to isolate learners. However, with advancement in technology and new improvements in instructional technologies such as message boards, chats, e-mail, and teleconferencing, this potential drawback is reduced. Yet critics argue that the magical classroom bond between teacher and student, and among the students themselves, cannot be replicated through communications technology.

Types of Online Learning

Most community colleges and universities that offer online courses through World Wide Web deliver their classes in three main formats: hybrid, web-enhanced, and online.

Hybrid Classes: This is a format that combines both classroom and online learning where students complete some class hours via internet while other class hours take place in an on-campus classroom setting.

Web-Enhanced Classes: In this format, students meet in the classroom for all required classroom hours but make use of the internet for downloading study materials, including research, and learning resources, submitting out-of-class completed assignments, and communication. Similar to Hybrid, it is a combination of both live classroom and online learning environment. The only difference is that students must attend live classroom for lectures.

Online Classes: This format allows students to complete their course work through the internet. Before the students begin their online education, most schools require students to attend a live classroom online learning orientation on the main campus.

SOME TYPES OF ONLINE LEARNING MANAGEMENT SYSTEMS

The two main types of online learning management systems commonly used by many colleges and universities include but not limited to Desire to Learn (D2L) and Blackboard. The two management systems described below contain similar platforms and learning tools but with different formats. Students should get familiar with the type of learning management systems provided by their schools through orientations, learning the systems, and following the school established guidelines for student access/use.

Desire to Learn (D2L)

A learning environment founded in 1999 by John Baker, President, and CEO of D2L in response to the challenges faced by his engineering class to look at the world in new ways by coming up with questions that no one had ever asked before. Mr. Baker realized that despite all the technological advancements, his university campus appeared to be out of touch with the momentum generated by the changing times. His quest to find a way to use technology to dramatically transform learning led to the founding of D2L. Mr.

Baker believed that one of the most important things we can do to help each other is to ensure that everyone has access to the best possible learning opportunities. Today, D2L is working with many schools around the world to help learners at an unprecedented scale that was hard to imagine before 1999. D2L's technology is currently being used by K-12, higher education, healthcare, government, and the corporate sector. D2L contains distant learning tools that allow faculty to add learning resources for students to access online, such as assignments, links to websites containing materials for research, bulletin notices, discussion boards, etc.

Blackboard Learn

Blackboard Learn is an application for online teaching, learning, community building, and knowledge sharing. The Learning Management System (LMS) is a virtual learning environment and course management system developed by Blackboard Inc. It is a Web-based server software which features course management, customizable open architecture, and scalable design that allows integration with student information systems and authentication protocols. A Blackboard system is also an artificial intelligence application based on the blackboard architectural model. For this reason, Blackboard systems are used routinely in many military C4ISTAR {Command, Control, Communications, Computers (C4) Intelligence, Surveillance and Reconnaissance (ISR)} systems for detecting and tracking objects. With a Blackboard artificial intelligence (AI) system, in the military, Advanced C4ISR capabilities provide an advantage through situational awareness, knowledge of the adversary and environment, and shortening the time between sensing and response. Another example of current use is in Game AI, where they are considered a standard AI tool to help with adding AI to video games. Like D2L, Blackboard Learn is a tool that allows faculty to add resources for students to access online, such as assignments, links to websites containing materials for research, bulletin notices, discussion boards, etc. Its unique learning environment provides educators with the autonomy to deliver the inclusive, consistent educational experiences learners desire, while operating alongside the current tools and integrations. You can use any theory or model for teaching your online course because Blackboard Learn is open, flexible, and centered on student achievement.

VIDEO CONFERENCING SERVICES & THE MOST COMMONLY USED TYPES IN TODAY'S BUSINESS

The 2020 pandemic with massive spread of the novel coronavirus (COVID 19) has led companies around the world to accommodate remote working, helping to reduce the spread of the virus as they struggle to limit the impact of lockdowns on productivity. Advancements in technology has created reliable video conferencing which has become accessible and affordable, and can easily serve the modern workplace. The most commonly used video conferencing services by business organizations, educational institutions, and federal/state governmental agencies include but not limited to the following platforms:

Zoom

Zoom was founded in 2011 by Eric Yuan, a former Cisco executive. It was built upon Cisco WebEx web conferencing platform which remains a competitor in the conferencing space today. It evolved very quickly with the service launching in 2013; Zoom had one million users by the end of the year. By 2017, the company had a billion-dollar valuation and became a publicly-traded company in 2019 growing into one of the biggest video conferencing solutions in use today. The COVID-19 pandemic of 2020 brought more users from education sector into Zoom community; more teachers use it to teach and reach their students at various locations during COVID-19 lockdown as the coronavirus raged on. Currently, research shows that Zoom is the most commonly used conferencing tool ahead of similar solutions like Google Meet, Crisco WebEx, Microsoft Teams, and Skype. Zoom is a cloud-based video conferencing service that can be used to virtually meet with other people at any location around the world either by video or audio-only or both, while conducting live chats. It also allows the host to share computer screen with other participants during live meetings. One unique feature of Zoom is that it lets you record those sessions to view later making it the most commonly used web conferencing platform for audio and/or video conferencing. Other main features found at the bottom of the meeting window include options for managing meeting on your computer such as **Mute, Stop Video, Chart, Share Screen, # of Participants** in the meeting, and **End** or leave the meeting. See **fig. 8.7** below on how to use these features during meetings. To start your own calls or meeting for up to **100** people, you need a free account; paid versions can support up to **1,000** people. If you are using a free Zoom account, your meeting time is limited to **45 minutes**; paid Zoom account comes with unlimited meeting time. You can make unlimited phone calls, hold unlimited meetings, and record both. A typical Zoom window is show in the image below:

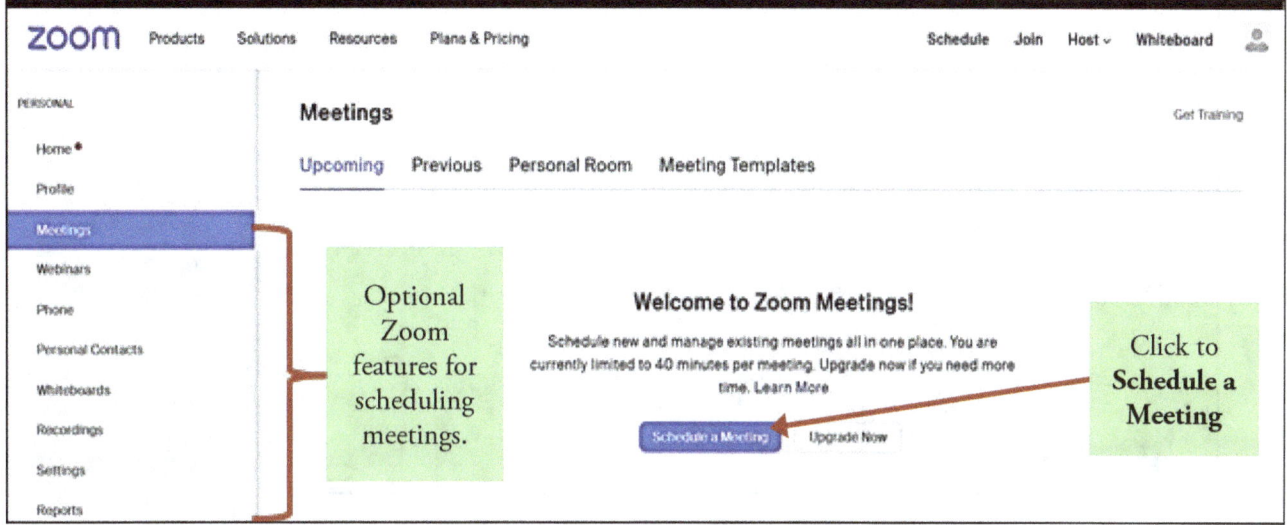

Fig. 8.1   **A typical Zoom Window**

How to Schedule a Zoom Meeting:
In meeting scheduling, you don't have to start your meeting immediately. Zoom allows you to schedule a meeting for a later day or time. To schedule a meeting follow these steps; view **fig. 8.1** above and **figs. 8.2 – 8.7** below.

1. Open a browser and log into your Zoom account.
2. At left pane of the Zoom window, click the link: **Schedule a New Meeting**.
3. Follow onscreen instructions to complete the **Schedule a Meeting** form to set up a meeting name, description, date and time, and other required details.
4. When you've completed the meeting setup, click **Save** at bottom of the page.
5. To the right of **Join URL**, click **Copy the Invitation**, open your email inbox, and paste the copied meeting information into an email message. Use your favorite email app or account to send the message to whomever you want to invite to the meeting.

All-in-One Beginners Guide to Computer Proficiency | 417

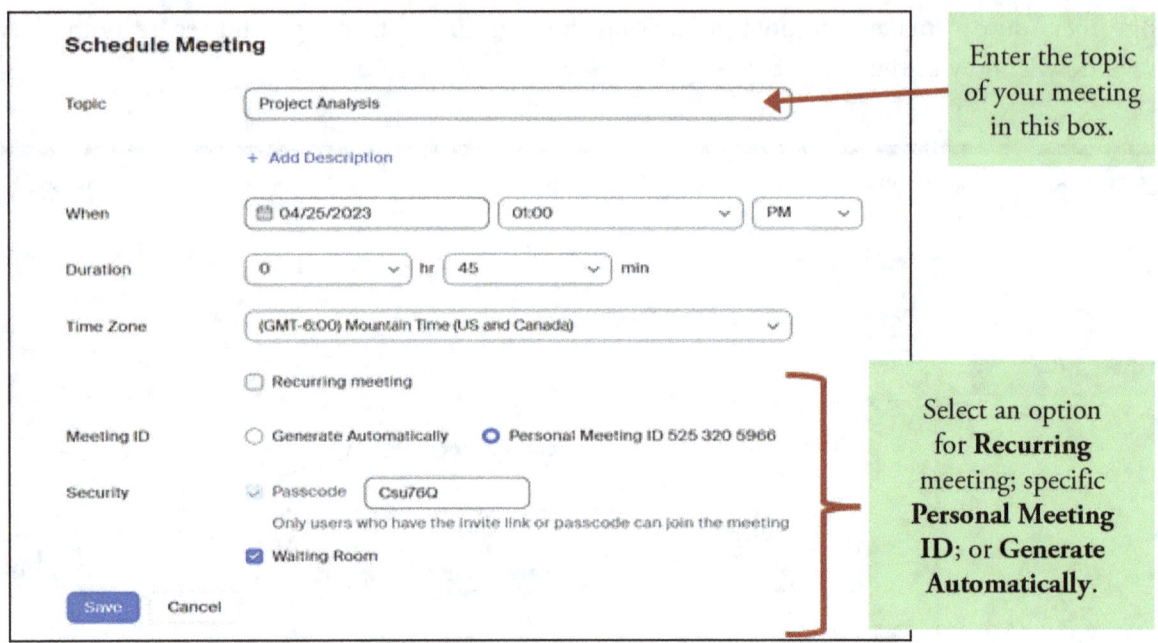

Fig. 8.2 Schedule a Meeting Window

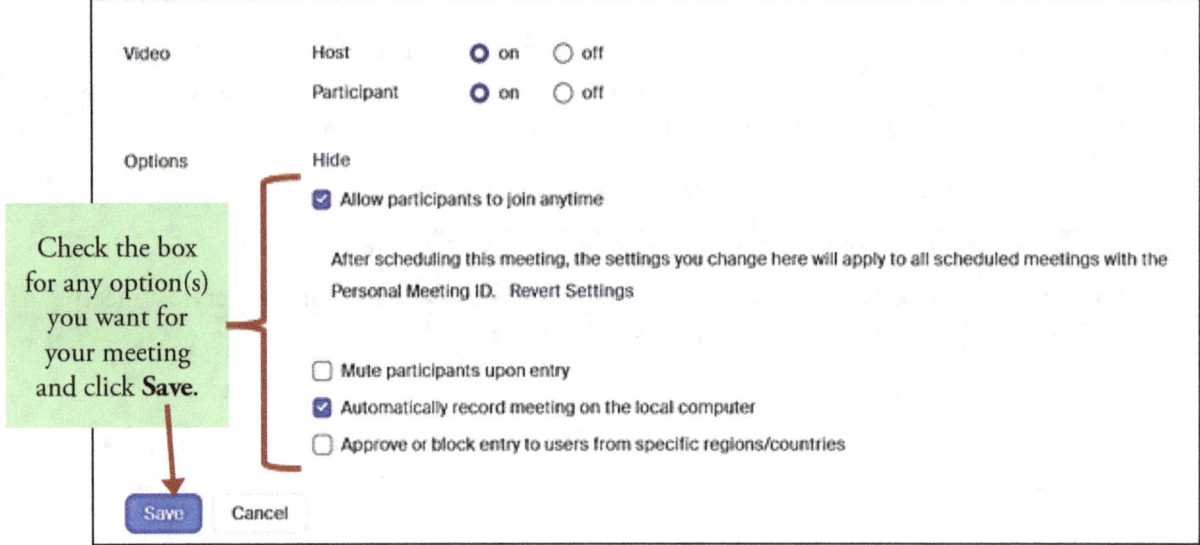

Fig. 8.3 Lower Portion of Schedule a Meeting Window – Select Meeting Options

418 | *Basic Computing Concepts*

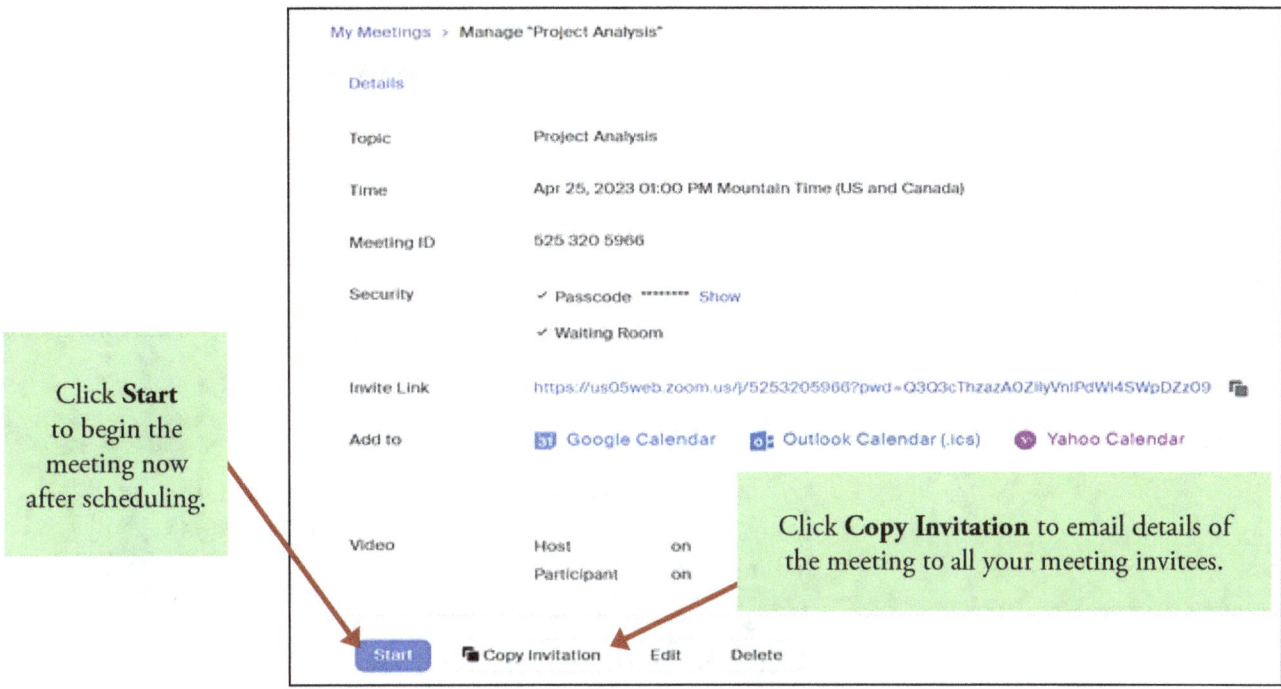

Fig. 8.4   **A Scheduled Meeting Window**

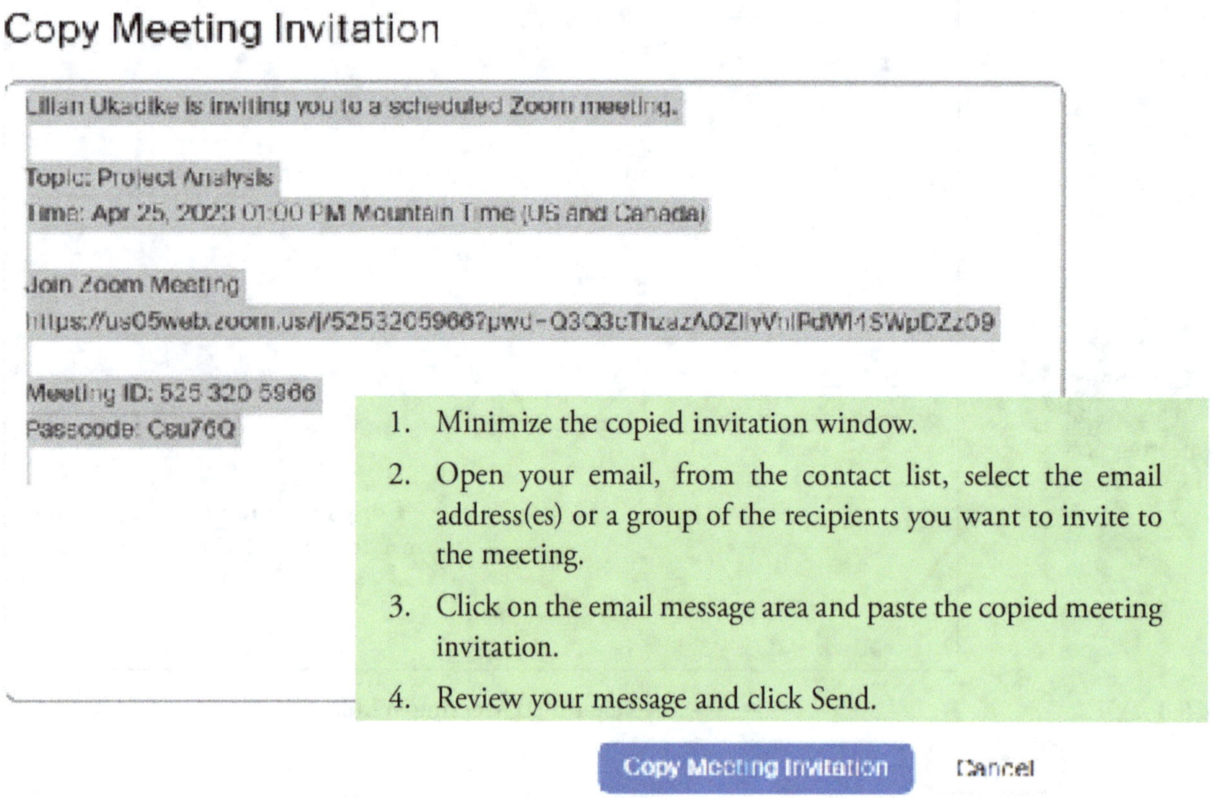

Copy Meeting Invitation

Lilian Ukadike is inviting you to a scheduled Zoom meeting.

Topic: Project Analysis
Time: Apr 25, 2023 01:00 PM Mountain Time (US and Canada)

Join Zoom Meeting
https://us05web.zoom.us/j/52532059667?pwd=Q3Q3cThzazA0ZIIyVnlPdWl4SWpDZz09

Meeting ID: 526 320 5966
Passcode: Csu76Q

1. Minimize the copied invitation window.
2. Open your email, from the contact list, select the email address(es) or a group of the recipients you want to invite to the meeting.
3. Click on the email message area and paste the copied meeting invitation.
4. Review your message and click Send.

[Copy Meeting Invitation]   [Cancel]

Fig. 8.5   **Copied Meeting Invitation Window**

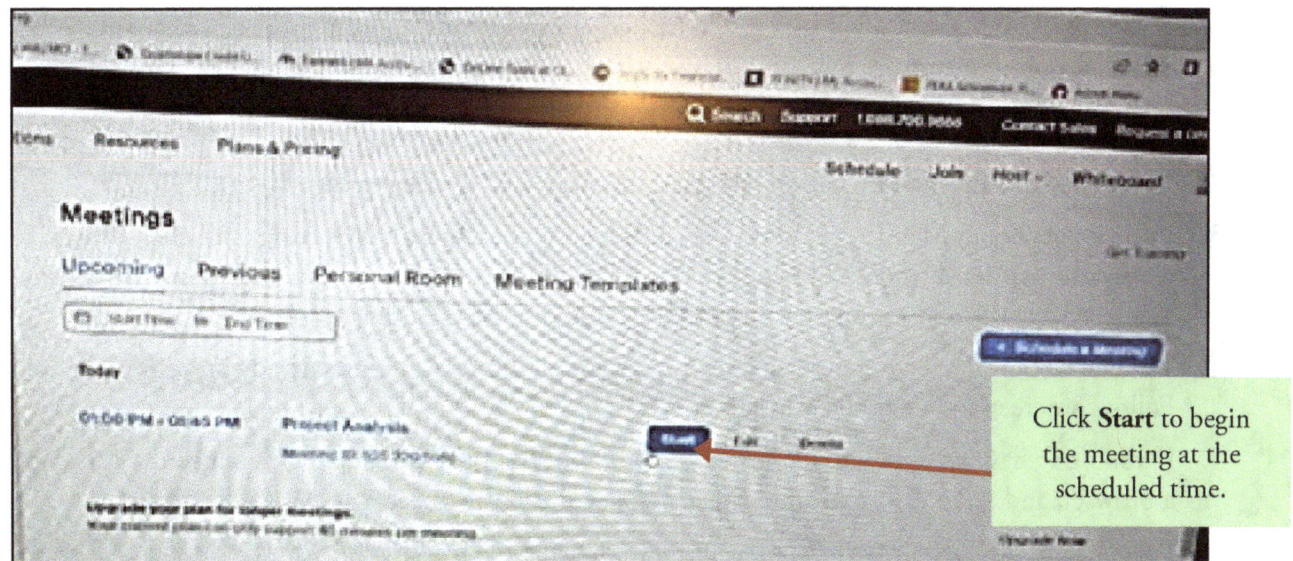

Fig. 8.6   To Start Meeting Scheduled for a Later Time

Fig. 8.7   Tabs Found at the Bottom of a Zoom Meeting Window

How to Join a Zoom Meeting: Whether you are joining a Zoom meeting from a PC, Mac, or mobile device, or using any type of web browser, the process is essentially always the same.

1. In most cases, you will be joining a scheduled zoom meeting using an email invitation.
2. If you received an email invitation, click the link provided in the message by the organizer.
3. In the open **Zoom Meeting** window **(fig. 8.8)** below, click **Launch Meeting**, and click **Join with Computer Audio** in the small window that follows allowing you to hear sounds in the meeting. You also have the option to test your computer audio to make sure it works fine.
4. You will be prompted to open the **Zoom** app, or install the app if it's not already on your computer. Follow onscreen instructions to install it.
5. If you don't have an email invitation with a link, but has been provided with a meeting ID, open a browser, and go to **Zoom's Join a Meeting** page. Enter the meeting **ID** and click **Join**.
6. Follow steps described in **fig.8.7** boxes above to manage the meeting on your computer or laptop.

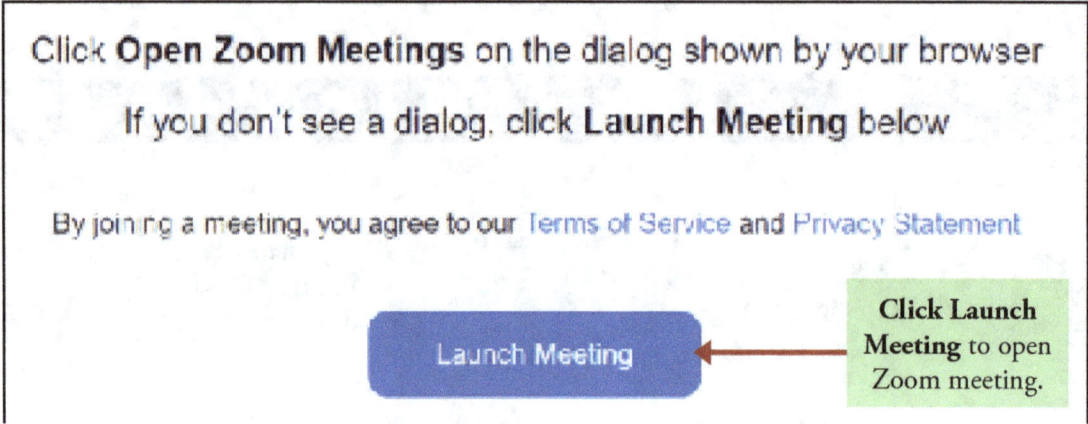

Fig. 8.8   Zoom Meeting Window

How to Host a Zoom Meeting: This is not the same as scheduling a Zoom meeting. Hosting a Zoom meeting allows you to start an unscheduled meeting online with or without video or screen share only. You must have a Zoom account before hosting your own meeting. If you already have a Zoom account, sign in. Otherwise, open a browser and go to **Zoom.us**, then click the link at the top of the web page captioned **Sign Up, It's Free**.

1. To complete the signup process, you will need to enter an email address and confirm that it is your email address by clicking the **Activate Account** link in an email that Zoom sends to you. After your email is confirmed, finish the signup process by entering your name and creating a password.

2. Once you submit your name and password, Zoom will ask you to invite colleagues. This is an optional step; if you choose not to do this. Click **Skip this step**.

3. After account setup, go to the **Zoom website** and make sure you're logged into your account using the link at the top of the page.

4. Hover your mouse pointer over **Host a Meeting** and choose **With Video On** or **With Video Off**. After a moment, you should see a prompt to open the Zoom app, click **Open Zoom**. If you don't see the prompt, make sure you install the app before proceeding.

5. The easiest way to do this is to click **download & run Zoom**, then follow onscreen instructions to install the app on your computer.

Google Meet

Google Meet is a free video conferencing service that enables people to join virtual meetings via audio, video, chat, and screen sharing with up to 100 people. You can start a meeting or join a meeting from any modern browser on your desktop or laptop and enjoy secure, high-quality video meetings and calls available to everyone on any device. There is no additional software to install, and like Zoom, the free Google Meet has a limited meeting time of **60 minutes** with no more than **100** participants. Paid meeting plans enable up to **250** or more people to join a call or meet at once. Additionally, for more than a decade, Google Company has also introduced a free app known as **Google Docs** that works similar to application programs used to create documents, manage financial information, and make presentations. Today, this free app is being used by teachers and students worldwide for teaching, learning, and doing school classwork or homework.

Google Docs: This app was first released in 2006 by Google LLC. It is a free web-based app that mimics the features of the most commonly used MS Office suites – Word, Excel, and PowerPoint. It can be used as a word processor to create and edit documents. However, unlike MS Office suites, Google Docs is not a software that you can purchase and install on your computer and must always be accessed through a web browser. To use Google Docs, login to the browser on your computer, or simply download the app on your Android phone or tablet. Then click on a Google Doc template and start typing your document right in your web browser. The document you create is stored as part of the Google Docs Editors suite of free web applications but you cannot save it on your computer as your own file. Usually, it may require some advanced computer tasks to save Google Doc on your computer, if at all possible. In using Google Docs, your documents are automatically saved on iCloud and updated whenever you log into the browser and work on it. On the other hand, with MS Office suite installed on your computer, you can save your documents in any location of your choice on your computer. In addition, documents you create are also automatically stored and updated in Microsoft OneDrive installed on your computer which you can access as needed without logging onto the Internet.

One of the main benefits of using Google Docs is that you can share files and folders with people and choose whether they can view, edit, or comment on them. Collaborators can also see the revision history of any changes made to Google documents and when those alterations were done in the revision history. A major disadvantage of Goggle Doc is that to use the app, you must be connected to the Internet. If your Internet is down or you live in a remote, rural area where Internet connection is difficult, you cannot work offline. Unlike Google Doc, with MS Word, Excel, and PowerPoint you can continue working offline on your computer even when not connected to the Internet. Google Doc cloud-based productivity platform that represents MS Office suites are called Google Doc (MS Word), Google Sheets (MS Excel), and Google Slides (MS PowerPoint). Further, compared to MS Office suite, Google Docs seem like a temporary quick fix to creating documents and storing on iCloud. It does not teach high school students who use the app the details of basic computer technology that will be useful to them as they prepare for college and take their first steps towards a career. Google Docs is more suitable for people who are already proficient with computer technology and MS Office fundamentals not for beginners in basic technology.

Crisco WebEx

WebEx is a multi-functional desktop Video/Audio Conference call application that allows people to **meet** with anyone, anywhere, in **real time.** People can meet from their offices or home powered by Internet access on the computer or availability of **WebEx** mobile app installed on their iPhones, iPads, Android, or Blackberry. It is a cloud-based suite of productivity tools that keep teams connected. The package includes WebEx Teams, WebEx Meetings, and WebEx Devices. This suite merges the web conferencing platform and the Spark team collaboration tool from Cisco into WebEx video conferencing. An important and powerful feature of Cisco WebEx is desktop and file sharing tool. With video meetings, file sharing, and team messaging, the suite allows for unified communications for any business from small business to enterprise-wide needs. With WebEx, all meetings within a company can be supported by either Cisco WebEx Meetings or WebEx Teams apps. Currently, WebEx has been optimized for rapid sharing of content. You can share files, attachments, photos, videos, GIF (Graphics Interchange Format), desktop, and desktop screenshots. The host sets the file-sharing permissions and can assign this control to any participant.

Microsoft Teams

This is a web collaboration and video conferencing service that enables staff within a workplace to communicate from any location via text chat, voice call or video conference. It enables users to schedule video or audio meetings with a single person or a team. Administrators can also organize webinars and large meetings with up to 10,000 participants. Full integration Microsoft Teams with Microsoft 365 enables meeting organizer to schedule calls and invitations which are shared among the organization, and allowing external guests to join from their web browser without downloading the application. As a leading video conferencing software provider Microsoft Teams also provides the full range of features, including screen sharing and call recording, live captions, background blur technology, and chat functionalities. Integration with Microsoft 365 makes this platform the market leader in video conferencing and digital workspace integration. The platform's powerful video conferencing software is complemented by hardware options that enable users to join calls from almost anywhere. When you're working alone or on the go, mobile devices, desktop computers, and Bluetooth conferencing headsets can power communication. When you're working collaboratively, Microsoft Teams devices enable some of the team to meet face to face, while remote participants are able to call in.

Skype

Skype was introduced to voice and electronic communications platform in 2003 during the early days of Voice over IP. Skype is a VoIP (Voice over Internet Protocol) that enables people to make and receive free voice and video calls using a computer connected to the Internet web browser or mobile phone. VoIP uses communication methods similar to the standard landlines and cellular plans. Skype appears to be less popular these days as VoIP communication has become mobile. Other apps and services have been more successful on mobile devices than Skype, like WhatsApp and Viber. To use Skype, install the app on your computer or laptop. Using the camera on your device, located at top of your desktop monitor or laptop, you can communicate with people all over the world and see them on your computer camera. Skype provides a variety of services for business, personal, and creative needs, including the following:

- **Meet Now**: This service is used for quickly creating and sharing meetings. Just clicking a button creates the session and gives you a shareable link that you can send to the people you want to talk to.

- **Skype Manager**: For people who own businesses or manage Skype usage for their households, Skype Manager helps to allocate credits (used to make non-Skype calls) and control which features are available for members of their group.
- **Skype with Alexa**: Skype can also be used with Alexa, the digital assistant that comes with Amazon Echo devices. Alexa responds to voice commands and talks too.

ADVANTAGES & DISADVANTAGES OF ONLINE LEARNING

Advantages

Clearly, the growing movement towards online learning is motivated by the many benefits it offers. However, regardless of its many benefits achieved through innovations in technology, it is important to note that computers will never completely eliminate human instructors and other forms of educational delivery. The main thing to keep in mind is that individuals should know exactly what e-learning advantages exist and know when these advantages outweigh the limitations of this medium of learning.

1. **Convenience:** This is the most important benefit for students who juggle full-time job while trying to obtain college education especially adult learners often referred to as "non-traditional" students. We live in a fast-paced world and if people can work education into their busy schedules on their own terms, they are more likely to see online learning as an attractive offer. As more and more professionals decide to further their education and obtain college degrees, the number of online students will continue to rise.
2. **Location:** With online learning, you don't go to the classroom; the classroom comes to you wherever you may be at any time. You can view lectures at your own time, anywhere – in your bath rope and in your bedroom without the pressure of being late for class. You do not need to be in the classroom at 8:00 am in the mornings or every night at 6:00 pm for the next five years in order to get the same degree in education. Online education comes to you wherever you can connect to the Internet. Whether you are at home, at work, or your favorite Internet café you can have the convenience of taking your work with you and enjoying the environment while you work.
3. **Flexible Schedule:** You chose how you want to handle your online class schedule as long as you meet required deadlines. You can even do your homework during your lunch break, while

the kids are practicing soccer, or while cooking dinner (depending of course on how well you multitask). This flexibility should not be confused with irresponsibility. As in any classroom setting, assignments have deadlines that must be met, and the same penalty for late submissions also applies to online learning.

4. **Individual Attention:** Online education allows students to have more one-on-one interaction with their professors than students in a classroom. The online classroom is virtual education and every correspondence is through email, instructors respond to email one student at a time and address particular issues as it affects that student. In addition, for those students who are too shy to ask the instructor questions in a classroom setting, email remains a comfortable means of communication. The individual attention allows instructors to know more about each student's learning patterns and needs more than they know about most of the students they see two or three times a week in their classrooms.

5. **Inexpensive:** You save money on convenience meals away from home, childcare expenses, and gas guzzling trips to a college campus that may be over thirty minutes away. Compared to all other incidental educational expenses, the small expense for Internet access seems like such a small price to pay.

6. **Improved Computer Proficiency:** If you have a little bit of experience with computer, online learning will help you to improve your skills. In an online learning environment, everything you do is done electronically, such as downloading and submitting assignments, sending email, using the bulletin boards, performing online research, and countless online activities. As you continue with your online education, your computer and internet skills are also improving.

Disadvantages

While a few benefits exist for online learning, you should be aware of the downside to taking your classes online. Before making the decision to school online, carefully weigh the benefits against the drawbacks to identify potential problems and make plans on how to solve the problems before taking the plunge.

1. **Bandwidth/Browser Limitations:** Bandwidth or browser limitations may restrict instructional methodologies. For example, if an instructor's teaching materials contain a lot of video, audio, or intense graphics and all students are not on T1 line (one of the fastest internet speed), online learning will frustrate some students. Limited bandwidth means slower performance for sound, video, and large graphics, or images.

2. **Added Cost of Education**: Some students who cannot afford to buy all that is needed to meet the system requirements for online learning cannot take advantage of this form of learning regardless of how badly they need it. This limits online education to just a privileged few.
3. **Limited Connectivity:** High speed internet connection is not available in certain areas of the country and the only choice for students living in those areas is dial-up connection which is very slow in downloading files or uploading completed assignments. The time required for downloading applications may take longer than usual and will frustrate the students.
4. **Reduced Social Interaction:** Online learning lacks human contact, too impersonal, and suppresses communication mechanisms such as body language, and eliminates peer-to-peer learning that are part of a learning environment.
5. **Time Limitation:** Unlike a classroom setting where a student gets immediate response to a question from the instructor, responses, feedback, and comments from instructor via email may not come as quickly as the students wants it.

TECHNOLOGY REQUIREMENTS FOR ONLINE LEARNING

Computer System Requirements

Computer system requirements for online learning include hardware that many computers are already equipped with. Students who already own a computer or a laptop should refer to the checklist of items below to make sure that they have all required items. First of all, the computer memory may need to be upgrade to make it run faster. The current Microsoft Office software may also have to be upgraded by installing the newest version. Online learning involves communication and printing certain research items; a printer and valid email address is a must. It is also recommended that students should have a monitor that is at least **1024 × 768** resolution to allow images to be seen clearly at all times. During online classes, students may be asked to view documents that have been scanned into the computer. These images may need to be blown up in order to see them clearly and monitors must be able to handle the images. Because online classes rely on computer-generated images, it is important to have a monitor, speakers, video, and sound cards. These are valuable resources that will be needed to complete most classes. Instructors may send audio lectures and visual worksheets that may further emphasize a point or be used in another assignment. While students may get away with not having a printer, it is recommended that the computer have the correct amount of memory storage. Since classes are taught online, there will be a lot of written correspondence in the form of tests, worksheets, notes, spreadsheets, and assignments that will take up a lot of memory. Having a CD burner or flash drive to store information will also be an asset to many students. Below is a checklist of computer system and software requirements:

- **Software Requirements:** Microsoft Office Word, Excel, PowerPoint, Anti-virus software, and Web browser.
- **Minimum Hardware Requirements:** 256 MB RAM, 20 GB Hard Drive, Cable modem/DSL, Sound Card, CD-ROM Drive
- **Equipment:** Computer or laptop, monitor, keyboard, mouse, speakers (with newer technology, most computers and laptops now come with in-built speakers), printer, and flash drive or CD.
- **Operating System:** Windows 10, Windows 7, or Windows 11 (latest version).
- **Connectivity:** High speed internet access with basic familiarity with Internet web browser.
- **Learner's Requirement:** A high dose of discipline and personal responsibility.

Technology Proficiency Requirements

1. Be proficient with the use of a computer and the use of basic Microsoft Office programs (Word, Excel, and PowerPoint). Before enrolling in online courses, make sure you have taken at least an introductory course in computer technology covering computer basics and the study of MS Office applications.

2. Know about file types such as what a PDF file is, and how to save a Word file in PDF format. **PDF (Portable Document Format)** is a file format developed by Adobe as a means of distributing compact, and platform-independent documents. Similar to a Web HTML file; a PDF document may contain images and text, as well as hyperlinks. Originally, a document in PDF format is read-only and can neither be edited nor modified. However, advancements in technology has made it possible to perform specific edits on PDF document, such as add texts/notes or comments, check marks, add signatures or initials, insert images, and various forms of editing; but it does not allow changing texts that are already written. To save any Word, Excel, PowerPoint, or Publisher document in PDF format, make sure that Adobe program is already installed on your computer. To save the document in PDF format, follow these steps:

    a. Display the **Word** file to be saved.

    b. Click **File** button, click **Save As**, and click **Browse** to select a location to save the PDF file.

    c. In the open **Save As** window, click **Save as type** down arrow, navigate the displayed menu, and select **PDF**, and click **Save.**

    d. The newly converted **PDF** file will display on the screen.

3. Know how to download a file from the home page into your computer and upload a completed assignment onto the learning environment. This is how information will be shared from you to the instructor and between you and your classmates.

4. Know how to compose and send an email with an attachment in the learning environment. Email is the main communication vehicle for remote online learning.

5. Be familiar with some troubleshooting tips and do not panic when you have a computer glitch. Be patient and work through it or wait until tech support provides help.

6. Know how to use various search engines **(Google, Yahoo, or Bing)** to conduct research online to write your term paper.

7. Know what a social network is and how to use it. Depending on the preferred means of communication, some online instructors may require you to use **Twitter and/or Facebook** as part of the course communication requirements.

OVERVIEW OF ONLINE COURSE MANAGEMENT TOOLS

Many schools and colleges that offer online classrooms have different learning environment application specific to their needs and to the needs of their students. These applications work differently from one school to another depending on how they have been programmed to operate by the school. However, regardless of how schools choose to use their online learning environment, the one element they may have in common is the course management tools. These tools are designed to facilitate interactions between students and instructors and among students enrolled in the online courses. How these tools are used may differ from one educational institution to another. The proceeding sections of this chapter contain a list and descriptions of the most common type of course management tools typically found in an online learning classroom. To be a successful online student, you must understand how your school uses these course management tools and know how to use them effectively. In general, the following term is very common with any type of online learning environment:

Learning Management System (LMS)

This is a term used to describe the entire process of online learning. It is a virtual learning environment (VLE) software system designed to support teaching and learning in an educational setting to create a distinct Managed Learning Environment (MLE). This type of learning environment typically takes place through the Internet and provides a collection of tools such as assessment, communication, discussion boards, uploading of content, return of students' work, peer assessment, administration of student groups, collecting and organizing student grades, questionnaires, tracking tools, and so on. The system contains some features that allow it to automatically grade exams, quizzes, or tests in the form of multiple-choice questions, and it applies students' grade in their grade books. Course management systems (CMS) were originally created to facilitate distance education, but they are now most often used to supplement traditional face-to-face classroom activities in a Web-enhanced format commonly known as **Blended Learning**. The virtual learning environment usually runs on servers to serve the course to students' multimedia and/or Web pages.

HOW TO PARTICIPATE IN AN ONLINE COURSE

Online classes may be offered either wholly or partially through the World Wide Web with some requiring classroom attendance while others may be delivered entirely online. Depending on the school policy, students may be required to attend an on-campus meeting for orientation of online learning. Most online learning systems are designed to be interactive and allow students to review class lectures, do assignments, and take quizzes, tests, or exams from any computer with Internet access. In an online learning environment, learning takes place through a combination of instructor-assigned readings; class discussions, group projects, case studies, research and writing assignments, including email and faculty feedback to students. Online courses are the same as classroom courses; the only difference is that students do not interact with the instructor or with other students in person. As an online student, you will receive individualized attention and guidance from your instructor and interact with other students through a discussion board or online chat. In addition, students may log into the Internet and view an instructor's recorded lecture online. On one form of video-recorded lecture, students can actually see the instructor online and, on another form, only the instructor's voice is heard on the video.

Participate in an Online Course

1. The five things to do before taking an online course are:
   a. Register for your courses
   b. Pay for your courses
   c. Purchase your textbook or E-book
   d. Login to the online course home
   e. Create your username and password
6. Log into the course on the first day of class and introduce yourself to the instructor by posting your biography on your **Course Home Page** account, and upload your picture (optional).
7. Read welcome message from your instructor posted on the **Bulletin Board Home Page**, if any.
8. Once you have logged in, click the **Content** tab, and download/print your instructor's Bio
9. (an introduction file where the teacher introduced his/herself), the course syllabus, course assignment schedule, and all other required information for the online course.
10. Make sure you read all pertinent information you downloaded about the course including your instructor's bio to know who your teacher is. Since you probably won't be seeing this instructor in person, what you read about him or her is all you have to go by; at least you get to know something about the teacher.
11. Download, print, and read all required reading identified on the assignment schedule.
12. Click the **Discussion Board** tab and respond to the discussion questions posed by your instructor.
13. Be sure to also read responses from other students and their comments; respond to the discussion questions, and post your response on the discussion board.

Course Management Tools on Desire to Learn (D2L)

D2L is the most commonly used platform for many colleges and universities with learning tools located in the home page of the virtual learning environment (VLE). These learning tools allow students to manage their online courses; download assignment questions; upload completed assignments; communicate with the instructor and other students; download research materials; take exams/quizzes/tests; and view their grades to monitor their performance in the course. These course management tools include but are not limited to assessment, communication, discussion boards, uploading of content, return of students' work from instructor, peer assessments, administration of student groups, collecting and organizing student grades, questionnaires, tracking tools, and so on. They typically appear in the form of small tabs at top on the VLE home page, and students can click on the tabs to open additional webpages. The open webpages contain a variety of course activities uploaded by the online instructor to facilitate the learning process.

The style and format of D2L learning environment may differ from school to school. However, as the most frequently used platform, listed below are the basic course management tools commonly found on most D2L platforms and instructions on how to use them. Depending on how each school decides to use these tools, the steps described below may be different from your school's platform or similar. The instructions provided in this section is intended to serve as general guidelines to give new beginners in online learning some idea of what to expect when they decide to register in an online learning classroom. Ultimately, online students must confirm to the online course management protocols and policies provided by their schools.

Course Home: The home page for your course. It contains news items and other information about your course. It is also known as **My Course Home**.

Course Content: This is where all the coursework for the semester is located. The link contains the course syllabus, assignment schedule, links to online research, all other course materials and learning resources. Occasionally, the course content includes information about your online instructor (an introduction file).

Access, View, Save or Print Course Content:

1. On the **Home Page**, click the **Course Content** link to display a list of information relevant to the online course.
2. Click your selected item or file to display file contents.
3. View content of file, save, or print as needed.

Class List: Located on the **Home Page** of the learning environment, the class list button contains a list of all students enrolled in the online course, including the instructor's name. Students can click on a fellow student's name or the instructor to compose an email message and send.

Email & Class List: The communication system of an online learning environment is located in the email and class list. This is one of the primary means of communication between the instructor and the students, and among students and their peers. When you click on the email tab, it opens the mailbox window that allows you to send and receive email to/from your instructor and fellow students. You can also use this system to send your completed assignment as an attachment to your instructor. To send an email with attachment to your instructor or student(s) in your class, follow these steps:

1. From the **Home Page** of the online course, click the **Communication** tab, click **E-mail,** or click the **E-mail** tab at top of the screen on the **Navigation Bar**.
2. Click the **Class List** tab to display a list of all students in the class including the instructor.
3. Check the small box to the left of the name(s) to select the recipient or recipients if you are sending to a group.
4. Click the **Email** icon above or below the list to open the **E-mail** window.
5. Click the **Compose** button to begin typing your message or you can start typing your message once the **E-mail** window opens in **step #4** above.
6. Click the **Browse** button, locate your file in the open **Browse** field and click to select the file.
7. Click the **Open** button to attach the file, and click **Send.**
8. To attach additional files, click the **Add** button under attachments or click another **Browse** button underneath to **Browse** to attach more file(s). You can add several files in one e-mail message by repeating steps **6 & 7** above.

Note: *Your school's learning management system (LMS) may have a specific size of file it can successfully transmit at a time in one e-mail message. Be aware of this before sending very large files in one e-mail.*

Drop Box and Assignment Link:
The drop box contains a list of all your assignments and projects for the course. This is where you download assignments from your instructor and upload the completed assignments. All assignments along with the related files uploaded by the online instructor are located in the assignment tab. Many colleges that offer online courses may have different names for the assignment tab, it may also be referred to as the **Drop Box.** Students must click the drop box to open it and download any required files for the assigned project, and also submit their completed assignment into the drop box.

Download Assignment Files and Save on Your Flash Drive

1. On the **Home Page** of the learning environment, at top of the screen on the **Navigation Bar**, click the **Assignment** tab or **Drop Box**.

2. In the open **Assignment** window, click the **Chapter Assignment** link to open a list of files relevant to that assignment including the instructions.

3. Click the files you want to download, in the **Open/Save** dialog box, click the **Save** button to download the files one at a time into your flash drive.

4. Alternatively, click the **Chapter** file name, click the **Save** button to save the entire file under that chapter in a **Zip Folder** in your flash drive.

5. When download is complete, click the **Close** button.

Submit Completed Assignment(s)

1. Click the **Assignment Link** or **Drop Box** tab at the top menu to display the relevant chapter assignment information.

2. In the open **Chapter Information** window, under **Submit Files**, click the **Add a File** button to begin attaching your file(s) for upload.

3. Click the **Browse** button and locate your completed assignment in your flash drive or any location saved on your computer, and click the **Open** button.

4. If you have additional files to upload, click the **Add** button, click **Browse** button, and select the file you need. Repeat this process until you have attached all your files, then click the **Upload** button.

5. Back to the **Chapter Information** window, under **Add a File**, in the **Comment Field** area, enter any comments you may have for your instructor about the assignment, and click the **Submit** button.

6. If you want to upload more files, click the **Upload More Files** button, and repeat steps **3 – 5** above.

Note: *Just clicking the* **Upload** *tab does not submit your assignment. To submit your uploaded file(s), you must actually click the* **Submit** *button.*

Quiz/Exam Tab: All the scheduled quizzes or exams for the online course are located on this tab. To take a quiz or exam click on the relevant tab, select the assigned quiz or exam, complete the task, and submit.

Take a Quiz or Exam Online

1. On the **Home Page** of the course, click the **Navigation Bar** to display a list of pre-assigned quizzes, and click on the **Quizzes or Exam** link at top of the screen
2. Click on the **Quiz** title you want to take.
3. On the open **Quiz** window, click **Start Quiz** button to open quiz window.
4. Begin your **Quiz** or **Exam**, which is timed. Make sure you keep an eye on the timer, and click **Save** after each question.
5. Each time you save a question, the question button is darkened. As you save, check to make sure the question button is darkened indicating that it is really saved.
6. When finished with all the questions saved, click the **Submit Quiz** or **Exam** button on the lower right of the quiz window, and the window automatically closes.
7. Click on the **Quizzes/Exam** link at top screen of the **Navigation Bar.**
8. Click the **Submission** icon to the right of the quiz/exam you have taken. This icon looks like a question mark.
9. Click the displayed number of attempts to view your score on the quiz or exam.

Student Grade Book: This holds all the grades you earned from project assignments, discussion topics, quizzes, and final exam grades on the course. In an online learning environment, grades that students receive from submitted assignments, quizzes, and exams are all recorded in the grade book. When students log into their online account, they are able to access the grade book to view their scores on various projects, assignments, and exams. The grades received enables students to evaluate their performances in the online course. To view your grades in the grade book, simply click the **Grades** link at top of the screen on the **Navigation Bar** to display your grades on each chapter of the course. When you access the grade book, it displays in the form of a spreadsheet with boarders.

Discussion Board: In addition to email, discussion board serves as another communication vehicle between the instructor and the students. It is used to respond to posted discussions by the instructor or your online classmates. The instructor posts discussion questions (topics), the students respond, the instructor grades their responses and put grades in the students' grade book. To respond to any discussion, you must click the discussion link first.

OVERVIEW OF ONLINE DISCUSSION BOARDS & HOW TO USE THEM

A discussion board is an asynchronous communication tool that allows one individual to post a comment or question online. It is the most important aspect of online learning and serves as a communication vehicle among all students enrolled in the course and the instructors. Asynchronous means that discussion occurs at all times but not in real time. Discussions occur by way of posts, and other individuals who are members of the same discussion board may read that comment/question and respond with their own remarks over time. In any online learning environment, the discussion board is a must. It is the most important aspect of online learning and serves as a communication link that connects all members in the course. Unlike the traditional classroom settings where students and instructors interact with each other in person, in an online learning environment (a virtual classroom), they cannot see each other; the only two means of communication are email and discussion boards. Therefore, it is imperative that students learn what the discussion board is, and how to use it to learn online. From the instructor's standpoint, the discussion board serves as an assessment tool. Discussion boards make online learning very enjoyable because when you exchange ideas with other students through the discussion boards, the coursework becomes more engaging, and you will become both a self-learner and a collaborator with your peers. Discussion boards, discussion forums, bulletin boards, and message boards typically refer to the same type of online learning management system. Students should be careful not to confuse discussion boards with live chats. Live chats provide for synchronous communication (all at the same time), whereas discussion boards provide for asynchronous communication (discussion over time).

The Terminology of Discussion Boards: When you learn online, you must speak the language of online learning. The same words used in a traditional classroom setting assume a different name in an online forum and students should have a good understanding of the terminology used on the discussion boards. Note the following discussion board terms:

Thread of Conversation: The term used to describe a situation where a student posts a question and one or more other people post answers to that question. It also includes questions or discussion topics posted by the online instructor and responses to the posts by students. Thread of conversation maintains a long string of messages in the form of discussions, opinions, questions, and answers or responses from students and instructors.

Thread of Discussion Board: This is commonly referred to as threads of conversation; each focused on a particular topic or question (e.g., "Where is the link to online research?"). Discussion boards, discussion forums, bulletin boards, and message boards typically refer to the same type of online learning management system.

Types of Discussions Posted on Discussion Boards

1. **Directed Discussions:** As the name suggests, this type of discussion is often directed by the instructor (the moderator) inviting students to discuss a specific topic or item from the textbook chapter, a novel, or a Web site, including a case study. Although students are required to think and respond freely with their own opinions, the instructor or moderator guides and leads the discussion to cover a range of issues related to the objectives of the course. The instructor's comments directs the students to which way to go with the discussions, for example, "*You made a good point here, but consider this factor as well . . . ,* " or "*Good point, but how about . . .* " To begin a directed discussion, the instructor typically throws out a question to kick off the discussion. As students respond to the instructor's question, they may begin to ask their own questions leading to an expanded insight into the topic of discussion.

2. **Critiques:** Discussion boards can also be used as a forum for evaluation and feedback on students' projects. For example, a student tasked with the responsibility of developing a Web site may share the project or media with other students for review and comments. The instructor may kick off the discussion with a "**thread of conversation**" for each student, with other students posting comments and suggestions for a particular student within their individual thread.

3. **Mentoring:** This involves a situation in which students use discussion boards openly without overt moderation by the instructor. In mentoring, students use the discussion boards as a tool to ask questions of their peers throughout the semester; for example, "*Does anyone know how to create a formula that references another cell in an Excel spreadsheet?*" Once the question is posted, students with an answer to the question may begin to post their comments in a "thread of discussion."

4. **Debates:** At the instructor's discretion, he or she may decide to add a twist to the format of the discussion by turning it into a debate. To facilitate the debate, the instructor may divide students into two or more teams and require each group to research different perspectives of a specific issue. Often the topics of discussion in a debate are controversial issues, either social or political in nature. For example, in a Sociology class, the issue may be (arguments for or against), "*Should sex education be taught in our nation's middle high schools?*," a "position statement" generated by parents and various groups in our country. As the debate continues, differences of opinion may exist in which case students can ask others to explain their reasoning or defend their views. The moderator typically helps students to develop a consensus position agreeable to all parties.

How Discussion Board Works in Online Learning Environment

Usually at the beginning of the course, students receive information from the instructor about requirements for using the discussion board. Use of a discussion board occurs in three basic steps:

1. **The Instructor Begins the Discussion:** The online instructor opens the floor for discussion by posting a thought-provoking question or inquiry from the textbook about a specific topic. The purpose is to help the students develop an understanding of the coursework. As students respond to the issue posited in the discussion, they gain a better understanding of the coursework.
2. **The Student Responds and Contributes to the Discussion:** In responding to the posted discussion, students are expected to follow the six main netiquette rules of online communication discussed later in this chapter. Students are also responsible for reading the required material in the textbook as in a traditional classroom setting and posting educated responses that are logical, well thought out, and that make sense relative to the main objectives of the course. As an online student, you must take your responses seriously because your performance on the course will be assessed by the type of responses you provide. Feel free to interact with other students online who have the same opinion as you, be open, and be willing to listen and share.
3. **The Instructor Grades the Posts:** The instructor uses student responses to the posts to assess communication, writing, and language skills, including logic and reasoning. In most online classrooms, students are evaluated and graded just for participating in discussions; the ability to use the forum; and how often a student uses the discussion board. Depending on the instructor's policy and as part of the course requirements, students may be required to post or respond to a post at least twice a week or more, and some instructors may even require a daily post from students.

How to Respond to a Posted Discussion

1. On the **Home Page**, click the **Discussion** button to open a list of discussion topics.
2. Click the topic you want to respond to and open a list of responses from other students.
3. Click the **Reply** button and begin typing your response to the posted discussion, and click **Send** to post it.

Quick Tips to Posting a Discussion

1. Read what others have written on discussion topic, reference it in your posts, but try not to repeat it.
2. Check back after you've posted your discussion to see if anyone has responded.
3. Keep your posts brief, direct, straight to the point, and very professional.

Benefits of Discussion Boards in an Online Classroom

1. Allows students to move beyond just listening to a lecture to developing their own thoughts and engaging them in well-articulated argument and critical reasoning.
2. Strengthens students' ability to be creative thinkers by prompting them to recognize the need for external research in order to provide adequate response to a specific discussion topic. Students typically reference and bring external sources of information into the conversation and provide the source of their information (e.g., "according to this website . . . counting with the quotes………..").
3. Provides an opportunity to extend the allotted class time for discussions beyond regular class time to allow for in-depth reflection on comments.
4. Provides an opportunity for all students to participate in an open discussion without feeling intimidated, especially those who sometimes feel reluctant to speak in the presence of others in a traditional classroom setting.
5. Provides an outlet for students to pose their questions and receive feedback from not only the instructor, but also other discussion board participants.
6. Stores records of past discussion topics and responses for future reference by students.
7. Instructors may also use the discussion board to:
    a. Create quizzes relevant to the course content and the discussions.
    b. Plan projects for group assignment (collaboration).

c. Add case studies and review of coursework, and post podcasts or PowerPoint presentations (online lectures).

   d. Add **RSS** feeds—these feeds are continually updated and the instructor usually expects students enrolled in the online course to read them. **RSS (Rich Site Summary)** is a format for delivering regularly changing web content. It allows people who regularly use the web to easily stay informed by retrieving the latest content from the sites they are interested in. It saves them time by not needing to visit each site individually. Most business organizations with news-related sites, such as weblogs and other online publishers, syndicate their content as **RSS Feeds** to whoever wants it. Online instructors often use Twitter to add feeds to the discussions.

IS ONLINE LEARNING FOR EVERYONE?

Learning is a lifelong process that will have a major impact on your future. Online learning requires a lot of discipline from the student, and definitely not for everyone. As in a classroom setting, you will be required to have the discipline to stay on track with assignment schedule, complete assigned tasks on time, and meet deadlines. The same school policies on traditional classroom setting also apply to online learning. You have to study as hard as you would if you were taking your classes in the classroom, and work even harder to figure some things out on your own because the teacher is not standing in front of you to give you the answers ready-made. Therefore, before enrolling in online classes, you must first do a self-evaluation and ask yourself: "*Do I have the type of discipline an online education requires?*" As you make the decision whether to enroll in online education or traditional classroom learning, take a personal commitment inventory of yourself by answering the following questions.

Personal Commitment Inventory for Online Learning

1. Do I have the strong discipline and perseverance it takes to commit to tasks from inception to completion no matter how hard it gets?

2. Am I a self-starter? How well am I at learning on my own? Can I develop a good study habit in order to complete my online education successfully?

3. Do I have the strong will and determination it takes to continue pursuing my educational goals even when things become difficult or should I run once I approach a challenging task online? Should I be a quitter or someone who latches on and fights back when the going gets rough so as to finish what I started?

4. Do I have the ability to balance the demands of daily life with that of online schooling?

5. Can I manage my time adequately and devote enough hours in the day to commit to reading, studying, and writing? Online coursework requires a lot of reading and writing.

6. How supportive is my family in my decision to learn online instead of the traditional classroom they mostly believe in? Do I have the support of my family/spouse to help me through this journey? Because you are at home on the computer, your family may not view going to school online as really being in school. Family support is a big part of your educational process.

Take a good look at your inner self, search your soul, and be honest to yourself in answering the above questions. If you feel confident that you can be successful in completing your courses online in this type of learning environment, then enroll for the classes. Online learning when done properly can be a very rewarding experience you will truly enjoy because of the flexibility it brings to the educational process. Once you decide to learn online, the following guidelines will help you succeed.

General Guidelines for Virtual Online Education

1. Introduce yourself to the use of technology by enrolling in an elective course offered over the Internet. Generally, elective courses require less commitment to time and study and will give a "first timer" an idea of how well you will do in future classes. This is a way to test the waters. After this test, if online learning is not for you, then you should focus on traditional classroom learning environment to achieve your educational goals.

2. Until you become proficient with learning online, "*do not bite more than you can chew*" This means taking few classes at a time (perhaps one or two) and take the rest of your classes in the classroom.

3. Learn to use your time wisely. Online learning requires a high degree of time management skills which are needed to ensure success. This is by far the most important ingredient for a successful online education. Because online classes tend to circumvent scheduling problems by allowing learners to make choices as to where and when they study and participate, students tend to put off studying with all the freedom technology provides. When you do this, you let time get away; you put things off; and you fail the class.

4. Learn to be a responsible learner and be responsible for your self-learning. Your instructor in the online environment serves as your coach that facilitates the learning process; you, the student must find your own way to learn and succeed. You must take responsibility for your own learning, and

complete assigned tasks on time. In this virtual classroom, how well you do at learning on your own will have a significant bearing on your overall performance and eventual success.

5. Learn how to use the World Wide Web, search engines, Newsgroups, FTP sites, and e-mail for research. These are all part of the necessary tools a student should possess to succeed in an online learning environment. Practice your internet skills over and over by navigation the web using the free demo time provided by Internet service providers. Remember, practice makes perfect. Ability to use a variety of search engines and database managers is a prerequisite for most courses.

ON-LINE INTERACTION & COMMUNICATION

The word **Netiquette** was formed from "network etiquette" and is considered to be a set of socially acceptable conventions that facilitate interactions over the Internet. Just like people learn to follow the simple rules of etiquette when interacting with people in the workplace, at school, at social gatherings, they are also expected to apply the same netiquette rules when communicating online. The netiquette of cyberspace covers not only rules to maintain civility in discussions but also special guidelines unique to the electronic nature of forum messages we read on the Internet. Since online education has become a big part of our lives today, it is imperative that online students adhere to certain rules when communicating online. In an online classroom, you will be communicating with both fellow students and instructors; therefore, it is important that you communicate effectively and professionally. Ultimately, as in a classroom setting, the same golden rules of etiquette remain the same in an online learning environment: *"do not say or do anything online that you would not do or say offline or in person."* In most online communications, both sender and receiver do not see each other; all messages are subject to interpretations based on individual perceptions and preferences. When communicating online always remember to adhere to the six netiquette rules of online communication.

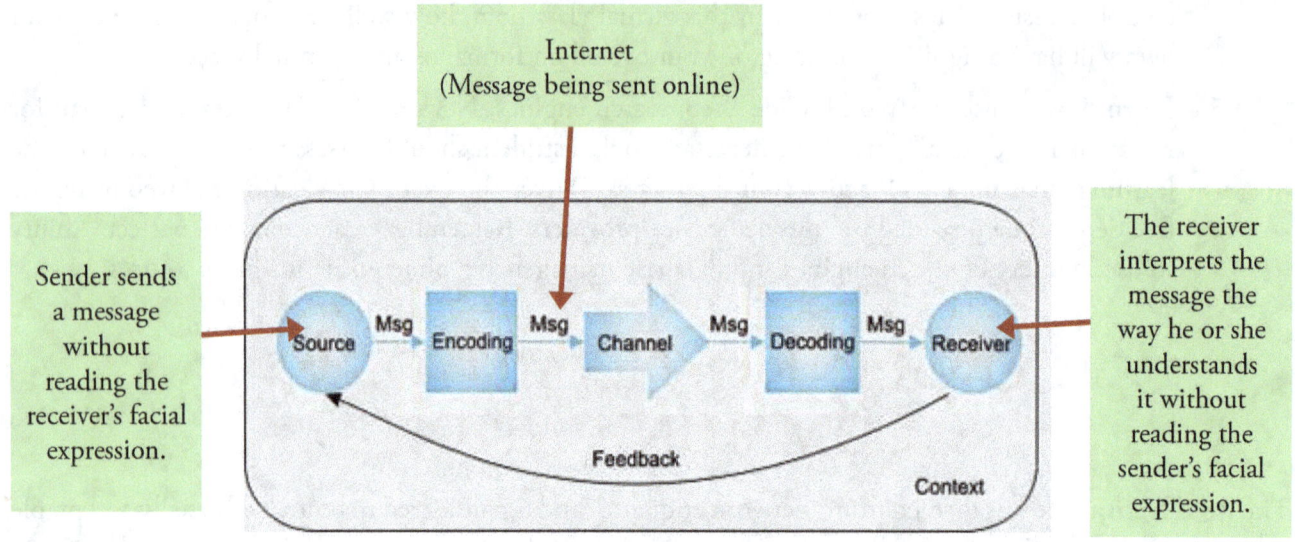

Fig. 8.9   **Online Communication Process**

THE SIX MAIN NETIQUETTE RULES OF ON-LINE COMMUNICATION

1. Always Maintain the Same Standards of Behavior both Offline (in person) and Online

What we view as "standards of behavior" may be different in many areas of cyberspace. Regardless of the differences, one thing remains clear; we should not expect those standards to be lower online than they are in real life. Generally, in real life, most people are fairly law-abiding members of our society, either by disposition or because they are afraid of getting caught if they break the law. On the other hand, in cyber- space, people's law-abiding instincts often give way to recklessness as the chances of getting caught appear to be slim. It would be wrong for people to think that a lower standard of ethics or personal behavior is acceptable in cyberspace since they can't really see the person on the other side of the network. As an online student, you cannot forget that the person on the other side of your computer is also a human being and deserves respect. Therefore, the same golden rule applies here – "d*o not say or do anything online that you would not do or say offline or in person.*"

2. Use Proper Language and Titles Appropriately

Address your online instructor as **Dr., Mrs., Miss.,** or **Mr.** to show respect, and if you are not sure, ask your instructor how he or she would like to be addressed. **NEVER** address your instructor by his or her first name and assume that it is okay. This is not okay in a traditional classroom and certainly not okay online unless it is acceptable to the teacher. Avoid using slang or even profane words in an online learning environment, even if they are words you normally use with your friends in real life and consider, "not so bad," as those words may sound offensive to the reader. In addition, sometimes our writing styles may suggest certain things to the reader. For example, if you use caps lock when writing to someone, it may insinuate yelling. The way you choose to write could hurt someone's feelings and possibly give the person a wrong impression of you.

3. Communicate Effectively

Effective communication comes from practice and requires careful thought. In sending messages online, use **Standard English Language (SEL)**, write clearly using correct spelling and grammar, and avoid using big and unfamiliar words. To be an effective communicator, you must speak and write clearly, logically, be concise, and write straight to the point without confusing your receiver or listener. Before you submit an assignment to your instructor or respond to a posted discussion question, review it first, define and restate your words where necessary, and correct misspelled words or grammatical errors right away. Read your message out loud to yourself, *"how does it sound to you"?* Chances are, if your message sounds bad to you, it may also sound that same way to someone else.

4. Display a Friendly, Positive Attitude and be Self-Reflective

The old adage, *"think before you speak"* also goes with *"think before you write,"* and always holds true in almost all real-life situations. When communicating with other people online, avoid using innuendoes, sarcasms, or belittling words because once you click the **Send** button, your message is gone to your receiver, and you cannot take it back. The message may be printed and filed as a record by the receiver. No matter how upset you are with someone, do not use hurtful words, and always strive to remain professional in person or online. If you are too upset to write the message, **STOP** until you have calmed down and had a chance to think about it. Write down your thoughts, wait, then come back and read it. When you do this, you may find that you no longer feel the same way as you did when you wrote it because you have had time to reflect on the situation. In addition, when you feel a criticism is necessary in your message, say it in a positive and non-belittling way. When people don't know you, or cannot see you online, all they have to go by is what you write, so be careful how you express yourself.

5. Maintain Professionalism

Most young people today speak and write in short hand or text message format just like they do when sending text messages to their friends. For example, the letter **"U"** means "You," **"B4"** stands for the word "Before," and **"IDK"** means "I don't know." In an online classroom, instant message abbreviations are not acceptable forms of communication. When you write your message, do not include characters like smiley faces; your friends may like it, but chances are your professor may not, and may interpret your message as childish or too casual for the online education environment. Use capital **"I"** when referring to yourself instead of small letter **"i."** Lastly, always say please and thank you when appropriate.

6. Ask for Clarification

As in a real-life classroom, when you don't understand your instructor's directives, or you are unsure of what was said, ask for clarification. Do not sit in silence and try to guess or pretend to understand for fear that your instructor might be offended or think that you are stupid. It is difficult to imagine that any teacher, whether in a traditional classroom or online, would refuse to answer a student's questions. Your instructor will appreciate your responsiveness and maturity. A polite and simple way to do this is to say (or write), *"I did not understand..."* always keeping the responsibility for the misunderstanding on yourself.

Fig. 8.10   Using Text Language to Communicate with Online Instructor is Inappropriate

CONDUCT ONLINE RESEARCH EFFECTIVELY

Conducting research to find information for a school term paper is not a new thing for students but doing the research effectively is another thing. With all the resources available on the World Wide Web, you can find anything you want on the Web, ranging from documentaries, scholarly journal articles, and to electronic books. It is important to note that although these resources are openly out there, they are not freely available to anyone, and that there are rules as to how to use them. These rules include avoiding **plagiarism** by giving credit to materials obtained from other sources through **citations**, and listing your sources on a **reference page.** To be successful in an online course, students must understand how to find and use reliable information. Despite the explosive growth of the Internet over the last two decades, the popular idea that *"you can find anything on the Web"* remains a myth. Depending on your research topic and your instructor's requirements, you may need to supplement Internet research with a visit to a library to find the right materials for your project. In addition, beware of freely-available Internet resources because they may not be as good as you may think, and therefore unsuitable for your research.

Plagiarism

Plagiarism is the presentation of another person's work as one's own work. Plagiarism is a form of academic dishonesty that involves passing on the work of someone else off as your own and it's often subject to disciplinary action. It is a practice that is condemned by scholars and professionals around the world. In addition, failure to properly document sources may raise suspicions of plagiarism and students who are found guilty of plagiarism may find their college career in jeopardy. Almost all colleges in our nation have rules in their **Student Handbook** that explains the school's policy on plagiarism and how violation of such a policy is handled. You may wish to refer to your **Student Handbook** for policies regarding plagiarism at your college. In business environments, plagiarism can significantly damage a person's professional reputation and can even lead to lawsuits.

Tips for Avoiding Plagiarism

1. As you find helpful resources, take good notes, and summarize as you read.
2. Use standard formats to cite sources so that readers can easily track down your facts and quotes.
3. Do not overuse direct quotes; and if an exact quote is needed, be sure that your reader will know where the quote was originally printed or spoken.

4. **NEVER** submit a paper that you have not written yourself. Everyone has a unique writing style, and most instructors can tell when a student submits work that is not his or her own. Some instructors also use electronic tools to detect plagiarized work.

Citations

This is the process of giving credit to sources from which you obtained the information used in your report. By law, when you write a report or research paper using information from other sources that are not your original work, you are required to give credit to the sources of your information. Instructors provide a specific citation format to students when writing research papers and expect students to use standard methods in making citations on information used in their research papers. An instructor may require a citation format where students have to state the name of the book, name of the author, year book was published, and page number within the body of their reports. For example: *"The Fight for Women's Voting Right in America,"* Chris Holmes (2002), pp.315. Another citation format may require placing the sources of your information as footnotes in a numbered format. The two most commonly used citation formats in schools and colleges for writing research papers are: APA Style (American Psychological Association) and MLA Style. APA is used for writing research papers mainly in the areas of social sciences, such as psychology, anthropology, sociology, including education and other fields. MLA (Modern Language Association) is most commonly used to cite sources within the language arts, cultural studies, and other humanities disciplines. If your sources are obtained from the Internet, your instructor will provide you a standard format for citing sources obtained from websites. As a general rule, always adhere to the citation rules provided by your online instructor for citing your sources. Writing good citations ensures that you avoid plagiarism, and proves that you can formulate your own ideas using the ideas of others and creates a path for readers to learn more about your research work.

Reference Page

This is the last page of your research paper and typically contains a list of information about the source used in your paper. The type of information found on this list includes name(s) of the author(s), the full title of the work, the year of publication, and other publication related information. Follow the reference listing format provided by your online instructor.

LOCATE RESOURCES FOR YOUR RESEARCH

Giving the multiple options available to students for finding information, obtaining materials for your research is now more accessible than ever. To perform online research, students often turn to Internet search engines. While the Internet offers many resources, it also offers pitfalls such as outdated, incomplete, and biased information. For this reason, don't overlook resources that libraries have to offer. Most libraries offer much more than printed books. You may discover that your college or public library offers a wealth of premium information that can be accessed from any Internet computer at any time of the day. Usually, all it takes to get started is a password from your librarian.

Decide Where to Find Your Sources

To conduct a successful search, think before you search and decide whether to use a library catalog, an online database, or the open Internet. Wherever you decide to find your sources, make sure you follow the rules of performing online searches described in the following sources:

Internet Resources: This is the easiest and most inexpensive way to obtain research information online. It allows students to search for materials using search engines such as **Google.com, Yahoo.com and Bing (Microsoft Corporation)**. Refer to **chapter 7** of this beginner's guide to read about how to use search engines to find the information you need on the website. In using this method, be careful and very selective when using information found on the open Internet because some sites may not be reliable and some may even be outdated. To conduct your research online effectively, you should be concerned not only with finding information, but also with finding quality information that is accurate, complete, and current. Students should be critical of all web sources especially websites that are freely and openly available via the Internet. To determine the reliability of an online source, students should ask the following questions:

1. **What Does the Website's Address Tell Me?** Websites with addresses ending in **.gov** (government), **.edu** (educational), or **.org** (organizations) may be more reliable than sites with addresses ending in **.com** (commercial).

2. **What Do the Creators of this Site Expect Me to do – Believe, or Buy Something?** If a website tries to persuade you to do something or only represents one point-of-view, then it is biased. It may be okay to use biased sites in your research as long as you recognize the bias and consider other

points of view. Most often, if you are required to buy something before getting the information you need, the source is probably not reliable.

3. **Is the Web Site Current?** Look for dates and other clues that indicate when the site was last updated. For example, if a site still refers to Barack Obama as President of the United States today, even though US has a different President – Joe Biden, then you may need to find more recent information. By using a source that is outdated, you risk writing a paper that is not accurate because you have used old facts that are outdated. Check to see the last time the source was updated on the website and always use the most recent date.

4. **What Do I know about the People or Organization Offering this Website?** Investigate the person or group who sponsors the website. Do some checking about the company putting out the information and particularly read about the author of the article containing the information. Then ask yourself: *Is the author an expert on the topic? How long has he or she been in the field? How many articles has he or she written on this topic?* Expertise of the author and consistency in writing style means reliability of information provided by the author.

5. **Is Information Presented Professional?** Most reputable organizations want to provide serious websites that reflect positively on the work that they do. Signs of an unprofessional website include excessive advertising, poor design, spelling and grammatical errors, and distracting sounds or animations.

6. **Does the Website Provider Acknowledge Sources?** Unlike writers of research papers, web site authors do not necessarily have to list sources on their information; however, a site that does list quality sources is probably a good place to turn for information.

7. **Does the Website Meet My Assignment Requirements?** Depending on your course, your instructor, or the topic that you are researching, you may have to rule out websites that do not provide **scholarly** or **peer-reviewed** information. These two terms refer to sources that have been reviewed by a panel of experts before going to publication. These questions provide a guide not concrete rules for finding good resources. Do not feel that you must cast aside a website because it does not pass all of these tests. Simply remember that if there is any doubt about the quality of a site, you should look for other resources that confirm or validate the information you have found.

Electronic Resources: Many online colleges have library subscriptions that allow students to access a wealth of online information that they would not be able to access through the open Internet. However, for students enrolled in online courses, they may be required to log into their courses with a user name and password before they can access the college library. This protocol is for security reasons ensuring that the person using the online college library is actually a student of that school. For students enrolled in traditional classroom and physically present on campus, passwords may not be required to access electronic resources from a college computer. The three most commonly used electronic resources in online research are research databases, electronic books, and online videos.

1. **Online Research Databases:** These are collections of research information stored on a college database. Several online colleges provide their students access to many online databases through their library that include citations and/or full-text articles from thousands of journals and magazines. Some databases also include resources such as business reports, encyclopedia articles, and government documents. Databases are easy to search and generally contain a large body of full-text information that is more reliable than many resources on the free Internet.

2. **Electronic Books:** Commonly referred to as E-Books, these books are electronic versions of college text books. Through the library, online colleges offer their students various collections of full-text e-books. E-books are searchable by title, subject keyword, or full-text, and like databases, provide information that is generally more reliable than information from the open Internet. Additionally, some E-books have interactive tools such as linked tables of content and searches for finding words or paragraphs within the E-book.

3. **Online Videos:** College libraries also offer services that provide access to several thousands of online videos. Students can search or browse for videos that are generally more reliable than free sources of Internet videos.

Perform Online Searches

A good researcher is concerned not only with finding information, but also with evaluating its quality. The researcher must also ensure that appropriate credit is given to other sources used in writing the paper. Always take a little time before you search to consider various words that describe the information you need. For example, all of the following search phrases could potentially turn up information on the same topic: teen drug use, drug addiction in teenagers, substance abuse and adolescents. Note that by adding more words to your search, you actually limit the number of results you will have. For example, *"drug addiction"* will turn up more results than *"drug addiction in South Carolina,"* but the longer search will be more specific. Remember that you can also connect your search terms with the words *"and, or* and *not"* to ensure that you get the results you want. If your first search does not return the results you expected, try others. You may have to perform several searches before you find what you need. How successful you are in finding the information you need often depends on how you build your search. Think before you search! Whether you are using a research database or the open Internet, take a little time to consider various words that describe the information you need. The following tips may help you search successfully:

1. **Do not Limit Yourself to One Search Term:** Make a list of different ways to search for information. For example, you may find that all of the following search phrases, though similar in meaning, turn up completely different sets of resources – *teen drug use; drug addiction in teenagers; substance abuse and adolescents.*

2. **Consider the Length of Your Search Phrase:** By adding extra words to your search, you actually decrease the number of results you will get. Recall the earlier example in the paragraph above: a search for *"drug addiction"* will turn up more results than a search for *"drug addiction in South Carolina,"* but the longer search phrase will give you more specific results.

3. **Use Connector Words:** Words such as ***and, or*** and ***not*** may be used between your search words to ensure that you get the results you want. If you search *"bacon and eggs,"* any website that appears will have both words on the page. Using the search *"bacon or eggs,"* you will get more hits since you only require that one of the words appears on the page not both.

4. **Use Quotation Marks Around Search Phrases:** Visit an Internet search engine, and search for *Greenville South Carolina*. Take note of how many results appear. Now, compare the number of results that you get when you use quotation marks to search for *"Greenville South Carolina"* instead. You should see fewer, more meaningful results. Quotation marks ensure that search terms are in order and next to each other on a page.

5. **Do not give up Too Quickly:** The best tip for online searching is not to give up. If your first search does not return the results you expected, try others. You may have to perform several searches before you find what you need.

MANAGE YOUR TIME IN AN ONLINE COURSE

A major advantage of online learning is the flexibility it offers to the students, especially working professionals who have little time to attend classes in a traditional classroom setting. You chose how you want to handle your online class schedule as long as you meet required deadlines. Because balancing study, work, and family life can be very stressful, many adult learners choose to school online, allowing them some control over how they allocate their time among study, school, family, work, and social life. However, this flexibility should not cause you to lose sight of your own personal responsibility to effective time management. As in any traditional classroom setting, assignments have deadlines that must be met, and this same principle applies to online learning, including penalty for late submissions. Although this form of distance learning gives you the flexibility of planning your learning schedule at your own pace, you must treat it seriously, learn to manage your time, and allocate time to complete assigned tasks on time. To succeed in learning online, here are some tips on how to manage your time effectively:

Figs. 8.11   **Day Planner**   **Electronic Organizer**

Use Your Assignment Schedule Effectively

On the first day of your online class, print the assignment schedule for the course; read it thoroughly and take note of assignment due dates. Get yourself an organizer with a calendar, then using the assignment schedule as a guide, create a weekly schedule on your organizer showing how you would study to complete assigned projects on time. On your study schedule, make sure you put a deadline that is at least **three days** before the official deadline on every assignment. This gives you a cushion and allows you enough time to do a good job on the project without the pressure of rushing when you are running out of time. For example, if a project is due 04/30/202 on the assignment schedule, on your study schedule, put a due date of 04/27/2021. When you set the date, make sure you stick to it. After your first day of online classes, you should know your teacher's expectations with a good idea of how much time it will take you to finish assigned task.

Create a Study Routine

Based on the items on your assignment schedule, create a routine of logging into your online course every day or as regularly as necessary to review the discussion board and respond to any posted questions; work on any assignment nearing a due date; and read your text book or any required materials for the course.

Although you choose to learn online, you have to see yourself as routinely being in the classroom every day, just like you go to school every day in a traditional classroom setting. The routine is to place yourself in the classroom during your study time because you are in school; the only difference is that your school is online, not in a physical setting. As an online student, your study time is your classroom time in a traditional setting.

Learn to Prioritize Activities

Sometimes you may experience **"crunch"** time in your schedule – that period of time when everything in your life seems to be coming at you all at once, especially during final exams as the semester draws to a close. You may have projects from more than one course due at the same time, and additional pressure from the demands of daily life. Your ability to effectively prioritize demanding activities in your life will enable you to get through this crunch time successfully. To prioritize your time, follow these rules:

   a. Set your study schedule in order of importance and study or work on projects or exams nearing their due dates first. Then consistently adjust the schedule as needed to accommodate the time you need to work on the most important things first and the less important ones later.

   b. Take an inventory of activities in your life, and ask yourself, *"What items can I put off for later?"* Unless it's a life and death situation, some things can wait.

   c. Put off socializing until the semester is over, and use the socializing time to study. With time saved from your social life, increase your study time to at least three to four hours daily.

   d. Take good care of yourself by eating right, getting enough sleep, and relaxing as regularly as you can to avoid undue stress on your body and burning out. If you allow yourself to burn out, you may not be able to complete your online course.

Allocate At Least Two Hours Daily for Online Study

To keep yourself focused on things you need to study first, plan your study activities into your daily routine so that it becomes something you are used to doing at the scheduled time. As a distance learner, it is very easy to forget about your online study when you get too busy with your work. If you integrate your online study into your daily routine at least two hours a day just to focus on study, the studying will turn into a habit that you are used to doing daily.

Work Ahead of Scheduled Deadlines If You Can

Although your assignment schedule shows project due dates, it is always a good idea to work ahead of schedule if you understand the subject matter well enough to do so. This gives you better control over unforeseen events such as illness, computer failure or family emergencies. Working ahead of schedule is like having an insurance policy that you don't have to use unless you really need it.

Use Free Time Wisely

Use the most commonly recognized benefits of online learning which is location to your advantage. Distance learning allows you to login into your course on your school's online learning system at any time of the day, from any location with internet connection. Most companies and Internet cafes offer broadband connection these days; you can utilize your leisure time with your laptop. You can login to download assignment files; complete a project you've been working on; search for research materials on the internet, or log into your school library to find information you need. Although most distance learning programs allow you to complete assignments at your own pace, it is important that you stay on task and be productive.

EFFECTIVE TEST-TAKING TIPS FOR ONLINE LEARNING

Before the Exam

Most online testing may be open book where you are allowed to use your text book while taking the exam. But don't let yourself be deceived by thinking that since the exam is open book, it must be very easy. To pass the online exam with a good grade, you must study as hard as you would study if you were taking a closed-book proctored exam in a traditional classroom setting. The online exam is usually timed and you will be automatically logged off when the time expires. Keep in mind that even with an open-book exam, if you did not study hard in preparing for it and rely on flipping through the pages of your text book to find the answer to a particular question while the clock is ticking, you cannot complete the exam. You will run out of time, and you may fail the exam. Therefore, be wise, study very hard and cover all required materials, whether the exam is open-book or closed-book. Follow these steps to prepare for your online exam:

1. Your online instructor would probably provide you some hints on what will be covered on the test; the format of the test (multiple choice, true-false, short answer, matching, essay questions etc.),

and what to expect. Find out from your instructor whether there will be partial credit for essay responses.

2. Use the information provided by your instructor wisely to design your study plan and review for the exam. Know your materials thoroughly; identify the specific objectives or standards that will be tested, and review them over and over again.

3. At least a week before the exam, make a commitment to spending about an hour each night reviewing the exam materials. Don't wait until the last minute to study everything the night before the exam. In the midst of exam pressure, you may be unable to retain information you studied. Lack of sleep, exhaustion, and inability to remember topics covered in the course may cause you to fail the exam because you waited until the last minute to study.

4. Work the end-of-chapter practice questions in your textbook and practice answering the types of test questions you expect to encounter on the test.

5. Focus more on understanding the subject matter of the course such as basic concepts and the logic or reasoning behind the study of the course than just memorizing the answers to essay questions. If you don't understand the important things about the course and cannot remember what you memorized, you will draw a blank and may not complete the exam.

6. Get a good night's sleep and be well-rested the night before the exam. Studies have shown that cognitive performance declines with fewer than eight hours of sleep. Some experts recommend getting at least eight hours of sleep each night during exam periods.

During the Online Exam

You have worked very hard preparing for this test; be confident, stay relaxed, and maintain a good attitude. Remind yourself that you are well-prepared and you are going to do well. If you find yourself anxious, take several slow deep breaths to relax. Then log into your online course to take the exam and follow these guidelines:

1. Answer questions in a strategic order by answering easy questions first to build your confidence while mentally orienting yourself to the vocabulary and concepts of the covered materials. Sometimes this may also help you make associations with more difficult questions when you get to them.

2. In answering the multiple-choice questions, first eliminate those answers you know to be wrong, or are likely to be wrong, don't seem to fit, or where two options are so similar as to be both incorrect.

3. Throughout the test-taking process keep a watchful eye on the test timer, but do not let yourself be obsessed with the time clock. Otherwise, you will lose your concentration.

4. In answering the essay questions, make your answers short, concise, and straight to the point. Answer exactly what the question requires and avoid unnecessary details.

5. As you wrap up the test, resist the urge to end the test as soon as you have completed all the items. Most online tests give you the opportunity to click the review button to review your answers. Take some time to review your answers and check that you have not missed any questions, or that you did not mismark answers or make simple mistakes.

6. Proofread the essay questions by checking your spelling, grammar, punctuation, decimal points, and make corrections as needed.

7. If you still have time, after making corrections, review again before submitting your test. Complete the review, submit your exam, end the exam, and log off.

INTRODUCTION TO SOCIAL NETWORKING

Social network is a social structure consisting of a set of social actors (individuals or organizations) connected by a complex set of dyadic ties. It is a form of interpersonal communication that refers to the quantitative quality of a communication relationship between two people. The study of these structures through social network analysis helps to identify local and global patterns, locate influential entities, and examine network dynamics. There are specific sites on the Internet known as social network sites where someone can connect with other people through online communication, exchange ideas, or simply have a chat. Those sites are commonly referred to as social networking sites.

What is Social Networking?

There is no one-size-fits-all definition of social networking as many people may define it based on the way it helps them do what they do. However, according to popular opinions, social networking may be defined as the process of exchanging information, personal or public, through a variety of technological methods, such as the Internet, cell phones, and other socially acceptable means of online communication. The presence of social networking sites on the Internet provokes extreme reactions among people from different works of life. Some people don't care so much about it and most can't do without it. Regardless of how certain people feel about social networking, one thing is clear, you either like it or hate it; there are no in-betweens. Social networking sites have become the fastest growing communication tool on the internet. The rise of social networking sites has been phenomenal and widely accepted by majority of young people and a good number of adults partly because of the freedom it affords. While the internet has brought the world together in a global village, social networking sites brought our communities within the four corners of our walls and the world at large. Sitting in your home in front of your computer, with the stroke of keys you can make friends, interact with them, and get to know the various cultures and places around the world. These social networking sites have been known to help people share information with friends and relatives, and to advertise their businesses with very minimum cost. Facebook, Twitter, Linkedin, and Instagram are all examples of social network sites.

Types of Social Networking

Facebook: Introduced in February 2004; operated and privately owned by Facebook, Inc., is a popular free social networking website that allows registered users to create profiles, upload photos and video, send messages and keep in touch with loved ones and acquaintances around the globe. Joining Facebook or becoming a registered user is very easy by following simple steps on the website: **www.facebook.com.**

Twitter: This is a blogging and social networking tool where registered users can post small updates known as tweets of up to **140** or fewer characters. As a free online social networking and micro blogging service, it enables its users to send and read text-based messages. Twitter is referred to as a **Weblog**; a blog is a type of website where people make entries in the form of a diary or journal fashion. It can be described as an electronic diary where millions of people record their thoughts and opinions on every issue from political, controversial, down to what's for dinner. Some blog provide commentary on particular subjects such as social issues, economy, politics, the environment, national security, etc. Political consultants, news services, and political candidates often use blogs for outreach and opinion surveys. Depending on the type of message being posted, blogs primarily contain all text but some may also contain photos, videos, and other graphics relating to the posted message. Some examples of blog websites include but not limited to these: **www.blogger.com/start** *(for blogger),* **www.livejournal.com** *(for LiveJournal).* To create a Twitter account, log into **www.twitter.com** and follow onscreen instructions

Linkedin: A social networking site specifically designed for professional people in the business community. Registered members use the site to establish and document networks of people they know and trust professionally. LinkedIn was co-founded by Reid Hoffman, a former Executive Vice President in charge of business and corporate development for PayPal. The site was launched in May 2003, and currently has over 60 million members from over 300 countries, representing over 200 industries. The main advantage of Linkedin is that it helps jobseekers connect with people in the network and allows them to post their resumes for other registered users to view and contact or recommend them for possible job opportunities. According to Reid Hoffman, 27% of LinkedIn subscribers are recruiters. On LinkedIn site, you can create your profile page to include information about your employment history and education for recruiters to view and contact you or for other users who know you to recommend you to recruiters they know. With basic membership, you can establish connections with someone you have worked with or known professionally (online or offline) or has gone to school with. Unlike other free social networking sites such as Facebook or Twitter, LinkedIn requires connections to have a pre-existing relationship. Linkedin doesn't have all the fancy and attractive layout that other social networking sites have, but it really works to serve its core purpose of connecting professional people around the world. Basic membership for LinkedIn is free and network members are called **"connections."** To create an account on Linkedin log into **www.linkedin.com** and follow onscreen instructions

ETIQUETTES OF SOCIAL NETWORKING COMMUNICATIONS

Internet social networking etiquette is guided by the same principles applicable to real life "*treat others as you want them to treat you.*" These etiquettes are intended to facilitate efficient interaction so that networking sites are not turned into a war zone. There are no known specific written rules that govern the **'netiquette'** of social network; people are generally expected to use their sensibilities when communicating on social network sites. In this new world of cyber space, social networking sites have grown to a tremendous level and the need for Internet etiquette has become very imperative in order to protect users. Because it is difficult to convey politeness on Internet social networking since neither sender nor receive can see each other, people should learn the etiquette of social networking sites before using them. Here are some guidelines to follow:

1. Be careful when adding friends on Facebook. Make sure you are safely adding the people you already know and want to connect with them through Facebook. If you have to add other acquaintances, be selective by adding only people whose profiles are of interest to you.

2. The photos of yourself that you post on the site should be decent to display a positive image of you as a responsible person. Remember that a picture says a thousand words about you; it is your online presence and helps to build your reputation.

3. Never post photos of other people without their permission.
4. Think about the language you use online and not post negative comments that may hurt other people because once the sent button is clicked, there is no way to retrieve it back from cyberspace. When you later realize that your nasty comment was unwarranted there is nothing you can do to change that.
5. Never post links of adult websites or any other illegal sites and don't upload videos and photographs which are obscene and offensive.
6. When entering details of yourself on your profile, tell the truth and avoid providing false information that may mislead other people as to who you really are and what you do. User profiles are an important part of social networking sites that provide basic background information which other people rely on to make connections.
7. Be careful what you say about other people; do not spread malicious rumors for it can be very hurtful and destructive. Slandering other people on social networking sites is bad manners and may have legal implications. Everyone you are connected to can read what you post. Do not write nasty remarks about others. People form an opinion about you based on your interactions on the social network. You may run the risk of embarrassing yourself and others.
8. Do not send spam to other people; it is irritating and in bad taste.
9. Don't continue to be requesting people you don't know to add you as their friends, it is dangerous. You may be unknowingly inviting serial killers as friends.
10. To be an effective member of social networking site, update your posts as needed and participate in discussions. Post daily and comment on other people's post.
11. You can use smile face images to denote a tone but use it sparingly and for people you know really well to avoid sending the wrong message unintended.
12. Do not use all caps in your message posts because using all caps is viewed as the online version of shouting or yelling.
13. If someone posts you a comment make sure you reply; failing to reply is rude.
14. Always use correct **Standard English** language in posting your messages. Avoid using text writing and abbreviations so that people can read your posts and understand what you are saying.
15. Make sure your posts are as brief as possible and straight to the point. People do not have the time or patience to read page long ramblings.

16. In case of any arguments, focus on the issues rather than the people involved. Keep an open mind and don't get involved in online message wars.

Advantages of Social Networking Sites

1. It is the most cost-effective way to keep in touch with friends, family, relatives, classmates, and professional colleagues around the globe where geographical locations are no barriers to staying in touch.

2. Social networking sites remove the boundaries placed on people by geographical and cultural differences. They serve as a melting pot for people from all works of life regardless of culture. Users meet and connect with a variety of people with different and similar interests to theirs.

3. The sites are very interactive and allow you to see and know what your friends and relatives are up to through exchange of messages, uploading photos, and videos.

4. It allows people to build a professional network for employment purposes (Linkedin) and interact with a lot of recruiters at the same time.

5. Most business people use social networking sites to promote their businesses, services, products, or websites. The presence of social networking site remains a tremendous advantage to advertisers.

6. Users of social networking sites (especially recruiters on LinkedIn) provide information on a variety of subject matters that are useful in business, employment, education, and social life.

Disadvantages of Social Networking Sites

1. The most troubling disadvantage of social networking sites is the risk of identity theft and fraud. User's personal information may be used by dubious individuals for illegal activities. Information like the e-mail address, name, location, and age can be used to commit cyber-crimes.

2. With online communication where both sender and receiver cannot see each other, it is possible for people to pretend to be someone they are not. These types of people with bad intentions will prepare their online profiles with false information in order to dupe unsuspecting users.

3. The risk of sexual exploitation by child molesters is very common in social networking sites where these criminals pretend to be someone they are not online for the main purpose of luring minor children into their traps. They end up either sexually molesting the child and/or taking nude pictures for illegal global business that trade pornographic photographs of young children.

4. Because the social networking sites are very poorly regulated, it is often a fertile ground for people trying to get even with one another. These individuals can spread malicious rumors among friends, including uploading embarrassing photos of the victim for everyone to view.

Addiction to Social Networking

With the many advantages of social networking sites, the potential for addiction remains a big concern in our society today. Before the growth of Internet social networking sites, an average person's daily routine may include: wake up in the morning, brush teeth, get ready, go to work, and begin work. These days it is not unusual to see that some people may log into their favorite networking site immediately after waking up – after their morning coffee, before starting actual work in the office for the day, or even in the restroom with Wi-Fi support. This type of habit can only breed one category of people in our society–**"Social Networking-Aholics."** who cannot function well without their daily dose of poking their cell phones to post messages online, upload pictures, play various games or answer one of the various online quizzes. This situation gets out of control when the addiction begins to creep into one's normal lifestyle and begins to affect healthy human relationships with 'real people' not virtual individuals. While it may be difficult to get rid of this addiction, here are some suggestions to help you avoid social networking addiction:

How to Avoid Social Networking Addiction:

1. **Choose a Short List of Cyber Friends:** Most people get so carried away with the fun of social networking sites that they end up having a long list of Facebook friends, Twitter followers and so forth. They befriend too many people over the internet and cannot take time out for work or family. This usually happens when some of those friends keep posting, and you feel a compulsive need to respond to every post they send. Often a few of your 300 friends may post pictures of their birthday parties and you feel compelled to see it. Another one of such friends may answer a quiz and would have sent you an invitation to play the same game and you feel the need to take a look; before you know it, you are hooked online. Do not allow yourself to be stuck online responding to every single post. Choose very few online friends and be very selective who you accept as a friend. Follow the etiquette of social networking already outlined in this chapter; be wise, and stay safe.

2. **Logoff from Social Networking Site:** Make it a habit to always log off from social networking site after each use and turn off the computer to minimize the temptation and frequency of usage. Do not keep social media sites open in your web browser at all times to reduce the ease of media accessibility and limit your interaction to the site. If the computer is turned off and you have more important things to do, you may be more likely to attend to your daily tasks than turn on

the computer; wait for it to start; log onto the Internet; wait for it to start; and then log onto your favorite social networking site. As you calculate all the time it will take you to get to the social network site, you would probably want to start working on your things-to-do list than waste your time on the Internet.

3. **Set Limits of Usage for Yourself:** Most people get addicted to Internet social networking sites over time because once they log into the site, they don't know when to stop, log out and turn their attention to something else such as family and work. The most important aspect of setting limits of usage is personal discipline. You must challenge yourself and stick to a specified login and logout out time from the social network site. It is irresponsible for anyone to compromise on the day's work at the office to make time for social networking until the behavior turns into a full-blown addiction. Setting limits of usage may be difficult at the beginning but over time, you will become accustom to sticking to the time limit. If possible, set an alarm for about 30 minutes at the onset of logging into the site and log off as soon as the alarm goes off. From this point on, you can discipline yourself to stick to the **"30 minutes per usage rule."** Always remind yourself that you have better things to do with your life than just waste it socializing over the Internet.

4. **Make a Daily Schedule:** Generally, the average person, especially married people with children may have full day with so many things to attend to including a full-time job. If you can schedule your day such that you spend only a limited time preferably half hour a day networking over the internet, you will be able to avoid addiction. When you make your daily schedule, place network Internet socializing last on the list after you have done all your important things for the day. Even if you end up not getting to that last item on the list for the day, the world will not stop, and you will be okay; you can socialize the next day. To stick to this schedule, you have to ask yourself, *"How important is it that I log into my favorite networking site daily?"* If the answer to this question is *"not that important"* then you can live without it for one day or even more. On the other hand, certain items on your schedule, such as your child's doctor's appointment or picking up the kid from the daycare cannot be compromised for social networking.

CHAPTER SUMMARY & KEY TERMS

Remote online learning classroom may be referred to as artificial intelligence applications that serves as a virtual learning environment designed to support teaching and learning in an educational setting to create a distinct managed learning environment. To be successful in online learning, a student must be proficient in with the use of a computer and the use of all Microsoft Office programs (Word, Excel, and PowerPoint). Before enrolling in online courses, make sure you have taken at least an introductory course in computer technology covering basic computing concepts, the Internet, and Microsoft Office applications. Being technology proficient is imperative to online learning because it provides a strong foundation for students to build on in learning how to navigate an online classroom using the course management tools. Proficiency in application programs is necessary because most online instructors require students to do their assignments in Microsoft Office applications.

The first five things to do before you can learn online are: (1) Register for your courses, (2) Pay for your courses, and (3) Purchase your textbooks, (4) Login to online course home and (5) Create your username and password. The Home Page of an online learning environment consists of learning tools that allow students to manage their online courses, download assignment questions, upload completed assignments, communicate with the instructor and other students, download research materials, take exams/quizzes/tests, and view their grades to monitor their performance in the course. It is also important to adhere to the netiquette rules of online communication such as using Standard English language, being professional, being friendly, positive, and assertive, and asking for clarification when necessary.

To succeed in online learning, you must know how to perform searches on the Internet to obtain reliable information you need for your school research paper. Depending on your research topic and your instructor's requirements, you may need to supplement Internet research with a visit to the library to find the right materials for your project. In addition, beware of freely-available Internet sources because they may not be as good as you may think, and therefore unsuitable for your research. When you write that paper, do not plagiarize. Plagiarism is a form of academic dishonesty that involves passing on the work of someone else off as your own and is often subject to disciplinary action. Although distance learning gives you the flexibility of planning your learning schedule at your own pace, you must treat it seriously, learn to manage your time, and allocate time to complete assigned tasks on time. Learn to use your study time wisely, and practice effective test-taking techniques. Internet social networking etiquette is guided by the same principles applicable to real life *"treat others as you want them to treat you."* There are no known specific written rules that govern the 'netiquette' of social network; people are generally expected to use their sensibilities when communicating on social network sites. With the many advantages of social networking sites, the potential for addiction remains a big concern in our society today. Do not let yourself get addicted to social networking sites; use it wisely and follow the rules of correct discipline.

KEY TERMS

Citations
Compose
Course Content
Course Home
Computer-Mediated
Distance Education
Discussion Board

Drop Box
Forum List
Linkedin
Netiquette
Plagiarism
Portable Digital Format (PDF)
Post

Reference Page
Thread of Conversation
Thread of Discussion
Twitter
Virtual Online Education

Demonstrate Your Knowledge & Skill

CHAPTER 8 SKILL-BASED PRACTICE PROJECTS INTRODUCTION TO REMOTE ONLINE LEARNING

Short Answer Questions: Open a Word document entitled **Remote Online Learning** at top page, and center title. Demonstrate your knowledge and understanding of remote online learning by answering the following short answer questions. Please use correct Standard English in your responses and keep your answers brief, clear, and straight to the point.

Required:

1. What is the difference between Web-enhanced classes and online classes?
2. Describe the **Course Home** of a learning environment.
3. List three items found on the **Course Management Tools**.
4. List any three of the six "netiquette" rules for a successful online education.
5. In terms of technology proficiency requirements, list at least four things you must be proficient in before you can enroll in an online class.
6. What is the purpose of the course management tools in the online learning environment?
7. Describe the three steps for responding to a posted discussion.
8. Describe the three quick tips to posting a discussion on the discussion forum.
9. What is Plagiarism? Why is this practice condemned by scholars and professionals around the world?
10. In writing a research paper, why would you need a reference page? What is the correct location of the **Reference Page** in a research paper?
11. Save your Word file in the preferred location on your computer as **8_RemoteLearning_Firstname_Lastname** using your first and last name. Submit your completed assignment (the Word document) following the instructor's preferred method – electronically or printed hardcopy for grading.

GLOSSARY OF TERMS & DEFINITIONS

A

Action Center: A single area found on Windows 7 desktop that collects important notification messages about security and maintenance settings.

Activation: The process of registering installed software on the computer by providing a Product Key as part of Microsoft anti-piracy technology designed to verify that software products are legitimately licensed. The purpose of activation is to verify that the Product Key, which you must supply to install the product, is not in use on more personal computers than are permitted by the software license. Activation also ensures that the installed program continues to function as expected.

Address Bar: The bar that is displayed in a browser window, enabling you to type the address of a Web site to visit.

Adware: Software that gathers information about a computer user's Internet travels without the person's knowledge.

Animations: Visual effects that give your PowerPoint presentation slide a unique appearance. They are features that allow you to add movement and eye-catching elements on your slide to draw attention from your audience.

Animated Banners: A series of rotating or changing text and images embedded within the Web page – colorful images used to attract attention and stimulate interest to a Web site.

Anonymous FTP: In an FTP web site, this means that permissions are set so that anyone on your network can log in using a password such as **"guest"** or **"justme"**.

Antispyware Software: Software that removes spyware from a computer system.

Antivirus Software: Software that searches a computer system for computer viruses, removing any that are found.

Asymmetric DSL (ADSL): A type of DSL that uses existing phone lines, providing fast downloading but slower uploading.

Arithmetic Logic Unit (ALU): A part of the system CPU that performs all the arithmetic and logic functions of the computer, which includes addition, subtraction, multiplication, division and also makes logical comparison decisions.

Attachment: An electronic file created in a Microsoft Office program or other applications, saved on your computer, and included in an e-mail message. The attachment could be a document, spreadsheet, picture, or other graphics.

Authenticated Feeds: A new feature of Internet Explorer 8 that automatically platforms authentication on the RSS windows without user interaction.

B

Back Button: A backward arrow used to return the user to the home page.

Background: The part of the screen not occupied with displayed characters or graphics, particularly on the Windows desktop.

Backspace Key: A keyboard key that removes text from the screen one character at a time to the left of where you want to insert a word (insertion point). To use backspace key, position the cursor to the Right of the word(s) you want to delete and press the backspace key until all the words are deleted, then type the new word(s).

Backup System: A way of saving your data and files from your computer.

Bit: Binary digit; the smallest binary component, which can hold only a zero or a one.

Black Theme: A Microsoft Excel feature that allows you to change your Office theme simply by clicking File>>k Account>>the Office Theme drop-down arrow and selecting the theme you want. The theme you choose will be applied across all your Excel Office apps.

Blended Learning: A traditional face to face classroom activities in a Web-enhanced format.

Blog: Also referred to as a Weblog, a blog is a type of website where people make entries in the form of a diary or journal fashion. It can be described as an electronic diary where millions of people record their thoughts and opinions on every issue from political, controversial, down to what's for dinner.

Bookmarks: A stored URL address for quick retrieval at a later date, sometimes called a *favorite*; as a user visits Web pages and finds favorites to be visited later, the URL can be saved as a bookmark which can be revisited.

Booting: Powering on a computer.

Broadband: A high-speed transmission type that carries several data channels over a single cable.

Browser: Software that allows a user to access the Internet.

Browser Add-ons: Programs such as multimedia add-ons, search bars, or other items that usually appear on your browser's toolbar during downloads unsolicited, and can also cause slow performance problems on your computer.

Byte: A unit of measurement for computer memory and disk space; the byte is the lowest unit of measure.

C

Cable: Connects a computer to a cable TV service that provides Internet access.

Caps Lock Key: Located under the Tab key, this key makes typed letters appear in all uppercase when pressed. Green light indicates the caps lock is on, pressing the key again turns off the cap locks and typed letters returns back to lowercase.

CD: Compact Disk; an optical disk storage device used to store programs and archival data that doesn't often change.

CD-R: A recordable compact disk; an optical disk that can be written to one time and read from many times.

CD-ROM: Another portable disk drive which stands for compact disk.

CD-RW: A rewritable compact disk; an optical disk that can be recorded, erased, and re-recorded.

Central Processing Unit (CPU): Also called the CPU or simply, the PC. This is what makes a computer work. It is like the brain of the computer, and contains the disk drives and hard drives the computer uses to process information. The power switch must be turned on for the computer to work.

Citations: This is the process of giving credit to sources where you obtained the information used in your report.

Close Button: The red X located in the top right corner of the window that is clicked to close the window.

Column Chart: Also known as vertical bar charts, it is an Excel data visualization method where each category is represented by a rectangle, with the height of the rectangle being proportional to the values being plotted. The purpose of column chart is to compare the values of each category.

Computer: A programmable electronic device that can input, process, and store data. A computer processes data and converts it into information. The definition of a computer is derived from its four basic functions also known as the **information processing cycle (IPC).**

Contents Pane: The right side of the Windows Explorer window that lists the files and subfolders in the current folder.

Content Advisor: An Internet Explorer feature used to control the types of Internet content that can be viewed on your computer.

Cortana: Windows feature that uses audio and speech to interact with a user when searching for information.

Constant: A constant is a value in Excel that is not calculated; it always stays the same. For example, the date 08/9/2010, the number 325, and the text "Quarterly Earnings" are all constants.

Contact List: Also referred to as an address book in an email window that contains a list of your contacts; the people you maintain email communication with on regular basis.

Cookies: Data files stored on a user's computer that identifies the user and keeps track of preferences.

Course Home: Displays upcoming assignments under.

CPU: The processor of the computer, which consists of electronic circuits that accept, evaluate, and act on instructions found in software programs; the CPU also communicates with all peripheral devices.

Crawler: Software used by a search engine to search for Web pages whose content matches criteria specified by a user.

Course Content: A D2L link located on the navigation pane that contains course syllabus, assignment schedule, and all other course materials and learning resources for the course.

Cursor: A special symbol, usually a rectangle or a blinking underscore that indicates where the next character will be displayed.

Cyber Squatting: Registering or using a domain name in bad faith, with the intent to profit from the name at the expense of another person or company. People who engage in this type of act are often referred to as "Dot.Com Grabbers."

D

Data File: A file that is created by a user when working with an application program; can contain just about any type of information, such as documents, spreadsheets, or photographs.

Delete Key: Located above the Insert key and used to delete typed characters. Highlight the word or words to be deleted and press the delete key to delete them.

Desktop Computer: A personal computer in which all the components, including the keyboard, mouse, monitor, and system unit, easily fit on or under a desk.

Desktop Publishing: The use of a personal computer to create documents for publication.

Desktop: The background of the Windows display that appears when the computer is turned on and the user has logged. It is the first screen you see when the computer starts up. The desktop has several icons that can be used as short-cuts to a program or file. You can also save your information on a desktop.

Details Pane: A pane that displays details and metadata about a selected folder, such as file name, size, and author.

Dialog Box Launcher: A button found at the bottom right corner of most ribbon groups found in a Microsoft Office 2007 window, which, when clicked, causes a subsequent dialog box to be displayed.

Dialog Box: A special-purpose window that provides the current status of a program or operation and accepts input or directions from a user.

Dialup: Method of connecting to the Internet; the slowest method for connecting since it uses a standard modem and phone line.

Digital Camera: Camera that does not use film, but stores images digitally.

Discussion Board: A asynchronous communication tool that allows one individual to post a comment or question online.

Disk Cleanup: A utility program that removes files from the Recycle Bin (the temporary holding area for deleted files), deletes temporary Internet files, and compresses old files.

Disk Defragmenter: A Windows tool that rearranges data on a hard disk to connect fragmented files and

Disk Drive: A device that reads data from a magnetic disk and copies it into the computer's memory allowing data to be used by the computer. It also writes data from the computer's memory onto a disk for storage.

Diskette: A magnetic disk enclosed in a plastic case. It is an external storage device for saving your documents, such as 3.5" Floppy Disk.

Domain Name: Name of the Internet service provider and refers to the address of the Internet server on which the Web page resides.

Downloading: The process of copying a file from a Web server to your computer.

Driver: A program that manages the functioning of a peripheral device, such as a printer or scanner.

DSL (Digital Subscriber Line): A high-speed Internet connection that uses existing telephone lines, but in such a way that data transmission is fast and does not tie up the telephone line.

DVD (Digital Versatile Disk): An optical storage device that has much more data capacity than a compact disk. DVDs come as DVD-R and DVD-RW as well.

DVD ROM: Portable disk drive that stands for digital video disk and holds more information and images than the CD.

DVD-R (Digital Video Disk Recordable): An optical disk that can be written to one time and read from many times.

DVD-RW (Digital Video Disk–Rewriteable): An optical disk that can be recorded, erased, and re-recorded.

E

Electronic Books: Commonly referred to as E-Books, are electronic versions of college text books.

Electronic Business Card: A view of specific information about a contact, in a format similar to a paper-based business card that can be inserted into an Email message.

Electronic Mail (e-mail): Sending, receiving, storing, and forwarding messages in digital form over telecommunication facilities.

E-mail Client: The e-mail user who sends and receives e-mail.

E-mail Server: Computers dedicated to the task of managing and passing along e-mail on the Internet.

E-mail Account: A profile that contains basic personal information about you, data files, and account settings where your e-mail is stored.

Email Attachment: An electronic file created in a Microsoft Office program or other applications, saved on your computer and included in an e-mail message.

Encryption: Encoding technology used by Web servers to code the transaction so that outside parties will not be able to read the data; particularly important for purchases and other monetary transactions.

End Key: Located under the Home key. Press the End Key to move the cursor from left to the right of your document.

Error Checking: A utility program that examines a disk for data storage errors, from physical defects on the disk surface to weakened areas that might cause that space to be unreliable.

F

Favorite Center: Located at the toolbar, the favorite center contains a list of the websites visited most frequently. Stored URL addresses for quick retrieval at a later date are also called bookmarks.

File Compression Software: A program that stores data in a format that requires much less space than usual, such as WinZip, PKZip, or StuffIt.

Firewall: Hardware or software that is designed to prohibit unauthorized access to computer resources and files.

Flash Drive: External storage device that is neither magnetic nor optical and has no moving parts; used in notebook computers, digital cameras, and other portable computer devices.

Floppy Disk: A magnetic disk that is removable and enclosed in a plastic case (also called a diskette).

Folder Pane: Located on the left side of My Computer window and displays the hard drive, all other drives in the computer, including removable storage devices, folders, and subfolders.

Folder: A holding area on a disk storage medium, designed to organize files and subfolders.

Folders and Documents: Folders help organize the files you save on the computer. Each item you save is called a document or a file.

Font: Character design; also called type or typeface; the most common fonts or typefaces are Arial and Times Roman.

Forward Button: Becomes available once the Back button has been used. This button is a forward arrow that takes the user to the next Web page that has previously been viewed before going backward.

Forward: An action that sends a selected e-mail message to another recipient.

Fragmented: A file that is that is broken apart as it is saved, with pieces of the file being stored in any available free disk space.

FTP (File Transfer Protocol): A Web page protocol that supports the transfer of files from one computer to another.

Function Keys: These are keys labeled F1 to F12 are located at the top of the keyboard. When pressed, they perform certain actions in the programs. For example, pressing F1 will open the help window. Each program uses different function keys for different purposes.

G

Gadgets: Mini-programs typically located at a Windows 7 desktop sidebar that offer information at a glance and provide easy access to frequently used tools.

Gigabyte: One billion bytes.

Gigahertz: A unit of measure for the processing speed of a CPU; a frequency of a billion times a second

Graphical User Interface (GUI): A component of Windows 10 that uses graphics or pictures to represent the commands and actions on your computer that allows you to see document formatting on the screen as it will look like when printed on paper. Graphical user interface, the icons.

H

Handheld Computer: Also called a PDA; a personal computer that is small enough to fit in the palm of your hand.

Hard Copy: Physical copy printed from the computer.

Hard Disk: A magnetic disk for storage housed in the system unit that has much more storage capacity than a floppy disk (also referred to as the hard drive).

Hard Return: A non-printing, invisible character created when you press Enter.

Hardware: This is the name for the physical parts of your computer, which includes: the central processing unit (CPU), monitor, keyboard, mouse, and speakers.

Help and Support: A feature built into Windows operating system software that enables the typing of a search word or phrase related to the operating system, which in turn provides information related to that phrase, if possible. The help and support center can be activated by pressing F1 key or by clicking the question sign (?) at the upper right corner of the window.

History List: A listing of Web pages on the Internet visited during a specified interval of time that is maintained by a Web browser; the History list can be set to maintain history for a designated period of time (one month, two weeks, and so forth).

Home Key: Located between the Insert and Page Up keys. Press the **Home Key** to move the cursor from right to the left of your document.

Home Page: The first page that displays every time Internet Explorer is started. The default home page is installed when Windows is set as a Microsoft site because Internet Explorer is a Microsoft program. These home pages, including MSN, act as portals or launching sites to other Web pages.

Hotmail: A free Web-based e-mail service provided by Microsoft.

HTML: Short for Hypertext Transfer Protocol, this is the document format used to display Web pages in newer/other versions of protocols are called XML, SGML, DHTML.

HTTP (Hypertext Transfer Protocol): Communications protocol used to connect to a server and then transfer HTML pages to the computer user's browser.

Hybrid Class: A learning format that combines both classroom and online learning where students complete some class hours via internet while other class hours take place in an on-campus classroom setting.

Hyperlinks: Images or text on a Web page that you can click to move to other Web locations; also called a link.

I

Icon: A small picture that represents a program, document, file, folder, or shortcut in Windows.

Ink Jet Printer: The most popular type of printer for home computer users; affordable, with high quality, and color capability.

Input: The computer devices that accept commands from a user and transform them into a form the computer can use, such as a mouse or a keyboard. Data entered into the computer is referred to as an input.

Insert Key: Located at upper right of the keyboard next to the Home key. Press the **Insert Key** to insert a word between words in your document. Press **Insert Key** again to release it from Insert mode.

Insertion Point: The blinking vertical line that indicates the position where text will display.

Installing: Copying a program onto a computer hard disk (C drive.

Internet Corporation for Assigned Names and Numbers (ICANN): The organization responsible for certifying companies as domain name registrants.

Internet Explorer: A Web browser developed by Microsoft, available as a free download.

Internet Service Provider (ISP): A company that allows you to connect to the Internet through its host computer.

Internet TV: Internet service that uses a set-top box to connect a TV to the Internet; also called Web TV or MSN TV.

Internet: A global network used to access and send data; a group of interconnected networks that spans the world. It is a system which connects worldwide computers.

Intranet: An internal network for a company.

K

Keyboard: The primary input device for entering data into the computer keys consisting of all letters of the alphabet (A-Z) used to type documents, numeric key pads (1-0) for When the scroll lock is turned off, the arrow keys can neither move up or down nor right or left.

Kilobyte: 1,024 bytes; usually calculated by rounding to 1,000 bytes.

L

Landscape: Printing a document across the wider side of the paper; landscape orientation is wider than it is tall.

Laptop Computer: A notebook- or briefcase-size portable computer usually weighing less than 10 pounds.

Laser Printer: A type of printer that provides the highest print resolution and speed.

LCD: Liquid crystal digital format with clearer view and better pixilation.

Line Graph: An Excel graph used to show data that changes over time identifying the trends (movement) of data over a period of time. Line graphs are plotted using several points connected by straight lines. The line graph comprises of two axes known as 'x' axis and 'y' axis. The horizontal axis is x-axis while the vertical axis is known as the y-axis parts of a line graph. Line graphs can include a single line for one data set, or multiple lines comparing two or more data sets.

Links: Images or text on a Web page that you can click to move to other Web locations; also called a hyperlink.

Live Preview: A feature found in Microsoft Office applications; by pointing to various formatting choices, you can instantly see the effect on selected text.

M

Malware: Software, including spyware, worms, and viruses, developed for the purpose of being harmful.

Maximize Button: A button that causes the windows to fill the screen; the maximize button is found at the right side of the title bar and is the middle button if the window is not already at full size.

Megabyte: One million bytes.

Megahertz: A unit of measure for the processing speed of a CPU; a frequency of a million times a second.

Memory: The temporary storage of data and programs that are currently in use.

Menu: Choices across the top of the screen.

Microcomputer: The smallest and least expensive class of computer (also called personal computers).

Microprocessor: The basic arithmetic, logic, and control elements required for processing (usually contained in one chip); the Pentium is a common microprocessor chip.

Microsoft Office Professional: The complete Microsoft Office software package that contains Outlook, Word, Excel, Access, PowerPoint, and Publisher. It is are very expensive and most commonly used by business organizations and large corporations.

Microsoft Office Home and Student: The Microsoft Office package that contains only Word, Excel, and PowerPoint. It is less expensive than the professional package, and the most commonly used at homes and at schools because of its affordability.

Microsoft Word: A word processor program that works like a typewriter except that it contains features that allow you to edit typed document, copy, move, save, and delete text.

Minimize Button: Reduces the window to a button on the taskbar without actually closing the window; the minimize button is found on the right side of the title bar and is the leftmost of the three buttons; the taskbar button can be clicked at any time to return the window to the screen.

Mini-Toolbar: A semi-transparent toolbar in Microsoft Office 2007 containing formatting options that can be applied to selected text; using the mini-toolbar, a user can work with fonts, alignment, colors, indent levels, and bullet features.

Monitor: Similar to a TV screen, it is the primary output device of a computer on which data is displayed while being entered.

Mouse: The second most common input device; used to select commands or objects on screen, activate a program, or move items on the screen. The mouse is also used to navigate around and across the computer screen by moving the cursor to desired locations. It allows you to: click, double-click, click and drag, and right-click.

Multifunction Printer: A printer that also functions as a photocopier, fax, and scanner in one unit; popular in homes and small offices.

Multilingual User Interface (MUI): The name used to describe Microsoft technology for Microsoft Windows, Microsoft Office and other applications that allow users to install multiple interface languages on a single system.

N

Navigation or Arrow Keys: These are arrow keys located at the lower right of the keyboard. Press these keys to move the cursor to the beginning of a line, to the end of a line, up the page, down the page, to the beginning of a document, or to the end of a document.

Navigation Pane: The column on the left side of Microsoft Office program window that contains a list of folders that are contained within the current folder; also includes the results of searches and favorite links.

Netiquette: Common rules (etiquette) that provides guidelines on the appropriate ways to communicate with other people online.

Notebook Computer: A computer smaller than a laptop that can fit inside a briefcase

Notification Area: An area on the right side of the taskbar that contains a clock and icons representing programs currently running in the background, such as antivirus software; also provides information on such settings as wireless connections and local area networks.

Numeric Keypad (Num Lock Key): Located at top right of the keyboard, above the keyboard numbers. The num lock key allows you to type numbers only when it is pressed and turned on. A green light.

O

OCR Software: Software used to scan images or print into the computer.

Office Button: Replaces the File menu of earlier Microsoft Office versions and contains some of the same selections, such as open, close, and print.

Offline: Describes a situation in which a computer is not connected to the Internet.

Online Class: A learning format that allows students to complete their course work through the internet. Before the students begin their online education, they are required to attend a classroom online learning orientation on the main campus.

Online Service: A type of ISP that provides a wide array of services; for example, America Online.

Outline View: In PowerPoint the outline view displays your presentation as an outline made up of all the titles and main text from each slide. The Outline View is located in the Presentation Views group at top ribbon of an open PowerPoint program.

Operating System (OS): The operating system controls the entire operation of a computer and tells your computer how to act. It can change the way things appear on your screen or desktop.

Operators: Excel feature that defines the type of result that you obtain from the formula you create. The Excel operators perform actions on numeric values, text or cell references.

Optical Disk Storage: A disk storage device that uses a laser to read and write, in some cases, to a disk (like a CD or DVD).

Output: Information produced by the computer, such as text, numbers, graphics, and even sounds.

Output: Raw data processed into useful information.

P

Page Down: Located directly under Page Up. Press this key to move the cursor to the end of your document.

Page Up: Located at top right next to Num Lock. Press this key to move the cursor to the top of your document.

PDF (Portable Document Format): A file format developed by Adobe as a means of distributing compact, platform-independent documents. A document in PDF format is read-only and can neither be edited nor modified.

Pie Chart: A type of Excel data representation chart that contains different segments and sectors in which each segment and sectors of a pie chart forms a certain portion of the total percentage. The total of each data segment must always equal 100% of the pie taken as whole. To work with the percentage for a pie chart, the data must be categorized, total calculated, categories divided, and converted into percentages. The purpose of a pie chart is to show what percentage of the total (100%) is contributed by each segment of the pie chart.

Peripheral Equipment: All the input, output, and secondary devices attached to the computer.

Personal Computer (PC): A microcomputer designed for individual use, providing access to the Internet and allowing users to work with programs of interest.

Personal Digital Assistant (PDA): A personal computer that is small enough to fit in the palm of your hand (also called a handheld computer).

Phishing: The act of sending an e-mail to someone falsely claiming to be a legitimate financial institution, in an attempt to collect personal identifying information.

PKZip: A file compression software program.

Plagiarism: Plagiarism is the unacknowledged use of any person's work into one's own work.

POP3 Protocol: Post Office Protocol: a method of transmitting e-mail; mail is stored on the e-mail server, downloaded at the user's request, and removed from the server.

Pop-Up: A small web browser window that appears at top of the website you're viewing.

Portrait: Printing a document across the narrow side of the paper; portrait orientation is taller than it is wide

Primary Button: Mouse left button.

Print Preview: A feature that enables you to preview a file so that you can see how it will look when printed.

Printer: A secondary device attached to the computer that allows it to produce a hard copy document.

Processor: The hardware unit that controls all system activity (the brain of the computer).

Program File: File that causes a program, or application, to run on a computer.

Protocol: An agreed-upon format for transmitting data between two devices.

Protocols: Hardware or software standard that coordinates data transmission between computers; and provides additional space in your computer.

Public Folder: A folder used to save files to be shared by computers on a specific network.

Q

Quick Access Toolbar: A feature very common with all MS Office products; it is located at the very top left of MS Office programs: Word, Excel, and PowerPoint window. As the name implies, this feature allows you to perform quick actions such as Save, Undo, and Redo.

Quick Launch Toolbar: A toolbar that appears at the top of Microsoft Office application windows and includes buttons for commonly accessed commands such as Save and Redo; the toolbar can be customized to include additional functions.

R

RAM: Random Access Memory; the volatile memory of a computer.

Recycle Bin: A folder on the hard disk that serves as a temporary holding place for deleted files and folders until the user chooses to either restore the contents or empties them.

Reduced Functionality Mode: The condition of installed software on a computer where it behaves similar to a viewer if not activated upon installation. In this mode, you cannot save modifications to documents or create new documents, and functionality may be reduced. No existing files or documents are harmed in Reduced Functionality mode but you cannot create a new one either.

Relative Cell Reference: In Excel, relative reference is the type of reference which changes to another cell number when the same formula is copied to any other cells or in any other worksheet.

Reference: A reference identifies a cell or a range of cells on a worksheet, and tells Excel where to look for the values or data you want to use in a formula.

Reply: An action that sends a message back to the person who sent you the selected message.

Resolution: A screen setting that determines the sharpness of the display and the size of the screen elements. The number of pixels displayed on the monitor's determines the sharpness of the images. The higher the number, the higher the resolution and the sharper the image.

Restore Button: Appears as two overlapping boxes that returns a window to its original size when clicked

RSS (Rich Site Summary): is a format for delivering regularly changing web content. It allows people who regularly use the web to easily stay informed by retrieving the latest content from the sites they are interested in, and save them time by not needing to visit each site individually.

Ruler Bar: A bar above or to the left of the document area in Microsoft Office programs that marks the measurements of the document and displays the margins and tab settings.

S

Scanner: Peripheral input device.

Screen Saver: A moving picture or pattern that appears on your screen when you have not used the mouse or keyboard for a specified period of time.

Screen: Face of the monitor, part of the computer used to view information on the screen.

ScreenTip: A small note, activated by holding the pointer over a button or other screen object, which displays information about a screen element. It identifies the Web page that will display when you click the button.

Scroll Lock: Located at the top right of the keyboard, the scroll lock controls the movement of the arrow.

Secondary Button: Mouse right button.

Search Bar: Enables the user to search for any item on a computer system, such as a document or folder, by typing all or part of the file name or identifying key words in the Search bar; the Search bar is located to the right of the Address bar in a Windows 7 folder window.

Search Box: Files and folders on a computer system can be located by typing any part of the file name or an identifying key word in the Search box; the Search box is located on the Windows Vista Start menu.

Search Engine: Software that searches the Internet for data based on search criteria specified by the user; examples are Google, Yahoo, and Ask. These sites allow users to search for information on the Internet with questions, keywords, or terms.

Sectors: Pie-piece shaped areas of storage on a disk in which data can be stored for later retrieval.

Slide Show & Presentation: In a PPT presentation, these two terms are used interchangeably because they each represent the overall document you create in the application. Slide Show view occupies the full computer screen exactly the way your presentation will look on a big screen.

Slides: A slide layout contains formatting, positioning, and serves as a placeholder for the contents of your presentation. Placeholders are displayed as dotted line containers of presentation texts. Each slideshow in a PPT represents a page in a book. For example, if you are writing a school term paper that will contain multiple pages, each page you fill with words is a slide from PPT standpoint.

Slide Master: Located in the View tab at the ribbon of a PowerPoint window, Slide Master is a feature that allows you to choose the option you want for printing your presentation handouts.

Service Pack: A collection of updates, corrections, or enhancements to the software program installed on the computer.

Shift Key: Located at the left of the keyboard, below the cap lock key. It is used to type a word in upper case and to highlight a group of typed items. To type the first letter of your sentence in uppercase, hold down the shift key and type the word. To highlight a group of words in your document, hold down the shift key and use the arrow keys to highlight those words.

Shortcut Menu: Appears when an on-screen object or area is right-clicked; the options displayed on a shortcut menu are completely dependent on the object or area of the screen that a user right-click.

Shortcuts: Pointers to programs or data files, sometimes represented as desktop icons, which when double-clicked, open the associated file or program.

Smart Screen Filter: A feature that provides protection from socially engineered malware by tracking every website and download to check against a local list of popular legitimate websites, if the site is not listed the entire address is sent to Microsoft for further investigation.

Soft Copy: Copy of data or information saved on the computer.

Soft Return: A line break created by the program due to word wrap.

Software: Instructions or programs that run the computer.

Spam: An electronic equivalent of junk mail, which is unsolicited and usually unwanted e-mail

Speakers: Computer peripherals that allow you to hear sounds from your computer.

Spreadsheet: Excel software that allows users to organize data in rows/columns and perform calculations.

Spyware: Software that is often included with free downloads; its purpose is to send information about a user's Internet travel back to the computer from which it originated.

Start Button: Appears in both Windows XP and Windows Vista as a button at the left-bottom side of the window near the task bar that gives users access to programs and system resources.

Start Menu: A list that displays when the Start button is clicked and acts as the guiding route to running programs as well as to shut down a computer system. It is usually launched from the Start button, found at the left side of the taskbar.

Status Bar: The horizontal bar that appears at the bottom of the application window, indicating the current document settings.

Status Indicators Keys: Included with the numeric keypads are two other keys that perform different functions when turned on, indicated by green lights.

Streaming: Downloading audio and video content from the Internet.

Style: A combination of formatting characteristics in MS Office, such as font, font size, and indentation, that you name and store as a set.

Subfolder: A folder within a folder.

Surge Protector: A device that filters out short surges of high voltage so they don't damage electrical equipment.

System Unit: The hardware device that houses the motherboard, disk drives, memory chips, processor, and ports of the computer system.

T

Tab: A grouped area identified by a descriptive title.

Task Pane: Provides quick access to commonly accessed tasks or to those that are applicable to a currently running application.

Taskbar: The horizontal bar usually found along the bottom of the desktop that displays the folders, applications, and documents that are open.

Template: A preformatted document model that remains the same, allowing multiple new copies of the same type of document.

Title Bar: The top bar on a window, which displays the name of the program as well as containing the minimize, maximize/restore, and close buttons.

Theme: A combination of pictures, colors, and sounds on your computer that includes a desktop background, a screen saver, a window border color, and a sound scheme.

Trackball: A type of keyboard with an input device similar to an upside-down mouse that helps to reduce hand movements required for a mouse.

Tracks: Storage channels on a disk or tape.

Transitions: These are animation-like movements that occur when you move from one slide to the next during a PowerPoint presentation. It is added to a presentation to bring it to life. Using a transition in your presentation makes it stand out to your audience and gives it a dramatic effect.

Trojan Horse: A program that appears to be harmless, but performs some destructive activity when it is run.

U

Uniform Resource Locator (URL): A unique Internet address, defining the path to a file (page or document) on the Web.

Uninstall: The process of removing unwanted programs from a computer.

Updates: Modifications to software to address possible flaws, security risks, or simply to enhance software performance.

Upgrade: A newer version of existing software.

Upload: The process of copying a file from a local PC to a Web server.

USB: Portable disk drive (jump drive).

User Account: A set of permissions associated with a user name. The account that comes with your computer is created by Windows 10 at installation; it is set at the administrative level allowing you complete control of the system as the owner (Administrator).

Users: People who use computers.

V

Virus: A program or code, intentionally written, that causes damage to a computer or is an annoyance.

View Tab: A feature located at top ribbon of all Microsoft Office programs that allows users to view document in several different layouts' formats, and sizes. Click view and select an option.

W

Web Authoring: This is software that simplifies Web page programming by allowing Web developers to specify the design of a Web page without actually writing the supporting code.

Web Page: A document on the World Wide Web that displays as a screen with associated links, frames, pictures, and other features of interest.

Web Scripting: Programming language, such as Java and HTML, used to specify a set of instructions for a Web page.

Web Site: A group of related Web pages published to a specific, unique location or Uniform Resource Locator (URL).

Web TV: Internet service that uses a set-top box to connect a TV to the Internet; also called Internet TV or MSN TV.

Web-Enhanced Class: A learning format where students meet in the classroom for all required classroom hours but make use of the internet for downloading study materials, including research and learning resources, submitting out-of-class completed assignments, and communication.

Window: Screen box in the Windows operating system.

Windows Explorer: The Windows file manager, with which a user can copy, move, delete, create, and rename files and folders.

Windows Registry: A database included in a Windows installation that records configuration information.

Windows Search: A Windows XP and Vista feature that enables you to search for files, folders, e-mail messages, and other data to find items that match criteria that you indicate.

Windows Update: A service provided by Microsoft Corporation to Windows users for updating the Microsoft Windows operating system and its installed components.

Windows Security Center: A Windows feature that makes a computer more secure by providing alerts when security software is not updated and identifying possible security threats.

Windows Sidebar: An important tool in Windows 7 that keeps information and other Windows tools readily available for use. It allows you to display news headlines right next to your open programs. This feature makes it easy for you to keep track of what's happening in the news while you work, you don't have to stop what you're doing to switch to a news website; everything you want to know is there at your fingertips while you work.

Windows Firewall: A bidirectional firewall that prohibits unauthorized access to a computer and stops many kinds of malware before it can infect a system.

WinZip: One file compression software program.

Wireless: A method of connecting to the Internet that does not use cables for connection; instead, electromagnetic waves carry the signal over part or all of the communication channel.

Wizard: A program feature that provides guidance through a process step by step.

Word Processing: Software program that lets you write, revise, manipulate, format, and print text for letters, reports, manuscripts, and other printed matter. The most commonly used word processing software is Microsoft Office Word.

Word Wrap: A word processing feature that carries the text to the next line when it reaches the right margin.

Worksheet: The rows and columns in an Excel spreadsheet are collectively called a worksheet.

World Wide Web (WWW): A subset of the Internet in which a system of Internet servers supports documents (pages) formatted in HTML.

Worm: A special type of virus that can replicate itself and use memory, but cannot attach itself to other programs.

REFERENCES

Microsoft Corporation, *Microsoft Windows 10* (2016). *Microsoft Office Application Programs* (2019), https://www.microsoft.com/store.

National Center for Education Statistics, *Trends in High School Dropout and Completion Rates in the United States* (2013-2017). https://nces.ed.gov. Last updated January14, 2020

My Food & My Family Journal Article. https://www.myfoodandfamily.com/. Last updated February 25, 2021.

ABOUT THE AUTHOR

Ms. Lilian Ukadike is a former Instructor of Business and Information Technology at Piedmont Technical College (PTC), Greenwood, SC, where she taught computer technology and business courses for 5 years (2007-2012). She obtained her Bachelor's degree in Accounting from Lander University, Greenwood SC, (1993), and Master's degree in Business Administration from Ashworth University, Norcross, GA., (2007). Prior to becoming an educator, she spent 18 years in corporate accounting, governmental, and nonprofit accounting where she worked as a Controller, Director of Accounting, and General Manager. Despite her passion for accounting, while in graduate school, she spent a significant amount of time in advanced research and studies of instructional computing technologies, management information systems, business oriented application programs, and technical writing as part of her chosen program of study. Determined to pursue her interest in technology, upon obtaining an MBA Degree in 2007, she left the corporate world and joined the faculty and staff at PTC as an Instructor to teach the business and computer courses she had been passionate about. During her time at PTC, in delivering her daily lectures, she saw first-hand, how her students struggled with the current text book in use at the time, which had incomplete instructional steps for performing basic computer tasks. With her strong desire to help her student learn common basics of technology, she decided to write a very simplified book on basic computing to facilitate easier hands-on learning for the new beginners. She provided her students handouts at the end of each class session with complete steps to help them do their homework. Before each class lecture, she would go through each chapter of the school's textbook and broke it down, added the missing steps, and provided the handouts to students. She said,: T*his process was very excruciating and time consuming but the students became very motivated to learn and were excited to come to class." This is mission accomplished, that was my big reward."*

The effectiveness of Ms. Ukadike's handouts to students as a learning tool caught the attention of many student beginners in computer technology at PTC to the point that students who were not enrolled in her class section were sneaking into her class during lectures. Whenever she identified students she couldn't recognize as already being in her class and asked them why they showed up in the class section they were not registered in, they would respond: *"Our friends told us that you teach really good, break things down in detail so they understand it, and provide them handouts; we want that too."* Every semester, her class section was filled up above capacity as students kept registering in her computer class (CPT-101) section to the point that her class had to be divided into two or three sections at different time slots within a week (both day and night). At that time, word began to spread around campus, all the way to the Dean of Business Technology and Public Service, who invited her to her office and said: *"I've been hearing some positive things about your basic computer class and the handouts to students, what's going on?" "Please tell me about it."* After she explained the problem with the current textbook to the Dean, the Dean had Ms. Ukadike's handouts reviewed by her peers, which was followed by the Dean commissioning Ms. Ukadike to write a custom textbook for the school. The collective handouts she had written over a period of one year became the foundation upon which her first manuscript was written. This was how she became a writer and today a published author, although an Accountant by profession.

The first edition was a seven-chapter book on basic computing skills aimed primarily at non-traditional students who were brand new to computing. It took her a year to complete the book *"Basic Computing Concepts: A Simplified Approach"* 1st Edition, based on Windows XP. The book was published as a custom textbook for the college by McGraw Hill Learning Solutions in 2010. Shortly after that, Microsoft came out with Windows 7, Ms. Ukadike, began work updating the first edition with new technologies to create a 2nd Edition of *"Basic Computing Concepts: A Simplified Approach"* based on Windows 7 which was also published by McGraw Hill Learning Solutions in 2011. Thus, the 1st and 2nd editions of her custom books were driven by her strong desire to help her students learn the simple basics of computer technology, be able to perform everyday basic tasks on the computer, and become computer proficient. The two custom books were inspired by her students, and written for her students. Her students also inspired her to become a writer and gave her a voice to speak out to the world on the issues of computer illiteracy.

In July 2012 Ms. Ukadike relocated to New Mexico following her husband's acceptance of the position of a Judge with NM State Government. She secured a job with New Mexico Taxation and Revenue Department (NMTRD) first as Cash Control Manager (Dec. 2012–Feb. 2015) and later promoted to the position of Assistant Bureau Chief (Feb. 2015–Dec. 2022). While in NM, unbeknown to her, the two custom books she wrote for PTC in SC were already getting the attention of a representative from Tate Publishing Enterprise, a vanity publisher based in Mustang, Oklahoma, who wondered why such good books should be confined to one college alone while many beginners in our society continue to struggle with computer illiteracy. In 2013, the Tate representative who reached out to Ms. Ukadike insisted that with the good quality of the book contents, and so many people continuing to struggle with computer literacy, the book should be made available to everyone in the national market where there was a good market it. Tate convinced Ms. Ukadike to write a 3rd edition of the book which she hesitantly agreed, and the 3rd Edition of *"Basic Computing Concepts: A simplified Approach"* was published in 2014. That edition was sold on Amazon, Barnes & Nobles, other online bookstores, and in store front bookstores, including the Hasting's stores in Santa Fe and Albuquerque, New Mexico. Tate Publishing later went out of business, but Ms. Ukadike's book continued to attract attention, specifically from Martin and Bowman, a Delaware-based literary agent/publisher who persuaded her to write a 4th edition of the book. This time, Ms. Ukadike researched five competing books in the marketplace, most of which bite off small pieces of beginning computing. She was determined to include what she thought was missing in those books with thorough, complete steps to performing basic computer tasks. She also decided to go comprehensive and included chapters on fundamentals of Microsoft Word, Excel, PowerPoint, and online learning platforms for beginners. As with previous editions, that meant exhaustive step-by-step testing on every function she covers plus creating graphics, so users get visual representations of what they are learning. *"This is practical computing in real time"* she said. *"As I perform the functions on the computer, I write them down step-by-step, to create the learning materials."*

Before writing the 4th edition, through research and inquiries, Ms. Ukadike became aware that students and teachers in the New Mexico public school system were struggling with computer illiteracy and some were unable to perform everyday basic computer tasks. She decided to conduct a research on the New Mexico Public Education Department (NMPED) curricula. As part of her research, she interviewed high school students, teachers, computer science teachers, school principals and vice principals. The findings from her research show that there was no basic computer technology course listed on the curricular of any of the top ten high school, and 2-year colleges she reviewed. Instead, they teach students Adobe Shop, Robotics, Photo Shop, Info Tech, Basic Keyboarding – all these courses have no value for students to help them build solid foundation in basic computer technology as they prepare for college. Her findings also revealed that many high school students and teachers in public schools were not computer literate. In addition, the NMPED schools do not have a basic computer textbook; there is no budget for it every year because basic computer technology is not a core course (it's an elective). Further, teachers use Google and YouTube training videos online as training materials to teach students basic computing which do not contain complete steps in basic computer training. When Ms. Ukadike began work on the 4th edition in March 2019, she was also conducting her research on computer illiteracy in New Mexico state, the findings of which were her inspiration for writing the 4th edition of her book. She completed the manuscript in June 2021; additional work continued with the publisher—editing, graphics formatting, and book cover design—for an additional year, including delays caused by COVID lockdowns. Finally, on July 19 2022, *"Basic Computing Concepts: All-in-One Beginners Guide to Computer Proficiency,* the 4th Edition was released on Amazon and Barnes & Noble, and available on 22 online and storefront bookstores in the United States. Shortly after the book was published, Ms. Ukadike submitted a comprehensive 35-page report of her research to NMPED titled: *"The Current Computer Science Program in Public Schools Does Not Meet the Requirements for Introduction to Basic Computer Technology. Find out How in this Report."*

In her role as a Tax Accountant with NMTRD (Dec. 2012–Dec. 2022), her writing skills and classroom teaching experiences placed her in a position to also function as organizational policy/procedure writer and trainer. She wrote standard operating procedures for the Department and also participated in providing employee trainings during implementation of new technologies and new work processes. Ms. Ukadike is an Accountant by profession, a job she loves, and has enjoyed doing for the past 28 years. However, she also loves to write and teach; explaining that she feels very passionate about helping people learn new things; make them feel empowered; and get excited about acquiring new knowledge. As a former teacher who has witnessed firsthand how individuals struggle with computer technology, Ms. Ukadike approaches the learning process from the eyes of new beginners and wrote the 4th edition of her book *"Basic Computing Concepts–All-in-One Beginner's Guide to Computer Proficiency."* from their point of view to make it easier for them to grasp.

The computer industry is very dynamic as technology creators and program designers continue to introduce new and updated program features for school, home, and business computing. In this constantly changing technological environment, new beginners continue to struggle to learn how to perform basic computer tasks and face the challenge of adapting to the ever changing computing world. With tremendous empathy for beginners in computer literacy, Ms. Ukadike poured her heart and soul into this 4th Edition: *"Basic Computing Concepts–All-in-One Beginner's Guide to Computer Proficiency."* Her goal is to capture the essence of today's technology with authenticity in practical system functionalities, and in real time, to ensure that beginners can learn with ease. In her own words: *"People need to learn with enthusiasm, excitement, and feel the empowerment that comes with new knowledge."* The book also contains beginners guide to the most commonly used Microsoft Office application programs to help beginners become proficient in basic computing as well as build strong foundation in MS Office programs that will enable them progress to intermediate and advanced levels if they so desire. Ms. Ukadike is married to Dr. Kenneth Ukadike, currently a retired judge from the State of New Mexico. Together they have raised four grown children. She is also retired from New Mexico Taxation and Revenue after 10 years. She is currently focusing her efforts on writing, promoting her book, raising awareness to the problem of computer illiteracy in the state of New Mexico, and operating her accounting and tax business as a Retired Accountant.